The Vintage Book of Canadian Memoirs

Edited by

GEORGE FETHERLING

The

Vintage

BOOK *of* CANADIAN

Memoirs

Vintage

Canada

VINTAGE CANADA EDITION, 2001

Copyright © 2001 by the contributors. Introduction © 2001 by George Fetherling. All rights reserved under International and Pan-American Copyright Conventions. Published in Canada by Vintage Canada, a division of Random House of Canada Limited, in 2001. Distributed by Random House of Canada Limited, Toronto.

Vintage Canada and colophon are registered trademarks of Random House of Canada Limited.

Pages 581–582 constitute a continuation of the copyright page.

National Library of Canada Cataloguing in Publication Data

Main entry under title:

The Vintage book of Canadian memoirs

Includes bibliographical references.
ISBN 0-679-31062-2

1. Authors, Canadian (English)—20th century—Biography.* I. Fetherling, George, 1949–   .

PS8083.V56 2001   S810.9'0054   S2001-930126-X
PR9186.3.V56 2001

Text design: Scott Richardson

Printed and bound in the United States of America

www.randomhouse.ca

2 4 6 8 9 7 5 3 1

TABLE OF CONTENTS

Preface VII

PREFACE

Book prizes for Canadian authors have grown phenomenally in recent years, both in number and size (forming a pool of money that helps to compensate writers for the virtual dismantling of the arts council grant system). Anyone reading the newspapers' book sections can see that a disproportionately large percentage of these honours go to the genre that's usually called the literary memoir. People may not agree on what a literary memoir is but they know one when they see it, and they have created a demand, which writers and publishers rush to satisfy. The more acclaim or controversy such books attract, the greater the quantity of them sure to follow. This anthology, although only a sampling and a rough survey of the field, leaves no doubt that Canadian writing has been undergoing such a boom. But the text itself can't answer some of the questions that hang in the air, such as "Why now?" and "Is Canada's interest in the genre different from America's or Britain's?" So I use this space for an awkward attempt to suggest a few possible answers.

Putting the matter simply, literary memoirs are not necessarily memoirs by or about literary people (though they can be, surely) but rather ones that use accepted literary techniques to tell their stories. We would never call the autobiography of a politician or other professional public figure a memoir. Such books are too formal to fit the distinction, following as they do the straight conventions of non-fiction; too determined to cover the subject's entire life or career and show him or her in the most favourable light. A memoir is more tightly focused, more daring in construction, and (its author hopes) more penetrating. A memoir can be of one's self or of other people or of a particular decade—or of a particular place. It's no coincidence that literary memoirs started to become popular in the 1970s and 1980s, at the same time the great revival in literary travel books began, for remembering is a kind of travelling and the one form tends towards a type of prose that's also common in the other. Armchair travellers read travel narratives to transport themselves to places they're unlikely to visit in any other way. Similarly, people read literary memoirs to travel inside the luggage of somebody else's life. The finest travel books and the finest memoirs have other qualities in common too. For one thing, they're works that are lived rather than researched.

For another, they're not morally bound to remember details exactly as they were or to recount events in precisely their true order. They answer to a higher, more impressionistic, more fictive type of truth. This is one of the ways in which a literary memoir earns its adjective. The distance between an autobiography and a memoir, then, is essentially the same as that between a diary and a journal, in that they're done in different ways, for different purposes, under the weight of different responsibilities towards what happened. If formal autobiographies display the writers to their best advantage, private journals, if honest, show them at their worst and most human. Memoirs fall somewhere in-between.

Wayson Choy begins his *Paper Shadows: A Chinatown Childhood*, an excerpt of which is included in this anthology, with the following note to the reader: "This memoir is a work of creative non-fiction. In order to recreate past times and personalities, I had to select details and various points of view, and I am solely responsible for these choices. No doubt, other views and opinions exist about the same persons and events. This book is, however, about the people and stories as I remember them—from my own life." Such explanations or disclaimers are common but also increasingly unnecessary, as readers know the rules of what they've selected to read. Still, Choy's words provide a pretty fair description of the inner-workings of a literary memoir. In addition, they point to one of the central questions of concern to anyone writing today, whether in fiction or non-fiction: the need to find a third means of discourse that is neither lying nor telling the truth, that balances journalistic literalness (or plausibility) with imaginative freedom. No doubt this is one reason why memoirs are so popular now—because writers are struggling hard to find personal solutions to this challenge. This is another reason, perhaps only one of many, why Canadian memoirs have a different tone from those similarly popular in the United States or the United Kingdom. Canadian writers have a head start in solving the professional puzzle because they have a certain tradition of literary mythomania from which to draw.

Think about it. In the 1930s, the naturalist writer Grey Owl had the world convinced that he was a Canadian Native, not, as he actually was, an Englishman named Archie Belaney. That he fooled an entire generation by his books, utterances, and actions strikes me as extraordinary, now that I've seen newsreels of him that make it perfectly plain that he looked exactly like an English tobacconist, was less than expert at entering a canoe, and had a habit of hamming it up for the cameras by putting the fingers of his right hand to his brow and scouting the horizon in what he presumed was aboriginal fashion. His contemporary Frederick

Philip Grove, the author of *Over Prairie Trails*, *The Master of the Mill*, and other creaky staples of many a syllabus, was actually Felix Paul Greve, a German con-man, ex-convict, and *littérateur* who came to Canada after faking his own death and eventually wrote a made-up autobiography. A more recent and non-criminal instance is John Glassco's *Memoirs of Montparnasse*, another work represented in the pages to follow; after the author's death, scholars such as Louis Dudek and Michael Gnarowski had a fine time separating the actual from the imagined. The latter category seemed to take in many of the most fascinating parts of the book. Only a few years later came the death of the poet Milton Acorn, who, except for being born in Prince Edward Island as he claimed, lived an almost wholly fictitious past in which, according to the moment and the mood, he had been a craftsman, a communist agitator, a dedicated member of the working class, and the proud bearer of Native blood. In fact, he was a former civil servant from a family of same who died in the Anglican communion and had no aboriginal ancestry. The difference between how the exposure of Belaney, Grove, and Glassco was received (shock! horror!) contrasted sharply with the indifference that greeted the news about Acorn as revealed by various biographers. Certainly, Acorn's case was different from those others, because he was a paranoid schizophrenic and because he didn't set down his memoirs on paper, preferring the medium of the beer parlour boast. But another reason is that between Glassco's death in 1981 and Acorn's in 1986, the literary memoir had come into its own and such imaginative use of one's past was seen as permissible—more permissible, I think, than in the United States or Great Britain, where I believe greater store is laid on verisimilitude (though I can't prove this).

In the United States, the title of Thomas Wolfe's *You Can't Go Home Again* has entered the common language. In Canada, one would be more accurate to say *You* must *go home again*. Returning imaginatively to one's home in order to choose what to keep and what to dispense with in departing memory is an important aspect of literature by Canadians, whether those born here (Margaret Laurence is an excellent example) or those from Away (Rohinton Mistry could be used to represent scores of writers who, during the past decade especially, have found themselves by confronting their own pasts, in distance as well as in time). Both these cases are quite different from the American tradition of lighting out for the territories, recreating oneself a little farther west, as measured by either the map or the mind. All of these seem to be more difficult in Britain where history lies under every footstep and threatens to drag writers down to the depths like the mythical sea monsters taking sailors to their deaths.

Yet there are also countervailing forces at play that make the memoirs produced in Canada part of a more global phenomenon. One is the present dominance of deconstructionist theory over literature itself in the universities of all the English-speaking nations and the European mainland. Teachers of theory, for whom *privilege* is a verb not a right, acknowledge that theory privileges memoirs, because criticism is a personal act and reading is contextualized through individual experience. In this milieu, writing about one's experiences is a way of reclaiming them, of reasserting one's ownership of memory and reaffirming one's identity to oneself in a designer age that forces anonymity on us all—a way of laughing in the face of received history (which would be represented by the sort of political autobiography mentioned above).

As a convenience for the readers of this anthology, I have grouped the selections under four thematic headings. I have done so, aware of how the merging of fiction and non-fiction (essentially, the journalizing of the one and the dejournalizing of the other) has tended to make questions of genres, subgenres, and themes less important than in the past. Less important but by no means obsolete, for new categories have arisen to consume the old. One of the most studied fields in literature today is life-writing, a blanket usage for a phenomenon that is also gaining ground in the non-literary world, where it is often tied to some form of therapy (or is a therapy in itself). Life-writing is the general term whose specifics include autobiography (about one's public self), memoir (frequently about others but with oneself as a thread), diary (a day-by-day record), and journal (a discontinuous and often more private or intense product of the same impulse to record). Many argue compellingly that life-writing today is popular because it's connected to the traditional realistic novel in which a recognizable world is created in a recognizable manner through the telling of a story. Fictional characters are flesh-and-blood figures whom their creators care about passionately, but they're essentially inventions. Memoirists or other life-writers create from actual experience but allow themselves the fiction writer's freedom of rearranging and telescoping in order to make what happened worthy of being called a tale.

A vast literature on the subject of memoirs and other life-writing has grown up in the past few years. As an aid for the reader I have appended to this anthology a short list of Canadian articles and books on the subject. In the hopes that this collection will stir people's interest, I have also included a selected bibliography of some other recent Canadian literary memoirs.

Part One:

At Home & Abroad

A Sense of the Ridiculous

MORDECAI RICHLER

Mordecai Richler was born in 1931 in Montreal, the setting of his most famous novels such as *The Apprenticeship of Duddy Kravitz* (1959), *St. Urbain's Horseman* (1971), and *Solomon Gursky Was Here* (1989). But he lived abroad from 1954 to 1972, mostly in London but also, briefly, in Paris, as he recounts in this memoir of restrained and ironic nostalgia. The piece first appeared in the *New American Review* in 1968.

NOTES ON PARIS 1951 AND AFTER

For Mason Hoffenberg and Joe Dughi

In the summer of 1967, our very golden EXPO summer, I was drinking with an old and cherished friend at Montreal airport, waiting for my flight to London, when all at once he said, "You know, I'm going to be forty soon."

At the time, I was still a smug thirty-six.

"Hell," he added, whacking his glass against the table, outraged, "it's utterly ridiculous. Me, forty? My father's forty!"

Though we were both Montrealers, we had first met in Paris in 1951, and we warmed over those days now, *our* movable feast, until my flight was called.

A few days later, back in London, where I had been rooted for more than ten years, I sat sipping coffee on the King's Road, Chelsea, brooding about Paris and watching the girls pass in their minis and high suede boots. Suddenly, hatefully, it struck me that there was a generation younger than mine. Another bunch. And so we were no longer licensed to idle at cafés, to be merely promising as we were in Paris, but were regularly expected to deliver the goods, books, and movies to be judged by others. At my age, appointments must be kept, I thought, searching for a taxi.

Time counts.

As it happened, my appointment was with a Star at the Dorchester. The Star, internationally known, obscenely overpaid, was attended in his suite by a bitch-mother private secretary, a soothing queer architect to keep everybody's glasses filled with chilled Chevalier Montrachet, and, kneeling by the hassock on which big bare feet rested, a chiropodist. The chiropodist, black leather tool box open before him, scissor-filled drawers protruding, black bowler lying alongside on the rug, was kneading the Star's feet, pausing to reverently snip a nail or caress a big toe, lingering whenever he provoked an involuntary little yelp of pleasure.

"I am ever so worried," the chiropodist said, "about your returning to Hollywood, Sir."

"Mmmnnn." This delivered with eyes squeezed ecstatically shut.

"Who will look after your feet there?"

The Star had summoned me because he wanted to do a picture about the assassination of Leon Trotsky. Trotsky, my hero. "The way I see it," he said, "Trotsky was one of the last really, really great men. Like Louis B. Mayer."

I didn't take on the screenplay. Instead, on bloody-minded impulse, I bought air tickets and announced to my wife, "We're flying to Paris tomorrow."

Back to Paris to be cleansed.

As my original left bank days had been decidedly impecunious, this was something like an act of vengeance. We stayed on the right bank, eating breakfast in bed at the Georges V, dropping into the Dior boutique, doing the galleries, stopping for a vin de maison here and a Perrier there, window shopping on the rue du Rivoli, dining at Lapérouse, le Tour d'Argent, and le Méditerranée.

Fifteen years had not only made for changes in me.

The seedy Café Royale, on Boul. St. Germain, the terrace once spilling over with rambunctious friends until two in the morning, when the action drifted on to the Mabillon and from there to the notorious Pergola, had been displaced by the sickeningly mod, affluent le Drugstore. In Montparnasse, the Dôme was out of favour again, everybody now gathering at the barn-like La Coupole. Strolling past the Café le Tournot, I no longer recognized the abundantly confident *Paris Review* bunch (the loping Plimpton in his snap-brim fedora, Eugene Walter, Peter Mathiessen) either conferring on the pavement or sprawled on the terrace, dunking croissants into the morning café au lait, always and enviably surrounded by the most appetizing college girls in town. Neither was the affable Richard Wright to be seen any more, working on the pinball machine.

4

Others, alas, were still drifting from café to café, cruelly winded now, grubbiness no longer redeemed by youth, bald, twitchy, defensive, and embittered. To a man, they had all the faults of genius. They were alienated, of course, as well as being bad credit risks, rent-skippers, prodigious drinkers or junkies, and reprobates, and yet—and yet—they had been left behind, unlucky or not sufficiently talented. They made me exceedingly nervous, for now they appeared embarrassing, like fat bachelors of fifty tooling about in fire-engine red MGs or women in their forties flouncing their miniskirts.

The shrill, hysterical editor of one of the little magazines of the fifties caught up with me. "I want you to know," he said, "that I rejected all that crap Terry Southern is publishing in America now."

Gently, I let on that Terry and I were old friends.

"Jimmy Baldwin," he said, "has copied all my gestures. If you see him on TV, it's me," he shrieked. "It's me."

On balance, our weekend in Paris was more unsettling than satisfying. Seated at the Dôme, well-dressed, consuming double Scotches rather than nursing a solitary beer on the lookout for somebody who had just cashed his GI cheque on the black market, I realized I appeared just the sort of tourist who would have aroused the unfeeling scorn of the boy I had been in 1951. A scruffy boy with easy, bigoted attitudes, encouraging a beard, addicted to T-shirts, the obligatory blue jeans and, naturally, sandals. Absorbed by the tarot and trying to write in the manner of Céline. Given to wild pronouncements about Coca-Cola culture and late nights listening to Sidney Bechet at the Vieux Colombier. We had not yet been labelled beats, certainly not hippies. Rather, we were taken for existentialists by *Life*, if not by Jean-Paul Sartre, who had a sign posted in a jazz cellar warning he had nothing whatsoever to do with these children and that they hardly represented his ideas.

I frequently feel I've lost something somewhere. Spontaneity maybe, or honest appetite. In Paris all I ever craved for was to be accepted as a serious novelist one day, seemingly an impossible dream. Now I'm harnessed to this ritual of being a writer, shaking out the morning mail for cheque-size envelopes—scanning the newspapers—breakfast—then upstairs to work. To try to work.

If I get stuck, if it turns out an especially sour, unyielding morning, I will recite a lecture to myself that begins, Your father had to be out at six every morning, driving to the junkyard in the sub-zero dark, through Montreal blizzards. You work at home, never at your desk before nine, earning more for a day's remembered insults than your father ever made, hustling scrap, in a week.

Or I return, in my mind's eye, to Paris.

Paris, the dividing line. Before Paris, experience could be savoured for its own immediate satisfactions. It was total. Afterwards, I became cunning, a writer, somebody with a use for everything, even intimacies.

I was only a callow kid of nineteen when I arrived in Paris in 1951, and so it was, in the truest sense, my university. Saint-Germain-des-Prés was my campus, Montparnasse my frat house, and my two years there are a sweetness I retain, as others do wistful memories of McGill or Oxford. Even now, I tend to measure my present conduct against the rules I made for myself in Paris.

The first declaration to make about Paris is that we young Americans, and this Canadian, didn't go there so much to discover Europe as to find and reassure each other, who were separated by such vast distances at home. Amongst the as yet unknown young writers in Paris at the time, either friends or nodding café acquaintants, there were Terry Southern, Alan Temko, Alfred Chester, Herbert Gold, David Burnett, Mavis Gallant, Alexander Trocchi, Christopher Logue, Mason Hoffenberg, James Baldwin, and the late David Stacton.

About reputations.

A few years ago, after I had spoken at one of those vast synagogue-cum-community plants that have supplanted the poky little *shuls* of my Montreal boyhood, all-pervasive deodorant displacing the smell of pickled herring, a lady shot indignantly out of her seat to say, "I'm sure you don't remember me, but we were at school together. Even then you had filthy opinions, but who took you seriously? Nobody. *Can you please tell me,*" she demanded, "*why on earth anybody takes you seriously now?*"

Why, indeed? If only she knew how profoundly I agreed with her. For I, too, am totally unable to make that imaginative leap that would enable me to accept that anybody I grew up with—or, in this case, cracked peanuts with at the Mabillon—or puffed pot with at the Old Navy—could now be mistaken for a writer. A reputation.

In 1965, when Alexander Trocchi enjoyed a season in England as a sort of Dr. Spock of pot, pontificating about how good it was for you on one in-depth TV discussion after another, I was hard put to suppress an incredulous giggle each time his intelligent, craggy face filled the screen. I am equally unconvinced, stunned even, when I see Terry Southern's or Herb Gold's picture in *Time*.

I also find it disheartening that, in the end, writers are no less status-conscious than the middle class they—we, I should say—excoriate with such appetite. As my high-school friends, the old Sunday morning scrub team, has been split by economics, this taxi driver's boy now a fat suburban cat, that tailor's son still ducking bailiffs in a one-man basement factory; so we, who pretended to transcend such matters, have, over the demanding years, been divided by reputations. If our yardstick is more exacting, it still measures without mercy, coarsening the happy time we once shared.

Paris.

It would be nice, it would be tidy, to say with hindsight that we were a group, knit by political anger or a literary policy or even an aesthetic revulsion for all things American, but the truth was we recognized each other by no more than a shared sense of the ridiculous. And so we passed many a languorous, pot-filled afternoon on the terrace of the Dôme or the Selecte, improvising, not unlike jazz groups, on the hot news from America, where Truman was yielding to Eisenhower. We bounced an inanity to and fro, until, magnified through bizarre extension, we had disposed of it as an absurdity. We invented obscene quiz shows for television, and ad-libbed sexual outrages that could be interpolated into a John Marquand novel, a Norman Rockwell *Post* cover, or a June Allyson movie. The most original innovator and wit amongst us was easily the deceptively gentle Mason Hoffenberg, and one way or another we all remain indebted to him.

Oddly, I cannot recall that we ever discussed "our stuff" with each other. In fact, a stranger noting our cultivated indifference, the cool café posture, could never have guessed that when we weren't shuffling from café to café, in search of girls—a party—any diversion—we were actually labouring hard and long at typewriters in cramped, squalid hotel rooms, sending off stories to America, stories that rebounded with a sickening whack. The indifference to success was feigned, our café cool was false, for the truth is we were real Americans, hungering for recognition and its rewards, terrified of failure.

The rules of behaviour, unwritten, were nevertheless, rigid. It was not considered corrupt to take a thousand dollars from Girodias to write a pornographic novel under a pseudonym for the tourist trade, but anybody who went home to commit a thesis was automatically out. We weighed one another not by our backgrounds or prospects, but by taste, the books we kept by our bedside. Above all, we cherished the unrehearsed response, the zany personality, and so we prized many a bohemian dolt or exhibitionist, the girl who dyed her hair orange or kept a monkey for a pet, the most defiant queen, or the sub-Kerouac who wouldn't read anything because it might influence his style. Looked at another way, you

7

were sure to know somebody who would happily bring on an abortion with a hat pin or turn you on heroin or peddle your passport, but nobody at all you could count on to behave decently if you were stuck with your Uncle Irv and Aunt Sophie, who were "doing Europe" this summer.

Each group had its own conventions, which is to say we were not so much non-conformists as subject to our own peculiar conformities or, if you like, anti-bourgeois inversions. And so, if you were going to read a fat Irwin Shaw, a lousy best-seller, you were safest concealing it under a Marquis de Sade jacket. What I personally found most trying was the necessity to choke enthusiasm, never to reveal elation, when the truth was I was out of my mind with joy to be living in Paris, actually living in Paris, France.

My room at the Grand Hotel Excelsior, off the Boul' Mich, was filled with rats, rats and a gratifyingly depraved past, for the hotel had once functioned as a brothel for the Wehrmacht. Before entering my room, I hollered, and whacked on the door, hoping to scatter the repulsive little beasts. Before putting on my sweater, I shook it out for rat droppings. But lying on my lumpy bed, ghetto-liberated, a real expatriate, I could read the forbidden, outspoken Henry Miller, skipping the windy cosmic passages, warming to the hot stuff. Paris in the fabled twenties, when luscious slavering American schoolteachers came over to seek out artists like me, begging for it. Waylaying randy old Henry in public toilets, seizing him by the cock. Scratching on his hotel room door, entering to gobble him. *Wherever I travel I'm too late. The orgy has moved elsewhere.*

My father wrote, grabbing for me across the seas to remind me of my heritage. He enclosed a Jewish calendar, warning me that Rosh Hashanah came early this year, even for me who smoked hashish on the sabbath. Scared even as I smoked it, but more terrified of being put down as chickenshit. My father wrote to say that the YMHA *Beacon* was sponsoring a short story contest and that the *Reader's Digest* was in the market for "Unforgettable Characters." Meanwhile, the *New Yorker* wouldn't have me, neither would the *Partisan Review*.

Moving among us, there was the slippery, eccentric Mr. Soon. He was, he said, the first Citizen of the World. He had anticipated Gary Davis, who was much in the news then. Mussolini had deported Mr. Soon from Italy, even as he had one of our underground heroes, the necromancer Alistair Crowley, The Great Beast 666, but the Swiss had promptly shipped Mr. Soon back again. He had no papers. He had a filthy, knotted beard, a body seemingly fabricated of Meccano parts, the old clothes and cigarettes we gave him, and a passion for baklavas. The police were always nabbing him for questioning. They wanted to know about drug addiction and foreigners who had been in Paris for more than three months without a *carte d'identité*. Mr. Soon became an informer.

"And what," he'd ask, "do you think of the poetry of Mao Tse-tung?"

"Zingy."

"And how," he'd ask, "does one spell your name?"

My American friends were more agitated than I, a non-draftable Canadian, about the Korean War. We sat on the terrace of the Mabillon, drunkenly accumulating beer coasters, on the day General Ridgway drove into Paris, replacing Eisenhower at SHAPE. Only a thin bored crowd of the curious turned out to look over the general from Korea, yet the gendarmes were everywhere, and the boulevard was black with Gardes Mobiles, their fierce polished helmets catching the sun. All at once, the Place de l'Odeon was dotted with communist demonstrators, men, women, and boys, squirting out of the backstreets, whipping out broomsticks from inside their shapeless jackets and hoisting anti-American posters on them.

"RIDGWAY," the men hollered.

"*A la porte*," the women responded in a piercing squeal.

Instantly the gendarmes penetrated the demonstration, fanning out, swinging the capes that were weighed down with lead, cracking heads, and smashing noses. The once disciplined cry of *Ridgway, à la porte!*, faltered, then broke. Demonstrators retreated, scattering, clutching their bleeding faces.

A German general, summoned by NATO, came to Paris, and French Jews and socialists paraded in sombre silence down the Champs Elysées, wearing striped pyjamas, their former concentration camp uniforms. A Parisian Jewish couple I had befriended informed me at dinner that their newborn boy would not be circumcised, "Just in case." The Algerian troubles had begun. There was a war on in what we then called Indo-China. The gendarmes began to raid left bank hotels one by one, looking for Arabs without papers. Six o'clock in the morning they would pound on your door, open it, and demand to see your passport. "I am a c-c-c-itizen of the world," said Greenblatt, at that time something called a non-figurative poet, now with Desilu Productions.

One night the virulently anti-communist group, Paix et Liberté, pasted up posters everywhere that showed a flag, the Hammer and Sickle, flying from the top of the Eiffel Tower. HOW WOULD YOU LIKE TO SEE THIS? the caption read. Early the next morning the communists went from poster to poster and pasted the Stars and Stripes over the Russian flag.

9

With Joe Dughi, a survivor of Normandy and the Battle of the Bulge, who was taking the course on French Civilization at the Sorbonne, I made the long trip to a flaking working-class suburb to see the Russian propaganda feature film, *Meeting on the Elbe*. In the inspiring opening sequence, the Russian army is seen approaching the Elbe, orderly, joyous soldiers mounted on gleaming tanks, each tank carrying a laurel wreath and a portrait of Stalin. Suddenly, we hear the corrupt, jerky strains of "Yankee Doodle Dandy," and the camera swoops down on the opposite bank, where the unshaven behemoths who make up the American army are revealed staggering towards the river, soldiers stumbling drunkenly into the water. On the symbolically lowered bridge, the white-uniformed Russian colonel, upright as Gary Cooper, says, "It's good to see the American army—even if it's on the last day of the war." Then he passes his binoculars to his American counterpart, a tubby pig-eyed Lou Costello figure. The American colonel scowls, displeased to see his men fraternizing with the Russians. Suddenly, he grins slyly. "You must admit," he says, lowering the binoculars, "that the Germans made excellent optical equipment." The Russian colonel replies: "These binoculars were made in Moscow, comrade."

In the Russian zone, always seen by day, the Gary Cooper colonel has set up his headquarters in a modest farmhouse. Outside, his adorable orderly, a Ukrainian Andy Devine, cavorts with sandy-haired German kids, reciting Heine to them. But in the American zone, seen only by night, the obese, cigar-chomping American colonel has appropriated a castle. Loutish enlisted men parade enormous oil paintings before him, and the colonel chalks a big X on those he wants shipped home. All the while, I should add, he is on the long-distance line to Wall Street, asking for quotations on Bavarian forest.

Recently, I have been reading John Clellon Holmes's *Nothing More To Declare*, a memoir that makes it plain that the ideas and idiom, even some of the people, prevalent in the Village during the fifties were interchangeable with those in Paris. The truculent Legman, once a *Neurotica* editor, of whom he writes so generously, inevitably turned up in Saint-Germain-des-Prés to produce his definitive edition of filthy limericks on rag paper and, incidently, to assure us gruffly that the novel was dead. Absolutely dead.

Even as in the Village, we were obsessed by the shared trivia and pop of our boyhood, seldom arguing about ideas, which would have made us feel self-conscious, stuffy, but instead going on and on about Fibber McGee's closet,

Mandrake's enemies, Warner Bros.' character actors like Elisha Cook Jr., the Andrew Sisters, and the Katzenjammer Kids. To read about such sessions now in other people's novels or essays doesn't make for recognition so much as resentment at having one's past broadcast, played back as it were, a ready-to-wear past, which in retrospect was not peculiar to Paris but a fifties commonplace.

At times it seems to me that what my generation of novelists does best, celebrating itself, is also discrediting. Too often, I think, it is we who are the fumblers, the misfits, *but unmistakably lovable*, intellectual heroes of our very own fictions, triumphant in our vengeful imaginations as we never were in actuality. Only a few contemporaries, say Brian Moore, live up to what I once took to be the novelist's primary moral responsibility, which is to be the loser's advocate. To tell us what it's like to be Judith Hearne. Or a pinched Irish schoolteacher. The majority tend to compose paeans of disguised praise of people very much like themselves. Taken to an extreme, the fictional guise is dropped and we are revealed cheering ourselves. And so George Plimpton is the pitcher and hero of *Out of My League* by George Plimpton. Norman Podhoretz, in *Making It*, is the protagonist of his own novel. And most recently, in *The Armies of the Night*, Norman Mailer writes about himself in the third person.

This is not to plead for a retreat to social realism or novels of protest, but simply to say that, as novelists, many of us are perhaps too easily bored, too self-regarding, and not sufficiently curious about mean lives, bland people. The unglamorous.

All at once, it was spring.
One day shopkeepers were wretched, waiters surly, concierges mean about taking messages, and the next, the glass windows encasing café terraces were removed everywhere, and Parisians were transmogrified: shopkeepers, waiters, concierges actually spoke in dulcet tones.

Afternoons we took to the Jardins du Luxembourg, lying on the grass and speculating about Duke Snider's arm, the essays in *The God That Failed*, Jersey Joe Walcott's age, whether Salinger's *The Catcher in the Rye* could be good *and* a Book-of-the-Month, how far Senator Joe McCarthy might go, was Calder Willingham overrated, how much it might set us back to motorcycle to Seville, was Alger Hiss lying, why wasn't Nathanael West more widely read, could Don Newcombe win thirty games, and was it disreputable of Max Brod to withhold Kafka's "Letter To My Father."

Piaf was big with us, as was Jacques Prévert's *Paroles*, the song "Les Feuilles mortes," Trenet, and the films of Simone Signoret. Anything by Genet, or Samuel Beckett was passed from hand to hand. I tried to read *La Nausée* in French, but stumbled and gave it up.

Early one Sunday morning in May, laying in a kitbag filled with wine, pâté, hard-boiled eggs, guiches and salamis and cold veal from the charcuterie, cheeses, a bottle of Armagnac and baguettes, five of us squeezed into a battered Renault quatre-chevaux and set off for Chartres and the beaches of Normandy. Nineteen fifty-two it was, but we soon discovered that the rocky beaches were still littered with the debris of war. Approaching the coast we bumped drunkenly past shelled-out, crumbling buildings, VERBOTEN printed on one wall and ACHTUNG! on another. This moved us to incredulous laughter, evoking old Warner Bros. films and dimly recalled hit parade tunes. But, once on the beaches, we were sobered and silent. Incredibly thick pill boxes, split and shattered, had yet to be cleared away. Others, barely damaged, clearly showed scorch marks. Staring into the dark pill boxes, through gun slits that were still intact, was chilling, even though gulls now squawked reassuringly overhead. Barefoot, our trousers rolled to the knees, we roamed the beaches, finding deep pits and empty shell cases here and there. As the tide receded, concrete teeth were revealed still aimed at the incoming tanks and landing craft. I stooped to retrieve a soldier's boot from a garland of sea-weed. Slimy, soggy, already sea-green, I could still make out the bullet hole in the toe.

Icons.

We were not, it's worth noting, true adventurers, but followers of a romantic convention. A second *Aliyah*, so to speak. "History has not quite repeated itself," Brian Moore wrote in a review of *Exile's Return* for the *Spectator*. "When one reads of the passionate, naïve manifestos in Malcolm Cowley's 'literary odyssey of the 1920s,' the high ambitions and the search for artistic values which sent the 'lost generation' to Paris, one cannot help feeling a touch of envy. It would seem that the difference between the American artists' pilgrimage to Europe in the Twenties and in the Sixties is the difference between first love and the obligatory initial visit to a brothel.

"Moneyed by a grant from Fulbright, Guggenheim, or Ford, the American painter now goes to France for a holiday: he knows that the action is all in New York. Similarly, the young American writer abroad shows little interest in the prose experiments of Robbe-Grillet, Sarraute, and Simon; he tends to dismiss Britain's younger novelists and playwrights as boring social realists (*we finished with that stuff twenty years ago*), and as for Sartre, Beckett, Genet, or Ionesco, he has dug them already off-Broadway. It seems that American writers, in three short generations, have moved from the provincial (*we haven't yet produced any writing that could be called major*) to the parochial (*the only stuff worth reading nowadays is coming out of America*)."

Our group, in the fifties, came sandwiched between, largely unmoneyed, except for those on the GI Bill, and certainly curious about French writing, especially Sartre, Camus, and, above all, Céline. We were also self-consciously aware of the twenties. We knew the table at the Dôme that had been Hemingway's and made a point of eating at the restaurant on rue Monsieur le Prince where Joyce was reputed to have taken his dinner. Not me, but others regularly sipped tea with Alice Toklas. Raymond Duncan, swirling past in his toga, was a common, if absurd, sight. *Transition* still appeared fitfully.

Other connections with the twenties were through the second generation. David Burnett, one of the editors of *New-Story*, was the son of Whit Burnett and Martha Foley, who had brought out the original *Story*. My own first publication was in *Points*, a little magazine that was edited by Sinbad Vail, the son of Lawrence Vail and Peggy Guggenheim. It wasn't much of a magazine, and though Vail printed four thousand copies of the first issue, he was only able to peddle four hundred. In the same issue as my original mawkish short story there was a better one by Brendan Behan, who was described as "27, Irish ... Has been arrested several times for activities in the Irish Republican Army, which he joined in 1937, and in all has been sentenced to 17 years in gaol, has in fact served about 7 years in Borstal and Parkhurst Prison. Disapproves of English prison system. At present working as a housepainter on the State Railways."

Among other little magazines current at the time there were *Id* and *Janus*. ("An aristocrat by his individualism, a revolutionary against all societies," wrote Daniel Mauroc, "the homosexual is both the Jew and the Negro, the precursor and the unassimilable, the terrorist and the *raffiné*....") and *Merlin*, edited by Trocchi, Richard Seaver, Logue, and John Coleman, who is now the *New Statesman*'s film critic. *Merlin*'s address, incidently, was the English Bookshop, 42 rue de Seine, which had once belonged to Sylvia Beach.

In retrospect, I cannot recall that anybody, except Alan Temko, perhaps, was as yet writing fantasy or satire. Mostly, the stories we published were realistic and about home, be it Texas, Harlem, Brooklyn, or Denver. Possibly, just possibly, everything can be stripped down to a prosaic explanation. The cult of hashish, for instance, had a simple economic basis. It was easy to come by and cheap, far cheaper than Scotch. Similarly, if a decade after our sojourn in Paris a number of us began to write what has since come to be branded black humour, it may well be that we were not so much inspired as driven to it by mechanics. After all, the writer who opts out of the mainstream of American experience, self-indulgently luxuriating in bohemia, the pleasure of like-minded souls, is also cutting himself off from his natural material, sacrificing his sense of social continuity; and so when we swung round to writing about contemporary America, we could only attack obliquely, shrewdly settling on a style that did not betray knowledge gaps of day-to-day experience.

For the most part, I moved with the *New-Story* bunch: David Burnett, Terry Southern, Mason Hoffenberg, Alan Temko, and others. One afternoon, Burnett told me, a new arrival from the States walked into the office and said, "For ten thousand dollars, I will stop in front of a car on the Place Vendôme and say I did it because *New-Story* rejected one of my stories. Naturally, I'm willing to guarantee coverage in all the American newspapers."

"But what if you're hurt?" he was asked.

"Don't worry about me, I'm a paraphrase artist."

"A what?"

"I can take any story in *Collier's*, rewrite it, and sell it to the *Post*."

New-Story, beset by financial difficulties from the very first issue, seldom able to fork out the promised two bucks a page to contributors or meet printer's bills, was eventually displaced by the more affluent *Paris Review*. But during its short and turbulent life *New-Story* was, I believe, the first magazine to publish Jean Genet in English. Once, browsing at George Whitman's hole-in-the-wall bookshop near Notre-Dame, where Bernard Frechtman's translation of *Our Lady of the Flowers* was prominently displayed, I overheard an exasperated Whitman explain to a camera-laden American matron, "No, no, it's not the same Genet as writes for the *New Yorker*."

Possibly, the most memorable of all the little magazines was the French publication, *Ur, Cahiers Pour Un Dictat Culturel*. *Ur* was edited by Jean-Isador Isou, embattled author of *A Reply To Karl Marx*, a slender riposte hawked by gorgeous girls in blue jeans to tourists at right bank cafés—tourists under the tantalizing illusion that they were buying the hot stuff.

Ur was a platform for the Letterists, who believed that all the arts were dead and could only be resurrected by a synthesis of their collective absurdities. This, like anything else that was seemingly new or outrageous, appealed to us. And so Friday nights, our pockets stuffed with oranges and apples, pitching cores into the Seine, scuffling, singing *Adon Olam*, we passed under the shadows of Notre-Dame and made our way to a café on the Île Saint-Louis to listen to Isador Isou and others read poems composed of grunts and cries, incoherent arrangements of letters, set to an anti-musical background of vacuum cleaners, drills, car horns, and train whistles. We listened, rubbing our jaws, nodding, looking pensive.

—*Ça, alors.*

—*Je m'en fous.*

—*Azoi,* Ginsberg. *Azoi.*

Ginsberg was the first to go home. I asked him to see my father and tell him how hard up I was.

"Sometimes," Ginsberg told him, "your son sits up all night in his cold room, writing."

"And what does he do all day?"

Crack peanuts on the terrace of the Café Royale. Ruminate over the baseball scores in the *Herald-Tribune*.

We were all, as Hemingway once said, at the right age. Everybody was talented. Special. Nobody had money. (Except of course Art Buchwald, the most openly envied ex-GI in Paris. Buchwald, who had not yet emerged as a humorist, had cunningly solved two problems at once, food and money, inaugurating a restaurant column in the *Herald-Tribune*.) We were all trying to write or paint and so there was always the hope, it's true, of a publisher's advance or a contract with a gallery. There was also the national lottery. There was, too, the glorious dream that today you would run into the fabled lady senator from the United States who was reputed to come over every summer and, as she put it, invest in the artistic future of five or six promising, creative youngsters. She would give you a thousand dollars, more sometimes, no strings attached. But I never met her. I was reminded of the days when as a kid in Montreal I was never without a Wrigley's chewing gum wrapper, because of that magic man who could pop up anywhere, stop you, and ask for a wrapper. If you had one with you, he gave you a dollar. Some days, they said, he handed out as much as fifty dollars. I never met him, either.

Immediately before Christmas, however, one of my uncles sent me money. I had written to him, quoting Auden, Kierkegaard, *The Book of Changes*, Maimonides, and Dylan Thomas, explaining we must love one another or die. "I can hear that sort of crap," he wrote back, "any Sunday morning on the Manischewitz Hour," but a cheque for a hundred dollars was enclosed, and I instantly decided to go to Cambridge for the holidays.

Stringent rationing—goose eggs, a toe-nail size chunk of meat a week—was still the depressing rule in England and, as I had old friends in Cambridge, I arrived laden with foodstuffs, my raincoat sagging with contraband steaks and packages of butter. A friend of a friend took me along to sip sherry with E. M. Forster at his rooms in King's College.

Forster immediately unnerved me by asking what I thought of F. Scott Fitzgerald's work.

Feebly, I replied I thought very highly of it indeed.

Forster then remarked that he generally asked visiting young Americans what they felt about Fitzgerald, whose high reputation baffled him. Forster said that though Fitzgerald unfailingly chose the most lyrical titles for his novels, the works themselves seemed to him to be without especial merit.

Unaccustomed to sherry, intimidated by Forster, who in fact couldn't have been more kind or gentle, I stupidly knocked back my sherry in one gulp, like a synagogue schnapps, whilst the others sipped theirs decorously. Forster waved for my glass to be refilled and then inquired without the least condescension about the progress of my work. Embarrassed, I hastily changed the subject.

"And what," he asked, "do you make of Angus's first novel?"

Angus being Angus Wilson and the novel, *Hemlock and After*.

"I haven't read it yet," I lied, terrified lest I make a fool of myself.

I left Forster a copy of Nelson Algren's *The Man With The Golden Arm*, which I had just read and enormously admired. A few days later the novel was returned to me with a note I didn't keep, and so quote from memory. He had only read as far as page 120 in Algren's novel, Foster wrote. It had less vomit than the last American novel he had read, but....

At the time, I was told that the American novel Forster found most interesting was Willard Motley's *Knock On Any Door*.

Cambridge, E. M. Forster, was a mistake; it made me despair for me and my friends and our shared literary pretensions. In the rooms I visited at King's, St. Mary's, and Pembroke, gowned young men were wading through the entire *Faerie Queene*, they had absorbed *Beowulf*, Chaucer, and were clearly heirs to the tradition.

All at once, it seemed outlandish, a grandiose *chutzpah*, that we, street corner bohemians, kibitzers, still swapping horror stories about our abominable Yiddish mommas, should even presume to write. Confirmation, if it were needed, was provided by John Lehmann, who returned my first attempt at a sub-Céline novel with a printed rejection slip.

"Hi, keed," my brother wrote, "How are things in Gay Paree?", and there followed a list of the latest YMHA basketball scores.

Things in Gay Paree were uncommonly lousy. I had contacted scurvy, of all things, from not eating sufficient fruit or vegetables. The money began to run out. Come midnight, come thirst, I used to search for my affluent friend, Armstrong, who was then putting me up in his apartment in Étoile. I would seek out Armstrong in the homosexual pits of Saint-Germain and Montparnasse. The Montana, the Fiacre, l'Abbaye, the Reine Blanche. If Armstrong was sweetening up a butch, I would slip in and out again discreetly, but if Armstrong was alone, alone and sodden, he would comfort me with cognacs and ham rolls and take me home in a taxi.

Enormous, rosy-cheeked, raisin-eyed Armstrong was addicted to acquired Yiddishisms. He'd say, "Oy, bless my little. I don't know why I go there, Mottel." 17

"Uh huh."

"Did you catch the old queen at the bar?"

"I'm still hungry. What about you?"

"*Zut.*"

"You know, I've never eaten at Les Halles. All this time in Paris...."

"I don't care a tit if you ever eat at Les Halles. We're going home, you scheming *yenta.*"

Armstrong and I had sat next to each other in Political Science 101 at Sir George Williams College. SYSTEMS OF GOVERNMENT, the professor wrote on the blackboard,

a. monarchy   c. democracy

b. totalitarianism   d. others

Canada is a _____

Armstrong passed me a note. "A Presbyterian twat."

At Sir George, Armstrong had taken out the most desirable girls, but I could never make out. The girls I longed for longed for the basketball players or charmers like Armstrong and the only one who would tolerate me had been the sort who read Penguins on streetcars or were above using makeup. Or played the accordion at parties, singing about Joe Hill and *Los Quatro Générales*. Or demonstrated. Then, two years ago, Armstrong had tossed up everything to come to Paris and study acting. Now he no longer put up with girls and had become an unstoppable young executive in a major advertising company. "I would only have made a mediocre actor," he was fond of saying to me as I sat amidst my rejection slips.

Once more I was able to wrangle money from home, three hundred dollars and this time I ventured south for the summer, to Haut-de-Cagnes. Here I first encountered American and British expatriates of the twenties, shadowy remittance men, coupon-clippers, who painted a bit, sculpted some, and wrote from time to time. An instructive but shattering look, I feared, at my future prospects. Above all, the expatriates drank prodigiously. Twenties flotsam, whose languid, self-indulgent, bickering, party-crammed life in the Alpes-Maritimes had been disrupted only by World War II.

Bit players of bygone age, they persisted in continuing as if it were still burgeoning, supplying the *Nice-Matin*, for instance, with guest lists of their lawn parties; and carrying on as if Cyril Connelly's first novel, *The Rockpool*, were a present scandal. "He was only here for three weeks altogether, don't you know," a colonel told me.

"I'm only *very* thinly disguised in it," a lady said haughtily.

Extremely early one morning I rolled out of bed in response to a knock on the door. It was Mr. Soon.

"I have just seen the sun coming up over the Mediterranean," he said.

In spite of the heat, Mr. Soon wore a crushed greasy raincoat. Terry Southern, if I remember correctly, had given it to him. He had also thoughtfully provided him with my address. "Won't you come in?" I asked.

"Not yet. I am going to walk on the Promenade des Anglais."

"You might as well leave your coat here, then."

"But it would be inelegant to walk on the Promenade in Nice without a coat, don't you think?"

Mr. Soon returned late in the afternoon and I took him to Jimmy's Bar, on the brim of the steep grey hill of Haut-de-Cagnes.

"It reminds me most of California here," Mr. Soon said.

"But I had no idea you had ever been to California."

"No. Never. Have you?"

I watched, indeed, soon everyone on the terrace turned to stare, as Mr. Soon, his beard a filthy tangle, reached absently into his pocket for a magnifying glass, held it to the sun, and lit a Gauloise. Mr. Soon, who spoke several languages, including Chinese, imperfectly, was evasive whenever we asked him where he had been born in this his twenty-third reincarnation. We put him down for Russian, but when I brought him along to Marushka's she insisted that he spoke the language ineptly.

Marushka, now in her sixties, had lived in Cagnes for years. Modigliani had written a sonnet to her and she could recall the night Isadora had danced in the square. Marushka was not impressed by Mr. Soon. "He's a German," she said, as if it was quite the nastiest thing she could think of.

I took Mr. Soon home with me and made up a bed for him on the floor, only to be awakened at 2 A.M. because all the lights had been turned on. Mr. Soon sat at my table, writing, with one of my books, *The Guide For The Perplexed*, by his side. "I am copying out the table of contents," he said.

"But what on earth for?"

"It is a very interesting table of contents, don't you think?"

A week later Mr. Soon was still with me. One afternoon he caught me hunting mosquitoes with a rolled newspaper and subjected me to a long, melancholy lecture on the holy nature of all living things. Infuriated, I said, "Maybe *I* was a mosquito in a previous incarnation, eh?"

"No. You were a Persian Prince."

"What makes you say that?" I asked, immensely pleased.

"Let us go to Jimmy's. It is so interesting to sit there and contemplate, don't you think?"

I was driven to writing myself a letter and opening it while Mr. Soon and I sat at the breakfast table. "Some friends of mine are coming down from Paris the day after tomorrow. I'd quite forgotten I had invited them to stay with me."

"Very interesting. How long will they be staying?"

"There's no saying."

"I can stay at the Tarzan Camping and return when they are gone."

We began to sell things. Typewriters, books, wristwatches. When we all seemed to have reached bottom, when our credit was no longer good anywhere, something turned up. An ex-GI, Seymour, who ran a tourist office in Nice called SEE-MOR TOURS, became casting director for extra parts in films and we all got jobs for ten dollars a day.

Once more, Armstrong tolerated me in his Paris flat. One night, in the Montana, Armstrong introduced me to an elegant group of people at his table, including the Countess Louise. The next morning he informed me, "Louise, um, thinks you're cute, boychick. She's just dumped Jacques and she's looking for another banana."

Armstrong went on to explain that if I were satisfactory I would have a studio in Louise's flat and an allowance of one hundred thousand francs monthly.

"And what do I have to do to earn all that?"

"Oy vey. There's nothing like a Jewish childhood. Don't be so provincial."

Louise was a thin wizened lady in her forties. Glittering earrings dripped from her ears and icy rings swelled on the fingers of either hand. "It would only be once a week," Armstrong said. "She'd take you to first nights at the opera and all the best restaurants. Wouldn't you like that?"

"Go to hell."

"You're invited to her place for drinks on Thursday. I'd better buy you some clothes first."

On Thursday I sat in the sun at the Mabillon consuming beer after beer before I risked the trip to the Countess's flat. I hadn't felt as jumpy or been so thoroughly bright and scrubbed from the skin out since my bar mitzvah. A butler took my coat. The hall walls were painted scarlet and embedded with precious stones. I was led into the drawing-room where a nude study of a younger Louise, who had used to be a patroness of surrealists, hung in a lighted alcove. Spiders and bugs fed on the Countess's ash-grey bosom. I heard laughter and voices from another room. Finally a light-footed American in a black antelope jacket drifted into the drawing-room. "Louise is receiving in the bedroom," he said.

Possibly, I thought, I'm one of many candidates. I stalked anxiously round an aviary of stuffed tropical fowl. Leaning against the mantelpiece, I knocked over an antique gun.

"Oh, dear." The young American retrieved it gently. "This," he said, "is the gun Verlaine used in his duel with Rimbaud."

At last Louise was washed into the room on a froth of beautiful boys and girls. She took my hand and pressed it. "Well, hullo," I said.

We sped off in two black Jaguars to a private party for Cocteau. All the bright young people, except me, had some accomplishment behind them. They chatted breezily about their publishers and producers and agents. Eventually one of them turned to me, offering a smile. "You're Louise's little Canadian, aren't you?"

"That's the ticket."

Louise asked me about Montreal.

"After Paris," I said, swaying drunkenly, "it's the world's largest French-speaking city."

The American in the black antelope jacket joined me at the bar, clapping me on the shoulder. "Louise will be very good to you," he said.

Azoi.

"We all adore her."

Suddenly Louise was with us. "But you must meet Cocteau," she said.

I was directed to a queue awaiting presentation. Cocteau wore a suede windbreaker. The three young men ahead of me, one of them a sailor, kissed him on both cheeks as they were introduced. Feeling foolish, I offered him my hand and then returned to the bar and had another whisky, and yet another, before I noticed that all my group, including my Countess, had gone, leaving me behind.

Armstrong was not pleased with me, but then he was a troubled man. His secretary, a randy little bit from Guildford, an ex-India Army man's daughter, was eager for him, and Armstrong, intimidated, had gone so far as to fondle her breasts at the office. "If I don't screw the bitch," he said to me, "she'll say I'm queer. Oy, my poor *tuchus.*"

Armstrong's day-to-day existence was fraught with horrors. Obese, he remained a compulsive eater. Terrified of blackmailers and police *provocateurs*, he was still driven to cruising Piccadilly and Leicester Square on trips to London. Every day he met with accountants and salesmen, pinched men in shiny office suits who delighted in vicious jokes about queers, and Armstrong felt compelled to prove himself the most ferocious queer-baiter of them all.

"Maybe I should marry Betty. She wants to. Well, boychick?"

In the bathroom, I looked up to see black net bikini underwear dripping from a line over the tub. Armstrong pounded on the door. "We could have kids," he said.

The medicine cabinet was laden with deodorants and sweetening sprays and rolls of absorbent cotton and Vaseline jars.

"I'm capable, you know."

A few nights later Armstrong brought a British boy home. A painter, a taschist. "Oy, Mottel," he said, easing me out of the flat. "*Gevalt*, old chap."

The next morning I stumbled into the bathroom, coming sharply awake when I saw a red rose floating in the toilet bowl.

21

After Armstrong had left for work, the painter, a tall fastidious boy with flaxen hair, joined me at the breakfast table. He misunderstood my frostiness. "I wouldn't be staying here," he assured me, "but Richard said your relationship is platonic."

I looked up indignantly from my newspaper, briefly startled, then smiled and said, "Well, you see I could never take him home and introduce him to my family. He's not Jewish."

Two weeks later my father sent me enough money for a ticket home and, regretfully, I went to the steamship office at l'Opéra. An advertisement in the window read:

"liked Lisbon, loved Tahiti. But when it comes to
getting the feel of the sea ..."
give me the crashing waves and rugged rocks
give me the gulls and nets and men and boats
give me the harbours and homes and spires and quays
GIVE ME NEW BRUNSWICK
CANADA

I had been away two years.

Memoirs of Montparnasse

JOHN GLASSCO

When the young Mordecai Richler posed as a Paris bohemian, he was of course following in the almost mandatory footsteps of the expatriate writers of the 1920s, the sort chronicled in *Memoirs of Montparnasse* by John Glassco, of which the following (an account of an evening at Gertrude Stein's) is a taste. "Buffy" Glassco (1909–81) was a poet, translator, and pornographer. *Memoirs of Montparnasse*, when it appeared in 1970, might be said to have begun the present vogue for Canadian literary memoirs: *literary* in the sense of being about the world of books and writers but also in the sense of employing fictional techniques. That Glassco was actually writing, or at least talking about writing, a book-length memoir while living in Paris in 1928 is supported by a reference in Morley Callaghan's satiric short story "Now That April's Here," in which Glassco is fictionalized as a character named John and his friend Graeme Taylor as one called Charles. John, Callaghan writes, "had been writing his memoirs of their adventures since they were fifteen, after reading George Moore's *Confessions of a Young Man*.... Johnny's memoirs, written in a snobbishly sensationalistic manner, had been brought up to the present and now he was waiting for something [else] to happen to them." But literary historians later proved that most of the handwritten manuscript of the *Memoirs*, as preserved in the Glassco papers at the National Archives in Ottawa, was in fact composed in the 1960s. This fact may rob the book of some of its preciosity but not of its charm.

"Today we're meeting the white hope of North American literature," said Bob next morning. "His name is Callaghan, and he's just come to town with a pisspot full of money from a book called *Strange Fugitive*. Have you read it?"

"No," said Graeme. "But I know his stories in *The New Yorker*. Very fine and sophisticated. Just like Hemingway's, only plaintive and more moral."

"Well, Fitzgerald says he's good, so he's probably lousy. Anyway he has a lot of dough, so we might get a dinner out of him. He's Canadian too. What do you think he's like?"

"Well," said Graeme, "I see him as tall, thin, blond, cynical, in a pinstriped suit. It's the way he writes anyway."

"Rats," said Bob, "that doesn't scare me. I know these sophisticated *New Yorker* types. They're just a bunch of *arrivistes*."

However, he shaved carefully, running the razor up to his eyes, shined his shoes with his socks, and put on a new polka-dot bow tie before going to meet Callaghan at the hotel room he was still keeping on the rue de Vaugirard.

"Join us in the Coupole Bar around four," he said. "I'll have him softened up by then. *Sophisticated*, what the hell! I've handled John Barrymore in my day. But look, for God's sake, both of you get your hair cut."

Graeme and I went to a barbershop and then idled around the quarter until four o'clock. We looked into the Coupole, the Dôme, the Select, and the Rotonde without seeing Bob; by five o'clock we had also done the Dingo, the College Inn, and the Falstaff, still without success. Coming from the Falstaff we saw Bob sitting with a couple at the little *tabac* on the corner. He hailed us and we sat down.

Morley Callaghan was short, dark, and roly-poly, and wore a striped shirt without a collar; with his moon face and little moustache he looked very like Hemingway; he had even the same shrewd little politician's eyes, the same lopsided grin and ingratiating voice. His wife was also short and thickset, and wore a coral dress and a string of beads. Both of them were so friendly and unpretentious that I liked them at once. It was like meeting people from a small town. We apologized for not finding them sooner, saying we had looked in the Coupole.

"I didn't like that Coupole, it's too much of a clip joint," said Callaghan. "The drinks here are just as good, and a lot cheaper. Eh, Loretto?"

"Yes, about 15 per cent less, Morley. And you have just the same view here. My, this is a lovely city, but the French are right after you for all they can get. You find that, Mr. Taylor?"

"Yes," said Graeme. "You get used to it."

"Like hell we will," said Morley. "Right now we're looking for an apartment. The hotel we're at charges like the dickens." Suddenly changing the subject, he asked, "Say, how do you get to meet James Joyce? McAlmon, you know him, I'm told."

"You're damn right I do," said Bob. "But what do you want to do in Paris, go around like a literary rubberneck meeting great men? I'm a great man too, for God's sake. And here I am. Ask me your questions. I'll even give you my autograph."

"You're a good writer," said Morley, all his strength of character appearing, "but you're not Joyce—not yet. What the hell," he went on, "this guy Joyce is great. *Ulysses* is the greatest novel of the century. I wouldn't compare myself to him. Why should you?"

"Oh," said Bob, "now you're getting modest. Well, you can't fool me. You think you're one hell of a writer, why don't you admit it? Why do you give me all this crap about Joyce? You're more important to yourself. If you think so much of Joyce, why don't you write like him instead of your constipated idol Hemingway? Lean, crisp, constipated, dead-pan prose. The fake naïve."

"Now, McAlmon, let's go into this properly. First thing, I don't write like Joyce for the simple reason that I can't, it's not my line. But I can admire him, can't I?"

"No, you can't. You can't admire Joyce and write like Hemingway. If you do, you're a whore."

Morley reddened. "You're a funny guy. I don't know if you're talking seriously, but let me tell you I write as well as I can, and though you may not like my stuff ..."

"I've never read your stuff. I don't read *The New Yorker*."

"Well then what in heck are you talking about? Perhaps you haven't read Joyce either."

"Right! I haven't read Joyce or Hemingway. I don't have to, I know them— and I know you too, Morley, and I like you. Especially when you get mad. I know you're a good writer. The test of a good writer is when he gets mad."

"Are you boys all through arguing?" said Loretto. "Shall we all go and have supper somewhere?"

"Sure, but none of these clip joints. McAlmon, where's a good cheap restaurant? Fitzgerald told me you know Paris inside out."

"My generation doesn't eat supper," said Bob. "I'm having another drink. Waiter, five whiskies and water!"

The conversation continued in the same way. Bob was unreasonable and outrageously rude; Morley remained patient and serious. At last things became boring and I let my attention wander.

A little old man in rags came by, holding up a sheaf of pink papers. "Guide des poules de Paris!" he cried in a shrill quavering voice. "All the girls in Paris, only ten francs! The names, the addresses!" He broke into a tittering singsong, smacking his lips. "Ah, les jolies pou-poules, fi-filles de joie de Paris! Achetez, achetez le Guide Rose! Toutes les jolies petites pou-poules de Paris! Dix francs, dix francs!"

Two Americans sitting nearby began to laugh. The little man pounced on them, fluttering his pink sheets.

"All the girls in Paris for only ten francs," one of them said. "It's a bargain." He held out a blue ten-franc bill, the little man seized it, peeled off one of the pink sheets and ran away. The two men bent over the *Guide Rose* for several minutes. "Say, this is the real thing. Listen: 'Pierrette gives aesthetic massage.' 'Chez Suzy, everything a man wants.' 'Visit Mademoiselle Floggi, in her Negro hut: specialities—'"

"Boy, where do these girls hang out?"

"Here are all the phone numbers—"

"Man, these are just numbers—they don't give the exchange ..."

They both studied the sheet carefully, then one of them pointed to the foot of it in disgust. "No wonder there's no exchange! Look, this goddamn thing was printed in 1910."

"Well for Christ's sake. The little bastard!"

Loretto Callaghan was shaking her head at me. "Now isn't that just like the French," she said. "Always cheating!"

"Well, there goes your sophisticated *New Yorker* type," said Bob when Morley and Loretto had left in search of a cheap restaurant.

"They're both very nice," said Graeme. "He's got brains and determination and a devoted wife. He'll go far."

"Rats, he's just a dumb cluck, an urban hick, a sentimental Catholic. All he's got is a little-boy quality."

"I'll bet he works like a dog," I said. "I wish I could."

"Don't you ever work like he does, kid! Hard work never got anyone anywhere. A real writer just keeps on putting the words down! He gets the emotion *straight*, the scene, the quality of life—the way I do. Nuts to all that literary business."

I thought of the inchoate maunderings of *The Politics of Existence* and said nothing. I was thinking that if Bob would only condescend to work, his books would be very fine. I see now, of course, that if he had done so they would be still worse than they were.

"All this literary talk is boring," said Graeme. "It's almost as bad as the chatter of poets—they're all so earnest, smelling trends, clawing or kissing each other—"

"Keep your skirts clean," said Bob. "That's all a writer has to do.—Hello, Caridad, sit down and have a drink."

"Yes, I will. Graeme, my dear pussycat, you look very serious. You all do!

You must stop it at once. And you must all come to a nice party tonight with me—a real party of poets and painters and writers."

"Not me," said Bob. "I know those lousy parties."

"Oh but this is a very distinguished party—and very, very wealthy. Our hostess will be the great American lady writer, Miss Gertrude Stein."

"That old ham! You three go there and lap up the literary vomit. Not me."

"Let us have dinner first anyway," said Caridad. "You will have to pay for mine because I haven't any money. But please, Bob, let us not have one of those awful ducks at the Coupole. We'll go to a nice cheap place like Salto's where I can eat a lot of spaghetti."

We went around the corner to Salto's, just above the Falstaff, famous for the size of its portions and its coarse red wine. Here the food was good; there was always a minestrone that was a meal in itself and a wonderful *gâteau maison* made of some kind of yellow cake filled with raisins and drenched with Marsala. Caridad ate her way through a plate of anchovies, a bowl of minestrone, a mound of spaghetti, an osso buco, and the *gâteau*, chattering all the time; Bob toyed with a veal cutlet; Graeme and I had a fine spicy rabbit stew made with green peppers, celery, and lima beans. We went to the Dôme for coffee.

27

"Now," said Caridad, pouring a ten-cent rum into her coffee, "we shall go soon to Miss Gertrude Stein's and absorb an international culture. Her parties are very well-behaved and there are always plenty of rich men—which I find very agreeable. A girl must live. Bob, you must show yourself there—you, celebrated man of letters, publisher, man of the world. It will also make my own entrance so much more impressive—with three cavaliers. Come, it is only a few streets away—"

"Rats, I know the place. I've been to her parties. Never again. Gertrude paid me to publish her lousy five-pound book and we've never been the same since. She thinks I held back some of the proceeds. No, you three run along."

Although neither Graeme nor I cared for Gertrude Stein's work, we really wanted to see the great woman. I was thinking too of how I would write my father about meeting her, and that (once he had checked her credentials with the English department at McGill) he might just raise my allowance. The business of living on fifty dollars a month was becoming almost impossible: we were always short of money, we were never able to eat or drink enough, and while Bob was often generous it was apparent his own resources were running low and he would soon have to make another requisition on his father-in-law. As foreigners we could take no regular work, and while Graeme's skill with the poker dice seldom failed, it often took him over an hour to win 100 francs and obliged him to endure as well the conversation of the dreariest types of American barfly; the worst of it was that he had to spend almost a quarter of his winnings drinking with them during his operations.

Accordingly we set off with Caridad down the boulevard Raspail in the plumblue light of the June evening, arrived at the rue de Fleurus, and were greeted at the door by a deciduous female who seemed startled by the sight of Caridad.

"Miss Toklas!" Caridad cried affectionately. "It is so long since we have not met. I am Caridad de Plumas, you will remember, and these are my two young Canadian squires to whom I wish to give the privilege of meeting you and your famous friend. We were coming with Mr. Robert McAlmon, but he is unavoidably detained."

As she delivered this speech she floated irresistibly forward, Miss Toklas retreated, and we found ourselves in a big room already filled with soberly dressed and soft-spoken people.

The atmosphere was almost ecclesiastical and I was glad to be wearing my best dark suit, which I had put on to meet Morley Callaghan. I had begun to suspect that Caridad had not been invited to the party and all of us were in fact crashing the gate. But Caridad, whether invited or not, was in a few minutes a shining centre of the party: her charm coruscated, her big teeth flashed, her dyed hair caught the subdued light. She paid no further attention to Graeme or myself, and I understood that she was as usual looking for rich men.

The room was large and sombrely furnished, but the walls held, crushed together, a magnificent collection of paintings—Braques, Matisses, Picassos, and Picabias. I only recovered from their cumulative effect to fall under that of their owner, who was presiding like a Buddha at the far end of the room.

Gertrude Stein projected a remarkable power, possibly due to the atmosphere of adulation that surrounded her. A rhomboidal woman dressed in a floor-length gown apparently made of some kind of burlap, she gave the impression of absolute irrefragability; her ankles, almost concealed by the hieratic folds of her dress, were like the pillars of a temple: it was impossible to conceive of her lying down. Her fine close-cropped head was in the style of the late Roman Empire, but unfortunately it merged into broad peasant shoulders without the aesthetic assistance of a neck; her eyes were large and much too piercing. I had a peculiar sense of mingled attraction and repulsion towards her. She awakened in me a feeling of instinctive hostility coupled with a grudging veneration, as if she were a pagan idol in whom I was unable to believe.

Her eyes took me in, dismissed me as someone she did not know, and returned to her own little circle. With a feeling of discomfort I decided to find Graeme and disappear: this party, I knew, was not for me. But just then Narwhal came up and began talking so amusingly that I could not drag myself away.

"I have been reading the works of Jane Austen for the first time," he said in his quiet nasal voice, "and I'm looking for someone to share my enthusiasm. Now these are very good novels in my opinion. You wouldn't believe it but here— among all these writers, people who are presumably literary artists—I can't find anyone who has read her books with any real attention. In fact most of them don't seem to like her work at all. But I find this dislike is founded on a false impression that she was a respectable woman."

"Jane Austen?"

"I don't mean to say she was loose in her behaviour, or not a veuhjin. I'm sure she was a veuhjin. I mean she was aristocratic, not bourgeoise, she was no creep, she didn't really give a darn about all those conventions of chaystity and decorum."

"Well, her heroines did."

"Oh sure, they *seem* to, they've got to, or else there'd be no story. But Austen didn't herself. Who is the heroine, the Ur-heroine of *Sense and Sensibility*? It's Marianne, not Elinor. Of *Pride and Prejudice*? It's the girl that runs off with the military man. What's wrong with *Emma*? Emma."

"You mean Willoughby and Wickham are her real heroes?"

"No, they're just stooges, see? But they represent the dark life-principle of action and virility that Austen really admired, like Marianne and Lydia stand for the life force of female letting-go. And when Anne Elliott falls for Captain Wentworth—you'll notice he's the third W of the lot—it's the same thing, only this time he's tamed. It's a new conception of Austen's talent which I formed yesterday, and which was suggested to me by the fact that Prince Lucifer is the real hero of *Paradise Lost*, as all the savants declare."

This idea of Jane Austen as a kind of early D.H. Lawrence was new. Never had the value of her books been so confirmed as by this extraordinary interpretation of them: it was a real tribute.

"Do you happen to know if there were any portraits of Austen made?" he asked.

"A watercolour by a cousin, I think."

"Good! I guess it's lousy then," he said with satisfaction. "Because I've been thinking of doing an imaginary portrait of her too. I see her in a wood, in a long white dress. She's looking at a mushroom. But all around her are these thick young trees growing straight up—some are black with little white collars and stand for ministers of the church and some are blue and stand for officers in the Royal English Navy. I'm also thinking of putting some minia-ture people, kind of elves dressed like witches and so forth, in the back-ground—but I'm not sure."

"It sounds good."

"The focus of the whole thing will be the mushroom," he said. "It represents the almost overnight flowering of her genius—also its circumscribed quality, its sug-gestion of being both sheltered *and* a shelter—see?—and its e-conomy of structure."

"An edible mushroom?"

"You've got it. That will be the whole mystery of the portrait. The viewer won't know and she won't know either. We will all partake of Jane Austen's doubt, faced with the appalling mystery of sex."

We must have been talking with an animation unusual for one of Gertrude Stein's parties, for several of the guests had already gathered around us.

"You are talking of Jane Austen and sex, gentlemen?" said a tweedy Englishman with a long ginger moustache. "The subjects are mutually exclusive. That dried-up lady snob lived behind lace curtains all her life. She's of no more importance than a chromo. Isn't that so, Gertrude?"

I was suddenly aware that our hostess had advanced and was looking at me with her piercing eyes.

"Do I know you?" she said. "No. I suppose you are just one of those silly young men who admire Jane Austen."

Narwhal had quietly disappeared and I was faced by Miss Stein, the tweedy man, and Miss Toklas. Already uncomfortable at being an uninvited guest, I found the calculated insolence of her tone intolerable and lost my temper.

"Yes, I am," I said. "And I suppose you are just one of those silly old women who don't."

The fat Buddha-like face did not move. Miss Stein merely turned, like a gun revolving on its turret, and moved imperturbably away.

The tweedy man did not follow her. Leaning towards me, his moustache bris-tling, he said quietly, "If you don't leave here this moment, I will take great pleas-ure in throwing you out, bodily."

"If you really want," I said, "I'll wait outside in the street for three minutes, when I'll be glad to pull your nose."

I then made my exit, and after standing for exactly three minutes on the side-walk (by which time I was delighted to find he did not appear), I took my way back to the Dôme. Graeme joined me there fifteen minutes later.

"That's the last party we go to without being invited," he said.

I Come with My Songs

ELSA GIDLOW

Whereas John Glassco would leave to be an expatriate, his fellow Montreal poet Elsa Gidlow (1898–1986) remained in Canada and tried hard to build a literary bohemia around herself: not an easy task, given the nature of Canadian society at the time (and the fact that Gidlow was probably Canada's first openly lesbian writer). Eventually, Gidlow forsook Montreal for Greenwich Village and San Francisco. Significantly, though, her long-term relationships appear to have been mostly with other expat Canadians, with whom she kept returning to Canada for long periods. Until the end of her long life, most information about her came second-hand. The American poet Kenneth Rexroth was a great friend, for example, and devoted a chapter to her in his book *Excerpts from a Life*. But then, just before her death, she published a memoir, *Elsa: I Come with My Songs*. The straightforwardness and simplicity of its style may derive from the fact that Gidlow dictated the work, as she was perilously ill at the time. Indeed, the publishers had to rush an early copy to her before she died, an act reminiscent of the famous "death bed" edition of Walt Whitman's *Leaves of Grass*. In addition to her memoir and her collections of verse, she published *Ask No Man's Pardon: The Philosophical Significance of Being Lesbian*.

RAILWAY EXPLORER

Observing how a railroad operated fascinated me. In 1916, it was a new achievement to link unimaginably vast Canada coast to coast. We skirted lakes like seas, climbed mountains that made me shudder with awe. We crept sightless through long tunnels smelling our engine's smoke and steam. I had expansive time in the travelling days to think of puny human accomplishments. Little was mentioned then of the exploitation of those who gave their sweat and blood to the railroad. I became aware that it was a domain of men. All men. Only men. I watched, listened to their shouts, taunts, and laughing camaraderie against the clang and grind of metals. Looking back, I realize how unique my experience was for a girl of fifteen. Given my rebellious nature, it was inevitable that my dawning feminism should be fed. I had plenty to compare the life of my mother with as we travelled.

With much pushing, pulling, grinding, our car would be set at a siding, a helpless segment cut off from the iron dragon, the head puffing, belching, whistling away as if glad to be free of the burden. I can still hear the eerie, long-drawn whistle waking me in the night, the accelerating chant of wheels on the tracks to which I sleepily made poetry. Wherever we stopped, there was the coupling and uncoupling of cars, the shock and shudder of their junction. I observed the cleaning and servicing of the monster, water fed to it from towers and coal shovelled in. Food and supplies were brought for us when we were coupled to a passenger train. Daily fresh laundry, immaculately white sheets and towels, sent my thoughts back to Mother's laborious washing.

It was novel to be served meals I had had no part in preparing. There was more than we could eat of everything, and the work was all done by the manservant, Moses. I was shocked to see how much food was wasted. I kept thinking of the excellent soups and stews, potted meats, and meat loaves that Mother would have made from the meat and vegetables that went into the garbage cans. Father had grown used to it and was not troubled. When I spoke of it, he explained that his work associates or visitors might come aboard for a meal. Moses had to order enough to be prepared.

The land itself was almost too much to absorb. Hitched behind a freight, one had the full impact travelling slowly enough for its detail and magnitude to be grasped. How vast was the pure water of the Great Lakes! The pairs of rails converged on infinity over the hypnotic monotony of the prairies. A distant forest fire at night blazed a backdrop for stark trees. Changing sky and weather! Near Calgary an electric storm split the universe asunder, illuminating it with infernal fires while we were stopped at a siding. I was very conscious of being encased in and surrounded by conductive metal.

The magnificence of the Rockies made beauty a weak word. As we crept with two engines over steep passes, I knew that avalanches of snow or earth could crash down and wipe our crawling metal caterpillar off the face of the cliff in an instant. Father told me that more than one train had been buried with all its human freight beyond possibility of rescue. He dreaded the hazards, especially in winter. I could share the sense of terror. That could happen to us, now, this moment, any moment.

34

For relief from the overpowering grandeur and its menaces, I would turn to the lacy cascading falls, trying to ignore the depth of the canyons into which the waters plunged. But these had a feminine delicacy: their melting and shifting mists, pure white in the mornings. I tried not to be fully conscious of the rearing rock above that made insects and toys of humanity and its works. I felt the Earth as alive, in wait to take back what was Hers from the arrogance of men. Yet I could not help but admire some of man's attempts.

One nightfall, the groaning, whining iron serpent of freight cars at the end of which we were coupled came to a halt at a solitary depot. Water was taken on, and wheels checked for the next slow climb. I liked it when we were attached behind a freight train as the last car because we could use our observation platform. I stood there alone. The altitude, the stillness, the twilit green sky, induced a sense of exaltation not disturbed by the clang of metal on metal, a kind of music in itself, as men went the length of the train tapping each wheel for soundness. The groans and bumps of the freight's slow starting was by now too familiar to disturb the wild isolation of the scene. The engine's whistle intensified it. As did a solitary human figure in oil-stained shirt and pants standing on a flatcar on a siding beside a water tower. He was small and insignificant in the dim light against the massive mountains.

I heard a light whistle. It pierced the steady groan of the starting, stopping, backing, and restarting of the freight. The whistle had the tender quality of a bird on its first note, and I imagined it was one, listening for a repetition to identify it. A wholly different sound succeeded it. Human.

"Psst. Psst—!"

I related it to the forgotten man on the flatcar. When he saw that he had my attention, he unbuttoned his trousers, took his penis in his hand and pointed it at me, working it vigorously. I rushed inside.

Father was seated at the window of the lecture hall with a man and a young woman, Bob and Ethel, who had joined us at Winnipeg. The woman was supposed to provide some company for me. Had he, had they, seen the man? They could have if they had glanced out. But they were intent on a game of cards, talking, drinking ale. I did not look to see if the man was still there.

This was not my first experience involving exhibitionists, adults we children were supposed to respect. There had been several in early childhood: in the bush when we went berrying; in any solitary spot where one walked to be alone. Once on a haywagon, a farmer from whom we often bought apples offered me a lift home with my heavy bag of groceries. After helping to haul me up, he set the horse to trotting, and I, eleven years old, laughed, thrilled by the ride and getting home quickly to surprise Mother.

Then I noticed that with his free hand, the farmer had undone his overalls in front to expose the thing that seemed so stupid to me. Then he thrust his hairy hand under my dress. Gripping the bag of groceries, I fell away from him to the wagon's far side and started to clamber out. He yelled, stopped the horses, grabbed my dress. I tore free and rolled over the side, falling, skinning my knees and bursting the grocery bag. I had to gather up the scattered contents and carry them in my held-up skirt, limping the rest of the way home. I was afraid to look back to see if he was coming after me. To Mother's questions, controlling my shaking, I said only, "I tripped and fell." How could you tell your mother a thing like that?

The train had finished its shunting and pulled away from the depot. I sat where Father made room for me and accepted a glass of ale. He had always let us children sip a little when he was drinking. At Christmas and other festive occasions, we were allowed our own small glass of port wine. It seems to me now a good practice, removing the aura of the forbidden and undercutting the lure of curiosity. Sipping the ale, I sat silent, looking out at the snowy peaks, letting their remote grandeur replace the image of the small, silly human and his ugly act. Disgust and indignation finally merged with a sort of pity for the man.

Used to my silence, the others paid no attention after acknowledging my presence. They discussed plans for a stopover at Banff, at Emerald Lake, and an extended stay in Vancouver, later at Victoria. Father had to organize new classes, put instructors to work, give lectures to get the workmen interested. In between, an itinerary was planned to allow time for sightseeing. He wanted me to see as much as possible.

"What better education can you have than travel," he remarked, as if apologizing for my having not the kind I yearned for. "And along with the fun, you learn to be my little secretary." Mellow from the ale, he put an arm around me and rubbed my cheek with his rough one. I always drew away when he did that.

Education? More and more I was finding it an ambiguous term. What would he have thought if he had seen the man on the flatcar exhibiting his sex? Would he have been angry, ready to defend my "innocence"? But how often had I seen him sitting with his dressing gown open, legs apart, as if he, too, wanted to be seen? Why did men do this? By then I knew that tube not only spouted pee but could put seed into women that caused them to have babies, whether they wanted them or not.

I did not know how babies got out once they had grown inside their mothers. No matter how hard I thought about it, there seemed no aperture large enough for six, seven, eight pounds of infant to emerge. One morning when I was taking my sponge bath in the washroom of the jolting car, I thought I had it solved. I was carefully drying my navel. What was it for? It must have some use? It looked as though it wound inward to the interior of the abdomen where babies were carried. A flash! It must expand, somehow stretch and enlarge to let the infant out. Pleased with having thought this problem to a conclusion, I stood back from the inadequate mirror to survey my body, straight and curveless but lithe, hips narrow, small breasts just budded.

I could see I was not pretty. By Mother's standards, my mouth was too large, but well-shaped over excellent teeth. None of us had ever been to a dentist. My features were even, face oval, complexion olive. I was not pink and cream and golden like all the younger children, except Ivy who had dark hair and eyes. How had I come to be so different? My mass of shining chestnut hair down to my waist was nice. Father became angry when I said I was going to cut it as it was too much trouble to put up and be a young "lady." Most of the time, I still wore it in a heavy braid down my back tied with a piece of ribbon, occasionally in two braids coiled at my ears, or in a big coil at the back of the head. But it was so heavy and always falling loose if I was active. Not being considered pretty did not bother me. I would rather be clever.

At home there was no large mirror so I had never studied my entire body. The privacy was also lacking, with all children in the same bedroom. I craned to see my back, the rounding but still small-girl buttocks, and noticed a pair of dimples. A silly couplet came to mind and made me giggle:

> Dimple in the chin, living coming in,
> Dimple in the cheek, living to seek.

What did dimples in the buttocks portend?

I surveyed my mound of Venus; somewhere in poetry I had found that pleasant phrase. It was lightly covered with silky hair a little darker than that on my head. I looked at the lips between and spread my legs to see deeper. "It's like the inside of a flower." I touched lightly but withdrew my hand, alarmed at my excitement. Many times I had been aware of sensations arising there, but something held me back from experimenting with touch. I had never heard the word masturbate, nor had I received any warning about it. I remembered when very young, rubbing against one of my sisters lying beside me or a pillow or face down sometimes on the bed. I liked the sensation. It was pleasant and soothing, like having your hair brushed or being stroked as I stroked my cat.

This childish self-initiation into the voluptuous had subsided. But adolescence revived the waves of electric energy that flowed through my body and fired my mind. I felt like flying. In dreams, I often did fly with a sense of nourishing power and delight. It felt more like swimming through the air, around a room or over the heads of the crowd. I wonder if such dreams are prehuman memory of a time when we were all sea creatures? The dreams certainly added colour and excitement to hard, uneventful dailiness. I saw ships on jade seas, treasures of flowers in the secret woods and gardens; I visited paradise in sleep.

Leaving fantasy, I prepared to dress after a last quick survey of my body. I had a deep conviction it never would be swollen with another body growing in it. I felt big with another sort of life, inspired by the reading of Plato's *Symposium*. I had become entranced by Socrates' debate on love with the wise woman Diotima. I cherished Diotima saying that there were those who were more pregnant in their souls than in their bodies. "And they conceived what is proper for the soul to conceive ... wisdom or virtue ... and such creatures are poets and all artists who are deserving of the name inventor." I longed to meet a woman like that.

Almost late for breakfast, I quickly finished dressing. I had no creams, powders, perfumes. I had never used any sort of cosmetics, hardly knew of them other than the rumour of their use by "fast" women. When our hands cracked from the cold and chilblains in winter, Mother rubbed them with Vaseline. I kept fingernails trimmed with a scissors, but hated to have them too short because the tips were intolerably sensitive.

Between breakfast and lunch each day, I usually attended to whatever work Father needed done, mainly answering or writing letters, copying lecture notes or occasionally an article he had written about his work for the newspapers. There were long hours while we travelled when I was free to read, to write in my diary, work on poems, and to think. When we stopped somewhere and did not sightsee in Father's free time, I wandered by myself in towns, cities, about the depots where the railroad men might be brought together for instruction. Home was not missed, but often I found myself thinking of Mother, tied down, always working, with no respite or recreation.

What if Mother had realized her dream to become a singer as I expected to realize my dreams? What if she had not married, not had children, or married someone else? *In that case there would have been no me.* It was shocking and painful to face the fact, as I wrote in my diary: *Mother's not realizing her dreams, her hopes, means that I am here. If she had done what she wanted, I would not be.* What then would have become of the essence, the elements, whatever it was, that now constituted "Elsa"? Would a potential something have remained unborn as potential children of mine would remain unborn? I tried to think that through: myself, them, unborn. I felt ready to burst; my head ached, and I hurt all over. Had the essence, the elements that were to comprise "Elsa" been waiting somewhere out there? Were they determined to be embodied, compelling my parents to come together and give me flesh? Was all that converged to the unique event of me sheer accident? Or part of a total obscure design? Is it a will to self-validation that I have always had the conviction that "I" wanted to be born? Before I had any real knowledge of Eastern philosophy, which later was to play a large part in my life and provide a more credible world view than Christianity, there was the haunting sense of some unbodied Consciousness "choosing" to enter the bit of protoplasm that became me. But who, what was that "*me*"? That ego? It was decades later that I contemplated the Zen koan, "Before your Mother and your Father, who were you?" Today at eighty-six, I ask: Before the flaming amaryllis in the garden burst from the dormant bulb and bare stalk, where was its colour, its perfume? I have found no answer. My answers now, as then, are mainly more questions.

39

Did Mother mind her role in my design? It seemed dreadful that I did not know. Beyond any doubt, I did know that I would find my Mother's life intolerable. Was Mother living it so that I, Elsa, would see and be warned to shape my life differently? Was Mother unhappy? Again it was painful that I did not know. Usually she appeared cheerful, making the best of what she could not alter, singing over her work. How often she said, "You children will have it better." She appeared to believe it. Was that belief, or hope, enough to justify to her her own life, its deficiencies, and absence of pleasures? Or were there satisfactions I could not guess?

And Father? Parenthood sat lightly on him, except for some economics of the responsibility. His contact with us was limited. When he was not travelling, he insisted that the younger children have their supper and be in bed before he got home from the office. They were glad when he was "on the road" since they had more freedom. I shared that feeling, although I was treated as a sort of assistant parent. When he was away, we were spared the parental quarrels. Mother sang more. We were all on her side in domestic conflicts.

I did not know why Father favoured me. I never catered to him, always evaded his hugs and kisses smelling of beer or whisky and strong cheese. I defended Mother and the younger children when his wrath exploded against them. People said I "took after him." He liked that, admiring my independence of spirit for which he took credit. It is true that in an English family the first-born is privileged. The first-born girl of the royal line has the right to reign as monarch despite the subsequent birth of boys. Such traditions can affect individuals even of humble estate. I was being fully aware of my status as the eldest. I gave Father credit for his vision, energy, and ambition with a sort of detachment that did not include daughterly tenderness.

There were times when I felt hatred for his treatment of Mother and his absence of feeling for the children other than myself. He was happiest living away from us like a bachelor. The obligations of our economic support were dutifully fulfilled, but without depriving himself. True, the "burden" of a wife and seven children is no light load. Perhaps, "it just happened" to him as well as to Mother. But I was beginning to grasp the overwhelming odds against women exercising power over their lives, and I did not feel compassion for him as I did for her. Why was he letting me see his life? Could it be to inspire me to "better" myself in my turn? Or to boast to me? Possibly both.

He took me to the company's grand hotels, where he had expense accounts, when we stopped in one of the cities on his itinerary. Periodically our car was laid up in the yards for cleaning and servicing. We had our meals in the imposing hotel dining rooms of elegantly set tables, spotless napery, sparkling glasses, more sorts of cutlery than I had ever seen. Father would guide me if I took up the wrong fork. Some of the obsequious waiters knew him. I observed that he left them large tips, more money than I had for my entire monthly allowance.

Once or twice we stayed in a hotel overnight. I had a luxurious room and bathroom to myself. My first real bathtub since we left England! I luxuriated in the hot running water. What a contrast to bathing in the wooden wash tub in the kitchen. But the sumptuous, padded hotels made me feel suffocated, alien. The expensively dressed people idling about did not look real. My interest in the novelty soon was replaced by a sort of distaste.

After one such excursion, I asked Father if he shouldn't give Mother more money to make things easier for her and the children. It was not easy to raise the question. He took unkindly to implied criticism from his family. What he did was right and not to be questioned. After a startled glance, he said he did not have more to give her.

"But don't they pay you more now that you do all this ... important work?"

"Not much. They figure it's enough with the private car and an expense account. And the kudos, I suppose." After a silence, dark of face, he added. "She has all she needs. If I had more to give, she'd waste it."

I could not let that pass. I flared into indignation. "You know that is not true! Mother is extremely careful with money. She has to be; there is never enough. She should have things to help her in her work. She does all the washing for everybody without even a wringer. Have you ever looked at what it does to her beautiful hands?"

A case of champagne appeared on board the car the next morning, later the same day a case of Scotch and one of White Rock mineral water. When an opportunity presented itself, I inquired quietly where it all had come from. "Gifts from our guests." Possibly recollecting our earlier conversation, he added, "I did not spend money on it."

It struck me that my Father was getting fat from drinking and eating too well; he didn't exercise. I was almost his height, five feet five. Once his body had been lean as mine. I had thought him rather good-looking with his shortcut black hair and lively, cheerful blue eyes. His general appearance was one of good nature. He had a pleasant mouth and strong chin and wore a short moustache, greying slightly like the hair at his temples. The expanding middle body and fleshier face did not trouble him; jocular remarks gave one the impression he thought it made him look successful! It wasn't a success I envied. But I knew I must go deeper, further, know myself before presuming to put bandages on others faults or ills. I must explore that "pregnancy of the soul" of which Diotima had instructed Socrates. I must find my kind of people. Who were they? Where were they? It was no use trying to explain any of this to Father. I could not tell him that I found most of his associates without imagination, dull, and superficial. He would be insulted, as if I thought the same of him. He seemed satisfied with them as "good fellows," jolly drinking companions, their women pretty and cheerful, like the young woman Ethel he thought would be a companion for me.

She was eighteen, wore stylish clothes, was sociable with everyone. She spent much time in the washroom doing her face and training curls over each cheek with egg white. She appeared content to play cards (solitaire if there was no one for a game), watch the scenery as we travelled, and make up the fourth member of our party. Bob, a salesman with a company that supplied first-aid materials for Dad's work, was large, hearty, and outgoing. I learned that he had placed the champagne and Scotch on board.

41

A dictionary, Coleridge's collected works, and the plays of Shakespeare were the only books I had with me. I read and reread them. There were no books on board except Father's first-aid and other reference books. I read them too, as well as magazines and newspapers brought in by visitors. One day a number of pamphlets appeared near the stack of first-aid manuals. One was *The Menace of White Slavery*. Another, *Coffin Nails*, spelled out the horrors of cigarette smoking. Two others dealt with *Social Diseases* of which I'd never heard. These tracts detailed the consequences of leading an evil life, with warnings against frequenting prostitutes, whom one gathered were the main source of the infections. But how had *they* become diseased? There were also cautions against public toilet seats. It seemed that life's needs and temptations all had red "Danger" flags attached to them. I wanted to know more specific information. Who to ask? Ethel? She'd be shocked.

Not Father. It struck me he might have left those pamphlets for me to pick up because he could not bring himself to speak of such things to me. I'd have to wait until we got back and I could explore in the library.

How hungry I was for people, even one person, with whom I might frankly raise the questions that continually presented themselves to my ignorance. In my young arrogance, the adults who were Father's associates seemed "impossible" to me, yet I still observed each new one intently. Seated silent at a meal or with a book held as a shield, I watched and listened. Is anyone *real* there? Behind the talk I tried to read their lives in eyes, gestures, tones of voice. I looked for aliveness, joy, signs of knowledge beyond the superficial and beyond mine. Occasionally, I would inject a remark, either because I could not contain my disagreement or to see if controversy might be provoked.

Once I tossed some sparks into a discussion of the young men dying in the terrible war in Europe. Nearly all the middle-aged friends of Father's had sons there. They were proud to have sons fighting the wicked Germans. Flushing, I burst out, "The Germans are just like us." Didn't I have two German grandparents? What about the British Royal family?

"Eh?" A startled silence.

"People shouldn't kill one another. It's *wrong*."

"You'd let the Kaiser overrun Europe? Next thing, the Huns would be in Canada, Elsa."

"And what about honour, my girl?"

"We're not fighting for honour. Killing isn't honourable." My heart was beating harder with the effort of overcoming self-consciousness.

"What do you think we are fighting for?" from Bob.

"So the Germans won't take away Britain's markets." I had heard Mother and Father say something of the sort and also come across such a suggestion in my newspaper reading. It made more sense than honour.

Bob and Ethel looked to Father. "Do you give her ideas like that?"

"Elsa thinks for herself." He thought that too; why didn't he say so?

A small, blond man who was one of Father's instructors asked me where I went to college.

Before I could decide what to reply to such an absurd question, Dad spoke jocularly, "Here. I'm teaching her my work."

"Lucky young lady," from the blond man.

"You couldn't learn anything more useful," the man's wife approved. "I'm having Archie teach me. It will stand you in good stead when you are married and have a family."

"I'm not going to get married."

They all stared at me as at a strange species. Bob sighed. "That's what comes of educating girls, burying themselves in books instead of looking after babies." My impulse was to reply that I already knew too much about looking after babies. Why bother arguing with such hidebound men? He had already turned to Ethel who was patting her egg-stiff curls, flirting to bring attention to herself. She murmured sweetly, "A woman's place is in the home." The social atmosphere was restored. Smiles turned to laughter and scornful exclamations when the instructor's wife mentioned "those dreadful women, the Pankhursts and their kind, chaining themselves to lampposts and breaking windows, attacking bobbies, *demanding* the vote." I found it hard and painful that a woman took this attitude.

I was ready to burst out. "They are right. They are wonderful, courageous women; we must have the right to vote." Father's uneasy attention stayed me. I did not wish to embarrass him. Holding myself silent, I felt a small, hot core of anger. The distance between me and the human beings seated opposite widened and grew chilly. It seemed an unbridgeable space then, that painful sense of aloneness, of belonging nowhere....

LES MOUCHES FANTASTIQUES

Absorbing in my scant leisure what was available in the city of affordable concerts, plays, the few art galleries, I soon began to realize that my friends were justified in their complaints that Montreal was—at that time—culturally provincial. I was excited by it at first, enjoying the beauty of Mount Royal or wandering about the streets full of life, diverse and sometimes clashing mixes of peoples (British Canadian and Canadienne Francais). There was a gaiety I did not then appreciate; it struck me when I visited later after living in New York City.

The physical city itself was a contrast to the laughter and talk on doorsteps in the humid summer nights or music from open windows. Sombre and solid with high-walled convents and omnipresent churches, the banks and massive public buildings were built of handsome grey sandstone quarried from its own Mount Royal. It spoke to me of the power of a commerce confidently male and a religion inimical to my being. Lacking standards of comparison, I did not realize that the city was magnificently planned and built for its founders' ambitions and needs.

It was even then a mercantile metropolis, seat of banking and trade. A land and waterways transportation hub, Montreal was Canada's gateway to the world via the vast St. Lawrence River and tributary waters. The early men, their sights narrowed to commerce, trade, expanding industry, had not considered the higher needs for educational facilities beyond the (separate) Catholic and Protestant schools for the young. The merchant-dominated provincial government of Quebec had provided no funds for a university. The subsequently famous faculties of McGill University, its handsome campus and library, grew out of the vision and endowments of private individuals.

Those same early men apparently did not feel that literary, musical, and dramatic arts were of primary importance. Claiming, conquering, "developing" the new continent came first. Any urges to philosophy or the spiritual were satisfied by the dominant Catholic religion whose hierarchy benefited from the blessing given by trade.

Samuel Butler, a bitter commentator on Victorian hypocrisies, was reported to have summed up his view of its cultural limitations in the exclamation, "Oh God, Oh Montreal." We intolerant young rebels looked to France, to London. Canada seemed not to take root in me; it never became "my country" despite my formative years there. This was partly due to climate, to which neither my body nor my spirit ever accommodated. I am not physically or temperamentally a northerner.

In some ways, the overwhelming maleness of Canadian society was most oppressive. In heavily churched Quebec, patriarchy was the warp and woof of daily existence. Would there ever be one of my own sex to whom I might turn in love or for the comradeship Roswell and his male friends enjoyed? Had it all been buried for women in the Island of Lesbos? Whatever my feelings, voiced mainly in poetry, I schooled myself to endure and make the best of what was possible. I had a natural gaiety of spirit. One lived with what one had until better could be won.

Before long I had to realize that while beauty's shrine was safe in my own heart, I separated myself from the rest of humanity at the peril of my integrity. Without the support, the genuine friendship, of intermediate and other noncon-forming men, I should have been isolated indeed. Looking back on those associa-tions they seem to me to represent a happier, more healthy situation in some ways than prevails today, when the polarization between lesbians and gay men often generates distrust and competitiveness.

As a woman struggling to hold my own in the society at large, I had every evidence that my opportunities, my potential recognition and rewards for equal contributions, were not equal. But in those personal relations with chosen male companions, I felt myself to be an equal. There was no evidence that they ever regarded me otherwise. Was it the non-discriminating camaraderie and solidarity of those who knew they were outside of the mainstream society? I did constantly wonder if there was or could ever be a community of women such as appeared to exist to some extent for men, perhaps in Europe, most promisingly Paris. There we heard that people like us were simply taken for granted. In Germany and in England too, we were eventually to realize the climate for variants was better.

The somewhat rarefied lesbian coteries overseas remained hidden from me. Even if I had known of the salons, the literary and artistic circles of women in Paris, London, Berlin, in my economic circumstances, dependent on working continuously at a subsistence job, I should not have had access to them. Although we "bohemians" were not "class-conscious" in today's terms, I was well aware of my "working-class" state economically. On another level, I felt that as artists we transcended "class."

Closer to home, what of Mother, my sisters? Ought I to be staying home try-ing to make life easier for them? Remember, in that second decade of this cen-tury, it was hardly questioned that daughters stayed with the family to be help and solace. Even after we became breadwinners, it was shocking for a "good girl" to be on her own. In contrast, I thought of parent birds encouraging their fledg-lings to leave the nest when it is time for them to fly. The mother feline pushes her kittens out after teaching them to fend for themselves. Shouldn't humans be as sensible? Eventually I alleviated any tendency to guilt by believing I might do more for the younger family members by my example and by sharing what I learned. But sorrow for my Mother's condition was a wound in me as well as a warning.

45

These doubts and hesitations nagged against my persistent desire to have a place of my own, however modest. I would visualize a cell with a cot, a table or desk for writing, a cupboard or chest of drawers for my few essentials, a shelf for books. Life pared down to necessities appealed to me like a religion. I craved a refuge of peace and solitude where I might get to the core of myself. Such a place presented itself.

The artist Gershon Benjamin had a studio in a building not far from the college campus. He intended to move into a larger studio with a better light for painting. The McGill College Avenue place was a house whose upper floors had been converted to single rooms for students. A Scotch woman whose husband was fighting in Europe lived with her small son in one part. A tiny room was for rent for $10 a month. With beating heart and the sense of commencing another rite of passage, I put down a $2 deposit. I could not afford it immediately, having had to spend most of what I had saved in recent months on a winter overcoat, underwear, a dress or two, and other items to keep me presentable for employment.

I told no one of the deposit on the room. My immediate intention was not to entirely "leave home" but to use the room as a place of retreat, going home for meals and most of the time to sleep. Father was starting on another of his long trips, which made it easy not to tell him until it was an accomplished fact. I did not intend total independence until I had a better paying job and was twenty-one. Whether Father would try to force me back home if I left, I could not guess. I knew he had the socially sanctioned and legal right to do so. I was inwardly preparing myself, making the cutting of the family cord real. Although I did not feel that Mother would oppose me, I had not yet the heart to tell her. Then something unexpected happened to make it easier.

Full of joy, Mother told me Father had promised that as soon as the family moved into a larger flat he was going to get her the piano she had longed for these many years. Also, he had increased the household budget. He never revealed his actual financial circumstances. Each month he simply brought home the money for the regular expenses, and it was up to her to manage as best she could.

Father bought the piano. He always kept a definite promise, but he insisted on a player piano. Having heard one, he realized he too could produce music with it. When he was home, after a beer or two, Father would sit running his fingers over the keys as if he was playing the delightful sounds while the perforated rolls unwound. To all of us, it was magic to hear Wagner's "Flying Dutchman," waltzes by Strauss, "Murmurings of Spring" and "When It's Apple Blossom Time in Normandy," playing themselves, as Thea said. We giggled to see Father, looking dreamy and sentimental, pedalling to "put expression" into the mechanical productions.

In that improved atmosphere, I had the courage to tell Mother I should like to take a little room downtown where I could have quiet and solitude to write and study in my spare time. She had been proud when I showed her that *The Canadian Bookman* had published some of my poetry and an article. I was going to do occasional book reviews for them; I had just done something on William Butler Yeats.

"There's another reason I would like to have the room," I bargained, "so I won't have to spend time and carfare taking the long trip home if I'm out late. I could sleep there sometimes. There is a bathroom on the same floor as the room I have in mind. It's close to the McGill campus. I am thinking of taking their extension course in journalism in the evening. B.K. Sandwell, the editor of the *Bookman*, teaches it." She sighed but raised no verbal objection.

I never did ask Father's permission. He was travelling so much now that at first he did not realize how much I was away. He too was proud of my work getting into print. Mother colluded with me up to a point in not mentioning the room; she told me when he was expected to be around. I would show up, be present for the meal, sleep at home. Time enough, I decided, to make an issue of it when I was twenty-one and ready to strike out entirely on my own. Paris being for the present unattainable, I was beginning to dream of New York City. The custom that a daughter should remain in her father's house until he "gave her away" to enter a husband's was looking more and more anachronistic. In my journal I wrote: *I'll give myself away if there is any giving. I belong to myself. No one has any rights over me that I do not of my own will concede.*

47

In all my years since 1914, human consciousness has been steeped in blood and horror. Each new generation has believed itself worse off than any before it. But I doubt that any succeeding generations have had their lives more disrupted, their values more explosively assaulted, their career prospects more damaged, than the sensitive young adults during World War I.

We know from the histories, novels, the art, poetry, music, what it did to the young of Europe. Less is known of the effect on Canada. The war's long shadow fell on everyone; particularly the young, irrevocably changing our lives. We were pressured, virtually compelled at work to buy war bonds; the payments were deducted from our already insufficient wages. Roswell told of being insulted in public places by people who inquired why he was not in uniform "over there." Our fledgling adult consciousnesses were lit from the start by war's murderous phosphorescence. Every previous value we had absorbed became suspect. Whatever rebellion we had felt against the restraints of society or the unexamined conventions of our elders, the war's subversion of the very bases of existing order left us no stable pivot from which to establish our own orbit.

During girlhood I had been superficially and uncritically patriotic, even writing a heroic poem or two when war was first declared. But how could I continue to feel patriotism when, by mid-1918, ten million men from nearly every country of Europe, Canada, and the United States had been slaughtered? Twice that number were maimed—physically or emotionally—all "to make the world safe for democracy." In the process of saving democracy, democracy was being destroyed. This is old news now—it continues today. How many in the subsequent wars have had to try to reconcile similar contradictions? Young women and men debated and revolted during the Vietnam horror, now against the Central American one, as we did in the early part of the century.

48

Roswell would argue: "We have sacrificed those young men in this holy war against militarism, while we ourselves became militaristic. Can't people see the trap? What is gained if we become like those we call the enemy?"

I remember my bitter reflections: "If it is against the laws of God for A to kill B, why is it not against divine law for A Country and B Country to kill millions? Is it wrong for C and D—you and me—to covet and steal one another's meagre goods, but right for Nations C and D to covet and steal each other's territory, or raw materials, or markets?"

In what could we believe? To what give allegiance? Not anything as suspect as Christianity's Ten Commandments. I was not alone in my skepticism towards churches and their priests whose hypocrisies smelled of self-interest. Each side called upon "The One God" to give the victory. Was God supposed to toss a coin? Or play favourites?

The explosion of the Russian Revolution added to the bewilderment. A new Russian dictatorship must be countenanced and the "liquidation" (a disinfected new term) of individuals justified. These were supposedly necessary first steps to a sunrise of freedom and plenty for all humanity. The dragon to be slain was not militarism, but capitalism. Again the graces and amenities of life—not to mention life itself—must be sacrificed. The outcome promised little more than a change of oppressors. Couldn't betterment be achieved without holocausts?

These positions and others were debated far into the night in one another's rooms in the house on McGill College Avenue. Roswell had a room there now, as did Louis Gross and artist Regina Seiden who believed that art was the only saving grace. Towards the end of one heated evening, I exclaimed during a pause of general exhaustion: "I believe I am an anarchist." Emma Goldman had dawned on my horizon.

Her writings and brave life shone with the warm light of genuine heroism; yet I must admit that neither I nor my companions were ready to take to the streets, soapboxes, or brave jail. We were profoundly skeptical that values we could espouse would flower from "the masses." We could not see salvation in any brand of politics. Our abiding faith was in art, in the fruits of the spirit, in personal integrity and responsibility to one another. There could be no ultimate allegiance except to the voice within. Against the horrors and the chaos without, we set the frail barriers of our personal commitments and loyalties, developing a high fever in the process. With so much of society around us also running a fever, we were exceptional only in harbouring a wilder strain of the virus. I wonder now if this spiritual fever did not result in the terrible influenza epidemic of 1919.

Inspired by a group in New York who published their own newspapers and magazines and were known as the Amateur Press Association, I spoke to Roswell about doing the same. "We are not exactly amateurs," he said, "I'm paid for my work on *The Star* and am considered a pro. You have been paid for your stuff in the *Bookman* and other rags. Why not? We could bring out a mimeographed paper for the fun of it." Mrs. Reid, the poet Alfred Gordon, a new acquaintance, Harcourt Farmer, an actor who also wrote, and one or two others liked the idea. We formed a group, myself named president, and planned a publication. Roswell and I were the co-editors. Someone knew of a mimeograph machine we might use that produced somewhat smudgy-looking, glaring purple type.

My recollection is that much of the matter was also purple. We were by intention iconoclastic, mocking hypocrisies and smugness. Our first few issues were named *Coal from Hades*. Later, at Roswell's instigation, we changed the name to *Les Mouches Fantastiques* (The Fantastic Flies). About half of the material was written by Roswell and me. Besides our poetry, he contributed translations from Verlaine, articles on "the intermediate sex," and one-act plays sympathetically presenting love between young men. My poetry was obviously addressed to women. My editorials satirized what I saw as society's stupidities and injustices and the wrongness of the war. The hundred or so copies went locally to our friends and the amateur journalists ("AJ'ers") in various parts of the United States.

One day I was surprised to receive a letter from a woman in Havana, who wrote that a correspondent of hers had sent her a copy of *Les Mouches*. She was impressed by its quality, its awareness of society's wrongs, its idol-breaking, and wondered if we had seen *Pearson's Magazine*, published and edited by one Frank Harris in Manhattan. I wrote back that I had not seen it. From my correspondent I learned that *Pearson's* had been held up by U.S. Postmaster Farley on the ground that it contained "seditious" material. (The United States was now in the war.) But she would get copies to me.

I discovered that the magazine was not permitted to enter Canada, and so advised my correspondent in Havana, regretting I should be unable to see the publication. Several weeks passed and there came to me in the mail a copy of *The Ladies' Home Journal*. Folded inside was *Pearson's*. Subsequent copies safely reached me in the same way.

With excitement, I devoured each issue of *Pearson's*—there was nothing like it in Canada. I was thrilled to find views I was daring to formulate and express voiced in print by an individual of literary eminence. We learned that Harris had been a famous and controversial editor in London, a literary figure noted for his *Portraits* of poets and other writers, which I was able to find in the libraries as well as his *Man Shakespeare* and *Life of Wilde*. I resolved that if I got to New York I would somehow get to know this man who appeared to be fearless in crusading for what he thought right, even in the face of persecution and financial loss.

Another "star" of a different sort rose on my horizon. Roswell obtained passes for a reading by William Butler Yeats, whose nostalgic and lyric early poetry I had begun to read. We went together. Never had I felt more transported than by Yeats's sonorous voice chanting the poetry I was beginning to love. He appeared in his flowing cape, winning me to the cause of Ireland. Ireland's heroic poetry gave me courage when I was most depressed by the slavery of my job.

To compensate, I stole hours from the night for reading and writing, never sleeping enough. I also neglected eating. I was beginning to feel a revulsion against meat, but the vitamin industry did not exist in 1917. We had never eaten much meat at home, unable to afford it often. The impulse to abstention resulted from my having to pass an abattoir on my way to work unless I went by a roundabout route. The bellows and screams of the cattle and pigs, the stench of their fear, the blood and death haunted me. How could I eat the result of that ugly cruelty? I forgot to look to the material of my shoes and purse.

Careless eating and lack of sleep no doubt were responsible for my swings between utter, almost-suicidal dejection and transports of ecstasy when I would stay awake half the night writing. In addition, I fell in love, and this time I knew what it was.

MARGUERITE

One evening Roswell gave a reception at which a number of people new to me were present, including two women. Regina Seiden was having a first exhibition of her paintings. Gershon had brought her. Marguerite Desmarais, a French Canadian pianist of great charm, came with a teacher of music, Adelard Brunet, handsome despite a pockmarked countenance, a common affliction then. Another woman, Estelle Cox about thirty-five, also a pianist, was accompanied by the young actor, Harcourt Farmer, who was trying to organize a group for amateur theatricals.

Estelle immediately caught my attention with something in the glance of her grey, almond-shaped eyes that I could not decipher. Wherever Estelle was in the room I found my eyes following her, tantalized as if by a memory. Her skin was very fair, her hair dark, almost black. Slight of figure, she appeared both delicate and strong. Later when she was playing Chopin at the piano, I observed that her hands gave the same impression.

The evening was filled with music, Roswell's short play, light conversation, and a pleasant effervescence helped by the sloe gin in soda water and little sandwiches. Then I noticed that Estelle was no longer in the room. A sense of loss came over me. Had she left? I went into the bedroom to find my handbag holding some new poems I had requests to read. Estelle was at the mirror rearranging her hair which had come loose during her energetic performance accompanying parts of Roswell's playlet. She turned to smile at me.

"I read your poem in the *Bookman*—beautiful! I thought you must be older to write about love with such sophistication."

I felt my face begin to burn, stammering, "Maybe one is born knowing some things, knowing how they feel."

"You sounded experienced."

"I—I'm afraid I am not."

"You're a sweet girl." Estelle turned from the mirror and kissed my mouth, a light, warm kiss. Dizzy, I had a hard time keeping myself from falling as I forced myself to speak.

51

"They—Mr. Farmer—are asking me to read—" Blindly, I pulled the manuscripts from my purse and fled the room. Now Abelard was playing the piano. I was grateful for the opportunity this gave me to regain my steadiness before reading. The sensation of the kiss stayed on my lips as if branded.

The next day I asked Roswell about Estelle.

"I noticed you did not take your eyes off her all evening. She is married"— I felt stabbed—"to a handsome old scrooge who runs one of Montreal's important lithography concerns. They do beautiful work. He is, or was when he was younger, quite an artist I am told. He's thirty years older than she is. They've been married about fifteen. She has a thirteen-year-old daughter."

"She—does she—care for him?"

"Lord, no, she hates him. By now I imagine it's mutual. They barely speak. Leave notes for one another if they must communicate. I don't know what happened except that, according to her, he wanted her to do 'unspeakable things' in bed although in public he is a pillar of rectitude and conformity. She has long since denied her sweet body to his corrupt caresses and he punishes her by giving her not a penny above minimal household expenses. She has to play piano in the Park Cinema to get a little money for herself. He keeps a mistress but is so jealous and revengeful towards Estelle that she cannot have her friends to the house when he is likely to appear."

"How sordid."

"Yes. She is gay and lighthearted by nature and would love to entertain. She dances beautifully, but he would never tolerate her dancing—another man might touch her. It's depraved exhibition to him. I imagine it was her refusal to cater to his exotic sexual tastes and her supposed frivolity with younger men and women that began the rift. She is stubborn and refused to bend to his will. They live in a big handsome house, each with their own quarters, as in an armed camp. She calls the house 'The Morgue.'"

I listened with chilling horror. "Why doesn't she leave him?"

"On what? For one thing she loves her daughter and is concerned for her future. She would not surrender the child—little Lorna hates her father. How could she afford to bring her up decently, not to mention pay for her education on the pittance she can earn playing piano in cinema houses? He is not in good health and can't live forever. I gather she is resolved to sit it out so that she and her daughter can benefit from obligatory inheritance for wife and offspring, even under Quebec's medieval laws."

My feelings for this woman were now complicated by compassion. How might Estelle be rescued from such a living hell? I was moved to my depths by indignation and heroic fantasies. I sighed: "She seemed so gay and lighthearted last evening. I loved her laugh and her musical voice."

He replied, "I thought it would be Marguerite who would captivate you. She is unattached, approachable. What did you think of her?"

"She seemed charming—I hardly had a chance to find out more, she disappeared so early."

"A call from a friend she left looking after her sick mother. I've never encountered the old lady but the rumour is she's sort of—*non compos*—not all there, almost entirely paralyzed following a stroke. Marguerite supports her, giving music lessons, acting occasionally, doing part-time work in some office. She never speaks of her difficulties, never complains. I know she has a hard time but creates beauty around her for herself and others. She thought you exquisite."

"Exquisite! Me?"

"What she said to me was, '*Elle est exquise, votre petite amie*; I must know her.' Don't look so skeptical. You really were lovely last night. Do you ever look in the mirror?"

I had worn the new, long, green velvet gown and piled my hair on top of my head for a dramatic effect, encouraged by Roswell, who had insisted on making up my eyes and touching my lips with rouge. "It's like play-acting," I laughed, but entered into it for the party.

"Well, you must know Marguerite. She is the most female creature I have ever met, secure and confident in realizing it. I imagine if she found herself in the situation Estelle is in, she would cleverly conquer that old codger with one little finger using the rest of her two hands to give caresses to whomever she pleases."

"At the eye of the hurricane," Roswell declared one evening serving Russian tea in glasses with jam, "love and music become the only verities."

"Why are you all so serious and cynical tonight?" Estelle reproached. "I escaped from The Morgue hoping to find some lightheartedness."

I said passionately, "How is it possible to live in happiness? The most we can expect is joy after agony. I do believe in the possibility of joy in love and poetry. If I could not *live* poetry as well as live for it and write it, life would have no meaning."

"How young she is," Gershon murmured.

Closer to my ear, more softly spoken, a gentle, accented voice: "My Elsa, you have reason." It was Marguerite, thinking in French and with her engaging accent speaking in English. Quietly she had moved from a chair to seat herself near me on the couch, as Louis had left my side to refill his tea glass.

Marguerite whispered, "Can you come to me tonight?"

"I—I am not sure—" I was anxiously trying to guess, after a quick glance, whether Estelle had observed Marguerite's move and if she was affected by it. She had barely acknowledged my presence. Marguerite's hand feeling for mine, her body close against me, started shivers of desire. I was confident she would not play with my feelings as Estelle, I suspected, was beginning to do. I whispered: "Yes, Marguerite. I think I can. Let's meet outside."

I did not wish Estelle to see us leaving together.

"... Elsa ... Yes! Ah-h *Quelle delire* ..." Marguerite pressed her lips against my neck in passion. It took me by surprise. I had not anticipated being effective with so experienced a woman—or was she acting a little to encourage me? Her hands, her mouth, her tender responses were guiding me. Yet I was aware of my shyness and did not feel quite adequate. It was a miracle to be held in the arms of a loving woman. Deep within I felt a tremendous emotional release. Genitally, I was still to learn the totality of orgasm, but I did not feel the lack, so much of me was satisfied by her caresses. But suddenly a sob rose in my throat.

If only it were Estelle holding me, clinging, with that cry of ecstasy! Estelle's kiss, so lightly given, had seared my lips so that I still felt it. That single kiss was like an infection that had invaded my blood. *She did not mean it. Why did she do it?*

"My sweet, you have tears. Two little tears falling on me like dew from a flower. Sometimes much love does that also to me."

I felt ashamed for the ingratitude, the disloyalty of my thoughts.

"Marguerite, you are so beautiful. And generous."

"I do what I cannot help doing, and so do you."

"It surprises me that you wished to make love with me."

"Why should something so natural surprise you? You must know you are beautiful."

"I have never thought so."

"Ah, but yes." Her hand caressed, her lips strayed over my body, awakening with touch and words, more profound responses. "Yes, let me know all of you, how deeply you can feel. You are a remarkable woman, *passionné, si sincere, exquisement poetique* ... oh, how is it possible to make love in English? I listened to you this evening. For me, you are poetry. Why should it surprise?"

"Partly—because I thought you, like—(I checked the name Estelle) like all women, could love only men."

"*Mais oui*, men, yes, until now I have loved only men. Oh, to my friends I have given a few kisses. Only kisses. Until now I have not loved a woman except for friendship. But love must not be explained. One loves. *C'est tout.*"

"But you will not cease to love men. I could no more keep you for my own than hold an armful of moonlight."

"We cannot hold moonlight because it does not need to be held. We have it now. Isn't that enough? And moonlight can return. I can." She stretched slowly, catlike, a laugh in her throat like a purr.

"If I am able to satisfy you."

"I have never been so satisfied."

"I should apologize for my—my failure—that first time."

"It was not failure, *ma chere*. That time is for me a sweet memory. The green scent of the mountains from outside, the stillness, the sun through the little cabin window; such a little window, but the sun could find us on the bed. You were still asleep, but your hand moved and touched me as if you knew I desired love from you."

"I was not very fast asleep. I was—afraid—too shy—"

"Had you not learned about the body a little with that Frances who hurt your heart?"

"How did you know about her!"

"Roswell told me a little."

"Such a gossip. No, Marguerite, I did not even know it was that kind of love tormenting me. But knowing would not have helped. I have learned since that Frances is quite conventional. But so lovely. I can't regret knowing and loving her. You are the very first to touch all of me with love. I have wished to tell you, Marguerite; I felt badly about being so inept with you that morning."

"That morning" was the second one of a weekend in the Laurentian Mountains. Someone had loaned Roswell a cabin. With seduction in mind, he had invited Louis Gross and Marguerite and me for reassurance or perhaps kindly matchmaking. The cabin had two small bedrooms; we had chosen a sunny loft. I was tired and not in a sociable mood. With Estelle's image between me and the indifferent

55

mountains and Estelle's kiss haunting with unfulfilled promises, I had left the others after supper to walk by myself. I went to bed early to dream of Estelle and, dozing, pretended to be fast asleep when Marguerite slipped in beside me. At dawn Marguerite had drawn me into her arms, gently kissing and touching my breasts. Suddenly aroused and aching with the years of hunger, I had clung in return. But I did not know what else to do. Marguerite must have been unappeased.

"Do you forgive me, Marguerite?"

"Forgive? For what?"

"That I seemed to reject you, or not welcome your caresses. I was in a poor mood and nervous."

"Oh," Marguerite laughed, "I quickly understood how innocent your body was. But your mind, dear, was not so innocent. Your poetry tells me you were dreaming of all kinds of *volupte*.... I imagined perhaps you preferred to keep your kisses for The One who had not yet arrived. Before I met you, I never desired a woman's kiss. But I did not wish to conquer you over yourself."

"And now you have my full co-operation."

We made love again, her responses and words instructing me. Her pleasure contributed to my self-confidence.

I realize today, how fortunate I was to have had Marguerite as my first lover at eighteen. That I was not "in love" with her may have been an advantage. Being "in-love," as I learned from involvements over the years, does not necessarily allow the most free erotic experience. Our most intense moments may not be the happiest. Dare one say they are perhaps "too serious"? With love that is not the "in love" madness comes a balance of detachment and involvement.

I did not know then that Marguerite's lovemaking was a sensitively cultivated, acquired art taken as seriously as her music. There was no artificiality, no affectation. Her loving came so naturally to her that I assumed love must always be that way. In another age, she would have been a *hetaira*, worthy, gifted, beautiful as any famed courtesan who was an erotic companion of artists and philosophers. That she made the most of what was available within the cultural limitations of Montreal in 1917 was her genius.

I am grateful to her for being entirely Woman—strong, with the power of water, yet in no way dependent. She contributed to my love and respect for women who do not feel they must imitate the least attractive qualities of men. In loving me, she did not expect or require me to be—or to fake—*"le male Sappho,"* as Pierre Louys put it in his *Chansons de Bilitis.*

In later life, recalling early events, we may tend to recreate them suffused in a rosier light. I have not done so with my memories of Marguerite. To make sure, I found and reread letters of hers received after I left Montreal. With her engagingly mingled French and English, they evoked the same mood I recollect of playful and yet serious erotic companionship—giving without demanding. One may call it flesh transfused by spirit. I wish for every woman as happy a first experience of the love of woman for woman.

But let us return to where I lay with Marguerite in that long-ago morning. We again made love. From the sleep that followed, I stirred at the sound of a thin cry, like a child's except for its querulous hiss. Marguerite roused instantly and almost before her eyes were open had on her dressing gown. She kissed me, whispered, "*A bientôt,* dear one," and closed the door behind her.

Our room was an island of life and health surrounded by sickness and creeping death. It was a bastion of beauty that Marguerite wore around her like protective clothing or armour. This room alone in the flat, perhaps in her world, was her fortress. She usually slept in another bedroom next to her mother's to be near if the old woman, helpless in the prison of paralysis, needed attention or comfort. Often, I had learned from Roswell, she would moan and cry all night. That night she slept with sedatives.

"For nights she has hardly slept," Marguerite told me. "The doctor said I should give her one of the little pills. He knew I needed also to sleep." When we came back together from Roswell's, Marguerite laughed softly, "Sleep, yes but more I need love." She arranged the couch in her studio as a bed.

The couch was across from the baby grand piano. During our first hour together she had played for me from Erik Satie's *Gymnopidies* and improvised from *Poeme de l'Extase* of Scriabin. She explained that these two contemporary composers were bringing a fresh spirit into music and told me to listen to the new sound and not be critical if at first it seemed strange. Far from wanting to criticize, I was enchanted.

This morning, with her gone from the room, I lay looking towards the long window where the early sun seeped thorough the drawn drapes. I visualized the grace of her strong figure at the piano, her movements as she played, the slightly bent neck where little curls of brown hair strayed loose. When she had finished playing from the *Poem of Ecstasy*, she murmured, coming to kiss me and tenderly bite an ear, "That is for you, for us, tonight."

The flat was in an old mansion in uptown Montreal. The high ceilings were adorned with cupids and other mythological figures. The walls, papered in a tapestry design, were almost entirely covered with reproductions of paintings and photographs of musicians and other artists. There was one large framed photograph of Brahms, a massive, masterful head, whom Marguerite especially admired and whose music she frequently played. There were statuettes and loveseats, two comfortable armchairs, a dainty rosewood desk, glass-enclosed bookcases filled with books and bound sheet music, and the couch in a corner voluptuously piled with velvet cushions when it was not converted as now to a bed. Half a dozen red carnations in a crystal vase gave off a spicy scent.

She seemed to be gone a long time. I floated in a dreaming lassitude of mind and flesh, yet my senses were alert. I imagined I could smell sickness at the far end of the hall through the walls. It mingled with the spice of the carnations and the perfume of love from my own and Marguerite's bodies. I heard the water closet flush, water run, kitchen sounds, early carts rumbling, the clip-clop of horses hooves on the macadam street outside the window. When I opened my eyes, every object in the room seemed to breathe with Marguerite's life. Each seemed a projection of her—sharp, shining, alive. And who may say that a room, its contents long suffused with the spirit of its occupant, does not impalpably breathe? Sensitized by the erotic, I felt the pulse of life in everything around me.

When she came in, Marguerite herself appeared to glow. She had changed into a dress of soft, grey-green material that brought out lights in her darker grey-green eyes. Her wavy brown hair was no longer hanging free as when she rose from bed but in shining coils at each ear. Eyes and mouth smiled as if she had not come from sorrowful duties. She bore a tray with coffee and sweet rolls and sliced peaches. Setting it down she knelt beside the couch where I had thrown back the covers to feel the air on my body; she ran her lips from my throat to my feet. She smelled faintly of a toilet water that made me think of flowering woods in spring.

"Marguerite, you make everything beautiful," I said, glancing from her to the silver tray set with delicate china and accepting the flowered kimono from her arm.

"There are some things impossible to make beautiful; but one can keep them from corroding the heart." Seeing the shadow cross her face, I stood quickly to embrace her. "I am sorry there is sadness."

"How can there not be? It is life. You would like the bathroom? I will show you where to wash." I felt her reluctance to let me out of the haven of this room. I attended to my needs quickly in the old-fashioned bathroom with its enormous tub on griffon feet and marble wash basin. The sickroom door was closed, but as I passed it, I smelled antiseptics, thinking of the poor old woman I had never seen.

Roswell had told me she was dry and brown-yellow like a leaf about to fall; incontinent, unable to move without help or to communicate except by cries and moans, she needed to be served like an infant.

"To make everything beautiful, one may suppose, is the function of the woman," Marguerite said, on my return, as if there had been no interruption to our remarks. "The brother, the son, goes singing to the war and is patriotic. He becomes a hero and gains decorations. The daughter who stays at home and lets her life be used will gain no medals."

It was the first and only bitter remark on the subject I ever heard from Marguerite. In a moment she was smiling, pouring coffee, passing the cream for the peaches. The drapes were open, the couch no longer a bed of love but a velvet-covered divan with plumped cushions. Sun poured in. I savoured the peaches, the pleasant bitterness of the coffee, the rolls spread with unsalted butter; food and drink had never been more delicious.

A hall's length from suffering and decay, life asserted her supremacy.

ESTELLE

Returning to my studio I found a note under the door from Estelle, evidently left there the night before. Electrified by the mere sight of the handwriting, I read: "Will you come to dinner with me at home Sunday evening? I shall be alone so The Morgue should be a little more cheerful than usual. Telephone if you cannot come. Otherwise I shall expect you—about half-past seven? Lorna is to spend the night with her girlfriend." Sunday—that was tonight!

I read and reread the note in a turmoil of emotion: hope, surprise, doubt, fear, hope again. Did this mean—No. I refused to allow that expectation.

In a hotel I found a florist shop open and ordered a mixed bouquet of flowers to be sent to Marguerite with an improvised bit of poetry. Counting my remaining money, I figured if I walked instead of taking streetcars and did not buy any lunches, I would have enough left to get three red roses for Estelle.

When it was nearly time to leave for supper with Estelle, I realized, heartstruck, that I did not have her address. One night Roswell and I had gone to pick her up, and I had taken no note of the street and number. The telephone directory was no help; there was no listing for Estelle and I did not know her husband's first name or initials. I tried calling Roswell and everyone at the studios. All were away.

I sank to the couch in my tiny room ready to cry with frustration. In my mind was a vague image of the house: solid, stone, two or more stories, over-shadowing maples, among a half-circle of similar houses in a court-like place. I determined somehow to find my way to her. Placing the roses back in their green tissue, I invoked memory of the night walk with Roswell. It was like a recurrent dream I had begun to have of walking streets, lost, seeking some unrevealed objective. My actual quest turned out to be rewarded. As if drawn on Ariadne's thread I came to the familiar location: the crescent-shaped court with the imposing houses, the maples, loomed out of the dusk. For a moment I hesitated over the house itself, recognized the particular maple reaching to an upper window on the side, a higher stoop than the other houses with a wrought-iron seat to the left, the door with a high, stained-glass window.

Heart thumping, I ran up the three steps, listened to the pressed bell peal inside. Estelle stood before me at the opening door. Too choked with relief to speak, I thrust the roses into her hands and followed her through the wide entrance hall. The room we entered was book-lined, with a fireplace in which a small coal fire glowed. I glimpsed a wide staircase winding upward, opaque glass doors partly open revealing what seemed the drawing-room of a mansion. A grand piano was partially visible at one end.

"The chill never leaves this house even in summer——the library is the least gloomy. I hole up here when I am not in my room upstairs."

The glowing fire was inviting, so was a small table set for two beside it. Exclaiming with pleasure over the roses, Estelle brought a vase with water and placed them. "Red roses—for love—. Sweet girl, thank you!" The kiss on the lips was as lightly given as the first one.

Tongue-tied, I stiffened, longing for the embrace I did not dare. *What does she mean? Can she not know what she is doing to me?*

The food was brought to the table with a small carafe of red wine. I do not remember what we ate or talked about. Near the end of the meal, she said that she could not count on being alone after eleven o'clock, clearly a warning that I must leave before that time. "He might be later, but I can't be sure. Old hypocrite. As if he could be at the office on a Sunday until eleven at night. Lorna and I both know he is with his mistress. Why does he lie?" She said nothing else about her domestic situation. When the meal was cleared away and we were at ease among cushions before the fire with the wine, she sighed, "This is so nice. Do you know, you are the first friend I have had in this house for months?"

This and the wine made me bold. I leaned towards her, took her hands and covered them with kisses. She did not repulse me, but disengaged one hand gently to draw the bone pins from the coil of my hair and let it fall loose. "Such beautiful hair," she ran her hands through it. Afraid of breaking the spell, I hardly dared move, glad that the fallen hair hid my burning face. The leaning position was awkward; one of my legs was going to sleep. The huge, dark house was so still that I was afraid to swallow to ease my constricted throat. A clock chimed, and I counted ten. Less than an hour before I must leave! Would there ever be another occasion of such intimacy? Desperate over the galloping minutes I drew myself up to Estelle's mouth and after the first deep kiss was no longer able to restrain my passion.

Estelle disengaged herself gently, her voice seemed to smile. "My *dear*—" Was it protest or surprise? "Such an intense little being!" I could not get out the words, "I love, love, I love you—" and I trembled from the incomplete embrace.

She moved from me, stood, saying, "Let us go upstairs." She quickly removed all evidence of dinner, handed me my hairpins, and picked up the vase of roses. "I'd best have these in my room, he never comes in there."

Although the clock was measuring the half hour, I blindly followed her up to the bedroom, hoping—if he never came in here.... Her next words exposed my naïveté.

"Do you need a comb to fix your hair?" I took the comb and restored my appearance, aware of her ear turned to every sound from the street. Resenting her anxiety, which was spoiling the remaining minutes, hating the man who was its cause, I knew she was telling me it was time to leave. Taking courage at the door, I flung myself into an embrace. I could not tell if it was welcomed or merely accepted.

Was Estelle a woman so used to men that she expected to be "conquered"? Was she putting out just enough provocation to entice, to lure, to hold? The doubts tormented me throughout a night of little sleep. Hypnotized under Estelle's fingers playing with my hair, remarks hardly noticed, now shouted out of the dark: "We missed you last night, disappearing right after I arrived, Roswell said you were with Marguerite—"

So, it did matter to her. Was that why she had invited me, to keep me from Marguerite? Did she, Estelle, want me? What game was she playing? I drifted in and out of sleep, in and out of dreams haunted by bright, mocking, almond-shaped eyes, by a mouth inviting yet denying sensuality, a kiss and a touch that promised and withheld.

61

Did Estelle have a lover? The thought was intolerable, but I allowed it to torment me. According to Roswell's gossip, there had been more than one man in the past. Her husband knew, and this was the reason she dared not sue for divorce; he could claim she refused him his conjugal "rights" but was unfaithful with other men. He would also win custody of her daughter. Under Quebec's marriage laws, it was unlikely that she would come out of a contest with anything other than scandal. "Estelle never could face that—or poverty," was Roswell's view of her.

What a trap! I ached with compassion, burned with indignation, lay tormented by her helplessness as if it had been my own. What solution could there be for her? Yet, as I saw it, anything would be preferable to living with no freedom in a house referred to as The Morgue, with a man she could name Death Himself. Poverty, any sort of struggle, appeared to me preferable. But, the daughter? A hostage. Perhaps it was not lack of courage or of will to face hardship, but of unwillingness to sacrifice the child. I wanted to see noble qualities in this woman to whom I was surrendering so much of myself.

Again, I contemplated the lives of women: Estelle, Marguerite, my mother, Mrs. Williams, her daughter Netta, married with one child and another coming. All were trapped. Marguerite alone, who earned her own living and could express herself in her art of music, appeared half free.

It was close to dawn when I slept, exhausted, to wake with some verses fully formed which I scribbled down by the light filtering through the drawn mauve drapes at the tall French windows.

Love's Acolyte

Many have loved you with lips and fingers
And lain with you till the moon went out;
Many have brought you lover's gifts
And some have left their dreams on your doorstep.

But I who am youth among your lovers
Come like an acolyte to worship,
The thirsting blood restrained by reverence,
The heart a wordless prayer.

The candles of desire are lighted,
I bow my head, afraid before you,

A mendicant who craves your bounty,
Ashamed of what small gifts she brings.

Those lines might have taught me how profoundly I needed the Religion of
the Goddess that I discovered so much later. At the time, they merely revealed
the difference between the power Estelle had over me and my feelings for
Marguerite. For three years of ecstasy and anguish, I never resolved whether
Estelle's magic was of heaven or hell. Perhaps only early youth can be held in
such bewitchment. I could in the end free myself only by flight. Years later, I
summed up the experience in "Region of No Birds."

Where the earth groans with earthquake
I know you,
Where the waters boil black
And the dragons are
You are immersed in me.
Beyond pleasure, where terror is kissed
And the small I's die.

In that region of no birds
One does not speak prettily of love.

63

What if Estelle had responded to my devotion with the intensity and passion I brought to her? For me, from the first moment, she was the physical manifestation of that Woman-Being who had entered my child consciousness and
haunted me since. Lifelong I've held an image of that form comprising a spiri-
tualization of a Woman/Man composite, but the vessel female. I have glimpsed
that image in paintings, in photographs, in human faces—and never ceased to
look for it.

Women say to me now that they become lesbians as a "political" act. In the
mood and context of today's awareness, I hear and feel the meaning behind that
statement. I was committed to the goal; but not able to see love as a weapon of
war. If I had felt magnetized towards any man, for all my commitment to the
struggle for freedom as a human person, I believe I should have found a way to
consummate that attraction in erotic union and still maintained independence. My
feeling for women is a need more profound and deep than the social, ranging from

the compellingly physical to and through the nourishment of the aesthetic to the transcendingly spiritual. I look back now on my journal and Estelle.

Estelle. Star. She knows now she has only to smile, and I follow. She does not refuse my devotion. On the contrary. If I compel myself for twenty-four hours not to telephone or make any attempt to see her, as if accidentally, she will find some way to make it happen that she will be where I am. Or if I cloak myself, withdraw, hold back expression of the love that never ceases to ache in me for response from her, she will make some advance. I hope again and am at her feet. Or she may be depressed, lonely, and invite me to be with her as if whatever despair or emptiness had opened up in her might be assuaged or filled by my devotion.

Seeing all this clearly, I still am powerless to stay away from her if she displays the slightest need for my presence. It isn't rare for her to initiate or accept an engagement with me and break it if her mood changes or something else comes up that she wants to do more. One night, for example, I invited her to my studio to read some new poems for her. I sometimes wondered if she enjoyed my poetry out of vanity; she knew she inspired so much of it. She accepted with seeming pleasure. Eight o'clock came and passed without her. I waited, suffering, until nine. She could not call me as no studios had telephones. Hurt and angry and worried, I finally resolved to take a walk and then telephone her. I took along a book to return to Harcourt Farmer. At the door of his studio I felt a peculiar, icy sensation. I stood still for a minute, heard murmuring. Harcourt was likely to have someone with him, man or woman; he loved them equally, in and out of bed. I gave a tentative knock, assuming if he wished to be alone he would not respond. Low murmurs continued. I started to turn and leave when Harcourt came to the door. After pausing elaborately, he drew me into the room with an embrace. He gave them casually and easily.

Dishevelled, Estelle sat on the velvet-covered couch, pulling her clothing to decency. The couch cushions were flattened, one on the floor. Estelle, usually pale, was flushed and her eyes sparkled. She was in one of her gay moods. If she was embarrassed she hid it, laughing, rising, and embracing me, something she usually waited for me to do. She took one of my hands and kissed it, put an arm around me. Ordinarily, that would have given me shivers of delight. But I stood, numb, looking from one to the other. I had

64

not noticed that Harcourt's pants were open until he reached down and fastened them as if that were the most natural thing to be doing.

I drew from Estelle's embrace and started blindly towards the door, "Sorry to have intruded." Harcourt brought me back by force, laughing as if there were a joke I could not see. "No intrusion, Dolphin, no intrusion." He gently pushed me to the couch beside Estelle, stroking me as if I were a ruffled cat.

Harcourt had a dark, slightly sullen, dissipated face, the plastic face of an actor, handsome at times, and a thin, nervous body that he handled gracefully. The few times I had been alone with him he had appeared lonely and had not hesitated to let me know he would have liked to make love with me. My lack of interest and response let our relationship settle into a pleasantly casual friendship. Usually, I liked him. At that moment I felt hatred.

Estelle drew me to her and stroked the back of my neck. I have let her know that undoes me completely. I tensed myself and sat stiffly, resisting feeling. It seemed incredible that she did not know when she was torturing me. In my fairest and most sane moments, I would tell myself she was incapable of realizing that one woman could feel for another what I felt for her. Erotically, she belonged to men. I must school myself to accept that, as well as what she accorded me of herself that I could not do without.

Harcourt came and sat on the other side of me. "I love to see you two together, cuddling and caressing: a sweet Sapphic scene." I still sat stiff and silent. "Why so glum this evening, Dolphin? You're not your usual playful self. Your new job a bore?"

The job, yes, the job, it was no worse than any other, I told them. I now worked in the office of a distributor of motion picture films with the manager, Mr. Horsefall, and a woman bookkeeper. In the rear was a large warehouse, a long wide table and paraphernalia for checking, editing, and preparing the films for the various theatres to which they were assigned. This work was done by a young woman and a young man, both French Canadian.

They talked together while they worked at great speed, joked, laughed, drank soft drinks, and munched candy. I liked hearing them. Even with the door to our office closed, their gaiety projected a refreshing sense of life enjoyed rather than endured. This changed when Mrs. Grundy stepped in. I entertained Estelle and Harcourt with the sequel, although I did not think it was funny. Dolphins are expected to be playful.

65

The pair, Gaston and Marie Rose, arrived at work at eight; the book-keeper and I at nine; Mr. Horsefall usually at a quarter of nine. One morning he walked in twenty minutes past eight to attend to some special request from a theatre. He went to the stockroom, found Marie and Gaston making love on the work table. Gaston admitted that this was not a rare occurrence; they found it a pleasant way to start the day, and worked better afterwards with lots of energy.

"And the boss fell off his horse?" Harcourt punned, "or did the horse fall on the lovers?" Harcourt and Estelle could not stop laughing. They wanted more. What then?

Well, when I got to work that morning, and noticed Gaston working alone, I inquired if Marie Rose were ill. Miss Curtis said, "No, fired. Mr. Horsefall sent her packing." He had given her no notice and no compensatory pay.

"Gaston is staying?" I was puzzled, shocked.

"Yes."

"But—why let him stay and fire her?"

Miss Curtis could see nothing wrong with Mr. Horsefall's action. "The girl plainly had no self-respect—pretty shameless—on the table—at eight in the morning—"

Having performed for them my playful Dolphin trick, I got up to leave. Estelle said she would walk back with me. The only excuse she gave was that she had stopped at Harcourt's to talk about her playing the piano for one of his skits—the time passed before she realized it. She came up to the room with me, was more affectionate than usual, praising the poetry I showed her, especially a piece written for her. How could I remain angry? She was so lovely, kind, and warm. Once again I allowed hope to overwhelm me. As soon as I became the serious lover, begging her to stay, unable to restrain my kisses which at first she had not rejected—up went the barriers. The impassable space opened between us. It was like the vision by the brook when I could not get into the cave to reach the beautiful Being.

I could not sleep that night. I wrote instead:

If she can love only men, why does she play this game with me? The real question I should answer: Why am I fool enough to go on? Why?

Because I can't stop. Because I love her. Because being with her, having only such whimsical favours as she grants, being allowed when she is in the mood to kiss, caress (just so far) is bribe enough for my pride to evaporate. Because her friendship, which I believe I do have, is too important to me. As long as I may see her, am with her, as is inevitable—we know so many of the same people, do so many of the same things socially—I desire her and crave the totality of her love.

The totality of love? What is that? To Marguerite I gave my bodily virginity. I treasure and cherish the sweetness of that first night with her and those since. Her tenderness, her artistry as a lover, are gifts I feel almost ashamed of accepting with Estelle always lying between us. Because Estelle is forever there, Marguerite cannot enter me or I her much beyond the periphery of pleasure, the release and comfort of assuaged bodily desire.

What I feel, although I do not know (in that region I am still virgin) is that in the totality of love there would be depths beyond depths of mutual surrender. Somehow, together, the beloved and I would have to enter that cave surrounded by rocks and black water, and dare a terror like the willingness to die. Surrender of self. I feel this. But do not yet understand it, voicing it only a little here and there in my poetry. It is obvious this can never be with Estelle. Maybe it is known to her with men. How can I know? Because of Estelle, it cannot be with Marguerite—and Marguerite, too, needs men.

In love, I am still going to school.

67

Barrelhouse Kings

BARRY CALLAGHAN

As he recounts in this excerpt from *Barrelhouse Kings: A Memoir* (1998), Barry
Callaghan (b. 1937) grew up in a complex relationship with his father Morley Callaghan
(1903–90), who was in his day the most famous Canadian novelist at home and
abroad—and who published his own literary memoir, *That Summer in Paris* (1963). Part
of what they shared was their cumulative and minutely intimate knowledge of Toronto,
where Barry Callaghan is today a poet, fiction writer, visual artist, small press publisher,
and all-round presence on the arts scene.

ONE

It was a bright July afternoon. I was about to become a reporter. On television.
I was standing in a small field that I had played softball on as a child, a field at
the foot of Casa Loma that had been used by Acme Farmers' Dairy to walk their
wagon horses. The dairy had converted to trucks and the field was now disused,
but I was standing there beside a horse. I was reporting for CBC news. It was
in 1958. Premier Khrushchev had just appeared on television at the United
Nations in New York, banging his shoe on the Soviet desk. I had been sent out to
interview the horse. It was a talking horse. One *whinny* meant No. Two *whinnies*
meant Yes.

"Did you see Mr. Khrushchev on television as he banged his shoe?"

"*Whinny.*"

"Do you approve of what he did?"

"*Whinny.*"

"Do you think the Soviet Union should be censured?"

"*Whinny, whinny.*"

The interview with the horse ran as the second item on the six o'clock news, after a feed from the United Nations.

"Great," my boss said, "and too bad about the kid."

Before meeting with the horse in the field I had spent the morning with a mother distraught by sorrow and desperation who was trying to raise money so that she could take her dying child to the evangelist Oral Roberts, hoping for a miraculous healing, a cure of cancer. The child—sitting in her lap—had screamed in pain and terror all through the conversation. The film editors had refused to edit the film for air.

"Without the screaming," my boss said, "it would have been great."

John Harasti, a young writer and actor, was a reporter at the CBC. I had met him at Canadian Press and he had found the job at the CBC for me. It was a wonderful place to be a young reporter. Those were the first days of television news. Nobody knew what they were doing, which meant almost anything could be done. As each show went live to air, anything could happen and so it was a forgiving newsroom. It had to be. Too many mistakes were made.

The executive editor took me aside. "You've got a weakness," he said. "You're trying to do too much, to do everything. You've got to learn to spread the mistakes around. Watch Harasti."

Harasti had a certain brilliance and charm, but had taken to drink. He had a bed at what became the Bohemian Embassy, a second-floor coffee house above shops on Yonge Street where writers like young Gwendolyn MacEwen and Margaret Atwood read their poems. He drank all day, coming in at six o'clock to put his feet up on a desk and watch the news. He always gave the show a warm round of applause. Our exasperated boss ordered him to interview a local alderman live in studio. Harasti, half-soused, sat beside the alderman. The rather snooty floor director counted down. Harasti didn't see the count. "Just relax," the home audience heard Harasti say to the alderman. "They'll signal us when to start." The floor director ignored the two men who sat side by side in "live" silence for a full minute. The floor director then threw Harasti another signal. He turned, looked at the alderman, and said, "What the fuck is your name anyway?" He stood up and walked off the set. The boss went berserk. I collapsed in a heap of laughter. The assignment editor said in Harasti's defence, "I can't remember his name either." Harasti was not fired. He was given a month off with pay and told to dry out, which he did. At the end of the summer, he came back and replaced the assignment editor (who was on holidays) and told me to work up a three-part series on crime on the waterfront. "But there's no crime on the waterfront," I said. "There's always crime on the waterfront," he said. "Don't you go to the movies?"

I decided to ask one of the older reporters what he knew about crime down at the docks. I dropped by his small spare flat on Cumberland Street, next door to the The House of Hambourg. "Come in," he said. He had a copy of Gorki's *Creatures That Once Were Men* in his hand. He whacked me on the shoulder with the book. I took it as a sign of affection between men who liked books. It was a bed sitting room: one chair, a bed, a desk, and a big heavy dresser. The walls were painted gold. He said the room had been previously rented by a high-priced call girl. He called the room his Winter Palace. To my utter astonishment, I found the newsroom's dwarf copy-boy sitting happily in the top drawer of the dresser, listening as the older reporter lectured him on Soviet Socialist Realism. He gave me a warm beer. We talked briefly about Sholokhov and *And Quiet Flows the Don*. It was a Soviet classic, he said. The dwarf said he liked to listen to the Soviet Army Chorus. He began to sing *Kalinka, Kalinka* ...

Several days later. I found a ship down around the Cherry Street docks that was unloading guns destined for Hercules War Surplus on Yonge Street. Thousands of old 303s. The Danish captain couldn't understand why I wanted to film the unloading of boxes of old guns but he not only let me film, he gave me two guns. An hour later, Harasti and I stood in the newsroom happily slamming the action bolts in and out of the unloaded guns. He was wonderfully pleased.

"Now what do we know about Hercules Sales?" he asked.

"I knew a graduate student last year who was so upset at failing his exams that he hid in Hercules and came bursting out through the window at midnight wearing camouflage gear and a gun in each hand."

"No kidding."

"Ran right into the arms of two cops."

"Too bad we don't have that on film."

The item on the unloading of guns ran at six o'clock, headlined:

GUNS ARRIVE AT TORONTO PORT

The real news, of course, was always covered and nearly always covered well—there were some excellent men there, like the young Morley Safer, and the seasoned, sometimes marinated and often brilliant Norman Depoe—but a slight loopiness was always in the air, at all levels.

Sometimes it was slapstick, as when Depoe's dentures slipped out of his mouth onto his desk in mid-sentence, or when Stanley Burke, in Zaire, told the nation: "Don't give me any more goddamn cues." Sometimes it involved incompetence: as when the federal Conservatives, convinced that the Toronto newsroom was not a hotbed of rest but a hive of Liberal animosity, ordered that a Convocation Hall speech by Prime Minister John Diefenbaker be filmed from start to finish. A newsman of Conservative bent who had just bought a camera was dispatched. He came back with rolls of film for processing. It turned out to be all black leader. He had forgotten to take the lens cap off the camera.

Sometimes matters were more insidious: as with the prominent city councillor who regularly extended "loans" to one of our City Hall reporters every time the councillor was on the news, but no one said anything until the reporter was suspended for being drunk and then the councillor showed up in a huff saying, "If my man is no longer working the City Hall I want my money back." The solution was to stiff the none-too-bright councillor, who slowly came to understand the position he had put himself in, and to punish the reporter by posting him to a plush job in the Caribbean.

72

This rawness was a godsend. If the newsroom was open to any approach, so was the whole network, radio and television. At the end of every afternoon I went across the road with Nina, who worked in radio, to drink at the Everene Hotel (known affectionately as the Neverclean) or the Celebrity Club, a serious watering hole for actors, agents, writers, raconteurs, singers, and vaudevillians of almost no celebrity. After a short word with Terrence Gibbs, a producer, I was asked to discuss books once a week on the national morning radio show. I said, "I'm still in school." He said, "So what?" So I started talking about Faulkner, Burroughs, Genet, Williams, Blais, Eustace Ross. Whatever interested me. Gibbs never once pretended to know what the audience wanted or wouldn't put up with. "That's for people who read chicken's guts," he said. I stepped out of a studio one day and there was Duke Ellington passing Kate Reid in the hall. Glenn Gould and Marshall McLuhan were in the cafeteria. Bob Weaver was buying fiction and poetry for broadcast on radio from writers all across the country, and serious dramas, classic dramas, were acted every week. The city—with the CBC at its core—seemed rampant with men and women doing things ... and none of it was conventional. Everything seemed possible as we turned the corner into the sixties. Nothing was charted, nothing preordained. Writing, good writing, the best writing, was important. Harasti, when he was sober, made me read *Watt* while listening to

Mahler. "There doesn't have to be a reason why," he said. "Every cripple has to have his own walk." The sophistication of radio, a sophistication honed during the War, had spilled over into television to combine with a reckless enthusiasm that only amateurs could afford.

I worked in the television newsroom and on morning radio for several years while going to the University of Toronto. After Windsor, the "Oxford-like" university was staid, even stifling. There were professors who seriously believed T.S. Eliot was too *modern*, too *contemporary* to be studied. There was, of course, no such thing as Canadian literature. At St. Michael's College, a young woman told me, as we discussed ethics, that she had worn "a Blessed Virgin bra" since high school in Boston. I longed for my "jiggler" in Detroit. A fellow I had known for years confessed with sudden passion that he prayed for my soul every morning at mass. His passion seemed sexual to me. His roommate believed the fluoridization of the water was a Communist conspiracy and there were several priests and young men who still supported Senator Joe McCarthy. At Trinity College, young men and women leading faux Oxford lives in black gowns lunched in "The Buttery." Marshall McLuhan was at St. Michael's, and he was certainly a whirly-gig of ideas, but the amiable, welcoming centre of the University for me—as it had been for my father—was Hart House, a stone and oak refuge for men—a hall of leather sofas and leather easy chairs. A place to educate yourself, as Morley liked to say. There were music rooms, debating rooms, a library, an art gallery, a theatre, all presided over by a former Deputy Commissioner of Penitentiaries, Joe McCulley.

He was a big-boned, ambling, articulate, well-read and hard-drinking bachelor in his fifties whose apartment in the Tower House was a well-appointed place for late night drink and banter. "The best men, the best minds," he liked to say, almost quoting Matthew Arnold as he lunged after a young man who had struck his fancy. He was homosexual and a couple of times at three in the morning he suddenly came crashing through his coffee table, arms open, seeking a kiss, but I didn't mind. No one minded. That was Joe. Some men wanted to sing at three in the morning. He wanted to kiss.

If he became a bit overbearing in his happy affection for me and my family (Morley still attended Hart House debates at the warden's invitation), I just said my goodbyes and walked out without regret or rancour, well-liquored and amused, and within ten minutes I would be sitting at one coffee house or another with friends, particularly painters, many of whom were also musicians: the

Village Corner (the first uptown coffee house, run by an English actor, John Morley, who launched Ian and Sylvia in Toronto as separate acts), the Purple Onion (where I first saw John Lee Hooker), the Mynah Bird (which featured the "first nude dancer in the city"—she was nude but not seen: she choked on the dry-ice smoke she swallowed as it engulfed her), the First Floor Club (Clarke Terry, Art Blakey), the Penny Farthing, the Riverboat (where Bill Cosby began his career), The Pilot (where young painters drank until midnight and then went to Jimmie Hill's after-hours bar), clubs where the house singers were Joni Mitchell, Gordon Lightfoot, Brownie McGhee and Sonny Terry, Neil Young, Phil Ochs ...

> Black night road,
> No moon or stars in sight,
> Don't you lead me way out there,
> My poor heart is full of fear ...

There was no fear in my heart, the black night road seemed a straight run towards the stars, and way out there was just around the corner.

74 The Penny Farthing, on Yorkville Avenue, was a place where summer runaways, gawking day trippers, hash peddlers (but not the speed freaks), and folkies hung out. It was slightly upscale, a coffee house of chocolachinos and fancy rye bread sandwiches. It also had a tiny swimming pool in the intimate yard-space behind the old brick row house. I knew the poolside: it was a nice place to sit at a table and read of a summer afternoon because the yard was usually always empty in the afternoon. But in the evening, a trim cluster of young Germans—fit and blond— had taken to sitting at the backside of the pool.

I often ran into Larry Zolf in the cafés. He was an extraordinary young man. So was his father, an ex-czarist draft dodger and ex-infantryman in Alexander Kerensky's revolutionary army—Yoshua Falk Zholf—who had drifted to Winnipeg and become a teacher of Jewish liberal-socialist values to Jewish children at the Isaac Loeb Peretz Folk School. Larry—youngest son of Yoshua—had been enrolled in that school and he had learned to read from a Dick and Jane—Max and Molly primer. He had first read *Huckleberry Finn*, *Rip Van Winkle* and *Moby Dick* in Yiddish. He had learned that Franklin Delano Roosevelt was God and Canada was a temporary penal colony for temporary undesirables in the Great Several States to the south. He was thrilled when Barney Ross boxed someone's brains in and Hank Greenberg beat the leather off a baseball. He drooled at the succulent beauty of

Miss America 1945, Bess Myerson. He and his father cradled each other and wept when Harry Truman gave Israel to the Jews. Yoshua Zholf then wept again when young Larry Zolf left home.

Larry went to Toronto. Having read Dickens and Dostoevsky in Yiddish he reread them in English. He became obsessed with Canadian history and politics. He married a *zaftig* girl from Newfoundland, Patsy. She was *zaftig* but she was not Jewish. He had a little paunch, a big bush of kinky hair and a very big, even bulbous nose. There was a wart on his nose. He became a stand-up comedian in the manner of Mort Sahl, though he was more mordant and more cutting than Sahl, who after all was only a Jewish Will Rogers.

In many ways, Zolf was the best of what I saw my city becoming, a place of acerbic loners entrenched in the lore of the country and the local politics, men who were self-absorbed but only so that they could be more public-spirited, men who were profoundly parochial but only so they could be entirely at ease in the world.

As my grandmother Minn would have said, "Zolf was forthright to a fault."

He believed we could be forthright and I believed we were astute enough to get away with it.

"Be careful," my father said, warning us.

"My father," Zolf said, "saw the American dream this way—to be Jewish and human was to be American. As I see the American Dream operating in Black America and Yellow Vietnam, I am forced to conclude that somehow to be really human is to be neither Jewish nor American. Today the Jewish community in America is indeed a participant and more than an equal in the power elite of White America. The Jews are close to the top in education, affluence, status. But to Black America the Jew is as much Whitey as anyone else. The American Jew lives in a white neighbourhood, worships in a white, cavernous temple, eats white kosher Chinese food at white Chinese restaurants, has white directors for his white bar mitzvah movies. He likes it that way and is sure everyone will understand.

"I must admit that my stomach feels queasy when I hear Nicholas Katzenbach gloating over the Viet Cong kill toll, the damned dead of American-style democracy. I must admit to a similar-type queasiness when I hear Jews gloating over Six Day War Arab losses, the damned dead of Zionist-style democracy ... It saddens me to see how the American Dream and the melting pot has coarsened and vulgarized my racial confreres. I prefer the schlemiel wisdom of Gimpel the Fool to the Sammy Glick-shtick of Norman Podhoretz."

There were Jews in Toronto who said Zolf was an anti-Semite. They were the same Jews who said Mordecai Richler and Philip Roth were anti-Semites.

One evening, I sat in the Penny Farthing as eight or nine young and beautiful Germans arrived for their usual aperitifs, the men all looking like my friend Dieter, from the tax assessment office. Then Zolf came through the narrow door to poolside. He waved hello. Behind him, his entourage. Wherever and whenever Zolf performed, he had his travelling entourage: one club foot (the painter, Gershon Iskowitz, who had survived Auschwitz), one dwarf (a comedienne), and two very fat women who never wore bras, letting their great breasts loll. The troupe trucked in and sat around a table at the end of the pool opposite the young Germans.

After coffees and chocolachinos, Zolf suddenly rose and in a high nasal drawl he intoned, at the top of his voice, "Auschwitz, Auschwitz, I know nothing of Auschwitz. I vork at Dachau."

It was as if the young Germans had been poleaxed.

No one moved.

No word was said.

Zolf sat down.

His entourage snickered quietly.

A moment passed, the Germans, trying not to glance over their shoulders, stumbled back into conversation.

Zolf rose.

They saw him rise.

They waited.

He intoned, "Vee Nazis and Jews must stick together."

There were gasps. The dwarf began to laugh hysterically. Half the Germans leapt to their feet and fled.

I thought, He's going to clean the joint out ...

There was a long silence. Hardly anyone spoke at either end of the pool. Iskowitz stood up. He had a sad face, a mournful smile. Dragging his foot, he got to the edge of the pool. He looked like he was going to jump in, but he stood staring at the iridescent turquoise water. What was he thinking, this man who had been a child in the camps, staring into the stillness of water? I realized I had never seen anyone swim in that water. I had never seen a ripple on that water. It was just there. The Germans were there. Zolf was there. He rose. He intoned, "Be ze first one on your block to turn in Anne Frank ..."

The Germans fled. Zolf's entourage laughed and giggled. In a little while, they left, too, but not before the owner chastised Zolf: "After all, they were too young to do what their fathers did."

I felt sad for the young Germans. I felt triumphant glee for Zolf and his entourage …

I laughed.

Iskowitz was the last to leave. As he turned to wave goodbye to me, he asked, "Hey! How's Bill?"

"Good," I said, "he's good."

TWO

Bill Ronald had grown up in the small town of Fergus, northwest of Toronto. It was Presbyterian country, Orange Lodge country. Squat, square-cut stone houses. The people had a purse-mouthed way of talking. Bill didn't talk that way. His father did, but he didn't. He had listened to the radio and had practised throwing his voice. He could talk loud and well and he told everybody that he wanted to be a painter. He came to Toronto, somehow persuaded the Home Furnishing Department of Simpson's department store to hang his "abstracts"—and in 1954 helped to found Painters Eleven. Then he went on to New York to study with Hans Hofmann. Ronald was brash, he had brilliance, and he sold a work to a well-known collector, Countess Ingeborg de Beausac. She introduced him to the Kootz Gallery. Shortly after, the Guggenheim Museum bought a large painting, and then the Rockefellers. His signature—RONALD—was often almost as big as the central image on his canvases. RONALD. He liked that. He painted hard, he was under contract to produce 18 canvases a year and he did so for seven years. Then his nerves frayed. Kootz cancelled the contract. A doctor in Princeton put him on uppers and downers. Confused, he came home in the early sixties, but being by temperament a man apart—expansive and certain of a destiny, an abrasive innocent who was wise enough to be paranoid—he did not settle in the central part of the city but on Ward's Island out in the bay. He had a friend on the island, an Anglican parish priest, Father Hopkins. He rented a house close to the small island church. He rested for a while, contemplated the calming waters and then he went on television as the host of an arts program, "The Umbrella." He heard me talking about Eustace Ross on radio and he asked me if I would like to come in out of the local rain and do all the literary interviews for the show, and I said sure. So we stood together under a geodesic umbrella—the stage set—and some people said, It's not raining, but I said, The little you know. Those look like thunder clouds to me. BOOM ...

Morley asked, "Why is it you go in for that boom and rain kinda stuff?"

"It's what I hear."

"The rain?"

"No. The clip-clop of the caisson, the horses hauling JFK's caisson. I hear it all the time, like rain on the roof, on top of my head."

Wearing silver cowboy boots and capes lined with satin, refusing to work with a prepared script, Ronald was a flamboyant presence on television in the staid Sunday afternoon time slot of old movies, hymn sings, and football. He was so honest he could be guileless, so intently serious he could indulge in slapstick, or, as he told me, "Warhol makes pop art. I *am* pop art." But at the CBC, some of the men with the pipes and English accents wrapped in ivy looked at him as if he were the backside of the moon: what he thought was pop art they thought was mooning—loopy conversations with Marcel Duchamp, pie-throwing with the hockey player, Eddie Shack, banter with the Goons, hobnobbing with Henry Moore, and the strippers—all his life he loved "exotic" dancers, insisting that their "nakedness" was their costume, that they wore their bodies as he wore his suits. But the cultural comptrollers said he was awkward, gauche, self-indulgent, flippant, outspoken, crass, tongue-tied, carping, elitist, hysterical, unresponsive, skittish, scatterbrained ... and perverse, because he insisted on painting his own set, surrounding *himself* with *himself*, a defiant reckless image of openness and vulnerability. As a still centre of turbulence, "The Umbrella" not only had an audience but one Sunday afternoon it actually outdrew professional football.

And I said, "What do you know today, Bill?"

And he said, "Boston hates Muhammad Ali."

He was listening to radio stations. He loved boxing and he loved radio. As a boy, he carried a rolled-up copy of *Ring* magazine in his back pocket. He listened to the *Look Sharp Feel Sharp Be Sharp* Gillette Blue Blade Friday night fights from Madison Square Gardens. He sat listening to the radio for hours. He talked on the phone for hours, to cities all over the continent. He was tuned in, I was tuned in, it's what we talked about, the whole of America's hopscotch game that had turned helter-skelter ... assassinations, riots, doobies, and draft-dodgers, the sardonic laughter in the songs (*Oh God said to Abraham, Kill me a son ... Abe says, Where do you want this killin' done? God says, Out on Highway 61*)—Rapp Brown and Ronald Reagan, Mayor Daley and Jerry Rubin, Dick Nixon and Norman Podhoretz and Timothy Leary, Black Panthers and Mortimer Snerd and the Maharishi Yogi, Ken Kesey and his Merry Pranksters, Herbert Marcuse and Ayn Rand, all of them— all shopworn gurus lying about like rubber dummies waiting to be inflated by some publicist, and then, when they rose up, once they were ambulatory, they followed Tiny Tim, alias Julian Foxglove, alias Deny Dover, alias Herbert Khaury, alias Larry Love, to the altar where he married the perfect Virgin, Miss Vicky ... married her *live* on the Johnny Carson show, a singer devoid of talent, fêted precisely because he had no talent, rescued from obscurity to sing the good old songs, all teeth and hook nose, burbling ... all of them burbling as they were introduced by their Master of Ceremonies, Ed Sullivan, hugging himself as he stumbled through the language, Ed Sullivan, who had single-handedly rendered the word *wonderful* meaningless; an opera singer was *wonderful* and so were the flea-ridden chimpanzees who followed her *wonderful*; *wonderful* acts parading on and off for a fee. They were total theatre. They were the revolution. They were the apocalypse. They were midnight skulkers. They were naked. They were banal. They were the Big public Show.

"I'm so tuned in," he said, "I tuned out McLuhan long ago."

I always found a tension in Bill between his love of discipline and his love for the ludicrous. Often, he seemed at odds with himself—sometimes ingrown, reticent, whining, and selfish, and then wide open, gentle, and courteous, with an extraordinary generous streak. He not only gave away his paintings and watercolours, but gave his time and compassion to people he knew would not only disappoint him but double-cross him. It was as if his generosity came out of a quiet despair: aware that there was so little generosity in the world, he proved its existence by giving ... and expecting little or nothing in return; and—with a determined, self-indulgent guilelessness—he insisted on imposing his style on the world around him, affirming himself ... so that he was able, with a straight face, to agonize over having no money while standing outfitted in a beautifully tailored brocade suit with lace cuffs. He was contemptuous of know-nothing radicals and mind wreckers, not because he was conservative—no, he wanted them to be more dangerous, more expert, more disciplined in their destruction, so that he could respect them enough to really hate them and to arouse within himself a fuller sense of triumph at his own individuality. He extended himself in all directions, as if he had no centre, yet tenaciously held on to his family, to his wife, his children, his women, as if it were possible to patiently organize not only his emotions, but the emotions of others. Outrageously public and always on stage, he was enormously private with only two or three close friends whom he seldom saw; and though he was sometimes preposterous and ludicrous in the way he left himself open to attack, he worried and fretted and was upset when anyone he knew strung himself out, even a little, in pain. But he himself lived in pain, arthritic pain, tendonitis, high blood pressure ... always alive at the ends of his nerves ... to ecstasy, work, rage ... MAINTAIN A STANDARD OF CHAOS, he insisted, slashing at the air with one of his silver-handled canes, as he had the pleasure of calmly contemplating his own distress ...

Inland, Larry Zolf had been hired as a political correspondent on the public affairs television program, "This Hour Has Seven Days."

He was like William Ronald, he was not "off-the-rack"—a perfect 42, a perfect 44, trousers cuffed.

He brought verbal energy, arcane anecdotes, scholarship, laughter, the capacity not just to see but to observe, to his televised conversations and his reporting.

He caused consternation.

A cabinet minister, Pierre Sevigny, was seen on film beating him about the head with a cane. Because he had asked an honest question.

Zolf had a future.

But McLuhan told me over coffee in Hart House that television could have no future. "It can't have a future, not as we usually use the term. Because it has no past. Everything on television is instantly forgotten. It has no history. How can it have a future if everything that has happened is forgotten?" He also told me that he believed there were angels on the planets.

"Angels!"

"Why not? They've been around a while."

"I guess so."

"Now they've got a future."

When I saw him again Zolf said, "Future, future ... I'll tell you about future. The fucking Israelis have killed my father's language, his whole culture, who I am ... Yiddish. They're killing off Yiddish. To them Yiddish is out. To them there's only Hebrew. That leaves me, my father nowhere ... what future? What culture have they got in Hebrew, you tell me that ... No culture. That's what they've got. No culture."

Zolf, a future?

"He'd better zipper his lip," Morley told me.

"Morley says you better zipper your lip."

"Morley says ..."

"This Hour Has Seven Days" had no future. It was taken off the air. The president of the CBC fired Zolf.

We met at night at the Riverboat. Brownie McGhee and Sonny Terry were on stage. Brownie sang. *My Father, my father said these words, followed me down through the years.* Zolf was upset. He had wanted to publicly denounce the Ottawa mandarins who had scuttled the program. *Believe half you see an' nothing that you hear.* I'd told him I was sure that the "stars" of the show—Patrick Watson and Laurie Lapierre—would gladly hang him out to dry for their cause. "Patsy's your wife's name but that's what they'll play you for. A patsy." Zolf talked it over inside his head with his own father, and then with my brother, and came to a grim conclusion. "This is one Jew who isn't offering anybody either cheek," he said.

"So what d'you want to say?"

"What I want to say is one thing, what I got to say is nothing."

Brownie and Sonny came down off the stage, a crippled man leading a blind man, singing *Walk on, walk on, got to keep on walking to make my way back home.*

There was a heavy downpour as we left the Riverboat. Larry went home. Lessons were beginning to sink in. Brownie and Sonny and I went to my brother's flat on College Street. It was a steady drumming rain that kept on all through the night. Then at five in the morning it cleared and in the milk-white hour, in a lean side alley under a folded steel fire escape, Sonny Terry, his wide-brimmed, stained fedora plunked on his head, shuffled along the cement alley, rapping his blind man's cane against the brick wall. Several paces behind, riding up and down in a hobble-step, was Brownie McGhee.

Brownie scowled.

As a child, polio-stricken at four, he had been hauled around by his brothers in a wagon as he tried to hide his stunted leg, a cripple whose mother had bought herself "a train ticket as long as her right arm," whose sharecropper father, Huff, a fish-fry guitar player, had told him, "You going to play guitar, you best learn to pick. Otherwise, you'll strum all your life."

Brownie had picked.

He had picked up and left Tennessee.

He had picked his words, picked his time, and he had picked his friends. For forty years, beginning in 1938, he and Sonny had sung together.

They had met in Burlington, North Carolina, working the textile mills, Sonny playing with Blind Boy Fuller, but Fuller had died, and Brownie and Sonny latched on to each other, moving to Harlem, with Brownie talking the talk and Sonny settling—wherever he was—into a hulking quietude. Brownie was suspicious and prickly and sometimes abrasive—with his magisterial head and a hobble he hated; keeping a journal of misspelt sayings and poems, aware of his own pain and hatred and how chameleon he was, and how he tormented those who loved him with a bewildering evilness of temper. He had a smile that could kill. He didn't trust anybody. Not on the road. But Sonny had to trust everybody. He was not only blind, he couldn't write and didn't know his numbers and carried an ink pad and a stamp: SONNY TERRY. He was all pockets—for his harps, his keys, his papers, his money. He tried to separate his money into pockets ... ones, fives, tens ... but people lied to him, took too much money from his open palm or short-changed him.

On this morning, both Brownie and Sonny were alert and laughing, though—sitting around in my brother's apartment upstairs—we had been quick on the bottles of Johnny Walker Red all night. Brownie held his guitar under his arm. He called out, "Walk on, Baby, walk on. Break clean, come out fighting," and he swung the guitar across his paunch, singing out as we came into the ordered emptiness of College Street on a Sunday morning:

I'm a stranger here,
Just blowed in your town
If I ask you for a favor
Please don't turn me down ...

A streetcar clattered by, pale mass-bound faces in the windows staring sleepily at two black men, one burly and blind, the other crippled, singing their way out of the narrow dead-end alley, followed by me, a white man with his shades on, black sunglasses. Sonny suddenly hollered, "Man, you see me do a buck and wing? You see me do that? Hold my cane."

"Watch that drainpipe, man."

"You watch your worried mind."

Sonny Terry was thick through the shoulders and arms, his hands meaty, and he moved his feet heavily in a carefree shuffle, staring straight ahead, a white film in his eyes behind glasses. He had a boyish smile and spoke with a country slur so thick that not everyone could understand him, and there he was, doing a buck and wing, big feet slipping back and forth—like a sandman dancer—and up and down, snapping his heels, and then he leapt into the air, crossed his legs and smacked his heels with his hands. After he took his cane back he said, "Man, I could do that the whole time 'fore I got the gout. Can't do nothing with the gout. Got me pills from a doctor in Washington, they hardly do nothing."

Sonny, Brownie, and I stood under the fluttering dying neon of the closed restaurant beneath my brother's apartment. It was too early for Brownie to go to his hotel, a shabby flop for rummies and roach peddlers, the Hotel California, where they padlocked and chained the doors at two in the morning—despite fire regulations—and didn't open again until seven, trapping anyone asleep inside, but, "Never mind, a man should have an official room to rest his head," Brownie said, "and I surely do." He often slept in his car. He thrust out his chin and turned his mouth down like a disapproving wry preacher, stepping back to say as he aimed his guitar at me, "Mother, when the great day comes ... I may just save you."

Suddenly, my brother appeared in the alley, buck-naked, loping towards us. Michael waved gaily to people in a passing streetcar as he came out onto the sidewalk, smiling broadly. "I forgot to say goodbye," he cried.

"Nothing I can do will save that boy," Brownie said as my brother threw his   83
arms around him, and they stood there, embracing in the morning light.

Sonny tapped his cane. "What's going on, man, what's going on?"

THREE

Decades later, my friend Austin Clarke—the novelist from Barbados who lived in Toronto—invited me to his home for a night drink with the pugnacious Norman Mailer. I said I was delighted to come. But in my heart I resented Mailer. I had resented him for years, ever since he had written an unfair and self-serving review of Morley's *That Summer in Paris* in 1963 in the first issue of *The New York Review of Books*. The big memorable scene in that book was Morley bloodying Hemingway's mouth and knocking him down. Mailer's review hadn't been about the memoir, it had been about Mailer. He had talked as if he knew about fighting, as if he could duke it out. He had belittled a wise and generous book. As I walked to Austin's house I got angrier and angrier. And all my resentment of self-serving reviewers who had cold-cocked me, too, rose in my throat. I knocked on the door. I told myself that I'd like the son-of-a-bitch to say just one smart-ass thing and I would clock him. I wouldn't tell him why. I'd just whack him in the head.

We shook hands. He was a little old guy who only came up to my shoulder. He looked like a tubby little *schlepper* in a tweed jacket. Fat Saul, who couldn't beat a rug, would have had him for lunch. I felt ridiculous, ashamed. What in the world had I been thinking? Mailer was affable and courtly to everyone in the room. He couldn't have been more charming. I sat in a corner of the sofa, stuck. What was to be said? Nothing. It went against all my inclinations, but I knew I had nothing to say so I stood up and said goodbye to Austin. He asked me what was the matter, why was I going so soon? I said, "Nothing, it's just that I've got nothing to say to Mailer."

Once I was out on the street, I thought, Shit, I should have whacked him in the mouth. Or given him a short shot to the ribs. Break a rib, I thought as I walked down the street, picking up my stride. Yeah, break a rib. A cat was running along in the shadows ahead of me. My mind began to play tricks, the cat drawing me into the darkness. I decided I wouldn't tell Morley that I had met Mailer. He would just get angry all over again, and after all, what could he say that he hadn't already said to me? What could he say? What could I say? Silence. I dropped my shoulder as if I were about to let go a left hook, and went on home alone.

The flashing eyes in the shadows, the snarling, then the glint of moonlight on the tiers of seats, made him draw back, and his mind played tricks on him. The whole arena seemed to come alive; it seemed to be there in a reddish glow as the fierce sun was strained through the giant coloured awnings on the poles around the arena; and the wild animals, the leopards, the wolves, the cheetahs and the tigers were there, circling around crazily, blind with fright, sliding frantically along the barricade, crashing into it, lashing out with their tails; and now waiting with wild glowing eyes, watching him because he was standing over the underground cells where the prisoners, doomed to be tossed out as meat, waited. The fear and the terrible anxiety of the prisoners was like a smell seeping through the ground to him, and there before him, waiting with glowing eyes, half-starved, the great cats.

It was a sunlit morning. About to cross the street before the light changed to red, I felt a searing pain in my right knee, burning wire drawn through the needle's eye of the joint; I couldn't breathe for pain. As I lay in bed in Wellesley Hospital my knee was swollen with fluid. "I've got goitre of the knee," I said. The doctor looked at me, smiled, and said, "That'd be easy to fix. You've got arthritis." My ankles were swollen, too, and there was a clamplike pain in the middle of my backbone. The doctor laid his palm on the taut skin around my knee. "Really warm" he said. "This'll hurt." The needle looked like a ballpoint refill. He pressed hard, driving the needle through the skin into the membrane. Pale yellow fluid whooshed out. "Terrific pressure," he said. "We'll shoot it with cortisone but we'll probably have to do this every day."

"How come I got this?"

"At your age?"

"Yeah."

"Arthritis hits babies. No surprise it hit you. You're in your twenties."

"It's a surprise to me."

"Look, I'll tell you something." he said. "Doctors'll talk to you all day about arthritis, and you've got three different kinds so far as we can figure, but fundamentally we don't know anything about it because we don't know why, we don't know why it is what it is, so we don't know how to cure it. Treat it, yes. Cure it, no."

Nothing had been more natural for me than running. The quick dart, the deceptive loping stride. Run. Run. Run. Now I was lying still on my back. The weight of the sheet on my knee was painful. The least movement, the least flex of a muscle was painful. A burning, gnawing pain. Breathing was painful. I thought I was having a heart attack. My heart was in a grip. The doctor told me pain travels, picks a muscle and travels, and sometimes you don't know where it's come from but you know where it's been and where it is. The inflammation was in my back, the pain was around my heart.

I lay still, as still as could be. Staring at the walls in stillness. Trying so hard to relax while in pain that I broke into a sweat. Then nurses and interns came with a razor, big bowls of water and plaster. They drained the knee, shot in cortisone, shaved my leg, and began to swathe the length of my leg, instep to inner thigh, in wet bandages. Encased, except for an oval window to the knee. So that I couldn't move the joint, so that the pain would lessen, so that I might sleep.

"Want us to do that too?" a nurse, her hands thick with plaster, asked as she drew the sheet up across my legs and belly. "Might save you some trouble." She laughed. It was a sad, friendly laugh.

My mother and father and Nina came to see me. My mother seemed stricken, to see her dancing boy so, and I was stricken that she should see me so.

Days passed.

Days upon nights upon days.

I practised holding my breath. I don't know why. Maybe to see how long I could hold it. I would imagine the secondhand on King Whyte's pocket watch, the night grandfather Tom was supposed to die. When I wasn't breathing I could listen to my body.

Pain seemed to be creeping through the whole of my body. I was sure I could hear it, feinting, receding, but travelling until one night around midnight I couldn't move. I felt a total silence. I could move my head, but nothing else. It was like my arms had been vacated. I felt a tear on my cheek. I was surprised. I didn't want to feel self-pity. I was afraid, and felt sorrow but not self-pity.

A nurse came into the room.

I said, "I can't move. Nothing."

She sat down and held my hand. She didn't say anything. She held my hand in the dark.

The nightlight was the only star in the dark.

At some early hour, in a half-sleep my arms lost their numbness.

In the morning, I was able to move my arms and left leg. My hips felt like the linchpins had been pulled, grinding, unable to bear weight. A young doctor came into the room and told me that I had to accept a couple of things: first, most people got a serious illness every ten years and I was lucky because mine was not cancer; second, I was going to be in bed for a long time, and being young, this would be hard on me, but more important—especially in years to come, I'd have to learn to absorb all pain, in fact, to forget, as much as possible, everyday pain and go about life like life was normal.

"You mean from now on pain is so normal it's not there?"

"Yes. If you can do it."

He left me alone to think and then came back to tell me that many arthritics could not drink liquor, it further inflamed the joints. He handed me a glass of Scotch. "Drink this," he said, "we're going to see what happens."

In the afternoon, after it was happily clear that the drink had not damaged me, he told the head nurse that I was allowed liquor in my room and he advised me to tell Morley and Nina to come with a bottle before supper, "a kind of small cocktail hour. You may be here for months."

I was. For months.

I decided to drink anything too thin to eat.

And that's when I was surprised at how easily I shut down the outside world, how seldom I even looked at the window, let alone outside. I accommodated myself to the bed, my narrow white boat adrift in white, like Pym, who had sailed into a great white womb of ice, wintering without committing myself to the walls, taking in everything in the room, the sudden apparition of faces, their stillness, the stillness of eyes and mouths suspended in the play of light on the walls, still waters, I had never known such stillness. Such refusal. That's what it was. A refusal that let me be free of everything that might impinge on me except my pain. A refusal in which I was learning to forget pain.

Of course, I also got drunk. At least once a week I drank myself to sleep. An amber sleep. I believed I could feel the amber in my bones. A balm. That left me smiling. I thought I was smiling in the dark. In silence. That silence the other side of the coin to my mother, her rice blossom face howling in pain. A sudden screech, a fierce silence.

A young but balding priest from Our Lady of Lourdes Church came to see me one morning. He wanted me to go to confession. I said No. I thought I had been through a period of purity, almost absolute. Not sexual purity, not that stupidity. But in the marrow of my mind. In the ice womb. I told this to the young priest. He smiled and smiled, bewildered. I felt sorry that I had talked to him like that, bewildering him. As he went to the door he said, "You're sure now, no confession?"

"No," I said. "I'd take the white wafer, but no confession."

"You know you can't do that."

"I know. But I would."

The blood rose in his face. He was angry and left.

Just before Christmas they took off the cast. My leg looked like it had been under water for a month, sickly white.

The pain had eased. I encouraged several nurses to massage my legs.

The bedpans had been cleared from their cabinet. A selection of single malts stood in place.

Nina had a drink at five, my father at eight, and two interns took to dropping by just before midnight.

Between Christmas and New Year's one of the interns wheeled me upstairs to a lounge where we drank pure alcohol. White lightning. We got pleasantly drunk.

"You know man is going to the moon soon," the intern said. "He's going to walk on the moon."

"Yes. Maybe."

"No maybe about it. He's going to walk on the moon. We're still going to be trying to figure out how to get you walking while somebody's walking on the moon."

"I don't think about the moon too much. Stars, yeah. I like thinking about the stars, but the moon leaves me cold."

"Standing there the guy'll look down and see how really small we are."

"You think about that?" I asked.

"Yeah."

We drank more white lightning.

"You think doctors are dummies?" he said. "We don't think about these things? Cut and stitch, cut and stitch?"

"Naw, I just like to know you keep your mind on what you're doing."

"You ever think about Medusa?"

"No."

"When they cut her head off, they did something terrible. She worshipped men, her hair was all snakes and snakes were like penises to those people."

"You sure?"

"Men who hated themselves cut off her head. Mass castration!"

"You're gonna be a surgeon," I said.

"Sure."

"Keep your eye on what you're cutting," I said.

He wheeled me back downstairs.

Within three weeks, after physiotherapy, my parents came to get me. Morley brought me Tom's hawthorn walking stick. I was learning to walk all over again on the one leg. I moved very slowly.

"Be careful," my mother said.

"This is how they'll walk on the moon," I said.

I didn't know if it was the stiff drink I'd had or whether I'd learned how to forget, but I felt no pain.

FOUR

In 1963, arranging my marriage was not easy. I was a lapsed Catholic and Nina—the daughter of people from Russian border villages, immigrants who had no affection for the Church, either its teachings or its randy village priests—had not been baptized. I went to a well-liked, white-haired old Irish priest, Father Kerridan, a man of deceptive affability, and asked him to marry us (that's when I learned I had a great weakness for assuming that affability was a sign of tolerance and generosity of spirit). Standing in the shadow of St. Basil's steeple, he dismissed me angrily, saying that I was lapsed—in a state of sin—that I was less than a Catholic, and the woman I was going to marry was nothing. "Nothing, you see. Nothing. The Church is not a recreation hall."

I phoned Father Fehr in Windsor.

"I made a mistake in talking to Kerridan," I said.

"No, no. I think we'll find that the Church is a little bigger than Father Kerridan," he said. He told me to call a Father Noonan, the pastor of St. Basil's Church, which was close to my office in the graduate school. "He's a priest who really works in the parish, he's gentle, he worries a little too much for his parishioners. Last week he was tipsy and walked through a glass door. You'll like him."

I met Father Noonan in his office and he said, as I sat down, "Do you know who a Catholic is?"

"No," I said.

"Neither do I," he said. "When would you like to get married?"

"In a couple of months," I said. I stood up.

"I'll talk to Nina a while. Instruction. Two or three chats. That'll be that."

"Good."

"Father Fehr says to say hello."

"Hello."

"Hello," another priest whispered, "hello, down here."

It was three o'clock in the morning, a month before the marriage. I was working late, my office light was the only light on close to the church grounds, except for the flashlight of the watchman who checked doors and kept an eye peeled for Father Teskey. It was Father Teskey whispering to me as I set out for home. He often whispered "Hello" to me, while he crouched down among honeysuckles and dogwoods, a little drunk, hiding from the watchman.

Father Teskey had taught me first-year Philosophy.

"Heraclitus and the boys," he'd said. "Up to their necks in the changing tides ... does any one have a rope you could throw to him that'd be worth hanging on to?"

He didn't teach anymore.

"Down here, down here," he said. The grass had been freshly cut, a sweet wetness was in the air.

"Would you come down and kneel for a while and have a drink perhaps, just a sip, mind, I've little to spare."

He was in his fifties, with close-cropped grey hair. "I've been watching you," he said, from behind a bush. He had narrow shoulders. "I sit in here waiting for the watchman and when he trots by I watch him. He's been told to look out for me, even found me once over by the tennis courts. He's a Scot, a bad breed, all calculating and no dreams and when they die, their mouths are holes. That's it. Holes. In need of a cork."

He held out a silver flask.

"One pull is what you get."

I took a drink.

He looked around warily. "The Boss ... he told them to keep an eye out for me, you know. What's a watchman for if he isn't watching, and I'm what's wrong. You know that?" He touched my hand. "They tell me I'm all wrong because I don't want forgiveness, none at all. Any time I think about it I end up ... You know what St. Teresa said God said to her? 'If I hadn't created Heaven for Myself, I'd have to create it for you.'"

The priest rose to a crouch.

"He's coming. I've got to beat it ..."

"Never mind," I said.

"What?"

"I'll take off ..."

I crouched forward, head down and bolted out of the bushes, half loping, half crawling up the slope of the lawn, a shadow in the moonlight. The watchman, running, called out, "Hold on there, Father, hold on ..." as I headed off between the trees, leading him away from the old priest hiding in the bushes.

On the day that we were married, Nina was driven to the church by Goffredo in his "Mayor of Motor City" black Cadillac and the car was daubed all over with white paper flowers made by his children. There were two priests on the altar in the stalls behind Father Noonan; Father Shook, the president of the Pontifical Institute of Medieval Studies, and Father Teskey. I was very touched to see Father Teskey there. I hadn't seen him in the daytime for years.

It was to be a simple mass, only the families and close friends, with two choirboys from the Cathedral Choir School. There was, however, a huge *corpus* in agony on the Cross on a side wall of the church. I worried a little about that. The first time Nina had seen it—at a Christmas midnight mass—she had begun to cry. "What's the matter?" I'd asked. We had both been drinking at a Celebrity Club party earlier on.

"He's in terrible pain. Someone should do something."

"What?"

"Take him down."

"You can't. He's God. He's got to be there."

"Take him down. Look at him. He's a man ..."

"He's God, and He has to die. You don't understand the story."

"That's terrible. I can't believe you don't want to do anything."

On Saturday afternoon, as Nina came up the aisle, she paid no attention to her man on the cross. The prayers were said. The songs were sung. Just before the vows, as I was about to be asked if I took this woman for my wife, Father Teskey stood up, crouched forward and hurried from the altar. I remember thinking, That's odd. My best man handed me the ring and I put the ring on her finger.

Years later, I remembered Father Teskey. I remembered the watchman and my taking off in the night in Father Teskey's stead: had he, at the wedding, taken off in my place? Had it been a signal missed? And if—as a signal—it had been taken, what would I have done? Nothing. I loved Nina. Still, signals are signals and maybe I had missed Father Teskey's as I had missed a signal my father had given me a year earlier.

Morley, Nina, and I had been talking in the living room about pain, my pain, and the meaning of pain ... and Nina had said something about "mind over matter" and overcoming pain and suddenly Morley said, "Of all the Greeks, the great old Greeks, who's the one who's most important to you, to society?"

"Sophocles," I said.

"Solon the Law Giver," Nina said.

"What!" I said.

"Why?" Morley asked.

"Because, if there is no law, everything falls apart. There's nothing without the law."

"You believe that?"

"Yes. I even wanted to be a cop once," she said.

Ever since my childhood jaunt to Woolworth's, I'd been uneasy about cops.

"But Sophocles," Morley said. "The artist is an anarchist."

"Sure," she said gaily, and gave Morley a kiss on the forehead.

A month before the wedding, Nina's father had asked me, "What do English people drink?" To him, anyone who spoke English was English. He drank vodka, the English drank ... Scotch, or rye, or gin; who knew? Some of my aunts didn't know what to make of my marrying a woman who wasn't of Irish descent, but a mysterious Slav ... a strange, unruly people. Paul Rabchuk was Russian, his wife

Ukrainian. While still young, he had gone from his village at the Polish border to Vladivostok and then had come back through Siberia to join the Polish army, and after he was mustered out and had returned to his village, he picked up a Canadian handbill. "I read it," he told me, "and it said 'Go to Saskatchewan.' I didn't know where it was, so I went."

My people didn't know anything about Nina's people, didn't know anything about Siberia, just as her family didn't know anything about the coffin boats, so no one knew what to expect. (I did enjoy explaining to Morley that many of Mrs. Rabchuk's friends thought Nina was marrying "down" by marrying outside their community.) All the English-speaking people gathered after the wedding mass at Morley's house, drank whisky and soda or rye and water and ate little white bread sandwiches. By six o'clock, when they set out in cars for the Russian reception in a big hall, they were all a little tipsy.

The Ukrainian band blared out the "Wedding March" as each guest arrived at the door. There were long rows of tables, seating for five hundred, a bottle of Scotch at every third place setting. My people had never confronted so much free drink. They carried my uncle Ambrose out before anyone sat down to eat. A dozen women came bustling from the kitchen, carrying trays heaped with food that my people had never seen: braised brisket, heavy with garlic (my father and brother hated garlic), roast chicken and potatoes, deep-fried meat on a stick, thick mushroom gravy, *kapusta*, *pyrohy*, *holupchy*, *rakusky* ...

By the time the meal was done and the tables taken up for dancing, Nina's 450 people were standing back against the walls, agape. The small band of "English," though they didn't know how to polka, had taken over the floor, turning themselves loose, twirling, hopping, whirling, trying to bound into the air like members of the Red Army Chorus ... and Morley watched in quiet awe as the long lineup of guests moved to toast the bride and groom, each person carrying an envelope stuffed with cash. Mr. Rabchuk warned me that I could not drink a shot-glass of whisky with each guest. "You will kill yourself. Drink water, pretend it's vodka." I danced with Nina, danced with my mother and then Mrs. Rabchuk said, "Time to count the money." We went into a closet filled with mops and pails. After the counting, Nina said, "That'll take us through Europe." (The bridal shower with Three hundred guests would help with the buying of our furniture.) As the dancing wound down, as the band played a last tune, the subdued Russians and Ukrainians shook their heads in amusement as the "English" straggled happily and hopelessly drunk out into the night, some picking up whisky bottles that hadn't been opened. "Obviously," I said, "the English will drink anything they can get their hands on." My friends and family, some singing at the tops of their voices, an unruly bunch at one o'clock in the morning, drove off in all directions, some going up onto lawns, around lampposts, totally delighted and dead drunk.

And that is how Nina and I crossed the cultural barriers and got to Dublin, London, Rome, and Paris.

Escape from the Glue Factory

JOE ROSENBLATT

Joe Rosenblatt grew up in Toronto at more or less the same time as Barry Callaghan, who now often publishes Rosenblatt's poetry and drawings. But their worlds were so far apart that their recollections show no similarity. Rosenblatt (b. 1933) won the Governor General's Award for Poetry for his 1986 book *Top Soil*. Some of his other collections are *The LSD Leacock* (1966), *The Winter of the Lunar Moth* (1968), *Dream Craters* (1974), and *Virgins and Vampires* (1975). He lives at Qualicum Beach on Vancouver Island. What follows is taken from *Escape from the Glue Factory: A Memoir of a Paranormal Toronto Childhood in the Late Forties*, published in 1985.

MY SHRINE BY NUMBERS

My mind roves sluggishly, then slices through birth water, propelled like a channel catfish, searching for the house where I was bar mitzvahed, that sanctified front room with its high pale green ceiling, a room on a tree-lined street, rows of embracing chestnut trees, and it seems like aeons since I was bar mitzvahed, a grey spot on the winding sheet of memory ...

The building on D'Arcy Street has vanished, gone like a shy creature into the fog. Some malignant force has nudged the house down the block or ripped it out, leaving a cavity, a parking lot in its place. The D'Arcy Street Talmud Torah is gone, and so, I'm sure, is Rebbe Noble. The neighbourhood has borne the strain of time, even the chestnut trees seem bent. I remember those trees when they were young, ragged and wild, the spiky green capsules falling, striking the sidewalk, cracking, the white flesh inside exposing a dark brown eye, and hundreds of those empty green shells torn apart by wind and rain ... brown eyes strewn on the lawn.

The chestnut trees spread over the lead-painted dwellings, proliferous leaves. Like some senior elephant, my shrine wore a russet skin and inside dwelt a plebeian Hebrew soul: ragged yellow wallpaper bubbling here and there from anxiety, the oak veneer floors covered by an inexpensive tile, in which an aquamarine floral arrangement swam against a creamy background, blending into a seeded gold and silver inlay ... asterisks glistened and had a quieting effect. I studied the rhythms of the surface of the tile ... eye alerted to the various gravities, hot and cold zones ... The tile had a will of its own and a penchant for stealing footprints from worshippers during winter.

I love an aging house, plasterboard showing through the chipped paint, a dwelling older than Noble, its ribs revealing the seamier side of growing old, paint applied to paint, unable to hide decaying liverwarts, an aged heart barely alive under freshly painted skin.

There was a mural in the tiny vestibule, a mural that seemed to have been painted by numbers. A pencilled outline had been left on the wall. Trees pencilled-in had been partially erased, but the perimeters had been left. The mural complemented the tile, giving off a sallow light and an odour of stale oil paint and turpentine ... the usual forest scene ... derived from European wall hangings ... the shaft of sickly yellow light ... dabs of ultra-golden sunlight ... exaggerated lightbeams on a mushroom ... and there, the familiar puzzled stag without testicles. Done by numbers ... a wilderness painting and this degendered creature in the landscape, in a patch of toadstools, lost, licked, and sucked by a mouth of bad lighting. The picture cried out for an androgynous youth ...

But wait: a brown moth is trying to dominate one area of this world of numbers. Did the painter stop and let his assistant continue? A brown moth resting in vigorous sunlight, a moth with a real stomach, who dominated and had intensity ... leaving a shadow, a surrounding blur ... Outside my shrine, green spiky planets fell from chestnut trees, splitting on the pavement, exposing their brown eyes.

BLOSSOMS IN THE SHRINE

If I could number my memories I'd paint myself into a corner. There wouldn't be enough good bourbon to wash the sadness of the brushes. Still, I remember a sweet time: one fall afternoon, when pain finally realized its bar mitzvah blossoms. Following the ceremony held at a store-front synagogue down the street from the D'Arcy Street Talmud Torah, guests marched down the hall to the back of the

house into a makeshift banquet hall and seated themselves at their designated banquet tables. Rebbe Noble, an inscrutable septuagenarian, banged a drinking glass
to get everybody's attention, and soon his absolute authority held the whole room
silent. He lauded the bar mitzvah boy, intelligence ... drive ... and announced I
was about to make a speech, in Yiddish.

I praised my beaming parents, my uncle sitting silently nearby, and Rebbe
Noble for his tireless instruction. Then, I ended my speech by thanking the assembled guests for attending my confirmation, wishing them a good appetite, which
was a cue for the kitchen staff to get the machinery in motion.

Thunderous applause ripped through the hall. A few among the hard-pressed
volunteer kitchen staff ventured out to contribute glee. The women, my mother
and friends, had prepared gefilte fish and laid out hundreds of evenly roasted capon
parts cooked in their own wild juices. Chicken parts faced lilliputian Prince
Edward Island virginal spuds. My attention was glued to salient islands of chicken
... tall thighs and legs bejewelled by their own frizzled grease, authentic Chicken,
not birds fertilized by artificial light. The food was heaped onto huge serving plates
accompanied by trays of baked egg bread, the twisted *chalah*, freshly glazed, braided, lightly tanned.

97

The guests were overwhelmed as I was: this was the first course. It beamed
on me that perhaps the guests had tolerated my youthful exuberance out of civility. The dollies arrived loaded with mounds of steaming food: an aromatic tide
swept the banquet room; kreplach, chopped liver, chopped raw onion, herring in
its skin of schmaltz, bowls of cabbage soup, cold beet borscht, more plates of
chopped onions, eggs, as a gastric seismograph recorded the ebb and flow of stomach acid, playing a glyphic arrangement on the mind, and my palate, abstracting
itself, became a wolf eel lusting after kishka, an intestine stuffed with onion, flour,
seasoning, and roasted to a deeply hued brown. This was no ordinary intestine,
but one taken from a bovine of delight.

Rebbe Noble clinked his glass. He proposed a toast to my folks ... Uncle
Nathan ... the janitor ... the cooks in the kitchen, whose names he had memorized so as not to offend, and before he tossed down a tumbler of schnapps, mumbled a blessing. Then the bread was blessed and appetizers leading to the main
course. I marvelled at the rebbe's alcoholic tolerance.

Nobody poured a shot for me. I had, after all, become a man and had earned
the right to a drink. The good rebbe turned down my request before I could even
ask for a drink. His eyes sparkled and he laughed softly into his shot glass. Turning

aside, I saw a private table dominated by an elite of grey beards who waved me away from their zone of influence, segregated from the others, a gerontocracy unto themselves. "Go Vey ... *gey avek*," they shouted in Yiddish and chopped English.

I was not to be denied firewater. I swiped a bottle of Canadian Club and in the privacy of my room at home drank it quietly, trying to outdrink Rebbe Noble in one sitting. As I tossed down a shot, a thought occurred: what had happened to those sealed envelopes pressed into my mother's hands ... the bar mitzvah gifts ... expenses were involved, of course, in putting the feast together ... the hall rental ... and the rebbe himself had to be paid for instructing somebody terminally hopeless ... but ... I blessed myself ... blessed the schnapps ... and the woozies struck. The booze sent me into a spin. By moonlight I saw the clock reverse its hands. My bedroom floor, a whirlpool, was dragging me down. I jumped around like a carp out of water. I flopped in panic. Soon, the whirlpool dragged me under into a deep, merciful sleep, a greenish state, and then clouds shaped like kishka drifted as I swam in a private sky.

Deep Fried Dream

The ferocious dream I had, whereby the woozies released me to demons of the subgalactic world:

I fall into a bog. The kishke clouds pass. I am staring at a silver screen illumed by a powerful prison lightbeam.

"Can I get you something, kid?"

The kid scrubs away a tear. The Father Confessor next to the kid bears resemblance to Rebbe Noble.

"Father, a nice onion pizza ..."

"I can't do it kid. It's almost time."

Father Love wants to tell the world they are all responsible for pulling the trigger, the kid didn't have a chance, born in the slums ... the school of hard-knocks ... his friends: pimps, prostitutes, perverts, drug addicts, cops on the pad. No, the kid didn't pull the trigger. It was hate, society, you and me, including Father Love. And now, they are playing God ... killing the kid ...

Eddy, con #9 on Death Row, thoughtful as a tick drilling for blood, would dearly love to tear the collar from Father Love's neck.

The film becomes grainy, crackles ... a cavity is present, a sepulchral silence.

The only sound in the theatre: popcorn rattling in buttery containers, as usual before a death scene.

The kid's upper lip quivers as though brushed by a religious firefly.

The dream ruptures.

"So why'd you do it, kid? All those nice goils ... aren't you ashamed, Eddy. Did you know your mother was a goil?"

In the '40s, every celluloid degenerate's name was Eddy. Every prison priest had the flush of the bagman's worldly goodwill.

The kid refuses to make eye contact. "Huh," he slobbers, guilt absent from his blue peepers. He is going to turn over those peepers to an eye bank ... maybe ... if Father Love can talk him into it.

"Eddy, and you being from such a decent family ... you could have done the college ting like your brother, Eddy, you could have amounted to somebody ... the president ... yes, Eddy, a fine ting ... democracy."

Eddy is boiling. Can he tell Father Love his mother was a whore ... a drugged wormy ...

"Back off ... screw ... you hear," he shouts.

"Eddy ... I'm not a copper ... Don't be mad, now. God will forgive you, in His Infinite Love ..."

"Don't call me Eddy ... only my pals call me Eddy ..."

"Okay, kid."

"I don't care about the Big Cheese up there. Maybe you'd like to meet that big Rat. Ha, ha, ha ..."

A hiss of air: "Help me, please ... I don't want to die." Father Love strokes the kid's hair. "Be brave ... I'll be with you ... so will He ..." The kid's face streaks with tears.

The kid starts giggling. He starts shivering and rubbing his hands together. He can feel the deeper chill entering his bones. He moans for his mother. The kid hates his mother.

"Please, please help me ..." It's time for one last confession. Not worth a nickel on Earth, maybe his soul has a little platinum. "Eddy ... let us pray."

The kid knows the game is up.

"You fruitbar ... I bet if I ripped that collar off your friggin' neck."

"Eddy, don't mock ..." The kid's bawling like there's no tomorrow, which is accurate. There's the rhythm of rubber footsteps down the corridor, the cries of prisoners on Death Row. "I ain't afraid," says Eddy.

"Thou therefore, my son, be strong in the grace that is Jesus Christ ..."

The bulls move in and put the handcuffs on the kid. "It's okay, boys, I'm ready." They secure their special cuffs and chains, leading Eddy down the corridor, the confessor at his side. They stop before a steel door, the one with the red light above it. Eddy hands the confessor a crumpled piece of paper. "It's for mum ... I want her to have a few things ... it ain't much ..."

"I'll make sure she gets it. I promise."

The guards, ex-linemen for a college football team, drag the kid over the threshold. "Sometimes they foul themselves," says one of the bulls. "They do it all the time. But this kid's different."

"Goodbye kid ... see you in Heaven ..." Father Love shouts as the doors clang shut. They strap Eddy into his high chair. "I ain't scared," he says, screwing his lips tighter, peaceful as eggplant. He turns his eye to the porthole where the warden, his boys, a reporter (who harbours a special hate for degenerates like Eddy) and the confessor are peering into this strange spaceship.

"Show them how to die, Eddy ..." I shout into my pillow.

In the cramped theatre, kids are squirming on the plush, the girls sobbing for Eddy. "He looks kinda cute ..." The closest girl is probed by her boyfriend, a blond chipper, trying to force his hand under her cotton dress, a punk with *wandering hand trouble*. "You're a wolf ..." she cries. The rutting boyfriend starts to wheeze like a young rodent in love ...

The bulls are placing a cheesecloth over Eddy's face. One squeezes Eddy's shoulder. It's Porky's way of saying goodbye. Porky used to buy Eddy his Old Gold and warn the kid about the "tubercules." "We all got to shove off some time, Porky," Eddy used to say, offering the guard a weed.

Eddy's lips are moving.

The confessor strains for signals from under the death veil: MUM ... is the Word.

A cyanide crystal ejected into a pail of sulphuric acid by remote control makes a sizzling sound, an Alka-Seltzer tablet in a glass of cold water. A bell starts ringing ... a red light flares ...

A ghost fills the bowl of Eddy's skull. The confessor is making small animal noises.

Big Red, the tough-assed reporter who said dirty rats like Eddy deserved a sulphuric enema, turns away.

Eddy starts vibrating, convulsing slowly, then rapidly. His chest heaves, as if there were some huge rat in Eddy's chest. Eddy is straining to inhale the final vapours.

The young girl slaps her boy friend's hand just as he drives his tongue with animal joy into her ear ...

Eddy is dead. They all know it. The girls in the theatre ... their tumescent boyfriends ... the confessor ... the warden ... Eddy's mother, still hooking on the street. Everybody knows Eddy is dead, except Eddy ...

The legs stop jerking against the steel bands, the rat in Eddy's chest is asleep, the fan on the wall is whirling, the confessor is crying. He knows Eddy's face has the colour of broccoli, fresh, and in season.

THE MEDITATION TANKS

Uncle Nathan reigned over a fish emporium on Baldwin Street, not far from the D'Arcy Street Talmud Torah. His dark fish tanks contained meditative creatures of sea and lake who stared vacuously at their closed perimeters before lapsing into a partial comatose state. The shop floor was inches deep in a carpet of sawdust to absorb gore, scales, and intestinal matter conglutinated with other intimate organs.

Every Friday, during the late forties and early fifties, a shade before sunset, I carried home packages of carp, pickerel, whitefish, and salmon-trout, selectively scaled, clipped and cut into generous portions by Nathan. Wrapped in layers of newspaper, the Neptunian confraternity appeared mummified. Fish blood, the ultimate glue, held the diversified corpus to the newspaper.

What disturbed me most was not the pieces of fish warming the mummifying layers of newspaper but Nathan's gusto in the quick dismemberment. His gusto had deep suspicious undertones, even to a blooming teenager. His violence revealed a disturbed sublimated sexuality. The pieces of fish virtually exploded on his hard oak operating table, spurting little blood geysers, raising anatomical sectors ... an eye here, and there a white lung ... a pink heart ...

It seemed an endless wet dream, but what stabbed my curiosity was his manner of fondling them, arousing their libido ... somewhere in a vague erotic area of their infinitesimal brains, a temporary pleasure principle was set in motion. Moments before their execution, they wheezed in a responsive anxiety while he sweated profusely.

The poor dwellers in those meditational tanks had the air of political prisoners, lipping out obscenities to their captor. Of course, depending on how religious or poetic one was, the odd torpedo carp or whitefish could just as easily have mouthed benediction. I like to think it was more a curse than prayerful utterance.

101

No one has ever lip-read a fish before, but I learned to decipher the messages: an extreme distortion, a lip bending over another, meant the creature was venting hatreds, and therefore, his anger, or perhaps, his displeasure at Nathan, or anyone peering into the holding tank. Nathan paid little heed to these fine details. He kept cold water flowing into the tanks so the tribes remained vigorous until that eventual hour when he snuffed the batch of finned ethnicity, snuffed without the use of local anesthetic. A blow on the head was his method, and sometimes it required several vicious strokes with a club specially designated (called by contemporary anglers a "priest"—but Nathan lived in the literal world: he never thought of calling his club a rabbi). His dispatcher's instrument was a small paddle. He rushed a wide butterfly net into the tank, scooping up a minor leviathan, dumping the beast on the terminal table, clubbing it into unconsciousness. I like to think the fish were dead when he clipped their fins, scrubbed their scales off their backs, and, wielding a miniature scimitar fish knife like Ming the Merciless, measured the meat for a few precious seconds, and then with the electric eye of a diamond cutter, split his tenants into even sections.

I assumed Nathan was courting a nervous breakdown, rebelling against ichtiocidal guilt by bashing that guilt out of existence. I recall the gasp of a creature not far from Death's fishing hole, a gasp microseconds before the animal was dismembered. Struck, the fish leaped off the surface of the sacrificial table but Nathan pounded it for good measure to ensure a swift demise, though sometimes he or she leaped again one last time. Another comrade followed, a fractured predecessor ... the knife and mallet readied in the restless tension of a Zen master ... the blade danced, another fish was stung ... fish after fish divorced from an alienated body ... it was all rhythm, sex, spontaneity ... a fish blood not nearly so red as our own, but more transparent, like ink in a cheap ballpoint pen ...

I developed an aversion to the fish blood from Nathan's emporium, and to this day I rub my hands together when the topic of blood comes up in lurid conversation, but as the blood gushed in every direction, Nathan darted a glance my way, and bashed his victim: it was all a process of the trade, sentimentality had no place in his establishment. The blow sent a shock wave through the shop, rattling the windows while the tub athletes flipped and were retired from active duty.

Nathan seemed inured to the slaughtering of his underwater legions. The question of launching his fish to the stars as an act of immorality never touched his heart and mind. A stronger point would have been: did he ever dine on his own fish? I never got around to asking him a few sensitive questions about the nature of the immutable and the noumenal, let alone fish and whether he felt that they had souls; and did mankind evolve from fish ... Nathan, tell me ... were you clubbing your prehistoric root ...?

In truth, Nathan kept his feelings to himself and eked out his livelihood. He appeared to enjoy his work and his attitude to his fish possibly would not have been any different than Joe the Fruitman in Kensington Market had you asked him in a moment when he was not busy serving his customers—what were his feelings about selling a large cabbage ...?

The difference was that fish to Nathan were living edibles who had lips which he never tried reading. They were temporary guests in his ponds. Nathan suffered no fish-induced anxiety attacks ... oblong shadows semaphoring in the tanks had absolutely no impact on him ...

Nathan would have assumed that a goldfish was the freak of the batch which arrived in the iced fish crates and had, as a result of the extreme cold been slightly discoloured, or were they?

Of course, they had little time to develop any rapport: none of the tribe survived longer than a week. Friday was terminal city. There was no governor reprieve. Nathan never succumbed to piscatorial liberalism. The complete hyperbole would have been Nathan closing the shop for a day and mourning their passing; the ultimate leap off-the-wall would have been Nathan opening a vegetable shop out of expiation (years later, after Nathan passed away, a mung bean health store opened on the same premises; the ghosts flip about after closing time ... fractions form into one solid fish ... they pout out their pain ...).

Nathan, depleting his fishy world, had a fishlike presence; while his heart wasn't grazed by guilt, his genes were. His psychic armour gave way at times to a deep brooding and a stillness came over him, like the quiescence of some channel fish. In Nathan's deep tubs thoughts bubbled up from the floor ... heavy thoughts ...

Like a carp, Nathan had wide, thick shoulders, and he was short and stout; it was the compactness of a wide-bodied underwater animal ... and while often praising carp, he had a dyspeptic expression, as though everything in life tasted bitter, since there was more sweetness in heaven. The physical Earth was merely a sub-station, one of many, in that long trek to parts unknown. In the meantime, we swam through life like bottom-feeders—a carp or flounder, and found satisfactory edibles on the psychic floor, more readily available than bait fish above. Nathan stayed on the first level and was, as a result, constantly dour, one who believed you had to suffer on the bottom before reaching a school of bait fish residing in one's dreams.

Nathan's fishlike qualities reflected not only his sombre state (I don't ever recall him smiling on any of the Fridays I picked up my fish) but in the karmic outcome of his cruelty: his skin pores were broken and bleeding, similar to the large scales of the carp he had murdered. Fish scales stuck to his inflamed hands. Fish blood had dried and glued a grisly pattern onto those murderous fists so wide and thick, and to complicate his life and trade, he had one bum finger—white from his endless uncrating, unpacking, and sorting of fish from the ice crates. He had developed what is commonly known by carpenters and others who work in inclement weather as a "dead finger." It appeared oyster white, as did his face, which had only the slightest flush of health in his ruddy cheeks. When he worked fast and furiously, a fog emanated from the crates, enshrouding him ... a spectre from the aquatic cosmos attacking his bones ...

It was his cold selection finger. Nathan plucked those chub, or whitefish that were still breathing through the ice slivers, and dropped them into the holding tanks where they gradually came out of their deep sleep. The other deep sleepers were displayed in the shop window. They were gruesome against the background of ice chips, exhibited in an open casket ... a ghoulish sense of humour on Nathan's part ... It was the embalmer in his personality. In truth, Nathan enjoyed his work, and if he indulged in rude display of his fishly wares, then he could be forgiven his indulgences. Every trade has an occupational hazard. He measured his fish with a deep sense of pride. He lived through his fish in the same way parents live through their children. The man never sold a bad fish to anyone and this was evident on Friday when his shop was crammed with customers. They expected the best and received the best of freshest fish, gutted, scaled ... A customer pointed to a carp and Nathan lowered his net ... his mood *concealed*. In his substance, a form of misanthropy dwelt: the misanthrope swam like a sardine-shark attacking some unsuspecting tourist in the tropics—the devil or devils enter the bowels of their victims, ripping them to pieces ... A psychic sardine-shock seemed to follow Nathan around in his shop as he mumbled incoherent words, totally alienated, until a shiny fish appeared ... and his detached grimace became something close to being a smile.

Nathan needed diversion. His energies needed to be channelled elsewhere, into something more creative. I'd have preferred him as a collector of bad debts, a phantom with the atomic particles of Al Capone, Scarface, Edward G. Robinson, the bonbon particles of Nathan, all adding up to Big Eddy and efficiency. Eddy runs an outfit called the Piranha Acceptance Corporation, or PAC, as it is known on the street. A defaulter has disregarded Big Eddy's final notice. The greaseball, a pimply-faced hustler who dominates a few hard street corners, won't pay interest on his loan, won't pay his fifty bills a week, and this has caused gas bubbles in Big Eddy's stomach. The punk has let it be known that the warning is worth less than asswipe: this has given Big Eddy heartburn. The only antacid is maybe chop a finger off, for good measure ...

The dirty little punk is picked up by Big Eddy's gorillas, a standard bunch in their two-tone pointed shoes and creamy white suits ... black shirts and white ties ... hair is pressed flat with Wildroot Cream Oil ... and they carry the skinny meatloaf along the street to a cream-coloured convertible. They drive away with their delinquent account, who is sweating in the back seat. He knows it is wise to say nothing. They would love to damage his body before handing it over to Big Eddy. The machine stops at an ugly semi-detached house. They are greeted by two nasty Doberman. The phantom blows a whistle, the two monsters disappear. The punk is again lifted by his elbows; fright sets in like rigor mortis. They carry him into Big Eddy's den with its phony fireplace. Big Eddy is staring into an aquarium. A rumbling noise issues from the tank, a thick-faced fish staring through the glass, the black torpedo opens his jaws—revealing a set of upper and lower needle works.

Eddy feels affection for his pet. He has fed it fingers, chicken, goldfish, and various strains of cat food ... concerned that his charge is missing a mixed diet ... too overweight ... arterial sclerosis, a heart attack ... he ... she ... certainly no eunuch ... as Big Eddy strokes his gold-edged razor, everyone is all ears, including the punk.

Then, a little appetizer before the morality play. Eddy is scraping hair off his hands, a ritual he's been through before. He plucks a hair from the back of his head, slices it as though it were greased in butter. Dorothy, his pet piranha, has not had her midday meal. She is Dorothy, though Eddy's never really determined the gender of his aquatic pal. Dorothy, in honour of his first wife, who wore Lamour-like sweaters and was also picked up at a drugstore counter, spinning on her stool.

"Schmuck, you missed a payment," says Eddy. The punk shrugs. "Screw you," he says. Eddy is in a meaner mood than Dorothy, the lunatical eating machine. The shine on those teeth ... the minty breath ... Dorothy of the clean gleamers, capped ... a dental surgeon's wet dream ...

There's an electrical glee in the fish.

"What did you say, punk?"

"You heard me," snaps the meathead, sneering into Eddy's face.

"I must be hearing things," Eddy says with a Dorothy-like leer. The boys nod like true robotons. Eddy grips the punk's wrist and gives him a burn. Those are worker's hands. Eddy used to butcher pork in a slaughterhouse.

"You heard me, SLIMEBALL," the punk says, playing the Big Bluff.

Eddy gives the punk a third-degree burn on the wrist. "Okay boys, let's make some pastrami out of this sucker ..." The punk feels warm piss trickling down his pant leg.

"Hey, wormface," Eddy screams, "you ain't never gonna use your pinkies on your broad again. Nobody shits on me and walks away ... nobody."

"Please ... Eddy ..." The punk's voice box is working but the voice doesn't belong to him.

"I'm gonna clip your little wee finger and feed it to Dorothy cause she loves them fingers." Big Eddy breaks out into a gust of laughter. Everybody's laughing but the punk. Dorothy is laughing in her tank. She has a tight Pepsodent smile.

The torpedos hold the punk down. "I'm just gonna chop that little finger, the one with the phony ice ..."

"Eddy, I can explain ... no ..."

The punk sees his pinkie and ring gobbled by Dorothy. He goes into a spin, passing out on the rug, his stump spurting red juice. Eddy has a red-hot curling iron to staunch the bleeding. Eddy fancies himself a finger specialist.

Dorothy chews, burps.

"You know boys, I love the sound she makes. That's real music, not the canned shit ..."

The punk comes to, smells the singe of burning flesh, and passes out again. Eddy shoves an ammonia vial under the punk's nose.

"Oh ... oh ... God ... oh MOM ..."

"Hey wormbag ... You must have chocolate ladyfingers. Dorothy likes you ... And it ain't Mom ... MUM'S the WORD."

There was a sleek little Dorothy in every customer crowding into Nathan's claustrophobic shop. There was a lot of piranha in Nathan, too. He knew how to deal with boisterous housewives maligning or molesting his fish. "That fish was stale ... such fish you should throw in the garbage ... to fool an old lady?"

Nathan endured the Friday Harpies. It was bad enough when they fondled his fish, but suggesting his fish were not fresh when he himself kept them under cold showers, and for no longer than a week in their tub, pressed on his heart. Jabbing a deadly finger, he dimmed their invective, continued his butchery, his place of extermination, sometimes flinging a fish head down on the table, splashing the women with blood. That had a cooling effect. The newspapers stacked to the ceiling were rapidly depleted. He pulled on a white cone of string suspended from the ceiling, yanking an arm's-length of cord, sweeping loops around each bundle, securing a favourite knot. A bundle of fish was shoved into his customer's hands, a flush of anger in his cheeks, but no sound came from his lips; his eyes were fixed on theirs and it was not a friendly entrepreneurial gaze, but a predacious force whose negative vibrations rattled the shop windows. Nathan, rather than endure an argument with a customer, generously added an extra fish body. Each paid and made for the door passing the antique cash register that he rarely if ever used. Nathan liked something more personal, an old cash drawer at the back of the shop. After his apron pockets were loaded with bills and coins, he pulled the drawer out and stuffed the money in, and if there was a free moment, he would clean the coins and bills, wipe off the fish blood, guts, and scales, handling the bills which he rolled into a tube and tied down with an elastic. He carefully stacked his coins: nickels, dimes, fifty-cent pieces, silver dollars; not a square inch of space was wasted. His accounting system was sufficient. It didn't impede his progress.

Nathan's sink was broken down. He stopped to scrub blood off his face, and wiped his hands on a soiled towel. A shard of mirror hung from a nail. He stared into the mirror, flicked away some scales, brushed his hair away and turned back to his chores. He had, along with his other implements, a special triton to keep the dead and dying at bay. Sometimes a fish head sought its severed body, a tail favoured a particular anatomical part, flipping towards union. Nathan brought his triton into play, pronging the piece to the surface of the table. It was ancient, it was magic.

He could have waved it at his cantankerous customers but his stare was enough ... an insult mumbled and regurgitated ... He regurgitated anger and it sublimated itself in his actions as he flung a huge cod head onto the antique scale, shifting the weights until the balance steadied in an even horizon while Nathan fried his customers with his eyes. The frame of the scales was cast iron and parts were bronze. He patiently waited for the correct weight and never rushed, although his fingers fluttered while the machinery was in motion.

Nathan always kept me off balance, in motion for a fist full of silver and, when he was in a more generous mood, a five spot. I had to clean the shop, sweep the floor and shovel contaminated sawdust into a bin along with offal and an assortment of guts. There had to be a fresh carpet of sawdust and the tanks had to be scrubbed and cleaned. Nathan had a steel scrub brush. He expected spotless scrubbing and sweat and rhythm, for no matter how much energy I put into the scrubbing, it was never quite enough. It was always blood he imagined he saw.

The sour-smelling sawdust and pails of offal were loaded along with broken fish crates onto an old railway wagon which Nathan pulled out of the alleyway next to his shop. Together, we piled fish crates and forced the pails in, pressing them into the wood, crushing the containers. I hauled the rusted creaking wagon down the road, turning the corner at Henry Street and at last going along a laneway at the back of the shop. I had to be careful pulling the load, piled so precariously, but somehow I managed to get the wagon down the lane, stopping at Nathan's yard. I tossed the crates over a high fence. Bits and pieces of offal mixed in sawdust fell back on me. A fish head would fly at my face ... some lung ... guts ... I reeked of decaying fish. I kicked at the cats meowing around my legs. I stood on a crate and peered into Nathan's yard, discovering sunflowers bending their heads, the tallest sunflowers in the neighbourhood ...

108

I dragged the wagon back to the shop where Nathan was still hosing down the tanks. A bundle of fish was on the table and an envelope of bills. Nathan was extremely generous this day. I didn't ask any questions. I thanked him for the fish and the money. He rarely replied. I was fortunate to be blessed with a grump and nothing more. I faithfully carried the palpitating bundle home, stripped the paper, dumped the fish into a sink of cold water, and the pieces took on a life of their own ... a fish head lipped an obituary ...

Under a lightbulb casting a sallow yellow light, Nathan moved in shadows, Nathan ready with his net, Nathan staring into the holding tank ... as the bubbling increases in the water, the carp smacking the water with its tail, staring walleyed at life. There is a form of thought transference taking place between Nathan and his fish. I view the fish as being a diminution of Eddy. They are all waiting for the red light bulb to flare. Their appeal has been turned down.

BIRTH OF A LIBERAL: 1947, 1948

A few teachers at Lansdowne Public School loomed larger than a summer flounder. They were veterans fresh from the battlefields of Europe, or British transplants who found themselves in a holding tank, or poor fish who dreamt of English barons pulling King John's elbows at Runnymede, June 15, 1215, extracting liberties ... politics as dentistry.

They suffered from Anglophilia, revering all things British. They believed in their long bones that Britain was the cradle of civilization. If you'd said that the Chinese invented paper and discovered gunpowder just when the tribes of Britain, painted a nice blue, were introduced to Roman lead plumbing, they'd have put your name in a dark book, a possible Bolshie ... in the Red bud ...

Mr. Chick, an endearing character who had the oily efficiency of a British drill sergeant, was my grade seven history teacher. He had a magnificent obsession, the Battle of Hastings. He chalked out the whole psychic relief map of the war between the Saxon defenders and Norman invaders on a blackboard under a massive headline: HASTINGS, 1066.

Mr. Chick was almost seven feet tall, or so it seemed to us munchkins, as he let his long arms wag while he chalked spasmodic X's or a swooping footnote. Needless to say, his heart was with the Saxons, but it was a wonderful bias; the man tried to be *frightfully* objective as a *historian*. Normans, those dastardly foreigners, had invaded Britain, landing on pure Anglo-Saxon soil, intending to make slaves of the peasant folk, get in a little bit of looting ... (Chick never dared mention rape—) and were met by King Harold and his lads "good and bold," battle-armed to the pearly white teeth (Chick's dentition shone as he waxed on about wonderful Harold ... tall in the saddle ... his men emboldened by example ...) and as a fair footnote to the Norman chieftain, Chick mentioned a tiny episode: the warlord had fallen off his horse, but being quick-witted and no slouch, scooped up a handful of sand: "Comrades, I've scarce arrived and already Britain is mine and yours." The sand trickled from his palm, his men cheered, and a bad fall had been converted into symbolic victory, a divine revelation (Oh, Eddy, Eddy, where was the handful of sand when you needed it?).

From the start, God was leaning over Harold's shoulder, bleaching his blond hair with Eternal Light; a vulturous shadow hovered over the invaders. This was no ordinary battle, but one between the forces of light and darkness. We were naturally with the forces of light, and to root for the Normans would have meant an after-hours detention for life. We were as quiet as carp.

Chick was doing a dance, his lanky body swaying to the rhythms of mortal battle, to death, to cowards in the rear, come on boys ... fight fight fight ... let them feel your blades ... hip ... hip for Harold ... hooray ... Chick never explored the theological ramifications of the battle's outcome. It was his blind spot, a source of anguish, and globules of sweat fell from Chick's forehead, vintage 1066 ... The room temperature went up, Chick reached his climax ... his blue eyes about to pop, caught like a mayfly on the riffles of a historic current and trouts of happiness were nipping at his wings. History sucked him into a whirlpool, he swayed in the grips of high emotion as he curiously cross-hatched the gory moments and then, ZAPPO ... wham-bang ... brave King Harold got stung full in the eyeball by a lucky and treacherous Norman arrow.

Chick stopped to emphasize the gaping vicious wound, the slender sleek arrow, grunting, and even moaning softly. We were terrified. I realized what this meant and how utterly demoralizing for England: the forces of light, and Harold's fighting comrades ... I pulled the arrow out of *my* eye socket ... a ruptured oyster ... with fibre ... bloody ... the pain intense ... lodged so deeply ...

Chick wheezed, his thin body swaying to some sun god ... Chick going through the agony of defeat: "Brave Saxons, throw down your weapons ... you have fought a good battle ..." Chick hauled at his eyeball, dragging that mental arrowhead out ... He took his time, twisting, pulling, and it was a lean arrow ... longer than usual ... it was his special exorcism ... and we dignified his psychic disturbance by listening and not making rude noises. Chick was dying for Harold. Harold and Chick were one. Harold died on the field for Chick ... the eyeball bursting ... I know that pain: once, while fishing at summer camp, I hooked a sunfish in the eye. The animal twisted on the hook. Chick twisted in his dance. Harold had twisted in his pain. My sunfish died in '47, Chick got his in 1066.

Chick's cross-hatchings filled the blackboard, arrows engulfed the sky. It was Chick's way of saying it would have been easier for a camel to enter through the eye of a needle than for some poor duck to fly through his sky of factotum. We never had a chance in that slivered atmosphere, the air was pregnant with arrowheads, just like the day Harold got his. The whole blackboard was an Erik Satie score to the gods ... Seismographically speaking, we were held by descriptions of carnage, thousands of corpses cross-hatched on the battlefield, Harold roaring in pain ... my eye ... God ... my eye. Chick was breathless, white as his catharsis. I meant to ask him how many horses had died that day ... But it would have been in vain. Being a captive audience, we had absorbed his shame and shock of defeat. In his defeat lay his dignity. Therein lies pure poetry, a powerful purgative in Chick's repressed landscape. Twenty years later, he and others would have worked it out through primal therapy. Chick sagged for a moment, spent, then straightened up, brushed back his hair, tucked his tartan tie into his suit coat and flashed a feeble smile.

"Never, *never* give up ... you are made of sterner stuff, lads," Chick said. Suddenly he broke into a wide, almost supernatural, smile; supernatural because it had little or no relationship to the rest of his face. A detached grin, extraneous, but a smile with its own integrity, a smile, to diminish mortal smiles ... "Never ... never ..." King Chick boomed. He puffed his chest out. "One battle lost does not a war lose ... Remember that, lads, when your time for lost battles comes."

"Yes Sir," roared the class. Chick marched the length of the blackboard, as though doing penance, moving back and forth, turning to shake his head in disbelief ... Oh Hastings, Hastings.

Chick's teeth seemed to be snowing. He had a hopeful smile. I had come to recognize phases of his smile, secrets in nuance ... humble, arrogant, playful, angry, all tributaries of a central smile. You kept your distance when the smile waned ... when he was in a state of thought transference, sitting silently at his desk facing his class, his spine straight as a British bayonet. Chick discovered I had a budding curvature of the spine: and something had to be done about my disorder, my spine somehow straightened. I was told to press a blackboard pointer to the small of my back and stand firmly at attention, chin up, eyes front. I stood at the back of the class and Chick kept his lights on me. "Chest out, lad," he roared, a friendly roar followed by an epiglottal laugh, trailed by a smile of encouragement. There was no damned way Chick was going to tolerate a hunchback in his group. Chick meant well and, alas, saw the shape of things to come.

"Godsakes, straighten up, lad ..." He marched by showing me how to straighten my shoulders. "Throw those shoulders back, eyes front, chin up ..." " Yes Sir," I snapped, straightening the pointer until it almost sang.

Chick had several other ants in his spiritual craw. For example, at the snap of his fingerbone, we jumped like tiny jacks out of some emotional box, dashing twice around our desks and down we'd blast into our seats when he snapped his fingerbone for the second time. I watched this disciplinary drill from the back of the room where I was doing my spinal exercises ... But no one resented Chick's drills. The man's eccentricities were a welcome relief. He was fair. Chick displayed no malice towards any child who failed his marching orders. There was only his displeasure smile, a slight droop of the lip, but no droop in his spirit, because he also had a fine brimstone fever. Muscle tone of the mind. He made us memorize Isaiah. First thing in the morning, someone would recite a particular passage ... the student delivering a line from memory and the class coming up with the following line ... *And they shall beat their swords into ploughshares*, and they sang *And their spears into pruning hooks.*

If a student faltered, and the silence became unbearable, Chick then boomed out the line. The students bellowed back. It was all angelic music to his ears. Chick was an ecstatic, his eyes shining like freshly minted dollars

Nation shall not lift up sword against nation

Chick beamed in the Creator's holy radium and raised his sonorous voice, his face calm, the flesh bright with rejuvenation, his blue eyes bluer

Neither shall they learn war anymore

How did these pacifist lines gel with glorification of the gore at Hastings? Chick had a fissure in his logic. Like many a man in his tweedy mind, he gloated over violence provided he took no part in any hairy war. The man was both mental warrior and lover of Biblic lambs, the contradictions of hope wherein

... the wolf shall dwell with the lamb,

And the leopard shall lie down

with the kid;

And the calf and the young lion

and the fatling together;

And a little child shall lead them.

There was a child in Chick, a little lamb, and some ham as well whenever he heard the Lord calling from over a high mountain

And the lion shall eat straw like the ox

And the sucking child shall play

on the hole of the asp,

And the weaned child shall put

his hand on the basilisk's den.

Gratitude rumbled up from his stomach, issuing from his pearly mouth. I had chanted Isaiah in the *Tenach* in ancient Hebrew, a language I didn't understand, written down in soiled Hebrew prayer books, but it was Chick, that eccentric Christian who led me to the illuminative poetry of the major Hebrew prophet, opening a place in my brainpan for the power of language and the meaning of poetics ... implanting the first sprouts on the bald pate of my muse ...

He was, you see, a liberal, and that took a certain amount of courage in a world of pain ... courage and cosmetics. He reeked of cologne while sweating profusely, furiously mopping his brow with a perfectly pressed handkerchief. Is this the fate of the liberal? Nervous twitching, a stiff-legged walk, an iron rod pinned through the spinal column, always on the verge of ecstacy or tears. Dead, perhaps the living dead ... never guilty of bad posture, and he really did wash behind his ears, so that they shone like his teeth, and his Lone Ranger smile matched his starched grey flannel trousers, and the light bounced off his leather elbow patches that matched his brogues, and his broadcloth shirt was laundered to death so that it sang in all its whiteness, shining, like a slug in sunlight, and only the fearful tartan tie broke the symmetry.

Neatness. Did it grow on his person like a fungus. Neatness. Life as a folded letter.

I was sure he boiled his spoons, wore white gloves in the evening to ward off *spiritis herpes facialis* … fatal kiss of a luna moth … and sure he was addicted to green soap … as the flypaper of dementia unrolled its long tongue and followed the man everywhere … shadowing him like a sad mist where tubercules sang out to him in the evening … ah, he was a liberal; he lived through wish fulfillment, an arrow in his soul, but in an era of schoolboy corporal punishment—which worked its way through the body politic with the ferocity of a maggot plunging into meat——Chick was a liberal luxuriating in the romance of gore, reluctant to harm the terrorizing fly, let alone a child. There was no strapping in his cloakroom … It was all logic … and pristine presentation … drills, drills, cologne, and a military liberalism … the voice of authority proved potent, a pointer pressed against the curved spine. The voice of the Empire, scrubbed behind the ears.

"A Chinaman Can Do It"

Anyone passing Crunchdale pissed their pants. Crunchdale, his face cratered by chicken pox, caught a nervous tick denoting mischief, grabbed a kid, tweaking his cheek into an involuntary smile on the spot. Tears meant his *medicine* was working, inducing fear, which translated into *respect*. Magically, Chick materialized after a tweaking, like a mortician warming up to a stiff, extending a pressed clean white handkerchief to a boy who had saved his tears, bursting into a sobbing gush as the monogrammed cloth passed before his eyes (the good cop, the third degree, and the degree of grace … Broderick Crawford, where were you then, where are you now?).

"Now, sonny … here you are …"

Sometimes for civility's sake, Chick and Crunchdale appeared in the halls chatting amiably, co-existing, respecting zones of influence. They kept their distance, two plague ships passing in the night: you stopped dead in your path when Chick clanged the school bell, and with a second ringing, you marched to the entrance and lined up quietly. Chick the dipstick cop, Crunchdale the hard-nosed meatball …

Chick was invisible whenever Crunchdale grabbed a student by the scruff of his neck, seized the shortest hair on the hairline, and began twisting that shoot ... twisting ... until his victim went into hysterics, howling, delicious music to Crunchdale. A pygmy dervish spun around ... and Chick was always nowhere when Crunchdale performed his hairy symphony: how many orthodontists ... lawyers ... nose-bobbers and nabobs ... real estate barons and buffoons had a twist, did a dance, and were shaped by Crunchdale's fingers, fear working like a sardine-shark nipping the bowels ... the boy mewing like a wounded lamb ... Crunchdale capped his hair-twisting with a backhander, a skilful blow that didn't draw blood, a rosy protrusion ... but no blood ... Crunchdale was particularly careful about ears. No ruptured eardrums, and no blow to the eyes ... nose ... mouth. He had a delicate sense of those who might make him twist in the wind, parents turned bloodthirsty by blood of their blood. He was a cheek man and expert in hairlines. And then a handkerchief appeared, Chick smiling the way Jesus smiled in all the Salvation Army posters ... Let Rome have its due ... taxes ... as the flesh was rendered unto Crunchdale ... Thus the cuffed boy gathered his marbles, his head singing like a canary ... it was hard to hold onto the balance wheel ... the blow had disconnected the cerebral wiring ... Some boys, stunned, made a slight woofing sound ...

Crunchdale loved dogs.

And then there was Miss Plover, who put her whole being into a good strapping. She had one arm; the other had been amputated at the elbow. Her one good hand was for holding up the Bible or laying on the leather. She explored a student's hand, read his palm for pain points. She stood back. The strap sailed, cutting the meat at the wrist-bone, and then another and another, her breath up and down like an asthmatic vole in heat. She pounded our meat. After a session with Stumpy Plover we washed our hands in cold water to keep down the bruises ... the throbbings ... the burn ... Bleeders were sent directly to the nurse's office. Hush. Hush. Ice in the office. But at least Miss Plover didn't tap you across the cheek for good measure. I still remember her swaying, some flautist playing *Aves* inside her skull, holding the Bible up with her good hand, emphasizing her point by wagging the stump ...

Sometimes Crunchdale cocked his head and stared scornfully at the one-winged warrior. Crunchy had the munchies for girls in transition between dolls and lipstick. He was a tit-feeler, and explored more than a few acorns, and so set his beams not on the Plover but on Gloria. A tropical flush seeped into the cratered flesh of his face. Oh, he never strapped a girl. He was a coddler, a cuddler. He loved dogs and little girls with budding acorns. Beaming at his child brides, his Gloria—who suddenly understood the power a flower has in opening to the sun.

"You can do it ... For God's sake ... a Chinaman can do it ..."

His hand was on Gloria's shoulder, then her neck, under the curled brown hair, massaging. "You can do it for God's sake ..."

Gloria smiled. The room sat still, suspended in Crunchy's tropical humidity.

"Add up that column ..."

I tried concentrating: should I carry the number over to another column.

"It's easy ... a Chinaman can do it," he growled.

Crunchy, I failed and you cuffed me, and I have carried your memory over to the next column.

MANNY

Every school has its lunatic: a child from a broken home, a budding psychopath lopsided in the brainpan. A time bomb, Manny had to be disconnected. He had a nasty habit, carrying razor blades into the classroom. The rub was, no bughouse in the land would store a junior lunatic unless he had *offed* his folks and gotten printer's ink in the way of news. There was talk about hauling him away to a special trade school (possibly the very institution some teacher had in mind for me), but that was only rumour and the loose lip. So, Manny—whose lip sometimes hung a little loose—kept on bringing razors to class, with a growth of peach fuzz on his face and a wild leer in his brown eyes. He smelled of urine and once in a while the teacher quietly opened a window when the whole room took on the tang of a washroom. Everybody kept their distance. They realized that the slightest remark could transform him into a demon ... frothing like a deranged animal and peeing in protest. Even Crunchdale avoided him; while he liked dogs, he was nervous about a demented boy whose unwholesome habit was biting—as his was hair-tugging. Manny's teeth were rotten, his mouth stank, and a bite was dangerous. A few boys regarded Manny as their secret weapon, their defence against pain, tagging behind him when they passed Crunchdale who pretended during class that the sighs, whimpers, and sobbings came not from Manny but from steam pipes along the walls and ceiling. And an almost indistinct hissing noise ... pee running along the aisle ... was a portent of inner lunatic pain, and Crunch was no fool ...

115

he left the leakage there. It was a lesson learned from a man who loved dogs: always be prepared to leave a little leakage. I wonder if Manny ever received a report card, and if he did, who did he show it to?

MAGIC VOYEURISM

I heard the steady hum of printing presses on Sussex Street. Like wolves who had come into their oestrus cycle, we moved over the bins where tons of *sunbathing* magazines had been discarded. We reached out for the solarography, pulling armfuls of printed pages still warm from the presses. They were discoloured, oily, some pages bound, others partially collated. We were minnows in life's filthy stream of smiling couples in the buff, their smiling brood in birthday suits.

I had no interest in the family unit ... they were less appealing than any carp with its immense scales swimming in one of Nathan's fish tanks ... carp so naturally filled out with a healthy lustre to their appearance ... and besides, whoever thought of carp being too thin, obese ... underdeveloped ... skin problems? The young twiggy women were succulent as speckled rainbow trout in season. A tall women with small breasts was the stuff of dreams priapismatic ... those glossy photos were as steamy as a Kensington Market bakery on Sunday morning. It took years to comprehend the implications of such haute voyeurism.

In a sense, the glossies were better than getting laid years down the road; they left something for the wicked imagination to probe, while the real McCoy dispelled every wild illusion. The feral creatures in the woods of my mind were laughing at me. You sucker, sneered the groundhog—pictures are worth more than a thousand words because everything eventually is stripped to the bone and the final result of stripping is the deep and easy sleep ... excitement is in the illusions we groundhogs lost with the first winter. Only the shadow really knows.

I hogged the magazines; they were my mental funhouse and very affordable. There the soul was trapped in the photograph and the nudist had given away his soul to the *public*. The savage in me thought the unprotected image of the self too vulnerable. What did nudists sell their soul for? Were they some evangelical cult for nudity? Did they do it for love? And now were their souls in cold storage forevermore? Nudists for God? And why in blazes were they always smiling as if they'd just been drugged?

Nobody was going to steal my soul because I wasn't going to join this zany crowd down at Buff Beach. I enjoyed cutting open the multiple pages, finding the ideal sex symbol, a young tanned woman straight as a teenaged willow with a modest Venus mound ... I could have steamed open those pages with my bated breath. I assumed decent folk were born into clothes as some animals naturally evolve into a glossy pelt. Benny had once confided to me that clothes were meant for humans in the same way a set of fairy wings belonged to a housefly. We were meant for clothes not because of torturous elements: ice ... snow ... rain ... frogs ... fish falling from the sky ... but because the flesh itself, in extreme modesty, craved clothes as dry bones need an adhesive agent to glue down the skin. Does a duck sunbathe nude? Wasn't Hoppy tall in the saddle in his sharp clothes? Only his horse was nude ... Carp, at least, have scales ... trout, a mucous membrane to protect its body ... They are natural flashers ... inoffensive ... fitting into the natural order ... melding into the ecological chain ... Nudists, crave *psychic clothes*, a suntan ... a dermal layer of clothes ... they are clearly exhibitionists who have gone over the flasher's horizon ... they've long ago discarded their trenchcoats ...

Fish have the decency to *hide* from public view.

The white folk flexed their muscles ... *bronzed* biceps ... they were body-builders for the glory of God ... muscles and a deep suntan ... but there was more ... the porphyroid flawless people became the bronzed family unit sucking-up to the sun as a bee to the sunny powder of a hollyhock ... health food ... essential golden pollen ... secret bread ... so what was the obsession with a bronzed body? The common denominator in those magazines, it seemed, was a fixation—the bronzed beautiful. A few abnormal sun fanciers were flung in among the pages: dwarves ... midgets ... the token hunchback ... an obese man or woman ... and even an androgyne ... a vague attempt to tone down the Apollo complex ... but in the raw ... the force of the meat was with the very well-hung male, tall and blond ... and his counterpart in the opposite gender: the wide-hipped and abun-dantly bosomed woman, also blond ...

There were a few narrow-hipped females, whippets in the *minority*, nymphets running around the beach ... close to the family unit, all linked in a ring of smiles ... fixed ... not only their personalities but their jaws had been anaesthetized for all eternity ... bronzed as some bronze their baby shoes ...

But there was a dark malevolent undercurrent in these solar-loving magazines: food for every brain: the gay-bi male and female could ogle the image of their choice ... and there was ammunition for the pedophile ... naked pubescence in the nuclear family ... And supposing you were a tri-sexual cannibal; then your eyes would run in glad glue ...

The photographic detail was impeccably clear and intimate from a safe distance: you did not have to *sweat* among these sun-lovers ... Nobody would laugh at your physical imperfections ... you could stare contemptuously as they made fools of themselves ... the mind has an intensity equal to the pulsing parts of the sexual economy—and it could be aroused to heights greater than the carnal. The brain with its billions of freeways and concession roads to an erotochemistry: that grey protoplasm is both projectionist and projector of stimulating images long after other portions of the body have completed their act; thoughts secreting themselves into the pores of the memory sponge ...

They glare at me still from those high-gloss pages ... they surface away from spouse and brood ... glaring at me with unblemished faces ... the blonde Aryanized woman with wide hips and large breasts ... her smile muscle-bound ... and the husband, his huge snake an entity in itself, hanging like a thick vine ... and the same smile ... detached ...

As for the boys at the print shop, the presses hummed but did their heads sing? The same question can be begged from a baker: do the enzymes scream when dough rises in the pans of heated ovens? Does wheat germ have feeling? Does yeast break down ...?

Perhaps the printer was a hunchback who resented all stiff-spined folk, all straight-haired freaks ... grinding away at his job, he has nothing against the solar system. He worships the moon. The phallus head of the Creator may impregnate the world, while our planet cooks in that sex ... crocuses bloom ... cabbages laugh under their many leaves ... and the *mother naked* crowd goes on tanning ... but the printer, he was alone, unmoved in his inky light.

Who among them, printer and nudists, cared about the Battle of Hastings? The only meaningful arrow in their skinscape was an erection faster than any speeding arrow splitting King Harold's lightbeam. This was the real stuff. They blew out Harold's eyeball because they meant business. War is the best jerk off of all. All those generals beating their steel meat, the deeper penetration of death. My mottled obsession with the unblemished, my voyeurism was healthier by far than any Norman arrow singing into a brain ...

Scott

Colonel Scott, he of grade eight literature, was a Tory, from thin pencil-moustache to pointed black shoes. He lectured us on the glories of the Empire, unrolling a global map from above the blackboard, laying his pointer upon the British Reich thickly blobbed in scarlet. His moustache flickered like a snail, and his grey eyes flared when he came to Bolshevism, the other empire, evil, Godless ...

Scott fulminated. His face paled, the blood ceasing to course, leaving him pallid while he pounded the pointer for freedom, family, church, God, and democracy—but not necessarily in that order.

There was another chart in the classroom and it stood next to the cloakroom. Its bucolical tones glued our attention: it had the appearance of a health chart, a balanced diet ... but that was a device, for this was a chart of a different stripe. Several cows stared out at the viewer: there were *cows* representing capitalism and freedom; there were fewer cows representing socialism; but the lone Bolshevik cow was the most pathetic of all ... lonely, thin, emaciated so that its rib cage protruded. This was the price of Communism; the state grabbed your cows ... your livestock was nationalized; the state took your individuality ... The red British Empire was protective, civilizing, but the dark empire ... the Red octopus was cruel ... barbaric ... Democracy, God, family ... and who among us would have challenged Britain's barbarism in India, Africa? Scott glittered like a banker, everything about the man starched. He, too, suffered from intense hygiene. He had a pinstripe contempt for the apathy of the unwashed and unknowing.

He smacked his pointer across his knee, instilling a love of Kipling in us, a love of patriotic poetry. The rhyming line and the thin Red line. A line of blood between barbarism and a jolly good show. I was all for the show, at the Alhambra or Midtown. One afternoon I went to the movies, to *Four Feathers*, a Korda production about a man who refused to join his comrades by volunteering to join General Gordon in the Sudan. He was deemed a coward and sent a white feather, a symbol of cowardice. To make up for that taunt, he took a more circuitous route so he could link up with his comrades who were under dire attack. I gasped as waves of Arabs and pygmies undulated across the desert and charged the Red Square. Breathless, I told Scott about the film. He listened politely. "They broke the Square, sir," I said.

"Who did?" Scott asked cooly.

Gasping for the words, I blurted out, "Why sir, the FUZZY WUZZIES" (I had it directly from a sergeant in the flick as he fell to the ground, a pygmy's spear upright in his gut: "Fuzzy ... ugggh Wuzzies ...").

Stony silence: Scott's blond hair was the sergeant's on the sand ... blood seeping ...

"Yes," Scott replied. "That's exactly how it happened." He smiled sadly and chewed a little lozenge to freshen his breath.

THE VAMPIRE

After the school day dissolved, we retired to the schoolyard where the action was marbles and fast silver. A kid steadied a fifty-cent piece against a marble and then stood well back from that mottled planet. Directly facing him, another boy directed a beam of concentration on the target which was worth half a week's allowance, a tidy fortune for a twelve-year-old, and an absolute disaster to lose. The boy behind the coin made immediate eye contact with the kid about to propel a bullet of a marble at the silver face. He was some thirty to forty feet away, behind a chalked line, concentrating his psychic stare, and the more his cerebral energy, the closer the coin and marble eyeball appeared. The banker kept eye contact, hoping to throw his opponent off by sheer willpower. It was a test of faith: one wave of electromagnetic force meeting another, bending it like a spoon, slightly ...

Kneeling behind the chalked line, the shooter hoped to be the executioner with his magic marble: the cosmic blast, the trigger-finger exercised, the knuckle snapped, and then the legal reach of the marksman's hand across the line. The entrepreneur of the shooting lane realized the odds were in his favour, but the possibility was there of losing his money, if not in the first shot, then the second: the shooter had purchased several marbles at approximately half the value of the coin he was going to send into an orbicular spin (they were larger marbles than those on the shooting lanes, fatter) ... and more veins seemed to reside under the surface of the marble: the odds were 60 per cent for the house and 40 for the player, and the odds increased substantially for the nervous little fellow facing the shooter. There were more nerves alive in the shooting lanes than in the ganglion in the marble ...

A glob of spit slid from a lower lip and fell to the pavement where it lay, a transparent glue. This marksman was not just any shooter, he was taking on the airs of a blood eater ...

He cracked his knuckles, stretched his finger taut, twinked his eye muscles, rotated his neck, and to everybody's amazement—and the entrepreneur's grief— a winning light surrounded him, a play of light in late March, glancing off the small shoulders of the vampire. Other boys, and a few girls, crowded around the vampire who was alone in his cerebral in-space, the marble firmly in the grip of his shooting fingers, and they were deadly.

For hours, the vampire had enjoyed the rhythm of nickels, dimes, quarters, and the surprising appearance of a fifty-cent piece. So, what was important to him was the natural roll of the marble, its resistance to friction and the fluidity of its movement; in short, he wanted a winner. The vampire tended towards the literal, and was meticulous in his selection of marbles, so that any vendor who sold him a soiled marble was anathema and dressed down as a worm and worse ... the vampire focused his orbic powers: the large silver coin was already singing around the marble ... it was already his before he released his trigger finger, and it gave him a special glow because he knew he could instill terror in his opponent. Some boys claimed the vampire could bugger a coin with his eyes; all he had to say was Leaping Lizards and a fifty-cent moon started waltzing. The only defence was to freak the vampire out, distract him at that split second when he aimed his murderously accurate marble ... The vampire fixed his gaze ... suffering was the sauce on his lips ... he made a note of the minuscule sphere glowing in the distance ... licked his lips and displayed a killer smile ... giddy, swimming in the hemoglobin of his success ... a quarter ... coins ... line up all the coins ... everybody's ... a quarter was a light pop on the surface of the skin as he drained one marble-monger after another ... the first shot was deceptive, close ... a tease ... the second sent the marble and coin into orbit ... the music of the spheres in that ringing coin ... a third was never needed ... the coin sang its sad song:

SOMEWHERE OVER THE RAINBOW

SKIES ARE BLUE

A few of the girls laughed, some giggled ... But what excited the exudation of saliva was not silver jangling in the spring air, but the roll of green dollars: marble-mongers playing nervously with wads of five, ten, and even a rare twenty mixed in with all that green. The germinal capitalist would try to hide the twenty; it was a stiff amount for a ninety-six pound weakling to carry around; he tucked the paper money into a deep pocket and rammed a safety pin into those heavy bills, securing it to his pant pocket, so that a mugger would have to rip out that pocket with a knife. Every kid playing the fast lane needed a bodyguard, a pal to stay with him. Green currency had filled the vampire's heart and soul with a hue of bilious envy (I had no jam for the marble game: because once, while I was playing outfield, a blow had sent the softball in my direction and as I ran to catch it I tripped, straining my leg, gimped to the ball, and in the meanwhile all runners headed for home plate. I had earned the hatred of my teammates, and for weeks I left school by the back door, running home because I had lost the game;

now, faced with fast marbles, I had come to the conclusion it was better to watch a war than to be in one).

The vampire cared little for the decorative aspect of marbles: green, transparent, speckled silver, gold, blood spots, a few veins rupturing ... the vampire detached himself from the aesthetic ... he was interested in the kill. The dizzy rollers in knee pants who ran the marble lanes never formed a cartel to keep the vampire at bay; instead, they encouraged the monster to eliminate their competition, thin the ranks and thus allow the strongest to survive, only whetting the killer's appetite as he waited. Each entrepreneur offered a better deal ... more marbles for your money ... a higher value in coinage to challenge one's predatory streak: lured by the challenge of confronting a fifty-cent piece ... mere sucklings salivating, because the shinier moon meant a package of Old Gold cigarettes ...

No matter. The vampire had long slender wrists like a gunfighter, loose as though a bone was missing, and then seconds away before releasing his miracle marble, they stiffened. The proprietor of the lane made his move in the microsecond before firing time. "You fucken' fairy," shouted the kid into eternity. "Move yer ass to the girl's line, fruitypie ..."

The vampire kept calm as a tombstone.

"Eat shit," shouted the boy. The vampire squatted down. The second was oiled. The killer lived in a closed economy, not unlike a perfect sonnet. He drew back his marble. The jelly defending his coin suffered. The marble supporting the coin shuddered. A psychic shave, nothing more. He let his arm hang loose, squatted, and drew back again, diminishing his prey, reducing the kid's ego to a teensy-weensy marble, a grape seed. The kid muttered a line about Harold. A mug like Harold would stomp on his trigger finger? But we knew Harold was in the vampire's pocket ... bought off, not with marbles but cash, paper cash, and coins ... Obviously, Harold had a three-pack-a-day habit, his nicotine weed. Where are the heros when you need them? Over a rainbow, somewhere, or grown up and handing out parking tickets. Harold ...

The vampire knew in his slime of a heart that the kids running the lanes could never keep him away. He had studied the scene like a yellow spider following the heat outline of a smaller insect inside the corolla of a wild orchid ... the prey perfectly outlined in ultraviolet ...

There was a poisonous substance in him that gave his skin an unhealthy softness and a slight discolouration. His malignant shadow passed over the shooting alleys and the marble elite squeaked. They melted away ... thinning their numbers, their only defence. To quit. He reeled about offering generous odds to anyone who would play a lane. "I'll step back a hundred feet. Look, you dorks, I can't give it away." He had become a leper among the marble set. An animal sound rumbled from his stomach. "Don't be a bunch of fried assholes ... look, you can keep your backsheesh ... Just let me play." Others faded away. The school ground, bustling with pushers, was now empty. The pale grey light of the bully alone with his shadow. They had fled like a biologic organism, an antibody dissolving before the pathogenic onslaught, and the invading force moved like a pulsation of infected light. Oh, the world is too, too full of shooting lanes, marbles, coin, and infected light.

THE INVISIBLE LINE

Shooting marbles, joyriding on somebody else's bike, salvaging sidewalk cigarettes: the next thrill was the invisible line game. Evening, a kid winds a black sewing thread around the stem of a door knocker, makes sure the thread is properly secure, pulls the line to see if the mechanism will rise and fall properly, testing it again and again, and then—like a skilful fly-casting fisherman—allows loops of slack on the line to fall across the road. The house has an unlit veranda. The street itself is badly lit. He has concealed himself in the darkness. A surge of confidence runs through the child. He stares at a starless sky: the conditions are ideal, pitch blackness, as black as the mischief in a boy's premature soul. Suddenly, he tugs on the line, once, twice ... and waits, his heart pounding, fear pissing through his body.

He cackles to himself. A man opens the door, stares out in disbelief, and closes the door. Only the wind knocking. The wind? There are unusual occurrences in the city. The child pulls on the string. The giant opens the door again. Suspicious, he peers into the street, scratches his head, sniffs the air, and steps onto the veranda. The night is tilted. Moonless. He steps back into the hallway, snapping on the porch light. He touches the doorknob, caresses the thread, seizes the line, carefully lifting it until he scans a direction into the dark, a radio wave from a distant star.

"You little prick," he shouts. He strides across the road, groping for the devil who ruined his supper. "Listen, I'm gonna bust your teeth ..." The kid realizes he hasn't tied onto a doorknob, but the knob of a psychopath who has been waiting a good part of his life to destroy some child in the night. He is stoked, the animal coals burn in his furnace. "I'll kill you ..." The boy is terrified, his young legs

123

carry him away from psychopathic pounding feet. Young legs sprint, fly, as he is racing ahead of his body; white lightning flaring front and back. He hears the gasping giant; every ounce of energy is being burnt away.

I ran so fast I thought my heart would burst. My ribs ached. The marrow went dry. I had run the whole block in a matter of seconds in metaphysical time. I had run right into the origin of experience, of the relation between things. My protective spirit had entered my limbs and carried me away from the giant towards first principles. Implosion and explosion. There were times I felt him breathing down my neck, his fingers clawing my shoulders. I knew the laneways of the night, zones of shadow, the one loose board in the fence, an eel-hole in the dark. I kept on moving until I knew I was absolutely safe because the lunch-bucket crowd didn't play around and were mean at supper time. It was the best run of my life. It sent bolts of electricity through my body, revved my tired spirit. A thought crossed my coarse mind. If I was going to live with the pack I had to be quick on the hoof. Slamming a door knocker, circa 1948–49, was not just a secret dark highway of sewing thread but a flow of electrons that provided the necessary jag to make me watch my flanks even in the daylight hours. For the door knocker had hit something more than wood. The man who answered the door (invariably, the person answering the evening call is the man of the manse or mansion) had not only been made a fool of by some street punk, but his castle had been profaned, his master's dinner—prepared so lovingly by his wife the homemaker—lay cold as a frozen rat. Something blew away under his lid, a valve so personal its nearest equivalent is the umbilicus attached to his mother's sacred navel. There he was, the kindest person on the face of the earth, a provider and peaceful monarch to his brood, metamorphosed into a raging killer, a timber wolf licking fresh ink from a croaked rabbit. And nothing is more illusive than safety. Safety's in numbers, not on the run. His pointed shoes hoofed my little bugger ribs, chest, and balls. Some numbing feeling from the very roots of my sexual organ travelled directly up to the roof of my feed bag, my gaping mouth. Again, he kicked the lump of meat, me. Caught in a white cocoon of rage, he was actually murdering a child, killing the future, delivering a horrible shit-kicking. Then, a shard of panic-stricken reason prevailed. Self-interest. Fear of consequences. A quiver of remorse.

"Hey kid, get up … Jeeez, I hope he ain't dead." Me, the quivering punk, tiny hands protecting minor manhood, holding my future, groaned.

"Don't hit me mister." That plaintive call of the meek and mild in wild country.

"Here, let me help you, kid. Look, you tell your mom to marry your dad, you hear? And look, you little peckerhead, next time you won't be so lucky, cause if I catch you playing with your little wire I'm gonna make sure you become a girl, you hear, you little piece of snot."

I shook, and scrubbed a tear from my lights. "Thanks, mister," I mumbled.

"Yeah, now keep your shit away from my door."

The householder felt good. He suddenly was wearing elevator shoes. He was feeling so wonderful he decided he'd give the child a swift kick in the butt. The boot made contact and the featherweight was lifted off the ground. Such is the art of levitation. I have flown; and staggered down the street where I stopped and leaned against a lamppost. I lit up a cig. The man stared. That sawed-off punk was actually smoking.

"Your mother is a whore," I shouted and darted quick as a switchblade down the lane. The breadearner stared incredulously as though struck by a wave of crud.

"What is the world coming to," he squeaked. "Shitheads. Little shitheads," he said, answering his own question, which gave him pleasure and the confidence to go on in an uncertain world.

WHEN MONSTERS SMOKED

There was a trick you could do with an empty package of Camel cigarettes. You folded the package into several parts, squeezed out the central image of the camel itself and then rolled the parts out until the beast seemed to move across the dunes: the mind drugged by cigarette smoke, drifting. We were blowing smoke behind my house on Major Street. Turning on with the weed, a soaring feeling of confidence, buoyed above the crowd. It took a number of cigarettes to get the habit going. It sizzled sometimes as the smoke shot up the wrong flue, but after a few practice bouts, my soul descended on a spiral. It had a calming affect, although when it went bad for me I would choke, gasp, and throw up spots of parakeet blood. I was determined to get the drift of it. I wanted to be like other paranormal people. In those days, everybody wore a cigarette butt in the corner of the mouth. Smokers were the toughest, the meanest, the truest romantics, and if they weren't killing they were loving. They loved and killed before or after the act. Sex seemed an excuse to have a smoke. They sometimes made love without fondling but only staring into each other's button eyes and blowing smoke into each other's faces. This was legal sex. Everybody smoked: detectives, poetroons, cowboys, buffoons, rich dudes, poor Okie folk ... it didn't matter, they had one thing in common: they smoked every damned chance they had: brains, manhood, courage, villainy, what did it matter; facing the last mile on death row you smoked, or stepping into the vortex of a cowtown you smoked before you smoked your shooting iron.

I smoked Camel, others smoked Black Cat ... which I think was a cigarette for sissies ... You smoked through your nostrils, your mouth, or simultaneously. I loved Frankenstein because he could smoke through his ears. He didn't smoke Old Gold ... he only smoked when he was being wired down and shot through with bolts of electricity ... the straps snapped ... his huge chest swelled ...

I was jumping up and down in my seat ... the monster's lips twisted and turned, and then his eyeballs (which weren't his) popped back into their sockets. Frankenstein, it seemed, was an electrical junkie ... somebody you could never trust in an electrical storm, who attracted bolts of lightning as a packing house attracts sewer rats, and there he was, the monster with a spike running through the *flat* on the forehead of his skull ... he gurgled words, or rather, he ate sound ... the same sound the mummy made when a deluded scientist unrolled his linen, a regurgitated, half-wormy sound ... urgg ghh murrrrRRRRRrrr

I stared into the gape of his mouth ... did he have natural teeth though made of spare parts? Who looked at his teeth? ... they were stubs ... they reeked of decay ... The monster jerked against the straps, his huge cement shoes jerked up with the zaps of electricity ... and finally the monster passed out, having climaxed with the last burn, and smoke poured out of his ears ... out of his skin ... His cheap trousers seemed to singe with every electrical fuck in the ear ... and the hands, they were huge ... the good doctor wiped the sweat from his creation's brow ... and the rag steamed ...

"Yes ... yes ... my son ... yes ..." assured the doctor. "You will live ..." and URRRRRG ... gurgled the monster ... urgggh ... and then the monster flaked out. A thought crossed through my mind: supposing I wired the wrong door knocker and the monster came to the door ... they would use parts of me to keep the creep together ... nobody screwed around at Dr. Frankenstein's door, only the police captain with one arm who had heard a rumour that the doctor was rejuvenating the beast who had ripped his arm off before in a vicious encounter. With his steel fist he pounded on the thick oak door. The captain didn't believe in knocking ...

I knew the monster was lurking around the coal bin down in my basement. My mother told me to go down and get potatoes. I was too frightened. The war was still on and there were blackout drills and by some freak coincidence, as soon as I mustered my nerves and went down, the lights suddenly went out. Half my body was steaming in fear. Lights flashed outside the basement window; it seemed my life was flashing away, and goosebumps rashed all over my skin: warm piss, goosebumps and a handful of potatoes, dirt still fresh as the grave ... earth apples ... musty ... Frankenstein's boneyard ...

I was crying and cringing and had anybody said boo I would have jumped out of my mouth. I dashed blindly up the stairs, stopping at the top to puff out my fear. I had gone through dungeons, my imagination yeasting with images of dismemberment ... ripping ... tearing ... choking ... clawing ... but never biting: neither the mummy nor Frankenstein's creation ever bit anybody: they tore off their hands, applied a choking hold, but certainly never bit anybody ... that was for the squeaky vampire who darted around in the early hours of the morning and materialized in a dusty coat, a nocturnal evening dress, a starched white shirt, as though the wearer had been sleeping in a crypt where only moths cleaned up after him. From that day on it was hellish to go down into the basement and sidle past the furnace room, past the hidden presence of the square-headed Frankenstein monster. I was sure he was concealed under the coal. Each shovelful brought me closer to the shuffler. I saw his outline in the flames, his grinding mouth and twisted face. Even monsters love to eat potatoes. He could have been hiding in a burlap bag. I kept away from the spuds and handled the coal shovel gingerly, selecting clumps of coal but not digging deeply into the earth lumps piled to the basement window. I dreaded the coal men lumbering up to the window at the side of the house, dumping sacks of coal onto a chute that ran up to the open window. Hands reached out from the grave, Franky's calloused hands.

The coal navvy pushed me aside as he swung another bag of coal down the chute, his face covered with grime, and as the man sweated he smeared the dirt across his brow as though he meant to convey how his life was a smear of coal darkness containing the gift of fire. To the householder it was different: it seemed the dirtier he was the more acceptable he seemed; the householder wanted his money's worth and felt elevated viewing a human being who worked with grime ground into his pores. The coal man was doubled over, one hand gripping the nape of the bag, the other supporting his hip and the small of his back, and he gripped the rear end of the bag and hoisted it above his waist, rolling the coal over his back. The coal roared down the chute. The coal man smiled, or at least, he always seemed to smile, and his features were made all hideous by the few blotches of white skin ... advanced leprosy ... and his teeth appeared ominous, and his peephole eyes. The coal man seemed to love his job, dumping coal without a sign of being disgruntled. A few of the labourers requested a glass of water, lapping the water like sick cats. What disturbed me most about their vocation was their lunch hour ... they munched on a sandwich ... ingested, dust and all, and to top off their meal, they sucked on a cigarette, the quick flow of digestive juices blending with dust and the tar from a Camel or Sweet Cap. Still, none of these actual creatures came close to Frankenstein, whose face—although it appeared clean—had its veneer of sickly light: the filth was on the inside. Frost chilled away at a coalman's face but the dirt acted as a protective layer. It was eerie to see a man with a blackened face not only sweating but exhaling a draft of warm bodily air against the savage nip of winter. They sweated, smearing lines of dirt across their face, and gurgled sounds like the monster, their lungs past repair, dust eating away the linings of their precious lungs ... and then sneezing, dust flying up their nostrils ... and then they laughed.

It was an honest living, more productive than attaching new parts to a monster who had a pair of size twenty shoes and whose head had apparently been flattened by a concrete ironing board. He walked through his dungeons with his hands stiff as wood, his shoulders broad enough to carry two bags of coal. He was at least five axe handles across the back and had bolts on his shoulders and tufts of black hair, transplants as well. The poor dumb bastard tried to form sounds but the only real sound was *MASTER* ... *master* ... *master* ... and it made the good doctor's day when his fear of fire singed his very soul, if he had one: *Master master* cried the monster, globs of tears and glue flowing along his jutting jaw.

What a poor dumb clot. He proved to be nothing more than the doctor's evil alter ego, uglier than a toad blowing marsh gas. The coal man had a set of shoes that went crunch crunch crunch melting the snow in their path, but even Frankenstein's shoes belonged to somebody else. Who? *Master Master* ... the mouth formed a harsh sound ... The doctor smiled at his creation. "Yes yes ... my son ... yes ... soon you will have a brain ... yes yes ..." Glue oozed and gurgled out of the monster's mouth at the very mention of a transplanted brain. The monster rammed a finger at the side of his head above his prominent ears: "Brrr aain ...?" Demented, a smile formed around his drooling mouth: the thought of a brain, the delicious watering of the monster's hole of a mouth ...

Another zigzag of electricity. The operating room was crammed with electrical devices and tubings, electrical panels and giant switches, motors with huge rubber bands and auxiliary engines. The monster, strapped against the table, which was itself on gears and pulleys, strained against his straps. Even the transplanted mat of hair on his flattened head appeared to smoke ... The doctor's assistant, usually a dwarf, tried to restrain the monster, fearing the beast would blow the spark plugs in his cranium. The fury of shattering electricity had brought on psychic orgasm, the monster's eyes blackened, jolts jamming through his body, smoking as well ... and then he lay back, passive ... all he needed was a cigarette ... as the dwarf turned up his bubbly eyes to the doctor, who calmed his twitchy assistant, stroking the poor soul's crooked hump, running his hand over the dwarf's heavy-set eyebrows. *EEeeegor ... all is ready ... soon I will prove that the fools were wrong ... I ... Doctor Frankenstein ... they laughed at me ... I'll show them ... I'll ... who are you staring at ... you fool ... you lump ... dirt ... away with you ... away ... hahahahahaha.*

"Yes master, yes ..." Eeeegor squealed, waddling away with his painful hump (at least two sofa cushions high). The hunchback appeared to move sideways, past the coal bin, and he waddled up a flight of concrete stairs. He squealed again, a fiendish cry ... something resembling a laugh, its frostiness melting into the shard of a twitter ... the monster clumps towards the doctor, his hands raised like one in a dream state, those eyes open, those peepers that don't belong to the creature ... planted as seeds of vision, fitted in, played around with, the pulps of eyes ...

There was a huge rabbit-like brain in a jar. Igor fondled the jar, staring like a child at its content ... brain ... brain ... he was transfixed ... "Give me that, you oaf," snarled the doctor, seizing the jar from the hunchback who raised his hands to ward off blows. "No, master ... no ..." The child in Igor had not yet fathomed the gravity of his act: to hold, to fondle, to fabricate, to flush another's brain ... that was to put the hunch on the back of life. That was power. The doctor set the jar on the marble table and connected the circuits. A jag of white thunder illumed the contents of the jar. The monster, supine and sedate, rolled his eyes and suddenly a knowing smile formed on his pale lips.

Unfortunately, there's always a rat's hair in the mills: the brain's former owner was an absolute degenerate, a sociopath, a destructive low-life. After all the soft hum of ozone sucking in a nitrogenous vapour ... glup glup ... and the gases liquefying ... with Igor silently watching in the background, full of hate, assuming that the brain was meant for him (a perverse love triangle here)—the vast bully grunted his approval, popped his eyes and pulled against the straps. Igor screamed, but it was too late, the monster had seized the doctor's wrist ... but it was only a gentle tug, playful ... and Igor, after a touching moment of reconciliation, served as a guide, a procurer for the monster, who huffed and puffed, emitting obscene noises at Igor ... kill kill kill ...

The village folk complained to the one-armed captain, the eyes and ears of the judicial system. Enough was enough. The village inhabitants mobilized for a torch-lit deputation to the castle, a lynching ... there was safety in numbers ... they carried pitchforks, shovels ... knives ... and only the one-armed power-tripping captain was in possession of a long piece of hardware, a revolver. It was curtains for the deadly trio: a frightened Igor hoisted above the heads of the mob ... the doctor stomped to death by the peasants ... and the monster chased into quicksand near the castle ...

Master, he cried out before he sank into the muck of the subconscious. The castle was torched and everybody but the dead was as happy as vampire bats strung out on a jugular vein. I charged up the basement stairs, my heart thumping. I knew he was down there, that he had pulled himself out of the quicksand. There was a spud in his mouth. He was smoking out of his ears, he was moving across the dunes of my mind leaving huge footprints, and who ... who had worn those huge cement shoes before ...?

"YANK ... YOU TALK ... NO?"

I sank into the plush of the LaSalle Theatre, distracted by flickering matches and tributaries of smoke turning in a lightbeam from a film projector. In that cavernous theatre, there was a deep harsh cough, a rattling of an addict's pipes, and he had coughed up a vital glue essential to his personality. The sick man's hacking symphony produced sympathetic coughing from others nearby and in turn, a rippling effect. Cough echoed cough through the whole theatre and the film projector's lightbeam vibrated. I caught the whiff of a sickly sweet smell, tobacco leaf or flesh cured in some wild secret sauce, and the leaf glowed just before it dissolved into a white ash that kept on burning, and noxious fingers of tobacco smoke wormed into the very bowels of that dark theatre, where, having inhaled those grey ghosts I slipped into a cloud, and I would have gone on counting white microbes if a hard slap a few seats over hadn't wakened me.

My preteen eyes detected a shadow hand moving away from a woman's dress. "You got some wandering hand trouble," a woman hissed at a man who bubbled for a word and squirmed in his seat. "Don't pout," she said, "you're behaving like a child. You're just oversexed," she whispered, "but that's OK." Then the controls snapped. "Bitch, bitch." The voice hovered overhead. "Stop it," she cried. "Shut up" somebody shouted. There were a few boos and then silence absorbed itself. A mood, sullen and perfumed, in a haze of smoke intolerably morbid, took hold as brutal images formed on the silver screen: a yellow foe who appeared to have human features ... a nose and eyes, became vicious and simian ... became sadistic, toxic ... the flesh of the face of the torturer, a Japanese colonel, his teeth pointed like a canine who had just dispatched a jackrabbit.

"You talk Yank ... no?" The sound of the underflesh of the dreaded sublime. Menace: the sexuality of menace. The camera captured the long tapered nails of the colonel, a feral beast, a raging clawish finger ... pointy teeth ... and those slanted eyes almost lidless ... no eyebrows ... eyelashes ... then that tight deformed smile ... contrived ... "Smoke ... Yank ... you like Lucky Slike? ... smoke ... you like?" The blond-haired Yank, heavy-browed and sweating, signalled with a nod. He needed a drag, a smoke. The whole human race needed smoke, was becoming smoke. The colonel suddenly took on the airs of an oily head waiter at a country club (but the Yank had his wrists bound together: not even Houdini could have gotten out of that bondage). The oil-can colonel puffed a fag into a glow and passed it gently into the Yank's mouth. The victim tightened a corner of his lips and sucked in smoke, blowing it partly through his nostrils, releasing the rest of the refreshing drag in slow streamers from his mouth. "You talk ..." The Yank spat out a goober. The colonel slapped the cigarette out of the poor devil's mouth. "You got wandering hand trouble," the woman whispered. The yellow toothy creature now forced the most hideous of smiles: its only resemblance ... a garter snake sucking in a tree frog, that smile of absolute satisfaction as the reptile orgasmed, and then grinned. The yellow blight of a colonel seemed, with every passing millisecond of film space, a degenerate who could eat your mother or, for that matter, everybody's mom. My imagination was alive with all possible features of exciting depravity: wooden splints under warmed up fingers ... a flamed-out blackened eyeball bursting like a sickly grape ... a ruptured eardrum ... But, strangely enough—no dental work. No choppers ...

131

"You talk ... *yes* ..." The colonel's nostrils flared, sweat beaded on his narrow forehead. He was in heat, a wired-out spider monkey ... only heavier boned, filled out around the biceps ... and his terrible fingers had grown in length ... they itched to rend something decent ... tapered like chopsticks, delicate ... The colonel struck a match with one long fingernail and in the flare of the flame I saw his face, it too seemed tapered ... and then the flame went out, and his hand disappeared as the man with hand trouble plunged under the woman's dress in the sepulchral light of the movie house. Her hand was on his ... my eyes shifted from the torture on the silver screen to the huffing of the pair ... a rising tide of breath, abruptive, a ripple of coughing, the sweet sickly smell of cheap perfume and the shave lotion of lust at the movies, a little low-life high on sexual energy and resigned to a sad fate, the result of the heat...a secret emission ... The friction of thighs pressed together ... a hot tongue in her cool ear ... she, biting on his lip. "Shut up." The slap that came was from the colonel. He struck the Yank with a blow that sent his blond head banging on the floor. Two stout, very short Japanese guards picked the man up. Everybody was sweating. The tortured soldier was clearly dead ... his face blotched with burns ... but water was poured into his mouth. The colonel stopped smiling ... smoking flesh in the air ... acrid smoke ... groans ... the Yank was a pool of stagnant water ... a muted voice trapped inside a frozen cry ... (A small dog struck by a car on the crescent across from the theatre: a sickening thud, a high squeal and the dying dog crawling slowly to the side of the curb to die. Some kids trying to comfort it as it lay with pathetic soft eyes staring ... a school girl sobbing while she supported the animal on her small lap. A boy had run to get someone but it was too late ... blood spurted out of its mouth and nostrils, the eyes getting colder ... the animal gazed and I saw a glassy expression, a fixed glaze that had the coldness of marble, a look locked on nothingness, the look of one resigned to dying that said everything that had to be said about suffering: even as life left the dog, it struggled for every second of intake until the final frost chilled its vital organs. The dog taught me more than all the would-be minuscule Napoleons who entered the pores of pedagogy. I had learned to read and write but had I learned to live? The beast, pitying himself in his canine soul, was weeping for us. Soon some janitor would wrap the dog in an oily blanket and dump the dead. But only children stood by the curb during the dying. Perhaps larger folk couldn't show their feelings on a short sleeve? A trickle of blood ... a dead dog. A dead dog, a dead heart, a dead dead thing. I seemed never slated for luck but was sensitive to its touch, the brush of a falling leaf on a November night. I felt more drained than the passing dog as I stared, locked in wonder, at the colonel, that overachiever. His English was broken but it was sufficient, so that like a good surgeon he smiled ...).

132

"I think you talk, no ..."

The colonel believed in his cause just as the dog desperately hung on to life.

Belief is power, the true believer is the thug in uniform, whether soutane or sweaty sergeant's jackboots. I didn't believe in anything. I played the game on their terms. The dog couldn't fathom the rules: crossing the street was like Russian roulette. No more tail-wagging. The boyfriend puffed on a cigarette. He believed in getting it off, a little tail, "The bitch," getting rid of heat.

"You talk, Yank ... no?" The Yank spit a goober of glue at his tormentor. The dog's glue was left a little while on the curb. The following flick had a mummy in it who struggled in a world of bandages. That bandaged freak was really angry, and no wonder: he was doomed to stand at attention for four thousand years. Chick's perfect student.

MUMMIES & MORE

In the twenties, Cantor Rosenblatt (no relation) had a voice comparable to Caruso's. An orthodox Jew, Yossele Rosenblatt, refused to shave his beard and conform, and so—unacceptable to Tinsel Land—the Hollywood moguls gave up on him. They cut him adrift in his own dreams. Nevertheless, he went on singing his heart out to a more appreciative audience. The Chaliapin of the synagogues. So the legend went in Yiddish films, his spectral image staring into his dressing room mirror, his beard white as his pallid shocked expression. It appeared he was on the verge of surrendering his soul ... distraught, clutching a telegram, or is it a letter, an ultimate tearjerker, and I couldn't stop crying, aching for the cantor. The dialogue was entirely in Yiddish, produced by an American Yiddish film company. A number of other sentimental Yiddish flicks—sweet, bitter, and blended with comedy—made the rounds in the forties at the LaSalle. Coming out of the theatre one day, I saw a man had been struck by a car and he lay still just like that dog. A crowd stared back. Locked on the nothingness that hung between them. Without trying to see who the dying man was, I dashed home to tell my mother that dad had been struck by a car. She dropped what she was doing and dashed down the street. Pushing her way through the crowd, she discovered the person lying still on the road was somebody else and was so relieved that my father was still alive that she forgot to smack me for scaring the wits out of her. I was prone to accident. There seemed to be accidents wherever I was ... a melancholic atmosphere feeding reels of silver melancholia to a hungry audience, or schools filled with student dread and fear of authority, all amounting to manic affairs and mental scars. A dead dog symbolized this phase of my life: trusting only

133

a few friends and a dead dog. Perhaps the accident victim had been at the LaSalle, and depressed by the newsreels, had wandered into the traffic, blinded by a veil of tears.

Certainly a veil of fear had enveloped Jewry, even as I saw Cantor Rosenblatt absorbed in gloom, studying his features in the mirror. My father had come to Canada from Lodz, Poland. He had worked at menial jobs until he scraped together savings enough to bring my mother over in 1932. My uncle Nathan, who eked out a meagre living from his small fish store on Baldwin Street (an enterprise he founded in 1926 and which sadly folded when he died in 1956) had assisted my parents as they'd settled down in their new life. Despite the horrors of the Great Depression, life in Canada, according to my father, was preferable to anti-Semitic Poland.

But hatred works by degrees. The political climate was inhospitable to immigrants competing with native sons for employment; as in Europe, anti-Semitism found fertile soil in the impoverished national psyche. Poverty doesn't link people together in mutual support; it agglutinates hatred, hatreds like barnacles attaching, each to another. Native eyes are directed at a scapegoat, a minority, and not at the ruling classes who are able to distance themselves from hateful fermentation. The poor hate the poor and the poorer you are the more you're hated. The mob, striving for social mobility, pins the poverty-stricken to the wall ... they fear being dragged down into the furnace room, their spare parts used to build up moral inferiors ... those chosen pieces attached to lepers, who serve the total monster (*Master, master*) the system itself: it is a culture of obsolescence, of spare parts and there is a perverse love affair here. Immutable, the blight grows and flourishes. Nurtured by perversity, it regenerates itself.

My parents settled in Kensington Lane a year before I was born. The rented cold water flat had only one water tap and a sink in the bathroom. They paid twelve dollars a month for the slum and often when I go past that laneway, I wonder where it was, exactly. Father earned two dollars a day when he worked. Like millions of people my parents suffered deprivation during the Depression and yet—because I was overprotected—I have no memory of hardships. Staring into a family photo, circa 1936, I see a fat child in short pants, dour between my smiling parents. I am seated on a family table, which is as polished and bright as I am melancholic, peeping out at a world making faces at me.

My parents moved out of Kensington Lane and settled on Markham Street, not far from the market. It is the house I recall during the war years: sirens wailing in the city ... practice drills ... people hurrying home although no bombs rained down ... but there was fear itself, and it invaded the psyche of a ten-year-old who would soon learn the dreadful truth about the Final Solution on that dancing beam of light in the La Salle Theatre. It happened at a regular Saturday matinee. That devastating feature changed my life in a matter of twenty minutes. The regular movie had ended, some inane flick titled the Curse of the Mummy, which had scared the juices out of me, and I was dry, or so I thought. The sights and sounds of snapping linen as the stiffs broke free from their bondage and bandages had had me leaping from my seat, and then had left me limp.

When this regular silver screen delight ended, the ushers told the kids that they had to leave. They waved droves of kids towards the exits. What was next on the bill was for a mature audience only, and ushers flashed their flashlights, bellowed out orders, looked under seats and moved us all in single files down the aisles. Teachers, ushers, single files. I ducked into the washroom to hide. I had no intention of missing Mickey Mouse with teeth or Minnie with tits.

The silence in the half-empty theatre gave it another dimension: the other side of the grave. A booming voice described the death camp survivors just liberated by the advancing British forces. Cadaveric sights flashed across the screen. I felt an icy presence, a chill: those hills of shoes scattered about immediately grabbed my lights ... I spotted a child's shoe, and then many children's shoes ... tons of sorrowful shoes ... stark black and white ... hills of corpses suddenly appeared to be moving ... a harvest of naked death ... skeletal dunes, twisted ... their bones falling apart ... skulls ... spare legs that had no flesh ... mounds of dead ... starved beyond death itself ... their eyes bulging in disbelief ... their mouths open ... screaming ... at whom? ... at the young Tommies, their young faces pallid, soldiers covering their faces ... the acid sweet smell of rotting hands, hearts ... sprawled ... flung ... a child ... a rhythmic flow of death ... the dead screaming in flecks of silver before my eyes ... as though static electricity had become the larvae of death ... but still, there were those among the dead who were reaching out at the living ...

The Tommies delicately carried a few skeletal children, their dangling chalky limbs moving ... and the flesh on their limbs ... what flesh? ... there didn't seem to be any ... flesh ... white loose skin ... a skein of terror ... the gritty quality of the film gave the elements a life form of their own ... a rain had fallen, giving the film a feeling there was dew clinging to it ... a wash to the permanent stain ... and now the whole mongrelized feeling was present ... a montage of superdeath ... the machinery, fresh ... no time to move the evidence, the technology that went

135

into this industry of death, fillings become bars of gold ... hair becomes mattress stuffing ... the doors of the ovens ... swung open ... white mounds ... the crematoriums for turning corpses into potash ... half-baked, hair still on the skulls in the narrow ovens ... Tommy groomed to a T, held a delicate handkerchief to his nose and explored the dead. A frightened gleam appeared in his eye, his face without emotion, his pistol drawn, leading a rigid SS officer dressed smartly in leather into the building. In the next shot, the officer had the glazed look of a marble.

I left the theatre before the newsreel ended. There wasn't anybody in the lobby. I had moved ahead of the crowd. In the street I felt suddenly strange, like a moth stormed by sunlight; I drifted, as a ghost would drift away from the surface of the planet.

The Friendly Giant

There lived a friendly giant on Major Street who kids loved to taunt and throw stones at, and they made vicious comments when he lumbered by, his blue eyes fixed upon an imaginary horizon that always existed, even when blanketing snow fell on the street. The children followed Harvey, a few demons tugging at his coat, pulling his suspenders. They threw snowballs at him, striking the side of his face, or a fattened snowball struck him full in the face, eliciting a large collective laugh as Harvey wiped away the shame and managed to smile while the children continued pelting him. Harvey reeled from the blows. He appeared cursed. Even as he pleaded in his own sheepish way, "Please don't hurt me ... you are bad boys," the mobs followed him down the street. The trouble was, Harvey didn't have a mean bone in his childish psyche. He wouldn't have harmed a blowfly feasting on his blood. Harvey, the poor giant, had wept many times surrounded by street gangs. He became their surrogate monster, their substitute Frankenstein creation ... and while it is true he didn't have a spike through his forehead, each foot deliberated as it hit the pavement, as though his shoes were casements of cement.

Actually, Harvey and the monster had few things in common. Frankenstein never stopped at a neighbour's picket fence and fondled a marigold or sniffed the hollyhocks, nor did he feel depressed about a damaged monarch or sigh as the sun struck a huge sunflower. He marvelled at the sunflower's construction, itself a lost plant soul manured in sheep shit—perhaps a living thoughtful plant in prayer? You would have thought so watching Harvey lean over the fence, stretching his neck to get a closer look. He always appeared to pull his neck out to study plants, people, and to gaze directly ahead, smiling at a horizon none of us ever saw. I liked Harvey: he appeared happy but somehow sad on the inside. In short, he was in constant pain and more miserable than me. Here was someone I could set my compass at, remind every particle groaning in me that there was someone sadder. I gazed on him as some people spy on birds. I followed him, and even years later—in the fifties—I chanced to find that he had become my neighbour in another part of the city. I began to hate the children who tormented Harvey, and yet I had become as helpless as he. When I made any defensive gestures on his behalf, they relentlessly showed how cruel they could be: someone zipped behind him and another suddenly darted in front, while a third evil creature shoved at his middle, and back he fell, three hundred and some odd pounds striking the pavement, wailing, crying, pleading, reaching desperately, calling for his mother and father. Sprawling on the sidewalk, all seven feet of him, Harvey rolled his eyes like a wounded animal slugged on the crown with a sledgehammer. He tried to lift himself and fell back sobbing while I ran to get the neighbours.

Harvey, in his thirties, not only suffered from giantism and slurred speech, but he had an eight-year-old mind locked away inside a huge skull. It sickened me to see him sliding on ice while, in his vulnerable state, some kids tied his shoelaces together. The neighbours, although shocked by Harvey's mistreatment, somehow never managed to catch any of the rascals. They accepted his sad state of affairs as a condition of life; nothing could be done to lessen the plight of the giant. Every morning, Harvey's dad fastened his suspenders to his huge pair of pants and stood on a chair to straighten Harvey's threads, his shirt and tie, and sent him out for a walk in the world, his smile concealing a hurt. It was Harvey's defence. He refused to show he was hurt. His huge shoes rose and fell with a heavy thud. He stared at the sky, at that horizon. It was a fixed blue stare, and he said nothing, as though his mouth were closed by ice.

A Winnipeg Childhood

DOROTHY LIVESAY

The poet Dorothy Livesay (1909–96), the daughter of a pioneer feminist and a nationally important journalist, attended private schools and enjoyed an elite university education that prepared her to assume her place in Canada's upper middle class. Instead, after moving to Toronto with her family in the 1920s, she became radicalized by Emma Goldman and others. Politically, she was by turns an anarchist sympathizer, a socialist, and a communist. The sequence suggests a growing authoritarianism, but this must be viewed in the context of her generation and of her vocational preferences (life-long poet and one-time social worker). Her first collection of poetry appeared in 1928, when she was eighteen, her last in 1986, when she was 77; what she published in between illustrates to a large extent the course of English Canadian verse in the twentieth century. The following samples from her 1973 book *A Winnipeg Childhood* demonstrate that she cultivated a simple, direct voice and technique in her prose that is quite different from those of her poetry. This was the result of her trying to recapture the experience through a child's eyes. Note that she gives herself a fictional name.

FATHER'S BOY

The year that father was overseas as a war correspondent was the year that mother took off "on a spree" and travelled to the West Coast to visit relatives. It was the first long train journey for Elizabeth and Susie; and their first view of the ocean.

When they returned to Winnipeg, it was July. Elizabeth moved into the deep of summer, the sun a great friend streaming warmth into her bones. And across the street there was Peggy come flying, her eyes more like cornflowers than ever as she opened them wide to hear the tales of Elizabeth's travels.

"And mother says," Peggy confided, "that I can invite you soon to come and spend the night at my house."

To sleep at Peggy's house! Elizabeth tingled; she felt a little aghast, but encouraged by Peggy's evident delight. She had never been away from her parents at night, unless it was at Granny's house.

Suddenly the special evening came. Susie went off on a visit to Granny's. Mother packed Elizabeth's nightgown in a little bundle and gave it to her, with her toothbrush. "Good night, dear. Have a nice time at Peggy's."

"Yes, mother." Elizabeth stooped obediently to kiss her mother, who was in bed herself. Mother had been sick ever since they got home from the West. "Be a good girl," mother said.

She nodded. She found Peggy on the front steps, impatiently waiting for her. "Mother said when it gets to be dusk, we can go to bed. Won't it be fun?"

They crossed the street, arms wound around each other's waist. When they got to the Green house there was no one on the verandah; and no one in the living room or kitchen.

"They've gone already," Peggy said.

"Gone?" Elizabeth was puzzled.

"Gone to a show. But they'll be back, you know. Mother said we could each have an orange and eat it in bed—see, here's my big bed out on the back porch!"

Elizabeth had never been upstairs in Peggy's house before. Mrs. Green didn't usually like Peggy to bring her friends in. Now Peggy had a friend to stay the night, but there was nobody to look after them! Elizabeth felt a dull cloud gathering in her heart.

"Maybe we shouldn't go to bed," Elizabeth said, "until your mother comes home."

"Sure we should, that's what mother said we should do. Let's race eh? I bet I'll be undressed before you." Peggy shook her nut-brown curls and began to undo her white button boots.

Elizabeth undid the buckle of one sandal, then the other. Doubtfully, she opened the paper bag and pulled out her nightdress.

"Oh, it's pretty, a pink one. Yours is pink, mine's blue!" And Peggy pulled her nightie quickly over her head, and giggled as she got caught in it. "Help! Help! Let me out." Elizabeth laughed too, Peggy looked so comical. But then her face sobered. She folded up her nightgown again.

"I think I'd better not stay," she said. "I better go home."

"Oh, no-o-!" Peggy was incredulous. "You can't do that, Elizabeth! What would mother say? You're invited to stay."

"I don't think my mother would like it. There's nobody here to look after us," she said stiffly.

"Why, I'm often alone. Or me and Jack, we're often alone while Dad and Mum and Rita go somewheres. It's safe as safe."

"What if a burglar got in, downstairs?" Elizabeth challenged.

"All the doors are locked."

"I know, but Will—I mean, a boy got in our house and stole my bank. Burglars don't get in doors, they get in windows." She looked apprehensively towards the windows of the porch, all screened in.

"We never had a burglar," said Peggy. That settled that. "And you can't go home, Elizabeth, you just *can't*! Your mother wants you to be here."

"Why does she?"

"I dunno. She just does. My mother says there was a doctor coming to your house tonight."

The doctor! A chill seized her. What if mother were very sick—what if she died? Elizabeth felt the tears forming in her throat.

141

"I got to go. I just got to go. I'm awful sorry, Peggy ... I'm going right home now!" And as Peggy lay in her nightie saying mad things and then crying too, Elizabeth got her sandals buckled again and left, running down the stairs fast, unbolting the front door, away across the street into the hurrying dark.

She found mother in bed, with the blinds drawn. A nurse in a white uniform was bustling about.

"Why, Elizabeth! What's the matter?"

Elizabeth sat gingerly on the bed, to make sure mother was just the same. She tried to keep the tears back. "There was nobody to look after us," she explained. "Mrs. Green's out ... Mummy. Do I have to stay there? Can't I sleep in my own bed?"

"Oh, I suppose so." Mother stroked her hair. "There, kiss me; and go right off to sleep now—no imaginings." Elizabeth looked at the nurse; she swallowed.

"I'll go right to sleep, Mum, honestly I will!" And for once she did.

When she awakened it was broad daylight. The shadows of people walking along the street were reflected on her ceiling, slow steady shadows whom she dressed up in her mind's eye, dreamed about. There was the thin man, hurrying off to work; and now the scrub lady; next the princess.

A sound broke in upon her storytelling. A strange sound, something like a cricket—no, a crow! squalling. Her heart began to beat fast, she held her breath, listening. "Ah-ah-ah" it quivered again.

"Mother!" she called, still in her bed. "Mother!"

"Are you awake, dear?" called mother, very happy. "Come and see the baby doll I've got for you—in your doll's cradle."

She had a swift picture of the dimity doll dress wrapped in mother's trunk. No, it couldn't be that. She knew now! She knew what she would find as she put a bare foot on the floor, felt around for her slippers. Nearly bursting with shock she tiptoed into mother's room.

The blinds were down still and the room had a greenish half-light, with the gold sun peeking in through chinks and cracks. There lay mother in the wide bed; and right beside the bed, on the floor, was Elizabeth's doll cradle, the one Willie had made for her.

"Come and look," mother smiled. Elizabeth bent over, peering in among the soft flannel blankets. All she could see was a tiny puckered red face, a sweep of fine black hair. Then the eyes opened, blue as Peggy's ... The little creature squalled, right into Elizabeth's face.

142

"Oh," she said, nearly crying; yet laughing too. "It's a brother!" mother said. "A baby brother for you, Elizabeth."

"A boy?"

"Can I hold him?"

"Yes. Lift him up in the shawl, see—very gently now; there, just like a doll, isn't he? Tiny as a doll."

She held him for a moment, a wave of feeling surging between her and the bundle. Then the nurse came in and Elizabeth was shown how to tuck the baby up again in his nest.

"Mother?"

"Yes, dear." Mother sounded tired.

"Is that why Susie went to Granny's and why I had to go to Peggy's?—Why didn't you tell me?" She was choking, puzzled, yet happy too.

"We weren't sure he would live, dear. The doctor said he might be born dead."

"Oh ... Well now he's alive, I guess Daddy'll come home quick, won't he?"

"We'll send him a cablegram. He'll be so excited about having a son! But he won't be able to come home, not yet awhile."

"Not even to see his boy?"

"No. Because the war is on."

The nurse began fussing around mother's bed and Elizabeth was told to run along now and go down and have her breakfast. Aunt Maudie would be there to look after her.

"Well, how do you like having a little brother, Elizabeth?"

"I don't know." She stuffed a spoonful of porridge in her mouth and seized a piece of toast as she heard the doorbell ring. It was Rita, come flying over to see mother. And after her came Peggy.

"I know what you've got!" Peggy said, her eyes saucer-sized.

"I bet you don't." Elizabeth was baffled; she did not know whether she was supposed to tell anyone about this new arrival.

"I do so! Can I see it?"

"What d'you mean?"

"What you've got upstairs."

"No. I'm supposed to go out and play."

"Oh." Peggy was disappointed. She sulked, and said she wouldn't play. She'd go right back home, so there. But before they got into a fight about it, Aunt Maudie appeared in the doorway. She was astonished that Elizabeth hadn't told her friend the great news. "Why, if I had a baby brother I'd be just bursting to tell everybody on the street."

Elizabeth did not bother to explain that she thought it was a family secret, not to be told to the neighbours. It had been kept secret even from Elizabeth. But now everything was all right, you could talk about it. She squeezed Peggy's arm. "C'mon, let's go over and play at your place."

"Can I see him soon, d'you think?"

"Maybe, when the doctor says so. He's coming back today."

"Oh, isn't it just lovely! I guess the doctor brought him last night, in his bag," Peggy began, as they crossed the street.

"I dunno." Elizabeth had other ideas, not to be divulged to Peggy. Sometimes Peggy seemed awfully silly, like now when she was chattering and chattering of how the baby brother would be a great thing for her brother, Jack, to play with.

"But why Jack?"

"Because Jack's lonely, he has no one to play with."

Elizabeth was doubtful. "But my brother is only a baby. He's too young to play with Jack."

"Oh, they grow up fast—before you know it," Peggy said, blissfully. And she took Elizabeth through her gate and into the back garden, where they cooled themselves by lying under the rhubarb plants—the huge leaves like elephants' ears, fanning their faces.

After lunch Elizabeth tiptoed upstairs as Aunt Maudie had told her to do, quietly; past the bedroom where mother was sleeping, and softly turned the handle of the bathroom door. That was where the doctor had ordered the baby to be— in the bathroom, snug inside his cradle, with a heater in the room to warm him. He was so small, the doctor said, it was a miracle he had been born alive. So nobody had expected him, and nothing was ready for him except Elizabeth's doll cradle.

She opened the door a crack, then crept in. There he was, just a snug bundle with a puckered-up red face. He was asleep. She gazed for a moment, then slipped out again; full of dreams now, like Peggy's. She would not have to take Willie Weeks out any more, she had a brother of her own to walk down the street with!

Next morning Susie came home, along with Granny; the clergyman came too, Mr. Goodall; and Elizabeth was called upstairs to come and hear the baby being christened. His name was to be Richard.

Elizabeth and Susie knelt down near Granny in mother's bedroom; but when the long prayers started Elizabeth felt the room too stuffy, and the praying too much like in church. She tiptoed out and ran downstairs to sit on the front steps. She could hear Mr. Goodall's voice droning on from the upstairs window. She felt much more comfortable where she was, though a little ashamed for having run away.

Mr. Goodall finally came down and passed her on the steps, patting her absently on the head. At the gate he turned, realizing who she was. "You should have stayed for the service," he said. "You should do what your mother says, not always having your own way."

Elizabeth flushed, darkly; she wanted to shout a taunting rhyme at him; but luckily for her, Susie arrived clattering down the steps and the house was again filled with the sound of voices, all released and happy now because the baby had become Richard and he was safe in the doll cradle.

That afternoon Elizabeth still felt full of excitement, with dreams of yearning to rock the baby in her arms. She tiptoed up to the bathroom and peeked in. The baby hadn't cried for a long time and the red of his face seemed bluish. She poked him. He did not stir. Frightened, she ran downstairs quickly and slipped like a ghost out into the sunshine.

"Elizabeth!" Aunt Maudie's voice wakened her from a sleep she had fallen into, on the lawn. "Elizabeth! Mother wants to see you."

Her heart pounding, her mouth dry, she climbed the stairs. The room was darkened again. Mother lay with swollen breasts. Her eyes were all red-rimmed, her voice was shaky. "I'm sorry to tell you, dear, the little baby has gone."

"Gone?"

"Yes, the doctor came and took him away. He had always said the baby would not live." Mother's voice cracked, the tears streamed down her face.

"You mean—Richard's dead?"

Mother just nodded. She couldn't speak any more, the tears were running so fast down her cheeks. Mother crying! Elizabeth had never seen her mother crying before. She could not bear it, but turned and ran from the room. Through the open door of the bathroom she could see her doll's cradle, the blankets all disturbed. The cosy nest was empty.

So father didn't get his boy, after all.

THE OTHER SIDE OF THE STREET

That day Elizabeth was trading "samples" with Peggy Green on the front steps. Spread out before them were old cardboard chocolate boxes full of tiny samples, miniature soaps and perfumes that father asked for whenever he went into a drug store. Direct morning sunshine brightened the trade. In the shade it would have been a quieter business, slow and cool. Instead, words were getting sharp. Her friend Peggy said:

"Well, then, I'll give you my Palmolive and the Zam-Buk for that new toothpaste tube."

"Both of them?"

"Uh-huh."

Elizabeth's arm moved. Gingerly, she picked up the toothpaste tube. She held its cool roundness, weighing its worth. And there, in the back of Peggy's box, she saw again that darling wee bottle of green perfume. She remembered yesterday's violent quarrel—

"I know what, Peggy!"

"What?" Peggy raised her eyes, cautiously.

"I'll give you the toothpaste, *and* my lilac powder tin—if you'll trade for that little perfume bottle."

"No," said Peggy.

"Aw, come on, Peggy, please! We can always trade it back again."

"When?"

"Oh, anytime."

"Tomorrow?"

"Maybe tomorrow. Aw, come on. Please, Peggy."

The barter was balanced there, almost ready to tremble in her favour. And then didn't Rita Green, Peggy's big sister, come and spoil it all. From the house across the street she came running; she pelted through the gate, letting the latch click behind her.

The little girls thought that Peggy must be called home. "Aw, do I have to go?" Peggy pouted. But Rita ignored her, ran past them both up these steps; and then through the open doorway into the dark hall, her pigtails flying. Rita was crying.

"What's the matter with Rita?" Elizabeth asked Peggy, leaning down in a whisper. Their trading was suspended. The cold cloud had come over Peggy's face.

"Oh, I guess it's just mother and Rita—they fight all the time. Rita cries. Rita wants to go in for being a nurse, but mother won't let her."

"Why not?"

"How should I know?"

"It would be nice to be a nurse," Elizabeth suggested conversationally. But Peggy didn't want to talk about it so she said nothing more. But upstairs, from the open window above the verandah, she could hear the low hum of voices. Rita was with mother, telling her troubles to this side of the street.

It had all happened before. Rita shouting an angry word to her own mother, Mrs. Green, and banging out of her own house; running across the street as if she really believed she lived in this house. It was wrong, somehow. Granny had said it was wrong, hadn't she? Telling mother she shouldn't interfere with the neighbours, no matter what trouble they were in. But mother lying upstairs sick all these weeks, with nothing to do, and Rita having no one who could understand how much she wanted to break away and try for a nurse; somehow Rita just had to come and talk to mother. But it seemed to upset things, to put a great black cloud between this house and the house across the street.

Long after the screen door had banged shut the two little girls sat in silence on the verandah steps. Elizabeth hardly dared look at Peggy; instead she fiddled with her samples; then scattered them roughly away.

"Aw, let's not play this any more," Peggy said. "Come on, let's skip!" Peggy picked up the rope and began chanting. "Bluebells, cockleshells——" but Elizabeth didn't feel like skipping or singing. She watched Peggy flipping the rope in flashes over her head. Then the twelve o'clock whistle blew, startling them.

"Guess I gotta go home for lunch." Peggy began picking up her samples, not without a quick glance at the upstairs window.

"Well, g'bye."

"G'bye." Peggy shrugged her shoulders and ran out across the street.

Then Elizabeth, too, moved indoors. It was cool and quiet. In the dining room lunch was ready, and mother was actually downstairs, sitting across the table from Rita.

"Hello, dear. The doctor said I could come downstairs today, for a little while."

Elizabeth slid into her place, saying nothing. Rita Green was silent also, her red eyelids lowered upon the plate of macaroni and cheese. But mother was busy. In between bits of macaroni and white bread-and-butter mother leaned over to where the telephone hung on the wall. She clutched at the receiver, calling numbers that she had torn out from the newspaper jaggedly, with her hairpin.

"Hello?—Yes, in answer to your ad—are you suited? No, it is not for myself. A young girl I know is anxious for a position. Yes, she is very good with children ... Seventeen ... Oh, very clean and competent."

Rita winced. Rita still kept her eyes lowered, pretending to eat, but not eating. She was really just listening, listening to the words on the telephone, her breath held in as if it got in the way of her hearing. Yet mother's voice was high-pitched, loud, and sure. Mother was trying to get Rita into somebody else's home. Away from her own home across the street. Away from Peggy.

Suddenly Elizabeth couldn't eat any more, either. Cornstarch pudding, on top of the macaroni and cheese, seemed too difficult a task. When mother had laid down the telephone and turned to her cup of tea, she asked: "Please, Mummie, may I be excused?"

"Why yes, dear." Mother seemed relieved to have her go, not noticing the untouched pudding.

"That one sounds like a good place." Mother began talking quickly to Rita.

Elizabeth went outside again, looked longingly across the street. The early afternoon swooned in the heat, dragged on; still Peggy did not come out to play. She was sure Peggy must be at home, but the house on the other side of the street had its blinds drawn down to keep out the sun. It looked forbidding, as if only

147

pretending to be asleep. At the least stir or poke, she thought, the eyes of Peggy's house would flash open, their hard light shooting through you. No, the eyes of that house had better be left alone, like the eyes of Peggy's mother ...

On the sidewalk in front of her own house Elizabeth began to play hopscotch by herself, lazily, without enjoyment. Then suddenly her heart skipped as she heard Peggy's front door opening. Out they came, Peggy and Mrs. Green. Peggy had on her pink dress, newly starched, and her flowery sunbonnet. She must be going downtown with her mother.

Out of the corner of her eye, she watched them flounce down their steps, pass by the low green railing they called a fence, then turn towards Portage Avenue. Peggy seemed to notice her, but didn't dare wave a hand. She bobbed along the street beside her mother, who took quick hard steps away from the house. Then, tossing her arm upward with a snap, Mrs. Green let her dark green parasol envelop them both.

Almost immediately from above the verandah a blind snapped upward. Mother's bedroom was awake again. She could not have rested very long! The low voices started again. Then silence. Presently quick steps sounded on the stairway and Rita came out of the front door in a great rush. She slammed the gate, making it click resoundingly like Granny's false teeth.

"Hi, Rita," she called to the big girl, tentatively. But Rita was already crossing the street to her own house. Rita tripped, and nearly fell into the pile of manure that lay fresh and unmashed on the curb. Fascinated, Elizabeth followed, sneaked towards the road to look. The milkman's horse had probably done it, while he stood nibbling the few sparse leaves of the boulevard tree. Poor thin little tree, she thought, beginning to feel the ache in her side. Poor little tree that never seemed to grow. Often she would have liked to push away the horse from gulping at the tree, but his huge glittering eyes frightened her. The driver never cared, even if his horse stepped right over the curb and onto the grassy boulevard ...

Now Rita had picked herself up, was heading for the side door of the Greens' house. Under a mat a key would lie hidden.

"Hi, Rita! Your mother's gone downtown," she shouted.

"Shut up," Rita's lips said, as she tossed her pigtails. But she must have been whispering, for the words made no sound. All the same, they bounced hard against her face. They made Elizabeth turn back into her own garden, fast.

What did she care anyhow if Rita Green was going to get heck? Rita had never cared for her—nor for Peggy, either. It was as if the big girl had cobwebs on her face, and kept stroking them aside, trying to see the world. Elizabeth was much smaller, but she could see the world clearly, the flawless sky, the sunshine a great golden roof vaulting the street. Nothing on the pavement but hot white light, ribboning the dull boulevard. Nothing moving. Only in the hollow concrete ditch near the sewer, some sparrows were having a dusty bath.

She sat down on the garden grass, trying to look for four-leaf clovers. She would be alone now, all day. No one to play with. Soon Rita would be coming out of the house across the street, quickly like a thief. Yes, there she was, straw hat on her head; old leather suitcase pulling her sideways as she struggled with it to the street. Then, when Rita reached the green railing she put her burden down for a moment, looked up towards mother's bedroom window and waved a gloved hand.

Elizabeth could not see her mother. She was lying inside the garden on the grass, pressing its dampness into a round nest. If she lay back, head on her arms, she too could get a squint up at the window. Yes, mother was sitting there, smiling but a little tearful. Her hand gave Rita a quick little wave. Cocky, mother seemed to be; yet underneath, not sure of herself. If *she* felt that way, it was because she had been bad. If *she* waved her hand like that, it was rapped sharply with a pencil.

But mother waved her hand and Rita nodded, very quickly as if someone might see her. Then she hurriedly picked up her suitcase, reeled around the corner. She was heading the opposite way, towards the park. She disappeared.

The afternoon hung so quiet now, it seemed to have stopped breathing. Rita was gone, and her own stomach had pain in it. Rita was gone; and Peggy would be gone too, never allowed to play with her any more. She knew. She *knew*. Best thing to do now would be go down the next block, across the street, down the lane, and see whether the Schulz kids were out playing. She moved that way slowly, but there was no one in sight. And so she hovered back and forth all day, not knowing which way to go, what to do. All the while her left side had a dull ache in it, full of the feeling of Rita; she wondered what Rita would be doing tonight, in a strange house. And so, to forget it, she would pick up her skipping rope and try skipping to a hundred, faster, faster. That was how she came to be out in the lane, still playing, when the cool of evening came. That was when Mrs. Green's flapping arms bore down on her.

"Well, child, where's my daughter—Rita?"

"I don't know." The hung head, the pounding heart.

"But you saw her go, didn't you?"

Silence.

"Didn't you? Didn't you? Tell me, you little imp!" Peggy's mother had an awful temper. She seemed to be near to grabbing her, shaking her.

"Yes." A scared gulp.

"Where did she go then?"

"I don't know." Her head hung, she felt the guilt and shame upon herself.

"You don't know?" The woman was nearly screaming. "But Peggy says you saw her. Rita was talking to your mother."

"You'll have to ask my Mummie."

"Your mother is supposed to be sick—not to be disturbed. But if she's been interfering with *my* family, I'll see to her, I will!"

Elizabeth stood there, paralyzed. Then suddenly it was over. The door slammed as Mrs. Green went into their house by the side entrance, dragging Peggy with her.

She turned and ran. Only as she drew near her own side of the street did she begin to lag a little. What was there to go home for? She opened the gate, hesitant, heard it click behind. There ahead of her on the steps lay the scattered "samples," never put away. She began to pick them up forlornly. The brightness of the morning—where was it? She looked upwards, loving always to look for the twilight creeping on, drawing veils over the face of the sky. But tonight the dusk came down fast, like a chill blind ...

It covered the street, and the other side of the street. And she couldn't see the house across the street any more.

THE END OF A WAR

If it hadn't been for father's letters "from the front" where, as Elizabeth had learned to say, "My Daddy is a war correspondent," the children would not have noticed the war very much. Without radio or television, with only black headlines in the *Free Press*, war did not seem important unless one was at Granny's house, watching her search those columns marked "Killed in Action" or "Missing." Or else war meant a parade, a Scottish bagpipe band, and young men with bright faces marching along Portage Avenue, their kilts flying.

Father's letters, too, seemed to make war an exciting, happy kind of a picnic. After supper, if a letter had come that day, mother would read the children "bits" written especially for them.

"It is rotten luck not to have my girls—my three girls, here, but except for that I am very happy and having a lovely time.

"I have what we call a bedroll and inside is a warm sleeping bag like a double duvet. Sometimes I sleep in a tent on the ground (and that is the best fun of all) but the past few nights I have had a real bed and mattress in a real house. My, what luxury! Next door is a pretty garden with roses just like in Victoria. On the other side is a small cottage and in it are two little girls, Annette and Pauline. 'Here is half a franc, my little children,' I say; 'Merci, Monsieur, thank you, sir,' they answer, and smile nearly as prettily as Peggy when she says she won't take ten cents but wants to very badly all the time. By the way, how is Peggy? Sometimes I look up in the sky and see her eyes and I look over the fields and see her hair—but I never hear her laugh, because the children of France do not laugh. They are sorrowful little children. Annette's and Pauline's father was killed in the war—'Many years ago, Monsieur'—by which they mean 1914. It is a long time to be without a father. Their brother is just seventeen and he has gone into the army. Their mother is working in a munition factory a long way off. They live with their grandmother—or perhaps their great-grandmother—she looks at least a hundred. There is no school here—the teachers went away when the Germans came so near. But now the Canadians have driven the Germans a long way off and school is open again. Always remember, dear girls, that it is our Canadian boys who won this great victory. If the people on each side of us had kept up to us we should have been at the Somme River on the fourth day (Sunday). I am going to draw you a map which I think you can understand. You will see how much further the Canadians went than anyone else ... There are no soldiers in the world equal to our Canadian boys and if we had a lot more of them nothing could stop them. We think we are on the way to Berlin."

But the children did not quite understand these messages and only really listened when father wrote, "I suppose when I get back you will be so tall and fat that you can't ride pigaback any more. 'Ugh! Ugh! Ugh!' That is Big Bear. 'Run, children, run, or he'll get you.'"

Those games seemed very far away now. But maybe, maybe, Granny said, the war would end soon and the fathers would come marching home. Meanwhile, here in Winnipeg, this was November, the grey season: no snow, not very cold. They had left their own street, their own house—rented now, for the duration— and were stopping at Granny's before moving to a rented apartment. Elizabeth was out playing, in the middle of a grey morning, when suddenly a mill whistle shrieked; then another! and another! until they were all baying like hounds. Neighbours rushed out onto verandahs, then down to the gate as if they could see, up the street, what the whistles were blowing about.

"Why it must be——! The war must be over!" Granny's neighbour burst into tears and ran back into her house. Elizabeth caught the excitement, spurted up the steps and into Granny's door.

"Mummy! Mummy!" Mother was at the telephone in the hall. "Mummy, Daddy's coming home! The war's over!"

"Yes, I heard it, dear." She put the receiver back on the hook. "That's what everybody says, Elizabeth, but it's just a rumour. I've phoned the office and they say it isn't true."

Not true! Elizabeth was crestfallen. Not true, and yet everybody was believing it! She turned and went outside again, to prove it to her own eyes. People were streaming into the street. She followed them a little way towards Main Street and saw that the stores had mysteriously brought forth flags, balloons, whistles, and horns. Grown-up men and women grabbed at coloured streamers, laughed, and threw confetti. The march began to the City Hall.

152

Elizabeth ran home this time, certain the war was over. "Gee, Mum, there's going to be a big, big parade! Can't we go? Can't me and Susie go?"

Mother explained that she had different plans. This was the day they had chosen for the family to move to the rooming house. Elizabeth knew, didn't she, that their own house was leased and all the goods and furniture had been sent on to the new address, in St. James. She told Elizabeth they would be going soon, on a streetcar.

"Take a taxi," Granny urged. "You'd be safer in a taxi." So mother phoned and phoned, but she could not get a taxi. "Humph," said Granny, "Commandeered."

"It's ridiculous," said mother. "The war isn't over!" But Elizabeth had only to go outside and listen, to hear the war being over. A lump formed in her throat as she heard the far-off tooting and shouting. If only they could be there, too, waving and shouting! But it was no use. Mother was going to move.

Later they did get to the corner of Main Street, carrying bundles and with mother holding the suitcases. On the platform they had to wait and wait until a streetcar came, not too loaded to get on. They stood together, jammed into the front of the car, while people all around loomed heavy and thick with excitement, towering over the children, stepping on their feet as they shouted, sang, and blew loud on cardboard trumpets.

Even above the din Elizabeth could hear mother saying, in a high voice: "Such nonsense. The war isn't over! There's no official word to that effect."

"You're crazy!" a man shouted. "Of course it's over. Hooray! Hooray! Hooray! The war's over. Bring the boys back home."

"Bring the boys back home!" the streetcar chanted.

"Bring the boys back home," Elizabeth prayed, under her breath. They had to get off at Portage and Main, to transfer. Elizabeth and Susie clutched mother's skirt, one on each side, as they wriggled their way off. Then Elizabeth tugged:

"Please, Mummy, can we have a horn?"

"Toot too-ot," said Susie.

"No," said mother, cross. "There's nothing to blow for. The war is still on!" And she marched ahead while Elizabeth and Susie tried to keep up, wading through the thick muddy pool of people. Elizabeth saw the streamers catching in mother's wide-brimmed hat, a balloon going off in mother's face, horns blaring in her ears. "Hooray! Hooray! Hooray! The war's over!" the crowd thundered.

Elizabeth and Susie watched as mother drew them close to her and took her stand on the next platform and signalled wildly for a streetcar to stop. It rolled on. Then another. And another. Above their heads flags were waving, horns too-tooting. Elizabeth longed desperately to have, if not a horn, just one little flag—one of those little silk flags on the black stick. But mother said no.

Finally a streetcar stopped. They squeezed on, somebody lifted Susie over his head onto the back platform. And that was as far as they could go, jammed to the outer platform and stuck there, scarcely able to breathe. "Hip-hip hoor-a-ay!" came the hoarse roar of the people. People whom Elizabeth couldn't be a part of, must move with, and yet be separated from.

"You're all foolish," mother shouted to those around her. "My husband is a war correspondent and the office says there is no official news at all. It's a false rumour. The war is *not* over."

"Boo! Boo! Boo!" shouted the people, as the streetcar swayed and rocked. Elizabeth felt dizzy, a sick empty feeling in her stomach. She tried to hide her face in mother's skirt so people would not notice her; so they wouldn't wonder why she too wasn't a part of this great moving mass of humans, swaying and singing, deliriously happy, chanting those words: "Bring the boys back home!"

At last they had left the roar of the city centre, they were coasting along into the quiet of St. James. Mother pulled a bell and they struggled off the car. Elizabeth felt bruised and bumped and terribly glad to be breathing the fresh November air.

153

"Are we here now?" asked Elizabeth.

"Yes, this must be the house, 278. Well, thank goodness that's over," mother said.

Two days later she showed Elizabeth the headlines in the newspaper. "*Now* we can be glad, see, dear! The war's really over now."

"Is it?" Elizabeth was putting on her rubbers and did not pay much attention.

"Here," said mother. "Here's a quarter so you can go to the store and buy a flag and horn for Susie."

She went up to the corner, but slowly, because there was no one out in the streets. The quarter felt sticky inside her woollen mitt and it was hard to get it loose when she came to the store. Elizabeth asked for a flag and a horn; but the man didn't have any left.

A WEEK IN THE COUNTRY

"Jenny's got a beau! Jenny's got a beau!" Elizabeth was chanting, beneath the dining-room window. As soon as Jenny's flushed, shiny face appeared behind the lace curtain, Elizabeth made off. It was fun to tease Jenny, but dangerous too; Dickon might get too embarrassed and just go away.

Elizabeth went around to the front and sat on the fender of his Model T Ford. She rather wished Dickon hadn't come to town with his car this week, so that he and Jenny could go for a jitney ride; and take Elizabeth with them. Now that there was a streetcar strike in Winnipeg many servant girls like Jenny took their half-day off by riding around town in a jitney beside their beaux—some of them young soldiers just back from the War. Elizabeth could think of nothing nicer than riding in a jitney, unless it was going to see Charlie Chaplin or Billie Burke in the moving pictures.

But that June there was much more excitement in store. As the weather grew warmer the news father brought home from the *Free Press* made the grown-ups' faces look cross and tired. People didn't laugh or joke any more about the strike. And Mother stopped going downtown. Father had seen a streetcar turned right over, on Main Street. Then, one morning, all the bread and milk wagons stood idle in the yards. Elizabeth and Jenny had to walk to a citizen's depot to get milk. "General Strike" they heard people saying, horrified.

Mother decided it was time now for Elizabeth to be packed off to the country. "It's nearly the end of the term, so it won't hurt her to miss school." She turned to Jenny with her plan: "If Dickon comes to the city this week, perhaps you could have a little holiday, and take Elizabeth to your folks' farm. Dickon wouldn't mind?"

"I guess not." Jenny didn't sound very eager.

"You'd like to visit with your mother for a week or so, wouldn't you?"

"Oh, yes. I'd like real well to see them. It's just ..."

"Just what?" Elizabeth demanded. Nosey Elizabeth.

"Oh, nothing ... sure, I'll ask Dickon," Jenny promised.

Elizabeth jumped up and down, not knowing what it was like "in the country" but imagining all of Jenny's family to be like herself, plump and rosy with shining nut-brown hair.

They were all ready that Saturday evening when Dickon came driving along the street in his floppity Ford. The top was pushed down and it seemed to bounce at every bump. Dickon drew up with a grinding sound and climbed out carefully. He wore a shiny black suit and a red striped tie; but his face, so rough and red from the sun, did not seem to fit his clothes.

"Hello, Dickon!"

"Hello, Liz." He had that kind of a smile that made her feel warmed up.   155

"We're already packed, Dickon! I'll tell Jenny!"

When they started out, waving goodbye to mother, Jenny held Elizabeth between her and Dickon. She had on her sailor hat, and a motoring veil that flopped in Elizabeth's face. As soon as they were out on the prairie, on the narrow black dirt road, Dickon stopped the car. "Tuck her in the back seat. She'll rest better."

"Oh, she's all right here, aren't you, Elizabeth?" Jenny squeezed, almost poked her.

"I don't care." She felt sleepy already. "There's a rug back there." And Dickon slid her over onto the slippery black leather. The top was still pushed back, and she could watch the sky slowly fading from blue and mauve into the long twilight.

It was pitch dark when she woke, hearing voices. The auto seemed to have stopped alongside a poplar bush. Ch-rump. Ch-rump. Frogs, was it? Overhead the sky was like a huge sieve, showering stars. Jenny's voice came to her, murmuring from the front seat.

"No, Dickon, please. Not now, please!" And Dickon the tongue-tied was saying, "What's the matter, Jen? You used to like a kiss."

"Not just now."

"Last year—"

"This isn't last year."

"Everything's just the same, to me."

"Well, I can't help it. I feel different. Living in the city ..."

"I see." He was quiet, and then he came out with it, strong: "You'd better tell me, Jenny! Is there another fellow?"

"No! There's never been anybody else but you that I've gone out with. Honest. It's not just that, Dickon. It's just ..."

"What?"

"Oh, I dunno. Maybe getting back to the farm ..."

Elizabeth felt the long silence stretching between them. Then the frog chorus arose and enveloped all the night. Dickon began to fuss with the engine. He had to get out and crank before they were off again, speeding into the cool country.

"Nearly home," Jenny murmured, leaning towards the back seat. But Elizabeth pretended she was asleep.

She was awakened with a bump. No sound of the engine. Darkness and voices. Jenny was shaking her, saying "Here she is, Bessie!" Small warm hands seized hers. "Welcome to the farm!" Someone held a lamp over the doorway and as she entered, wrapped in encircling arms she saw Bessie's golden brown eyes smiling into hers. Sleepily she felt her clothes being taken off. Soon she was lying in a big double bed with Bessie beside her.

"We can be downstairs in the best room," Bessie giggled, "'cause we're both nine. The rest of the kids have to sleep up in the attic." Then Bessie's candle was blown out and they lay alone in the surrounding night.

In the morning it was Sunday. Dolly, an older sister, pounced on their bed shouting, "Sleepyheads! Sleepyheads! Come on, Bessie. It's time to make the tea."

"Tea and crackers, Sunday treat," Bessie explained. And Elizabeth forgot to say, 'I'm not allowed to have tea.' She drank hers blissfully, dribbling the cracker crumbs all over the bed.

"Never mind," Bessie said. "We'll shake 'em out and air the bedding—you and me together, eh?" Bessie was only just nine but she knew how to work. Elizabeth's fingers trembled, she struggled all day to keep up. "Come on, Liz, it's easy," Bessie encouraged, carrying a pail of water from the pump to the trough. "And then I'll show you the new piggies, and my own baby calf. Fred's his name."

Chores and play, play and chores. It seemed all part of the same life.

Elizabeth, sniffing it up like some new comfort never before enjoyed, was astonished at the way Jenny complained: "All that work churning butter, ma! And in
the city you just run over to the store."

"Somebody has to churn the butter," was all Mrs. Moffat said, mildly. She
smiled tolerantly at Jenny, steaming over the washtub. "It's such hard work you
have to do, mother ... no washing machine. And it takes so darn long." Mrs.
Moffat just laughed, including Elizabeth in her look. Yes, it took time. Yet the
farmer found time, between his jobs, to tease the girls and to toss baby Laura high
in the air.

"Ouch! Rained in your pants again. Why don't you go out in the proper place
and water my seedbed, eh—you rascal?"

Laura was always wet, but nobody minded. Fun to be Laura, riding on the
manure sledge, pulled by a horse. Fun to be Bessie and Dolly, starting off Monday
morning for school, swinging their lunch pails. How they laughed and waved,
clambering onto the school wagon, pulled slowly up and over the hill by two
white horses.

Elizabeth was alone now, till nightfall. She hung around the kitchen for a while,   157
watching Mrs. Moffat kneading dough while Jenny stood by, sighing for baker's
bread "delivered right to your door." Elizabeth said nothing, just sniffed the yeasty
scent and thought of the moment when the knobbly crusts would burst from the
oven, filling the kitchen with fragrance. Mrs. Moffat paused long enough to put a
cookie in her mouth, and a book of fairy stories into her hand. Then Elizabeth
thought of the old deserted buggy beside the barn: a good place to read. She
climbed up into it happily, imagining herself a fairy princess on the way to a ball.
Lost in reading, it was a long time before she noticed the sun had climbed higher and was beating down upon her head. The letters danced on the dappled page,
sizzling heat strafed her head.

"That'll be enough of that there sun!" the farmer called, passing by with a
pail on either arm. "Come to the cool side o' the barn, girlie, and play in the dirt
with Laura."

In the evening the farm came awake again. After a supper of ham and fried
potatoes the children swarmed outside for games of tag, hide-and-seek, prisoner's
base. The excitement of games! Elizabeth found she had to run, shrieking and
panting, till her throat was as hot as a pipestem. She tried hard to catch the ball
thrown to her; but her fingers trembled, she missed. But no one said (as her own

father did), "Butterfingers!" And soon Bessie's arm was flung around her shoulder. "Let's go say goodnight to Fred." Gently they walked, arm in arm, cooling off as the prairie night wrapped itself round them.

"Let's just go tiptoe," Elizabeth dared to suggest, "and see if your calf is asleep." "They'll all be sleeping."

When they reached the barn Bessie unfastened the bolt softly and they slipped into the gloom, into the smell of straw and manure. Dull thud of a horse's hoof, cows chewing their cud: these were the only sounds. Bessie beckoned and Elizabeth followed on tiptoe to Fred's stall. Chuckling, they stooped to rub his nose. Elizabeth tripped and nearly fell over into the stall. Right away she was petrified by a voice from the loft above: "What's that noise?" Bessie stiffened, put a finger on her lips. Then they heard a man's voice murmuring, "Just the beasts below."

"It's Dickon," Bessie whispered, half giggling. She took Elizabeth's hand and they stood stock still, tight together.

Dickon spoke again. "Aw, please, Jenny, you don't have to go yet!"

They could not hear a reply, only a scuffling in the loft. Bessie could hardly hold herself in, trying not to giggle. Elizabeth was trembling, her mouth dry.

158 "It's a long way I walked from my place, just to go home again."

"But honestly, Dickon, Ma'll need me for the separating; I'll come back after," Jenny promised. "Now let me go, quick!"

Bessie, choking with laughter, seized Elizabeth's arm and led her on tiptoe to the barn door. "Hurry," she whispered. Elizabeth stumbled on the sill and nearly fell. They fled rocketing out the door and through the barnyard, running for dear life. In the first field they plumped into a haystack, exhausted, letting their laughter loose in the sweet prickly comfort of the hay.

When they could talk, Elizabeth choked, "Gee, what if they heard us?"

"It wouldn't matter," Bessie told her. "We kids used to peek at them last summer. Dickon lives all alone, y'know, on his Dad's old farm. He has nobody to look after him. But Ma says he's too shy to ask Jenny to marry him."

"He didn't sound shy tonight." That set them giggling again. But after they had crept home and slipped into bed Elizabeth whispered, "But why is Jenny so mean to him?"

"She's not mean!"

"She is so! She's always trying to get away from him."

"Is she? I dunno. I guess maybe she doesn't want to get married. She doesn't like the farm ... but I do!"

"So do I. And I'd marry a farmer!" Elizabeth smiled into the dark, where she could imagine so clearly the face of Dickon: red and crusty with sandy tufted eyebrows looming above such blue eyes. Blue as ... as cornflowers ... sky ... She fell asleep, still smiling.

When tomorrow came it proved to be a day for housecleaning at Dickon's farm. Jenny took the horse and gig, with Elizabeth and baby Laura up beside her. Ahead of them stretched the straight prairie road with upturned black loam stretching for miles on either side. All else was sky, blue, with puffs of cloud at the brim; and the sound of meadowlarks. It was a happy morning. Only Jenny sat heavily holding the reins, saying nothing.

Elizabeth looked up at her, hesitant; observing the rounded bloom of her cheeks, her ginger-coloured hair struggling to be free from the prim knot at the back; her brown eyes that could flash, her mouth that could pout. Why wouldn't she talk?

"Is it a long way to Dickon's house, Jenny?"

"About three miles."

"I'm glad we don't have to walk ..." Elizabeth watched the horse's tail twitch as he clopped along. "Is it a nice house—Dickon's?"

"Nothing to get excited about." Jenny pulled the reins tighter.

"Are you going to get engaged to him, Jenny?" As there was no answer she started to say it again, more loudly; but Jenny's clouded face choked the question. They did not talk again until they reached the poplar bluff that served as gateway to Dickon's farm.

The old frame house was sagging, crouched to the earth, unpainted and curtainless. But the barn looked stronger, sturdier, as if it knew the feel of footsteps, touch of hands. While Jenny went into the house to start a fire and clean up, the two children wandered about. Around the barn there were no animals to look at. The chicken house they peered into was empty and untidy; swallows swerved in the gloom of a shed. A tightness ... she felt a tightness in her throat. Poor Dickon, with no one to look after him! He was far off in the back field today, behind his team. He did not seem to know they were there.

"Is Dickon coming here for dinner?" Elizabeth asked, hungrily hanging around the kitchen door.

"No," said Jenny. "He takes his lunch pail out to the fields. Here, I brought some sandwiches for you and Laura."

They munched them, deep in the unshaven grass, pouring themselves drinks of water from the rusty pump. "Sp'ash, sp'ash," cried Laura, and Elizabeth obediently pumped great squirts of water over her bare feet. Then she jumped into the puddle herself, letting the mud ooze through her toes.

"Here," said Jenny, weakening. "You can take this thermos of tea to Dickon."

Elizabeth wiped her feet on the grass with alacrity, fumbled for her socks and sandals. Then she and Laura trotted off along a muddy lane, on and on through the shimmering sun to Dickon.

He was sitting in a bit of shade by a poplar bluff, eating his lunch. "Well," was all he said. "Well, well." And then, "Thanks, kiddies."

Elizabeth glowed, but she did not know what to say, standing stiffly before him. "Jenny is cleaning up for you," she offered.

"Yes," he replied. "Real nice of her, isn't it?"

"It needs cleaning," said Elizabeth.

"It does that."

"It needs a woman around, I guess." She half laughed, making it sound casual like. But he did not answer. He just looked a long way off across the flat fields. Since apparently that was all he was going to say, and he had finished his tea, Elizabeth picked up the empty thermos. "G'bye then."

160

"G'bye, Liz." He smiled his rare smile, his blue eyes crinkling. She went back to Jenny in a golden dream, scarcely noticing that Jenny asked no question about Dickon; nor did she look his way when the buggy, homeward bound, passed near his field.

Before Elizabeth's time was up, there was a picnic in the bush beside a creek; and a visit to a neighbouring farm. But most days curved in an arc of steady sun, black shade. In the evening, breathless after a game of tag, Elizabeth and Bessie would climb onto the field gate and swing slowly to and fro. Elizabeth always looked along the lane to see if there was anyone coming—a man in blue overalls, it might be, and a blue shirt. But Dickon never came.

"Jenny was cross as two sticks today," Elizabeth told Bessie. "I bet she's sorry she was mean to him."

"Jenny likes the city—shows, and jitneys and things," replied Bessie, who had never been there.

"And I like the country!" Elizabeth sang it out.

"I'm glad. Wisht you could always stay with us."

"So do I." Strange, she had not felt homesick yet.

But the day arrived when the farmer came driving his team home at noon, with Dickon beside him.

"Dickon!" Elizabeth ran to greet him; then hung back, shy. He really looked pleased to see her, and swung her up in his arms. Elizabeth blushed and kicked, so he set her down quickly, saying: "Why I do believe the kiddie's put on weight here!"

"You bet she has." Mr. Moffat smiled. "Too bad she has to go back."

"Go back?" Jenny echoed Elizabeth's question, suddenly appearing from the kitchen door.

"Yep. Strike's over," Dickon told them.

"They say things will be rolling again by Monday," said the farmer.

"'Bout time, too."

"Did the men win?" Jenny wanted to know.

"What's that to you? I dunno. Jones passed the word over the fence to Dickon. They've quit, that's all we know. Them ringleaders arrested."

"Well, I guess your mother will want you home again, eh, Elizabeth?" Mrs. Moffat patted her shoulder.

"Oh, I don't think Mummy would want me yet," Elizabeth asserted, casting a hopeful glance towards the farmer and his wife as they stood in the farmhouse doorway.

"Naturally Elizabeth will have to go back to her folks." Mrs. Moffat smiled firmly, putting an arm around her shoulder as they all moved inside. "Though I don't see why Jenny should have to go back so soon. She's entitled to a holiday."

They all turned to look at Jenny.

"I've had my holiday," she said.

Dickon, just inside the doorway, flushed red, moved awkwardly from one foot to the other. He managed to ask her, "Do you want me to drive you to Winnipeg tomorrow?"

"Yes, please," she said. Then she went straight to the stove and began carrying hot dishes to the kitchen table.

"Well, sit down, sit down, Dickon," urged the farmer. "Can't waste time eatin', this time of year."

On Sunday, after the heavy afternoon dinner, goodbyes had to be said. Elizabeth loitered through the barnyard with Bessie; then Bessie packed her suitcase for her and tucked into it a sprig of "everlasting"—"So you won't forget me, Elizabeth."

"Oh, thanks." She was almost choking.

"Maybe Elizabeth can come back some day," the mother said, softening and giving her a last hug. Then she was up into the front seat, between Dickon and

Jenny. Everyone waved white handkerchiefs, even little Laura in her daddy's arms. Bessie ran to close the farm gate after them.

"Don't forget, Elizabeth! Don't forget!"

Elizabeth felt dry and empty. Some day, she was certain, she would return to the farm and marry Dickon and really look after him. He wasn't really so old; only twenty-four! Sitting there in the car beside him, with Jenny on the other side, she felt as if Dickon really belonged to her. She began to chatter away faster and faster, talking to him about the farm.

"You don't like the city, do you, girl?" said Dickon. He called her "girl" now, not "kiddie." "Well, no more do I. No more do I." And he pressed his foot on the accelerator, hard.

Jenny said nothing, all the dusty way home.

THE UPROOTING

When they had returned to their second house, after the war, they saw clearly it could never be the same. Not only had it shrunk—the white clapboard that had seemed so high now looking like a doll's house set in a doll's garden—but the house possessed a secret air. The neighbours soon made known to mother what the secret was about. But even if they had not described the changes in the house, there was enough evidence, taken alone: taxis pulling up at night and unloading men; sounds of revelry; deep day silences—the house must have got used to all these, mother guessed. For the telephone would ring, at all hours: "That you, Flossie? Can I come up tonight?" Mother put down the receiver with a bang. Later she said (in front of Elizabeth) that she had thought it strange that father's steel engravings of Jove and Juno had been brought downstairs and hung in the drawing-room. Worse still, as far as Elizabeth was concerned—the blue elephant was gone. He had been a plush elephant sent by Granny—in England; and because he was so pretty he had always sat on the plate shelf, just to be looked at. Now he could never be played with. He had gone, with the tenants.

"There must have been some children here," Elizabeth argued. But no one chose to answer. From snatches of telephone conversation she gathered that "the nurse" and her mother, who had rented the house, were not really what they said they were, at all; but something queer. Probably Unitarians, Elizabeth thought.

And so the little white house had become, not father's any longer, but Someone's—nobody knew quite whose. Father blamed mother for having rented it while he was away; he wanted to sell it, and move. And then the great decision came, for him and for all of them. He was to go east! He was to have a big job to do in the newspaper world and they would live in a city called Toronto.

Leave Winnipeg! It seemed impossible. "But I can't leave Peggy!" Elizabeth said. Father just laughed. "Wait till you see the cherry trees in bloom," he promised. "And trilliums. Trilliums in Stoney Wood." Father was already reliving his youth, spent with relatives in the Ontario countryside. Enthusiasm lighted his face, he chuckled like a boy.

Cherry blossoms? She did not know. But Elizabeth had no choice. She had to go. She had to watch the little white house being dismantled; clothes and books packed; old toys thrown away. Father said they couldn't possibly take the doll's house; but Elizabeth and Susie insisted that they could, they must. The doll's house was a symbol, for them, of all their life in the larger house. Their loves and hates had entered into it; and each bit of furniture—the little coal scuttle that came from England—the tiny lamp—these objects had become as inseparable as their own hands. Mother saw this, and understood: and the doll's house was also given a ticket marked "Toronto."

It was different with people. Elizabeth, anguished, apprehended rather than reasoned that you could not take people with you. And that last morning, sitting on a suitcase on the front verandah, she felt desolate, a hollow feeling in her stomach. It was a cold spring day, nearly crocus time again. Wind blew the crows about, wherever it wished, in a grey sky: a lonely, unreal morning.

Across the street, Peggy could be seen, skipping. But oddly enough, it was not Peggy now whom she missed, whom she longed for. Peggy had changed. She stayed more at home, now that Rita had gone off to take her hospital training. And also, she played more with boys. Why, even last week Elizabeth had seen her chasing Robert, the new boy, and tripping him up—and then bending down, flinging her curls in his face, as if she were going to kiss him! This was too much for Elizabeth. She seemed to have lost Peggy, that very moment; so today it did not seem to upset her to see Peggy staying on the other side of the street, just waiting till Elizabeth's taxi came. Let her skip!

No. It wasn't her own friends Elizabeth was mourning for; nor the familiar shape of the wide street and the brown boulevard grass looking like a map, with its raised bumps of sooty, gritty snow. It wasn't the separation, even, from those beings who had watched over her like angels: Granny and Aunt Maudie. Especially Aunt Maudie, who had a way of sitting down beside you as if she knew you wanted her;

and of giving you a little hug: "Well, how's my sweetness?" and putting into your hand something she had made for you. This time it was a tiny farewell sachet, smelling so keenly of lavender.

"Oh, isn't it darling!" Elizabeth smiled, nearly crying. And she remembered all the ways in which Aunt Maudie had been like a mother to her: teaching her, so patiently, to knit; to sew; to make that spicy cottage pudding with the brown sugar sauce. Aunt Maudie never gave her a book, nor paintboxes, nor musical instruments; but she made her a white eyelet embroidery dress to wear at the Sunday School concert. And at all times Aunt Maudie took the warmest interest in her doll family, and made dolls' clothes and showed Elizabeth how to make them ... Why wasn't Aunt Maudie a mother, she wondered, suddenly; and feeling the closeness and warmth of this gentle person beside her, she burst out now with the question:

"Why didn't you ever get married, Aunt Maudie?" And Aunt Maudie smiled, without a tear in her eye. "Why, I guess I never met a man I liked well enough," she explained, simply. "I was always at home, you know; looking after your Granny."

164

"Oh ... Well, if you didn't want to marry, wasn't there anything else you wanted to do, Aunt Maudie?"

And the sweet mouth smiled, the weak blue eyes behind gold-rimmed spectacles lighted up. "Why, if I could have had the training, dear—I would have liked to be a chemist. A druggist, you would call it. I was always so interested in herbs, and drugs and their uses. How to cure people."

"A druggist!" Elizabeth looked at Aunt Maudie with increased curiosity. She could not imagine that white hair behind a counter, selling Zam-Buk ... perhaps she would fit in at the back, in the dispensary, fiddling about as she did in her own, terribly untidy pantry. But Aunt Maudie might so easily get the drugs mixed up, putting half-a-teaspoon of one into this saucer, and half-a-teaspoon of that into a cup. Oh, no! Elizabeth thought Aunt Maudie would have managed much better, as a mother ... and left it at that; only realizing long afterwards that Aunt Maudie had been a mother, after all; for she had taught Elizabeth what mothering was like.

But this farewell morning Elizabeth smiled, flung her arms around Aunt Maudie's neck. "I wish you were coming with us too, Aunt Maudie."

"I wish I was, dear. I wish I was." And the gentle, work-worn hand stroked her hair, gazed into her eager eyes. "Promise me you'll he a good girl, Elizabeth? And always do what's right?"

"Yes," said Elizabeth. "I promise!" Embarrassed, she jumped up, ran down to the gate to see if the taxi was coming. That car, could it be that black car in the distance? It was! It stopped at the curb in front of the gate.

"Are you going now? Are you going?" Peggy and Frances and other girls on the street, free on their Saturday morning, came dashing over to the white house. They all wanted to help the taxi man carry valises and boxes down to the car. Then mother came out of the doorway, in a wide-brimmed hat with an ostrich feather, and carrying all kinds of little parcels and bundles. "And have you got the lunch?" asked Aunt Maudie. And Susie ran out, carrying her rag doll; and last of all, father, turning the key in the lock though there was nothing left to lock; father, carrying a new walking stick with a carved knob at the top.

"Goodbye, goodbye!" they called back and forth, in high childish voices, till they were all piled into the taxi and the door closed. The engine whirred, the car moved forward, backed up a side street, then tore around to a flying goodbye, goodbye to Lipton Street.

So it wasn't Peggy, nor Rita, nor Aunt Maudie, nor the street itself; nor the little white clapboard house: it was something of all these, whose loss she felt; but it was more, more than that. What she experienced was the sense of separation, the knowledge that she was no longer tied to anything; but was a human creature walking alone, with only her own legs to sustain her, her own arms to pull.

She pressed her face against the car window and saw, high overhead, scudding along amongst soft spring clouds, the deep V-wedge of the geese. She could not hear them, but she knew their song.

Morning and It's Summer

AL PURDY

Al Purdy (1918–2000) was one of Canada's most admired poets, a true innovator, virtually without literary antecedents but rich in admirers (only in small part because he could not be imitated). In his later years, he turned increasingly to prose. One of his first ventures in this direction was this reminiscence of his childhood in a hard-scrabble region of Eastern Ontario, published in 1983 as *Morning and It's Summer: A Memoir*. The tale of his childhood makes an instructive contrast with that of Dorothy Livesay, who aspired to Purdy's lower social rank through radical politics while Purdy held no pretensions of climbing either up *or* down the social ladder and was by nature, as the writer Charles Taylor described him, "a folk tory."

When electricity came to our street in Trenton, around 1921 or '22, I was three or four years old. In late evening when lights flashed on for the first time, people rushed outside to see what the street lights looked like, each with an aureole of moths and flying insects. And there was a feeling of foaming lakes and rivers coming from far away, while the overhead wires hummed urgently.

Some people left their house lights burning all night, just for the novelty, and being so pleased at not having to use messy oil lamps and candles any longer. And the birds on our street kept on singing, probably thinking this new kind of daylight would never end, feeling hoarse and exasperated. Of course I was too young to remember all this, only a little; but my mother told me the rest.

When my father died and we moved from the Wooller farm into the red brick house in Trenton in 1921, it was already more than a hundred years old. The floors were sagging upstairs and down, as if the house was tired from all those years and couldn't stand properly upright any longer. Some of the doors wouldn't open or close without a struggle. At night when I was awake and listening, small noises came from everywhere: the sound of old floor joists, boards, and square-headed nails talking together.

The wooden barn was red as well, a cobwebby place of shadows that filled most of our backyard. There was still hay in dusty corners, and iron rings on walls where horses once had their stalls. In fact, our house and barn were probably part of an old farm. When you closed your eyes and made all the surrounding houses disappear, there was nothing left in your mind but green grass and flowering buckwheat and a hum of bees filled the air.

McLean's pumpworks stood just across the street from our house. The rusty tin-covered building was too small to be called a factory, but too large for a workshop. Old McLean, sandy-haired, sour-faced, and bad-tempered, made wooden pumps for farmers' wells. The pumpworks hummed with belts and pulleys, whirring lathes in pine-scented gloom, shavings piled deep on floor, small boys crowding the doorway, deeply interested in yellow-bearded McLean and the small men he made from wood.

That's what they looked like, small men. When chisels and lathes had done their work, and black metal bands encircled their four-foot bodies to prevent splitting, with an iron mouth and long wooden pumphandle attached, then by an act of magic a small man was created. Other men might be doctors and lawyers and storekeepers, but the men McLean brought to life spent their days lifting water up into sunlight. It was cold and sweet. It tasted of deep springs and wells and rivers under the earth.

I was about three years old. And still retain this almost mythical memory of an incident that happened then. I used the toilet, then called for my mother to button me up again, since the flaps and buttons were a complete mystery. She wasn't there. I wandered downstairs and out onto Front Street with short pants dangling around my knees, calling "Mother, Mother, Mother!" She wasn't there either.

A farmer and his wife were passing by in their horse-drawn wagon, on the way to market with a load of farm produce. They heard me bawling, stopped, tried to find my mother. But she wasn't in sight or sound.

Speculating that my mother might have gone to market herself, they took me onto their wagon. We clopped off to market while the farmwife tried to comfort me with soothing words. But I was not to be comforted so easily.

The market was jammed with people. Farm wagons piled with bright orange pumpkins, yellow onions, and brown potatoes were backed up at the market square. Puppies in cages awaited buyers. Chickens squawked in other cages. Some were dead and stripped clean of feathers, wearing bloody bandages where their heads had been decapitated. A big blue policeman with shining buttons strolled through the mob of townspeople: the Trenton market square also housed the police station.

It was terrifying. I squirmed out of the farmwife's grasp, dashing into a clotted mixture of vegetables and people, calling "Mother, Mother!" All I could see was legs legs legs, the bottom halves of people without heads. Maybe they had no heads, which might have been cut off like the dead naked chickens. I screamed and ran.

Then I was surrounded, in the middle of a circle. People with potato heads and potato eyes were looking down at me. People with pumpkin heads and pumpkin eyes, onion heads and onion eyes. The live chickens squawked, the dead ones swayed where they hung on cords by their feet. A tremendous wind roared through my own head, a sound like the end of the world.

I didn't, couldn't think. But I knew. I was all my other selves. For the first of many future times, you're in a situation that you don't know how is going to end. Whatever action you take might make it better—or worse. The temptation is to stand perfectly still, close your eyes, don't even think, because an unknown something might notice the flashing lights in your mind. If you moved. If you talked. If you didn't close the shutters in your head, while the alarm bells somewhere rang and rang. Which is sheer terror.

That is the memory, simple enough to explain and rationalize as you grow older. How my mother appeared and I was comforted. How the noises stopped. And so did terror. It was ended. But the memory doesn't end. It stays at the beginning of memory, hovering on the edge of consciousness, where the beasts with onion heads may still be waiting.

Trenton had a population of about six thousand in the 1920s. The town was divided into two halves by the wide, black Trent River flowing under an iron bridge; and dominated by an oversized molehill, Mount Pelion, with an old Crimean War cannon on its crest.

At the bakery a block away, I hung around to smell the bread baking, and played with the little girl who lived there. The B.W. Powers coal sheds filled nearly a whole block on the river side of our street. I watched great teams of

169

drayhorses struggling out of the sheds, their wagons loaded with canvas bags of coal, delivered by black-faced sweating men to the town stoves and furnaces.

At Simmons' Drug Store, at the corner of Front and Dundas, the town's two main streets, bottles of red, blue, and green coloured water with lights behind them shone from the store windows. When I owned a nickel or rare dime, I bought horehound candy and gazed longingly at the big red Chums books from England displayed there before Christmas every year.

Below the town bridge, the river widened and became the Bay of Quinte. In winter, when I owned my first pair of skates and kept falling down repeatedly, we chased an old tin can or lump of coal on the frozen river, batting at it with a broken board, or an old hockey stick if we were lucky. When the river was clear of snow, the game sometimes took on wider dimensions. A fast skater might stickhandle clear of the small boy ruck, making for the bridge and under it to the bay, a coloured screaming rabble of children pursuing him onto Quinte.

And far out there on the black ice, alone, in really cold weather the ice would rumble and crack with the sound of eternity. I'd stand there shivering, knowing there were monsters waiting, looking at me under the ice. See their shadows wavering back and forth behind the ice barrier, hungry. And notice also another boy watching me, red-nosed from the cold, lifting his hand when I lift my hand, uncannily like myself but not myself, reflected on the ice.

Farther north on the river road, Mayhew's Mill. The millpond covered several acres, fed by many shallow streams that froze quickly in winter. At night boys and girls of the town lit torches of bulrushes dipped in coal oil or gasoline, skating away and waving them over their heads, into the hinterland of creeks and winding little streams. As if the moonlit world had many doorways. Or they built fires at the pond edges, toasting marshmallows and hot dogs, or sitting silently in blankets while the daylight world vanished.

Reddick's Sash & Door Factory across Front Street overlooked the Trent River. Lumber and heavy planks were piled in sheds where thick-bodied willows leaned over the water, their red roots waving under the surface like drowned girls' hair. I went there to be alone, sitting on the sweet-smelling lumber, trying to get used to being alive. At that early time of my life, five, six, and seven years old, I still had the feeling of belonging somewhere else, having lately arrived without any explanations given. Even the colours of things, that later become so familiar, gave rise to questions in my mind. Aware of it for the first time, red was a phenomenon. Also green, blue, yellow, and orange. I wondered: are black and white things dead? And only coloured things alive?

I was a stranger in that world. Other people acted in such a way as would allow them to be comfortable and at ease while getting used to human existence. Some learned very quickly, others haven't even now. Some part of me still remains a child: sitting on a pile of lumber behind Reddick's Sash & Door Factory in 1924, trying to explain to myself how I got here and what I'm going to do about it.

Overhead, a bird goes "Wow-ee! Wow-ee!"—among willow leaves that gleam and gleam, having trapped the sun a million times in three-inch strips of green. Then another bird, one that sounds like a medieval musical instrument that I have never heard played. It is enough to hear them for this moment, to feel the mind stop thinking and join the mindlessness of red willow roots and mud of the blue-black river.

Later, days later or only hours, lying on my back in deep grass, watching clouds drifting towards the world's edge. And adjust their shapes slightly with my mind, so that they alter into fat faces, thin faces, or the body of someone you know. Grandfather, for instance, called "Old Rid" by his friends.

"Old Nick," my mother would probably have called him, since he had lived with us shortly after we moved to Trenton from the farm. Grandfather chewed tobacco, drank whisky, was personally careless and untidy of dress, used a few cuss words at judicious moments, and played cards with other ancients (he was about eighty in 1920) at a floating poker game in downtown Trenton. "Floating" meaning that the location of the game shifted whenever public or private criticism became strong enough to make them change the venue.

Grandfather's unregenerate character and my mother's religious one forced him out of the house shortly after his arrival. He rented a long narrow room, resembling a bowling alley, over a dry goods store downtown, where poker flourished and chewing tobacco decorated the greasy floors whenever it missed the spittoons.

I visited him there as often as I could, with the feeling of being slightly wicked. My mother permitted these visits, but I think she felt suspicious that he was corrupting me somehow. And I listened to his stories when he wanted to tell them, which wasn't very often, for he was a taciturn old man with cold watery blue eyes and a look of calm ferocity.

Grandfather was slightly over six feet tall. He weighed 260 pounds. His nose was a parrot's beak; his face had the look of youth, or remnant of youth—not of young and carefree days in the past, but the bullmoose time of being a lumberjack and backwood wrestler, barn raiser and don't-give-a-damn-about-anything stud and hellraiser. He was.

Grandfather tolerated me. And all the time something smouldered and burned inside him which I felt too, something out of the far-distant past. He was eighty years back of me in time, and seemed less a relative than a queer aging animal from forests where other animals had avoided him. My father had been fifty-eight when I was born, and my mother had been forty. My own connection with these people seemed many generations distant. All the world was old, this very world that was closest to me.

That ferocity, that smouldering and burning self, concealed or half-concealed in rotting flesh! His talk about wrestling the woods bully: no doubt he was a bully himself, although that never occurred to me. Barn raisings and booze, and "I wanted to get into her pants." Nothing softened or euphemized for me: he said what he thought and felt. Death was "I'll turn up my toes," and "You don't dast stop—" Or everything would fall down.

I pictured (later, of course) those 260 pounds of gaseous body and fatty muscles back at Canadian Confederation in 1867, when it was trim and sleek as a wolf, when it was young, but always having foretraces of being an old man living over a dry goods store in Trenton. The stench of stale food around him, dirty dishes in the sink, most of his friends dead: yet he exhaled power. And I am not mistaken.

I couldn't imagine his ever being defeated, physically humbled, whatever his age. When I walked with him to Tripp's Pool Room, holding onto his hand at age five, his great flat feet beating onto the concrete sidewalk towards earth beneath, I felt a thrill of pride. And partook of that power just by being with him. Myself a child, so weak and fearful of the dark, but joined to this strength extending back in time.

Old Rid, in his late eighties, with a heavy walking stick: the scarcely waning strength and huge body carried with it all the weight and majesty of the darkness I feared so much. Not just a fading physical power either. It was an aura, a feeling, even a rightness. I felt it like mental calories, infused through all my senses. And grew stronger inside this casual gift of knowing. And it was a casual gift from him, for it never occurred to him that he was giving. Perhaps I was too. While my mother worried.

Campbell's Tombstone Works was just next door, with dozens of red, black, and green granite tombstones, crated and uncrated, arriving there from all over the world. Every day but Sunday chisels pounded at stone. The names and dates of dead men and dead women were carved in granite, or those of living people anticipating their own demise. Later on, compressed air powered the chisels, and later still, sandblasting operations were installed. With that last innovation, choking clouds of stone dust floated inside and outside the building, a "pillar of cloud by day."

In moonlight, the tombstones next door were like a small cemetery; granite and marble seemed to attract a silver light around them. But I was never afraid for some reason, despite being terrified of darkness. Perhaps it was the familiarity of the headstones. And there were no human bodies buried underneath, no ghosts of the dead haunting our neighbourhood. It may have been that the noise of steel chisels and the roar of sandblasting kept them away. No ghost could stand such noise.

Bernard Campbell was my own age, and we played together, along with Jack Clegg, a distant cousin. My mother and Mrs. Campbell visited back and forth. At age five or thereabouts, I owned a little wooden wagon with rubber wheels and pedalled it along the sidewalks. Model A Fords were becoming plentiful at that time; the Campbells owned one. Scattered around in their garage were miscellaneous tools and junk that accumulates in such places. Also six or eight spark plugs. When I wandered into the garage, I knew that spark plugs had something to do with making Ford cars travel the roads, but not exactly how. And if they did that for automobiles, why not for my wagon? I installed them along the wagon railing, thinking that I now possessed something the grown-ups had, something to astonish everyone with the additional speed I could achieve.

Of course the spark plugs didn't add any speed to my wagon whatever. I left them in the wagon that night. Next day they were gone. I was slightly indignant and went to look for them again in the Campbell garage. Sure enough, my spark plugs sat on the window ledge in a shining row. Maybe I hadn't installed them correctly. The little gleaming bits of porcelain and steel must have a secret, some magical power that would make things go fast, faster, and fastest. I intended to find out what it was. Maybe if I put them under my pillow when I went to bed at night, like you did with a tooth when you lost one, then made a wish.... Something dark came into the garage from outside. The red-faced Campbell called Arnold loomed over me. "You little thief," he said. "You little thief!" He picked me up with one arm, so that I swung upside down and dangled there. He carried me in front of the tombstone works next to the street, tied me with thick hempen ropes to the block and tackle hook, used to lift tombstones from one place to another.

173

I bawled and caterwauled for my mother. As it happened, the ropes were tied loosely enough for me to have slipped out of them, but some part of my mind knew that escape would solve nothing. All the Campbells came out of their shop and house to look at me accusingly. "Thief," they said. "Thief!" My mother heard the racket after a few minutes, and came over to secure my release. "Don't you think he should be punished for being a thief?" the Campbells asked her. "Yes," she said, "and I should have the opportunity to punish my own son." I agreed with her, of course.

When grade school arrived, and secondary school later, Bernard Campbell turned out to be the smartest kid for blocks around. Perhaps in the whole town of Trenton. His marks were often the highest in his class, my class, any class. Eventually, a scholarship to university was mentioned. And for all those years, Mrs. Campbell arrived to inform my mother of her son's triumphs. These visits occurred fairly often, and sometimes I would listen behind curtains or door.

"Bernard topped his class again this week," said Mrs. Campbell. "Isn't that nice?" My mother agreed that it was nice, after which ensued a long silence from Mrs. Campbell. A silence that might be construed to mean: Why isn't your son as smart as Bernard? In fact, your son is just plain stupid. There was no possible answer to these thoughtful statements, since they were unspoken. But there was a faint sizzling in the air at times.

The calendar moves forward then backwards: and a memory so frail that any additional effort to add details might break a thread to the past: two small boys are standing looking at each other. Both are seven years old. Both feel terrible, with tears not far away. The other kid's name is Jack Corson. He has been accused of stealing at school, and was unable to defend his innocence to the satisfaction of school authorities. In fact, he may have been guilty. That didn't matter. The important thing was that we both felt so badly. It was like dying. We loved each other. Both felt what the other felt. All of human existence had narrowed down to two boys feeling an inexpressible sorrow for which there was no outlet, without beginning or end. Time, of course, covers everything with a cynical or sentimental overlay, but time had stopped for us at this exact moment.

At the age of two until perhaps ten or twelve, I was always conscious of living in a land of giants. The child me was anywhere from two to four feet tall during those ages, and being confronted continually with enigmatic doorknobs high over my head and difficult to open, kitchen and bathroom sinks made for towering monsters, winter snow piled into great chalk cliffs making mountain-climbing equipment necessary to scale them. And always, when you talked to an adult, or were talked at, you would be gazing just above or below a belt buckle, somebody's waistline, either fat or thin.

Adults talking to children don't address them directly very often, acting as if they were some kind of object about to be disposed of. Ada Kemp, my mother's old girlhood friend, used to look at my mother and say: "Alfred (I hated that first name), I think you should be helping your mother, doing more things around the house." And her bony face convulsed a little as if she had a bad stomach ache, but controlled it heroically. My mother would make a mild rejoinder, for she was a mild person despite the wildfire of religion raging in her veins. Sometimes she made me acutely uncomfortable, as if she wanted something from me, and yet took my response for granted. But I lived on different levels from hers.

When you were climbing a tree or hiding from the calling giants, small size was a positive advantage. The big chestnut tree in our driveway provided a leafy perch for hours, climbing to the slender topmost branches among flowery spring lanterns was as close to the sun as I could reach. Sometimes shaking the tree vigorously, sending a shower of prickly chestnut burrs tumbling down on the heads of people beneath. That was very helpful for my Lilliputian complex.

The darkness was worst of all. It was peopled with ghosts, goblins, and dead men with their throats cut and blood pouring from wounds. All these were-creatures of horror had once been living, some had had their blood drained out by vampires, whether animal or human. They often had gruesome physical deformities, hunchbacks, black flattened nostrils, twisted faces, insane minds. Children talked about these beings and their habits in hushed voices, collecting a pool of information about them. Whatever you knew about horror might be useful for protective purposes. All these discussions secretive and unknown to adults. In fact, adults were sometimes even listed in the catalogue of demons.

Sometime around 1925, an officer of the Trenton police force had died violently, from what agency I can't remember. He was a young man named Brown. On the night his body was "laid out" in a coffin on Division Street two blocks away, Jack Clegg and I had managed to evade the bedtime-calling voices, and were still playing in the streets.

It was a warm summer evening. We wandered to the death house, which had a funeral wreath hanging from a door that was slightly ajar. We could see the shape of a coffin through the curtains of the dimly lighted front room. One of us said, "Let's go in, there's nobody there." The other said, "You go in, I'll wait here

175

and keep watch." One of us said, "I dare you!" And the other said, "No you don't, I double dare *you!*" Unwilling to back down, both of us sneaked through the open door, but cautiously, ready to run if the corpse made any movement.

The coffin and waxen face of Constable Brown dominated the room, which was piled with flowers. They gave off a sick smell, advance notice of their own decay. The dead man's face had no expression, bore no marks of the violence that had killed him; the body lay there in a kind of unnatural repose, hands folded across the breast, in full policeman's uniform with glittering metal buttons.

It was quite different from finding the body of a dead cat or dog in the bushes where someone had thrown it. And brought to mind a fear that death might even visit someone I was close to, my mother, Uncle Wilfred, or even Grandfather. For this dead man was a symbol of authority and strength, who ought to have been safe from that other presence which was also inside the room.

We were uneasy and left quickly. There was no fear of the body itself, only from a fresh personal experience with something that had only been talked about among children before. Confirmed in that pale face there was something that walked abroad on the streets and roads, entered private houses and public buildings unseen, here and everywhere. It did not breathe, had no heartbeat nor specific shape, and yet possessed a form of reality, was in being, was a thing. It was there in that room with the body of Constable Brown, and is not certainly absent among these words which I am writing now.

The Follow

LINDA SPALDING

Linda Spalding (b. 1943) is an American writer who has lived in Canada since the 1970s and is an editor of the literary journal *Brick*. She has published two novels, *Daughters of Captain Cook* (1988) and *The Paper Wife* (1998), as well as *The Follow*, the unusual 1999 travel memoir from which the following is taken. *The Follow* led Spalding to edit *Riska: Memories of a Dayak Girlhood*, a rare memoir by a Borneo aboriginal. Spalding lives in Toronto.

orneo? It was only a suggestion by someone I'd never met, describing the unusual life of a woman who committed herself to a malaria-infested swamp and a group of endangered orangutans. The thought of the woman and the swamp and the forest around them reawakened thoughts that had been tormenting me for years. Thoughts about our connection to nature. We seem to be wandering outside it, but how can that be? Aren't we made of the same coils of DNA as everything living? Aren't our closest relatives the other great apes (chimpanzees, bonobos, gorillas, and orangutans)? Now only orangutans still live in the trees *whence we came*, wandering like nomads through the canopy, without permanent nests, the way we must have wandered once upon a time. Was it settlement that cut us off from nature? Are we human because we left paradise?

Orangutans were virtually ignored by naturalists until a young Canadian named Biruté Galdikas climbed out of a sampan in 1971 and settled in an abandoned forester's hut in the nature reserve of Tanjung Puting. As an anthropologist, she had a mission to study the tree dweller and to learn through this study more about the origins of human behaviour. In those days, Biruté—like Louis Leakey's other protégées, Jane Goodall and Dian Fossey—"followed" a primate for days, even weeks, learning what she ate, where she slept, how she raised her children, what mark her life in the forest made. It was a new kind of research, observation in situ, one for which Leakey found women particularly adept.

I knew nothing about orangutans or the rainforest where they live, but I knew enough to know it was going to be hard to follow Biruté. The trail was overgrown. And I am no athlete. Still, Rousseau's prescription for us, who have drifted so far from our origins, was to make two journeys: one to a place where life is still uncorrupted, and another into the self. And Biruté had written in her memoir, *Reflections of Eden*: "Every trip into the field is also a journey into yourself."

By following Biruté, perhaps I could accomplish both journeys.

My follow began in the north, in Toronto, where I live, but it took me deep into the rainforest and even deeper, into a tangled web of relationships and beliefs. I met snakes, frogs, scientists, and the man convicted of smuggling a group of baby orangutans called the Bangkok Six. I met the Dayak (the headhunters of Borneo), government officials, passionate ecotourists, and plenty of troubled orangutans. Each of them was a station along the way. Every footstep affects the forest, but a breath taken in or given out changes nothing, until the breath is *Homo sapiens's*. Until the breath is human, all that changes is the weather, the level of the damp, the season. There is swelling and subsiding, birth and death. Only we, the human finger on the primate hand, desire to hold, to save, to change.

178

Biruté and I are both children of the magical sixties, formed by that time when everything seemed possible, and the end justified the means. We no longer speak the same language. We chose different ways. But we have much in common. I knew nothing about the Bangkok Six and little about the new theories of our primate heritage, but those thoughts about nature and our place in it had been nagging at me. I was fifty and I was willing to see that as a defining moment. Even if Biruté is as elusive as the orangutans she follows, I thought, she might lead me to an understanding of how we *Homo sapiens* got ourselves thrown out of the garden and how we must look, in our exile, to the many eyes watching from the trees. Of course there was something else. A quest is as much about the seeker as the sought. We look in the mirror of another face to find ourselves. This is a signature act of all primates....

HOW TO GET THERE FROM HERE

What happened between the last strata of the Pliocene age, in which man is absent, and the next, in which the geologist is dumfounded to find the first chipped flints? And what is the true measure of this leap?

    —PIERRE TEILHARD DE CHARDIN

I went back to reading and waited for Biruté to call. I wrote her another letter. I made dates with the women I'd met who had travelled to Tanjung Puting, throwing questions at them about clothes and equipment. "Cotton, completely covered." "There's a new kind of pants at Mountain Co-op that dry in minutes." "Ziploc bags. Everything, all your paper stuff gets wet." "Get hold of Carey Yeager," Anne Russon advised me. "She's up the river studying proboscis monkeys, but she knows everything about the place. She used to work with Biruté. When she was doing her Ph.D." I made a date with a doctor who specializes in tropical medicine. We would need shots and malaria medication. I called the Indonesian consulate. We would need to renew our passports. From my perch by the phone I looked out at the melancholy weather. Snow, sleet, rain. My neighbourhood in Toronto is a mix of derelict houses and houses of the same vintage that have been fixed up by enterprising people. I guess it's a neighbourhood of enterprising people and not-very-enterprising people. There are men who sit on porches and men who don't have porches to sit on. They sit in the alleys that run behind the houses and their faces become familiar. In summer, they act as sentinels, but in March of 1995, their presence behind my house seemed ominous. Businesses were closing. There were no jobs. They had no place to sleep. And it was cold. While I was calling travel agents and consulates, I kept my eyes on a man who was mostly residing behind my house. He talked to himself. "I'm not so bad," he'd say. "I'm not a *bad* person." Sometimes he talked to my dog through the fence. "Don't worry, I like animals, I do. I'm a good person."

"How are you today?" I asked him one morning, as I went out the back gate.

"Bitter," he answered. And once he shouted, "Stay home!" as I went down our alley through the rain.

Leakey's study of the great apes was largely directed at research into behaviour as it relates to skeletal structure and habitat. Tired of basing all his theories about human prehistory on the fossilized remnants of *sapiens* and pre-*sapiens* who had lived thousands if not millions of years ago, he wanted to study people living much as he imagined the earliest humans had lived—modern hunter-gatherers— as well as our closest relatives, the other great apes. "Scientists were at last beginning to believe Charles Darwin's prophecy that the birthplace of both man and the great apes would be discovered in Africa," he wrote in *By the Evidence*. The idea that all hominids evolved out of the warm forests of Africa was radical, but eventually East Africa yielded remains of Hominidae, the taxonomic group that includes humans and apes, dated at twenty million years ago, when there were at least ten different species of apes living in the forest. In Olduvai Gorge in Tanzania and Koobi Fora in Kenya, two very different species of hominoid lived as neighbours for over a million years.

Finding the ever-narrowing bridge between ape and man depended on recognizing the first use of tools, the first attempt at speech, the first time, even, that a tool was used to fashion a tool. The Leakeys—Louis and Mary—studied chipped pebbles as well as fossils. And because the fossilized bones were also surrounded by fossilized seeds, insects, and plants, they were able to reconstruct the environment and to see how similar it was to the forested shores of Lake Tanganyika, which was inhabited by chimpanzees, whose habits might therefore provide clues to our own earliest history.

Leakey sent Jane Goodall out to study them.

Later he sent Dian Fossey to study the mountain gorillas.

And Biruté to Kalimantan.

I bought guidebooks and maps, and when Kristin arrived for a visit from Portland on a break from her work, we spread everything across the living room floor. An orangutan carries a mental map of all the trees in her range, including the state of ripeness of the fruits on each, but it must look quite different from the maps we studied. An adult male orangutan weighs around 180 pounds (eighty kilos) and has four times the strength of a human being. The problem is how to sustain that huge body on a diet of fruit and leaves, so along with the map goes a sense of timing that is absolutely accurate. If he arrives at a tree too early, the fruit will be inedible, and quicker animals will plunder it if he arrives too late. So orangutan mapping skills require a complex system of neural transmission and memory storage. But maps are anathema to me. I can't seem to associate the lines on a piece of paper with three-dimensional reality, and I have no sense of direction stored anywhere in my brain.

Borneo was certainly far away. Somewhere between Malaysia and the Philippines, it was big—the third-biggest island in the world—and had pieces of three countries in it: Malaysia (the parts called Sarawak and Sabah), Brunei, and the Indonesian part where we were going, which is called Kalimantan and has four provinces, West, Central, South, and East.

"We can't get to Borneo from Bali. Not by air," Esta said on the phone from Guelph, after talking to a travel agent.

"So we'll take a bus," Kristin decided.

"She hasn't written," I told my new friends (for what is a friend, I thought, but someone who has an interest in common?). They were priming me with stories of dangers and hazards as they were telling me what clothes to pack.

"She's testing you," they said.

"Loyalty," said Anne Russon, "is her big thing."

I dreamed that we were already there, that we were waiting at Camp Leakey for Biruté to arrive. Would she recognize me? When she finally came, she had many children at her side, but she had left me in charge of her smallest baby, and I stood there with the infant in my arms as she entered the room. The baby began to stir and cry and would not be stilled. She cried until Biruté came across the room and took her out of my arms. The moment was brief. Called to another part of the room, she handed the baby back, and I stood through the dream clutching a child I could not comfort, a child who wanted only her own mother. I was insufficient.

If the idea of travelling to the rainforest was new, my dreams of children were not. At night, my own are perpetually small. I am driving them through storms, up volcanic mountainsides, or I'm pulling one of them out of the sea. It's Kristin, my youngest, who always needs help in my dreams. She's having a birthday and I've forgotten the cake. I'm too busy or confused to do anything. Esta is the one who intervenes to save her, producing a cake and inviting the neighbours to a party.

Then one day in June, when Esta had finished marking final exams, she and I flew out of Toronto in the morning and arrived in Hawaii in the middle of the night, joining Kristin there for the first time since we'd all left together on a plane thirteen years before. I remember Kristin crying, her head down on the tray table all the way across the ocean. They were leaving everything *they* loved because I'd met someone *I* loved. I was moving them to Canada to live with him. It seemed, even to me, entirely unfair.

Now, Kristin and her father met our plane with 3 A.M. flowers, and within moments of entering the unforgettable humidity of our past, I was swept away to the small house where the father of my children lives on a hillside in Kaimuki. The house reminds me of our first one on the islands because of its painted redwood walls and the smell of earth coming up from outside and the cockroach in the laundry basket and the sense of this man I once loved now so near and so far away. But the words "once loved" make no sense to me. How is it possible to

181

stop such a force? That night Kristin and I slept in his bed and I lay at window level examining the leaves of a mango tree as I used to lie in my own bed on this same island after he left us, hearing the first rhythms of my own language become words I could put to a page.

Once again we were being parents of a sort—two parents under one roof for the first time in twenty-four years—and I wondered what was left of the people we had been then. ("Where shall we take the kids tonight, honey?" he had joked in the car.) I couldn't sleep, but it wasn't jet lag. It was something else. Excitement. Nostalgia. There was even a small seductiveness to this.

Where is the life that late I led?

We were on our way to Borneo by way of Honolulu, Bali, and Java. We had avoided the costly OFI tour and assembled a rough itinerary, and we were excited and stunned. In the morning we stood together in the bright sunshine, blinking at the chatter of birds in flowering trees. The ex had gone off to church. He's become a Christian, very certain in his faith, whereas I am uncertain in all things. Inside there were fat three-ring binders full of images of my children. And me. Young— younger—youngest. As if we had never dissolved as a family. In the old days I could never look in mirrors, but now I pore over pictures of the past, finding my own face and arms eloquent. Hands—they are the same! But different. They're part of a picture of someone who lives but no longer exists. I can see myself as I looked to his lens but not to his eyes. That will always be another of the mysteries.

Where is it now?

Utterly dead.

We can't re-enter our youthful bodies, but otherwise here, on this island, time seems almost to have stopped. The great ocean is below, making our hill seem simple, only geography. The cars on the highway circle the island at the rim of the ocean and the houses cling feebly to any land made available, as if they depend on claws. Swash of green watershed. Swash of human habitation. Swash of green again. Your eyes will be opened, says the serpent, and you will be like God.

All of this is strange, but strangest of all is the grown son who belongs to my ex and whom I last saw as a boy. This child is now the age we were when we met. Esta is older than I was when we parted. All that tragedy in lives so new. My foot in his jaw. Being swallowed.

After a day of circumnavigating our island, of stopping for "plate lunch" in Haleiwa, swimming on the north shore and crossing the Pali from the windward side at dusk, we flew out of Honolulu at 4 A.M., the hour of beginning and end,

182

amid blue-shirted surfers who pressed against us on the plane, big-boned, muscular, and feral. Esta stretched out on the floor to sleep. Kristin did crosswords. Nine-month sublet? Womb. Eye flirtatiously? Ogle. Care for, four letters? I woke to Mowgli on a movie screen directly in front of us—monkeys hoarding jewels and treasure—as if we'd already arrived in the forest. Why, I wondered sleepily, do we insist on seeing monkeys as devious?

Arrival in Denpasar was so sleep-deprived, so disorienting, that I only remember a long taxi ride into Ubud on a narrow crowded highway covered in smoke.The smell of a different land. In Bali, each village is arranged along lines of spirit, Brahma the wise, in the centre, Vishnu for life, and Shiva for death at either end. But Ubud is several villages grown together, and the lines there are complex. Durga, the goddess of Death, has a temple in the Monkey Forest at one end of town and our hotel, a place of bungalows and offerings of rice and flowers, was on the other side of this forest. As the consort of Shiva, Durga is not a goddess to pass in the night, but we knew nothing of this, as we knew nothing of anything yet.

That night—our first in Indonesia—we sat through part of the great Hindu epic *The Ramayana* on folding chairs in an open temple in the middle of town. Part One: *The Abduction of Sita*, and within minutes, I fell asleep, as two worlds, day world and dream world, collided. I was on the other side of the planet, and the rain had enclosed us in a wall of sound that drowned out even the clanging gamelans. Rama, god and prince, was exiled to the forest and Sita, his wife, went with him. Exile. The blackness of the night was a curtain behind which they journeyed, a blackness in which, all over Indonesia on different islands and different stages, parts of the old epic were unfolding, as they do every night—the prince being saved, in the end, by the divine intervention of Hanuman, the white ape.

In Bali, shadow puppets jerk and soar; live dancers imitate the shadow puppets; and on Java, wooden puppets imitate the live dancers. Hinduism was once the official religion on most of these islands. Now it survives in Bali and in bits and pieces on other islands. Now unassuming tourists sit under rain-drenched roofs and watch the epic in its many forms with its clearly defined oppositions. Evil and virtue. Battles of character and wiliness.

It was a night of no moon, no stars. Like sleepwalkers, stumbling and blind, we walked through the Monkey Forest to get back to our dry beds and more personal dreams. The white ape was a clue to something, but I was too weary to think. Thick trees over us and around us were ambiguous, and somewhere in the darkness were the monkeys we had seen on the morning movie screen and in the flesh in the afternoon, hugging their young and grabbing at tourists' bags in hopes of food. Descendants of Hanuman and acolytes for the ancient, inaccessible Durga, the monkeys must have been everywhere, but they are invisible at night. Nothing was visible, not even our hands. We had skirted the huge temple earlier, on our way into town, but now it was darker than the sky. I told myself that this was a first encounter with the great forest that once covered everything. With Durga, preserver, destroyer, mother, and origin.

Unusual fear. Thick silence. The three of us holding hands but moving single file following Kristin's voice. "There will be twelve stairs here," she whispered, although she had only traversed the path one time. "Watch out. Yes. Now a turn. That banyan will be ..." Kristin trained for many years as a dancer, and perhaps she remembers space through her feet. I hadn't noticed stairs or the length of the temple wall, but suddenly my youngest child—the one I dream of needing to protect—had taken the lead.

In order to get to an airport where there were flights to Borneo, the next part of our journey entailed a seventeen-hour bus ride into Java, ending in a mystic climb of Mt. Bromo at dawn. Esta had read about the Mt. Bromo experience, something that was going to take place on horseback, and "Wonderful!" she had breathed. So we signed ourselves up. The trip was a mere $20, including travel from Ubud to Semarang, which might have caused us to be suspicious, but we weren't. Seven hours, we were told. Your own jeep. Horses at the top. We did not even bother to pack lunch.

There was a procession of worshippers across the street as we climbed aboard the bus in Ubud. From the open window, I could see women in sarongs carrying baskets of fruit and other offerings on their heads. They poured out of an old stone temple and onto the sidewalk as if they were meant to guarantee the success of our journey, for now we were really moving into unknown space. Our hotel in Ubud had been recommended by Toronto friends, and we had had several sympathetic encounters there, including one with a travel agent named Hans Iluk, who knew all about Biruté and the orangutans. We had had access to a phone and a fax machine and a sense of connection to more familiar places. We had spent a week visiting the mother temple, the paddy fields, the pre-Hindu village of Tengganan and the town where white cranes come home each night to roost. Now, there was a short ride on a ferry across the Java Strait. There was the issue of where do we pee and when do we eat. Those were the things we had on our minds. Finally, there was a brief, brief halt in a roadside restaurant. That was it.

Seventeen hours, bolt upright.

Horrible music issuing forth.

Legs folded tight.

And Java is different. Even in the middle of the night, it's crowded, male, and Muslim. As a woman, one feels no vibration except of the sexual sort, which is not sympathetic but prevalent. The funny thing about this Muslim sexual vibration is that it's both curious and censorious. Hello, I love you, why are your arms so bare? It's not a good idea to be a woman, but to be a Western woman is worse. We offend with every breath and gesture.

Still, there was something miraculous about winding up a mountain at a snail's pace and being given two tiny rooms for two hours of sleep. At 3 A.M. we were wakened, given tea. We were to be taken up to the edge of the volcanic summit. "Where are the horses?" I asked, upon seeing our fellow-travellers boarding another bus.

"At the top, Madame."

"And where is the jeep mentioned in the brochure?"

"What jeep, Madame? What brochure?"

"The one in Ubud. The one we were shown at the travel office where we bought our tickets for this tour."

"That is there, not here."

I tried to convey the image I had of myself driving a jeep up the picturesque mountain at dawn. I said, "I paid for a jeep," with my usual uncertainty.

"Then you can have one. Madame."

As our fellow-travellers lurched away in their bus, we found ourselves being shoved into the back of a very small jeep. But I was triumphant. In a few minutes I was going to mount the smallest steed in the world to cross the high plains around the crater of Mt. Bromo in pitch-darkness. Boys carrying tiny lights lit the way and anyone with any sense—including my daughters—walked behind them through the perfect, pristine dust. But I, with my heels dragging, went at a little trot and I'll never forget it as long as I live, men and boys charging along in front on small steeds with scarves unfurled. It was magnificent.

Bromo is an active volcano over 6,500 feet high with a narrow stairway of 250 steps up one side, which we travellers ascended like angels from all corners of the earth. And at the top we sat down together in the dark and waited for the sun to rise. We were very quiet. Grateful for the company of other humans, we moved about very carefully when we moved at all and looked down the back side of our narrow ledge into a crater, which was smoking and sulfurous and which had swallowed a visitor in circumstances just like ours only weeks before. Then we turned towards the rosy side of the sky, or towards Mecca.

I suppose every person there was on some sort of pilgrimage. If I considered my own, it seemed unspiritual in the extreme. I was following a woman who did not seem to want my attention, hoping to find out whether she had fulfilled her own desires for accomplishment, what the cost had been, and whether she had managed, even in a small way, to leave a trail of meaning. Had we been other kinds of apes up there on Mt. Bromo, instead of *Homo sapiens*, we might have been watching the sunrise, but we would not have been thinking of Mecca. What would we have been thinking?

I do not remember leaving the mountain or entering Yogyakarta later that day, although I remember the place we stayed when we got there. In Yogyakarta, we walked through a family's kitchen to get to our rooms, which were on a narrow street full of roosters and restaurants. I remember eating in a place where baby chickens ran over our feet and going by *becak*, a rickshaw taxi, to see the water palace. Like the Hanging Gardens of Babylon, the palace, Taman Sari, once had lighted underwater corridors, subterranean mosques, gamelan towers, and bathing princesses. Now, there was an owl tied by its feet to an iron ring in an underground room and, nearby, a bowl for coins. Human droppings. His eyes stared at us as we passed.

The great pools where the sultan's harem had once swum were dry as bone but a guide explained how a woman would be chosen for an afternoon, picked out from the bathers and brought inside to a cool, brick room. We were shown the brick room and the brick bed upon which the woman and the sultan lay. There is still a descendant living on the premises. Unlike other Indonesian sultans, Yogyakarta's has retained some of the ancestral power because of his father's loyalty to Sukarno during the war of independence against the Dutch.

One of the odd things about this palace—at least the modern parts—is that photographs of its great hall look the same whether right side up or upside down. I can't explain this, but I swear it's true. There is such a glossiness about the ceiling, such a glossiness about the marble floor. There are pillars that extend from one to the other. And not much else. The past is more real than the present.

In Java it was like that: we wandered, we posed for each other's photographs and for the photographs of everyone else. We carried our cameras from one angle to another, looking for the perfect shot of history, and there were thousands of tourists just like us or different. They shouted, "Mrs., take my picture, please," or "My picture with you, Miss?" until, amazed at the pleasure I could so easily provide, I began to fake the little clicks of a shutter being released. I said, "Smile," and pretended to press, because what difference did it make? "May I take your picture?" became an excuse to smile and nod and hold each other close. "May I take your picture?" made us aware of ourselves. In Java we became outsiders, but our fragile triangle tightened, exactly as I had foreseen.

I was finding myself astonished by my daughters' abilities, and it was delightful to watch them interact. One will bargain over the smallest purchase until the cows come home. The other spends on impulse, with no thought of consequence. Both feel the morality of their convictions around money. It isn't important, but it is. Or it's important, but it isn't. It had been years since we'd been alone together for more than a day or two. Now we were sharing everything, every joy, every complaint, every decision. Even in the great expanses of Borobodur and Parambanan, we had nary an hour alone or apart. Only once or twice did we have separate rooms, and at those times I was reminded that I was the parent, that they were sisters, but otherwise we became, again, a single unit, functioning like a woman with six arms and six legs.

Finally, we went by bus to Semarang, where we could catch our Borneo plane and give ourselves one luxurious night in a hotel of several storeys with telephones and hot water. In the bar, someone sidled up to us and asked if we were with the OFI. It seemed incredible. "How could they be here?" I whispered, staring at my drink.

Esta said, "Don't be silly. Probably just a conference. Very common letters of the alphabet," and we retired to a room that was cool and a toilet that flushed and upon which one could sit. But when we unloaded our purses on the bed to examine our tickets, it seemed that Esta was scheduled to fly a day later than Kristin and me, which would throw the boat schedule off and leave us in separate disarray. So much for the luxurious room. Since there was a travel office in the hotel, we went back downstairs and spent the next two or three hours untangling our tickets with Air Garuda and the inter-island plane.

In the travel office, a stranger came to our aid. "Can I help? I'm sort of used to this ..." He turned out to be Eric, the very person I'd spoken to by phone at Bolder Adventures. So the OFI was the Orangutan Foundation International after all and we had all come, by some quirk of coincidence or fate, to the same hotel on the same day. The likelihood of this was just short of non-existent, but it had happened, and we were scheduled to take the same plane to Borneo the next morning! I wondered if I had wanted this in some corner of my unconscious. I'd known the dates of the OFI trip and forgotten them. But whatever my unconscious may have felt, my conscious wasn't pleased. We were surrounded by over-stuffed backpacks and egos. The atmosphere in the hotel restaurant swarmed with self-importance. Uneasily I began to see our trip through the eyes around us, as something frivolous and lighthearted.

The next morning, while the OFI group boarded an airport bus, we leaped into a taxi, speeding past them to get Esta into the ticket line first. Some of their tickets were also mixed up, but what hope had we, otherwise, against their tour guides? By the time they arrived at the Semarang airport, the smell of competition between us and them was already strong in the air.

Eventually all of us got on the same plane and flew over the same sea. Under us, there was the shadow of a plane on the water, a plane that now seemed to be going beyond the beyond. Crouched in the aisle of the plane was a woman named Giovanna who was too excited to stay in her seat. She was a teacher and she was making friends. She had spent all her savings to come on the OFI trip and I liked her short grey hair and intelligent face. "We're going to stay at Camp Leakey," she told us. "And work with Dr. Galdikas."

The OFI materials I had originally been sent described Biruté's research at Tanjung Puting as the longest, most detailed, uninterrupted study of wild orang-utans undertaken anywhere. "With the exception of four months, monthly observations have been continuous over nineteen years," it said. And in Biruté's words, apparently written for the volunteers the year before: *over the past twenty-two years I have systematically collected data on all aspects of orangutan behavior such as diet, foraging and ranging patterns, social organization, parturition, infant development, mother-offspring relations, reproductive behavior, vocalizations and tool use.* It was easy to understand why Giovanna might expect to see her. But I was sure she was mistaken. "Biruté's teaching in Canada," I almost said, but something silenced me. We were the oldest people on the plane and I felt drawn to her. Drawn because age was only one of a thousand things we had overcome to get this far.

Remember there will be insects, leeches, high humidity, malfunctioning machinery, fungus, toxic plants, creeping eruptions, malaria and who knows what else, the OFI materials had warned. But we all peered out of the little plane's windows eagerly. At last we were approaching that great thrill of green clinging by its roots to the island ahead of us, green that led away in all directions, borderless, astonishing, inarticulate. *Remember we are NOT in North America; we are in Borneo, one of the last wild places left on earth today.*

BLUE GUIDES

In Pangkalan Bun, the OFI group was met by Biruté's friend and assistant, Charlotte Grimm. "Someone just as interesting as I," Biruté had said, so I looked her over. There was a striking physical resemblance. Like Biruté, Charlotte has married a good-looking, younger Dayak and had two children by him. Her husband and Biruté's are nephew and uncle, so she sometimes introduces herself as Biruté's niece. But Charlotte came to Tanjung Puting for the first time in 1984, with her wealthy mother, on an Earthwatch expedition, and when Biruté paid special attention to them by taking them to lunch, Charlotte announced that she would be coming back. To stay. Now they live in the same village, although Charlotte spends part of each year on the big island of Hawaii.

There was a second group disembarking from our plane—English, younger than the OFI crowd and hardier, with long legs, clean faces, hiking boots, and rucksacks. They were volunteers for an organization called Trekforce and they'd come to work for Carey Yeager, whose research site is also on the Sekonyer River. Somehow they reminded me of myself at seventeen travelling to Germany to dig post-war basements with the Quakers. Another set of footsteps in the forest. Another set of good intentions. The Trekkers were met by someone from Yeager's station who had a letter for me. Since I'd had no word at all from Biruté, this small reception, with its apparent hospitality, was a comfort. In fact, since it seemed to confer official status on my arrival, it was a great relief.

There were other people waiting for us, too—a driver from the Blue Kecubung Hotel (with more mail and a car), a guide named Suwanto, who was connected to the hotel, and a young woman who had been contacted by Hans Iluk, the friend we had made in Bali. She was dressed in the uniform of a guide, but she was obviously too delicate, too *female* to take us upriver. I glanced at her waist-length hair, her city shoes, and smiled at her shyness. The young man looked altogether more reliable and seemed desperate to please, but as he went off to get the car, we discovered that two of our packs were missing and Riska, for that was her name, went about the business of reporting their loss and explaining that we would pick them

up when the next flight from Semarang arrived. The young man was outside waiting impatiently at the curb, but Riska was exuding something pleasantly cool in the
hot and crowded little airport. When she went off to find out about the next flight,
we followed her as if by instinct, and Suwanto and the hotel car disappeared.

The Blue Kecubung was not what we had expected from the guide books,
but nothing was. *Expect unavoidable, seemingly unreasonable delays, particularly in
Pangkalan Bun and Kumai.* Pangkalan Bun is a scrubby town on the coast. Two hundred years ago or so, the sultan of the old Kotawaringan kingdom moved his sul-
tanate from the banks of the Lamandau River to Pangkalan Bun on the Arut, which
is the next major river to the east. There, the local people converted to Islam and
became, like most coast-dwellers on the island, enmeshed in the vivid activities of
inter-island trade. The name itself means "landing stage/anchorage/depot for
munitions," and although it is not as close to the sea as Kumai, the river is wide
and navigable. There is a market strung along the riverbank and boats of various
sizes plying up and down. There is a steamy centre with two-storeyed buildings.
There are mosques and two or three banks.

The Blue Kecubung is owned by a lumber baron known as Pak Aju who has
used his plywood profits to build an edifice that seemed to go on and on—concrete hallways leading to gaping renovations and unfinished stairs. By the time we
arrived, the OFI group had taken over the half-finished lobby. Hot and excited
and hungry, they were waiting to be taken down to the basement restaurant, so
we chose the road and walked into the hot centre of town to "our best restaurant. Or at least," Riska added with a grin, "our most expensive one."

Her irony caught me by surprise, and I took a closer look at our quiet but
forthright companion. So far Riska had suggested nothing except lunch and a little help in preparing us for the river trip, but over our first bowls of *nasi goreng*
I asked her to consider coming with us. "As our guide. Would you like to? Would
your boss let you off?"

"Yes. I will ask him." An astonishing smile. Already I felt we could not make
the journey without this laugh, this quick step.

I told her that I had a letter from Carey Yeager promising me a twelve
o'clock appointment on Thursday and the best boat in Kumai.

"That will be the *Garuda II*," Riska said. "That's Mrs. Biruté's boat. I mean,
the one she always uses."

There was a check-in required by the local police (passports and photocopies),
and Riska offered to do the paperwork and check on our boat. But that night

Suwanto, the guide we'd ignored at the airport, sat down at our table in the Blue Kecubung restaurant and began to chew on our feet, regaling us with tales of his talents, flexing his triceps over our *mie goreng* and making it clear that we'd be better off if we did our travelling with him. He's a guy, after all, and he knows his way around. And Riska is ... well. There was a gesture that reminded me of the male gestures on Java.

"Were you born here?" I asked, because Riska had told us she was Dayak, born in a longhouse on the Lamandau River, and that seemed to me an excellent recommendation for a guide to the forest.

"I am from Java."

That settled it.

While he talked, he eyed Esta, as if his appreciation of her would guarantee her support, although in fact she was more irritated by his chatter than I was. Kristin wasn't listening. She was wondering about the *mie goreng*. Did it contain any meat? She was making friends with a cat. She was negotiating with the kitchen about dessert.

Our room had two narrow beds and a mattress on the tiled floor. Running water, hot and cold, a Western toilet, a TV and bedbugs. When Esta proved this by displaying bites and Kristin started to scratch, I got up, put on my clothes and began proceedings at the front desk with a phrase book. "*Ada serangga di kamar saya.* There is an insect in my room."

Blank stares. That night no one in the Blue Kecubung spoke a word of English or guidebook Bahasa Indonesian.

I tried the phrase again—"There *is* an insect in my room!"

More blank stares.

I rushed across the lobby and got on the couch, jumping up and down to demonstrate the jerky dance of a bedbug, snapping my jaws and prancing.

Soon the hotel boys were racing to the phone.

And whom did they call in this emergency but the helpful guide, Suwanto, who was asleep in his own bed in his own house and who, roused by the hotel's call, came cheerfully back to the Blue Kecubung to find out how he could be helpful.

"There is an insect in my room."

The guide very sensibly sent for a can of bug spray.

But I asked for new mattresses, mindful of the story of the princess and the pea and knowing we probably appeared to be prissy Westerners. Why did I want more mattresses when I already had three?

Eventually I took one of the boys by the hand, and together we found a closet where mattresses were stored, and then together we carried two of them through the halls. At one point I'm sure there were seven young men and five mattresses in our room, and I was repeating that there was an insect in my room until there was nothing to be done but make all our beds and lie on them.

With Riska, we took a taxi the next day to Pasir Panjang, where Biruté lives beside a hot, flat stretch of road. This was in order to pass the time while we waited for the police to give up our passports and in order to satisfy some compulsion I felt to see Biruté's house, even though she wasn't in it. I pretended it was research, but I wasn't very proud of myself as we pulled past the iron gates. Then I blinked. From her talks in L.A., I had thought that the house would be among Dayak villagers, but Pasir Panjang is a town with streets and curbs and satellite dishes with their heads in the clouds, and even so, compared with anything around it, anything within miles, the house looks very grand, set back amid trees and painted white with a red-tile roof. Stranger still is the wall surrounding the property—so white that it shines in the sun and so long that it looks like an example of perspective stretching into infinity. "I thought her husband was a farmer," I said, noting several women washing its many sealed windows.

"Not any more," Riska said.

"What is he, then?"

"A gambler." Riska giggled. "But don't worry, I am good friends with Mr. Jacki, who works here." She walked up the drive to the house and spoke to one of the women. The rest of us sat in the car. Later Riska told us that Pasir Panjang was established by the Dutch after a Dayak rebellion. This was surprising. Most Dayak live in the rainforest. But nothing in all of Indonesia had surprised me as much as the well-appointed house. A few blocks away we were to see a slightly smaller version when we passed the residence of Charlotte Grimm, but now a man appeared, as Riska came back, and she stopped and spoke to him. "Not Mr. Jacki," she said, when she got back in the car. "This man was one of Mrs. Biruté's workers, but he had a breakdown in the jungle." She sighed. "It's very hard out there. Now he's a little off. He can't get a job. I hope Mrs. Biruté looks after him."

Kristin pulled at my arm. "Let's go. Put your camera away."

"Nobody's home?" I asked Riska.

"There are some Dayak women and girls working, doing cooking and cleaning and taking care of the baby orangutans in the back of the house."

"Here?"

"Umm. I've been back there a couple of times. I asked one of the girls where the babies sleep at night, and she said, 'Just around here, on the trees.' And Mr. Jacki says they want to build a clinic. Maybe out here or maybe in Pangkalan Bun but there aren't many trees around and the road is so close. It's not a good place for orangutans."

I took another look at the house, and a thousand questions came to mind, but instead of asking them I asked Riska to ask the driver to take us back to Pangkalan Bun for our passports, then straight to the office in Kumai, where we could get our permits to enter the national park, our groceries for the ten-day stay and, I hoped, our bearings.

GARUDA

There were moments when one's past came back to one as it will sometimes when you have not a moment to spare to yourself.
—JOSEPH CONRAD

Kumai is a boat-building town and it sits right on the river of the same name near its mouth at the Java Sea. To get there from Pangkalan Bun, one drives across the land from the Arut River to the Kumai or one goes by boat around a pointy chunk of Borneo that sticks out into the Java Sea dividing two bays. The boats built in this seafaring town are enormous vessels made entirely of ironwood. Ironwood, hardest and heaviest of woods, floating here in preparation for great ocean journeys. Ironwood, which takes two hundred years to mature and which was once so prolific in the forests around Kumai that the seafaring Bugis came over from Sulawesi to build their famous and beautiful sailing ships. Many of them stayed. The ships are visible in several stages of completion in the water and on the riverbank, but before we got there we had still to walk through the hottest part of the day to the open market, which was shaded by blue plastic tarpaulins that cast a strange light over all of us, buyers and sellers.

Under those dark clouds I began to lose my connection to the others, who looked as unlikely in that place as the vegetables piled around them. But even my own hands and feet had begun to look strange. A group of little boys screamed when they saw us, as if we were monsters. The heat was an entirely different substance than it had been in Bali or Java. It was unbearable, oppressive, and ovenlike. Solid shapes wavered, melted. I was faint. We needed potatoes, cabbage, tomatoes, bananas, rice, water, canned fish. Riska kept urging me to walk, to make decisions, to count out my money and pay for our supplies while the little boys, at our slightest move, became frightened and ran into the racks of clothes their mothers were selling. I thought of Biruté's white house and understood the sealed windows. Air conditioning. On the point of tears, I knew I would never last out the trip. I was too old. I wasn't fit. I should have torn off all my clothes and leaped about to underline this: *Send me home.* I wanted to lie down in the filthy marketplace and quit. *I hate all this. I can't breathe.* The clouds were descending, as they sometimes descend. It was too late. I had gone past my limit.

The people who really needed me were on the other side of the world. Michael, my mother, stepchildren, old dog, old cat. What was the forest to me? I had no role to play in it and no energy to spare. There would be no phones where we were going. What if someone at home had an emergency? Since my brother's death, I am my mother's only child. I knew she would worry constantly, and now the whole trip seemed utterly selfish. Why was I trying to understand a woman who didn't want to be understood by me? My children would hate the trip. We would learn nothing useful or interesting. The boat we had rented would carry us away from everything we understood, everything we collectively believed. The last fine thread of our past would break.

It did not occur to me then that Biruté must have felt this in much larger doses as she'd set off, twenty-seven years before, for the remote, unbuttoned wildness of Tanjung Puting. For months she lived among strangers, or no one, with only her husband for familiarity. Long before she wanted to save orangutans, she left everything she knew and gave up everything she had in order to learn what she could about their lives in the trees. It did not occur to me because I wasn't thinking about Biruté any more. I wanted a fax machine. A telephone. Contact. I should have called Michael in Pangkalan Bun while I had the chance; now it was too late. I missed him. He might be worried. My nonchalance in the face of what was ahead had been stupid and prideful. Now I had to sit down, wipe my eyes and face. I wanted not here and now, but future and past. My own, not this.

Around me were people who saw me only as *outsider.* And how did I see them? Kumai's population is made up mostly of inland people who long ago moved to the coast. To *turun melayu* is to come downriver from inland Borneo. To me they were exotic, partly descended from the negrito Australoids who arrived in this part of the world forty thousand years ago, who swept out of Asia and into the shade of the great, already ancient dipterocarp trees, and partly from the Mongol Austranesians who came later. In the middle of our century, Tom Harrisson found a 35,000-year-old skull in the Niah caves of Sarawak—the oldest *Homo sapiens* skull ever found—but when it was the braincase for a living, breathing man, he had already forced his negrito cousins into the hills after taking a daughter or two back to his cave. His descendants are upriver Dayak like Riska's relatives and the coastal Muslim Melayu in the Kumai marketplace where I languished, miserably hot, and began to notice their faces: an old gentleman who squatted at eye level among his potatoes, a woman so beautiful that I asked Riska to ask her if I might take her photograph.

Riska said, "She doesn't mind."

"Are you sure?"

"She likes having her picture taken. Everyone wants to take it."

Deflated, I took the photograph. But looking through the lens was somehow a means of taking back my point of view. I began to feel better. If nothing else, even without language, I could see. And Borneo, as I framed it, would be what people at home would see, so I had to make choices. I could choose one face over another, and perhaps I could even select enough potatoes for our boat trip.

With a ten-day supply of food, we made our way to the offices of Perlindungan Hutan dan Pelestarian Alam or PHPA, the Ministry of Forestry's Nature Conservation and Forest Protection Agency. It stood at riverside, and we paid a secretary a small tip to hurry to the typewriter and compose our permits. "Look outside," Riska said, nudging my elbow as I stared at a hand-painted map on the wall. "Look, it's the *Garuda*." 195

Excitedly, we all ran to the door and saw at the end of the dock the bluest and brightest riverboat in the world. Riska waved. "It's Yadi," she said. "He's the best driver on the river. This is Biruté's boat—the one she always reserves—and he's her driver. He's always loyal to her."

Loyalty … I had heard weeks before … *it's her big thing*, and we carried our packs and boxes to the dock, where Yadi, a young man of twenty-three, stood waiting to stow them on the lower deck of the two-tiered boat. *Kelotoks* are the traditional means of transportation on Borneo's rivers, but they vary in size and age and condition. The *Garuda II*, which was to be home and transport for the next ten days, has a single engine, a seat on the lower deck for its driver and a kerosene stove. Otherwise, it is bare as the sky, and the same colour except for its trim, which is brilliant turquoise.

From the hand-painted wall map in the PHPA office, decorated with proboscis monkeys, orangutans, kingfishers, and giant hornbills, I had learned that the Kumai and Sekonyer rivers meet just south of town, where the expanse of water is so wide that our *kelotok* would seem minute. Now, engine puttering, we slid past the great ironwood ships, so raw and immense that they look prehistoric even as they are being built. Amazing that these great river hulks—shaped exactly like arks— can float, although one lay solemnly in the shallows as if expecting God's local creatures to march up the riverbank in pairs: two clouded leopards, a pair of macaques, a lone sun bear, then his reluctant mate.

The river takes half an hour to cross. Barges pass, a few boats, and the town quickly slips behind, out of sight. On the other side, angled through a thickness of trees, the Sekonyer was invisible until we actually entered it. Along its banks, great swaths of green connect water to land, and they rustled as the pressure of the *Garuda's* breath forced them back, making the sound of stiff skirts and a thousand women leaning together. Patient. Impatient. Pulling back on either side of us like curtains as we entered the narrow river and took our first scent of the forest.

There was the rustle of pandanus, the cry of nipa palms, but we were loud enough to provoke silence in everything else. In this way we were intruders, with our bright boat and our noisy motor, although we soon began to feel the rhythms of the river and its reeds seep into us and to feel the new rhythms of ourselves as a unit. We were four women now. There were two men aboard, but they were *them*, not us. There was boyish Anang, who stayed close to the stern, and Yadi at the wheel. Nevertheless, for purposes of conversation, decision and society, we were four. Women. A circle or a square but not a triangle. A shape for which a new balance had to be found. How and how much to include Riska in our thoughts, our jokes, our conversations. When and how often to explain ourselves in order to be neither condescending nor exclusive.

Riska was born in a village about seven days upriver, and the water is a different kind of trail for her than it is for us. For her it moves backwards, towards the place where her father was a hunter, her mother a teacher, towards the Dayak village of Kudangan, where she was born and spent the first seven years of her life. For Riska, this is the long road to her past and her history. The Dayak live along rivers, but depend on the water less than on the forest. Their animistic religion, Kaharingan, is so old, so aligned to the land and all its powers and secret places, that the Indonesian government has had to recognize it, although in order to put a good face on it, they have named it a branch of Hinduism, which is ridiculously inaccurate.

We were entering a landscape in which people have lived much the same way for thousands of years. Rattan for traps. Pandanus for baskets. All the necessities are guaranteed by the forest except for the rice grown in swidden or "slash and burn" plots, small sections of land temporarily stolen from the trees. On the river, narrow sampans skim the surface, nets and lines dipping, faces staring into the depths. Where river meets swamp, there are houses built of poles around which swim prawns and spawning fish.

The creator is male and female, upperworld and underworld, heaven and earthly water, hornbill and serpent, but lesser deities control the mundane affairs of human beings, and there are spirits, both friendly and malicious, who live in the forests and rivers, in stones and animals and trees. Even today the Dayak are relatively untouched by urban ways. Scattered over a vast area of intractable swamp and forest, these tribes have had little contact with the government except through the village elementary schools and sporadic, understaffed medical clinics. This is why Riska's mother was not allowed to stop teaching. The village officials did not want to lose her and forbade her to leave. "Escape," is how Risks put it. But one dark night, with only a few belongings, the family boarded a sampan and paddled for seven days. The children were fastened into cages on the little boat so they wouldn't fall overboard, a fact that Riska remembers vividly because of her fear that the sampan would capsize on one of the many sets of rapids and she would be trapped underwater in her cage. "I remember the night we left the village," she told us. "I did not know what was happening; nobody knew. But I saw my mother crying."

After a frightening time of poverty and displacement, Riska's mother found a teaching job in Pangkalan Bun, but even now she comes home from school every afternoon to an unemployed husband and son. When Riska mentioned this, she managed to convey her frustration without saying anything negative about either parent. She was twenty-five and not married, too old, she said, to be attractive to an Indonesian man. Saying this, she braided her waist-length hair and covered it with a cotton hat, worn to keep the sun off her skin.

For miles and miles we travelled with only the palms at our sides, though they were taller than the boat and provided a perfect unassailable screen. More animal groups live in these swamps than in any other part of species-rich Borneo. Here, fish climb trees and spit at flying insects. Here, land is born as seedlings root themselves to silt. Silt becomes mud. Mud becomes clay. Clay becomes earth as it mixes with fallen trees. Earth becomes forest and forest becomes peat. The soils have a pH range of 3.8 to 5.0 and the dark, tea-coloured water is anything but sweet. Tanjung Puting is a tiny part of the island, but it is big enough to be

197

visible on any map. *Tanjung* means "peninsula" and its levees are being built even now by rivers running over their own banks and leaving finer and finer particles of sand as they flow towards the sea. Where the particles rest, small depressions are formed. Sometimes gold is laid down by the water. But it is only one of a thousand things.

Conveniently, for anyone making Rousseau's twin journeys, in the Dayak world there are two souls. One lives in the body. One travels in the world of dreams. The *Garuda* was now transport for both, comforting in the harsh sunlight, when the upper deck created shade for anyone underneath, and comforting even in the rain, when two blue plastic wings were unrolled and let down over the open sides making a dark cocoon in which we could easily fall asleep. In fact, the effect of the water, the forest, and all that wavy blue became hallucinatory, so that I sometimes didn't distinguish between fact and dream.

Vishnu, the preserver, had ten incarnations. As Rama, he rode the wings of the sunbird Garuda during his exile. It seems strange that the great story of Asia involves exile *to* the forest, whereas in the Western tradition, we were thrown out of it. Now, like Rama, for the next ten days we would ride the *Garuda*'s back. Sitting on top, in the open breeze, we spread our wet laundry out, making flat, reclining bodies of our clothes after washing them every afternoon. Below we slept, sat, stored our things. Riska made coffee, tea, and meals in the tiny galley, and we ate above or below, depending on the weather. To lie on the green slats of that upper deck and watch the palms and sky slide by and an eagle sail between them was like ... being a god with a pair of wings. We would look for proboscis monkeys, the bulbous-nosed clowns who live along the riverbank in small tribes. We would look for kingfishers, and while we looked and talked and looked, our circle would change. I would be young or old. I would be one of four or a little alone, off to one side.

It was easy to slide into meditation. Aside from our bodies and the food to feed them, the lower deck had a stack of thin folding mattresses, pillows, and our overstuffed packs. This meant that when we were below, we sat with our legs tangled and our bodies half reclined. We spent several hours each day like that, and all of us slept in the cabin at night like seeds in a floating pod, the *Garuda* conveying both souls, one through dark, one through light.

At the rear of the cabin there was a door about eighteen inches high, through which we crawled to get to the galley or to a cubicle that stuck out over the stern in which, under cover of four shoulder-high walls, it was possible to pee or shit or bathe with a bucket of water, since there was nothing between the flesh and the river but a few wooden slats. The galley was a small space at the stern with a gas burner on the floor and a couple of pots, not unlike most kitchens in Indonesia, except that it was blue and required some careful balancing on the part of the cook. The food we'd bought at the markets in Pangkalan Bun and Kumai was stored in the cabin where we slept and ate and did whatever we did, which wasn't much because we couldn't move, except at a crawl, and how is it that a baby does that so easily? After a day, my knees felt swollen, chafed. When I crawled over the various six-inch thresholds between cabin and kitchen and the topless cubicle on slats over the river, I longed for knee pads. In other ways, too, it was awkward, being so much older than the others. I seemed to pee more often than they did, and the sound of my peeing seemed to reverberate off the water like an announcement of my difference. I caught myself groaning as I heaved myself up the tiny ladder and crawled onto the upper deck. I was graceless in the tiny bath cubicle and too shy to ask Anang, who might be hovering just outside, to pass me the soap I'd forgotten to take in with me. Since baths in the thin-walled box came from a bucket that was lowered into the river at the end of a rope, they weren't baths at all, but showers, or what Indonesians call a *mandi*. The water was icy cold but the air was hot. At four in the afternoon these buckets of water redeemed everything.

Yadi's father is a Bugis with three boats and two sons. Boat-builders and navigators for two thousand years, Bugis regard a son as irreplaceable, and Yadi was expecting one of his own. At twenty-three, he was already self-assured. He spoke no English, so being with him, one was physically accompanied and left mentally alone. Anang remained invisible. Mysterious, it was, to be on a twenty-foot boat with a silent driver and an invisible hand.

The sound of a *kelotok* is a loud putt-putt, a churning of the river, and it throws an echo against the trees and nipa palms along the bank. When we'd left the broad stretch of Kumai, we'd moved into the silence of the rainforest, and when the echo came back in a narrow channel the sound was deafening, as if we were at war, as if a helicopter were circling overhead. I kept thinking about Biruté in the early days. I imagined her first trip up this river. I thought about the tension and excitement she and Rod Brindamour must have felt and their separateness that day, which must have been more obvious than usual, as separateness always is when we come close to something important. I thought of Biruté young and determined. Age changes us, but character doesn't change.

As we moved up the Sekonyer and away from everything familiar, it began to rain, then to pour. Suddenly life, Riska, the four of us, this beautiful blue-and-green boat ... how had it all come together? A great joy hit me, as if it were part of this most ancient of airs. We sat below, above, below. Upperworld and under. Man world and woman world. We lay with our mouths open and drank in the sky. We sat with our eyes open and took in the rain that fell on the blue plastic wings that had been dropped to keep us dry. We sipped hot tea and smelled the river. Time went by and never moved. Two hours or four or ten of fleeting, eternal sky.

Part Two:

Getting Started

From Stage to Page

TIMOTHY FINDLEY

Most readers of Timothy Findley's novels, such as *The Wars* (1977), *Famous Last Words* (1981), and *Not Wanted on the Voyage* (1984), have forgotten, if they ever knew, that literature is Findley's third artistic career. He was a dancer until an injury forced him to turn to acting. He appeared in the first season of the Stratford Festival in 1953 and only gradually began dabbling in writing. His first book, *The Last of the Crazy People*, didn't appear until 1967. The following account of starting out as a writer comes from his 1990 work, *Inside Memory: Pages from a Writer's Workbook*. The "Stone Orchard" referred to at the beginning is an Ontario farm where Findley lived and worked for many years and which he describes in *From Stone Orchard: A Collection of Memories* (1998). He was born in 1930.

STONE ORCHARD
MARCH 1990

He is smiling. She is laughing. They are standing somewhere in limbo. People are the landscape of memory. Without the benefit of time and place, they are forced to play the scenery themselves. All the information they can give you is there in their faces and in their names.

Thornton Niven Wilder. Ruth Gordon Jones. I cannot think of one without the other. I met them both in the summer of 1954 and ever since, I have always imagined them standing side by side.

Ruth is small. She ticks like a clock—or, rather, like a watch. A ticking watch is less sedate and has more verve than a ticking clock. If a clock stops ticking, everyone rushes to wind it up. If a watch stops ticking, everyone runs for cover. You wait for the explosion. That was Ruth Gordon at her best—the pause between the ticking and the bang.

Thornton is big, until you measure him. He seems immensely tall and infinitely round—yet, alive, he was neither. Even his tailors could not define his shape. His suits were always cut as if Orson Welles had ordered them. The collars rose with a life of their own whenever Thornton sat down. He was forever leaning forward in his chair. His clothes were forever pulling him back. He favoured single-breasted jackets, vests, and suspenders. All his clothes were grey or blue or white.

He had impeccable taste, but he made no show of having it. He knew exactly how to present himself for every occasion; knew it, but would forget. He came down, once, to the lobby of his hotel in evening dress. Our meeting was pre-arranged and I was embarrassed when I saw him. I had arrived in slacks and sports jacket—quite inelegant.

"Aren't we going to the Savoy?" he said when he saw me.

"No," I reminded him. "We're going on a pub crawl."

"Oh," said Thornton. "Yes. I remember, now."

As he turned to go back to his room in order to change, he suddenly took in his surroundings.

"Good God!" he said. "I'm *at* the Savoy!"

204

After Thornton died, Ruth told how, once, he had asked her to marry him. This was early in the 1930s. Ruth and Thornton were relatively young. The proposal came at a time when her fortunes were low. She couldn't get a job—she couldn't pay her bills—and the man she had wanted to marry was not forthcoming. I suspect this man was Jed Harris, the father of Ruth's son, Jones.

Whenever Ruth Gordon told a story, she liked to drop a lot of names into it—*sort of like spicing up the sauce!* she said. But the only name she ever put in this story was Thornton Wilder's. The other players remained anonymous. Anyway, the long and short of it is—she turned him down. Not because she didn't cherish him. It was because she knew that Thornton's proposal had more to do with friendship than with love. He was offering a friend's way out of her predicament.

Ruth had a lot of practical courage. She took a look around her and decided that with friends like Thornton Wilder, she would survive the present crisis. Yes—she had begun to panic. But Thornton's proposal had calmed her. She had never been one to win her wars by doing what was expected of her. She did what she expected of herself—which was to be herself at any cost.

The subject of marriage between them did not come up again. Ruth went on to ever-brighter stardom and Thornton went on to take the theatre by storm. Jed

Harris, incidentally, went on to direct Wilder's masterpiece *Our Town*.

I take great comfort from this story. When I heard it first, it told me some-thing about independence I hadn't recognized before, which was: being cared for by someone doesn't mean you lose your independence. Under the best of cir-cumstances, you gain it.

Ruth said: *be yourself—but know who you are. Being yourself is not a licence. It's a responsibility.*

Not all that easy, when you begin as Ruth Gordon Jones or Thornton Niven Wilder. Not all that easy for anyone born with talent, once you have seen what must be done with who you are.

Ruth also said: *lots of people have talent, darlin'. But look how many people throw it away. It boils down to this: having talent is not enough. You also have to have a tal-ent for having talent.*

Ruth dropped the *Jones* from her name when she went into the theatre. But she kept it in her heart. It was the name she chose for her son. *But*—she said—*the name of Jones was not going to conquer the world when I came down out of Wollaston, Massachusetts in 1916!*

Thornton dropped the *Niven* from his name—but not the initial. When you got to know him—after a while, he would ask you to call him *T.N.* That was how he signed his letters: *cordial regards, T.N.*

I don't know why, but I never cottoned to this form of address and always—except in occasional letters, called him Thornton. He always called me *Timothy*—or *Findley*. He never cottoned, either, to my being called *Tiff*.

"It's my initials," I told him.

"Yes. But that doesn't make it your *name*."

He was adamant concerning names. "You can't call someone *Tiff*," he said. "It's a verb!"

"What would you call me if my name was Tiffany?" I asked.

"*Tiffany*," he said.

And that was that.

Most, but not all, of their major achievements were behind them when I met them first in 1954. Thornton had long since written *The Bridge of San Luis Rey*, *The Ides of March*, *Our Town*, and *The Skin of Our Teeth*. Ruth had already given what every-one agreed was the definitive performance of Nora in *A Doll's House*, adapted by

Thornton from Ibsen's play in 1937. There had also been *Abe Lincoln in Illinois*, in which Ruth played Mary Todd, the president's unhappy and unstable wife. And Natasha in the all-star production of Chekhov's *Three Sisters* in 1942. And there was more, of course—all the way back to Nibs in *Peter Pan*. *Seventeen* and *Clarence*. *Ethan Frome*, *The Country Wife*, and *Over Twenty-one*.

These were the legendary achievements that appealed to me, the young actor, who met Ruth Gordon and Thornton Wilder that warm July morning on the mezzanine of a West End theatre. I think it was the Globe, on Shaftesbury Avenue.

I was one of sixteen who had been gathered there to commence rehearsals of Wilder's play *The Matchmaker*. I remember now that, when I got the call to come and read for the producers, I had thought it was going to be a play about someone who manufactured wooden matchsticks. Turn-of-the-century tragedy stuff ... everyone freezing to death in the snow ... and then some character invents the safety match. Fires would be lighted—the human race would survive—and! ...

Mister Wilder had already written that one. He'd called it *The Skin of Our Teeth*.

In *The Matchmaker*, Miss Gordon played Dolly Levi. She played her in seventeen layers of pink organdy and seven shades of red hair. Her mouth was painted a mile wide and it didn't shut from the moment she came onstage until the final curtain. Her performance was a masterpiece of overstatement and vulgarity. Without any doubt, it was one of the century's greatest comic creations. Anyone who saw it will tell you so. Of course, when they made the movie, they gave the role to someone else. The real Dolly Levi went to the grave with Ruth, who probably had to drag her down and lie on top of her to make her quit.

The director of the play was Tyrone Guthrie. I had worked for him in Canada. That had been the previous summer, in the inaugural season of the Stratford Shakespearean Festival in Ontario. Wilder, who was a pal of Guthrie's, had come up to Stratford from Connecticut to see those first productions—*Richard III* and *All's Well That Ends Well*—but I had not been aware of his presence. On that morning, however, in July of 1954, his presence could not be denied. Though he tried his damnedest to play it in a minor key, he did not succeed.

He sat in a corner, more in shadow than not. The light spilled through the dusty windows and landed on his feet. He wore black shoes, I remember, but he wore them carelessly. One of his laces was undone. Balanced on his knees, his hands seemed disembodied. He constantly passed his cigarette back and forth between one set of fingers and another. Instantly, you recognized—not nerves—but energy. He always seemed to be at war with stillness.

The smoke from his cigarette curled up and obscured his face and all I could really see was the flare from his glasses and the pale grey tufts of hair that framed his head. I'm afraid I must have smiled at him from my place in the semicircle of actors' chairs. This was intolerable. He turned away and made a show of looking for an ashtray.

It was much too soon to say hello.

I nearly got fired that afternoon—the first of a half-dozen episodes in which I nearly got fired while playing in *The Matchmaker*. Life with Ruth Gordon was like that. Volatile.

That afternoon, I was reading the role I'd been hired to understudy. The part I was playing was Rudolph, the flamboyant waiter. The understudy role was Ambrose Kemper, a boy who was courting Mister Vandergelder's niece, Ermengarde. Mister Vandergelder was the misanthropic miser who had hired Dolly Levi to find him a wife. Ambrose was the character with whom Dolly Levi played her first expository scene.

Playing straight man in an expository scene is never much fun. I'd had my share of such roles over time and thought I had learned how to survive with my dignity intact. Every actor has to play the straight man at some point in his career, and the way to do it is to resolutely face out front and direct all your questions at the audience.

What is the point, Mrs. Levi? (Staring at the balcony.) *Married to you, Mrs. Levi?* (Staring at the mezzanine.) *What are you suggesting, Mrs. Levi?* (Staring at the box, stage left.) Et cetera.

In the meantime, upstage, Mrs. Levi is telling you her life story.

Books in hand, we set out to block the scene. (I was standing in because the actor hired to play Ambrose was unavailable that day.)

Tony Guthrie said: "all right, Findley—you're over there for this."

I stood *over there*.

Ruth at once said: "No, Tony. No."

"No to what, Ruth?" Guthrie asked.

"Mister Findley cannot stand over there," said Ruth. "He's much too far upstage."

Too far upstage? I was practically standing in the footlights. "Mister Findley," said Ruth Gordon—turning to me—"please stand further down."

207

I looked behind me and laughed. "You mean in the orchestra pit, Miss Gordon?" I said.

This was my big mistake. Ruth was not amused.

"You should be grateful, Mister Findley, that I didn't mean *the street*," she said. *Lesson number one: never play for laughs when the star is staking out her territory.*

We took a break and when we returned to the scene, I assumed the prescribed position—with my back to the house. I played the whole scene that way.

Miss Gordon was finally satisfied. Guthrie, however, was not. But he was crafty....

He clapped his hands when the scene was over and snapped his fingers.

"Very nice," he said. "Very nice." Then he looked at Ruth and added—deadpan—"Mister Findley has lovely wide shoulders, Ruth. *Very, very* wide shoulders. The audience will love them!"

Ruth bit her lip. "I see," she said. "Yes."

When the scene was finally blocked, Ambrose Kemper stood facing stage right—effectively turning him sideways to the house. I got to play this role quite often during the run. I was slimmer then, and I always wondered if I could be seen at all. Ruth, on the other hand, had no such worry. Playing to my paper-thin shadow, she was, to all appearances, the only person on stage.

"What is the matter with all you people?" said Ruth, one day.

We were on the road and playing in Manchester. This was prior to our opening in London and we had already played in Newcastle, Edinburgh, Glasgow, and Liverpool.

All you people meant people under thirty years of age and I was one of them. Twenty-three and loving it. I had never felt more alive.

We had been to see an exhibition of paintings, all of which had been created by artists in their twenties. It was called *The New Generation Shows Its Colours!* or some such thing. The colours were fairly uniform. Black, brown, and deep shades of blue. Many storms and a lot of *drang*. It was wonderfully depressing and, if you were twenty-three, profound as hell itself.

"Can't any of you people say *yes* to anything?" Ruth asked. "Say *yes* to one another? Say *yes* to life?"

"Well, yes," I said.

Ruth laughed. "I'll *bet*!" she said. "Your face is a sight, right now. You *loved* it in there, didn't you. Loved it and revelled in it! I was watching you. Oh—*you people!*"

We were walking in the street.

"I wish you'd stop saying *you people* like that," I said. "It isn't fair to lump us all together."

"*Lump* is a very good word, my darlin'," she said. "And *you* said it."

I was hurt by this. She obviously thought that mine was a generation of depressed defeatists. The exhibit of paintings had truly upset her. She did not believe in defeat. She did not believe in darkness. She knew, of course, that defeat and darkness existed—but she refused their blandishments. "Too easy, too easy," she said. "It's just too easy to accept defeat. You know what, darlin'? Laughter is the hardest thing in all the world to bring to your troubles. But it will save you. Get up! Stand up! And laugh!"

Get up. Stand up. And laugh.

"That should be your generation's motto," she said. This was the mid-1950s. Mine was the generation whose childhood had been interrupted by the war. We grew up through that time, deprived, one way and another, of normal life. Our fathers went to war. Our cities were bombed. And some of us went to Auschwitz. Our childhood ended with the dropping of the Hiroshima bomb. What darkened our moods—above all, I guess—was the vision we had been forced to endure of what people really do to one another—and, as children, we had been powerless to stop it.

I went home to my digs and thought about it. I thought about it for days— the juxtaposition of all those dark paintings and the darkness from which they had emerged.

It didn't come to me at once—but, finally, I caught a glimmer of what Ruth had meant by *get up, stand up, and laugh.* She had meant that after darkness, something must be done about the need for light.

If the future was just another dark place—then how could you ever hope to survive it?

Something like that.

I began to work it out—and to write it down.

I wrote Ruth a story. Fiction. I wrote about a woman who was afraid of storms and of darkness and whose way of "getting up and laughing" was to think of the storms and the darkness as salvation. It was loosely based on the story of a woman I had known when I was a child. She believed that Jesus would arrive to save the world from its wars and its other torments in a great, green storm—preceded by thunder and lightning. I called this woman Effie and I gave the story to Ruth.

"What's this," she said.

"I wanted to prove," I said—with an overdose of pomposity, "that some of us in my generation can still say *yes*."

This, of course, is not what I had written at all. It was what I had wanted to write. The story—called *About Effie*—was just as dark and just as depressing as any of the paintings in that infamous exhibition. Coupled with this was the fact that I had copied it out on plain white paper and the lines all fell away sideways towards the lower right-hand corner. My writing, at the best of times, is illegible—but I had no typewriter and had done the best I could. Every third word—on an average—could be read.

Ruth Gordon's dresser in England was a woman called Dodie. Dodie was blonde and wise and funny. And she was small. She was smaller, if that was possible, than Ruth herself. Everyone in the company was in love with her and we called her "The Bird." She had, however, one devastating mark against her.

The Bird was Ruth Gordon's messenger from hell.

The times to be wary of Dodie's arrival at your dressing-room door were during the half-hour call before the play and after the final curtain. Her fingernail knock and her whispering voice announcing that *Miss Gordon would like to speak with you* were downright chilling. If you asked The Bird why Miss Gordon was calling, her small round face would remain expressionless. *All I know is*, Dodie would say, *she wants to see you.*

We had already lost one actor this way.

The knock came for me with the half-hour call, the evening after I had handed Ruth my pages.

"Yes?"

"Miss Gordon would like to speak with you after the performance."

And me without unemployment insurance.

Had Ruth misinterpreted what I had written? *HOW DARE YOU SUGGEST THAT EFFIE IS LUSTING AFTER THE BODY OF JESUS CHRIST!* Had she been able to read my handwriting? *WHAT IS THIS INDECIPHERABLE GARBAGE?* (Throwing the pages in the air.)

What if she thought it was pornographic? *THAT WOMAN EXPOSES HERSELF TO JESUS CHRIST IN HER NIGHTIE!*

... Miss Gordon would like to speak with you.

All through the performances Ruth betrayed nothing of what her verdict might be. A person dared not approach her once she had stepped inside Dolly

Levi—and, once she had stepped inside Dolly Levi, she stayed there until her dressing room had been gained. Garson Kanin, Ruth's husband, told someone in an interview that life with Ruth had been relative hell while Dolly Levi trod the boards.

"She started being Dolly two hours before the curtain went up," he said, "and, most nights, we took Dolly home with us. I even had to sleep with her!"

Doubtless, this must have been exhausting. Eight hours of minor explosions— waiting for the big one.

The moment came.

Still wearing my costume, I approached Ruth's dressing room. My costume (this was Rudolph—the waiter) consisted of black trousers, white shirt, and a long, white apron. I wondered what to do about blood stains.

Dodie sat on her little chair outside Ruth's door.

"Can I go in?"

"Yes."

"*Should I?*"

"I don't know," said The Bird.

She stood up and went into the *sanctum*. I heard my name being spoken. There was a pause and The Bird returned.

She nodded at the open door.

As I went inside, I glanced at Dodie and said: "Goodbye."

The door closed behind me.

Ruth, still in costume but minus her wig, was seated at her dressing table. The back of her chair was tied with several little velvet bows. The smell of make-up and the warm, rich scent of Ruth's perfume eddied round me. Ruth was watching me in the mirror. Her eyes reflected light—a cat's eyes, brightly focused.

When she spoke, she had all her usual bluntness about her. "Oh, *darlin'!*" she said—and she got up out of her chair and threw her arms around me. "You must give up acting just as fast as you can!"

I stood there alarmed and paralyzed.

Ruth was weeping and smiling and she held on tight to the back of my neck— locking me in place as she looked up into my face. "Your story is wonderful!" she said. (There were many exclamation points that night.) "*Wonderful!*" She let go and went to her dressing table, where she picked up my pages and flourished them. "*This* is what you are! *This* is what you are! A writer—not an actor!"

I blinked—and I heard myself say: "Thank you."

But my heart was sinking. What had I done to myself?

There I was, twenty-four years old by now, and heading straight for stardom. Or so I had thought. But now this other thing—this writing—was standing in my way. *You must give up acting just as fast as you can.*

My talent for having talent was nowhere in sight.

"It was just an exercise," I said. "I didn't mean it to do any more than make a point...."

But Ruth wasn't listening. She was dragging out an old, boxed portable type-writer and putting it at my feet.

"The first thing you have to learn," she was saying, "is how to use one of these. I nearly killed myself trying to make out what you had written on those pages. So Garson and I—we just bought a new one—we're giving our old one to you."

Smith Corona.

Tap-tap-tap.

My acting career—to all intents and purposes—was over.

Or so I thought that night.

I had this image of Ruth sending messages to all the West End producers: DO NOT HIRE THIS MAN. HE IS NOT AN ACTOR.

But it was not to them that she sent this message. It was to me—and she didn't stop sending it for the next two years.

If writing *About Effie* was the beginning of the end of my acting career, Ruth's giving it to Thornton Wilder was almost the beginning of the end of my writing career.

He said: "Have you tried a play, Findley?"

I said: "No."

"Then let me urge you to try one."

He should not have said that.

If the play you are in achieves a long run, there are consequences—good and bad. On the positive side—*the money*. You can pay your debts. You can celebrate.

The first few weeks of this are heaven on earth. You begin to eat oranges again and you take home Twinings Earl Grey tea instead of flavourless tea bags. You eat in restaurants. You buy new records and books and presents for your friends. You get new trousers and a sweater. You have that extra piece of cake....

But, in time, this binge of spending ends and your comforts become more compatible with reality.

The Matchmaker ran forever. Or so it began to seem—and this is where the consequences took on a negative edge. I was not being stretched. The role I was playing was fun but it didn't offer much scope. Rudolph, the waiter, is an arrogant, angry piece of work—and while these qualities afford the actor playing him lots of opportunities for comedy, they do not afford him many opportunities for variation. To be more or less arrogant, more or less angry according to each night's audience was pretty well the end of it. That, and the necessary hold on technique to achieve the intricate moves required without screwing up the intricate moves of your fellow actors. The play is a farce—and Guthrie had asked us all to maintain a breakneck pace from start to finish. This required everyone to move like Olympic athletes. In essence, we went to the theatre every night and performed the decathlon. A person had to be in very good shape.

I kept getting calls to read for other plays—and, finally I wanted very much to be doing something else. My greatest heartbreaks were missing out on *Bell, Book and Candle* with Lilli Palmer and Rex Harrison (in which I would have played Palmer's brother) and a European tour and West End engagement with Gielgud and Ashcroft in *Much Ado* and *Lear*—in which I had been asked to play one of the Watch (superb comedy) and Oswald (the perfect villain). But Ruth would not let me go. She wanted her company kept intact and the producers bowed to her will. No one was released.

The weeks and the months stretched on. We played at one of London's oldest and most charming theatres, the Haymarket, and it was always a pleasure to go there to work. There was a ghost who appeared from time to time in one of the upper galleries. Not a rampaging ghost—but benign and rather sad. It was said he had been an actor and had died of a foiled ambition. There was also a book that everyone who had ever played the Haymarket had signed. *Everyone*—and in the long run, everyone included me. I wrote my name where Kean had written his and Barrymore, Gielgud, Ellen Terry, and Mrs. Pat....

Autumn came and went. And winter. Christmas. New Year's....

Now it was 1955.

Ever since Ruth had said *you must give up acting* and *this is what you are—a writer*, I had been trying to write more stories. Two of them, called "War" and "The Name's the Same," have subsequently been published. Nothing else I wrote then was worthy of publication—but it was all worth doing as an exercise. I began a novella which I then called *Harper's Bazaar*, and dedicated it to Ruth. This, in time, became *Lemonade*—but that was later.

I also wrote a play.

Perhaps there is such a piece in every writer's background—overwritten—over-serious—overbearing and over-everything! I called it, with what I thought was stunning understatement, *A Play*.

A group of actors are locked in a theatre with God....

That's right. A group of actors are locked in a theatre with God. They have been playing "God's play." It was their last chance to *get it right*—and they have failed. God has enemies everywhere. The actors try to encourage him—but God is very old and has lost the will to try again. Besides which, the enemies are coming to do God in. They surround the theatre—break down the doors and arrest not only God but all his actors, too—and everyone in the audience.

See what I mean?

Well. This was the play I offered to Thornton Wilder.

"Try one," he had said.

So, I tried one.

The poor man was honour-bound to read the thing. I got a card from Switzerland: *am reading play. We will talk when I return....*

Another card from Aix-en-Provence: *am reading play. Don't know what to make of it yet....*

And from Berlin: *have finished play. Hope the acting goes well....*

Then he was back in London: *greetings. Now prepared to discuss your play. Gird your loins. I talk tough. Dinner. Savoy. Sunday. T.N.*

I had, as every actor had, an audition suit. Blue. Somewhat baggy—but presentable. Late Sunday afternoon, I dressed for my "audition" for the Master. I polished my shoes and borrowed a better tie than the one I owned and I looked many hours at myself in the mirror. Would he approve of what he saw? Why should it matter? He'd seen me dozens of times already at rehearsal and in performance. *Yes*, I told myself—*but that was the actor he was looking at. This is the writer....*

Did I look like a writer?

Well?

What does a writer look like?

Thornton Wilder. Hemingway. Shakespeare. Emily Brontë....

No luck there. All I got back from the mirror was me—and somehow, that wasn't good enough.

Gird your loins. I talk tough.

What should I gird my loins with?

Three pairs of jockey shorts.

And Fowler's Extract. It keeps your bowels in place.

I was living then in Tedworth Square with Alec McCowen—an actor who played a leading role in *The Matchmaker*. Alec's friendship endures and we correspond and talk on the phone to this day. Whenever I go to London, it is Alec with whom I spend the longest time. He is one of the centrepieces of my life. *But this is not about that*—as Ruth would have said—*this is about the other. The other* being my meeting with Thornton Wilder.

Up from Tedworth Square, along Royal Hospital Road and then up to Sloane Square Station. I am going to Charing Cross on the Circle Line. None of my precautions are working. My stomach churns with apprehension—my blue suit shines with a dreadful gloss beneath the lights—my hair, which is cut in the Junkers style for my role in the play, is standing on end and crackling with electricity. My palms are sweating and my feet are cold. I have all the sophistication of a spotted disease.

I get off and allow the escalator to carry me further towards my fate. Here, in this place—or roughly, so I have been told—there was once a teeming mass of activity known as Hungerford Market. Now, there are all the gleaming tiles and the hollow silence of a tube station.

It was to Hungerford Market that Dickens, as a little boy, was sent to work in a blacking factory. The blacking factory had been right there—bleak in the shadow of the Hungerford Stairs, which climbed up out of the mud flats by the river to the Strand. The Strand was then much closer to the Thames than it is now, with all its hotels and shops.

Today and yesterday. Me and Charles Dickens. What was the point of thinking any other way? If you were going to be a writer, the only kind of writer to be—or try to be—was the best. That thought made me feel better. That and the thought that Dickens, on his way up out of the rat-infested blacking factory, had started further down at the bottom than I had ever been forced to go. My only connection to the blacking factory had been the polish on my shoes.

To achieve the foyer of the Savoy Hotel, you walk in off the Strand through a courtyard. By the time I got to the doors of Thornton's rooms, I had passed a lot of glass in which I could watch my ghost in the process of materializing.

Everything was going to be all right. Thornton Wilder was just another human being. He wasn't going to bite my head off.

I stood up taller and squared my "wonderful" shoulders. (These were my only visible asset.) The whole of me prepared to knock. But the door flew back, like a comedy door, before my knuckles had touched the wood. I was impelled into the light—fist raised and lurching. Somewhat blinded, I collided with my host and inadvertently forced him back against a table. All he said was:

"Timothy Findley, I presume."

He was laughing.

So was I. This was proof that, whatever he had to say about my work, I would survive it. With his laughter, I sensed I might already have been forgiven for its excesses.

Filet mignon. Roast potatoes and broccoli under silver covers. Shrimps on ice. Melba toast and a bottle of wine.

"*Eat!*" said Thornton. "You treat your body as if it was your servant, Findley. *You* are your *body's* servant. Feed it. *Eat!*"

The food had arrived on a cart about ten minutes after I had fallen through the door. Thornton had ordered it long before my arrival. If I had failed to materialize, he doubtless would have offered it to the waiter.

"You eat, I'll talk," he said. He never sat down once the whole first hour I was there. He didn't eat, himself. Perhaps he already had. At any rate—I sat there and ate alone while Thornton walked up and down the room and drank his Scotch and water from a stubby tumbler.

Beyond the windows, the sun was setting beyond the city, way beyond the visible skyline. London was still a mass of chimney pots then, and every chimney gave off smoke. The sunset colours infused this smoke with reds and yellows smudged with grey, and all you could see was colour and light and the gradual coming on of lamps as the darkness increased.

This fading light and growing darkness have remained for me an integral part of Thornton's presence and his words that night. But the darkness was neither threatening nor depressing.

"Be confident," he said, "that whatever I say is said as one writer to another. I do not mince words—but neither do I mince writers. You are a writer, Findley. That's a certainty. What you have written, on the other hand...."

What I had written, on the other hand, was everything I had feared it was and hoped it was not:

an intellectual forum in which your
characters talk their problems to death—
not an active exploration of their lives—
—an arrogant tirade, written from a
position of ignorance, not—as it should
be—an impassioned questioning written
from a position of bafflement—
The characters in a play must never know
what is going to happen next. In a play,
the moment is always now. Do you know what
is going to happen in the next five
minutes, Findley?
No, sir—
Well, then—

On the other hand, he conceded that I could handle dialogue.

—and some of your images are
good. Good enough to suggest that more good
images will be forthcoming—

All the while he spoke, he paced and smoked and drank. His cigarette ashes fell helter-skelter. Drops from his glass were spewed out over the carpet every time he turned his pacing in a new direction. But the words he spoke were spare and well considered.

He was always out of breath. His voice had edge—but the edge kept cracking.

He pulled at his tie. His collar wilted. He forgot—or seemed to have forgotten—where he was. He might have been on a hill in Athens five hundred years before the birth of Christ—he might have been blind, dictating to his daughters—he might have been sitting in an eighteenth-century drawing-room, wrapped in flesh and warts—he might have been musing out loud on the fate of roses in a Paris garden, circa 1910. He was all great teachers in one. The only assumptions he made were that knowledge was important and that I cared.

"Pay attention, Findley. Pay attention. That is all you have to do. Never, for an instant, leave off paying attention."

So it was. That evening, my attentions garnered the following:

I could write—but had written a travesty.
Talk is cheap—but you pay a hefty price
for the written word.
Come down from all high-minded places—no
one down here can hear you.
A writer—however good he may be
intrinsically—cannot communicate without
a sense of craft. In writing—the craft is
all.

After he had spoken and I had eaten, he gave me back my pages and urged me to put them away in a drawer.

"When you write again, write something new," he said. "Ordinarily, I say the wastepaper basket is a writer's best friend—but keep these pages as a reminder of how intentions go awry. Otherwise, forget it. Don't even mourn it, Findley. You've more important things to do than that."

He walked me to the elevator.

After I had thanked him, he wanted to know if I was going to go home on the bus or on the tube.

"I'm going to walk," I said. Which I did.

It took me about two hours. But every step was worth it. All the way home, I smiled.

You only have such an evening once in your life. There isn't room for two.

The relationship begun with Ruth and Thornton in London lasted through the years in places such as Berlin and Boston, Edinburgh and New York, San Francisco and Chicago, Washington, D.C. and Los Angeles. There was never a moment, for me, that wasn't rewarding—even when arguments, misunderstandings, and temperament stood in the way.

Thornton remained my mentor until he died in 1975. We wrote long letters often and saw each other on occasion. I never failed to pay attention.

The last time I saw Ruth, in person, was at the memorial service given for Thornton. This was in January 1976 at Yale's Battell Chapel. We all stood then, together, having come inside from the wind and snow of a New Haven winter and we sang the hymn from *Our Town*—"Blessed Be the Ties That Bind." What I remember most from that service is the enduring smell of melting ice and the sound of radiators cracking with heat as we sang. We stood in our boots and galoshes—overcoats over our shoulders against the draft and scarves draped round our necks. Ruth's opening words, when she got up to speak to all of us, were *have you got a minute?*

There it was—the essence of Thornton Wilder.

Have you got a minute? Have you got a lifetime?

Let's talk.

Late in the summer of 1955, Thornton and I went on one of our pub crawls. These could take place anywhere. You named a street—a district—a town—and you tried to drink in all its pubs and bars. Highfalutin hotel bars were out. You drank in them when you were on the road. A pub crawl was where you drank for pleasure—not for business reasons.

The pub crawl this time took us to Fleet Street.

"If you start at Temple Bar—which is where Fleet Street begins," said Thornton, "and end at St. Paul's churchyard, you can practically touch the whole of English literature...."

Daniel Defoe was pilloried there at Temple Bar—and across the road at Child's Bank, Samuel Pepys and John Dryden kept their money—Henry Fielding, William Congreve, Oliver Goldsmith, and William Makepeace Thackeray all were feted there in the Temple Hall—and this is where Charlotte Brontë was introduced to the London literary scene, riding in Thackeray's carriage along this street. Conrad wrote here. There—in the courtyard up that alley, is Doctor Johnson's house, where he created his dictionary....

On and on they went—the names.

"Know where you enter," Thornton said. "Know where you enter into the literature of your language...."

We stood, at the far end, having drunk many glasses of wine and many tumblers of Scotch—and, looking up at the massive doors of St. Paul's Cathedral, we devised a staging of the *Agamemnon* of Aeschylus. "The great doors open and Clytemnestra appears with her husband's body...."

We were like two excited children, suddenly falling on a world of life-sized toys.

This was a part of Thornton never to be forgotten. The joy he took in recognizing other people's joy.

"Shakespeare's publisher set up his stall in the churchyard, there," he said—pointing through the fence at the gardens. "How Shakespeare loved to come into this city! All this was food and drink to him, Findley. The great trees that would have been here then—the sellers' stalls—the people buying books—the colour of it all—the dawning of universal knowledge—and he was at the centre of it. God—he *was* the centre!"

Thornton tooted every horn but his own.

One last image of Ruth.

This is in New York.

I have rejoined the cast of *The Matchmaker*, having stayed behind in England when the production was moved to America. This would be sometime in 1956. Perhaps October or November.

The mails have brought me a copy of *The Tamarack Review*, from Canada, in which "About Effie" has been published. This is my first publication, anywhere, ever, of anything.

I am sick with excitement.

I tear the envelope open and look inside. There it is. There is even an illustration.

Ruth must see this. Ruth made it happen. This is how it all began.

I clattered down the stairs—tying the strings of my apron—holding the magazine in my mouth.

I race along the hall and around the corner. There is The Bird.

She rises from her little chair.

"No," she says. "Don't!"

Heedless—I rap just once on Ruth's door—and fling it open.

Goodness....

Ruth is standing there, wearing her slip and pulling on her stockings. She has—at sixty—the most beautiful legs I have ever seen.

She looks at me and yells with a terrible loudness: "GET THE HELL OUT OF HERE!"

I fling the magazine onto her dressing table and lunge for the doorway.

I go somewhere and hide.

Now—for certain—I will be fired.

Nothing happens. Dreadful silence ensues. The first act plays and I am not in it. I lock my dressing-room door.

At last, the call comes: *Act Two beginners, please.*

I go down onto the stage.

Since everyone is in this scene, the whole company is now assembled. Ruth will come—and fire me in front of all my friends.

She sweeps out onto the stage. The curtain is down. We can hear the audience.

"Listen, everybody!" Ruth says. "I have something to tell you all about Mister Findley...."

Oh, God.

She turns towards me and smiles. The whole shebang. She has the kind of smile that kills.

"Darlin'," she says. "I want them all to know."

Then she turns and says to the others: "Tiffy has been published! And here it is, in my hand!"

She shows the magazine and turns back to me and pulls me down and kisses me on the top of my head.

"Next time you're published darlin'—I only hope I'm stark naked!"

Gone, now. Both of them.

Whirlwind and teacher.

STONE ORCHARD

MARCH 1990

Another memory from London in the mid-1950s: I had just been up on the top floor of Harrod's—I can't remember why. What I do remember is coming down in the elevator. Reaching the third floor, the elevator stopped and the doors opened.

There stood—unmistakably—Beatrice Lillie: Lady Peel.

She was wearing her famous toque hat, her leopard-skin coat, and a pair of dark glasses.

I was the only passenger in the lift.

Miss Lillie paused. I can still see her eyes behind those tinted lenses. She was looking at me sharply.

I was thinking: *how wonderful! I adore this woman: she's probably the funniest human being alive. I come from Toronto. She comes from Toronto. I am an actor. She is an actress. What a delightful conversation we will have!*

I smiled.

Miss Lillie raised her glasses for a better look. She swept the length of my body with her eyes—and then:

"No thank you," she said.

She lowered her glasses and folded her hands.

The elevator doors closed.

For weeks after that, I studied myself in the mirror—but I couldn't work it out. In fact, to this very day, I'm stymied. Perhaps—somehow—she guessed I was from Toronto.

STONE ORCHARD

MARCH 1989

I was twenty-four years old—an actor still, before my writing days—and working London's West End. The play I was in was called *The Prisoner*, written by Bridget Boland and starring Alec Guinness and Wilfrid Lawson. I had earlier worked with Guinness at Stratford's first summer, in 1953. After an evening performance in March of 1954, Guinness called me to his dressing room and asked if I would be willing to play the role of Charles Surface in a rehearsal of the famous screen scene from Sheridan's *School for Scandal*. The occasion of the ultimate performance of this scene was to be a gala celebration in honour of Dame Sybil Thorndike, who was then arriving at one of the major mileposts in her long and distinguished career.

The screen scene was to be performed by Guinness, Paul Scofield, James Donald, Paul Hardwicke, and Vivien Leigh. I was being asked to take part because Scofield, who was to play Charles Surface, could not attend the initial rehearsal and the director, John Gielgud, needed a body to move around the stage in his place. Mine was the body chosen. The only problem was—the body had lines to speak.

"You can carry the book, of course," Guinness had said at his invitation. "We'll all be carrying the book—so there's nothing you have to learn. Just read the words and walk the moves...."

Hah!

I wore my blue "audition" suit and looked okay—but I was dreadfully nervous. John Gielgud—Vivien Leigh! To say nothing of Guinness. He took me to lunch at Prunier's to soothe my nerves. It didn't work. Sir John was a god—Miss

Leigh a goddess. So there I was, standing in for Paul Scofield (another god) and very much a mortal.

The gist of what Charles Surface has to do in the scene revolves around why it is called "the screen scene" in the first place. Lady Teazle (Leigh) has been caught in Joseph Surface's (Donald) rooms by the sudden arrival of her husband, Sir Peter (Guinness) and she seeks a hiding place behind an ornate Chinese screen. Once Sir Peter is onstage, *he* is surprised by the sudden arrival of Charles Surface (Scofield—me)—whom he does not wish to see. Sir Peter hides in a closet. On comes Charles—slightly hungover—to castigate his immoral and conniving brother, Joseph—catches the sound of a cough from Sir Peter—reveals him by throwing open the closet door—and then catches the sound of movement elsewhere and throws over the screen to reveal Lady Teazle. Woe! Disaster! Humiliation! Charles then throws down the gauntlet in a rather wonderful speech (he is in love with Lady T., himself) and sweeps off. That's it.

Now, all you need to add is that we were to rehearse this scene on the set of *The Big Knife*, because they had no matinee that day and the stage was "free." The modern furniture was pushed back against the set's walls and room made for the screen.

Hearing my cue, on I came. Guinness was "hiding" in his "closet"—watching me closely. I was his protege and must do him honour. Miss Leigh was ensconced with a crossword puzzle behind the screen—but watching, I was aware, what I was up to.

I did my initial number—quaking, book shaking, voice hoarse—and castigated James Donald, who was singularly unmoved and unperturbed. I then revealed Guinness—(who muttered: "you're reading too fast! Don't garble the words!") and moved upstage to throw down the screen.

Terrified of maiming Miss Leigh for life, I somehow managed to avoid her—and down went the screen with a satisfying *crash*! There I was, face to face with Scarlett O'Hara....

Oh god.

I worshipped her. She was lovely, she was kind. She *touched me*. Her fingers gripped my arm.

I finished the wonderful speech—addressing it to Vivien Leigh and Guinness—beginning to have the faintest sense of triumph. I hadn't bumped into Guinness—I hadn't crippled James Donald by walking on his toes—but, above all, I hadn't killed Vivien Leigh with the screen. In fact, at one moment I think I saw her mouth her approval to Guinness: *he's very good!*

I finished my speech and turned to "sweep off"....

Disaster.

There was the yellow chair.

How big it was. How well-made—formidable—and present it was. As if it had made an entrance especially to block my way.

How successful it was.

I went into it—*bam!*—and tipped it over, sending both it and a nearby table crashing to the floor. And me, of course. I went crashing, too.

I lay there in ruins. My humiliation was absolute. Done in forever by a yellow chair.

Scarlett O'Hara turned to the masterbuilder of the *Bridge on the River Kwai* and smiled her enigmatic smile. "Who was it who said: *just learn your lines and don't bump into the furniture?*"

"Spencer Tracy," said Guinness, as he offered to help me to my feet. "And worth remembering," he added, laughing kindly. "You did very well, till then," he muttered.

I looked at Vivien Leigh.

"Don't worry," she said. "One day you'll play Charles Surface—and you'll tell this story to break the ice."

She was more than kind.

I never did play Charles Surface. But now, I have told the story. And I can only add: *beware of yellow chairs.* For myself, I won't allow them anywhere near me.

STONE ORCHARD
FEBRUARY 1990
RADIO

My memory keeps delivering the past in brown-paper parcels done up with string and marked "address of sender unknown." One such parcel arrived the other day. Winter. Early evening. Not quite dark, but dark enough to turn on lights.

I had gone upstairs. The parcel was in my bedroom—waiting to surprise me. Not by saying "boo" and flinging itself at my feet in order to trip me up. Nothing like that. No *bangs*. No lurching shapes. It was a gentle, undemonstrative surprise.

I don't know how it arrived—I don't know why. But slowly, as I moved about the room adjusting lamps and thermostats, I was gradually overwhelmed by a certainty that someone was about to speak.

The noise, my dear. And the people....

The words were only in my mind, but the voice was very clear—distinct as any living voice.

Ernest Thesiger—wraithlike enough while still alive—pulled in and out of focus as I closed my eyes and tried to conjure him. *Ernest, tied with string and wrapped in brown paper.* Where was he coming from? Why was he being delivered now?

The noise, my dear—and the people.

This was Ernest's best-known pronouncement, his reply when- -returning from Flanders in 1917 with his hands so badly mangled it was thought they must soon be amputated—he was asked to describe the horrors of the battlefield.

The noise, my dear.

And the people, he said.

But why had I thought of that now?

I hadn't seen Ernest Thesiger for over thirty-five years—and he'd been dead since 1961.

Ernest Thesiger. Actor. Eccentric. Friend.

Well. What else was in the package? I sat on the bed and lighted a cigarette. Outside, the sky had almost completely blackened. A wind had risen—cold and menacing, promising snow. The world was disappearing, whiting-out in the dark.

Moscow. That was it. Part of it.

I had gone to Moscow with Ernest Thesiger in 1955. We had arrived there long after nightfall, in a blizzard. The storm had been so bad and our landing had been delayed so long that the plane was running out of fuel. We thought for certain we would be killed. And out of the silence created by our fearfulness, Ernest had asked in an offhand manner: *does anyone remember the Russian word for ambulance?*

He made us all laugh.

He always could—if he wanted to.

Christmas was not far off, that winter afternoon, and I realized with pleasure that Ernest would soon begin turning up again on the television screen, making his annual appearance in *Scrooge*. I mean in the best of all possible versions of *A Christmas Carol*—the one with Alastair Sim. Thesiger plays the conniving undertaker plotting the acquisition of Scrooge's possessions after Ebenezer "dies" in one of his nightmares. It is delightful. The undertaker's role gives him an opportunity to put on display what might be called "the essential Thesiger." Swathed in scarves and dressed in black, with his hands in fingerless gloves, he gives the impression of a cadaver's cadaver, just as, in life, he was an actor's actor.

225

I hadn't thought of Ernest Thesiger in such a long while. It was a comfort, sitting there in the lamplight, bringing him back into focus. I had been aware of him long before we met—aware of him even before I knew his name. He was the man whose appearance always made you smile with anticipation: something interesting was bound to happen if he turned up. His appearance had the same effect as a music cue.

Often, what happened was sinister. For instance, if it was a "costume film," the minute Ernest turned up, you knew the hero was about to be caught in a diabolical trap. Whereas, if the setting was contemporary, the presence of Ernest Thesiger signalled comic complications. He was rarely sinister in modern dress—and I've no idea what that meant, except to say it must have had to do with his physical appearance. Robes and ruffles gave him somewhere to hide—a business suit could not begin to hide him. Hidden, he could be frightening—but revealed, he caused a riot. Ernest Thesiger was a *provocateur*—in life as well as his career.

Tucked in the parcel of memories beside him, there was a ring, an autograph, a sewing needle, and a bicycle.

I recognized them instantly. These were Ernest's signs and symbols: his accumulation, over time, of the keys to his personality; his signature.

The bicycle on which, in his youth, he had ridden to Tite Street and tea with Oscar Wilde had become the symbol of his destiny. The sewing needle was a sign of patience. The autograph was his signature imposed on yours. The ring was his symbol of disguise.

There was always a sense, in Ernest's company, of being drawn into a charming conspiracy. The autograph game was his way of introducing himself.

"Give me your signature," he would say. "Put it on a large sheet of paper."

Once you had complied, Ernest would stare at your name for a moment, in much the same way a medium would stare at whatever talisman you might have handed her in order to acquaint her with your karma. He would turn the autograph upside down and sideways—hold it up against the light and run his eye up and down its shape. Then he would say: *most interesting ...* as if your name had spoken.

You would watch all this with growing fascination. His own concentration augmented yours and, this way, he could create an alarming sense of tension. *What was he going to find in what you had written?*

Then, with pursed lips, he would say to you: *give me your pen.* And he would begin to mark your autograph with what, at first, appeared to be hieroglyphs and runes. But they were not.

When he was finished, he would hand you back your pen and the sheet of paper on which *you* had written and *he* had drawn—and, instead of your signature, there would be a human figure or a tree—a vase of flowers or a gargoyle. Mine was a young Edwardian dandy—wearing a boater and sporting a walking stick. *That's you*, he said. *Or one of you....*

He had not known that I had played such a character on Canadian television long before I had gone to England and longer still before I had met him.

I have said that Ernest's hands were all but destroyed in the First World War. They were crushed when a building he was hiding in was blown to pieces during a bombardment. A whole wall fell on Ernest, smashing his hands and almost tearing his arms from his body. "I lay there, waiting for rescue, almost all of one day," he said. "I could not see my arms or my hands—and the only thing that informed me I had not lost them was the pain. I was almost reassured by this, until I dimly remembered what friends had said to me when they had lost their legs and arms—which was that you go on feeling as if they were still with you—long, long after they have gone. *Ghost pains*, they call this. I got in a dreadful panic then, and prayed that I would die. I could not imagine, you see, my life without arms. I had wanted to be an artist and an actor—and how could I be either one without my arms?"

The noise, my dear, and the people.

His arms and his hands were saved—but it took a great long while for Ernest Thesiger to recover their use. This is where needlework entered his life—as a therapeutic activity by which he could regain control of his dexterity. It is also where the ring, as a symbol of disguise, took its place in Ernest's consciousness.

His hands, as he found them even after two or three years of therapy, had not recovered their "beauty."

"Very ugly they were," he said—and held them out for me to see. "Worse than you see them, now. I could not bear to look at them. They made me weep."

Until the day of his death, it is true, his hands—in repose and stripped of gloves and other masquerades—were not the best a person could hope for. The fingers were delicate and bent and the knuckles as bony as those of any victim of arthritis. Still, he had beautiful fingernails and skin and he hid what he could of the wounds with rings.

Silver rings were his favourites. Never gaudy and always intriguing, each ring had a story. One I remember in particular. It was shown to me on a winter evening in 1955—much like the evening thirty-five years later on which I had been ambushed so unexpectedly by Ernest's ghost in its brown-paper wrappings. The ring was one of the many Ernest wore—a heavy silver ring with an opal set in a lion's claws. He showed it to me at his flat in London, after we had returned from Moscow. He was giving a cocktail party on a Sunday afternoon—the favoured day for actors' parties—and we sat on a blue velvet sofa under lamplight.

Ernest's voice, as I remember it, crackled and wavered somewhere between his nose and the back of his throat. He always seemed to be about to expire. It was a quavering voice with amazing strength....

"This ring," he said—and he held it under the lamplight—"belonged to Lucretia Borgia...."

I asked if I could touch it and he said: "You may, but not before I show you something. Here—look at this...."

He placed the ring on the little finger of his left hand, removing another ring in order to do so.

"Give me your drink," he said.

I gave him my martini.

He placed the glass on a small round table between our knees and waved both hands above it—the right hand touching the left hand for the briefest moment.

"There," said Ernest, sitting back and smiling invitingly. "Take it now and see what you think."

I lifted the glass and drank. My martini was suddenly inexplicably sweet. I made a face.

Ernest laughed.

"You're dead," he said. "I've poisoned you!"

"You've also ruined my drink," I said.

"It's only sugar," Ernest explained. He removed the ring and showed it to me again—giving the opal a gentle tap with his fingernail. "The poison goes in here, beneath the stone, you see." He pushed against the opal, revealing a tiny compartment underneath. "I fill it with sugar from time to time, for amusement's sake," he said. His eyes were shining. "I poisoned the Prince of Wales with it, once," he told me. "It was quite a triumph!"

Ernest lifted another martini from a passing tray and gave it to me. "Whenever I dined with the Prince of Wales after that, he used to inspect my rings before we sat down. It became our joke. He asked me, once, if I would lend it to him, but I told him: *not, sir, unless you tell me who the intended victim is going to be.* My brother George, he said—meaning the late Duke of Kent—and I said: *Oh, sir, you cannot want to kill the Duke of Kent!* And he said, yes, because he has more fun than I do...."

Ernest became quite suddenly serious.

"You know," he said, "the strangest expression came into the Prince's eyes when he told me that. He was joking. Of course, he was joking. But ... a look of anguish— of *sadness* overcame him—just for a moment—and he could not prevent it. Poor man. Deep inside, he really did feel trapped, I think. And the Duke of Kent—*well, he,* ..." Ernest laughed, ... *"was another story!* The Prince of Wales was right. Quite right! His brother George had a great, *great* deal more fun than anyone!"

We looked again at Lucretia Borgia's ring.

"Put it on," he said. "Go ahead."

But I had lost—I don't know why—my desire to wear it.

"No," I said. "Thank you."

Ernest looked at me.

He could see that his story had sobered me, as perhaps he had intended. Hidden inside what appeared to be a harmless anecdote about regal foibles, there had been a tender message of sympathy. He had seen in me a young man who shared the same crises and misgivings that he had endured when he was young. 229 Ernest had found his courage long before Flanders, when his mentor, Oscar Wilde, had been humiliated, arrested, and sent to gaol—losing everything in one rash gesture. We never spoke of these things in so many words. But much was implicit through various other words and gestures. Ernest, in spite of public mockery, had gone on to become, most emphatically and fearlessly, himself—and he was always urging me to do the same.

It wasn't easy.

Nonetheless, when he heard me say that I no longer wanted to wear Lucretia Borgia's ring, he looked at me carefully before he spoke—and then he said: "Never mind, never mind."

Then he put the ring away.

"But I was so looking forward to hearing about your intended victim!" he said.

His empathy could be wicked.

Ernest was not alone in the package I received that late afternoon. Perhaps in some ways it was inevitable that in my memory, especially, he should always keep the company of another with whom, in real life, I doubt very much he would have kept company at all.

This is one of the better tricks that memory plays. The crowd inside is made of disparate players whose swords may have crossed more often than their lives. I find it very hard to imagine Ernest in possession of a sword—but I think he might have armed himself with one if he had known who would share the package with him that day....

It was another British actor and quite an unlikely one, at that. His name was Wilfrid Lawson and my first memory of him was when he played Alfred Doolittle—Eliza's father—the dustman, in the 1938 film of George Bernard Shaw's *Pygmalion*.

As implied by his name, Doolittle's constant excuse for not getting very far in life was that he was always being thwarted by *middle-class morality*. Doolittle's complaint is fairly descriptive of any actor's life—certainly of Wilfrid Lawson's life, though for quite different reasons. And of Ernest Thesiger's life—and my own—though again, for entirely different reasons.

Middle-class morality has probably driven more actors into the theatre than it ever reached in and pulled out. But that's another story, too, and not what this is about—though middle-class morality would not have approved of Wilfrid Lawson any more than it approved of Alfred Doolittle.

Wilfrid Lawson—flailing and wiry—driven by an excess of bottled energy—dances into view. His voice, which always faltered, was like a singer's voice gone mad. He pitched his words up high and tried to catch them when they fell. His speech was made of glottal stops and choking—undelivered roaring—endless lapses into tenderness. He never spoke—like Molière's Bourgeois Gentilhomme—in prose. It was always some kind of poetry.

I made a journey with Wilfrid Lawson, too—not so great a journey as with Ernest in terms of miles, but greater in terms of intimacy. I was Wilfrid Lawson's keeper, in a way. It was my responsibility, on tour, to share his digs and get him to the theatre on time.

Of course, one immediately thinks of Alfred Doolittle's song in *My Fair Lady*—the musical based on *Pygmalion*. But, getting Alfred to the *church* on time was done with a band of a dozen burly dancers. I had to do it without a band and I was decidedly un-burly. A flyweight, you might say, pitted against the heavyweight champion of the world.

Wilfrid Lawson's drinking was legendary. I knew all about it long before I knew him. But he had good reason to drink—if such a thing can be said—and I guess, in Wilfrid Lawson's case, it *must* be said. He did not drink for the fun of it. Nor because he wanted to drown his sorrows. None of the classic reasons fitted Wilfrid Lawson's relationship with alcohol. He drank to stifle pain. Real pain—not imagined. Not occasional pain—but constant.

He took to drink with cold deliberation. He knew very well that, in the end, it would kill him. Perhaps, because of the pain, a part of him wanted that. I cannot say. But in the meantime, waiting for his death—drink would enable him to function.

The pain was caused by a metal plate in his skull. Like Ernest, Mister Lawson had been dreadfully wounded in the First World War and the plate had been placed in his skull in an effort to save his life. His life *had* been saved—the surgery had done that—but life itself had been made intolerable. The plate did that. He was crippled forever after.

Given that, at the time the surgery was performed, the techniques were primitive—and given that science had not yet provided the sophisticated painkillers we have today, Wilfrid Lawson had little choice in the matter of whether or not he could deal with the pain. We are not talking here of something that fortitude and aspirin—in whatever combinations—would ameliorate. Morphine and alcohol were all that would help.

Wilfrid Lawson chose alcohol because he knew that if he had chosen the more desirable morphine to deaden his pains he would also be choosing a drug that would prevent him utterly from pursuing his career as an actor.

Later, as he himself often said, other drugs presented themselves from time to time—especially during and after the Second World War—that might have helped. He did, in fact, try some of these—in tandem with attempts to withdraw from his regimen of drink. But by then, the drink itself had become a kind of food to him— a habit to his system from which there could be no permanent recovery. He began to go on and off the wagon like a mechanical toy that had been doomed to repeat the same process forever, until it burned out and dropped. Doomed and damned.

We were in a play called *The Prisoner*. It had been written by Bridget Boland and was loosely based on the brainwashing torture suffered at the hands of Hungarian Communists by Cardinal Mindszenty. Alec Guinness played the Cardinal. Wilfrid Lawson played his keeper—his jailer. I played a clerk in the office of The Prosecutor who succeeded in turning the Cardinal's mind.

We went on a lengthy tour in the winter of 1954, prior to opening in London early that spring. Edinburgh, Liverpool, Manchester, Leeds, and Cambridge. I was not put in charge of Mister Lawson until we got to Liverpool.

The rehearsal period prior to the tour had gone quite well. It was a tough, unrelenting and exhausting play to rehearse—let alone to play. Alec Guinness had alternate scenes with Wilfrid Lawson and The Prosecutor, played by the late Noel Willman. Guinness, once on, was virtually never off again until the final curtain. It was a punishing role and it took every ounce of daring and concentration to pull it off.

Everyone was nervous of Mister Lawson.

Would he—*could* he—sustain his current regimen of sobriety and pills for the run of the play? Everyone hoped so—and everyone wanted it to be so, not only for their own sake, but for Mister Lawson's sake. He was such a splendid actor— greatly admired and loved—and he needed a success. His last performances, in the title role of Strindberg's *The Father*, had been a triumph for him—but a triumph that ended badly when he started to drink again.

At any rate, there were only one or two incidents during rehearsal—a missed afternoon when Mister Lawson returned late from lunch and his lunch had been mostly liquid. That was difficult. Guinness—who adored Mister Lawson and gave him total respect—was nervous, nonetheless. So much of his onstage time was spent with Lawson as the jailer—and, in bad rehearsals, the outcome could be a nightmare of undelivered cues and rambling speeches, barely audible, stringing Mister Lawson's performance together.

Serious consideration was given, at one point, to hiring a replacement. But Lawson came through—and off we set.

By the time we got to Liverpool and I was living in digs with Mister Lawson, the drinking was on its way to becoming chronic. The bottle of ale was never far from his hand.

We had the loveliest landlady there. I can see her still: tiny—sweet—and very old. She adored Mister Lawson—and he had been her house guest for thirty years or more—whenever his plays had brought him to Liverpool. She always provided his favourite jams and jellies—she knew exactly how to cook his eggs— and she was expert at stashing the great green bottles of Bass on which he thrived between his rounds of hard liquor.

We did not share a room. It would have been intolerable. Mister Lawson always went to bed sodden and all night long he would be dragged from one nightmare to another—often yelling—more often screaming—very often struggling physically to free himself of impeding bedclothes and threatening shapes in the shadows.

His voice had a liquid quality at times—as if his vocal chords were being stewed—and he would sound as if he were drowning.

"Help! Help! Help!" he would shout—and sometimes, he would pound against the walls. "Help! Help!"

The noise, my dear—and the people.

It wasn't funny.

It was a horror story.

I would have to rise and go to his room and Mrs. Whatever would beg me to go in and save him.

"A *man* has to do it," she would say. "He will not tolerate a woman being his saviour."

So, I would go in.

To darkness.

I was always afraid. He could be so violent.

He didn't mean to be.

I felt so helpless with him—knowing that, from his point of view, I was always coming for him out of flames and battle-sounds and the cries of other people dying. What did it mean that a crazy young man in pyjamas was coming to save him from his fallen aeroplane and the horrors of the mud?

And so, in spite of calling *help! help! help!* he would then do battle with me—trying to beat me off. *Don't! Don't!* he would say. *Don't! Don't! I cannot bear it!*

Neither could I.

Often, I would have to lead him away—at last—from his wrecked and mined bed—his aeroplane—and get him from that wreckage, down the hall through no man's land—first to the WC and then to the bathroom, where, in the dreadful light of naked bulbs, he would let me wash his face and hands and adjust his uniform.

Mrs. Whatever, by then, would have a tea tray in his room and I would sit and watch from near the doorway, while Mister Lawson topped up his tea with something from a bottle.

Next day—every day—he would call me into the parlour on the first floor and he would be sitting in the corner—lit with delicate, forgiving light, and he would say to me: *all right, Findley, stand at attention and give me your report.*

I stood—like a soldier—looking over his head, and—arms pressed in against my sides and thumbs facing forwards—I would tell him that nothing untoward had happened in the night.

233

Going to the theatre, we always walked—unless it was a great way off—and Mister Lawson wore a tweed deerstalker and an Inverness overcoat with a cape.

We more or less marched. It was supposed to be good for our lungs. *Take in lots of air, Findley. Take in lots of air!*

My nightmare was that he would spot a pub and want to go in. That never happened. I guess it didn't need to. Primed before he left the digs—his dressing room was pub enough to welcome him up on arrival.

When Mister Lawson dried on stage, he would put a matchstick into his mouth and chew on that to force his concentration. Alec Guinness used to count the matches.

On a bad night, he would say, as he made his way to his dressing room: *Wilfrid ate two dozen matches tonight.*

The record was thirty-five.

They came—already old—into my young life. They left an indelible and wondrous impression—and they gave me the gift of their company whether for good or ill.

234

I never lost respect for Mister Lawson. He was—and he remains in memories—a superb performer—a giant among the actors of his time.

He worked to the very last year of his life—when, in 1966, he appeared in a glorious farce on film: Bryan Forbes's production of *The Wrong Box*. See it, for heaven's sake, if you can. Besides its other joys and delights—the masterful comedy of Ralph Richardson being chief among them—there is also the wonder of Wilfrid Lawson's bug-eyed scarecrow of a butler—with his collar askew and his white gloves torn with his nervous chewing on the finger ends—brushing other visions away with an impatient hand—pointing at a packing crate lodged, immobilized, in a doorway and pronouncing with infinite wisdom: "That is stuck. That is what that is."

His voice alone is worth the price of admission.

The only time I worked with Ernest Thesiger was in a production of *Hamlet* in which I played Osric. All through rehearsals, I was tormented by the director, Peter Brook, who had decided—for reasons of his own I will not go into—that I was this year's whipping boy. He would simply not let me rehearse. Every time we came to Osric's entrance, he would say: *Stop! May we have the next scene, please.*

It all began about one week in, when, moments after I had made my first entrance, Peter Brook called from the darkness: "Mister Findley—what do you think you are doing?"

These words were said with a chilling glaze of illogical anger. Hearing them, you might have thought I had come on riding a bicycle and juggling oranges.

Well—it got worse. Since I really hadn't done anything other than what we had so far decided I should be doing, both I and everyone else on stage knew perfectly well what was happening. I had been chosen. The knife had fallen and it was lodged in me.

I had seen this happen to other actors in other productions. It is just the way some directors are. Even the greatest of them—as with Peter Brook—may need, for whatever reason, to put someone away. They never fire you, under these circumstances. And your resignation would not be accepted. The whipping boy must stand his ground and make his way alone.

In the long run, the other actors and I worked out our own blocking and simply got on with the scene by rehearsing it, during breaks, in dressing rooms and corridors. Peter Brook didn't even let us do the scene at the cue-to-cue rehearsal when we first got onto the set—nor at the dress rehearsal. The first time I actually played it on the set was opening night in Brighton.

Some weeks later, we all flew to Moscow— where the production was a huge success. This was in 1955 and it was an auspicious occasion. Stalin had only been dead for two years—Burgess and Maclean had defected in the relatively recent past—and the Cold War was at its height.

Ours was the very first visit of any British company of actors since the Revolution of 1917. Hamlet was played by Paul Scofield, Gertrude by Diana Wynyard, Claudius by Alec Clunes and Ophelia by Mary Ure. Ernest played Polonius. All these actors, excepting Paul Scofield, are now dead—wrapped in their own brown-paper parcels—but Ernest was my favourite. When we got, at last, to Moscow, he had to be restrained. He was determined that he was going to sneak out one night from our hotel across the road from the Kremlin and write—in chalk—on its historic walls: BURGESS LOVES MACLEAN!!!

I wish he had.

Kenneth Tynan once described Ernest Thesiger as a "praying mantis." It was an apt description. He often held his hands before his breast with just the fingertips touching and all the rings showing nicely. He marcelled his hair and tinted it. The

235

length of his nose, which was immense, was often powdered to hide its redness. He was something of a fashion plate. His clothes were always impeccably cut and he wore them always with a sense of style. He favoured Prussian blue ties with polka dots—and sometimes wore a handkerchief neatly tucked into his sleeve....

The brown-paper package is nearly completely undone—its string is lying untied on the floor. Wilfrid Lawson makes one final appearance—dressed in the Inverness coat and with flying wisps of hair. He has been on a binge and we have got the understudy into costume and ready to go on. Where is Wilfrid? Where? Where? Where? We are playing in London now—at the Globe on Shaftesbury Avenue— backing into twisting alleys—the alleys filled with Soho pubs and restaurants.

Suddenly, the doors of the scene dock—enormous doors on pulleys—fly up to heaven and there is Wilfrid Lawson—roaring—literally....

WHERE IS MY THEATRE? WHERE IS MY STAGE?

He is clothed in coat and hair—and little else. The overcoat flies open revealing Mister Lawson's long johns and boots.

236

I WANT MY THEATRE! I WANT MY STAGE!

The understudy went on.

Mister Lawson went to sleep.

It was, for a change, a sleep without nightmares.

Ernest's final symbol was a sewing needle. Under the tutelage of his therapists, he had become so proficient in needlepoint that, less than twenty years later, he was one of Queen Mary's favourite sewing partners. She and Ernest would sit at either end of the carpet she was making and stitch away whole afternoons and mornings. Ernest, by the way, began to dye his hair around the time of the carpet—a time when he was also severely depressed and it turned, in Oscar Wilde's words, *quite gold with grief!* In the long run, Ernest Thesiger and Queen Mary began to look like one another—and, over the years, as the aging dowager explored other colours, other rinses, so likewise did Ernest. By the time I knew him in the mid-1950s, soon after Queen Mary's death, his "grief" was tinted blue. "She was, in many ways, my dearest friend," he told me. "I sensed that her silence was made of the same ingredients as mine. She endured a kind of private mourning, from time to time. And so did I. It had to do with the lives we would have preferred to live but could not because of who we were." He thought about this for a moment—then he added: "I do not mean who we were when we were born. I mean the people we became by necessity, rather than by desire...."

The wind blows now—the sky is black—the snow arrives. My windows—unshaded—are filled with reflections of the lamplit room. I think of Ernest's wondrous, crazy face and his broken hands and I think: *it is true that beauty is only skin deep*. But Ernest's lack of it cut to the marrow of his heart. Not, of course, that he ever said so. It was just the way he survived it: smiling.

He used to come, every night, dressed as Polonius, his needlework held in his hands, and he would stand in the wings and watch as I went out to play Osric. All through the sequences he would stand there—every night for weeks, in all the towns we played in England—and in Moscow—and, finally, in London. Watching—just watching—saying nothing.

At last, the scene began to play and, in spite of all the problems it had presented, it became a joy to go on stage. One night, just as I made my exit, there came a round of applause. That had never happened to me before, under any circumstance. I was stunned.

Ernest, in the wings, was beaming.

He put out one hand and took my arm.

He didn't say a word. When we came to his dressing room, he went inside, turned around and said: "*Thank you.*"

Upstairs, in my own dressing room, I cried. Not because there had been applause—but because I was overwhelmed all at once with the knowledge that Ernest had stood in the wings all those weeks to show me that in spite of Peter Brook he had believed in me. And he stayed there until I got it right. Until I believed in myself. After that, he never appeared in the wings again.

The package is now completely undone—and I am left with its fragmented contents—Ernest and his symbols—Mister Lawson and his icons: sewing needles, rings, and autographs—dark green bottles of Bass—beds wrecked as aeroplanes—Inverness coats and thirty-five matchsticks, chewed and ruined—thirty-five fires that Wilfrid Lawson never got to start.

As I go to the window, it seems that all I can see is the darkness outside and a few reflections. But way off—out beyond the reach of any normal light that any normal lamp can throw—I can just discern the shape of Ernest on his bicycle—

237

making his way, aged seventeen, along the Chelsea Embankment until he comes to Tite Street, where Oscar Wilde has invited him to tea.

Ernest is about to discover the importance of being oneself—no matter what.

He arrives at Oscar's door on a day long before my parents are born—before Mister Lawson is born—before I am even thought of. And yet, I see him standing there. And, in between that day and this....

The noise, my dear....

And....

The people.

I wave—and he is gone.

But not forever. Other parcels will arrive, in time. In time, I will remember more.

STONE ORCHARD

JANUARY 1971

RADIO

238 I can remember, some years ago, walking down a particularly arid city street, making my way from the apartment where I lived to the office where I worked. This was in Los Angeles, and out there, the smog makes your eyes water so that you can barely keep them open to see where you are going. After you've been there awhile, you realize that Angelenos don't wear sunglasses to avoid the glare of the sun but the plague of the smog.

Anyway, there I was walking along whatever street it was, having just come out of one concrete monstrosity, passing by others and heading for the one I worked in. Little plastic trees had been set up in tubs at intervals along the sidewalk. And as I made my way, I looked down at my feet and then up at the invisible sky, and was aware of the concrete that hedged me in—and I thought: but I wasn't born into *this*. My *body* wasn't born into this *place!* I was born *alive*; yet this is where I'm asking my body to function. What is the matter with me?

And I looked at all the people going past. And I thought: I don't and will not ever know who these people are. And they do not and never *will* know me. And I thought: but when I go up in the elevator in the building where I work, then I'll be able to nod at the elevator operator. Yes. And I will say "good morning" to Miss Gregson, who sits at the front desk. And when I get into the executive section, then I'll be able to see one or two movie stars, perhaps, discussing contracts—and even if I don't know them personally, at least I'll know their *faces* from the silver screen. Then, getting further into the bowels of the building, I will come upon the writers' section and in there I'm allowed to nod at Rod Serling, who is not allowed to nod back because I'm a junior, junior dialogue writer and such people do not get nodded at by senior, senior superstar writers like Rod Serling. And so I anticipated my daily ration of contacts in the city and this was the highlight.

I can nod and be nodded at by Miss Queeg, and I can even go so far as to ask her to type a few pages for me, which means we will have the following "conversation."

"Miss Queeg?"

"Yes, Mister Findley?"

"I have these few pages here—not very many...."

"Thank you, Mister Findley."

"Thank you, Miss Queeg."

Bang.

The bang is my little door, shutting. Shutting me into my four-by-four euphemism for an office. And there I would stay until my agent called—an event that took place every day at 12:15. Stanley and I really did know each other, to the full extension of the telephone wire, and we even knew the intimate details of one another's lives. I knew the name of his wife and he knew that I came from Toronto, Ontario, up in Canada. Intimate details like that. Anyway, following my conversation with Stanley, which consisted of remarks about the number of pages I had managed to work, and whether I had enough money for lunch, I would go out through the bowels of the building, past Miss Queeg's desk, along about twenty-six windowless corridors, to a staircase.

Down the stairs, out into a cemented courtyard bounded on three sides by high blank walls and on the fourth side by a wire fence, through which, not too distantly, you could catch glimpses of the Farmer's Market. In the courtyard you sat on wooden benches under an occasional canopy and ate cheese sandwiches that were sprayed with plastic and drank milk that was flaked with wax. If you were tremendously lucky, as I *once* was, you got to sit down right *exactly* where Angela Lansbury had been sitting two seconds before. If you were *not* lucky, you got to sit down where Miss Queeg had just sat. And you stared at the secretaries and junior, junior directors and super-junior executive producers while they stared back—all of you wondering what you could do for each other—all of you knowing the answer was: *nothing*. Not in this place; not in this city; not in this existence.

239

Then back inside and more slavery until five or five-thirty, and then out through the bowels of the building, past the executive suites and the elevators and along twelve miles of totally *un*impressive "impressive driveway" to the boulevard, and blindly along the boulevard to the Plastic Food Mart where you bought the plastic pork chops and a plastic head of lettuce and went home.

In my apartment—(hah! Oh, well, it was called an apartment and I went along with the gag)—I had made a very close relationship with a fly.

No kidding. This fly and I lived together for almost three months, until one day he got drowned in the tin shower stall—and I have often thought about that, and been reasonably certain it was suicide. I was so fond of that fly, I actually wept. And in a dream I thought I found his little towel and six neatly matched tiny slippers at the edge of the shower, and a note that read, "This is for the best, Tiff. City life is not for me. Good luck from your best friend, Buzz."

I left Los Angeles shortly after that, saying to myself, "This is for the best, Buzz—city life is not for me."

I had done forever—I swore it—with killing my feet on concrete slabs and had done forever with having to anticipate my conversation with Miss Queeg as the high point of my day. I had done forever with being stared at by the junior, junior superstar execs. And I had done forever with my best friend, Buzz—who died, to show me the way.

Now, I live on the outskirts of a town. And I can walk in on a Saturday morning at 7:30 A.M. and be the first one all the dogs bark at—and stand around under real trees eating real cheese sandwiches. I can wander in the park and see kids—little children—who know me by name just because I live close by. And I can visit several friends—if I want to. And I can buy my groceries from Mister Huyck and Mister Curie, and we *know* each other. And I can walk out under the trees and head for home along a dirt road made for human feet. And I can touch and know the reality into which I was born.

So. The towns and farms and country roads will save us. You see, I don't mind being seen as that kind of reactionary. *Let* people tell me I'm crazy and that city life's the greatest thing invented. For me, it's a hoax. Why, even a fly can tell you that. Look at Buzz. He knew. Maybe he didn't drown. Maybe he floated through the drain and is somewhere safe at sea.

The Last of the Terrible Men

HEATHER ROBERTSON

Heather Robertson (b. 1942) is one of the relatively few people to make the successful transition from newspaper reporter to serious author of both fiction and non-fiction. Some of the most important of her many books are *Reservations Are for Indians* (1974), *Willie: A Romance* (1983), and *Igor: A Novel of Intrigue* (1989). One of her most recent is *Writing from Life: A Guide to Writing True Stories* (1998), in which she cautions aspiring non-fiction writers to eschew any technique that smacks of the experimental. Yet in the case of the following memoir, her experimental adoption of a hard-boiled urban persona from the industrial age, as a means of mocking the values behind it, is what makes the piece memorable. "The Last of the Terrible Men" appeared in *Saturday Night* in 1980.

PUBLISHER CHARGED IN SEX CRIME CASE
Richard C. Malone, publisher of the *Winnipeg Free Press*, appeared in provincial judges' court today to face six charges in connection with a police investigation of alleged homosexual activities involving juveniles.

Malone, 37, of Oxford Street, has been charged with three counts of buggery and three counts of gross indecency ...
WINNIPEG FREE PRESS
February 22, 1979

The *Free Press* ran the story on page one. So did *The Winnipeg Tribune*. "Not the brigadier!" I squawked when I heard the news. Brigadier Richard S. Malone, OBE, had been called many things, most of them uncomplimentary, in his thirteen years as publisher of the *Free Press*, but faggot wasn't one of them. No, this was Brigadier Malone's golden son, who had inherited the *Free Press* when papa left for *The Globe and Mail* in 1974. Malone was the eighth prominent man to be arrested as part of a homosexual "ring"; the police had cruelly released the names one by one. Winnipeg was in an ecstasy of salacious speculation. The whirr of John Dafoe spinning in his grave could be heard from the corner of Higgins and Main to the outer reaches of River Heights.

A great story. And it got better. Out on bail, Malone arranged to meet one of the boys in Flin Flon. When he arrived at the Flin Flon airport, an RCMP officer disguised as an airport employee generously offered Malone a ride to a local motel. Malone checked in; the RCMP checked into the next room, water glasses no doubt pressed to the wall. The boy turned up; the lights went off. The RCMP crashed in and found the two naked in bed. Malone was charged with another count of gross indecency and with obstructing justice by attempting to persuade the juvenile witnesses not to testify, an infinitely more serious charge than the morals rap.

The *Free Press* hit bottom. People were laughing at it; the *Tribune* was breathing down its neck. The *Free Press* was ugly, old-fashioned, dull; the *Tribune*, which had been born again in 1975, was lively, trendy, bright. The *Free Press* had quietly taken down the famous sign—In Winnipeg it's the *Free Press* 2–1!—on top of its building. It quietly removed Richard C. Malone as publisher. People whispered that the *Free Press*, once called the greatest newspaper in Canada, would soon be Number Two in Winnipeg.

On October 23, 1979, Richard C. Malone was sentenced to a year in jail. The ghost of John Dafoe was laid to rest.

High time, too. Its withering hand had rested on the *Free Press* for thirty-five years, turning it into a sepulchre for dead ideas and stale prose, a terminal-care ward for the aged and infirm, a place to crash for drifters and bums, a jumping-off point for green young hustlers headed for *The Globe and Mail*. That's where I came in. Like hundreds of prairie kids I got my first real job as a reporter with the *Free Press*. It was 1963 and I was twenty-one.

The *Free Press* has always had a penchant for young people. We came cheap. I got $50 a week; copy boys made $35 a week. I had no experience worth anything and if the *Free Press* was prepared to risk printing the consequences of my ineptitude, it was doing me a favour. This attitude of noblesse oblige was a legacy of the Siftons, although the family, like the paper, had lost some of its sheen. Sir Clifford Sifton, a prairie Genghis Khan, had bought the paper at the turn of the century and hired Dafoe as editor. By the time of Dafoe's death in 1944, he had, with subsequent generations of Siftons, built the *Free Press* into the cornerstone of a powerful publishing empire. With their ruddy faces and tweedy clothes and stiff upper lips, their country estates and racing stables, the Siftons were Canada's last gasp of the Age of Chivalry. Their political views were as feudal as their style, but when it came to newspapers they were pure capitalists: the *Free Press* made a piss-pot full of money.

It was the smell of the *Free Press* that hooked me, that insidious narcotic made up of newsprint and ink, hot lead, cold coffee, floor wax, stale sweat, cigars, yesterday's sandwiches, sharpened pencils, dust, developing fluid, old linoleum, bad whisky, and fifty years of dirt. It was the smell of news. I knew it the minute I stepped into the newsroom—battered oak desks, ancient typewriters, blinds sagging at half-mast, swivel chairs worn smooth by a million bums—it was *The Front Page* right down to the paunchy men in suspenders bellowing "Copy! Copy!" as if the world were on fire. Even the typewriter ribbons were worn out.

The staff seemed about the same vintage, although given the ghostly pallor most newsmen develop by the age of thirty, they may have been much younger. I was handed a sheaf of press releases to rewrite and assigned a desk next to a gaunt, weathered, sad-eyed woman with bright orange hair, bright orange lipstick on one side of her mouth and a cigarette in the other. She was doing exactly the same thing. She rattled hers off in an hour, stubbed out her cigarette, and left. She was, I was told, the widow of a *Free Press* reporter killed in the Second World War; the *Free Press* kept her on out of charity, paying her a tiny wage for token work. The newsroom was full of these people, widows, old girlfriends, meek, battered women who came and went so silently, so humbly, their presence, or absence, was scarcely noticed. Was this where I would be in forty years, an eccentric crone with hennaed hair and nicotine fingers sitting at the same desk doing rewrites? They scared the hell out of me.

They weren't as scary as the freaks. As former *Free Press* copy boy and film critic Martin Knelman puts it: "The staff looked as if it had been hand-picked by Fellini." Dwarves, cripples, editors with tics and stammers, a fat woman with a terribly scarred face, reporters with wooden legs and wooden heads, ancient alcoholic elevator boys who never, never stopped the elevator exactly at the floor but jiggled it up and down half a dozen times, refugees, drunks, the retarded, the neurotic, misfits and has-beens, the wounded of the world. The *Free Press* newsroom was so bizarre that nothing I could encounter in the real world would ever shock me. I realized that newspapering was a dangerous business; the fact that the deepest, most painful wounds were invisible didn't come to me until I was at the *Tribune*.

243

Everybody had a story, like the news editor who had been sent to the coronation by a Toronto daily, got drunk, slept through the whole thing, and had been blacklisted across Ontario. The best stories had been passed around so long they had become legend: the classic *Free Press* story, how sports writer John Robertson had constructed what turned out to be his last column so that the first letter in every paragraph, read vertically, spelled "Fuck you everybody!", was not exactly true. Robertson did it, all right, but not at the *Free Press*. No matter; the *Free Press* staff wanted to believe it, so it did. The story expressed with perfect simplicity the reporter's eternal frustration, contempt, and desire, just once, to fuck management.

It didn't take me long to get the point that the *Free Press* didn't know, or particularly care, what it printed. If it was in the *Free Press* it was news. The staff was large, the news hole small; if we all had filed a story a day most of it would have ended up in the garbage. So we goofed off. Nobody seemed to mind. As long as we turned up from time to time, like guests at the Mad Hatter's tea party, we could stick around forever. Some people did. Nobody ever told me what a news story was, how to get it or how to write it, much less how to write it well. If I came back with a story, fine; if not, fine too. Nobody mentioned the *Tribune*. The *Tribune* never beat us; if it was in the *Tribune* it wasn't news.

It was no accident that Marshall McLuhan grew up reading the *Free Press*. The *Free Press* looked true. It oozed money. It oozed authority. It was as smug and condescending as the Colonel Blimps at the Manitoba Club where, since the days of Dafoe, editors had taken what they believed to be the public pulse. Founded on the holy trinity of Free Enterprise, Free Trade, and the Free World, the *Free Press* was more a church than a newspaper; Winnipeggers believed in it. News, regarded by pre-television readers as revealed truth, was judged on the basis of its conformity to dogma; by the mid-1960s the relevance of this dogma to reality was very tenuous indeed. The *Free Press*'s response to radicalism was an almost paranoiac campaign of smear, slander, and vilification directed against anyone the *Free Press* considered to be a Commie-creepo-hippie-dopefiend-fag. This definition took in almost everyone from Ed Schreyer, who was premier then, to CBC broadcaster Barbara Frum, and included specifically university professors, hippies, CBC employees, and members of the New Democratic Party, which in 1969 formed the provincial government. A successful libel suit against the paper helped staunch the flow of mud, but by the time the *Free Press* discovered a creepo-fag in its own publisher's office the greatest newspaper in Canada was little more than a sleazy, small-time rag.

Red-baiting isn't new to the *Free Press*: John Dafoe could spot a "bohunk" or "Bolshevik" at a hundred feet. It has always been a partisan newspaper. Its inflated reputation under Dafoe rested on its incestuous connection with the Liberal Party, first through Sir Clifford, a member of Laurier's cabinet, later through Ottawa correspondents Grant Dexter and Bruce Hutchison, who were close enough to Mackenzie King and Louis St. Laurent to have been cabinet ministers. It's easy to get the inside story when you write the script. As Hutchison made clear in his autobiography, *The Far Side of the Street*, they saw nothing dubious or disreputable about this *liaison dangereuse*. Liberalism was the truth; they reported it. The *Free Press* was a political newspaper in the old style. As the propaganda arm of the Liberal Party it helped build the Liberal empire in the West and, in the paper's increasing hysteria and irrelevance, helped destroy it. It was certainly no place for a left-winger heretic like me.

I was saved by demon drink, hired away by the *Tribune* at $90 a week over a beer at the press club. Everything important at the *Tribune* happened at the press club, a cosy, dark watering-hole in the basement of the old Marlborough Hotel, where a perpetual poker game ran in the backroom and the bullshit flowed as fast as the booze. We girls, as we were called then, weren't allowed to join the press club, but we were welcomed guests and the men were generous with the rounds; it helped make up for the fact that they were paid more—for the wife and kids, it was said—although the press club sucked in most of that extra money as eager young brown-nosers stood endless rounds for editors with unslakeable thirsts.

245

I didn't much like beer at first. I learned fast. A 4 P.M. drink at the press club was so much a part of my *Trib* routine for two years that the habit is still compulsive. The *Tribune* floated on beer. It was pickled in Scotch. I usually left by 6 P.M. but many stayed half the night, not infrequently stumbling back to the paper at 7 A.M., pale and reeking, to put out the next day's news. The benders were colossal: a mild-mannered desk man threw chairs around the newsroom at night and threatened to murder fellow staff members; reporters set off for police court in the morning and phoned up, ten days later, from Moscow or Inuvik; a political columnist was found sleeping it off, unscathed, between railway tracks. There was no distinction between work and play: the mood in the *Trib* newsroom was as cheery, cocky, and profane as at the press club. The *Trib* was fun. It was a part of life. Hell, it *was* life.

The press club was a parody of the Manitoba Club, which Winnipeg *Tribune* editor Eric Wells, unlike his predecessors, had refused to join. Wells was probably as good an editor as Dafoe had been thirty years before but absolutely different: a newsman, not a pundit; an adversary of the Establishment, not an accomplice; a political man but not a partisan. Corny as it may sound in this cynical age, Wells believed that the fourth estate was the eyes, ears, and voice of the people. He was independent, irreverent, and intrepid. He hated bullshit more than bolshevism. The press club's power grew out of Wells's implicit assumption that a good journalist has no friends—except other journalists. In his years as editor of the *Tribune* he gathered around him a fraternity, a brotherhood of young, clever, feisty newspeople who still saw themselves in a romantic tradition: hard-drinking, thick-skinned mavericks whose vulgar, profane conduct was a constant rebuke to the forces of respectability. My former managing editor, Al Rogers, calls them "the happy warriors," a fiercely loyal, aggressive band of guerrilla fighters engaged in mortal combat against deceit, conformity, and injustice.

They raged and swore and drank and landed in jail and played the most appalling practical jokes on one another. One Christmas Eve, as John Robertson and Al Rogers were putting the *Tribune* to bed, a story came in about a young man named Oliver who had been stabbed in his vital parts by his wife. Robertson headed it "You Should Have Seen Oliver Twist." Come on, said Rogers, cut the funny stuff and we'll go for a beer. Robertson rewrote it. Later at the press club Rogers casually asked Robertson what he'd written. The headline read: "She Decked the Halls with Balls of Ollie." They dropped their beers and rushed out, tearing down the snowy streets to the *Tribune*'s composing room, where the headline was being set in type. They caught the headline and rewrote it. They were terrible men.

It was, of course, mostly play-acting, an extension of the lewd comedy sketches at the press club's annual Beer and Skits night, social pinnacle of the *Tribune* year. The *Tribune* itself was an eminently respectable newspaper, a community paper, a family paper. Its political reporting was as dull and predictable as the *Free Press*'s; it was big on education, medicine, and community service. No tits and ass in the *Trib*. Even the juicy crimes were buried back of page three. God knows it was smaller than the *Free Press*—80,000 to 126,000 when I was there—thinner, and casual, even chatty in tone. It was obviously Number Two, the brash, aggressive adolescent trying to muscle in on big brother. It was considered the working-class paper. Nobody in Winnipeg really took it seriously, which gave us wonderful freedom. What was there to lose?

I skipped into work like Maggie Muggins disguised as Lois Lane, blissed out by the fact that each day brought new stories, new places, new people, *news!* We worked hard. We could work twenty-four hours a day if we wanted, and sometimes we did. We were paid in praise, which was parsimonious, and the chance to work harder on better stories. I got to be drama critic and television columnist as well as general reporter; I covered everything from Rotary lunches to police court and the Manitoba Legislature. I spent my first summer lurking in the corridor outside the office of Premier Duff Roblin, a man so constipated in his public relations I swear he locked himself in his toilet to avoid me. I felt very young and very dumb. I was. A healthy respect for my own ignorance was the first thing I learned at the *Trib*. A good reporter knows nothing. You ask. You listen. You make sense of it. If you can't make sense of it you keep at it until you do. It was the most valuable lesson of my life.

Maybe that's why Wells hired so many girls. Innocent we were, but curious, hungry. We were babies in the *Tribune* family, spoiled and scolded, dismissed by the old hands with amused contempt, sheltered by the city editor from the indecent predations of the terrible men and the jealousies of the women's editor, from whose red-lacquered clutches we had miraculously escaped. We were loyal to the *Tribune* and it stood by us. Wells fought off the outraged politicians, flacks, and advertisers who went for our heads after a critical story, like the president of the Manitoba Theatre Centre who wanted me sacked for criticizing John Hirsch's productions (Hirsch was a Jew, therefore I was anti-Semitic).

Women reporters—sob sisters, as we used to be called—have always been able to get certain stories more easily than men. The sympathetic smile, the quivering lip, the naive question have traditionally been used to get the grisly story (with photo) of a child's murder out of the sobbing mother or to seduce the straight dope out of hardened criminals, maniacs, and politicians. I'd turn up in a cabinet minister's hotel room at 9 A.M., bright-eyed, pencil poised, perched on the edge of the unmade bed while he slouched nervously in the single chair, eyes glazed, the thought going by like tickertape "Christ, they've sent a *girl!*" When he saw the headline the next day he'd phone up and scream that I'd got it all wrong; I'll bet he remembered nothing but the shape of my thigh.

We were different from the newspaperwomen who had preceded us. We had no tits. It had been customary to measure the talent of female staff members at the *Tribune* by the size of their bra cups: the women's editor was a statuesque 38-D, columnist Ann Henry a stunning 36-triple C. We were all As. We were different

247

in other ways too. We preferred sex to booze. We preferred money to compliments. We preferred a good book to a dull party. We were cool, university-educated daughters of the middle class, confident, ambitious, tougher in many ways than the terrible men, most of whom were grizzly bears with bunny-rabbit hearts. Refugees from marriage and the tedious female professions of school teaching and social work, we weren't there because we needed a job, or knew how to type, or even because we wanted to write: we were looking for excitement, independence, power. We were the first of the formidable feminists.

We scared the hell out of the terrible men. We wanted to change the script. We *had* to change the script. Women were not promoted to editorial positions at the *Tribune*; women were not hired by the Southam Bureau in Ottawa. (One was, briefly: she was the daughter of the president of Southam Press.) What was in it for us? Goody Two-Shoes assignments until we turned into wizened old ladies in flower-pot hats with a shopping bag full of stale buns from Rotary lunches? Superbitch hatchet jobs the men were too crafty to do? It was easy to get sucked into being a hearse-chaser or a vamp; if you're good at it you get to *be* hard-nosed and callous. You get to be one of the boys, like famous *Free Press* agricultural reporter E. Cora Hind who tramped the wheat fields in high leather boots, suit jacket, and Stetson.

That's why the boys drink. It's not just the daily deadline, seeing yesterday's byline in today's garbage can, the isolation of the professional *voyeur*, the humiliation of constant compromises with crass commercialism; it's the daily encounter with pain and sadness, the stupidity, corruption, and horror of human life, the encounter that demands that you leave a little bit of yourself in print for the world to see. News tends to be bad news. It gets you down. Booze provides some forgetfulness; play-acting, like the Dumbells in the First World War, helps shore up the barricades against despair. Despair was as palpable at the *Tribune* as Dafoe's ghost at the *Free Press*.

We all knew the fix was in. The editors never admitted it but there was a gentleman's agreement between the *Tribune* and the *Free Press* to preserve the status quo. The deal had grown out of the emergence of the rival Winnipeg *Citizen* during a bitter printers' strike in the 1940s. The two older papers had pooled their resources to break the strike; they broke the *Citizen* too. The existence of the deal was common gossip around the newsroom. Why else did *Tribune* circulation drives mysteriously peter out when subscriptions started rolling in? Why was the publisher nervous about big, headline-grabbing stories? Why did the *Tribune* remain so conservative, so safe? The answer was simple: the *Free Press* got upset when *Tribune* circulation edged over 80,000; everyone knew that in a circulation war the *Tribune* would lose. Or so they thought. Even the size of the news hole was regulated: 112 daily column inches for the *Free Press*, 108 for the *Tribune*. The managing editor counted them up every afternoon and got shit from the *Free Press* if he was over quota.

The news didn't really matter anyway. Everybody bought the *Free Press* for the classified ads. It was twice as fat as the *Tribune*. A bargain. My family subscribed to both papers for a while, the *Free Press* for the ads, the *Trib* for editorial. Without ads the *Tribune* couldn't increase circulation; it couldn't get ads without bigger circulation. For years the *Tribune* struggled along in a break-even situation with an excellent editorial staff but neither the money nor the management moxie to break out of the bind. Southam Press seemed satisfied with this arrangement.

The news side *was* play-acting, an elaborate charade to convince ourselves that all our talent and hustle really mattered. They didn't. We were just filling in the white space between the ads. The *Tribune* bought a million-dollar press to print the Safeway ads; I was making a hundred a week.

The curtain came down in 1965 with the arrival of a new publisher. Ron Williams was brought in from the Vancouver *Province* to clean up the *Tribune*. He was very keen on cleanliness, Ron Williams. Our copy had to be clean. Our desks had to be clean. *We* had to be clean. No long hair. No dirty shirts. No booze in the office. He issued the management little red vests with brass buttons to wear, like used car salesmen. Our minds had to be clean. One of his first acts was to send those editors who wished to a weekend course on psychocybernetics, a trendy scam run by a fly-by-night snake-oil salesman on Dale Carnegie principles. So here they were, these tough old buggers with the fried-egg eyes, standing in front of the mirror in their little red vests with brass buttons, smiling and saying to themselves, "Every day in every way I'm getting better and better." Like hell.

Clean minds made clean news. No more shit-disturbing. "Everything merry and bright," the city editor used to chirp cynically at us in the morning. The *Tribune* was going to be a Good News paper, a community booster, a force for moral rectitude, which was another of Williams's enthusiasms. He had countless enthusiasms and saw no reason why he shouldn't use the *Tribune* to promote them. "I'll put what *I* like in this paper!" he'd yell at the editors. He'd tear through the

249

newsroom several times a week waving something he'd just clipped out of *Life* or *Reader's Digest*, bellowing "Hey, this is great! Let's do this!" One of his ideas was a massive photo series on the smelly smokestacks of Winnipeg. The photographer stuck his camera out the *Tribune* window at one of Winnipeg's biggest, smelliest smokestacks, which just happened to have a big, black "E" for Eaton's on it. That was the end of that.

Like Mr. Clean, Williams was everywhere. He wrote editorials. He redesigned the office. He spent six months tinkering with the masthead. He wrote cutlines. He told the photographers how to print and crop their pictures and, on occasion, what to take: during the blizzard of March 4, 1966, he spotted some kids with cardboard boxes over their heads and insisted the *Tribune* get a photo. For all I know he sold the ads and swept the press room. He was inconsistent, unpredictable, interfering, a man of great charm and terrific rages who had us all nervous, angry, and miserable within weeks. Sure we'd done our share of puff pieces, flack stories, "publisher's pets," but we'd been taught to treat them with contempt. Suddenly fluff and flackery were to be the very stuff of the *Tribune*. When an advertiser sneezed, a hurricane blew through the newsroom.

250   The crunch came when the introduction of the new Canada Pension Plan increased reporters' anxieties about their financial security. Could they get their money out of the old *Tribune* pension? they asked Eric Wells. Wells told them they could. Fearing a run on the treasury, management told Wells to shut up. As long as he kept quiet, Wells was told, he and other senior editors would be allowed to take their own money out of the fund. It was the last straw. Eric Wells quit. Alan Rogers quit. Half the copy rim quit. Most department heads quit or were fired. The brotherhood was smashed; those who hung on were frightened or sad. The happy war was lost. It was the end of the terrible men. It was the beginning of corporate journalism. I quit.

The *Tribune* got cleaner and cleaner. Shorter stories. More white space. Big pictures. Big type. Contests. Gimmicks. Simple news. It looked like a colouring book. Circulation dropped from 85,000 under Wells to 69,000. By 1975 the *Tribune* was on the ropes. The plan appeared clear: to merge the *Tribune* and *Free Press* along the lines of the Vancouver *Sun* and *Province*. Ron Williams had other ideas.

Williams, to his credit, was not a gentleman. He was a fighter. He persuaded Southam to fight it out. His weapon—free personal classified ads. In deepest secrecy the *Tribune* was dramatically redesigned. A Toronto ad agency was hired to do a saturation media promotion; Southam agreed to put up about $5 million over five years to cover the cost. It was a smash hit. One day in November 1975, *Tribune* circulation broke 100,000.

But by the end of 1979 the *Tribune* had been stopped in its tracks. The *Free Press* dumped Malone and came up with a sexy new design and circulation drive. In June 1979, *Free Press* circulation peaked at 153,000. It has levelled off at about 141,000, still 35,000 more than the *Tribune*. The *Trib* is still Number Two by almost the same margin as in 1965.

The papers look flatulent but familiar, a couple of maiden aunts who have gained an alarming amount of weight. Both Saturday editions weigh in at a pound-and-a-half, and total a hundred pages, not counting flyers, funnies, and supplements. One has dyed her hair. One has had a facelift. Their big, smudgy colour photos only remind me of the pathetic old news hen with smeared lipstick at the *Free Press*. The *Free Press* is still fighting the Cold War: the *Tribune* is still running headlines like "City Suffering Great Decline in Cleanliness." Still merry and bright. Still no tits and ass in the *Tribune*. No investigative reporting either. The market survey that formed the ideological base for the reborn *Tribune* revealed that Winnipeggers considered the old paper to be chintzy and bland; they wanted more variety, more controversy, more hard news—precisely those things Williams had dumped with such enthusiasm in 1966. They got "Lifestyle" instead; it's hard to burp in Winnipeg without being the subject of a full-length, in-depth interview in the *Trib*.

The editorial staff at the *Tribune* has increased from seventy to ninety-five, but it still forms less than one-third of the total staff. The news hole has doubled, but most of that extra space is taken up by wire copy from New York and Hollywood—even book reviews are taken off the wire. Some wire stories in both papers appear one to seven days later than in Toronto. The bulk of the news is soft: cooking, entertainment, horoscopes, Ann Landers. The *Tribune* is still superb at local coverage; the *Free Press* has a better international news sense. Both have gone heavily into columnists whose opinions range from middle-right to middle-left. One *Trib* columnist has been writing for the paper for fifty years. Weddings, written up in painstaking detail by the bride's mother, are still big news in Winnipeg; a good obit will run ten inches, with photo.

Underneath the makeup and the silicone implants the formula, like Mae West, is the same. Eric Wells calls it "the oppressive hangover of looking for things considered important rather than interesting. That heavy hand of 'what's important' which the news desk tried to counterbalance with goofy yarns about nudist camps and Christmas cheer was the curse of newspapers in my day, and basically that trite formula hasn't changed. Sure, we get some good stories, but there is no sign of news judgment in the load of lard that just goes in automatically. And you won't find any newspaper willing to do something about it."

Reporters at both papers are unionized now, although the *Free Press* is still stonewalling on a contract. Wages are equal for men and women. A reporter starts at almost $300 a week, plus overtime. The *Tribune* staff is keen, hardworking, professional. They drop in at the press club occasionally, sip a single drink, and scoot off home at five o'clock. They read books and go to plays and build sailboats in their basements. They worry about pensions and seniority. They don't write "She Decked the Halls with Balls of Ollie." The editor wouldn't appreciate a practical joke. She is young and formidable.

Where are the terrible men? Some of them have gone into television, raking in big bucks as hosts and pundits, anchormen and investigative journalists. They've dried out. They drink Perrier water. They've lost weight. They jog. They've quit smoking. They ski. They write books. They don't screw around. Some have found God. Some have found Joe Clark.

Some are still out there, scattered across the country, ornery as ever, noses twitching at the scent of bullshit, stubborn, smart, rude, still fighting after all these years. Here's to them.

Part Three:

Uprootedness & Family

Baba Was a Bohunk

MYRNA KOSTASH

In memoir-writing, the search for family is often the search for self. In Canadian memoir-writing particularly, the quest is often bound up with the immigrant experience—either the writer's own or that of some not-too-distant kin. Myrna Kostash (b. 1944) has written a number of acclaimed and highly personal books on social and political issues, starting with *All of Baba's Children* (1977): a piece of reportage about Ukrainian-Canadians that seems to have grown out of this memoir, published in *Saturday Night* the previous year. Her most recent books are *The Doomed Bridegroom: A Memoir* (1999), and *The Next Canada: In Search of Our Future Nation* (2000). She lives in Edmonton where she was born.

There are ways in which my grandmother and I are more like each other than either of us is like the generation between us—my parents, her children. Baba is incontestably Ukrainian or "Galician," as she called herself in 1914 when she came to Canada—it took the combined efforts of Old World intelligentsia and Ukrainian-Orthodox priests and her own Canadian-born children to persuade her to discard the provincial designation "Galician" and adopt the nationalist "Ukrainian." And I am a Canadian. Unhyphenated. She has acquired enough English to make her way with shopkeepers, bus drivers, and me. I have sponged up enough Ukrainian to be courteous with priests, great-aunts, and her. We share a mutual but mystified curiosity about the conditions in which the other was bred and a respectful astonishment that the hardship and bedevilment of the one life underlie the jubilation and ease of the other, mine. We are tourists in each other's history, and conduct ourselves accordingly. In each other's country, we do not try to pass as natives.

With the generation between us it's a different story. Baba's children went to school with heavy accents (the short English "e" was consistently pronounced as the broad Ukrainian "a" so Edmonton became Admonton), and came back home memorizing lines from the Alexandra Readers about Empire, British manliness, and the duties of a good citizen in a democracy. Parent and child had to co-exist, but what was the one to make of the other? Baba grew up illiterate under a regime of Polish landlords, believing in the efficacy of prayer and garlic against mundane evils and in the hopelessness of protesting an arranged marriage with a fellow villager who had already left for Canada and built himself a house to contain her. Now she was raising children who learned not only algebra and grammar but also notions of racial inferiority and cultural shame. If her children ecstatically waved the Union Jack at the parade of George VI and Elizabeth, and identified passionately with the Duke of Wellington, it was not so much out of positive acceptance of Anglo-Saxon virtues as out of negative repudiation of their parents' Slavic character, deemed unworthy.

It would have been impossible for the immigrants to protest: they had learned servile behaviour in the oppressively feudal Old Country. And there was a sense of insecurity in the New, where an alien could—by a flip of the Immigration Act—be deported for subversive or immoral behaviour, or even for being too poor. No, Baba bit her tongue and kept her own counsel even when Canadians ran behind her in the street bleating at her back (she still wore a sheepskin coat), even when her children sat around the dinner table teaching her table manners and talking to each other in English, making her a stranger in her own kitchen. But, she reminded herself, she had come here to grubstake an economic existence. Its indignities, she felt, would ultimately be cancelled out by the financial gains of her children as they made the transition from peasant to lower middle class. And if lack of respect for her Galician habits and reflexes was the penalty she had to pay, she would pay it.

However, it wasn't a simple "lack of respect" that was confounding the children. All but the most opportunistic and craven of them endured a muddle of loyalties and an agony of appraisal symbolized by the hyphen-shaft of dual identity. On the one hand, their sense of decency and their sentiments showed them that Baba was the salt of the earth. She worked hard for little. She always fed and clothed them ("We may be poor but we're clean"). She encouraged their intellectual appetites even while she continued to console herself with superstitions and proverbs delivered in an ungrammatical version of the Ukrainian language. She formed part of the horde of European peasants without whom there would have been no economy on the prairies except for the Hudson's Bay Company, native hunters, and the CPR. For all these things, Baba was to be respected and admired. And so she was, sooner or later.

On the other hand, on the other hand. The children also knew that in exchange for the good fortune of being Canadian-born they were expected to do the decent thing and anglicize themselves. If the native-born Canadians tolerated the sudden influx of European peasants and all their strangeness, it was only because within a few years the whole tribe was sure to assimilate and be indistinguishable from the law-abiding, orderly, and Protestant Anglo-Saxon Canadians who represented the acme of Western culture. Even the redoubtable J.S. Woodsworth, future founder of a socialist party, was moved in 1909 to confess in his book *Strangers Within Our Gates* that "the idea of a homogeneous people seems in accord with our democratic institutions and conducive to the general welfare."

Assimilation was a loaded proposition, however. For one became "English" only through a process of defining "un-English" as bad, disgusting, and unstable. The trick for Baba's children was somehow to appear to be "English" in spite of the accent, the funny clothes, the so-called unpronounceable name, the childhood memories of Ukrainian food and music and festivals. So they polished up their English, changed their names, joined the United Church, moved out of Eastern European ghettoes and into suburbs, and ate turkey on December 25, just like everybody else. For this chameleon's talent they were appropriately rewarded: they could enter the bottom of the middle class.

This was it, then, Baba's raison d'être: to raise sons and daughters who would become teachers in one-room schools outside the cities, grain buyers in Ukrainian-speaking villages, and butchers in ethnic districts of the city. The hyphenated Canadians who became lawyers, doctors, and professors were the exceptions that proved the rule: the fuss made about them within the ethnic community was fantastic.

And then an interesting thing happened. It became obvious to these models of a success appropriate to their hyphenated status that in spite of all their attempts to "pass" as average citizens, the real power and influence in the country still resided with the Anglo-Saxon elite. It became obvious that nobody in this elite had ever been fooled into thinking Baba's children were anything but the second-class progeny of bohunks. At that point, the children became hostile. In their chagrin and disappointment, they defiantly resurrected the left-hand side of the hyphen. The Ukrainian-Canadian was born. And the subculture of ethnicity took off.

257

It was fuelled by a number of noisy intellectuals who had refused, throughout the pioneering era, to take their lumps as second-class citizens. As lawyers, members of legislatures and Parliament, schoolteachers, and newspaper men and women (in the ethnic press), they had consistently urged their compatriots to insist on their rights as *Ukrainian*-Canadians and not as some soulless, assimilated facsimile of an Anglo-Saxon. They had pressured the Establishment to open its ranks to the non-WASPs instead of keeping them huddled among the farmers and proletariat. These spokesmen were invariably polite and suggestive rather than nasty and aggressive in their demands, but they *were* sticking out their necks while all about them were meekly blending into the Anglicized woodwork. They are now vindicated, in their terms at least, by the next generation, which is middle class and acceptable while also observing the Ukrainian holidays and keeping their last names intact.

You have a right, those intellectuals argued, to both upward mobility *and* ethnic identity. But in the process of upward mobility the Ukrainian *as* Ukrainian vanished, to be replaced by someone like me: someone socialized by Anglo-American institutions, with English as a mother tongue, with culture and values vastly more dependent on what my generation is doing from Vancouver to London than on the past accomplishments of desperate muzhiks and Cossacks along the Dnipro some time ago. I have to ask that first generation of hyphenates: now that I'm successfully Canadian—a condition you demanded for me—how on earth can I also be Ukrainian? Is eating *pyrohy* and claiming William Kurelek as one of "ours" all it takes? If you mean something deeper, why are you so intent on being so innocuously colourful?

In this "ethnic revival," this cavalcade of pseudo-folkloric forms and sentimentalized rituals, the ethnics have received considerable support from the very elite they are reacting against, particularly from the Liberal government. So one has always to ask who and what are really being served by the revival. One has, in other words, to remain skeptical of the ethnics' claim that in their picturesqueness they are resisting the Anglo-Saxon hegemony even while the Anglo-Saxon is signing the cheques that make the multicultural extravaganza possible.

Ukrainian Day at the Vegreville Ukrainian Festival, sixty miles east of Edmonton in the middle of a densely Ukrainian district. I have been ten years away from this sort of intramural celebration, and I notice some changes. When I was a girl, I had been sometimes embarrassed by my ethnic origins. "Greek," I would say to

my friends, "I'm Greek," unwittingly reproducing a hierarchy of ethnic undesirables in which, to my mind at least, Greeks were less undesirable than Ukrainians.
I would have said I was German, if I could have gotten away with it. In those
days, what we did as an ethnic collective to remind each other where we came
from was purely an introspective and almost covert act. A series of ritualized
encounters—dance, song, poetry, speeches—in the church basement with none
but ourselves as witnesses and consumers. The fact that the rituals were incom-
prehensible to an outsider was the very essence of the act, and the exclusive use
of the Ukrainian language was evidence of that introversion. It occurred to me,
years later, that since I didn't understand the language very well either, I too was
systematically excluded, along with non-Ukrainians, from socialization into these
Ukrainian mysteries. This more than anything marked the gap between first- and
second-generation Canadians.

So, in Vegreville, in 1975, I, second-generation Ukrainian-Canadian, socialized Anglo-American, English-French bilingualist, confronted a festival organized
from the consciousness of the first generation. I was amazed. It was obvious that
the first generation had grown more self-confident, not to say boastful, and was
now assuming that the Ukrainian-Canadian "fact" was of interest to all Albertans.
No more church basements for them; the festival was held at the exhibition
grounds. It was this generation which had erected last summer a monstrous, aluminum *pysanka* (decorated Easter egg) near the Yellowhead Highway in Vegreville,
and dedicated it to the RCMP. (How short their memories are: it was the police
who had broken up their hunger marches in the 1930s, closed down their
Ukrainian-language concerts, spied on them in their Labour-Farmer Temples.) It
was these same people who had scattered throughout Vegreville signs in shop windows saying "Vitayemo," meaning "Welcome," and innumerable plastic and china
knick-knacks decorated with Ukrainian motifs. They operated concession booths at
the festival selling *kubassa*-on-a-stick and T-shirts emblazoned with "Drink Molson's
Ukrainian" and "Kiss me, I'm Ukrainian." The message seemed to be that anybody
could be a Ukrainian; it was implicit that somebody would *want* to.

As it turned out, however, the message was only teasing. For the core of the
program was the content familiar to me from twenty years ago when Ukrainians
were a *racial* tribe. The mysteries were the same, with few concessions to the fact
that now there were fewer than ever pioneers in the crowd and many more third
and fourth generation Canadians (the 1971 census lists 580,660 Canadians of
Ukrainian origin). Use of the Ukrainian language among the young is limited to

259

"Hello, how are you?" for Baba's benefit; their use of the culture amounts to changing out of blue jeans and into ethnic costume because the dancing is fun and easy to learn. The "National Hymn" was announced and I was taken by surprise that it wasn't "O Canada" they sang but the European (and pre-Bolshevik) anthem, "The Ukraine is Still Not Dead." In fact, I was impatient with this, and my impatience escalated to irritation when references in speeches from the MC and the Alberta minister of education to the "mother tongue" were to Ukrainian, not English.

I watched this sea of Ukrainian-Canadians singing mightily, meaningfully, the patriotic anthem of a country they have never seen, and which, since their parents' departure, has become a Soviet Republic. Their nostalgia is for a Ukraine where peasants in gorgeously embroidered, hand-woven linen shirts and bright red boots eat *pyrohy* under thatched roofs. Where they tremulously take their braided bread to the priest for blessing, respect their elders, detest the Jew and the Catholic Pole (tavern-keeper and landlord, respectively), and die, uncomplaining, in a slaughter or famine. Or so they would have me believe through their anthems and icons, their eulogies and dedications. And if it wasn't like that, why don't they tell me the truth?

The fact is, none of them really knows. They are Canadian by birth and experience, and their nostalgic zeal is not meant to function as history but as mythology. They were raised and socialized within a racist society whose message was that Slavic farmers and their families were "yokels." A columnist in the Vegreville *Observer* wrote: "In view of their education, ideas, moral standards, and mode of life, we justly regard them as inferiors. We are not prepared to be bossed by them … and it is unlikely that white men in this Province will stand for it," thereby raising the proposition: the Ukrainian as nigger. As objects of slander, they did the psychologically normal thing. They revised their past so they'd look better to the ruling class. This had its happy side effects: it instilled a racial pride where there had been apology, a sense of worth and a community where there had been self-disgust and alienation. It offered a position from which to dispute the calumny of Anglo-Saxon bigots.

But it performed a disservice as well. For one thing, it gave the lie to the experience of the pioneers who left Europe precisely because their lives there were intolerable, squeezed mercilessly between landlord and priest, between service in the imperialist's army and service for a pittance on his land. They left because they were hungry and crowded and had no pasture for cows or acres to inherit;

they had to scrounge for firewood and, according to some accounts, gave precious food to the priest who, overladen with such gifts, tossed it to his pigs.

It gave the lie, as well, to their Canadian experience, for the mythologizing process extended forward to the history of what happened to them in the New World. They were in a double bind. On the one hand, they prettified their European past in order to maintain dignity in the face of racism. On the other hand, they had also to dress up their Canadian experiences in order not to be further oppressed for making trouble about the very conditions they were protesting.

It was a touchy situation for them, in the 1930s for example, when the Depression hit only a few years after they had achieved a modicum of economic security as farmers. Their first five years as homesteaders had been gruelling, with the man usually away half the year working on the railroad or in coal mines to earn some cash for the oxen and plow and seed, the woman and children left on the land to feed themselves, somehow, and to ward off illness and staggering loneliness. By the time the husband returned to work the land, his family had already cleared an acre or two by hand, and the first crop could be sown. Inch by inch the bush was beaten back, the oxen traded for horses, the sod hut abandoned for a two-room log house. In the meantime, women died in childbirth, children died of diphtheria, men were killed in accidents—the nearest doctor was still too far away—crops were lost to early frost and creditors, Ukrainian-speaking teachers were dismissed by the department of education, male relatives (holding Austrian passports) were interned in camps during the First World War, and daughters were sent off to town to work as housekeepers in well-to-do homes. During the Depression, the Communist Party was disproportionately successful in organizing among non-Anglo-Saxon farmers and labourers through groups like the Ukrainian Labour and Farmer Temple Association, and Ukrainian communities in Alberta like Myrnam and Hairy Hill and Two Hills mounted several farmers' strikes and hunger marches. During the Second World War, Ukrainian Communists like John Boychuk and Matthew Popovich were arrested and imprisoned for "seditious activity," and ULFTA halls were shut down.

I make a point of listing these catastrophes because, parallel with them, was a consistent attempt on the part of some of the Ukrainian-Canadian intelligentsia to muffle the complaints and disguise the rebelliousness of their compatriots. English-speaking citizens were assured that the Ukrainians were rapidly and enthusiastically becoming assimilated, as in the speech of the lawyer, George Szkwarok,

261

to a Rotary Club in 1930: the Ukrainian-Canadians "will like your ways and customs, and they will assimilate them if they find them good. They will abandon their own if they are bad. They will learn of your ideals and will follow them," etc. In 1928 a federal member of Parliament, Michael Luchkovich, blamed the economic problems of his constituents not on their vulnerability to the excesses of capitalism but on their lack of character: "I have seen many run up a debt and then leave their farms because they would not live within their means. True patriotism, I insist again, also includes persistence and frugality even under trying circumstances." And my own great-uncle, a community leader and pedagogue, wrote in the Vegreville *Observer*: "We hear quite often that Ukrainians do not respect the law of this country ... If they do fight, assault or murder anyone it would be their own countryman, as they have great respect for the English or any other people." (But not, presumably, for their own.)

The self-hatred implied in these statements is painful. So is the transparent self-abnegation in assurances that Ukrainians "did not care for their own comfort," that centuries-long exploitation made them, not seditious, but "enduring, self-reliant, hard-working, and thrifty" and that, in the words of an amateur poet, Michael Gowda:

> A new horizon opens to our eyes
> Majestic vistas spread from shore to shore
> Our new-found home in a new promised land
> With freedom bordered and fair justice bound.

One struggles to imagine the pressures brought to bear on these people to deny in such sycophantic prose what was as plain as the nose on their face: that immigrants and the children of immigrants had to sweat and heave against exploitation for every penny of their prosperity and that, denied it, not a few would fight for it. One begins to understand such "patriotism" as a survival tactic, a manoeuvre to deflect the repressive reflexes of the ruling classes against the grumbling mass.

So, watching them last summer in Vegreville sing and dance and speechify— "Such days as today are very valuable for the patriotism of this country. You should first of all be the best possible Canadians and express thanks and gratitude to this country"—I wondered if this process were still in effect. Are declarations of Canadian patriotism still a political necessity for ethnics? Further: where are the art forms and contents, after all these years in Canada, that reflect the Canadian experience? Why are teenagers in 1975 still dancing the Arkan and reciting poems about the Motherland ("Ridna Maty Moya") and singing ditties about linden trees they've never seen?

The explanation is that the Establishment came under pressure during the 1960s from various dispossessed groups, including "ethnics," to spread its power around. In response, the federal government concocted multiculturalism for the verbal and articulate ethnic middle class as a make-believe participation in power-broking and a sweetener to help bilingualism go down. So we put on our costumes and invite John Munro to deliver his homilies about our "cultural and spiritual values" and make demands for Ukrainian-English bilingualism on the grounds of a fallacious comparison with Quebec, believing miraculously that such actions somehow decrease the distance between us and the board of directors of Capitalist Enterprises, Inc. Now that we are securely assimilated into our appropriate slot in the vertical mosaic—now that, in our habits and speech and values, we are indistinguishable from the mass of Canadians—it's no skin off the Establishment's collective butt to toss us a few dollars for a festival. We're so cute in our getups!

We see ourselves that way, too. Ask most Ukrainian-Canadians why they are proud of their heritage and they'll respond with a list of folk arts—Easter eggs, cross-stitch embroidery, cabbage rolls, the *kolomeyka* dance—which are characteristically described as "colourful" by a society inured to the tedium of assembly-line artifacts and metropolitan-based mass-culture. The ethnic as aesthetic relief.

There is an irony here, and it is that the skills displayed by these folk arts are themselves largely a product of North American, middle-class lifestyle; no peasant woman, either in the Ukraine or frontier Alberta, had the time or energy to spend on infinitesimally patterned eggs or microscopically embroidered clothes or laboriously braided breads. No work-exhausted farmers had the leisure to create choreographed dances or five-part harmonies. One must assume that what we take to be the popular arts of the Ukrainians of all classes and generations are in fact either the crafts of the Old World burgher class or the contrived and intellectualized products of a self-conscious Canadian middle class with the benefit of education and leisure time.

Ethnicity, then, is homage to a variety of icons, emblems of who we imagine ourselves to have been and are no longer. Ethnic culture as a hobby. Aluminum Easter eggs, cross-stitched tea cosies, *holubsi* dished up in a drive-in restaurant: surely these aren't signs of an indigenous culture crafted from our experience within the stewing pot of native, nomadic European-peasant, and

Anglo-Saxon-urban ways of life. They seem rather to be transplants grafted artificially onto a stem of nostalgia, cut off from its sources and able to survive only as a carnival souvenir.

It has all happened so fast. On the prairie, lifestyles barely evolved disintegrate at shocking speed. Within the space of ninety years our history has included the incarceration of the Indians, the surveying of land into quarter-sections, the cultivation of virgin sod, the erection of log buildings, churches, and grain elevators, the laying down of track and spur-lines, the closing down of spur-lines, the abandonment of log buildings, churches, and grain elevators, the overlaying of cultivated soil with cement, and the subdivision of quarter-sections into suburban developments. The people who dug holes in the ground as their first shelter here and walked fifty miles to Edmonton to get flour are still alive, living in high-rise old-age homes and shopping at supermarkets.

I grew up in Edmonton, my father on a homestead. The speed with which the transition was made from pre- to post-industrial culture shows up in the pile of rubble that marks the place where he was born. The farm is a ruin, a northern parkland version of a postbellum Louisiana plantation.

The road into the barnyard is a horror of weeds, a treacherous path of nettle and thistle. The barn is still there but, oh, such a modest, insecure structure compared to the cavernous building I remember! The loft into which my father and uncles pitched bales of hay is filtered through with sunlight. Barn swallows pass in and out through holes, and mice are at home. The roadway from the barn to the fields, down which they drove the team of Clydesdales, has reverted now to the prairie it was hacked from. The pathway from the barn to the house is so overgrown with bush that we make our way through it now like Stanley to Livingstone. The house burned down several years ago, after having been looted of junk that passes now for antiques. The site is grassed over. Somewhere to the right, under the bushes, is where the garden and flowers used to grow. Some of the perennials still bloom. To the left are the pig sheds, collapsed in their middles, a mess of weather-beaten wood, silent, hidden, and unregarded.

In one generation the materials of daily existence have become obsolete and unrecognizable. At the Shandro Ukrainian Pioneer Museum I had to ask the elderly warden over and over again, "What is this? What was it used for?" as he handled the churns, flails, spindles, and sheaf cleaners. They would have been familiar to my ancestors two hundred years ago. Fifty years after their manufacture, they are mysterious to me.

The graves I've seen: Marx, Dumont, El Cid, and now also the resting place of antecedents who came and went with nothing to mark their adventure except tombstones with their photographs sealed into the cross—stone-faced old ladies and jaunty, middle-aged men standing cross-legged in hats and old men posed defensively in front of their log houses. "This is me, this is where I was alive, and this was my condition"—while a mile down the road the homestead decomposes. Well, it's what they came here for. The disappearance of their generation and all its works into merely nostalgic memorializing is a measure of the success they've had in sidetracking their descendants from the land, as much from the CPR quarter as from the *kolkhoz*. One should then perhaps be more indulgent about the sentimentality surrounding their sacrifice: heaven forbid that the ethnic should be an ingrate.

Running in the Family

MICHAEL ONDAATJE

One of Canada's most prized writers domestically and internationally, Michael Ondaatje was born in 1943 in what was then Ceylon and is now Sri Lanka, where his family, a mixture of Tamil, Dutch, and Singhalese, played an eccentric role in the colourful local society. Or so Ondaatje portrays them in his fictionally crafted 1982 book *Running in the Family*, which the writer, in a note to the text, describes as "not a history but a portrait or 'gesture'"—in other words, a memoir. Ondaatje, a poet and novelist, lives in Toronto.

WHAT WE THINK OF MARRIED LIFE

TEA COUNTRY

"The thing about Mum was—she was a terrifically social person. And he came down to Colombo and swooped her up and took her to the tea estate. OK. They were in love, happy with each other, they had kids. But later there was nothing for her to do there."

Tea country. The sleepy green landscape that held her captive. And now, forty years later, in early May, on the verge of monsoon weather, I have come here to visit my half-sister Susan and her husband Sunil. The green pattern of landscape and lifestyle almost unchanged.

The one-hundred-mile drive from Colombo took us five hours. The gearshift was giving trouble, the horn was fading, and the engine heated up so fast we had to stop every twenty minutes to cool off and refill the radiator. We came along a road that climbed five thousand feet in thirty miles. Eventually the transmission broke in second gear, and the last miles were driven praying we wouldn't have to stop, not for oncoming trucks and buses, not for the numerous May Day parades along the mountain roads. The car stalled a mile away from the house and we walked under the thunderclouds that made the dark tea bushes brighter, through the lines of pluckers, Sunil carrying his Colombo whisky and Susan and I some bags of food.

In a wet shirt and with a headache it was good to walk. Twenty degrees cooler up here than in Colombo. And a sourceless light that seems to brighten the landscape from underneath, as if yellow flowers in the garden are leaking into wet air. Dampness hangs over the house, while three of us and one servant rattle around this huge long bungalow from which all furniture has been sent to be upholstered save for a few cane chairs, and where the loudest noise is the excited breathing of two dogs.

An hour later I am standing in the hall with Susan when I hear a pistol shot. Blue waves of flame. The house—hit by lightning, hit at the fuse box on the wall just above my head. I am so shaken I act calmly for the rest of the afternoon. Lightning has never touched this house before even though, perched on top of a tea estate, it seems an obvious target. The bolt is a signal for the end of quietness and the weather bursts open windows and steps into hallways. During the long evening we play scrabble, shouting out scores, almost unable to be heard over the stereophonic field of the rain.

We wake to a silence. Now the long quiet mornings. Susan moves up and down halls to the kitchens, organizing meals, reorganizing after the chaos of the first monsoon storm (burned out fuse boxes, knocked down telephone wires, chicken wires, dismantled gardens).

The dining-room doors open to the wet lawn and the francisco bushes. Their blossoms, like torn blue and white paper, release perfume into this room. When the dogs bark, eight or so parakeets swerve out of the guava tree and disappear over the cliff of the hill. Across the valley, a waterfall stumbles down. In a month or two the really hard rains will come for eighteen hours a day and that waterfall will once again become tough as a glacier and wash away the road. But now it looks as delicate as the path of a white butterfly in a long-exposed photograph.

I can leave this table, walk ten yards out of the house, and be surrounded by versions of green. The most regal green being the tea bush which is regal also in its symmetrical efficient planting. Such precision would be jungle in five years if left alone. In the distance the tea pickers move, in another silence, like an army.

The roads weave and whorl away—bright yellow under the grey sky. The sun, invisible, struggles up somewhere. This is the colour of landscape, this is the silence, that surrounded my parents' marriage.

"WHAT WE THINK OF MARRIED LIFE"

She is very gentle, Susan, my half-sister. Almost utterly humble. So sitting here with Susan and Sunil I find myself surprised they are younger than me. She has this calmness and quietness as opposed to the anger and argument that I see in myself, my brother, and two sisters.

I have been thinking that if she has Ondaatje blood and no Gratiaen blood then obviously it is from my mother's side that we got a sense of the dramatic, the tall stories, the determination to now and then hold the floor. The ham in us. While from my father, in spite of his temporary manic public behaviour, we got our sense of secrecy, the desire to be reclusive.

My father loved books and so did my mother, but my father swallowed the heart of books and kept that knowledge and emotion to himself. My mother read her favourite poems out loud, would make us read plays together and acted herself, even running a small dance and theatre school that people still remember in Colombo. Her reading out loud demanded the whole room, and while young her grace and dancing caught everyone's attention. Later it was her voice, her stories with that husky wheezing laugh that almost drowned out the punchlines. She belonged to a type of Ceylonese family whose women would take the minutest reaction from another and blow it up into a tremendously exciting tale, then later use it as an example of someone's strain of character. If anything kept their generation alive it was this recording by exaggeration. Ordinary tennis matches would be mythologized to the extent that one player was so drunk that he almost died on the court. An individual would be eternally remembered for one small act that in five years had become so magnified he was just a footnote below it. The silence of the tea estates and no doubt my mother's sense of theatre and romance (fed by vociferous readings of J. M. Barrie and Michael Arlen) combined the edited delicacies of fiction with the last era of a colonial Ceylon.

My father's actions were minimal and more private. Although he tormented his own father's rules of decorum he simultaneously and almost secretly valued the elements of honour and gentleness. He reportedly couldn't stand his mother-in-law, Lalla, for what he saw as her crudeness, although the stories about my

269

father are closer in style to those about Lalla than anyone else. While we used to love rushing around the house and estate at Lalla's insistence to catch the dog Chindit, who had run off with her false breast, my father would retire to a book or his office acutely embarrassed. Either that, or, and of this we were never sure, he would secretly train the dog to torment his mother-in-law by such acts. We know he encouraged Chindit to fart whenever possible in her vicinity and by raising his eyebrows would surreptitiously make us feel it was she who made us recoil to the other end of the room.

My father's dramatic nature pleased only himself and sometimes the four of us. Or he would tell a hilarious joke in everyone's presence that would convulse just my mother and himself.

My mother loved, *always* loved, even in her last years long after their divorce, his secretive and slightly crooked humour. It bound them together probably more than anything. They were in a world to themselves, genial with everyone but sharing a code of humour. And if there was to be drama in their lives my father preferred it to be just between the two of them. My mother on the other hand would somehow select the one action that would be remembered by everyone in the vicinity of the tea estate and would reach Colombo in twenty-four hours. On one of the last occasions that my mother left my father, after the tirade that was brief, loud, alcoholically one-sided, she told him she was leaving him at 11 P.M. She bundled us all up and, after my father grabbed the car key and threw it into the darkness of a hundred tea bushes, she got four servants and with each of us on a pair of shoulders, marched off through tea estate and dense jungle in utter darkness to a neighbouring home five miles away.

It was she who instilled theatre in all of us. She was determined that we would each be as good an actor as she was. Whenever my father would lapse into one of his alcoholic states, she would send the three older children (I would be asleep—too young, and oblivious) into my father's room where by now he could hardly talk let alone argue. The three of them, well-coached, would perform with tears streaming, "Daddy, don't drink, daddy, if you love us, don't drink," while my mother waited outside and listened. My father, I hope, too far gone to know the extent of the wars against him. These moments embarrassed my older brother and sister terribly; for days after they felt guilty and miserable. Gillian, the youngest of the three, threw herself with eagerness into these one-act plays and when they returned to the living room my mother would pat her on the back and say, "Well done Gillian—you were by *far* the best."

Her motive was to cure my father of manic alcoholic consumption. Those were moments of total war as far as she was concerned. During all the months of soberness the two of them were equals, very close and full of humour, but in his moments of darkness she drew on every play she had been in or had read and used it as a weapon, knowing that when my father sobered up this essentially shy man would be appalled to hear how my mother had overreacted. Her behaviour in his drunken moments was there to shock him in his times of gentleness when he loved muted behaviour. Whatever plays my mother acted in publicly were not a patch on the real-life drama she directed and starred in during her married life. If Mervyn was to humiliate her she could embarrass him by retaliating with some grand gesture—whether it was a celebrated walk through the jungle or actually holding her breath until she fainted at the Kitulgala resthouse when she saw him beginning to drink too much, so that he had to stop and drive her home.

His victories came when he was sober. Then he would discover some outrageous thing she had done and begin to mend fences. Within a week, by his charm and wit, he would have made my mother's behaviour more ludicrous than his— a bomb to disturb a butterfly, till he seemed the more sane of the two. In this way an incident, which most had felt could never be surmounted and which no doubt would destroy the marriage, was cemented over. Rather than being jealous, my mother was never happier and for the next six months or so they were delightful company, wonderful parents. And then with the first drink, after which he could almost never stop, the wars would begin again.

Finally, when it all came to an end, she played her last scene with him. She arrived at the divorce court in a stunning white dress and hat (she had never worn a hat in her life before) and calmly asked for a divorce, demanding no alimony— nothing for her and nothing for the children. She got a job at The Grand Oriental Hotel, trained herself as a housekeeper-manager and supported us through schools by working in hotels in Ceylon and then England till she died. The easy life of the tea estate and the theatrical wars were over. They had come a long way in fourteen years from being the products of two of the best known and wealthiest families in Ceylon; my father now owning only a chicken farm at Rock Hill, my mother working in a hotel.

Before my mother left for England in 1949 she went to a fortune teller who predicted that while she would continue to see each of her children often for the rest of her life, she would never see them all together again. This turned out to be true. Gillian stayed in Ceylon with me, Christopher and Janet went to England.

I went to England, Christopher went to Canada, Gillian came to England, Janet went to America, Gillian returned to Ceylon, Janet returned to England, I went to Canada. Magnetic fields would go crazy in the presence of more than three Ondaatjes. And my father. Always separate until he died, away from us. The north pole.

DIALOGUES

(I)

"Once he nearly killed us. Not you. But the three older children. He was driving the Ford and he was drunk and taking the corners with great swerves— and you know those upcountry roads. We began by cheering but soon we were terrified. Yelling at him to stop. Finally on one corner he almost went off the cliff. Two wheels had gone over the edge and the car hung there caught on the axle. Below us was a terrific plunge down the mountainside. We were in the back seat and once we calmed down, we looked in the front seat and saw that Daddy was asleep. He had passed out. But to us he was asleep and that seemed much worse. *Much* too casual.

272

As he had been driving he was on the right-hand side—the side which was about to tilt over, so we all scrambled to the left. But if we climbed into the front seat and got out then he would have gone over by himself. We didn't know what to do. We had passed some tea pluckers a few hundred yards back and the only hope was that they might be able to lift the car back onto the road. We decided the lightest one should go but Janet and Gillian got into a fight as to who was the lightest. They were both sensitive about their weight at the time. Finally Gillian went off and Janet and I tried to pull him towards the passenger seat.

When he wakened the car had already been lifted and moved to the centre of the road. He felt better, he said, started the car up and told us to hop in. But none of us would get into the car again."

(II)

"I remember when Daddy lost his job. He had just been sacked and he was drinking. Mummy was in the front seat with him, you and I were in the back.

And for the whole trip he kept saying 'I'm ruined. I've ruined all of you. All of you.' And he would weep. It was a terrible trip. And Mum kept comforting him and saying she would never leave him, she would never leave him. Do you remember that...?"

(III)

"When I left for England, god that was a terrible day for Mum. We were all at Kuttapitiya and she drove me down to Colombo. Left early in the morning. She had to move fast. He was drinking such a lot then and she couldn't leave him for too long. So when we boarded the ship, *The Queen of Bermuda*, that was about the time he was waking up and she had to get back before he got into trouble. She knew he had already begun his drinking as she said goodbye to me."

(IV)

"Remember all the pillows he had to sleep with? Remember how he used to make us massage his legs? Each of us had to do it for ten minutes...."

273

(V)

"To us he was an utterly charming man, always gracious. When you spoke to him you knew you were speaking to the *real* Mervyn. He was always so open and loved those he visited. But none of us knew what he was like when he was drunk. So when your mother spoke of the reasons for the breakup it was a complete surprise. Oh I did see him drunk once and he was a bloody nuisance, but only once.

Anyway she told us things were rough. Their servant, Gopal, would not obey her and would continue to buy your father bottles. So we suggested the two of them go up to 'Ferncliff' in Nuwara Eliya. They stayed there a week but that didn't work out and they returned to Kegalle. He had lost his job by then, so they were at home most of the time. Then your mother got typhoid. Paratyphoid, not the most serious kind, but she had it—and he wouldn't believe her. She said he hit her to make her get out of bed. Somehow she convinced Gopal how serious it was, and while he always obeyed your father he went into town and phoned us. We drove her down to Colombo and put her in Spittel's Nursing Home.

She never went back to him. When she was released she went and lived with Noel and Zillah at Horton Place.

Anyway, a few years later we decided to work on the lawn at 'Ferncliff' which was turning brown. So we arranged to have some turf delivered from the Golf Club. And when we started digging we found about thirty bottles of Rocklands Gin buried in that front lawn by your father...."

(VI)

"I don't know when this happened or how old I was. I was lying on a bed. It was night. The room was being thrown around and they were shouting. Like giants."

(VII)

"After leaving him she worked at the Mount Lavinia Hotel and then the Grand Oriental Hotel, that's called the Taprobane now. Then in the fifties she moved to England. She had a rough time during those early years in England, working at that boarding house in Lancaster Gate. She had one small room with just a gas ring. Noel's daughter, Wendy, was boarded at a private school at the time and she was wonderful. Every weekend she'd tell all her Cheltenham friends 'Now we must go and visit Aunt Doris,' and she'd drag these posh English school girls, about six or seven of them, and they'd crowd into that small bed-sitter and cook crumpets over the gas ring."

(VIII)

"I had some friends who played tennis. My best friends in London. And they were invited to Ceylon for a tournament. They were there for two weeks. When they came back to England I didn't contact them. Never answered their calls. You see I thought they would have found out what a disgraceful family I had come from. Mummy had drummed this story into us about what we had all been through there. I had this image that the Ondaatjes were absolute pariahs. I was twenty-five years old then. When I went back five years later to Ceylon to see Gillian I was still nervous and was totally surprised that everyone remembered him and all of us with such delight and love...."

(IX)

"In the end he used to come to Colombo every two weeks to bring me eggs and fertilizer for my garden. He was subdued then, no longer the irrepressible Mervyn we used to know, very kind and quiet. He was happy just to sit here and listen to me gab away.... I never met his second wife, Maureen, until the day of his funeral."

(X)

"You know what I remember best is how sad his face was. I would be doing something and suddenly look up and catch his face naked. And full of sorrow. I don't know. Long after the divorce I wrote to him. I'd just been to my first dance and I complained about all the soppy songs the boys sang to us, especially one they played constantly, which went 'Kiss me once and kiss me twice and kiss me once again ... it's been a *long long* time,' and he wrote back saying he just wished he could kiss us all once again.

... The sections you sent me made me very sad, remembering him and all those times. Of course I was always the serious one among us, with no sense of humour. I showed what you had written to someone and they laughed and said what a wonderful childhood we must have had, and I said it was a nightmare."

275

(XI)

"When I used to meet him years later he was always a fund of wonderful stories, never dirty, never mocked a woman. Anyway, one day I ran into him in the Fort and that night your mother, who was visiting Ceylon at the time, came to dinner. So, playing the devil's advocate, I told her who I had seen that morning and I said, *you* should see him. I remember she was very silent and looked down at her empty plate and around the room, somewhat surprised, and said, 'Why should I have to see him?' And I don't know why but I kept pushing it and then gradually she began to be interested. I think she almost gave in. I said I could easily reach him by phone, he could come over and join us. They were both in their sixties then, hadn't seen each other even once since the divorce. For old time's sake, Doris, I said, just to see each other. Then my wife thought I was being too cocky and made me change the subject and suggested we eat, that dinner was ready. But I know she was nearly persuaded to, I could tell that more than anything else. It was so close...."

BLIND FAITH

During certain hours, at certain years in our lives, we see ourselves as remnants from the earlier generations that were destroyed. So our job becomes to keep peace with enemy camps, eliminate the chaos at the end of Jacobean tragedies, and with "the mercy of distance" write the histories.

Fortinbras. Edgar. Christopher, my sisters, Wendy, myself. I think all of our lives have been terribly shaped by what went on before us. And why of Shakespeare's cast of characters do I remain most curious about Edgar? Who if I look deeper into the metaphor, torments his father over an imaginary cliff.

Words such as *love*, *passion*, *duty*, are so continually used they grow to have no meaning—except as coins or weapons. Hard language softens. I never knew what my father felt of these "things." My loss was that I never spoke to him as an adult. Was he locked in the ceremony of being "a father"? He died before I even thought of such things.

I long for the moment in the play where Edgar reveals himself to Gloucester and it never happens. Look I am the son who has grown up. I am the son you have made hazardous, who still loves you. I am now part of an adult's ceremony, but I want to say I am writing this book about you at a time when I am least sure about such words.... Give me your arm. Let go my hand. Give me your arm. Give the word. "Sweet Marjoram" ... a tender herb.

THE BONE

There is a story about my father I cannot come to terms with. It is one of the versions of his train escapade. In this one he had escaped from the train and run off naked into the jungle. ("Your father had a runaway complex" someone has already told me.) His friend Arthur was called to find him and persuade him back. When Arthur eventually tracked him down this is what he saw.

My father is walking towards him, huge and naked. In one hand he holds five ropes, and dangling on the end of each of them is a black dog. None of the five are touching the ground. He is holding his arm outstretched, holding them with one arm as if he has supernatural strength. Terrible noises are coming from him and from the dogs as if there is a conversation between them that is subterranean, volcanic. All their tongues hanging out.

They were probably stray dogs that my father had stumbled on in jungle villages, he had perhaps picked them up as he walked along. He was a man who loved dogs. But this scene had no humour or gentleness in it. The dogs were too powerful to be in danger of being strangled. The danger was to the naked man who held them at arm's-length, towards whom they swung like large dark magnets. He did not recognize Arthur, he would not let go of the ropes. He had captured all the evil in the regions he had passed through and was holding it.

Arthur cut the ropes and the animals splashed to the ground, writhing free and escaping. He guided my father back to the road and the car that his sister Stephy waited in. They put him in the back seat, his arm still held away from him, now out of the open car window. All the way to Colombo the lengths of rope dangled from his fist in the hot passing air.

"THANIKAMA"

After the morning's drive to Colombo, after the meeting with Doris —tense, speaking in whispers in the hotel lobby—he would force himself to sit on the terrace overlooking the sea. Would sit in the sunlight drinking beers, which he ordered ice-cold, and finishing them before the sweat even evaporated from the surface of the bottle. Poured out the glasses of Nuwara Eliya beer. He sat there all afternoon, hoping she would notice him and come down to speak with him properly, truthfully. He wanted his wife to stop this *posing* at her work. Had to speak with her. He could hardly remember where the children were now. Two in school in England, one in Kegalle, one in Colombo....

Till 5 o'clock, he sat out on the blue terrace with the blaze of sun on him— determined to be somewhere where they could be alone if she changed her mind and came down to him—not with the other guests and drinkers in the cool shadows of the lobby of the Mount Lavinia Hotel. He recalled everyone. Their crowd. Noel, Trevor, Francis who was dead now, Dorothy who ran riot. All burghers and Sinhalese families, separate from the Europeans. The memory of his friends was with him in the sun. He poured them out of the bottles into his glass tankard and drank. He remembered Harold Tooby from his school days and his years at Cambridge where the code was "you can always get away with more than you think you can get away with...." Till Lionel Wendt accidentally told his father of the deception. Lionel always guilty over this, who gave him and Doris a painting by George Keyt for their wedding. He still had that in any case, and the wooden statue of a woman he had picked up at an auction which everyone else hated. Objects had stayed and people disappeared.

At five he got into the white Ford. She had not come down to him. And he drove to F. X. Pereira in the Ridgeway Building and bought cases of beer and gin to take back to Kegalle. Then he parked near the Galle Face Hotel, old haunt, and crossed the street to the bar where journalists and others from Lake House sat and talked politics, talked rubbish, talked about sport, which he was not at all interested in now. Did not mention Doris. Drank and laughed and listened, till eleven at night at which time they all went home to their wives. He walked down Galle Road and ate a meal at a Muslim restaurant, sitting alone in one of the frail wooden booths, the food so hot it would sear back the drunkenness and sleepiness, and then got into his car. This was 1947.

He drove along Galle Face Green where the Japanese had eventually attacked, by plane, and disappeared into the Fort whose streets were dark and quiet and empty. He loved the Fort at this hour, these Colombo nights, the windows of his car open and the breeze for the first time almost cool, no longer tepid, hitting his face with all the night smells, the perfume of closed boutiques. An animal crossed the road and he braked to a halt and watched it, strolling at its own speed for it was midnight and if a car would actually stop it could be trusted. This animal paused when it reached the pavement and looked back at the man in the white car—who still had not moved on. They gazed at each other and then the creature ran up the steps of the white building and into the post office which stayed open all night.

He thought, I could sleep here too. I could leave the car in the centre of Queen's Road and go in. Other cars would weave around the Ford. It would disturb no one for four or five hours. Nothing would change. He lifted his foot off the clutch, pressed the accelerator and moved on through the Fort towards Mutwal, passed the church of his ancestors—all priests and doctors and translators—which looked down on him through a row of plantain trees, looked down onto the ships in the harbour docked like enormous sinking jewels. He drove out of Colombo.

An hour later he could have stopped at the Ambepussa resthouse but continued on, the day's alcohol still in him though he had already stopped twice on the side of the road, urinated into darkness and mysterious foliage. Halted briefly at Warakapola where the dark villages held the future and gave a Tamil a lift, the man striking up a conversation about stars, and he, proud of that mutual ancestry, discussing Orion with him. The man was a cinnamon peeler and the smell filled the car, he did not want to stop, wanted to take him all the way past the spice gardens to Kegalle rather than letting him out a mile up the road. He drove on, the cinnamon blown out already by new smells from the night, drove dangerously, he couldn't quite remember if he was driving dangerously or not, just aware of the night breezes, the fallout from spice gardens he skirted as if driving past vast kitchens. One of the lamps of his car was dead so he knew he was approaching stray walkers disguised as a motorcycle. He weaved up the Nelundeniya U-turns, then into the town of Kegalle. Over the bridge into Rock Hill.

For about ten minutes he sat in front of the house now fully aware that the car was empty but for his body, this corpse. Leaving the car door open like a white broken wing on the lawn, he moved towards the porch, a case of liquor under his arm. *Moonless.* The absence of even an edge of the moon. Into the bedroom, the bottle top already unscrewed. Tooby, Tooby, you should see your school friend now. The bottle top in my mouth as I sit on the bed like a lost ship on a white sea. And they sat years ago on deck chairs, young, going to England. In the absurd English clothes they surprised each other with. And then during the heart of the marriage sailed to Australia serene over the dark mountains in the sea, the bed of the ocean like a dragon's back, ridges and troughs and the darkest eye of the Diamantina crater. This too was part of the universe, a feature of the earth. Kissed in the botanical gardens of Perth, took the Overland train east across the country just so they could say they had seen the Pacific. His Colombo suit fell off him now to the floor, onto its own pool of white and he got into bed. Thinking. What was he thinking about? More and more he watched himself do nothing, with nothing. At moments like this.

He saw himself with the bottle. Where was his book. He had lost it. What was the book. It was not Shakespeare, not those plays of love he wept over too easily. With dark blue bindings. You creaked them open and stepped into a roomful of sorrow. A mid-summer dream. All of them had moved at times with an ass's head, Titania Dorothy Hilden Lysander de Saram, a mongrel collection part Sinhalese part Dutch part Tamil part ass moving slowly in the forests with foolish and serious obsessions. No, he looked around the bare room, don't talk to me about Shakespeare, about "green hats."

279

The bottle was half empty beside him. He arose and lit the kerosene lamp. He wanted to look at his face, though the mirror was stained as if brown water and rust hung captive in the glass. He stepped towards the bathroom, the yellow pendulum of lamp beside his knees. With each swing he witnessed the state of the room and corridor. A glimpse of cobwebs quickly aging, undusted glass. No sweeper for weeks. And nature advanced. Tea bush became jungle, branches put their arms into the windows. If you stood still you were invaded. Wealth that was static quickly rotted. The paper money in your pocket, wet from your own sweat, gathered mould.

In the bathroom ants had attacked the novel thrown on the floor by the commode. A whole battalion was carrying one page away from its source, carrying the intimate print as if rolling a tablet away from him. He knelt down on the red tile, slowly, not wishing to disturb their work. It was page *189*. He had not got that far in the book yet but he surrendered it to them. He sat down forgetting the mirror he had been moving towards. Scared of the company of the mirror. He sat down with his back against the wall and waited. The white rectangle moved with the busy arduous ants. Duty, he thought. But that was just a fragment gazed at by the bottom of his eye. He drank. There. He saw the midnight rat.

280

MONSOON NOTEBOOK (III)

A school exercise book. I write this at the desk of calamander looking out of the windows into dry black night. "Thanikama." "Aloneness." Birdless. The sound of an animal passing through the garden. Midnight and noon and dawn and dusk are the hours of danger, susceptibility to the "grahayas"—planetary spirits of malignant character. Avoid eating certain foods in lonely places, the devils will smell you out. Carry some metal. An iron heart. Do not step on bone or hair or human ash.

Sweat down my back. The fan pauses then begins again. At midnight this hand is the only thing moving. As discreetly and carefully as whatever animals in the garden fold brown leaves into their mouths, visit the drain for water, or scale the broken glass that crowns the walls. Watch the hand move. Waiting for it to say something, to stumble casually on perception, the shape of an unknown thing.

The garden a few feet away is suddenly under the fist of a downpour. Within half a second an easy dry night is filled with the noise of rain on tin, cement, and earth—waking others slowly in the house. But I actually saw it, looking out into the blackness, saw the white downpour (reflected off the room's light) falling like an object past the window. And now the dust that has been there for months is bounced off the earth and pours, the smell of it, into the room. I get up, walk to the night, and breathe it in—the dust, the tactile smell of wetness, oxygen now being pounded into the ground so it is difficult to breathe ...

LAST MORNING

Half an hour before light I am woken by the sound of rain. Rain on wall, coconut, and petal. This sound above the noise of the fan. The world already awake in the darkness beyond the barred windows as I get up and stand here, waiting for the last morning.

My body must remember everything, this brief insect bite, smell of wet fruit, the slow snail light, rain, rain, and underneath the hint of colours a sound of furious wet birds whose range of mimicry includes what one imagines to be large beasts, trains, burning electricity. Dark trees, the mildewed garden wall, the slow air pinned down by rain. Above me the fan's continual dazzling of its hand. When I turn on the light, the bulb on the long three-foot cord will sway to the electrical breeze making my shadow move back and forth on the wall.

But I do not turn on the light yet. I want this emptiness of a dark room where I listen and wait. There is nothing in this view that could not be a hundred years old, that might not have been here when I left Ceylon at the age of eleven. My mother looks out of her Colombo window thinking of divorce, my father wakes after three days of alcohol, his body hardly able to move from the stiffness in muscles he cannot remember exerting. It is a morning scenery well-known to my sister and her children who leave for swimming practice before dawn crossing the empty city in the Volks, passing the pockets of open shops and their light-bulb light that sell newspapers and food. I stood like this in the long mornings of my childhood unable to bear the wait till full daylight when I could go and visit the Peiris family down the road in Boralesgamuwa; the wonderful, long days I spent there with Paul and Lionel and Aunt Peggy who would casually object to my climbing all over her bookcases in my naked and dirty feet. Bookcases I stood under again this week which were full of signed first editions of poems by Neruda and Lawrence and George Keyt. All this was here before I dreamed of getting married, having children, wanting to write.

Here where some ants as small as microdots bite and feel themselves being lifted by the swelling five times as large as their bodies. Rising on their own poison. Here where the cassette now starts up in the next room. During the monsoon, on my last morning, all this Beethoven and rain.

Honey and Ashes

JANICE KULYK KEEFER

Here is a selection from *Honey and Ashes: The Story of Family*, a 1998 work in which Janice Kulyk Keefer, like Myrna Kostash the Canadian-born child of immigrants from Eastern Europe, comes to terms with the relationship between family and ethnicity—in this case, Polish. The writer, a prolific and much praised novelist, is also a critic. She was born in 1952 and teaches at the University of Guelph.

DEPARTURES, ARRIVALS: STAROMISCHYNA—TORONTO

"Travel": same word as "travail"—"bodily or mental labour," "toil, especially of a painful or oppressive nature," "exertion," "hardship," "suffering." A "journey."
Bruce Chatwin, *The Songlines*

BLUE STONES, BANANAS, THE IMMIGRANT SHUFFLE

Towards the very end of 1935, just before her thirty-third birthday, Olena receives a letter bearing Polish, not Canadian, stamps. It contains a notice that three third-class prepaid tickets from Gdynia, Poland, to Halifax, Canada, have been secured by one Mr. T. Solowski of Toronto, Ontario, for three adults (children are defined as being under ten years old). The notice includes the price for the family's "Total Ocean Fare"—$384.00—and Canadian railroad fares—$53.88—between Halifax and Toronto.

The receipt for the tickets looks a little like an old-fashioned theatre bill:

THE POLISH TRANS-ATLANTIC SHIPPING
COMPANY, LIMITED
owners of
GDYNIA—AMERICA LINE
Polskie Transatlantyckie Towarzystwo Okretowe, Sp.
Akc. Linja Gdynia-Ameryka
NOTICE TO PASSENGERS issued in connection with
Prepaid ticket No. 07173
Date of Issue Dec. 10, 1935

[Not good for Transportation]

    The **GDYNIA-AMERICA LINE** will furnish all necessary instructions and will deliver a ticket from the port of embarkation for transportation.

    Passengers MUST NOT leave their homes for the port of embarkation until advised to do so by the Line, but whether or not such notification has been issued, the Line assumes no responsibility as to the length of time passengers may be delayed prior to sailing, nor as to expenses for maintenance or otherwise incurred by passengers because of such delays.

Which must have left the mass of soon-to-be passengers—emigrants who'd spent their life savings on tickets for themselves and their families—in an anxious mood. Those booked to enter the United States were also warned that their rights were subject to "the act of Congress approved May 19, 1921, entitled 'An Act to Limit the Immigration of Aliens into the United States.'" The instructions are reprinted in Polish, Ukrainian, German, Finnish, Lithuanian, Latvian, Romanian, Czecho-Slovak [sic], Serbian and Croatian. There's also a text in Hebrew letters, labelled "Jewish." So no one could possibly claim they hadn't understood the conditions; could demand reimbursement for expenses incurred due to the regrettable necessity of having to eat and sleep all through the days, even weeks, when the ship lingered in port for reasons known only to the owners of the Polish Trans-Atlantic Shipping Company, Limited.

When did Olena finally admit that her husband would never come back to live in

Poland? After Tomasz left Staromischyna for the second time, in the autumn of 1932, it took her almost four more years to decide to join him. Even then, she set out with an eye to coming back. Looking at her life from the pieces of paper she left behind, the contracts for sale and rental of land, the buff envelope containing a surveyor's map and inscribed with the words *moyeh poleh*—my fields—I recall the depth and endurance of her passion; how on her deathbed she spoke of the loss of her fields with sorrow and bewilderment still. And yet despite this passion for land, despite her neighbours' warnings that she'd perish in the ice and snow of Canada, she sold her house and most of her goods, packed up the rest and left. Perhaps she was moved by fear—fear that she would lose Tomasz forever if she stayed another year in Staromischyna; fear that if she stayed, she would lose herself, that alloy of pride and aloofness that defined her.

What did she bring with her to Canada? The sky-blue can in which she used to carry cream to Helka's store. A handful of photographs, a miniature cupboard with a tilting mirror. Goose-down quilts and cushions; lengths of homemade cloth. Kilims woven with patterns of large and startling roses. A wall hanging of a golden fox, chain-stitched against a black background. And a long, slender *poyas* that she'd woven herself, out of wool dyed in stripes of blue and green and white, against an earthen red. This *poyas* is meant to be wrapped tightly round the waist, marking off the gorgeously embroidered blouse from the intricately woven skirt in which, of course, each of Olena's daughters will be married. And which, of course, are nowhere to be seen when Natalia and Vira sit for their photographs in white satin and tulle and orange blossom.

She took with her, too, a sheaf of documents signed and stamped at a municipal office in Skalat, the *Syndykat Emigracyjny* in Ternopil', a Warsaw commissariat. There's a Testament of Moral Standing, in which the mayor of Skalat attests that Olena Solowska and her daughters Natalja and Wira are known by him to have behaved irreproachably in every way. Certificates of Belonging carefully, even elegantly, signed by Natalja and Wira Solowska, pin them to the most minute of maps: the Republic of Poland, the province of Tarnopol, the region of Skalat, the township of Kaczanowska. There's a marriage certificate, and certificates of birth and death for the twins, Ivan and Marusia. And a notice written in Ukrainian that on March 19, 1936, an agreement was drawn up between Olena Solowska and Myhailo Pankevych whereby he would rent her fields in Staromischyna for a period of five years only, paying the rent in advance and ceding all rights to this property on Olena's return.

285

Arranging all this must have been a horrendous business: in the photo fixed into Olena's passport she looks sadly careworn, though this may be a trick of the light, of overharsh exposure. Her daughters stand on either side of her, Natalia a robust fourteen, Vira paper-delicate, her cropped hair and short bangs making her look far younger than twelve. In each face, blankness: a mask tied over fear, confusion, misgivings.

Other things are lost forever, ephemeral or expendable by their very nature. There were doctor's forms that must have been surrendered at Halifax, forms vouching for the perfect health of these immigrants, at least at their initial point of departure. For just after they set out from Staromischyna, Natalia's eyes turn red and watery, and by the time they reach Ternopil', her lids have started to twitch. Olena takes her daughter to a physician, who diagnoses trachoma, that long-standing bane of immigrants, as can be seen from the front page of the *Halifax Herald*, April 4, 1903. An article reporting the arrival of over a thousand immigrants on the Hamburg-American steamer *Armenia* declares that of the 160 Canada-bound passengers from Eastern Europe, fifty to sixty were held up for trachoma.

Chlamydia trachomatis is its proper name, the one Vira looks up for me now in her medical books. It's a highly communicable disease afflicting vast numbers of people in the dry, dusty areas of the tropics and subtropics—it is also present to some degree in southern Europe. In endemic areas the disease is commonest in children: Vira says she has never seen a single case in her fifty years of pediatric practice. The problem with trachoma is that it can cause blindness if left untreated—and it often is, since the onset of the disease is "insidious," the textbook says, and may pass unnoticed until the sufferer's vision begins to fail. I think of the steamer *Armenia*, of fifty to sixty passengers with watery, twitching eyes, their corneas already scarred: I think of the Halifax officials, panicking at the thought that with each boatload of immigrants, dozens of people soon to be blind will be loosed onto the streets of Canada. I think of my grandmother's determination to have her daughter's eyes cured so that nothing will stand in the way of their journey. Nowadays a course of tetracycline will easily dispatch a case of trachoma; in 1936 a doctor in Ternopil' prescribed this treatment: rubbing the girl's eyelids with blue stones and a special crayon.

What Natalia remembers of her time in that strange city is that the treatment, however odd and painful, lasted only a day—and that it worked. By the time they made their way back to the railway station to take the train to Gdynia, where a representative of the Canadian immigration bureau would pronounce her fit to travel, Natalia's eyes were clear enough to let her glimpse a marvel in a shop window. A pale yellow fan of oblongs made from some waxy substance she'd never seen before, and which would mystify her for some time to come.

When I ask them what they remember of the months and weeks and days lived through in the knowledge of leaving, they can't respond. In the same way children have such difficulty understanding what death means, Natalia and Vira couldn't understand all the *never agains* that would have shadowed their simplest, most ordinary acts—fetching water from the pump down the lane, or running to that same pump to press their hands against its icy metal, hands stung by their uncle's bees. Vira has only one vivid memory of leaving: she and her sister sitting on the gate of their house, kicking their heels, bawling their eyes out as their cow, Helka, and her twin calves were led down the road by the man who'd bought them.

On a morning near the end of March, a secular form of religious procession makes its way down the streets of Staromischyna: Olena, Vira, and Natalia, the priest and the schoolteachers, all the neighbours—everyone in the village except Yulia and her family. I imagine it as the first fine day after a spell of storms: the buds on all the branches magnified by raindrops, the mud thick as stew along the roads. One of the leave-takers neither walks with the procession nor waves as it goes by. This is Bohdan, the boy with the smashed spine, who is leaning against the gate of his father's house. His eyes never leave the face of the fourteen year-old girl he has watched walking home from school each day, the girl who'd spoken kindly to him while the others jeered. And because he can only stand straight by jamming his hands in his pockets, he can't even wave goodbye.

When they reach the road leading to Pidvolochys'k, where the train station lies, the villagers say farewell and turn back. Perhaps Myhailo Petrylo has loaned Olena his cart to carry her baggage: the driver helps the woman and her daughters up, secures their bundles and then sets off to town. He finds nothing to say to his passengers. They no longer need to care about the planting or harvest in this small corner of Poland; though he's seen or talked to this woman and her children nearly every day of his life, they've already become strangers. It's a relief to them all when they reach the station. The train pulls in so quickly that there's barely time to load their baggage before the whistle blasts their ears and a whoosh of steam carries them away, perhaps for five years, perhaps forever.

Five hundred miles or more between Ternopil' and Gdynia. On their way to the coast they would have passed through Lwow, Lublin, and Warsaw before the train headed north through a string of small towns to reach the sea. They'd have had German names then, these towns today called Swiecie, Tczew. But my grandmother and her daughters travelled without the luxury of maps; neither Vira nor Natalia can recall the places through which the train passed, or which lay along the coast skirted by the MS *Pilsudski* once it left Gdynia. Past Copenhagen and round the tip of Denmark; perhaps a stop at Bremerhaven and again at Rotterdam; through the English Channel, with a last call at Le Havre, and finally the open Atlantic.

It's impossible to keep romance out of this reconstruction. Perhaps I shouldn't try: Natalia and Vira would have breathed it in along with the stink of vomit and overflowing toilets down in steerage. For while Olena, tortured by seasickness worse than any migraine, lies in her bunk the entire voyage and prays to die, her daughters run the length of the ship, dance to the sailors' accordions, devour the oranges served up in the enormous dining room. That these oranges are woody and tasteless hardly blunts their pleasure. For this is the first time since their infancy that every moment of their day hasn't been burdened by household or farmyard labour, by school or churchgoing. The only hindrance to their freedom is the shoes on their feet, shoes they must wear every day from now on, instead of just on Sundays. Each morning they wash their mother's face, offer her a few sips of water she can barely swallow and leave her to the care of the women who haven't succumbed to seasickness. Then they bolt up the iron stairs to the decks outside, standing at the railing with their mouths open like sails to catch the fresh, salty air. A boy from Warsaw offers them the first mints they've ever tasted; they name the candy *whirlwind*, for the delicious storms it makes on their tongues.

On April 6 they catch their first glimpse of the Newfoundland coast. *Kanáda, Kanáda*, they cry out, as if expecting their father and the great city into which he's vanished to rise up out of the rocks and trees. When they reach Halifax Olena staggers up from the berth she's lain in for the full nine days of the crossing—she's been too ill to move even for the ship's obligatory fire drill. Freshening the clothes they've worn day after day, clutching their hand luggage, they totter down the gangway into what looks like a gigantic barn. They're deloused and bathed, their clothes fumigated, their bodies intimately searched for signs of communicable disease. Men in one section, women in another—all of them naked. Natalia stares at the older women huddling as far as they can from the tables of doctors and officials. At first she thinks they've hidden their nakedness with pale leather aprons, and then she understands:

the aprons are their breasts and bellies, sagging after years of child-bearing. She takes her turn shivering at the table, being pushed and prodded, until she's finally permitted to put her clothes back on. Vira, being younger, seems less shamed: to the doctor examining her, she blurts out her only words of English: "wan, too, tree!"

The train on which they endure the journey from Halifax to Toronto has bare wooden benches. At first they watch everything that flashes past them through the windows: cars, roads, dingy towns, then evergreens and rock cuts making a blur of green and grey. But long before nightfall, when the windows give them nothing but their own drained faces, they've had their fill of something too strange to call scenery. Vira strikes up a conversation with a man sitting across from them, a Polish man returning to Toronto from Lwow, where he's been visiting his family. When Vira tells him of the puzzling yellow objects they'd seen hanging from hooks in a Ternopil' store, the man calls to a porter passing by and buys for each of the girls one pale, unspotted banana. He explains how to twist the stem and peel back the skin, and watches as they take their first bites of a fruit far more exotic than oranges. Because he's watching, they can't make a face as their lips go numb; they must eat every inch of the unripe fruit that furs the insides of their mouths and chills their stomachs. When I first read Colette's description, in one of the *Claudine* novels, of how her heroine is initiated into sensual delights by eating the blackest of bananas, fruit so ripe its flesh has gone murkily translucent, I couldn't help thinking of my aunt and mother. Eating green bananas, smiling at the gentleman who'd treated them, and the gentleman beaming back because he'd authored this tremendous pleasure.

289

The train jolts on and on; the children fall into a tense, smoky sleep. They wake up next morning to another full day's ride until finally someone calls out, *Toronto, Toronto next stop*, and they push down the aisle with all the others, through the open door and into the night. The man walking up to them on the platform is not their father, or at least is not the same father they'd last seen four years ago. He limps under the pain of a wrenched back—only days before he'd been in hospital, in traction. They see the worry climbing back into their mother's face; they keep their heads down, stumbling behind their parents, sweat covering them like a clammy bandage.

Only when they step outside the station into the street do they stare up at the one thing that has stayed the same throughout this whole astonishing journey. But instead of being packed with stars, the sky is blinking out Polish words they've never seen before: *Tsotsa-Tsola, Tsotsa-Tsola*. Letters they'll learn to pronounce differently in English, turning them into the name of a dirt-coloured drink that scrapes and fizzes their mouths. The taste of sweetness here, this harsh soft drink called Coca-Cola.

Tomasz had come to Union Station with a friend, Mr. Moroz, who'd offered to drive the Solowskis home in his beat-up Ford. To the children, for whom rides in lumbering wooden carts had been a treat, that Ford racing along Front Street to Spadina, past brilliant-coloured lights and glinting sparks from streetcars, must have seemed like the chariot of an angel.

Home, the first home, was Antler Street, one small room that Tomasz had furnished with two beds, four chairs, an enamel-topped table, and the indispensable orange crates. Later they found better lodgings on Queen Street West, with another Ukrainian family. Somehow they all fitted into an apartment over a store—on hot summer nights the children would sleep on the roof, watching the stars rise or the sun come up through grids of telephone wires. "Which store was it?" I ask my mother. She can't remember: besides, it changed hands long ago. Walking back and forth along Queen, I try to guess which of these tall, narrow houses it might have been, houses at whose gingerbread gables I used to stare when having my teeth drilled in my father's office. It's hopeless. The street has changed so much even from the time I knew it best, working for my father as a teenaged receptionist, trying to interpret the Ukrainian and Polish of his patients, many of them old men with stooped shoulders and cloth caps, women bundled up in shawls and kerchiefs, a fragrance of poppy seed and dill about them.

Hopeless. Yet one day, only months ago, walking along Queen past Bathurst, past fashionable cafés and punk clothes boutiques, I happened to glance down a side street to find a large sign saying Charles G. Fraser Public School. This was the very school my aunt and mother had attended more than sixty years ago. I walked down the side street and inside the school's front doors. The buzz of lights, the intimidating height and width of the corridors—this my aunt and mother would have recognized from 1936. These stained-glass scenes of children having tea parties or flying kites—they would have been here, too, their content as opaque to Natalia and Vira as the lessons they were sitting through.

It's the end of the school day, most of the children are gone, there's nothing for me here. But still I walk inside the office, making my way past teachers, telephones, newspaper articles pinned to the wall praising the school for its success in acculturating immigrants—Asian, these days, rather than Eastern European. It cheers me to see these clippings and the photos that accompany them; they're a connection to my family's past. But when the secretary at the desk—a woman who wouldn't have been born when my aunt and mother first were students here— responds to my question by pulling out file cards from a cabinet, I am astounded. They are dated 1936, and they give me the very information that I need:

Solowska, Nataljia. Solowska, Irena Vera. Last School Attended: Poland. Present Address: I. 716 Queen Street West. II. 29 Manning Avenue. III. 94 Manning Avenue.

The immigrant shuffle, moving from rooming house to rooming house, apartment to apartment, each in a slightly better neighbourhood, with fewer roaches and more and more gestures towards gardens—pots of geraniums, even a patch of rank grass outside the front door. After Queen Street, two rooms on Manning, and then two larger rooms on Shaw. Tomasz and Olena, Vira and Natalia used the hallway as a kitchen and shared the house's one bathroom with half a dozen other families. Olena would take her turn lining up for the bathroom with the other women, lock herself in—it was the only room in the whole house where she could be alone—and cry her eyes out for the five minutes or so before a timid knock would signal the next woman's turn to go in and weep.

From a thatched and clay-floored cottage to a downtown rooming house; from the quietness of carts and horses to the screech and slam of city traffic— how do Olena and her daughters survive these sudden, stunning leaps? How do they know who or what they are anymore? Nothing here gives them back their true reflection. To those who own this place they are incurably foreign; if they're overheard speaking to someone in their own language, slurs like *bohunk* will be tossed their way. Not the colour of their skin, but the width and slant of their cheekbones, the very shape of their tongues mark them out as different, danger- ous—why else would English people—the *Angliky*—go to such lengths to keep clear of them as they walk down the street? "It will pass," Olena's neighbours tell her. Or else, "You'll get used to it."

But for a long, long while they think they'll never get used to anything here. The first time Vira sees her father come home with a paper bag holding eggs, milk, bread, she feels a shock that sixty years haven't stilled. The shock that money must be paid out for the food you put into your mouth each day, money that's always been so scarce you're terrified to spend even a little of what you've struggled to save. At home the only things you needed to buy were what you couldn't make yourself: sugar and salt, coffee and tea. Soap you brewed from ashes and fat, oil you got from hemp seeds pressed at the mill. Even when paying the hired man after harvest, you gave him sacks of wheat, not money.

Not just at night, but all through the day, Vira dreams of home, the cow whose warm, frothy milk her mother would squirt from the teat straight into a cup for her to drink, the walnuts shaken from the trees, the deliciousness of sour cream dribbled over lettuce pulled tender from the garden. The fourteen fragrant loaves of rye bread her mother would bake each month, pulling them out of the oven with long-handled paddles; the *kvas* that was their version of a soft drink, made from fermented buckwheat flour. The pigs slaughtered after Christmas, every inch of their shaved, skinned bodies boiled or salted down to make sausages, blood pudding, headcheese. Home is the place where she never went hungry. But here, if her father's back doesn't heal, if her mother's eyes stay so inflamed from sewing that she can't go to work, what can they do but starve? The government offers relief in the form of free oatmeal for something called porridge, but Olena is too proud and too fearful to claim it: she's heard that those who sign on for relief are shipped right back to where they came from.

And so Olena walks her mile and a half each day to and from the shirt factory: partly to save the fare to buy bread, and partly because the jolting of the streetcar reminds her too much of her ocean crossing. Mr. Rosmaranovich, a neighbour who works at a dairy, brings them outdated milk, cream, and butter for their table. Tomasz finds temporary work at a bakery, rescuing whatever's too stale to sell—I imagine the family sitting down to dinners of curdled cream and three-day-old chocolate cake and wonder what Vira and Natalia made of this new, forced luxury. Later, they'll live off soup bones and rhubarb; they'll even be able to laugh at things. Like the family downstairs, whose six sons play—most of them hopelessly—the violin. For exactly half an hour, each boy practises, handing the instrument to the next brother down as if it were a piece of chewed-out gum.

At first Natalia accompanies her mother to the shirt factory, but by the end of the summer Olena starts to earn enough—$3.50 a week—for Natalia to join Vira at school. This improvement in her wages Olena owes to the Russian woman who's the only person on her shift with whom she can communicate. "They're paying you less than anyone else," the Russian says. "They know you can't talk with the other women and compare wages. Don't let them get away with it— don't let them stick you with all the big sizes that take so long to sew." Somehow Olena makes herself understood, and the foreman, reluctant to lose such an expert seamstress, pays her the paltry sum per shirt that's considered fair. It's a small victory, but enough to give Olena the assurance she can hold her own here, just as she'd done at home.

It's the kind of assurance Tomasz lacks, by temperament and by experience. He had to borrow money to prove to the authorities that he could support his family once they came to Canada; now he's disabled and in great pain. If his back doesn't heal, he may never work again, even if by some miracle there's work to be had. He wanted to welcome his family to Toronto with a whirl of presents; all he can manage is to swear off cigarettes, after having chain-smoked all the years he was alone. But he quits cold turkey and manages to keep his temper, too, the best part of the only gift he can offer his wife. As for his back, Olena contrives to save up the price of a chiropractor. After one appointment Tomasz comes back dancing; finding Olena sewing in their room, he swings her round as lightly as he'd done when they first met. Instantly his back gives out and Olena has to help him into bed. He returns to the chiropractor, who effects a more permanent cure, but never again does Tomasz trust himself, or fate, enough to dance up a set of stairs.

Nights are Olena's *bête noire*, literally. Of the four of them it's she who wakes at 2 A.M., covered with red, swollen bites. After airing the mattresses, they carry the iron bedsteads out into the yard, pour gasoline over them and light matches, listening to the bedbugs pop in the flames. But the next night the bugs are back, as bad as ever. Tomasz suggests his wife sleep on the wooden table in the middle of the room, but when they switch on the light the next morning, bedbugs are massed on the ceiling over the table; the hardier among them have, of course, dropped down during the night onto Olena. It's only when the Solowskis acquire a home of their own that Olena can sleep undisturbed once more.

293

What was it like living all together again? My mother once told me that her parents' reunion, after all the years apart, had been saddened by something that was other people's doing. In Staromischyna Olena held her head high in the midst of talk that Tomasz had abandoned her; in Toronto she held herself back from her husband. The signs of such holding back—how obvious and yet intricate they must have been in those conditions, husband and wife and children in one small room, haunted by other rooms unreachably distant and yet always there. Finally Tomasz persuaded his wife to tell him what had gone wrong. Again, as in the orchard sixteen years ago, his tenderness embraced her pride, disarmed it. But something, my mother says, was spoiled in her parents' first days together: a joy refused, to return only slowly, and in altered form.

There were no arguments, no scenes. Perhaps my grandparents were so busy trying to survive each day that they had no energy for shows of emotion. Except once, when a letter arrived for Olena. A letter from the Old Place, a rare enough event, but the handwriting on the envelope, the mere fact of the letter's having been written at all, makes it all the more conspicuous. Olena's at work when the mail's delivered. Tomasz accepts it from the postman's hand, takes it inside to their room, where Natalia's trying to make some kind of meal out of stale rolls and rancid butter. There's a look on her father's face she's never seen before, even when his back was causing him most pain. She sees the letter he doesn't open but keeps turning over in his hands. She, too, recognizes the handwriting, and only a fast wire of courage lets her keep her head when her father asks her, softly, what she knows. She shakes her head, and he, too, shakes his, leaving the room, the house, still grasping the letter in his hand.

When he returns, long after Olena has come home, he makes no mention of what has kept him, where he's been. He's as gentle as ever with his wife, his oldest daughter, who knows enough to keep the letter, and the wordless conversation she's had with her father, a secret.

294 Community is the one luxury they possess. In this sense, despite electric light and automobiles and department stores, Toronto becomes an extension for them of the Old Place. Among Ukrainians, hospitality is a religion: even those just scraping by will offer guests a cup of tea, a spoon of sugar, advice on where to buy fruit at a good price, which butchers to avoid. One of the first things Tomasz does once his family joins him is to buy an enormous enamel pot. To repay the many meals he's been given here, he explains to Olena. Somehow, without telephones, without specific invitations issued or answered, up to thirty people come by after church, or after sleeping in on the one day a week they can do so. All Sunday morning Olena labours over two burners set up in the hallway, dropping the *varenyky*, for which her daughters have peeled and mashed endless potatoes, into the vat of boiling water. Lifting them out with a slotted spoon, dropping them into a pan glistening with buttery onions, and onto plates that empty faster than she can fill them.

Ten years later, in her own kitchen on Dovercourt Road, she will cook these meals for the classmates my aunt brings home from medical school, among them Amala Ramcharan from Trinidad, who'll invite Vira back to her place for an initiatory curry dinner so strongly spiced that Vira will sleep with a pail of water by her bed. But now Olena repays the hospitality shown to her husband. And with sign language she shows Natalia's first friend in Canada, the daughter of the one black family in the neighbourhood, how to make *varenyky* and *holubtsi*. But something goes wrong in transmission: the girl, when she cooks these dishes for her family, ends up baking what should be boiled and boiling what should be baked. I say "the girl" because my mother, sadly, cannot recall her name, only that for this one black family, things were even harder than they were for her own. "They were fine people," my mother says; yet their neighbours, who should have seen this fineness, made life so unhappy for them that the family quickly left the area, never to be heard from again.

But Natalia still talks of Stella, whose mother finally allowed a crew of immigrant girls into her home each week to listen to Lux Radio Theatre—if they took off their shoes and sat, not on the sofa, but in a semicircle on the floor. She talks of Mary, the pale girl with a tumour on the brain, whose neck was so stiff she could only walk with great pain and effort. Mary and my mother would creep the few blocks to and from school each day, their conversation as slow as their footsteps. Yet Stella and Mary, and the classmates Vira met at school, became something unknown in Staromischyna: *girlfriends*.

Even now, talking of women in their seventies or dead long ago, this is the word Vira and Natalia use in a way that seems so brimmingly sweet for them, and so foreign to me. I'm remembering my 1960s adolescence: how any girl who showed she had brains would be spurned by the prom queens, the cheerleader corps. And if you did find someone with whom you could talk about other things than Maybelline or miniskirts, someone who, like you, had vowed never to learn how to run a washing machine or iron a Brooks Brothers shirt, then you did your best to forget the fact that you were girls at all.

Looking at my mother's and my godmother Anna's albums, all the photos of girls and young women, heads crowding together, laughter and whispers still on their lips, I'm filled with nostalgia for what I never knew. In Anna's albums there are even more pictures—some small as postage stamps, others full-sized studio portraits—of girlfriends. Sunbathing on Centre Island, baking themselves, cooling off, baking again, so that at night their skin was puffed crimson and sore to the touch. Or sitting out in small backyards in the two-piece suits that seem so chaste, today, in the sunlight that once seemed so healthy. Girls talking together, the future in their eyes like a flotilla—which boat will come to carry you off? Will you board it, or at the last moment hang back and let it sail on without you?

And then the albums change: breezy snapshots give way to the formal spell of

295

wedding photos, in which the girlfriends out on double dates metamorphose into bridesmaids. Hordes of them; sometimes eight or ten at a go—sometimes girls the bride hardly knows but has to include in the wedding party—because they're going out with her brothers. Sometimes a girl and boy coming from different places out west meet in Toronto and decide to marry: "They couldn't afford to bring their sisters and friends from Saskatchewan, so you'd be asked to join the wedding party just for the look of it," Anna tells me. "I was always in great demand as a bridesmaid," my mother laughs. "I worked in the rag trade on Spadina; I could get the material for bridesmaids' dresses wholesale."

What happened to the girlfriends who never became brides? The beautiful girl no one will name for me, the one whose father beat her so badly she was always hiding out at a girlfriend's house. She ended up on the streets, my mother tells me, alcohol the slow fuse that burned her alive. I think of a song I learned almost on the sly at summer camp: "Mala Ya Muzha Piyaka." About a woman whose drunken husband does nothing but beat her; how she threatens to leave him with the children and run off, clear across the Danube. We used to sing it laughingly, tauntingly, over illicit campfires. Never once thinking of the song as a lament, as anything that could touch our own lives here.

What happened to the brides themselves, the radiant young women with their pompadours and platform shoes? They walk inside the whiteness of their wedding gowns and vanish, like trees in mist.

SCHOOLING: THREAD AND INK

Tomasz and Olena had their educations cut short by disease and war; they were determined their daughters would fare better.

My mother started school when she was seven—the village school in Staromischyna. To this day she finds reading not difficult, but largely unnecessary. The poems and folk songs she loves she knows by heart; she is fluent in all the shades and textures cloth can assume, and she can design, cut out, and sew a complicated dress or coat faster than most people can leaf through a pattern book. Vira, on the other hand, was a born scholar, quick at sums and letters. Because she was so small, her teacher made her sit at the very end of a classroom bench crammed with a dozen or more children. A huge, hefty boy would sit in the very centre, a boy who could never answer the simplest question. He would shake and wriggle, causing a general jellyquake that ended by tossing Vira clear off the bench and onto the floor. This would always happen during religion class; the priest would haul her out to the yard, grab her by the collar and hit her with a switch. But she'd always twist and pull away so that her skirt and not her backside took the brunt of the beating.

Somehow money was found to send her, aged eleven, to a *gimnazium* or high school in Pidvolochys'k, where the town children made fun of her country ways, and where she was seated among the Jewish children with their perfectly straight, perfectly black, chin-length hair. It must be at this school that Vira's given a poem she doesn't understand, a poem that the older children order her to copy out and pass to someone in the row ahead of her. She finds the words impenetrable, despite her fluent Polish. The teacher intercepts the note; recognizing the handwriting, she tells Vira she expects to see Olena at the school that evening. And so Olena, after a full day's work, dresses in her Sunday clothes and walks the few miles into town to meet with the teacher. When she returns at last, she picks up a galvanized tin pail, lifts it high over her head and flings it so hard against the floor that it crumples. Nothing more is said about the incident, and it's not till the next day that Vira learns, from one of her schoolmates, what the note had been about.

"And——?" I ask. Vira is seventy-three and I am forty-five; for the longest time my aunt can't answer me. And then, half-blushing, half-laughing, she answers. "It was about a painter who used his penis for a brush."

But Vira got her own back at that school she must have both loved and hated. Not long after, she stood up and announced to her class that the king had died. "What king?" the teacher asks scornfully. Poland, after all, is a republic. "King George the Fifth," Vira replies, proud of this knowledge she alone possesses and that has come to her from across the sea. "We are going to Canada," she continues, "because the king is dead, and now life will be so much better." She sits down with a flourish, having summarized the anti-royalist sentiments expressed by her father in his last letter home; not knowing how greatly Tomasz has underestimated the colonial mentality of Canada. How the teacher responded, I don't know—the point of this story is this: for the first time in her life, Vira didn't have to care.

As for their Canadian teachers, Vira and Natalia fell in love with them, entirely, eternally. Not at first sight, but over the first few weeks and months spent in the company of the maiden ladies who taught them at Charles G. Fraser Public School. Miss Ferguson, who took charge of Vira; thin, tall, fine-boned Miss Sinclair, who

297

became Natalia's mentor. I remember being taken with my sister on visits to Miss Sinclair's house on Duplex Avenue; sitting in her sunroom, playing with a matrioshka doll and being so good it hurt. African violets on crocheted doilies, a silver teapot and porcelain cups, the smell of winter light—a smell not of dust, but starched lace—from these few memories I try to understand what they were like, Miss Sinclair and the other spinsters who taught my mother and her sister.

What must they have been or done to earn the devotion of those silent or stammering immigrant girls, terrified by the enormous school with its harshly lit halls, coached by their schoolmates in four-letter words they'd proudly repeat as proof they were finally learning English? The true courtesy they possessed, Miss Sinclair and Miss Ferguson, invited to the clean, bare room on Shaw Street, sipping tea from enamel mugs and not once betraying surprise or disgust that, as a mortified Natalia noticed, small beads of fat were floating at the top. She'd had to use their only pot to boil the water, the pot in which soup had been made that morning, and no amount of scrubbing had banished the traces of chicken fat. But the teachers sipped their tea till it was gone and even asked for one more cup.

What I take to be cruel, arrogant behaviour on the school's part, my aunt and mother see as normal, necessary. Natalia, at fourteen, put in a kindergarten class, feels like a goose among goslings. In the classroom the teacher draws a picture of a rooster on the blackboard. Rapping it with his pointer, he demands that the big, shy, foreign girl tell him what the creature's called—something anyone out of diapers must surely know. And Natalia, who could have answered him in Ukrainian or Polish or even Russian, is laughed down when she comes up with the only answer she can manage: "Chicken's father." As for Vira, she goes crimson when asked questions in this language she can't understand; she crawls under her desk until the teacher finally persuades her to come out again. Vira ends by staying after school each day to practise her English: so great is her longing to learn that after only a year she jumps up six grades.

School helped them forget the enormity of what they'd left behind, of what they'd come to; it also helped them to understand that their lives were full of entrancing possibilities, not just worries and dangers. Their teachers did far more than point out these possibilities. Miss Sinclair, who taught home economics, gave Natalia her old clothes to make over into dresses for herself. The fabric was excellent, my mother recalls, Liberty prints, but the styles hopelessly old-maidish. Natalia restyled them with Peter Pan collars and puffed sleeves. Her teacher was so impressed that she loaned her the fee for a couturier's course at the Toronto

School of Design. "If she hadn't taken an interest in me," my mother insists, "I would have ended up with a factory job like my mother's."

Miss Ferguson, Vira's science teacher, took her aside shortly before her grade eight graduation to ask which high school she'd be going to. Vira, trying to fold herself into the coats hanging in the cloakroom, answered, "Central Tech." She was going to do what so many immigrant children did: learn the clerical skills that would get them an office job—one step up from the meat plants and sweatshops where their parents worked, if they were lucky. "You ought to be going to Harbord Collegiate," Miss Ferguson announced. And she gave Vira the then-considerable sum of five dollars to help her buy the textbooks and supplies she'd need for such a venture. It was Miss Ferguson, too, who took Vira on her first visit to the Royal Ontario Museum; she had to pry her away at closing time, so intent was the girl on seeing, knowing everything the "castle" contained. A cup of hot chocolate at Diana Sweets was the inducement to leave, and Vira still can't tell which of the two experiences she savoured most.

Abiding affection and endless gratitude, this is what Vira and Natalia feel towards their teachers, those fabled names I heard throughout my childhood: the names of empresses in countries of the mind and heart. Miss Ferguson and Miss Sinclair.   299

I. NATALIA. THE STORY OF A DRESS

As soon as her firstborn was old enough to thread a needle, Olena sent her to learn the art of sewing from a village woman living near St. Nikolai's. My mother can't remember the name of this woman with jet-black eyes and brows and hair, the most beautiful person she had ever seen. The most beautiful and the most mysterious, for although she was well past girlhood—twenty-five, even thirty— she let no man near her. The teacher lived with her widowed mother, who did all the household chores while her daughter sewed by hand. Delicate work, feather and satin and cross-stitch, drawn thread and fringe work for the embroidered towels or *rushnyky* indispensable to weddings and christenings and funerals. In the afternoons she'd sew by the window; at night by a lamp with a large glass shade, painted with flowers and fine ladies.

All the time her teacher threads the precious needles, or separates the long silk of embroidery thread, or as she straightens up from the table she's been leaning over, gently tugging the edges of her jacket so they hang just so, Natalia is falling in love. This passion is different from the curiosity that drove her to fiddle with sticks and string, inventing for herself the art of knitting, unknown in Staromischyna. It's connected to the cutting of her grandmother's black skirt, for which she was so severely punished. It has to do with something you could call style, flair—appearances. The way her teacher looks, walking so elegantly down Staromischyna's thin, muddy lanes, transforming them into something her pupil hasn't got names for yet: avenues, boulevards, promenades.

Only a few months ago I asked my mother something I'd never wondered about before. "What kind of clothes did you wear in the village?" I hadn't been curious because I'd always known that people in the Old Place dressed in some simplified form of regional costume. Youths in hemp trousers and cross-stitched homespun shirts; maidens with flowery ribbons in their hair, brilliantly embroidered blouses, heavy strands of glass beads or else *koralyi*, strings of fleshy orange corals. Now I discover that I'd dressed up the whole village in a lie. For except at Easter, when they put on a child's version of their regional dress, Vira and Natalia wore the low-waisted dresses of the twenties and, later, simplified versions of 1930s frocks.

Plain cotton or woollen dresses sewn on Olena's machine, with plenty of tucks and pleats to be let out over the months these dresses had to last. To soil, never mind rip, a school dress was a disaster. How then to explain what happened when, one morning on her way to school, Vira climbed the plum tree, the one with the branch half-broken off? Shimmying up the tree after one especially fat and gleaming plum, she slips and finds herself suspended, her skirt caught on the splintered branch. For a moment she hangs immobile until, inch by inch, the dress lets go of her, pitching her bottom-first into the nettles. Overhead, the perfect circle of the skirt, impaled; by her side, holding a broom, her mother. Inexplicably, Olena keeps the broom to herself and merely chides her daughter. "You've still got your eyes, you've still got your legs. What are you wailing for?"

In Toronto Olena and her daughters had to dress in whatever they could find, until a neighbour, a woman from Staromischyna, loaned them her sewing machine. In my mother's album there's a photograph of some social gathering, perhaps an anniversary party held shortly after she came to Toronto. At either side of a phalanx of adults stand Vira and Natalia, wearing matching dresses of some pale, filmy, ruched material, with sleeves like little clouds and slender belts drawn through shiny buckles. They may have been eating stale bread and sour milk, but they look, as one of those Depression sayings goes, like a million dollars.

In a memoir of life in working-class Carlisle, novelist Margaret Forster writes of the significance of dress in her own "respectably" poor family. Describing the custom of "getting dressed for Easter," on which families would spend their last penny, Forster explains the importance of having smart as well as decent clothes. "They showed the world you respected yourself and had made the effort to be as immaculate as possible. They showed that however hard your circumstances, you could rise above them." And one of the most moving chapters of the book has to do with her mother's outfitting herself for a brief return to the clerical job she'd had to give up in order to marry. The pleasure she took in buying new clothes so as to arrive appropriately dressed for the work she delighted in—brain work rather than bruising physical labour. The guilt she felt at buying clothes for herself and not her children.

At what point did Natalia outstrip her mother, making suits and dresses for herself and Vira; sewing Olena's clothes? Was there never a moment when she doubted her talent, mistrusted her ambitions—or simply wished she'd been born for something else? It's not a question a child can easily ask a parent, and for answer I can only go by something she told me once, when I was thirteen, fourteen. Arriving home from school one afternoon, I found my mother sitting in the living room we so rarely used. I waited for a moment, then joined her on the sofa, under the painting of an English countryside she'd never seen but that reminded her, a little, of the land round Staromischyna.

301

She sees my school bag, picks up a botany textbook, thumbs through it looking for the diagrams. She tells me how, in her last year at public school, she'd been asked to make a whole set of botanical drawings. How she'd spent the happiest hours of her life choosing the colours, designing the placement of seed and flower and fruit on the page, deciding how words and text would fit together. It took her months to complete them, but the pictures, she tells me, hung for years and years on the classroom walls. My sister may be sitting with us as well that afternoon, my sister who already knows that when she's through with grade thirteen, she will not follow our mother's urging to study something practical, but will go on to art school. The battles about how Karen expects to support herself, about what she will wear to her studio classes—not the ladylike dresses my mother has sewn her but *jeans*—lie a few years into the future, yet my sister's vocation must have been sitting with us, too. For suddenly my mother's confessing how she'd always longed to be a painter. How, if there'd been money for art school, to buy her equipment, to cover the time it would have taken to establish herself, she'd have—

The telephone rings, and by the time she returns she's someone else. Not the fifteen-year-old, drawing dozens of botanical specimens; not even a woman who remembers with her whole heart a longing that she'd had to surrender even as she formed it. But our mother, who needs us to peel potatoes and carrots, to run the vacuum cleaner before our father comes home. The wife and mother who knows how painful, how dangerous it is to untie her apron and step back, even for a moment, into that most Cinderella-like of ball gowns, her former skin.

How does she do it, what elixir turns the pudding-faced girl of the Polish passport photo into a young woman so slender that people tell her not to stand sideways, lest she disappear?

Just before I turned sixteen, when I still had a moon-shaped face and a chubby, blundering body, I left home for the first time, fell in love, had my heart broken and forgot to eat. The girl who returned at the end of a summer in Winnipeg was unrecognizable to her family; her friends, even herself. I'd lost twenty pounds and my hair had grown long enough to change the shape of my face, which, having shed its puppy fat, was acquainting itself with its cheekbones. Sixteen-year-old Natalia didn't have the luxury of living away from home, or of heartbreak, for that matter: she was too intent on helping her family earn a living. But she must have gone through a similar crash course in possibility, learning she could alter the shape of her body as she altered the cut of Miss Sinclair's Liberty prints.

What are the stages in this journey Natalia makes from immigrant grant schoolgirl to independent working woman? Fourteen when she arrives in Toronto in 1936; fifteen by the time she acquires enough English to get a grade six diploma and enter the Toronto School of Design. Sixteen when, in the fall of 1938, she starts work as a designer. Eighteen when she begins the most dazzling and demanding part of her career: travelling to New York City, staying at five-star hotels, window shopping on Fifth Avenue, sitting dressed to kill at fashion shows. Memorizing every flare and flounce, every detail down to the number of buttons on a sleeve.

I think of her on that first trip to New York, this girl who has never spent a night away from home, never slept in a room by herself. It's late at night, she's sitting at a table by the window of her hotel room, overlooking the brilliant lights, the traffic roaring far below. She has kicked off her skyscraper heels and changed into pyjamas; she's sketching everything she's seen on the runway that day. Once or twice, when there are noises in the corridor—a woman with a champagne laugh, a waiter wheeling a trolley past—she glances up at the door. It's locked,

of course, and the chest of drawers she's dragged across the floor to make a barricade is still in place. *Men are like that.* Like what? She still doesn't know.

One other, less glamorous, point in this journey. It has to do with a joke
told, for once, by the immigrant instead of the oldcomer, a joke at the expense
of all the givens of "English" culture. Natalia is shopping at one of Toronto's better department stores whose windows she hardly dared glance at only two years
ago. She buys a great many outfits, the design and cut of which she'll pore over
before sending them back and making her own improved versions. She asks for
all these purchases to be delivered to her home. "Of course, madam," says the
shopgirl, deferential to this stylish young woman with her elegant hat, her soft
leather gloves and her good shoes (all of them bought wholesale, through contacts,
though for all the shopgirl knows they come straight from Sak's Fifth Avenue).
"What name?" she asks.

Natalia's so tired of spelling out S-O-1-O-W-S-K-A; of hearing, "What kind
of a name is *that?*" So she tells the shopgirl, "Sloane." Thinking nothing more of
it till the next afternoon, when she comes home from work and finds her father
shaking his head over the huge package someone tried to deliver to their door, a
package destined for the zoo. It takes Natalia a moment to catch on to what's happened: that when her father read the delivery slip, what he saw wasn't Miss N.
Sloane, but *slon'*—the word, in Polish and Ukrainian, for elephant.

303

The sixteen-year-old girl is nervous, spotlit, stranded in front of all these people;
when she tries to smile, the cold sore she'd woken up with—the bloom of
panic—bursts, and blood spills down her chin. She and a model supplied by
Simpson's, along with the material and a seamstress and presser, share a satin-
draped stage at one of the ersatz palaces at the Canadian National Exhibition, illus-
trating what is billed as "The Story of a Dress." In front of packed rows of watch-
ers, without a single error or wasted movement, she sketches a design, makes a
pattern out of brown paper, cuts out the slippery, shining cloth and hands it to
the seamstress. After a whirr of basting, the seamstress hands the cloth to the
model, who, retiring into the wings, emerges with the idea of a dress wrapped
cloudlike round her. And now the designer deftly, swiftly, continues her work,
so that the cloud, bristling with pins, can be sewn up on the industrial-sized
machine and handed, limp as a fainting child, to the presser. Who does her part,
steam gasping from the iron whose pointed nose she expertly guides along this
line, that fold. The presser hands the dress to the model, who disappears once

more; then pivots round the stage, her skirts shimmering as she links hands with the designer and seamstress and presser to receive a rapture of applause.

Natalia is far from rapturous—she's faint, and furious. When Mr. Sinden, the teacher who'd chosen her from all his students at the design school to put on this display, comes up to congratulate her, she turns on him. "If *he's* here tomorrow, then I won't be!" "He" is the man who sat front row centre, never taking his eyes off her hands, and at every stage in the "story" calling out questions, interrupting the plot. "He," Mr. Sinden explains, handing her a Dixie Cup of the coldest water he can find, "is one of the few designers who's hiring these days, and he wants to give you a job."

The Toronto School of Design, once at 1139 Bay Street, no longer exists: its function has been taken over by Ryerson University. To my mother it had been a little hothouse heaven: she'd passed the course in half the time it was supposed to take. A young model named Gay was her partner in the design course; to honour that friendship, my mother gave my sister the middle name of Gay, despite the disapproval of her father-in-law. (He found the baby's first name, Karen—chosen by my father—equally impossible: Carrots, he thought it was.) To me, it's one of the freest acts of my mother's life, this naming of her first child after a state of happiness.

Going to work for Harvey Webber, on the other hand, was far more than heavenly. The paycheque Natalia earned went straight to her parents, to help buy groceries and medicine, and, later, to pay off the loan for the house they'd bought on Dovercourt Road. If she'd failed, if she'd simply been let go—and in 1938 designers were still a dime a dozen—it would have meant disaster. Yet she never faltered; she was even strong enough to hold her own against a group of zealous Baptists when Mr. Webber sent her, along with his daughter Margaret, to a Muskoka Bible camp. "Come, you sinners," called the preacher to the row of girls sitting on the rustic bench before him. Before anyone else could reply, a voice with a Slavic accent yelled, "No way!"

Once through the door of the huge brick box on Spadina Avenue, Natalia had nothing like an office to herself—she worked at the end of the shop where enormous rolls of fabric were piled. She was one of forty or fifty people employed by Mr. Webber: cutters, steam pressers, seamstresses, finishers, examiners, shippers, office staff—a lot of the work was contracted out for trans-Canada sales, for the big chains. Natalia designed evening jackets exclusively for Simpson's, and later casual outfits for Alton Lewis, discovering there really was an Alton Lewis, "a true gentleman," who'd take her out for lunch from time to time.

In designing clothes, my mother explains, you've always got to outdo the competition. You follow the line, whether it's pleats or flares, V-necks or princess collars, but then you have to add something different, you have to gussy things up. At a shop along Spadina, a sewing supply wholesaler's, she finds boxes of specially finished nailheads in all kinds of colours. She buys handfuls from each box, taking them home, experimenting, and showing up a week later with evening jackets and crepe de Chine tops on which the nailheads, gleaming green or red or blue, cluster into peacock feathers, fireworks of leaves and flowers. Mr. Webber is ecstatic, taking them home to show his wife and daughter. They beg him not to take them back to the office, they are so beautiful. The jackets and tops sold, my mother adds, like hotcakes—business picked up in spite of hard times, and her career was made.

By the time my mother left Harvey Webber Designs to get married, she'd been offered a line of her own. She always said she turned it down because she hated the name of it—the "Nat-line." Her boss took her out to lunch the day she told him of her engagement. "Don't do it," he pleaded. "You're just about to make the big time. You can have a house in California, a house in France. You can have everything you want on your own—why do you need to get married?" A question that must have rung in her ears a few years later, when she was lugging round pails of dirty diapers, cooking enormous meals for in-laws, sitting up all night with a feverish child. Or later still, when her children were all safely at school and she suddenly had time on her hands in the large house in a quiet suburb away from all the grit and hustle of downtown.

She was often asked to go back to work; once she toyed with setting up a small design company of her own. But none of it came to anything. She sewed for her children, her mother, her sister, for friends who had "challenging" figures. Later she worked on theatrical shows, designing costumes for Odessa sailors and market women, or for a Poltava wedding. Making the rounds of wholesalers, renewing acquaintances in the rag trade after so many years away, my mother bloomed, despite the long hours, the frequent obstacles and frustrations and—of course—the fact that she was being paid for all her work in nothing but applause. She didn't expect anything else, and yet after the show was over it must have been hard to go back to being just a wife of long-standing, a mother of children well past the tractable charms of infancy.

We had arguments all through my last year of high school, arguments only superficially to do with what I'd study when I got to university. What was really at stake was whether I'd become a mirror to my mother, or a door. I chose to be a door, thinking, perhaps, that doors can swing open after they've been slammed. My mother wanted me to study dental hygiene: she wanted me to marry a dentist, to have a life as safe and solid as she'd made her own. But I was in love with lost possibilities, and the closest I could come to what my father might have been if he'd run off with his violin to New York all those years ago was to study literature. Metaphors would be my guiding stars; through them I could trace connections between the most painfully disparate things, peel back the cloudy skin over my eyes, become real, at last.

The heated kitchen debates as to what I should do with my life were finally resolved by my father: "Let her study what she loves." I moved away to university; two years later I was married—not to a dentist, but to a graduate student in English literature and, what was worse, an *Anglik*. When we moved into a shabby downtown apartment, gloriously our own, my mother came to visit. All she could say to me was, "This is the kind of place we had to live in when we came to Canada. Don't tell your Nana—it would kill her."

306

Twenty-five years have passed since then: my mother and I have come to accept one another, the different lives we've fashioned for ourselves. And yet I want more than acceptance, the bread and butter of family love. I want to cut the stitches that keep my mother and me from knowing each other as equals and as strangers, too, the way all our friends were once strangers. I want to meet, in my mother, that sweet-toothed child so full of mischief and need, that young woman, hardly out of girlhood, setting off for New York to mingle with people who'd never guess in a million years that she grew up in a place where women soaked flax and dyed wool with onion skins. And I want her to see me as more than a daughter, known and named long before I could speak a single word for myself.

The closest I can come to any of this is by listening to and telling stories, such as the one I learned only months ago. When she was eight years old, walking through Pidvolochys'k with her mother—it wasn't a pleasure walk, they had cream and eggs to sell—Natalia passed a girl her own age. This girl was carrying a small green purse, a toy and thus doubly desirable. "I wanted that purse so badly," my mother sighs. I see her following the child with her eyes, memorizing the exact shape and shade of a purse that seems like a leaf plucked from a rare and lovely tree. Years later, my mother tells me—when she was working on

Spadina, or perhaps after she'd married—she saw in the window of a shop downtown a small green purse, walked inside and bought it.

It stops there, the story. And for once I don't want my mother to tell me anything more. I'm remembering how, when I was eight years old, I wanted nothing else in the world but the dog I wasn't allowed to have. Praying every night for two years, making countless bargains with a God who'd obviously forgotten that his name spelled backwards was the object of my longing. It would have made all the difference in the world to me, then, if I'd known about my mother's helpless passion for that small green purse.

When my mother was finally able to buy herself a green purse, when I finally bought a dog, not for myself but for our two sons, neither the dog nor the purse meant what they once had. I never came across the green purse in my childhood, although my mother tells me she still has it in a drawer in her sewing room, filled with buttons. It has come to remind me of how desire tarnishes. The dog I bought for my children is beautifully sweet-tempered, but I hold myself back from him. I can't wrap my arms around his neck, confiding all my dreams and griefs as I'd longed to do when a child. Just as my mother, a grown woman when she bought her child-sized purse, could never walk round with that bright green flag signalling from her shoulder.

Hope deferred maketh the heart grow—I can't remember the end of the adage. But desire deferred can turn the present moment, with all its possibilities for joy, into the smudge of ashes. We may know our true selves at the last by what we long for and can never have, but we must, just once, receive the objects of our longing—a dog, a green purse—if only to discover their insufficiency, and thus the true nature of desire. How it overflows the most precise outlines, the most lavish contours we can make for it. And how it stays with us a whole life long, the immense destination of our small, stubborn hearts.

II. VIRA. ACHES AND PAINS: THE TIME OF HER LIFE

When did she know she'd become a doctor, stitching up not taffeta and silk, like her sister, but split skin? Back in Poland, when she nursed dozens of goslings she'd found bleeding through their beaks? Or when she was given a precious orange to take to her sick grandmother, an orange that Melania refused, wheezing so badly from asthma she could barely breathe, moaning, "Eat it yourself, eat it yourself." And Vira did, her guilt and pleasure intermingling so that even now she can't peel an orange without hearing her grandmother fighting for her next breath. Or did her vocation find her long before, when she learned that her infant sister had died from the scarlatina she herself had brought into the house, and somehow survived?

Shortly after starting her last year at Harbord Collegiate, Vira gets a weekend job shelving cans at a corner store. One afternoon she overhears a conversation between the shopkeeper and one of his customers, a Mrs. Karmulska whose daughter Lilian has just been accepted into medical school at the University of Toronto. Mrs. Karmulska pronounces the ten syllables as if they refer to some vast, celestial empire. Vira stands clutching a tin of pitted cherries, saying over and over to herself, *Lilian Karmulska, Lilian Karmulska*. A girl with a Slavic name like her own, going on to medical school.

On the last day of grade thirteen Vira Solowska, wearing the box-pleated plaid skirt and matching waistcoat her sister has sewn for her, walks down Harbord Street to King's College Circle, where University College is laid out in all its splendid sham-Romanesque. She pauses in front of Convocation Hall, catches her breath and walks inside that grandly columned building echoing with its own importance. For it's here that decisions are made as to who will be allowed to enter the University of Toronto in this year of God and War and Study, 1944. Vira locates the Admissions Office, and finds herself before the desk of a maiden lady like the ones who taught her English and who came to her rooming house to drink tea poured through a film of chicken soup. But when this woman takes the application form and reads the name printed on it, she loses all resemblance to Miss Sinclair or Miss Ferguson. "Solowska?" she asks. "I hardly think so." And she hands the application back without reading any further.

In spite of Lilian Karmulska, Vira has scarcely dared believe she could become a doctor. How would her parents find the money to pay for her tuition and textbooks, how could they afford to keep her in school so long when she could be earning a salary, as her sister does? At the most, she might become a nurse, since the hospital would pay for her tuition. Or perhaps she could study pharmacy; she has often daydreamed about Tomasz and Olena working with her in her own shop, soda jerks in fresh white uniforms. When she'd revealed how expensive medical school would be, her parents told her to fret about her marks instead. She has those marks rolled in a tight cylinder in her hand, and somehow she finds the courage, after that icy, authoritative *I hardly think so*, to unroll the cylinder across the woman's desk.

Thirteen firsts on finishing grade thirteen. The woman reads through the figures twice, as if searching for something that doesn't add up; she stares at Vira no less haughtily than before. Yet this time she nods her head ever so slightly: Miss Solowska will be admitted to this year's class, one with a noticeably higher number of women, since so many of the men who would have enrolled are off fighting in Europe. A fact the professors will not let their women students forget. "Why are you here?" these men will complain. "You'll only marry and have babies and never use what we're letting you learn. Why are you wasting our time?" It was a question Vira answered by going on to practise full-time as well as marrying and raising three children. At the age of seventy-three she still sees patients, is still brought in for consultations by the large, prestigious hospitals.

When it comes time for Vira to be interviewed for that stark necessity, a bursary, she dances her way through the questions, until the key one comes round, the one on which her whole future hangs: *Why are you going into medicine?* She forgets about her hospital for sick goslings, the grave illnesses her mother somehow pulled her through. Instead, she blurts out a story of how, when she was very small and very ill in the Old Place, a doctor had come from town to see her, a doctor in a fine grey suit. He'd made her pee into a glass, and the pee, instead of being clear, was the colour of strong tea. That mixture of the fine and strange—this is why she wants to take up medicine.

309

She did get the bursary and plunged into her studies. It was the first ex-serviceman's year, and they crammed six years of learning into five: there was no time for holidays in the summer, no time even for a concert or a film. She graduated tenth out of a class of 178 in 1949. "So I must have done well," she tells me. "I don't know why—I just loved it so much." The fact that she was a brilliant student never enters the equation, it means nothing next to the warmth she still feels for her classmates, the gratitude to her early teachers. They attend Vira's graduation, two pale, proper ladies admiring an enormous bouquet of red roses given Vira by a young Irishman, who'd disappeared as soon as her parents came into view.

Even with the roses, the diploma, the borrowed mortarboard and robes, the stunning graduation gown confected by Natalia, the hurdles stay in place. When she is interviewed for a job at Toronto Western Hospital, one of the doctors on the interview committee—a certain Dr. Feesby—takes Vira aside to a window overlooking Bathurst Street. He's a well-built man in a pinstripe suit: his hand as it cups her elbow seems to be made of something far more durable than flesh and bone. He points to a building at 300 Bathurst Street, the Labour Temple to which

Vira's father belongs and where she'd played mandolin on the concert stage until medical school swallowed her every moment.

"*That* is where you grew up," Dr. Feesby says. "*That* is where you belong."

How he'd found out about her family's being Labour Temple, Vira never knew. But just as she'd found the courage to slap down page after page of glowing examination results at the Admissions Office, so she now detaches her arm from Dr. Feesby's grip. "I wouldn't work in your hospital," she says, looking straight into his eyes, "if you begged me on your knees." Later she'll tell the doctors who want her to join their pediatric practice in the Medical Arts building, the tony one at St. George and Bloor, that no, she will not change her name from Solowska to Smith so that her patients' parents won't have to know their children are being handled by someone from *that* part of the world.

(A few years later, at the hottest moment of the McCarthy era, my father, who had also refused to change his name to something more Anglo-Saxon sounding, will be denied entrance to the United States to attend that most subversive of all activities, a dental convention. The grounds for this refusal are these: as a boy, he played violin in the Labour Temple orchestra. Soon afterwards my sister, who has always spoken Ukrainian with her family, will be sent home from kindergarten with a warning note: if she keeps speaking "Russian" in the schoolyard, the authorities will have to be alerted. My parents stop speaking Ukrainian with both their daughters, and by the time it's politically safe for us to be sent to Ukrainian school—the one run by the cathedral on Bathurst Street—we have become strangers to the language, and will never find a way to make it home.)

In the Old Place there were no pharmacies, no hospitals, and no doctors, unless you were on your way to dying. The small child who peed into a glass for a grey-suited doctor had no hint of the world of grotesque and beautiful wonders to be opened to her by anatomy and physiology textbooks, by long hours in dissection rooms. All she knew was that aches and pains were cured with herbal teas, with massages performed by women skilled in the preparation of special oils, women with massive arms and shoulders.

To try to cure Bohdan, the boy with the cracked spine, the women of the village gathered twigs, needles, amber-coloured ants from the floor of the nearest pinewoods and steeped them in boiling water; a bath would then be readied for the boy from that same pungent brew. For bad coughs, for pneumonia, a woman would come round to the house with a special set of glass cups, a bottle of alcohol, a roll of cotton. She'd swab the inside of the glass, then heat it over the flame of a candle, putting the rim down over the place where the pain was worst. Vira would watch the skin rise inside the glass like a thick, tender bubble; watch as that skin took on the colours of a different kind of rainbow: yellow, green, purple, black.

Once, Olena developed a painful sty; from the river she procured a fat, black, slimy *piavka* to put on her eyelid. It was supposed to suck up the infected blood, relieve the swelling. But the leech, moving its powerful mouth back and forth, inched from the lid to the eye itself, the painfully sensitive cornea. Olena screamed; her daughters froze until, remembering the jar of precious store-bought salt, they ran to their mother with fistfuls to throw at her eye, making the *piavka* shrivel and fall away.

If you stubbed your toe in the woods, you'd look for a puffball, stick your toe into it, and immediately it would feel better. And should you be tormented by boils or a bad cut that wouldn't heal, you could salve it with any number of leaves, from nettle to cabbage. Band-Aids were unheard of—once, gathering clover from the field by the cemetery, Vira cut her finger so badly that the blood streamed. As she ran home, a woman, seeing the red glistening down her arm, grabbed her. She tore a strip from her underskirt and bound up the finger before Vira fell through the black pushing into her eyes.

We use the knowledge we gain in the present to visit the past, to puzzle through its mysteries. Vira has no sense of smell; when she was only a baby, she was told, a group of boys playing *kuchka* had hit her in the face with the can. Her mother's mother could never distinguish between a cut onion and a rose thrust under her nose; people said she'd been bitten on that nose by a horse when she, too, was very small. In her first year of medical school Vira learns of an extremely rare condition called anosmia, a minor congenital defect passed on through the female line that robs its sufferers of any sense of smell. Vira, but not her sister, suffers from anosmia: of Vira's children, the youngest will inherit the condition.

Though the horse bite makes a better story, there's a fascination in the existence of, the very name, *anosmia*. But no such Latinate precision marks the fate of one of Vira's aunts, Olena's sister, the second daughter of Melania Sikora and Ivan Levkovych.

Sometime during the First World War, on a raw November morning, Russian soldiers march into Staromischyna. Everyone is ordered out to the fields to dig trenches. Olena's sister, tired out with digging, sits down on the freezing earth, her legs and arms numb as stones. The soldiers leave her there until the other villagers have finished the work, then she is allowed to stumble home. That night the girl is made to sit with her legs in a pail of the hottest water she can bear. Melania keeps topping up the water so it stays just below the scalding point; the next morning her daughter's legs are swollen and discoloured and she starts to run a fever. By evening a doctor has been fetched from town. He prods the girl's legs with the tip of his finger as if they are mottled sausages he has second thoughts about buying. And then he turns to Melania and says—he is not a man to mince words—"The legs will have to come off at the knee, or she'll die."

For a moment no one replies: neither Melania, nor her husband, nor any of the neighbours who've come by to see what so important a person as the doctor is doing in Staromischyna. Olena watches her sick sister, who is staring at the floor and doesn't see the instruments the doctor's taking from his bag: the small saw, the many different knives. Olena's fifteen-year-old sister speaks clearly and slowly, just three words: "Then I'll die." The doctor waits for a moment till the girl's mother nods her head. She knows the truth of what her daughter's thinking: who would want a wife who can't walk, can't work, must sit in a chair all day? Who would feed, never mind marry, her? Perhaps the doctor knows this, too—perhaps it was only a little show he put on, taking out the polished instruments that he puts back now, wiping his brow with his handkerchief as if he's just finished the operation. He leaves with the proper number of zlotys in his hand; the priest is called. Some days later he buries Olena's sister in the cemetery of St. Nikolai.

It was the shock, my grandmother always said, that killed the girl—her near-frozen legs being forced into the painfully hot water, kept there till they turned the colour of beetroot. What she implied, but never said out loud, was that her mother caused this death, as much as any Russian soldier. But when I ask Vira, she tells me that what killed her aunt would have been blood poisoning, followed by gangrene. When the girl was digging, she must have grazed her legs with the edge of the shovel; when she sat down in the trench, she'd have gotten dirt in the wounds, contracted an acute infection. As simple as that.

Simple and appalling. Not so much that the girl would be allowed to die in a world without artificial limbs, rehabilitation centres, training programs—without the very concept of "handicapped." But that no one in my family remembers her name; that all we can call her is "the girl," the fifteen-year-old I imagine to be fair-haired like her younger sister, and delicate of build. So delicate that she would tire easily and, becoming clumsy, scrape her legs with a shovel so the blood ran down into the earth.

All through her twenties, despite the fierce pressure of study, the lack of anything like free time, and the absence sometimes of sleep itself, Vira had what she describes, in her seventies, as the time of her life. She and her friend Dorothy Shepherd were the first two women interns taken on by St. Joseph's Hospital; later they were joined by Hilda Vierkarter, daughter of the man called "the black shark" for having swum the English Channel. At 2 A.M. the three of them would make snacks with the toaster Hilda's mother had given her, only to be told off by the nuns, whose patients, fasting before major operations, were driven crazy by the smell of toasting bread. At other times the girls, as Vira calls herself and her fellow interns, would stagger to their room at 4 A.M. after finishing in the emergency wards. They'd be so tired they'd collapse onto their beds, shoes clunking to the floor. At breakfast the priest from the room below theirs would joke about how glad he was the girls weren't centipedes.

Gus, the young Irishman who brought Vira roses at her graduation, would come to see her at St. Joe's—a more welcoming place, just then, than the Dovercourt house. They would walk down to the lake, whose sunstruck waters could be seen from the hospital windows. Down to Sunnyside where they'd feast on doughnuts and hot chocolate and maybe go for a swim at the pool. "We would always take Dorothy along, my dear, dear Dorothy," Vira says. "She adored Gus, and he would never leave her behind—so you can see how romantic those dates would be. But anyway, we had a ball." *We had a ball*—the happy slang showing how much she's come to feel at home in her third language: the distance she's travelled between necessity and pleasure.

Vira was advised to finish her training in Detroit, under Dr. Wolfgang Zuelzer, a pathologist and hematologist at the Children's Hospital of Michigan. So off she went, aged twenty-six and on her own for the first time in her life. Her internship, it turned out, was mostly in gross pathology—there were so many dead children to deal with. When she came back to Canada and went on to the Hospital for Sick Children, she was prepared for things that doctors who'd done all their training in Toronto had never seen.

But it was intoxicating being in a new place, doing work that, however grim, endlessly intrigued her. For her work at the hospital she received the queenly sum of fifty dollars a month, out of which she bought for her newborn niece a lamp shaped like a duck. And she cajoled a fellow intern, Reuben, into taking her along on one of his home deliveries in one of the poor, black neighbourhoods. No sooner had Reuben spread newspapers over the floor than the baby shot from between its mother's thighs and straight into his arms—he almost hit the floor, catching it. To the grandmother frowning in a corner, her hefty arms crossed tight, Reuben stammered, "At the hospital we always jump up and down with them at least six times—it clears their lungs."

When Vira got her fellowship in 1954 and set up her own practice in pediatrics, she cleared exactly fifty dollars her first year after she'd paid the cleaner and the rent on the office. Sometimes her patients gave her cheques that bounced; at other times, when the ones who never had ready cash would ask, "How much, Doctor?" she'd feel like crawling under her desk. How could she charge a child for being sick? When she married, she set up a practice in her home, and her children learned to deal with a telephone ringing, day and night, with demands that the doctor drop everything to attend to this or that sick child. And the doctor always did. It was her way of answering those mustachioed men in their grey suits who had frowned from their lecterns at all the wasteful young women who'd only go off, get married, and have babies.

The Russian Album

MICHAEL IGNATIEFF

A portrait of one of Michael Ignatieff's ancestors, one of imperial Russia's great military heroes from Napoleonic times, hangs in the Hermitage in St. Petersburg. The author's grandfather was a minister in the last czarist government, his father a prominent Canadian diplomat and statesman. Ignatieff himself, born in Toronto in 1947 and educated at Toronto, Cambridge, and Harvard, came relatively late to an appreciation of his Russian heritage, as this section from his 1987 memoir *The Russian Album* testifies. The book won the Governor General's Award in Canada and the Royal Society of Literature Award in Britain, where Ignatieff has spent much of his time in recent years, acquiring renown as a public philosopher and liberal commentator, somewhat in the style of Sir Isaiah Berlin (whose biographer he is). Some of Ignatieff's other books are *A Just Measure of Pain: The Penitentiary in the Industrial Revolution* (1978), *Virtual War* (2000), and two novels, *Asya* (1990) and *Scar Tissue* (1993).

THE BROKEN PATH

Dwell on the past and you'll lose an eye.
Ignore the past and you'll lose both of them.
OLD RUSSIAN PROVERB

No one I know lives in the house where they grew up or even in the town or village where they once were children. Most of my friends live apart from their parents. Many were born in one country and now live in another. Others live in exile, forming their thoughts in a second language among strangers. I have friends whose family past was consumed in the concentration camps. They are orphans in time. This century has made migration, expatriation, and exile the norm, rootedness the exception. To come as I do from a hybrid family of

White Russian exiles who married Scottish Canadians is to be at once lucky—we survived—and typical.

Because emigration, exile, and expatriation are now the normal condition of existence, it is almost impossible to find the right words for rootedness and belonging. Our need for home is cast in the language of loss; indeed, to have that need at all you have to be already homeless. Belonging now is retrospective rather than actual, remembered rather than experienced, imagined rather than felt. Life now moves so quickly that some of us feel that we were literally different people at previous times in our lives. If the continuity of our own selves is now problematic, our connection with family ancestry is yet more in question. Our grandparents stare out at us from the pages of the family album, solidly grounded in a time now finished, their lips open, ready to speak words we cannot hear.

For many families, photographs are often the only artifacts to survive the passage through exile, migration, or the pawnshop. In a secular culture, they are the only household icons, the only objects that perform the religious function of connecting the living to the dead and of locating the identity of the living in time. I never feel I know my friends until either I meet their parents or see their photographs and since this rarely happens, I often wonder whether I know anybody very well. If we are strangers even to our friends, it is because our knowledge of each other is always in a dimension of time that my grandparents' culture would have considered inconceivably shallow. In the world of both the rich and the poor of even a century ago, one knew someone as his father's son, his grandmother's grandson, and so on. In the Russian style of address, first name and then patronymic, this kind of knowing is inscribed in the very way one names a friend or relation. To a Russian, I am Michael Georgevitch, George's son, a self rooted in a family past. In the non-Russian world I live in, I am known for what I do, for how I am now, not for the past I embody. Looking at someone's family album is a way towards a deeper temporal knowing of another. But nowadays, a frontier of intimacy has to be crossed before these photographs are shown even to friends. Within the family itself, photographs are not really icons, hovering presences on the wall. Styles of inheritance are now individual: we are free to take or refuse our past. Children have as much right to refuse interest in these icons as they have to stick to their own opinions. Yet the more negotiable, the more invented the past becomes, the more intense its hold, the more central its invention becomes in the art of making a self. Eventually there are few of us who do not return home one holiday weekend, go to the bottom drawer, pull out the old shoe box, and spread the pictures around us on the floor.

Father has his arm around Tereze
She squints. My thumb
is in my mouth: my fifth autumn.
Near the copper beech
the spaniel dozes in the shadows.
Not one of us does not avert his eyes.
    (Louise Gluck, "Still Life")

From its beginnings, photography was recognized as a new source of consciousness about the family past. As a contributor to *Macmillan's Magazine* wrote in
1877: "Anyone who knows what the worth of family affection is among the lower
classes and who has seen the array of little portraits over a labourer's fire place will
perhaps feel with me that in counteracting the tendencies, social and industrial,
which are every day sapping the healthier family affections, the sixpenny photograph
is doing more for the poor than all the philanthropists in the world" (quoted in Susan
Sontag, *On Photography*). In democratizing the privilege of a family portrait gallery,
the six-penny photograph deserves a place in the social history of modern individualism. With the coming of the photograph, poor families had a new kind of inheritance: six-penny tokens coded with the signs of their genetic legacy. If they could
not bequeath property, they could bequeath the history of the handing down of the
curve of a lip, the shape of a forehead, the set of a jaw. In giving silent presence
to vanished generations and in diffusing this presence throughout the whole culture,
photography has played a part in bringing the problem of personal identity to the
centre of cultural concern. The awareness that we must create ourselves and find
our own belonging was once the privilege of an educated elite and is now a gener-
alized cultural condition. For in helping to constitute identity in time, photography
also poses the problem of the freedom of the self to make its own present. To look
at an old photograph and to discover that one has inherited the shape of one's eyes,
to hear from one's parents that one has also inherited a temperament, is both to
feel a new location in time but also a dawning sense of imprisonment. The passion
for roots—the mass pastime of family history—represses the sense of suffocation
that family photographs can engender. That is one reason why the old photographs
get consigned to the old shoe box at the bottom of the drawer. We need them but
we do not want to be claimed by them. Because they bring us face to face with an
inheritance that cannot be altered, photographs pose the problem of freedom: they
seem to set the limits within which the self can be created.

317

The photographs in a family album bring us closer to the past and yet their acute physical tactility reminds us of all the distance that still remains uncrossed. As such, photographs have done something to create that very modern sense of the past as a lost country. My first impression of that sense came when I was very young. I was watching an interview on television with an old black man who was supposed to be the last American who had lived under slavery. In a whisper, he told how he had been born in what must now be Liberia and how he had been enticed onto a ship with promises of corn fritters growing on trees in a land where you never had to work all day. I can remember thinking that if this tiny man with his faint voice and papery skin were to die, the past of slavery, the chains and the chanting, would slide away from me like a cliff subsiding into the sea. I still cannot shake off the superstition that the only past that is real, that exists at all, is the one contained within the memories of living people. When they die, the past they hold within them simply vanishes, and those of us who come after cannot inherit their experience, only preserve the myth of its existence. We can mark the spot where the cliff was washed away by the sea, but we cannot repair the wound the sea has made. In my lifetime the last of the people born before the Russian Revolution will die. My father is the very last of that generation, aged four in February 1917, just old enough to remember the bayonets glinting like glass below the window of the house in Petrograd on the morning the soldiers stormed to the Duma and said they had had enough of hunger and war. His memory just bestrides this abyss dividing everything before and everything after the revolution. I in turn am the last generation to know his generation, the last to be able to plumb their memory, to feel the presence of their past in the timbre of their voices and in the gaze they cast back across time. Already I am so far away from what happened, so much a Canadian born of this time and place and no other, that I feel fraudulent in my absorption in the vanishing experience of another generation. Yet so swiftly does time move now that unless I do my work to preserve memory, soon all there will be left is photographs and photographs only document the distance that time has travelled; they cannot bind past and present together with meaning.

I am a historian and historians are supposed to believe that they can transport themselves in time to recapture experience swept away by the death of earlier generations. In even the most rigorously scientific history, there is a resurrectionary hope at work, a faith in the power of imagination and empathy to vault the gulf of time. To do their work at all, historians have to believe that knowledge can consummate desire—that our dull and patient immersion in the records of the past can ultimately satisfy our desire to master time's losses. The historical imagination emerges from loss, dispossession, and confinement, the same experiences that make for exile and migration. It is roused when the past can no longer be taken for granted as a felt tradition or when the past has become a burden from which the present seeks emancipation. It is a sense of fracture or a sense of imprisonment that sends historians back to the archives, the memoirs, the tape-recorded voices. Yet this relation between loss and the imagination is full of irony. History has less authority than memory, less legitimacy than tradition. History can never speak with the one voice that our need for belonging requires. It cannot heal the hurt of loss. Our knowledge of the past cannot satisfy our desire for the past. What we can know about the past and what we want from it are two different things.

Photographs of ancestors seem to capture this irony precisely. In the family album, my grandfather seems almost real, almost on the point of speaking. But his clothes, the frock coat, the hands held down the striping of his court uniform, mark him as a historical being irrevocably distant in time. The more palpable the photograph renders his presence, the more sharply I realize that the gulf that divides us involves both my mortality and theirs.

That it is *my* death that is in question, and not just his, becomes apparent when we look at photographs of ourselves. They awaken a sense of loss because they work against the integrative functions of forgetting. Photographs are the freeze frames that remind us how discontinuous our lives actually are. It is in a tight weave of forgetting and selective remembering that a continuous self is knitted together. Forgetting helps us to sustain a suspension of belief in our own death which allows us time to believe in our lives. At the end of his life, the French writer Roland Barthes gave a talk to an audience much younger than himself, and thought out loud about the hope—and the passion for life—that forgetting makes possible: "In order to live, I have to forget that my body has a history. I have to throw myself into the illusion that I am the contemporary of these young bodies who are present and listening to me, and not of my own body weighed down with the past. From time to time, in other words, I have to be born again, I have to make myself younger than I am. I let myself be swept along by the force of all living life—forgetting" (*Nouvel Observateur*, March 31, 1980).

Photographs do not always support the process of forgetting and remembering by which we weave an integral and stable self over time. The family album does

319

not always conjure forth the stream of healing recollection that binds together the present self and its past. More often than not photographs subvert the continuity that memory weaves out of experience. Photography stops time and serves it back to us in disjunctive fragments. Memory integrates the visual within a weave of myth. The knitting together of past and present that memory and forgetting achieve is mythological because the self is constantly imagined, constructed, invented out of what the self wishes to remember. The photograph acts towards the self like a harshly lit mirror, like the historian confronted with the wish-ful-fillments of nationalistic fable or political lie. Look at a picture of yourself at four or five, and ask yourself honestly whether you can feel that you still are this tender self, squinting into the camera. As a record of our forgetting, the camera has played some part in engendering our characteristic modern suspicion about the self-deceiving ruses of our consciousness. Memory heals the scars of time. Photography documents the wounds.

So it is not only the dead ancestors who seem as distant as stars but even the younger versions of ourselves who take up our positions in the family album. It is this double process of loss, the loss of them, the loss of oneself, which the struggle of writing tries to arrest.

> His pursuit was a form of evasion.
> The more he tried to uncover
> the more there was to conceal
> the less he understood.
> If he kept it up
> he would lose everything.
> He knew this
> and remembered what he could—
> always at a distance,
> on the other side of the lake,
> or across the lawn,
> always vanishing, always there.
> (Mark Strand, "The Untelling")

Yet loss is only one of the emotions awakened by exile and dispossession. There is also the "syncopal kick," the release of stored energies that Vladimir Nabokov describes in Speak Memory as being one of exile's least expected gifts. It was exile that made Nabokov a writer; it was exile that turned the taken-for-granted past into a fabled territory that had to be reclaimed, inch by inch, by the writer's art. Just as in the moment of flight exiles must grab the treasures that will become their belongings on the road into exile, so they must choose the past they will carry with them, what version they will tell, what version they will believe. From being an unconsidered inheritance, the past becomes their invention, their story.

Once the story has been handed on from first to second generation, the family past becomes still less a fate and ever more a narrative of self-invention. For someone like myself in the second generation of an émigré tradition, the past has become the story we write to give weight and direction to the accident and contingency of our lives. True, we cannot invent our past out of nothing: there are photos and memories and stories, and sometimes our invention consists mostly in denying what it is we have inherited. Yet even when we disavow it, we are inventing a past in our denials. The problem of invention is authenticity. In the second generation we are free to choose our pasts, but the past we choose can never quite seem as real, as authentic, as those of the first generation.

In my own case, I have two pasts. My mother's family, the Grants and the Parkins, were high-minded Nova Scotians who came to Toronto in the last century and made a name for themselves as teachers and writers. They were close to me as a child: as close as my grandmother's house on Prince Arthur Avenue in Toronto.

My father's past is Russian. My grandfather, Paul Ignatieff, was Minister of Education in the last Cabinet of Czar Nicholas II. His father, Nicholas Ignatieff, was the Russian diplomat who in 1860 negotiated the Amur-Ussuri boundary treaty that defines the border between Russia and China in the Pacific region to this day; in 1878 he negotiated the treaty bringing the Russo-Turkish War to a conclusion; and in 1881 he was the minister who put his name to the special legislation against the Jews.

My grandmother was born Princess Natasha Mestchersky on an estate near Smolensk bequeathed to her mother's family by Empress Catherine the Great in the late eighteenth century. In her family she counted a foreign minister of Russia, a general, and the first modern historian of her country, Nicholas Karamzin.

When my Russian grandfather was nineteen and choosing a career, the tramlines of his past ran straight into the future: he would enter a Guards regiment like his father, grandfather, and great-grandfather before him. He could then make a career in the army or return to the family estates and live as a gentleman farmer.

At some point in his life he would be expected to leave the estate and serve the czar, as his grandfather and father had done. He would "shoulder the chains of service." It is in these precise senses—a destiny inherited and shouldered without questioning—that his identity is irrevocably different from my own. My identity—my belonging to the past he bequeathed me—is a matter of choosing the words I put on a page. I am glad that this is so: his is not a fate or an identity that I would wish as my own. But it is a difference that makes full understanding between us impossible.

My grandmother's self was made within a frame of choices even narrower than those of her husband: to be a dutiful daughter and then a faithful wife. The fulcrum of her life, the one moment when fate could be heaved this way or that, was marriage. There would be some choosing for her to do, among the young officers with wasp-waisted uniforms who were allowed to dance with her at the Petersburg debutante balls. But she was a Princess Mestchersky and once her eyes had fallen on a man, his particulars "back to Adam and Eve" would be investigated and if they were found wanting, she would have to choose again.

Both of them were born into a time when their past was also their future. Life had a necessity to it: it was not a tissue of their own making. They grew up in a time measured by a protocol of family decorum. They ended their lives in the formless time of exile, a time with no future and a past suspended out of reach. When they landed in England in the summer of 1919 they were already too old to start again, too old to feel the emancipating energies of exile. My grandparents could only remember: they could no longer invent the present.

Between my two pasts, the Canadian and the Russian, I felt I had to choose. The exotic always exerts a stronger lure than the familiar and I was always my father's son. I chose the vanished past, the past lost behind the revolution. I could count on my mother's inheritance: it was always there. It was my father's past that mattered to me, because it was one I had to recover, to make my own.

My earliest memories are not memories of myself, but of my father talking about his ancestors. I recall being on board the *Queen Mary* during a crossing between New York and Southampton in 1953 when I was six and hearing my father tell the story of how his grandfather Nicholas rode from Peking to Petersburg in six weeks to bring the czar the news of the treaty he had signed with the Chinese emperor; and how when a blizzard struck on the Siberian plains Nicholas had formed his Cossack horsemen into a circle, bivouacked in the centre and warmed themselves through the blizzard by the breath from the horses.

Since my father was a diplomat who moved every eighteen months of my childhood, the things I came to count on as icons of stability were not the houses we lived in, since they changed all the time, but the very few Russian objects we carried with us from one posting to the next. There was a silver ewer and basin that stood on a succession of dining tables in a succession of official apartments, which had once been used by my maternal great-grandmother to wash her hands when she awoke at her country estate in the mornings during the 1880s. Objects like the silver ewer and basin, like the Sultan's diamond star that my mother wore on family occasions, were vital emblems of continuity in a childhood without fixed landmarks. Few of these were still left: some embossed volumes of Nicholas Karamzin's history of Russia, an icon or two on the wall above my parents' bed. Sometimes these objects turned up in family photographs. I still remember the pleasure I got as a child from discovering that a piece of jewellery my mother wore was to be seen in a photograph of my grandmother Natasha taken seventy years before. It was as if the little pearl and diamond brooch had flown free of its amber imprisonment in the photograph, vaulting all the time between me and her.

I heard very little Russian as a child: my father did not speak it at home. I went with him to the Russian church in the cities where I grew up—New York, Toronto, Ottawa, Belgrade, Paris, Geneva, and London—and I was moved by the service because I did not understand it. Standing beside him in the church, watching him light his candles, say his prayers, and sing in his deep vibrating voice, I always felt that he had slipped away through some invisible door in the air. Yet he kept his distance from the Russian émigré community, from their factional intrigues and antediluvian politics. He presented himself to the world throughout my childhood as the model of an assimilated Canadian professional. And to this day he is a much more patriotic and sentimental Canadian than I am. For him Canada was the country that gave him a new start. For me, being a Canadian was just one of those privileges I took for granted.

Father often met Soviet diplomats in his work and they always spoke Russian together. Yet the meetings were edgy. I remember one Soviet diplomat, dressed like a Zurich banker with a large black onyx ring on his finger, being introduced to both of us in a lobby of the United Nations building in New York. He doffed his astrakhan and in a great sweeping gesture said in English, "As the son of a peasant I salute you." Other Soviets treated the family past with the same mixture of respect and irony. In 1955, my father returned to the Soviet Union as part of an official Canadian delegation led by the foreign minister, Mike Pearson. The Soviet officials, led by Nikita Khrushchev himself, called my father *Graf* (Count) and took him aside and asked in all sincerity why he didn't come "home" again and continue the diplomatic work of his grandfather instead of serving the diplomacy of a small satellite state of the Americans. But my father didn't feel at home at all in the Soviet Union of the 1950s. Even the moments of memoried connection were brief, as when he was shown into his room at the Hotel Astoria in Leningrad, frozen in its pre-revolutionary decor, and saw on the writing desk two silver bears exactly like two little bears that had once stood on his father's desk in the same city forty years before. On that visit, he also realized how archaic his Russian sounded to Soviet citizens and how rusty it had become. He found himself stumbling in his native tongue.

Back home, family feeling on the Russian side was intense, but there were few actual occasions when we came together. Throughout my childhood, the Russian half of the family was scattered abroad. My father's eldest brother, Nicholas, had died in my childhood, and the remaining four were thousands of miles apart. When the brothers did come together for the wedding of my cousin Mika, we all made a little space for them apart and they sat on the couch, balding giants each over six feet tall, talking in Russian, while none of us understood a word. They had all married outside the Russian circle and so none of their children grew up in the Russian tongue. I never learned the language.

In my inability to learn Russian, I can now see the extent of my resistance to a past I was at the same time choosing as my own. The myths were never forced upon me so my resistance was directed not at my father or my uncles but rather at my own inner craving for these stories, at what seemed a weak desire on my part to build my little life upon the authority of their own. I wasn't sure I had the right to the authority of the past and even if I did have the right, I didn't want to avail myself of the privilege. Yet as one of my friends wryly says when I talk like this, no one ever gives up his privileges. So I used the past whenever I needed to, but with a guilty conscience. My friends had suburban pasts or pasts they would rather not talk about. I had a past of czarist adventurers, survivors of revolutions, heroic exiles. Yet the stronger my need for them, the stronger too became my need to disavow them, to strike out on my own. To choose my past meant to define the limits of its impingement upon me.

My father always said that I was more Mestchersky than Ignatieff, more like his mother than his father. Since he was more Ignatieff than Mestchersky, the statement underlined how complicated the ties of filiation really were between us. Inheritance is always as much a matter of anxiety as pride. If I was a Mestchersky what could I possibly make of myself? How could I ever master my temperament, that tightly strung bundle of fears and anxieties that seemed to have me locked in its grasp? From the beginning, the project of finding out about my past was connected to a struggle to master the anxiety of its influence.

I also found myself face to face with what I liked least about myself. My grandfather's favourite phrase was, "Life is not a game, life is not a joke. It is only by putting on the chains of service that man is able to accomplish his destiny on earth." When Paul talked like this, my grandmother, Natasha, always used to mutter, "The Ignatieffs would make hell out of Paradise."

Early on I learned that both my father and my uncle Nicholas had wanted to write a history of the family. My father had even been to Bulgaria to research the story of his grandfather's role in the creation of Bulgaria after the Russian defeat of the Turks in the war of 1877–78. Nicholas had had similar ideas, but he was dead and his manuscripts lay in his widow's basement. My father was a busy man and his project languished. So the idea of a history of the family had germinated: it was an idea I could bring to fruition if I wanted to. But I held back.

I was in my teens when I first read my grandparents' memoirs. Beginning in September 1940 in a cottage in Upper Melbourne, Quebec, my grandmother, Natasha, typed out a stream of free associations, beginning with childhood on the estate, her marriage to my grandfather, Paul Ignatieff, life in Petersburg, revolution, civil war, and escape. She wrote in the English she had learned from her governess, in the English she knew her grandchildren would grow up speaking. When she got to 1919—when she got to the moment they left Russia—she stopped. Everything became harder then, harder to say and all the period in exile she left in silence. By then there were over 250 pages, a jumble that my aunt Florence sorted and retyped after her death.

My grandfather, Paul, had written his memoirs in Sussex and in Paris during the 1920s. He wrote in Russian and only much later translated them into English with the help of a Canadian friend. My grandmother's recollections are a frank and faithful echo of the woman she was, put down just as she spoke in every meandering turn of phrase, but his dry, orderly, and restrained prose was, or so I felt, an exercise in discretion and concealment. He confined himself to his official career, as gentleman farmer, governor of Kiev province, deputy minister of agriculture and minister of education in the final Cabinet of the czar. It is a

325

restrained public document. Emotion cracks through the shell of measured phrases just once, when he describes his last meeting with Nicholas II in the final days of the regime.

Their memoirs were unpublishable, hers because what made them so alive also made them unreadable, his because they so meticulously excluded the personal and because the events he described had been so exhaustively retold in the deluge of czarist memoir. I decided, nearly ten years ago now, to retell their story in my own words. As a historian, I thought my first task would be to locate them in their historical setting, to distance myself from them as members of my family and to treat them instead as historical specimens, as objects of study. It took me some time to realize the unintended consequences of this strategy. I can remember a moment during the early days of my research when I was reading the proceedings of a Russian land-reform commission of 1902, searching for a mention of the family estates through spools of faint microfilm. Since my grandfather was a local marshal of nobility, he had to write a report for the commission. It was the first time I had read something by him that was not addressed to his family: the memoirs, the letters I had read before all had us as their intended audience. In this little report he was suddenly a tiny figure in a historical setting. The irony was that the process of tracking him into his historical context did not make the contours of his character come into sharper relief. The reverse occurred. The more I came to know about him as a historical being—as a quite typical member of the liberal service gentry, as a non-party constitutional monarchist—the more he began to slip out of reach. The sharper I drew his definition as a historical being, the more blurred he became as my grandfather. As an object of historical knowledge he could only be grasped in the plural; as an object of desire, I sought him in his singularity. In the process of finding him as an exemplary imperial character, I lost him as my grandfather. The historical way of knowing the past is to place a figure in the background of serial time; I wanted the opposite, to make him present in simultaneous time with me. Yet I always knew that this was an impossible desire and that even a history of their lives was doomed to failure. I could never recreate the past as my uncles remembered it or hope to conciliate the quarrels between contending memories. Even today the brothers still argue heatedly about some things and I could not hope to establish who was right. Most of all, I could not hope to bring back Paul and Natasha. Even the simplest physical detail about them, how she moved the hair off her face, how he used to snap a book shut when he had read it, required acts of painstaking reconstitution for me; for my father these details were such simple primary memories he scarcely bothered to mention them. It soon became apparent that the only portrait I could hope to paint of Paul and Natasha would always be a crude sketch, a study in the unbridgeable distances between first and second generations. For a long time I thought that if a history was doomed to failure anyway, I should abandon history and turn my grandparents' life into fiction. It was a tempting idea: my characters would be just sufficiently grounded in a real past to be authentic and yet they would do my bidding. They would wear my clothes, speak my lines, live out my dramas and fulfill my ambitions. In creating them I would create myself. In the end the idea of fiction foundered on the realization that such a novel would be peopled by characters neither real in themselves nor faithful to their originals.

It was years before I began to see Paul and Natasha apart from my needs for them. I learned that their lives were not an adventure that existed so that I could quarry them for meanings of my own. There were too many silences, too many things I could not know about them for me to ransack their experience for my purposes. Very slowly, it dawned on me that instead of *them* owing me the secret of my life, I owed *them* fidelity to the truth of the lives they had led. Fiction would have been a betrayal. I had to return and stay close to the initial shock of my encounter with their photographs: that sense that they were both present to me in all their dense physical actuality and as distant as stars. In recreating them as truthfully as I could, I had to respect the distance between us. I had to pay close attention to what they left unsaid; I had to put down a marker at the spots that had not been reclaimed by memory. I could not elide these silences by the artifice of fiction.

327

I went twice with my father to the Soviet Union to find their traces. There was a lot to find: until the fall of Khrushchev the folk drama of socialist reconstruction justified the levelling of palaces and the conversion of churches to printing plants or lumberyards. Only poverty and backwardness saved old buildings. A country too poor to replace them lived out the drama of the new in the tattered stage sets of the old. In the late 1960s and 1970s, the vandalism of Khrushchevian modernism produced a counter-reaction that reached back to national traditions untarnished by Communism. Now not just the great palaces and monasteries were regilded but anything with a patina of age began to reacquire authority. A new national past uniting pre- and post-1917 was constructed by artful elision of the revolution's destructive work. As a result of this ironic and uneasy attempt to recuperate the czarist past, in some ways it is easier to find traces of a czarist family past in the Soviet Union than it is in the West. In the leafy shade of the cemetery of Novodevichy convent in Moscow, near the graves of Khrushchev and Stalin's wife, we found the grave of the family renegade, Uncle Alyosha, who began his career as a czarist officer and ended it as a Red general. In Leningrad, we found the family house on Fourstatskaya street where my father had watched the first demonstrations of the February Revolution in 1917. It is now the Leningrad Palace of Marriages. In the ballroom where my grandmother once served tea, young couples were being married, one pair every ten minutes, by an imposing woman in a red ball gown and a sash of office. Downstairs in the school-room where my uncles used to take their lessons from their French tutor, Monsieur Darier, mothers with pins in their mouths were making last-minute adjustments to their daughters' wedding dresses. And down a small back hallway, with dim portraits of Lenin on the wall and an Intourist calendar of scenes from a Crimean resort, my father found the room that had been his nursery.

In Kislovodsk, a south Caucasus spa town between the Black and Caspian seas, one September afternoon, my father and I found the green gate of the garden in which stood the house he had lived in with his family during the civil war in 1917 and 1918. Several houses had been crammed into the garden since the family's wretched years there, but there were still apple trees and poplars at the back, just as there were in 1918.

Yet the apparent ease with which we picked up the traces of the family past inside the Soviet Union proved deceptive. I remember suddenly feeling the unseen distances separating me from my past while standing in front of the Matisse paint-ings in the Pushkin Museum in Moscow, all collected by czarist merchants before the First World War. For Russian visitors to the museum, the Matisses are a strange and discordant departure from the realism of Russian nineteenth-century genre painting; they are equally alien to the socialist realism that was to carry this tradition forward in the Soviet period. For Russians, the Matisses are thus frag-ments of modernism suspended out of reach of the European tradition that nur-tured them. For us the Matisse paintings are the founding canvases of our very way of seeing. As I looked at the sunlit ateliers, the bright deck chair, the bowl of flowers, the woman in the lustrous blue dress and looked at the dates of their composition, 1910, 1911, 1912, I realized that they were collected by my grand-parents' generation. This generation was the first to have successfully resolved the old dilemma of whether Russians were a European or an Asian people. Natasha spoke and thought in German and English; her dentist was an American who lived in Dresden; she bought her lingerie in Nice; she had Lyle's Golden Syrup for tea in her nursery. Paul was raised by French tutors and grew up thinking and speaking in French. Yet both were passionately attached to the religions, customs, smells, architecture, curses, and chaos of their native land.

They travelled across an open frontier to countries whose painting, food, and landscape they regarded as their own. Matisse's Mediterranean light was as much their own as the eternal summer light of Petersburg. They were the first generation to reconcile their European and their Russian identities, and they were the last. A border of barbed wire, searchlights, and gun emplacements has been sawed across a Europe they once believed stretched from Moscow to the Atlantic, and when I try to follow their footsteps across that frontier I am aware that I am entering a country that now seems more a strange new Asian empire than an old heartland of European culture. The distance that I now must try to cross between them and me is much more than the distance of time. It is the chasm marked by the no man's land of barbed wire that divides European culture into two armed camps.

My Soviet guides were often unsettled by my estrangement from their native land. They wanted to help my search for connections, phoning local history museums to find the new names of streets we knew only from their original names in the 1914 edition of Baedeker's guide to Russia, and helping us even to find the jails and interrogation rooms where my grandfather spent the loneliest hours of his life in 1918. The Soviet guides admired my father's slightly old-fashioned Russian, so much softer and gentler in enunciation than their own, and they were puzzled but polite when I said I understood not a word of my father's native tongue. There were a few sites that it was not possible to visit—Kroupodernitsa, the Ignatieff estate in the Ukraine where my great-grandfather and great-grandmother are buried, seemed to be off limits, though for reasons that were never explained. Yet the authorities sent a photographer to the village church and took pictures of the family graves, dressed with bouquets of fresh flowers. We were told the estate is now a village school. Of Doughino, the eighteenth-century estate near Smolensk where my grandmother grew up, there was no trace. It was burned to the ground in 1917. My father wept when he left Russia, and I left dry-eyed.

There must be something to the superstition that by returning to a place one can return in time to the self one once was in those places. My father was six when he left Russia in 1919, and his memories are few and indistinct. Yet he found a catharsis in returning, a rounding out of his life. For me, the trips to the Soviet Union redoubled my sense of the irrecoverable distance of my family past.

But by a paradox that must be at the heart of writing itself, the more distant everything became, the more urgent it became to get the story down before the death of my father's generation broke the last living links.

My father and his brothers gave me every kind of help but they could not conceal their misgivings. I was like an auctioneer sent to value their treasures for sale. Our long sessions together over the tape recorder were harbingers of their mortality. I often thought that it would be better if I left the project aside until they were safely dead and buried. Then I would be free to say it all. But what kind of freedom is that, the freedom to say everything one never dared to say in person? Who is not haunted by the silences, the missed chances for truth that slip between father and son, mother and daughter, the chances that slip finally into the grave? I do not want to miss my chance.

I have done my best to disentangle history from myth, fact from fancy, but in the end I cannot be sure of the truth, either of what happened or what is remembered. I wasn't there. I can only register the impact of their struggle to remember: I can tell them the wave did reach the shore. Because Paul and Natasha managed to remember what they did and passed it on, I owe to them the conviction that my own life did not begin with my birth, but with hers and with his, a hundred years ago in a foreign land, and that now as the last of the generation who knew what life was like behind the red curtain of the revolution begins to depart, it is up to me to pass on their remembering to whoever comes after.

After all these years spent searching for their traces, I can hear their voices at last as if they were in the room. This is how Natasha began her memoirs, her first sentence:

"I decide while I am still in my fresh mind to put down all dates and years of main episodes of our lives, my dear husband's and mine, so that when we pass into eternity our sons and their families may have a picture more or less of interesting episodes of our lives, colourful lives, thanks to so many striking events and in the middle age of our lives tremendous upheavals we had to pass through and which left a totally different side of our further existence."

THE LITTLE FOOLS

Natasha's *durachki*, her little fools, are now old men.

Last summer I went home to Canada to visit them all. Lionel lives in a nursing home north of Toronto. He is in his seventies now and looks like one of the studious saints on an Orthodox icon. I visit him in the Chinese café in a shopping mall many stoplights north of Highway 401, in the featureless sprawl of north Toronto. The café—and the whole mall—are owned by Hong Kong Chinese. Nothing but fields existed here five years ago.

"Hi, Uncle," the Chinaman says as Lino and I come in. "This your family from Russia?" "He's from London," Lino says slowly. "You must be happy man, he come see you." "I am happy," Lino says. His legs are bent and he shuffles to a booth and lowers himself down slowly. He wears a pith helmet. He shows me the initials on the hatband and says he checks them to know which way to put it on. He takes the bus to this shopping mall once a month to get his hair cut. "There is not much to cut," he says, rubbing his bald head. Afterwards he comes to this café and has tea and almond cookies. It is his major outing.

As a little boy, he grinned madly from the photographs in his father's arms in front of the wicker bathing hut at Misdroy. He is a Mestchersky like his mother but thinner, more finely featured than his brothers. The mad grin of childhood is replaced now by a whisper of a smile. He seems uninterested in the past.

I tell him I've been back to Beauchamps. "It must be overgrown by now." He smiles, takes a nibble from the almond cookies. I ask him whether he remembers the view of the sea from his bedroom window. He looks puzzled. "The sea?"

He says, "I have something called Parkinson's disease. Do you know about it? It makes my hands shake." He holds out his spidery hands. His mother's hands. They buzz with a barely perceptible tremor, like current humming through a line. "I also have had what they call depression. Here," and he points to a place on the top of his head. "I received treatments, you know."

My father had to sign the forms. They put the block between Lionel's teeth; they tied him down, they coursed the current through his limbs. They have stabilized his condition.

"In the hospital I met some exceedingly interesting people, people I would never have met in the world outside. They were depressed too." This bone-thin traveller, the mildest and gentlest of the brothers, has been in the locked wards. He was the one who paid the price.

"I ask myself many times. What is this depression? I think I know." He holds his coffee cup between thumb and forefinger and brings it delicately to his lips in a gesture from another time. There is Tina Turner on the radio. He is a long way from Petersburg. He says, "Depression is not having a purpose in life."

His brothers say he is the one who was hurt most by exile, by the breaking

331

up of the family in England, by the departure for Canada. He could have stayed in the Russian community in London; he could have continued to be an amateur actor in the dramatic society. Something went wrong. But if his illness is tenacious, so is he. After an early life of false starts—a marriage and a divorce—he got his doctorate and taught Russian literature at the University of Western Ontario in London, Ontario, until his retirement. I tell him I have been reading the Russian poet Anna Akhmatova. He spreads his hands out on the table to watch the tremor. "In translation. What a pity."

He looks at me. "Do you know *The Plain Truth?*" It is an American evangelical magazine. Lino watches evangelical television services from Pasadena, California, every Sunday. My father still takes him to the Orthodox services, but it is the electronic religion of California that has touched him deepest.

"Why were we born?" he asks me. "Do you know why?"

He should have been a monk: he missed his vocation, he never found a place of retreat. "We were born of the flesh. We have eaten of the fruit of knowledge. We have been banished from the garden." Neil Young is on the radio singing, "I've been searching for a heart of gold." The Chinese proprietor is tapping his finger on the counter waiting for the fries to fry.

332

"And why are we here?" Lino asks me. He looks out at a car wheeling around in the parking lot. "We are here to be sanctified. To be 'spiritualized.'" He says the word as if he were holding it with tongs. "To become of the spirit."

Exile took his purposes away, but now he has found them again. He looks at his watch. It is time to go back to the nursing home for lunch. The nursing home looks like other brown-glass corporate headquarters that squat along the ribbon of highway. In the lobby they are paging someone, and a bell sounds for lunch. Then Lino begins to sing.

> "In savage lands afar
> Heathen darkness ruleth yet.
> Arise O morning star
> Arise and never set.

"Savage lands *afar?*" he says and looks around the lobby. "Savage lands *here!*" He lets himself be kissed, shuffles determinedly to the elevator and is gone.

Alec and Marjorie Ignatieff's house on Reid Avenue behind the Civic Hospital in Ottawa is a small bungalow ringed by a picket fence on a street of houses much the same as itself. The television is on in the sitting room: Alec sits on the chintz sofa looking at the TV with his good eye. He is terribly thin, grey-faced, his blind eye misted over. Yet for all that he is still the most beautiful of Natasha's children. Eighty years of life have laid the Mestchersky bone structure bare. In the silent and wasted immobility of age, he is still her sailor-suited son. He lets himself be kissed and he says in a whisper, "I'm going down very fast." It has been a family joke that he has been going down very fast all his life. Marjorie says of him that he has a richly developed nunc dimittis mood. But when I look up, she does not wink as usual.

In a weak voice, he tells me about the Petersburg house, about the warren of corridors that led back to the kitchens and as he does so, he imitates the voice in his memory: "*Grafchik*"—little count—"what are you doing in the kitchen? You are gentry, you shouldn't be here!" I see the sweating cook in Fourstatskaya shooing him down the passageway.

When I ask him about Kislovodsk, he tells me about the time he saw a ragged soldier beating a gypsy woman and cursing her over and over: "You slut, the times of bloody Czar Nick are over!" He remembers going with his mother to a villagers' hovel outside Kislovodsk in the autumn of 1918 and hearing from inside a parched voice cry, "Boy, don't come closer. We've got the plague." It was typhus.

In the fading light of an Ottawa winter afternoon he goes right back to the beginning, to the light of the salon in Kroupodernitsa. It is 1910. He has been reprimanded by Aunt Mika because he has mispronounced something. What is it? He searches, bends his head. Aunt Mika was giving him his Bible lesson, getting him to repeat the words of the Gospel when Christ appears before Pilate. Alec was four: he kept pronouncing Pontius like *ponchiki*, the word for brioche. Then he was turned by his shoulders and placed in the corner. His clear eye stares out across time: "I watch through the window as the light fades to the left. A darkening sky." His words come out blurred, like a page of writing left out in the rain. Then there is silence, filled by the television news at six o'clock and the clicking of teacups. His memory reminds me of a film of an undersea wreck: here and there, amid the silt and gloom, there is a broken bottle, a shard, a doubloon.

He was the rebel son. "She wasn't kissable," he says of Natasha. "Sometimes she would kiss us on the forehead. She would sit Lionel and George on her knees. I'm damn sure I was never on her knees." He was the one who got out of 10A Oxford Road first, the one who slammed down his fists on the piano and refused to play another of Peggy Meadowcroft's infernal exercises. He went to the Royal

333

School of Mines, to tin mines in Cornwall, gold mines in Sierra Leone. The mines were right for him: the solitary one of the family, down in the earth, bent double in those dark shafts. After the war he came to Canada and ran the Department of Mines in the Ministry of Energy.

Alec is silent so his wife says, "He was always the odd one out in the family." "Why are you marrying this bad character?" were Paul's first words to Marjorie when Alec presented his bride to his father. "He was too hard on his sons," she says with a look of pain in her face. Alec laughs, a dry harsh laugh. Silence. I get up to go. With great effort he levers himself up. He used to be several inches taller, a thin giant at six foot four. Now I am taller than he is. I kiss him on his forehead.

In the driveway, Marjorie squeezes my hand and says, "You came too late."

I have a picture of Nick—the oldest brother—on horseback somewhere out west in the 1930s, tall and easy in the saddle, elegant in jodhpurs and a suede jacket, the sun lighting the high forehead, the deep eyes in shadow and an expression of irritation on his face as if he resents the camera's intrusion. He wanted to be a writer, but he made himself an electrical engineer to please his father. When he lost his job in the Depression, it came as a great release. He set off with a backpack through the bush country of northern Ontario, through little mining towns like Timmins and Cochrane, then across the prairies on the freights with the men who rode the rails in search of work. He wrote articles urging the opening up of the north for immigrant settlers, he wrote about the hobos he met on the rails and he thought of those months on the road as the happiest of his life. He slept under the stars by the northern lakes, in freight cars, on the front sofas of missionaries who combed the freight yards trying to convert the waifs and strays. He lived on a diet of raisins and bread, fruit and coffee. Tall, sunburned, athletic, slightly balding, with a natural authority that made him seem older than his years, he had a knack for making influential friends, for ending up in first class. His brothers in Toronto laughed when they got a telegram from their hobo brother telling them to put his dinner jacket on the first train north to Cochrane. He had met the president of the railroad at one of those northern sidings and the president had invited him to travel in his private car. All the way round Lake Superior, the big man smoked his cigars and listened while the young Russian poured out his schemes to open up the north to immigrant settlers. Nick was a man of schemes and dreams and speeches and projects and he always acted as if he was playing on a larger stage than the one he was actually on.

All of his life was a long reckoning with the Soviet experiment and with the failure of the beliefs and hopes his father had lived by. In 1936 he wrote an article for *Saturday Night* magazine in Toronto in praise of Stalin's new Soviet constitution. He tried to defend terror, forced collectivization, and the purges as the birth agony of a new society. In the coming war with Hitler, he said, Russia would be our ally again. It was always Russia he saw, eternal and unchanged beneath the carapace of the Soviet regime. His father thought him sentimental and naive and wrote a reply to the article saying so.

"'Land to the peasants! Peace! Soldiers back to our homes!' Where are those promises now?" Paul wanted to know. "The land belongs to the state; the collective farms are run by outsiders belonging to the new bureaucracy; the peasant is enslaved more than ever; while more soldiers are under colours now than ever before and the entire nation is militarized." Paul signed his reply, which *Saturday Night* published, "Your loving father and friend." Nick replied, "There is nothing more futile than to belong to a class which learns nothing and forgets nothing." And signed his reply, "Your otherwise respectful son Nicholas."

When World War II came Nick served in the Russian section of British intelligence in London. Once he was sent to Buckingham Palace to brief the King, George VI, on the new Soviet ally. As the war progressed he became ever more disillusioned with the way the Allied intelligence community came to withhold military information from the Soviets, and he argued fiercely with his brother George over the need to trust and assist their Russian brothers-in-arms. George was always more circumspect than his brother about the Soviets.

After the war, Nick returned to a wife he hardly knew and a son he had never seen. A solitary moody man, hard to live with, hard to forget, he became warden of Hart House at the University of Toronto, helping ex-soldiers like himself to return to the university, lecturing and writing all the while on Soviet affairs, fighting as best he could the McCarthyite tide of anti-Soviet hysteria. In March 1952 he was lecturing the Defence Staff College in Kingston on Soviet strategic intentions, insisting—in the wake of the news that the Soviets had the H-bomb—that a nation bled white by war had no interest in military aggression against the West. Again and again, he came back to the theme of the essential continuity between the autocracy of old and new Russia; the anti-Western Slavophilism of his grandfather, he said, was echoed in the Communist ideology of capitalist encirclement. He was already at work on a book to be called *The Eternal Crisis—Russia and the West.*

On March 27, 1952, he gave his annual speech to the students in the Great Hall of Hart House. By then, Russia past and present suffused his thoughts. He began his speech by recalling an autumn afternoon in 1918 when he had sat on a hillside in the Caucasus and had watched the Red and White armies in the valley below killing each other for possession of Kislovodsk:

> I was then fourteen ... I remember thinking acutely for the first time: what pitiful fools these grown men are to do this to each other on a day like this in a place like this. What blasphemy. All through those months and years of stress, excitement, misery, I was disturbed and refused to accept the authority of the explanations handed down to me by my elders and betters ... When my father and all our friends and relations said that Communism could only be fought by force and even to hang Communists was a service to society, I could not see the point and was haunted by the spectacle of a young mother who happened to be an active Communist and wife of one of their captured leaders, hanging for three days from a gibbet erected on a hill in the middle of the town.

336

I often wonder why this memory of the gibbet on the hill came back to him that night, why it seemed to fuel his sense of suffocation at the McCarthyism around him, the parochialism of student politics, the numbing geniality of Toronto life. Next afternoon, he was changing a tire in the parking lot at the base of Hart House tower. He had a heart attack and died instantly. He was forty-eight, an elusive romantic haunted by a country he never lived to see again.

From a phone booth in the echoing concourse of Montreal's Grand Central Station, I call Dima and tell him my train will be arriving at Richmond in an hour and a half.

"All present and correct to meet you, boy!" His voice booms: I hold the receiver away from my ear. The other brothers call him the Prefect.

The train journey from Montreal to Richmond winds southwest across the St. Lawrence River through small brick sunlit towns called Saint-Hyacinthe and Acton Vale, where now, on an August afternoon, men start sharing out the beer and lighting the barbecue and kids in Expo sweatshirts play scratch games on the lawns among the sprinklers. These towns are more French than they were in Natasha's time: all the signs that used to say Hardware now say Dépanneur, and the train man calls the names of the stops in French. In the car, the families down for a day's shopping in Montreal are munching potato chips and some of the children are asleep on their parents' laps. The fathers work in the Bombardier Ski-Doo factory, in the asbestos mines at Thetford, and on the dairy farms that dot the soft rolling countryside. The corn is ripening, the cows are wending their way to the barns.

When I smell the sulphur from the Windsor Mills pulp plant and catch my first glimpse of the St. Francis River and the railway bridge I know we are nearly there. Dima brought Paul and Natasha here in 1936 to a little brick bungalow they built on the shores of the St. Francis on land sold to them for a dollar by F. M. Robinson, the farmer for whom Dima had worked when he first came to Canada.

From the window of the train I see Dima striding up the platform searching the windows for my face and tapping the train windows with his stick. His hair is like steel wool and it rises straight up on the crest of his head; he is crooked like a great tree and he is wearing an extraordinary pair of bright green corduroy shorts. He is eighty-two years old. I tap on the window and he does a welcoming dumbshow, waving his stick and blowing me a kiss. When I step down on the platform he kisses me on the lips and bellows, "Say, it is good to see you, boy!"

They all know him here, the taxi drivers waiting for their old ladies back from a day's shopping, the retired schoolteacher waiting for his wife, the station master with the packet of express mail for Sherbrooke down the line. He is a kind of local seigneur, living in the big house on the edge of town, taking the annual salute at the Canadian Legion parade on Remembrance Day. He waves his stick at them all and directs Florence to drive us home.

Florence wears her glasses on a chain and drives hunched forward grasping the wheel tightly and squinting at the road. She keeps him going, keeps his voice down to bearable levels, teases him off his certainties and reminds him that he's told the same story before.

The car pulls off the highway up the curving driveway to Beechmore, a three-storey, steeply-gabled Victorian house with high ceilings and numberless rooms, a big kitchen where the wood stove burns all day and night and deep-carpeted rooms where the clocks tick on white marble mantelpieces. The house was built in the 1860s: there is a mezzotint of Sir Wilfrid Laurier in the hall and the furniture was made for the house out of Quebec maple 100 years ago. It is a house of the same size and vintage as "Beechums." The bungalow where Paul and Natasha

337

used to live was directly across the river: it has long since been sold. Beechmore is now the family's gathering place.

After downing his vodka and hot water and making himself comfortable in the huge armchair which has been built up to accommodate his gigantic size, Dima takes the notebook from my hand and draws the floor plan of the house at Kroupodernitsa, every room, every corridor, marking with an X the hole in the dining-room wainscot where Alec and he would hide the Jerusalem artichokes they hated but their grandmother commanded them to eat. Dima's return to this house he has not seen since Easter 1915 is effortless. He remembers everything as if it were yesterday: Mitro the coachman and the morning rides with his grandmother through the lanes of the estate; the servant girls carrying the steaming cauldrons of jam to cool on the veranda steps; the way his grandmother used to crack walnuts between her teeth and hand her grandchildren the pieces. To Dima it seems the most natural thing in the world that through the transmission of his memory to me, I am joined in time with a woman who dined with Disraeli, wearing the Sultan's stars.

I ask him why he never went back to Petersburg. He will not have anything to do with Bolsheviks. "The bastards," he says with relish. He has kept faith with his mother's convictions.

In the dining room, Florence serves us dinner from heavy silver dishes and she laughs when she recalls how Paul and Natasha would drive in together from Upper Melbourne to Richmond to do the shopping in the Buick they called Sweet Mary. Natasha would sit upright in the middle of the back seat in her hat and gloves and choker, and Paul would drive very slowly, tipping his fedora and bowing his head ever so slightly at the old ladies he passed in the street: "*Bonjour Madame*," he would say out of the window.

Natasha used to bargain with the butcher in Richmond, the mild-mannered Mr. Duluth. "Robber! *Cochon!* That's too much! I won't pay that!" None of his customers had ever tried to bargain with Mr. Duluth before and he rather liked it. In some region of her mind, she was still at the *Okhotnyi riad* in the old Arbat in Moscow. He got to like the game, and once when Florence came in with Paul and paid his price without complaining, the butcher looked startled, then winked at Paul and said, "The young one's not like the old one, is she?"

Natasha loved to rummage in the Rexall drugstore, particularly in the one-cent sale tubs, and she stocked up on soap, toilet paper, and laxatives as if preparing for a siege. There was never enough money: something from Dima and

Florence every month, an old American insurance policy that had matured, and a tiny bit extra that she used to put on the mining stocks. Her boys teased her about her stock market gambling, but she took it very seriously and managed to recoup every cent lost in the crash of 1929.

She was famous for her conversations on the party line with the few local friends she made: Mrs. Moray, the Swiss doctor's wife, or Mrs. Trigg, the bank manager's wife. Whenever her neighbours on the party line heard the tell-tale click that announced she had come on the line, they would pick up their receivers and hear her say her cleaning lady was "fat as five cows," or hear her call herself "the old crow."

I want to know whether my grandparents were happy in Canada. Florence says, "He was happy, I think." Paul worked the garden every day of spring and summer, growing kohlrabi and beetroot, digging the earth with a pitchfork, in rubber boots and an old cardigan, an old Russian gentleman with a distinguished moustache and a battered fedora for garden use. In the winters, he sat with Mr. Trigg, the retired bank manager, and worked on a translation of those even, sifted memoirs he had written sometime in the 1920s.

And Natasha? Florence knows what it is like here in the winter when the snow reaches the windowsill and every book has been read twice and for conversation you have to rely on Dima and your tender-hearted but slow-witted housekeeper. "You're fighting negative thoughts all the time. I mean, why not just give up?"

Then Dima says, "Just before I went overseas in 1940, I came back for the weekend to say goodbye and my mother took me aside and said, 'We must get out of here.'" The winters were too hard and lonely: she was perishing for lack of stimulation. All her sons were far away and she wanted to go out to Vancouver, where the weather was better and where she could be near Lionel, who was teaching school. Dima was furious. "I had brought them here, helped them to build the house. I refused, I told her they must stay there." He wants to explain, then he is silent for a time. "You see, that was the last time I ever saw her."

They say good night and leave me rummaging among the family papers stored upstairs in the bare rooms under the eaves. It is all a jumble, too confused for any sorting: Natasha's and Paul's Nansen passports with terrible strained photographs of both of them; Paul's bills from the hotel in the Square des Batignolles; correspondence in Russian from the Azov bank relating to his vanished industrial estates; even the catalogue for the sale of the house contents at Beauchamps, with

339

a price in some auctioneer's neat and pitiless hand beside every item. Sitting there at the top of a sleeping house, my hands black with dust from the documents, I wonder what possesses me to rummage through these traces of their mortality, why I must cover my hands with dust from the tomb of their dispossession.

When I come down to breakfast the next morning, Aunt Florence is in the kitchen making toast. She is talking about the times she used to visit Paul and Natasha during the war. "It was never Stalin or Hitler. Oh no. She always referred to them as Beast Stalin and Mad Dog Hitler. She would come down to breakfast and you would ask her what was on the news and she would say briskly, 'They've shot down 189 of those beastly planes of Mad Dog Hitler, thank God.'"

All through the war, Paul and Natasha felt a painful closeness to the course of the battle in the Soviet Union. A nephew, Nicholas Mestchersky, was one of those members of the White émigré community in Paris who believed after the fall of France that their best hope of a return to power in Russia lay in joining the German army and fighting on the Eastern Front. The Germans took him on as a translator. He expected he would be welcomed on Russian soil as a liberator and found instead he was interrogating dirty, frozen soldiers and peasants whose hatred of him and the army he served showed through even their terror. Letters arrived from the Smolensk area in early 1942 and then suddenly stopped.

His aunt Sonia Wassiltchikoff, by then dying of cancer, knew what had happened. She dreamed in her hospital bed that she saw Nikita lying face down in snow reddened with blood. In the spring, one of Nikita's fellow officers on leave came to the family apartment and told them that Nikita had been killed by sniper fire in a ruined estate near Smolensk. The officer apologized: the ground had been frozen solid and so they couldn't give Nikita a burial. They had laid him out in an abandoned barn and covered him with straw. And where exactly? the family asked, sensing they already knew the answer. The officer tried to remember. The estate was near a place called Sichevka, and the river Vasousa flowed through the bottom of the garden. It was Doughino, amidst the shattered columns of the Mestchersky home that Nikita Mestchersky made his return to Russian soil.

Paul's cousin Alexis Ignatieff had returned from Paris to Moscow and was lecturing at the Soviet army staff college and advising the military tailors who were reintroducing the epaulettes and shoulder flashes worn by the old czarist regiments into the Soviet army. In his apartment in Moscow his batman would answer the phone: "General Count Citizen Ignatieff at your service!" The family renegade, he had tired of the hatred of the émigré community for having backed Lenin in 1917

340

and sometime in the 1930s he returned to Stalin's Russia. The Kremlin made him a general and used him to bring back spit and polish and old-style drill. They even let him write his memoirs: *Fifty Years in the Service*. In the book, he dealt ironically with his poor cousin Paul, once a minister, once a millionaire, now "eking out his old age in poverty, supporting himself by the produce of his garden which he actually works himself, in far-off Canada."

As Germans and Russians slaughtered each other at the gates of Kiev, Paul must have thought constantly about his sister Mika, last heard from in the summer of 1918 alone in the path of the German army, and now again—in her sixties if she was still alive—in the path of an invading army. Then against all odds, in the middle of the war, they received a picture of her, out in the snow carrying a load of wood with a peasant woman beside her: Mika has turned and is smiling at the camera. How Paul must have stared at the picture of his sister, lost behind the veil of war, her hair grey now like his, her skin worn like his, flesh of his flesh irremediably out of reach, yet transmitting like a distant star the message she knew would mean most to him and which she scribbled in pencil on the back of the postcard: "They have not forgotten the village choirmaster."

There were grandchildren by then—Paul and Mika—brought down to visit by their mother Florence. Their grandfather towed them in sleighs and their grandmother made them Russian yoghurt sugared with maple syrup, and at night when they cried out in their sleep their grandfather would come to them and they would hear him say: "Is this a little bird I hear?" in his thick old Russian voice.

After breakfast, Dima leads the way up the stairs into the attic over the garage. The floorboards and the walls are made from massive rough-hewn planks—the unconsidered forest magnificence that grew on this site a century ago. We pick our way past boxes of children's clothes, old suitcases, toolboxes and sawhorses, spare lumber. At the end of the attic, lit by the cobwebbed light of the dormer window, stands a battered canvas trunk the shape of a loaf of Hovis bread, bound with leather straps. Her initials: NM for Natasha Mestchersky, the childhood self, then NI, the adult self, are visible on the top and when I shoo away the dust, all the stopping places of exile show up on baggage markings: a Canadian Pacific sticker for the "SS *Montrose*: Countess Natasha Ignatieff, Montreal, Not Wanted on the Voyage"; then in pencil on a sticker, "10A Oxford Road, Putney"; then in faint but legible blue chalk—like words seen in a dream—"Kislovodsk via Mineralni Vodi." We open up the top: the lining is white linen stretched on cane and on the inside lid there is the maker's stamp, E. Deraisme, 729 rue St. Honoré, Paris, 1902. It is quite empty.

It is as if I have followed a river course along an arduous climb and found at last the bubbling cleft from which the water springs. This is the source of all we became in Canada: everything from that other life which has haunted me since childhood was in this trunk, the icons, the embossed volumes of Karamzin's history, the square silver basin and the ewer in which my great-grandmother used to wash her hands every morning at Doughino; the photograph albums, the Sultan's stars. All of this has flowed from the trunk down the branching capillaries of a family that now stretches out from here to Australia, to England, to New Mexico and that still has branches, unknown, on Russian soil. Dima remembers the trunk going on board *La Flandre* in Constantinople harbour in June 1919, how the Turkish stevedore's legs trembled, how he sweated as he wobbled up the gangplank—all the weight of that past teetering on the brink of its passage to the present. But it made it: all the voyages of eighty years now make a circle back to me: Nice to Kroupodernitsa, to Petersburg, to Kislovodsk, to Novorossisk, to Constantinople, to London, to Montreal, to the lumber room of an attic in Richmond, Quebec.

Dima and I set off after lunch up the hill to the cemetery. In the fields the light skims over the top of the waving grain; on the rutted path he reaches over for a stalk of barley, takes the head and works the kernels loose with his fingernails. He was a soils chemist by training, a scientific farmer as his father had been. For thirty years Dima was a soils expert with the Food and Agricultural Organization, trying to improve the yields of rice paddies and peasant plots throughout Asia and Africa, issuing voluble instructions about nitrogens and phosphates and the dangers of night soil in the food chain, leading singsongs of "Alouette" at all the parties, *Oncle Merde* to his French colleagues.

"Would you rather have been a farmer?" I ask as he studies the barley. He shakes his head. "You have to be a mechanic, and you have to manage cheap labour. I would have been happy a hundred years ago." I laugh: "With the serfs."

He points his finger at me, and his eyebrows arch: "They weren't slaves, boy."

"Just people you could count on."

"Exactly."

He resumes walking: his vigorous, bent gait, the huge feet and hands and the tapping stick rolling forward. "None of this damn modern stuff."

"Equality, you mean."

"That's it, none of this damn equality."

He walks on in front of me, shouting over his shoulder as he goes, "I always knew I was a count. I always knew I had to take charge." He always took charge, this old man who conserves intact the open cheerfulness of a twelve-year-old boy.

St. Andrew's Presbyterian cemetery stands on a sloping hill high above the St. Francis River. Dima is on the cemetery committee and he checks that they keep the grass trim and the cypresses against the skyline shaped and fertilized. A highway has been built to within a hundred yards of the back fence and the occasional whine of a passing car makes him fret. For me it seems quiet and unchanged. All my memories flow together into one impression of the light upon the solid Presbyterian names cut into the marble, the cypresses at the top of the walk, the warm breeze off the fields and the glint of the river's course below.

Theirs are the only Russian names in the cemetery: "In loving memory, Count Paul Ignatieff, 1870–1945 Countess Natasha Ignatieff, 1877–1944." They share the same stone, the same earth. There is a large plot of grass around them. Dima spreads his hands out and indicates where our plots are: there is room for everyone, even for me. And then for an instant he seems old and frail. He makes the sign of the cross, and he says, "And this, my dear boy, is where I join them."

In August 1944, my father came back from London. He had been away nine years. 343 He had left for England in 1936 to study at Oxford as a Rhodes Scholar. He had been to Bulgaria to research a thesis about his grandfather and czarist policy in the Balkans; he filled folders with research notes; he saw his grandfather's statue in Varna's main square and spent long hours with his Uncle Kolya, finishing his days as a librarian in Sofia. He had been to Nuremberg, Munich, and Vienna in the summer of 1938 and had seen fascism first hand. In 1940 and 1941 he fire-watched on the roof of Canada House in Trafalgar Square and organized the evacuation of London children on the transport ships. He had been to the hospitals in 1942 to visit the Canadian soldiers back from the massacre at Dieppe. He had met and fallen in love with my mother. He was a boy when he left for England; in 1944 he returned to his parents a man.

When he arrived in Montreal, his father said he should come down to see them in Upper Melbourne as quickly as he could. The old man's voice sounded rattled. When George came into Natasha's bedroom, the cedar-panelled refuge looking out over the row of pines and the bright August fields, she said immediately in her deep voice, "Here I am in my bed dying."

Nick's wife Helen was with him and they sat Natasha up in bed and bathed her. The bones on her chest stood out unbearably, and there were deep cavities under her cheekbones. She was light as a child to lift, bright-eyed, feverish. In all those years of feeding others, she never seemed to feed herself. She would wander in and out of the kitchen, serving her men, nibbling on a biscuit or a prune, sipping from a glass of port, never joining in the eating. She was afraid of dying of cancer like her mother, and she believed cancer arrived in what she ate. So she ate as little as she could and now she was dying among other things of malnutrition, dying of her fear of cancer.

George sat up all night with her. Poised there, at the lip of unconsciousness, holding his hand, with the comical, heartaching directness that was always hers, she told him the most intimate secrets of her marriage: It was not his fault. I could not make him happy. Never blame your father. The blame is mine.

Mamenka, mamenka.

She confessed a sinful wish to die, to die before her husband. Her wish was granted.

They buried her in the cemetery on the hill overlooking the river on a bright August afternoon. Dima and Nick were still away at the war and Lino was in British Columbia, but George and Helen and Florence were there with all the people in Richmond and Upper Melbourne who had come to know them. Even Mr. Duluth, her butcher, came and stood on the other side of the cemetery gate with his hat in his hands.

When Paul was left alone, his daughter-in-law Helen went to live with him in the cottage through the autumn and winter of 1944–45. She called him Jedda. He called Helen his black beauty and there can be little doubt he bloomed in the presence of his tall dark-haired daughter-in-law, who skied into town when the cottage was snowbound and who shared with him the bright cheerfulness of her baby son, Nicholas. Once Paul told her about the time he went with his father to the Cossack villages in the Caucasus mountains to buy wild horses from the tribesmen. But that was all, just that story. He was not one to reminisce. In the spring he put on his old fedora and his cardigan and planted out his kohlrabi. He kept Natasha's garden weeded and her phlox and delphinium came up in abundance in August.

The night before the war with Japan ended in August 1945, my father was sitting with his father listening to the radio. The bombs on Hiroshima and Nagasaki had been dropped. A man born in the Russian ambassador's house above the Bosphorus in 1870, a man who had been treated by Charcot and had served the last czar of all the Russias, had arrived in the estuary of the new age. My father looked out the window at the darkening light among the pines and heard his father say that the Japanese would never surrender unless guarantees were given about retaining the emperor. It was with remarks such as these that they were closest, son and father; never talking about each other, but always about the news. My father turned to say that he thought he was right. His father's breathing had ceased.

Paul and Natasha died two years before I was born.

Someone once said devotion to the past is one of the disastrous forms of unrequited love. Like all loves mine feeds and grows on impossibilities. When I look at their final photographs in the family album, standing in front of the bungalow on a snowy afternoon, I want to be there to walk with them up the path to the house, to help them out of their coats, to make them a cup of tea and sit with them by the fire. I want to hear them speak, I want to feel the warmth of their hands.

Any love has its ambivalences, its feelings of suffocation. When I was younger, I wanted to be free of the unending stare of their portraits. But I also wanted them to mark out the path ahead, to help me make my choices, to guide me on the road. Now I have children and a family of my own and I have learned that you can inherit loyalties, indignation, a temperament, the line of your cheekbones, but you cannot inherit your self. You make your self with your own hands, here and now, alone or with others. There is no deliverance, no imperative in the blood. You cannot inherit your purposes. I know what I cannot have from Paul and Natasha and so we are reconciled.

I do not believe in roots. When Natasha was a little girl she believed she was a green shoot on a great tree descending into the dark earth. But I am the grandchild of her uprooting, the descendant of her dispossession. I am an expatriate Canadian writer who married an Englishwoman and makes his home overlooking some plane trees in a park in north London. That is my story and I make it up as I go along. Too much time and chance stand between their story and mine for me to believe that I am rooted in the Russian past. Nor do I wish to be. I want to be able to uproot myself when I get stuck, to start all over again when it seems that I must. I want to live on my wits rather than on my past. I live ironically, suspicious of what counts as self-knowledge, wary of any belonging I have not chosen.

I have not been on a voyage of self-discovery: I have just been keeping a promise to two people I never knew. These strangers are dear to me not because their lives contain the secret of my own, but because they saved their memory

345

for my sake. They beamed out a signal to a generation they would never live to see. They kept faith with me and that is why I must keep faith with them and with those who are coming after me. There is no way of knowing what my children will make of ancestors from the age of dusty roads and long afternoons on the shaded veranda deep in the Russian countryside. But I want to leave the road marked and lighted, so that they can travel into the darkness ahead, as I do, sure of the road behind.

A Passage Back Home

AUSTIN CLARKE

Born in Barbados in 1934, Austin Clarke immigrated to Toronto in 1955 and became one of the pioneering voices in African-Canadian literature as well as one of the key figures in the rise of African-American studies as an academic discipline in the 1960s and 1970s, as a visiting professor at such universities as Yale and Duke. Many of today's leading African-American writers, such as Henry Louis Gates, were once his students. In addition to his novels and collections of short fiction, he has published several memoirs, including *A Passage Back Home: A Personal Reminiscence of Samuel Selvon*, the Trinidadian writer, who died in 1994, the year the memoir excerpted below was first published.

347

I cannot remember how old those Sundays were and if the sun had travelled already over the Observation Post in Clapham, and was running over Britton's Hill, down into the Garrison Pasture, before night caught it, to plunge for that day, into Gravesend Beach, and end the light of Sunday. I cannot remember what time it was, when I first heard, either his voice or the magnificent acquainted language of his stories, sent back to us from overseas; and I did not, like all of us, consider it strange or characteristic of our cultural status, that our words spoken amongst us, in fragments and with no force of appeal, would be golden and acceptable portraits of our lives, *because* they were coming to us on these Sunday nights, from overseas: on the BBC's radio program, "Caribbean Voices."

My stepfather, Police Constable Fitz Herbert Luke, controlled the "private set," as he probably controlled the irascible men he had to arrest, with a wrist-lock, making their movements conform to his own obsessive views of obedience and order and lawfulness. And even if he could not precisely define these characteristics he had learned in the Barbados Police Force, (not yet "Royal"!), and in his own upbringing, I was not too small not to know that he meant those criminals were lacking in "Christian-mindedness." And this could be achieved only by listening to the sermons that came all day long, every Sunday, over the "private set," from the Andes Mountains. Luckily, we had passed that chapter that dealt with South American geography in the textbook written by Dudley Stampp, at Combermere School. I would be entranced as he was, sitting in the front house, with the cold glass of lemonade, in a colour I still cannot describe, with the chipped ice and the pith of the limes, swirling in it, as I listened to the voice and the chastisements and the thunder that summoned Sodom and Gomorrah, that gripped all of us into shuddering submission to those strange voices, those strange arguments, those strange men who through this mechanical device, the "private set," were able to enter our houses and occupy our minds, and scold us into this Christian-mindedness. My stepfather listened to these sermons on Sundays for more hours than I would spend any day at Combermere School.

But luckily for me, a message would come from the Married Women's Quarters, near the Garrison, from Captain Farmer, the Commissioner of Police, that something was wrong, and that "Mr. Luke was wanted." There was one telephone in our neighbourhood, the Yarde's; and one of the Yarde boys would have to walk the message from the Front Road, which all the boys journeyed, to Flagstaff Road.

348

And I would rejoice. The "private set" would be mine, after all. My mother's own feeling that we had been remanded from the onslaught of these religious sermons, from ten o'clock until the last leghorn fowl was on her roost, came out like mild blasphemy. "Praise God! He out o' the house!" She would have had her eyes on the part of the dial that brought Auntie Kay from Trinidad's Golden Network, with its own version of blasphemy over the seas to the sensibilities of Barbadians washed in Sunday properness of behaviour. "Playing tuk! And on a Sunday, to-boot?"; but it was the time of year when the new tunes were being tried by the talent of children; and we might be in for some musical wonder. But before the "tuk, and on a Sunday!" I would be permitted to roll the heavy knob of the ball-bearing tuning button along the waves of miles of the dial, passing countries in Latin America, moving over Holland (the "private set" was made in Holland!), through Europe's intractable languages, until by accident, I was plunged into the Mother Country. *Inglann!*

And a different kind of "tuk" would take possession of the airwaves. Caribbean Voices! And this is when I first heard the name, Samuel Selvon of Trinidad. It was, as Oliver Jackman would put it, a literary "federation" taking place. Our culture of Sundays, regular as our bowels on a first-Sunday; regimented as the dry peas and rice and baked chicken, sweet potatoes, pear, lemonade, and rum punch, was Rediffusion's recorded church services of ponderous, sonorous sermons delivered by Inglish vicars whose language was not the language of our miseries, and could not determine nor define what was contained in our hearts. They did not even know our sins. Or it would be choirs from Westminster Abbey, with which we joined in, demonstrating our own arrogant belief that Barbadians sang Hymns Ancient and Modern more better than anybody born. Or a chanced taped version of the same hymns, delivered by the men in the neighbourhood, at a Wake or a Sunday "service o' song." And of course, the interminable foreign-affairs chastisement coming from over the Andes Mountains, out of foreign mouths.

But to hear, all of a sudden about the breadfruit tree, the casaurinas, the names of flowers we had passed earlier that very Sunday, to and from Sin-Matthias or Sin-Barnabas, or even the Cathedral—those of us who travelled through the Pine, when it still had canes and was a plantation; through Government Hill, and saw them growing over the wall of the Convent—the Kiskides, Couva, Port of Spain, Gravesend Beach, and "Trumper": to hear these symbols of words, greater than words; greater than our recognition of them in everyday life, all this was to make us feel "we was people, too."

349

I cannot say that I understood all, or even most, of what was being transmitted back to me. I cannot say that I understand each poem about Sin-Lucia, Barbados, Guyana, and Trinidad, written by men of those "unknown" lands, who were so similar to me, and others who had passed these monuments in our respective neighbourhoods: the casaurina, the blue seas, the Sea Wall. I could not receive this "literary tuk" with an easy appetite because I had not been trained with tools that were Barbadian, to criticize it, or what is worse, to appreciate it. But I knew that something revolutionary, some "damn federation" was happening on those Sunday nights, when my mother and I, leaned close to the magnificent speaker of the linen-clothed mouth of the "private set" in the front house.

Samuel Selvon of Trinidad was one voice I heard over the radio. His works had appeared earlier, I am sure, in the small, tidy, impressive, and clairvoyant pages of *Bim Literary Quarterly*, assembled against greatest odds, money, and energy, by Mr. Frank Collymore, who taught me English more successfully than he could French, at Combermere School. But apart from that, apart from the privileged peeping into those pages, illustrated sometimes by gargoyles and monsters and "colly-beases," we would know of his existence in a more magnified, romantic way, in the weekly injections of "Caribbean Voices."

My little world of no more than thirty houses on either side of Flagstaff Road, stretching from the Corner where the Kendal Hill bus stopped, to the top of the hill leading down into the Saturday iniquity, as my mother would say, of Club Morgan, a club that catered to the tastes of white people only, and foreigners, and with a view of the commanding sea and ocean, over which earlier Samuel Selvon, along with George Lamming and Derek Walcott, A.N. Forde, and others had crossed in this new revolutionary and reversed "Middle Passage." There were the thirty or so houses perched on foundations of precarious blocks of coral stone mined by men from the same neighbourhood, with their sleepy windows adorned with rich window blinds of gold and silver, white and pink; this world which before these "voices," was littled in its Inglanned sensibilities regarding self, regarding dignity, regarding blackness and the variations of that blackness—lightness considered beyond the meaning of 'lectricity—regarding nationality and nationhood, regarding the new raging men, Cox and Adams; Barrow and Walcott; Mapp and Allder; Mottley and Talma, and others, many others; my world received the injection of those "voices" which in turn made sense of the diagnosis and the bitter medicine of ex-colonialism that these great men were ranting about, on the political platforms, and in rum shops throughout the island which was no longer small.

How could such magnificent, powerful brains be contained in only 166 square miles? How could we have amongst us, such big-brained men in various professions and vocations, the law, medicine, education, philanthropy—and women too—Henderson Clarke, Chris Springer, Mervyn Campbell, Beckles and Madame Ifill, and not wonder at their presence in our midst, and not bestow upon them, the glory and appreciation for this level of achievement measured, not in our own terms (for we had no way of measuring, we did not measure), but in Inglann's terms? Did not the BBC tell us, even if we were hard-mouthed about accepting this "federation" truth, that our "voices" were on the same level as those nurtured in the same Inglann; and that our apprehension of "fair daffodils," of Browning's "In A Gondola," and Tennyson's "In Memoriam," were not so aesthetically special and superior to George Lamming's early poems, (some say he is a better poet than novelist!), and now, for all to see and hear, "Omeros" by Derek Walcott who does not, thank God, need that validation from the BBC or the *Times Literary Supplement*? And did we not, on the pastures, on the beaches, the playing fields of Combermere, Harrison College, Lodge, and Foundation; roads rutted with rockstone, and any available space, on Sundays, bank holidays and "in tesses," see, before anyone else, Foffie Williams, Griff the fass-bowler, numerous Williamses, Smiths of two distinct tribes; Walcotts, Weekes and Worrell, and many others; and many others, still to come—with Sobers, Hall, Hunte, to name a few? And did we not applaud them on Saturday afternoon, forget them on Monday, put them in curing mothballed neglect and ignoring, until the Inglish came down, and *their* writers told *us* in the language of Oxford and reality, that this was another aspect of our greatness?

Why did we not, until these cricketing "voices," bestow upon our greatness our own acclamation? Is it because there are so many great ones that our conservative exuberance for praise was not generous enough to go around? I do not know the answer. But I do know that the calypsonian, that sharp-eyed historian of our greatness and our weakness, understood first, before any Tourist Authority, before any awakened Prime Minister to these axioms of greatness, before any struck committee, the calypsonians our living poets, with their apprehension of contemporary affairs, took notice of the enormity of the *event*. It happened at Lord's, didn't it? Could there be any other stage on earth, on which this dramatization of the battle between a known giant, and a contestant, not unlike the mythical Samson, could be more splendidly acted out? "Cricket, lovely cricket!" It was spoken, with more literary poignancy than the languorous and sometimes dulcet tone of John Arlott, himself a poet of some consideration. But it remained for our cultural historian, the caisoman, himself a "Lord," Lord Kitchener, to draw its historical, its social, and its cultural importance to our attention.

This, in another way, is what our "voices," pelted back to us on the BBC, and amongst which was Sam's, this is what Sam's voice did to me.

The dramatization of ex-colonialism and the building of a new sensibility, nationalism in its best sense; the disabusing of our minds from the position we had been schooled in: that we had no culture; that we had no models from amongst us, all this was vouchsafed in the language of Samuel Selvon.

There was no way, no fantasy large enough, no expectation that Sam would come into my life as literary model, as literary companion and travelling companion, and as friend, from the first journey of his "voice" over the BBC.

He had gone, like many immigrants in the fifties, to Inglann, not to be a writer, as most of the commentaries on West Indian writing argue. He had gone to Inglann to make a living, in circumstances perhaps more endurable and sympathetic than he felt he could live with in his Trinidad. He had gone with the grand emigration of

351

men and women looking for work. And if, as he discovered, he was able to work on London's Transport system, in hospitals as an orderly, at the Exchange, and still have time and money to indulge his desire to be a writer; to have the time to dream, and to capture with hairsplitting accuracy *the voice* of Trinidadians and West Indians and in a language that today, is being encouraged by academicians in Amurca, in various programs of Black Studies, and African-American Studies; to put into that language he had heard on the streets throughout Trinidad the ethnocultural etymology and raise it to a level of beauty, then his emigration was a blessing.

It was a Thursday in 1965, in London, in the Bible of literary justice, the *Times Literary Supplement* (TLS). On the front page. I can still remember the headline that spanned the breadth of the page, like a panoply over an artist's drawing of a typewriter. *New wine in old Bottles.*

The "old bottles" was the metaphor for the English language: tired, worn out, stiff, unable to cope with the changing realities of strangers upon the English landscape and their insistence, like the cricketers of Lord Kitchener's, "at Lords," that there was a new kid on the block, so to say.

The "new wine" was the literary assault that was being made against the bastion of a "canon" that had been our measurement, before one brave Englishman, Swanson brought about this "federation" of new writing on the BBC's "Caribbean Voices." The article praised the contribution of these new batsmen with words, who had injected into a tired way of saying things, the breath of the spice, the glitter and flash of a willow pointing a new ball, or an old ball, through covers; and as John Arlott said many times, about Worrell, about Weekes, about Walcott—and John Goddard—the beauty was in the speed with which the shot had been made, its execution like laser, and "not a *man* moved." Or as Shell Harris, in his own beautiful cultural vernacular described it, "Jesus Christ! Another four!"

The *TLS* article singled out the new great literary batsmen: stroke players of "Jesus Christ, prettiness!" There were stylists and magicians with the pen, as Ramadhin and Valentine "those two lil pals of mine," had done with the little red ball. It singled out Sam Selvon, it singled out George Lamming, it singled out V.S. Naipaul, it singled out Austin Clarke, and it singled out Dylan Thomas. But Sam's identification with this "new wine," is what concerns me here. It concerns me now, because, all we have left, after his sudden passing away in the land he loved, in which he was raised, and which he himself raised to an international symbol, through the language he used to describe it, through Trinidad's language, all we have left to do, is sit and read those words that are as invaluable as the calypsos by Sparrow or Lord Kitchener. I shall not recite any of his words here. I shall not compare any of his stories to those of any other authors. This is not intended to be a comparative criticism. It is simply a personal reminiscence, an appreciation of the wealth he has left behind. The wealth of words heard in the jammed streets of Trinidad, words that paint action, feeling, emotion, death, and above all, life. Words that I hear all the time; and heard even before I came face to face with him during this trip to Inglann in 1965.

I was there for the launching of my second novel, *Amongst Thistles and Thorns*; and my publishers, Heinemann, were putting on a party for the occasion. It was a Thursday. The *TLS* had just come out, and we were being praised. I was there also, because I was still a freelance radio broadcaster with the Canadian Broadcasting Corporation; and I had been commissioned to do a three-part radio series on West Indian immigrants in London.

Knowing the role of the artist in the defining of the people from which the artist has come, and among whom he lives, and taking the example of Lord Kitchener, I knew I would have to talk with writers, if I was going to understand the essence of the existence of these West Indians, newcomers, new batsmen upon the severe, grey, inhospitable landscape of Inglann and Lords, and London.

Had I not read "Waiting for Auntie to Cough," and pictured myself, through Sam's words palpable as taste, following and imitating the most minute movement of these men through the labyrinths of London and Inglann? It was not difficult to see the improvisation of that immigrant man, whether Trinidadian, Jamaican, or Barbadian, who through the exigency of racism or scarce employment opportunity, realizing that his own national culture did not put the same emotional value upon the life of a pigeon, flitting over Times Square in droves, and in eaves in greater droves, and spluttering the carefully laundered white shirt—perhaps, the only one—with shit; and knowing that if one was gone, it could not be missed in such great tragedy as the Inglish are wont to bestow upon the death of one of their pets. And who, in his right senses, would call a blasted stray pigeon, a pet! And *feed* him? And starve?

To put it into a 'luminium saucepan, and drop in some lard oil, pepper, salt, and curry—the bane to Inglish noses in the fifties!—and some rice, and have dinner! And who is more useful, more important, a West Indian evading death from hunger: or an Inglish pigeon?

In Sam's intention there was not supposed to be this severe, psycho-literary interpretation, riddled with symbolism. It was the mastery of the man's usage of language that through its easy comprehension, we, the reader, the critic, and the academician, were able to understand clearly what he was saying. We read into his words, so clear and single-minded, all the underlying serious implications that they suggested.

For years, Barbadians and West Indians have been leaving the islands on this journey, to live in Inglann. And it is either their blindness or their embrace of the Inglish ways that caused them to demonstrate through the immorality of silence, a profound deceitfulness about life in Inglann. From Sir Conrad Reeves, the son of a former slave woman, who must have encountered interesting resentments and disapproval when he was there, early in the nineteenth century, all down through hundreds of Barbadians who have endured the sojourn of students in the Mother Country; not one of them returned home with accounts of deprivation or prejudice or discrimination. We know now, years after, that life for those immigrant-students was not a bed of roses.

The Lonely Londoners is my favourite among Sam's books. In it I can smell the perspiration of the labouring West Indians. Can feel their resentment to their treatment at the hands of the "Mother." Can follow them through the dark, cold, dreary, and debilitating alleys on the way to their ambitions: a Barrister-at-law, a supervisor on London's Transport, a qualified teacher. And I can hear their pain. And most of all, sense their nostalgia, and their ambivalence about the wisdom of leaving Bridgetown or Port of Spain for Inglann. Sam gave me the blueprint to that "exile," an "exile" not always so pleasurable as George Lamming contended it to be in his personal brilliant commentary, *The Pleasures of Exile*, which dealt with his own life in Inglann.

When I arrived there, armed with a Nagra tape recorder and a huge per diem account, I was both prepared and unprepared for the blight I was to live with and in, during those two weeks in Inglann's "summer."

But the *TLS* had extolled beforehand, the excellence of this renaissance of writing, this West Indian literary force that dared to demonstrate the working out of the "new wine" in Inglann's backyards. George Lamming was at the height of his fame. V.S. Naipaul has just begun to court the Inglish and massage them into believing in his own nihilistic attitude. Jan Carew, living in a large house somewhere near Wimbledon, clothed in the huge skins of animals slaughtered or found dead, somewhere on the Steppes of Europe or the Latin American Pampas of boar-hunting, seal-hunting, or mink-hunting, and flitting from London to Moscow, and back many times, before the term "jet-setter" was invented and thrown into our lexicon. Andrew Salkey, whom I have christened "Handrew" in memory of his Jamaican Creole roots, buried amongst shelves and shelves of books reaching to the heavens in his prodigious study. Michael Anthony whose hands were calloused, and made harder, not from the solitary pounding on his manual typewriter, but from the labourer's job he held, for years, to put bread and butter on his table for wife and child. James Berry who persevered with poetry. And a man, later to be famous and notorious, for reasons that were not merely literary or political, Michael DeFreitas from Trinidad, later to be made more notorious even, by his countryman in the novel, *Guerrillas*; Michael DeFreitas later to be known as Michael X; later to assume a name more in keeping with his new religion, occasioned they say, through his meeting with Malcolm X, later himself to be known as Michael Abdul Malik. And in the company of my lifelong friend and "brother," more "brother" and more friend, Henry Moe, in Inglann to do Law at Durham University and teach part-time, at nights, I made the journey to some suburban district outside London.

I do not remember the name of the place. I do not remember whether we went by train, or by bus. I do not remember how long it took us to get there. I do not remember the disagreeable, disgusting, denigrating surroundings. Labourers, and those not in unions, must have lived there. It was "summer." But it was like winter. The houses were built from the same blueprint. There was no eye for beauty, no eye for individualism in the construction of this street of "brauhaus" deprivation.

Sam had captured even the smell of London's winter in his brilliant novel, *The Lonely Londoners*. And he had done something else. He had stripped them of the alienating hyphenation so common these days in the way we describe ourselves as minority ethnic groups living in a land other than our own. He christened them *"Londoners."* Not black Londoners. Not Trinidadian-Londoners. Not Black West Indians in London. Just Londoners. And he left it to the other tribes inhabiting that inhospitable landscape, to like it, or lump it. This distinction of definition is significant: for it describes not only the disposition of those brave men and women to the reversed direction of the "journey," but more than that, it expresses the ethnocultural philosophy of the man. Never once, during countless meetings, from 1965 until two years ago when we met at Brock University in St. Catharines, Canada, have I heard, even in jest, a word of implicit racialism come from this man's lips. And in hundreds of letters we exchanged between London and Toranno; and later on, between Calgary, Alberta and Toranno, there is no trace of enmity caused by his encounters with racism, (and he had many), that coloured his behaviour, his life, or his writing.

The house in which Sam lived at this time, was an ordinary house. Not outstanding in any of its dimensions. A house in which the Inglish put its underclass to live. It must have been the fatigue and exhaustion from the journey undertaken by Henry Moe and I that caused me to regret having taken this trip.

I remember he was wearing a sweater. And smoking. There might have been whisky. But his circumstances tell me that whisky could possibly not have been served. I do not remember eating lunch, or being offered any. The starkness of his surroundings and environment was not what I had imagined from his lively fiction in his short stories. This home was more in keeping with the lugubriousness of the life Edgar Mittelholzer wrote about in his autobiography. I could imagine the heavy strains of Wagner, which Edgar liked and listened to without taking a breath. I could imagine the locus of many of Charles Dickens' novels, except that this encounter was in the suburbs. I could imagine the garret and the woollened writer in darkness, no food, and the romantic prop of bottles of red wine, and burning candles drooping from a Chianti bottle whose mouth and basketted sides are drenched in dried tallowed sculptures. Not so this house.

But there was dignity. And human-ness. Sam had lots of that. The dignity of simplicity. His words exemplified that. I sat with him, in this minimalized surroundings, there was no music, no oil paintings, and we talked about London and Inglann for hours; and we talked not too successfully about his work and its place in the sphere of the "new-wined" renaissance of West Indian letters. And his self-effacing nature was the ethic, the nature, and the essence of the interview.

"Well, boy, I don't know, yuh know. I write my thing, and thing and thing ..." We talked about Notting Hill and the recent riots that erupted in the area; and Michael DeFreitas's name came into the conversation, as it should, because at this time, it was said that Michael was the "strong-arm" man for Rachmann, a rich Jewish gentleman who owned most of the dwellings in Notting Hill ghetto, and which he rented out to West Indians who had felt the pinch of prejudice against their renting rooms, basements, flats in the homes of the more genteel Inglish. And Michael and Rachmann both got bad names for their philanthropy and their extortion.

It was the day before, when I was in the basement of the CBC's studios in London, wondering aloud how I would meet this man, Michael DeFreitas, whose "reputation" had spanned the Atlantic and had reached me in Toranno, and which mentioned a Canadian woman with whom he was living in London, at the time. I expressed my desire to interview him; and the woman, another freelance broadcaster sitting beside me in the Editing Room, said, with the understatement the

Inglish are famous for, "I could arrange it, Austin. I live with Michael." My puritanism, fostered in Barbados, led me to conclude that she was his roommate; that they were living in the same flat; that she was paying her share of the rent, and he, his. But when I arrived at the imposing Georgian building, splendid in its appointments, I could not but conclude that the arrangement was a spousal one. He did not make any bones about it. And neither did she. I realized then, that there had been too much literary euphemism in the *Maclean's* magazine article that I had read as research, weeks before in Toranno.

And I think I asked Sam about his colleagues. Especially Naipaul, who had just made a mark for himself in world literature, if we may describe his success, in those terms. *House for Mr. Biswas*, perhaps his best novel, had just been published to great acclaim. But there was a problem. Was Naipaul really the son of a bitch that Handrew had hinted at? It was Handrew, after all, who had introduced Naipaul to his publisher, André Deutsch. And it was Naipaul, with the large publisher's cheque against advanced royalties, who could no longer remember Handrew's address on Moscow Road, London. Was all the rumour I was hearing, true? Were the recriminations about V.S. Naipaul, his nihilistic attitude towards black people, spread by his former friends, justified? I was convinced of his tremendous technical ability with the novel. I had not been able to separate this genius with structure, from the contents of his non-fiction, in particular, *The Middle Passage*. And years later, when he gave us the big book on his return to India, with the motto of Indian personality, "*The Indian defecates everywhere. He defecates on the street, in his temples ...,*" I asked Sam what he felt about *An Area of Darkness*, in which this nihilistic brand of satire appeared. I was expecting a personal commentary from a fellow Trinidadian. Something, though not so spiteful as the censure I had met, when the same question had been asked of other West Indian writers, the young nationalist intellectuals, and university students who did not necessarily read nor study Naipaul in their English curriculums—but something spicy. Perhaps, I was waiting to hear the latest personal gossip, to be able to bury this outstanding, money-making fellow author. Perhaps, it was too, nothing but plain envy and jealousy. For none of us had had Naipaul's wide and international attention. Not even George Lamming. Not Eddie Brathwaithe. And not, most certainly at that time, Derek Walcott.

I sat back, rubbing my two palms together, sipping the rum—or was it beer served too warm, which I do not like—waiting for the avalanche of what I felt would be justified disapprobrium.

357

Sam sipped his drink. Took a pull on the cigarette which was always in his mouth. And he said, in his voice that was so comforting in its soothing quality, like the voice of a dramatic actor who loves comedy; in a voice like the clown's, and the best of classical clowns, filled with wisdom beneath the humour; Sam said, "*Boy, Vidia is Vidia, yuh know. Vidia does-do his thing and thing, and that is Vidia. I ain't know nothing, eh, boy. I does-do my thing, and Vidia does-do his thing. Is so, yuh know, boy ...*"

There was no enmity, no jealousy, no recrimination. There was no hint of wanting to be in Vidia's shoes, and share in the enormous advances and prize money he had been having, no regret that he was not on the BBC television shows which lionized his countryman; no word of censure against the recognition given to Naipaul, in such large measure that it was felt in Inglann at the time, that Vidia was the only author worth noticing.

It taught me the essence about Sam, this great man, "no longer whinnying with us," as Dylan Thomas would have couched the words of his panegyric, had he too been alive, and had he not succumbed to the record-breaking transitory fame of drinking Scotches. "I think this is a record," Dylan is supposed to have said, when he drank others under the table, and himself, into the lamented coffin. "*Do not go gentle into that good night.*" It could have been said about Sam's passing in Trinidad on the 17th of April, as it was said about the passing of Dylan's own father.

"Do not go gentle in that good night." For it was night, when Henry Moe and I left this unnamed suburb in London's bowels, to trace our journey back to London itself, with the affect Sam had upon me, churning in violent conflict in my mind.

I did not expect to see Sam in such state and status. Meeting him, there was not the same dignity and magnificence that his prose had portrayed for me all those years before; his home was not distinguished in the way that his fiction's language had succeeded in distinguishing the English language. And I knew that the time he had taken away from his typewriter to talk to me, was golden. There was no wife at home. I do not know if I knew he had a wife in those days. But he probably had. For I think I remember there was a child, an infant. The voice was coming from a room I could not see. I knew, from what my eyes passed over, in his castle, that there were no T-bone steaks on Fridays, and roast beef and Yorkshire pudding on Sundays. That sherry was not served at five in the afternoon. That the car was not taken out in the Sunday evening dying sun, and driven into the country. I know that that time, all the time available, had to be spent over the labouring Underwood typewriter, and that late into the night, at the hour when even graveyards are quiet, that the working wife, and the infant, would hear the clacking-out of words in the new language he was fashioning into the "new wine" of the Inglish canon that determined the modern novel.

It was sad when I reached London. That night, because of my new reputation, I was invited to a discussion on the BBC's *Third Programme*. Anyone who knew Inglann in those days, can understand how the Inglish are able to differentiate "shavings" from the same piece of wood shaved on the workbench and give one piece meaning and worth, while the rest are relegated to the "shavings' box." It is typical of their process of selecting and elevating those selected. Three of us were selected for this program. I was selected. V.S. Naipaul was selected. And Anthony Burgess was selected.

I do not remember the name of the host. I do not remember exactly, the topic we discussed. What I do remember is the importance of the topic; it had to do with the novel of imperialism, or those novels written by Inglishmen during Inglann's period of imperial power; and how their works provided intentional or unintentional undergirding for the political and social philosophy of imperialism.

I can understand why I was selected: because I was a member of the new group of West Indian writers who were pouring this "new wine" all over Inglann's consciousness. Vidia was selected because, to me, his works had to a great extent, praised the idea of imperialism, while he dismissed any possibility that we West Indians and the West Indies as a whole, were capable of culture, had models and monuments worthy of sustaining, or worthy of emulation; and in the same breath was extolling the greatness of Inglann, meaning empire. Tony Burgess was selected because he had lived in India, the locus of the three books we were asked to discuss, and he had had first-hand knowledge about these things, in his capacity as a clerk in the Colonial Civil Service in India.

We were treated like young literary princes. There was a room in which we waited, and gathered our thoughts, and got to know one another, and bantered in an educated, Inglish civilized manner, encouraged in our words of sophistication and in our manner, the manner in which we were being treated, and the manner of our manners, by generous portions of whisky. I remember Vidia's appetite. He drank his as if he was accustomed to the best, and accustomed to drinking much of the best. Tony Burgess, hopping slightly, or rather, limping, through some injury, inflicted probably in India, and smoking one small brown

359

cigar, not much larger than a *Country Life*, after the other, holding the crystal glass in the proper Inglish manner, with the little finger free, and released from the thickness of the glass. And I, to some extent amazed to be included in this third-programmed company; understanding what it meant to me, and to Sam whom I had left earlier buried in the grime and greyness of suburban life, and to all other West Indians, students and labourers, who would tune in to this program.

I wondered how Sam would feel, placed between these two men? What would he say to Vidia? How would he have challenged Vidia's contention that *Passage to India* was a classic, and could provide to us, West Indian writers, a model of portraiture, a way of dealing with a permissive society, an example of brilliant language? And what he would have said to Tony Burgess, who had opened the innings with the same style and purpose of re-emphasizing the primacy of everything Inglish?

Their views did not sit easily with me. I must admit that I was not so conversant in the works of D.H. Lawrence, Rudyard Kipling, and E.M. Forster, which we turned to, in our discussion, precisely because I had been preoccupied, on my side of the Atlantic, by works of similar cultural rejection and "ethnical" degradation: Mark Twain's *Huckleberry Finn*, and Harriet Beecher Stowe's *Uncle Tom's Cabin*. When all five "inglished" authors had written their novels, there was no fervent and violent black intellectual opposition to them. Their opinions might have been accepted, even by black people, as the gospel, or worse still, as the correct definition of the persons they abused in their works. But when this *Third Programme* discussion was being done, it was 1965. The summer of '65.

And I have no doubt, that the same text of a novel read in 1935 must have a completely different impact upon the reader, if it is read in 1965. And this is so whether he is Inglish or West Indian to say nothing of the fact that he is black Amurcan.

That year, 1965, was the year of rising discontent in Amurca, which had taken over from Inglann all the power of ideas, strategies of twentieth-century abolitionism, and had begun to create a literature of greater excitement, if of lesser content and structure. We were all looking towards the *Amerika* of black nationalism, and of black cultural nationalism, for guidance. I, on this side of the Atlantic, found greater political and cultural identity with the black Amurcans than even with Sam Selvon, living in an Inglann that had coughed up the traumatic surprise of the Notting Hill Riots. The Notting Hill Riots were not so believable as the summers-long bashing of black people with high-powered hoses, police billy clubs, and

360

with pure, raw, brutal violence. And I had embraced the more reasonable position of the nationalists, that violence ought to be fought with violence, although for all of us nationalist adherents, we did not contemplate, nor did we have a strategy to bring about this redemptive violence of retribution by physical means. It was pure talk. Tough talk. Black power talk. The scent of blood on this side of the Atlantic was more inducive, than the smear left by a wound in a thousand Notting Hills. And Sam's "Londoners" were, in spite of their significance in the body of West Indian literature, nothing more than men trying to find something to eat; men trying to find a job; men trying to fit into the Inglish landscape with a minimum of social and personal dislocation. They were not men bent upon a dividing up of Inglann into a black one and white one. They had no such right of citizenship. And they were not contemplating at that time, a revisionist slant of history in the same way as the Amurcan blacks were. As a matter of fact, with the questionable leadership of Michael DeFreitas, they were themselves seeking political-intellectual leadership from Stokely Carmichael, Rap Brown, and Malcolm X, who was still with the Muslims in Amurca, and was still the protege of the Honorable Elijah Muhammad.

My point of view of these things racial; my realism constructed by the nearness of Amurca to Toranno, and my closeness to the realism that the black colour of skin was almost synonymous with death at the hands of the Ku Klux Klan, the policeman's hose and billy club, and the sheriff's enmity, did not therefore permit me to indulge even as a rising "new-wine" star, in the same leisure of intellectualism, in the beautiful language used by Vidia and Tony Burgess.

On this side of the battle, Richard Wright and James Baldwin and Malcolm X provided a more acceptable cataclysmic, bloodthirsty excitement of Armageddon, than could be found in Inglann and Notting Hill, if the writer is seeking models and ideas for repetition and emulation. I could not find these models and ideas in Forster, Lawrence, and Kipling.

I might have said this then, on the *Third Programme*, in the startled presence of Naipaul and Burgess. I cannot remember their rejoinders. I cannot remember how extremist I sounded. I cannot remember anything but our return, like three gentlemen of letters, back to the waiting room, where we poured ourselves even larger portions of the precious Inglish whisky, now that we had performed on the highest stage of Inglish intellectual and literary drama, and could, as the gentlemen we were, indulge in small talk and banter.

But Sam was still on my mind. I had seen his London and his *"Londoners"*; had seen the landscape against which he had painted them; had seen on my way from the flat of my host, my editor at Heinemann on Maida Vale, a large, imposing billboard, raw and conspicuous against the weak blue skies of "summer," the blunt painted *golliwog*. It was advertising a very famous and palatable marmalade. This marmalade with the golliwog on the jar, was served on every breakfast table in Inglann with the sausage and the kippers. It was served on my table, too.

My host had been living in Maida Vale for years, in a Victorian house in which he had a flat of some substance. As I went up in the lift, with its bellows of iron, I could imagine, as he had told me, over tea and over "the best whisky," a gift from his wife's family, who made "the best whisky" up in Scotland, I could imagine and live with the personages who had climbed in this elevator, when Maida Vale was the actual locus of murders for which Inglann is famous, in fact and in dramatization. He had travelled for years on the Maida Vale bus. And in all that time he had not noticed anything wrong with the large billboard, depicting the golliwog that advertised the same marmalade he and I had been eating each morning of the fortnight I was a guest in his home. He had grown accustomed to its presence, had accepted it most likely, as part of the London landscape which he loved, as part of the growing disgusting graffiti that was now littering his town, along with the strange presence of people from parts of the world similar to mine. He had read about them in adventure books. Now, they were on his sidewalk.

"You know, I never really *noticed* it!"

He had no power to pull it down. He had no power to change it. But he had the power to refuse spreading that brand of marmalade on his burnt toast and stiffened sausages. And he did that. The grotesque doll with staring eyes and fuzzy hair, haunted me no more on the breakfast table.

I mentioned this to Sam, when I called him to ask if he had listened to the BBC *Third Programme* with me and his countryman, Vidia, which is what Sam calls Naipaul.

Didn't I read his short stories, he wondered. Didn't I really understand the language of *The Lonely Londoners*? *"What happnin' to you, eh, boy? All-you not see it, write-down there in book, boy? What happnin' to all-you?"* It was a proper reprimand, to me, an author, concerned with the same aspects of the collision of black people and white people, upon the landscape controlled by whites. I wondered if Vidia had ever noticed these things? *"It have things here, boy, that all-you never hear 'bout ..."*

Handrew would know. Handrew would understand, in a flash: for it was Handrew who had been the most vociferous in his protest against these insulting monuments erected by the Inglish, in their facetious and frivolous broad-mindedness, which were intended to remind us, the "lonely Londoners," that even though we could "write book," as Sam put it in its essential rawness, "we is still blasted *wogs!*" Wogs we were. "Wogs" is the name they used, without apology, even in so-called polite society. And of course, the social scientists went wog wild with the usage of the term.

In this satirical, racist, and ironical manner, I was being elevated into the pale blue skies of London's summer, and made a monument, riveted with dishonour onto a billboard, reminding all of us, that even if there was something about us, about me, that was delectable, desirable, even contributing to the nutrition of Inglann, an essential part of the ritual of breakfast in Inglann, the symbol used, was to us, definitely not a pleasant one, nor one we ourselves would have chosen. And I wondered, without putting the suggestion either to David my host, or to Sam and Handrew, if there was one symbol, one metaphor, one stereotype that we held dear about the Inglish racial and imperialist depravity towards us, that any one of us would dare to erect, either in poetry or in fiction, and whether we could dodge the uppercut of being termed "reverse-racists"?

The "Londoner" amongst Sam Selvon's "lonely" ones was a man who lived in a room, in the basement or the attic. He was a man who encouraged others of similar plight to have the same address. And in the new world of shift work, this arrangement was possible and financially desirable. It showed improvisation, and it showed deplorable plight. But most of all, it showed this Londoner's ability to be creative in a world where creativity itself would have killed a person of lesser ingenuity.

And even though there is humour and sadness in the portrait of the man who holds his body precariously out the window in the attic, with his belt ready to attract the slippery pigeon, and dump it into his boiling pot of rice for dinner, it still is dinner. And the size of the bird, small for the four raging appetites of the inhabitants of the small room, is not far different from the size of meals I had seen in the homes of some Inglish.

The Inglish have been able to prolong the economy of food, rationed during wartime; and from this economy, it seems to me, there has come a daintiness, a skill of cutting and contriving, the ability to use an expensive carving knife made in Sheffield, from the finest steel, handled in the tusks of elephants plundered and shot in cold, illegal blood, in Indian forests, and with skill and civilized dexterity; and they can make a ritual of that carving, of that feast, of that present-day-feeding of five thousand, from a diminutive carcass of a bird.

363

If Sam had it, he would have placed the bottle of whisky upon the shiny linoleum of the table in the kitchen; placed two thick-bodied glasses made from cheapest glass; some ice, and we would have gone to town on the liquor. And when we rose, only the bottle would have been left—a monument to our appetite. But in this context, comparing ourselves with the Inglish, a monument to our gluttony.

In Toranno, we were like the Amurcans, obsessed with bigness: the steak I ate was one-and-a-half inches thick, and its oozing bloody dimension took up the circumference of the plate, and it would hang over the edge of the plate; and when the knife which was used to cut it into chunks large enough to fill the mouth at one feeding was put down, the fork used as a shovel to ladle the thick blood-curdling dead cow, from Alberta, into the gullet, all that was left was the bone in the rough shape of a T. And a belch would erupt, to signify that all was well with the world.

But in Maida Vale, the carving knife was sharpened on an instrument, and laid like an idle sword beside the two-pronged knife of identical manufacture in Sheffield; and the three plates edged in royal blue, the finest china, would have within their larger circumference, two smaller plates. Beside each "place" were two knives of different size, and a small one, for later; and on the other side, the *left*, three companion forks, varied some nights, if we were having soup. And when there was soup, a spoon large as a West Indian ladle. There was the light of candles. And platters large as coffins. And serving dishes, which reminded me, from their size, of the holes we dug into the ground after a downpour of rain. And of course, the napkin. You dabbed your mouth, in slow, delicate jabs, even though none of the meagre meal was left on your lips. How could any, from this small portion for three, have been left. There was hardly enough to fill one stomach.

I imagined, without the mind of the creative writer, holding the chicken that lay before us, a prize, a symbol of my present gracious living on Maida Vale, holding it by the plucked scruff of its neck, raising it to my mouth, and in a flash, devouring it like a child's magic, in two instalments of bites.

It was no larger than the pigeon that was oiled-down and flavoured by the curry of Sam's "Londoners." The rice they ate was more generous in the enamelled saucepan than the baked potatoes that looked like six golden, parsleyed golf balls.

"Oh God, pardner!" one of those diners, "lonely Londoners" would have said, as he raised the spoon to his lips, "this curry pigeon remind me of the time, back in Trinidad, when on a Sunday, it had real chicken! Chicken, for so!" And the memories would flow. And the nostalgia would, like the miracle of the Feeding of the Five Thousand, cause the food to increase; and in the chewing of the bones, the memories would flow. Who amongst *those* Londoners was expert enough with a knife to *carve* a pigeon with the dexterity of the Inglish, and have the skeleton left, ready for the pot of soup? They would have broken the pigeon into four; and if they were lucky in the hunt, and had brought down *two*; then they would been brek in half; and the only problem to arise would be based on status and rank. The provider of most of the other ingredients of the meal would have his status assured. The owner of the room in which they had met for this supper would have status. And the only problem left to be solved would be, who "going-get which half? You want the half by the head? Or the half by the pooch? And who getting the biggest half?"

And in a way, I wished I was in that room, in that attic, with that pigeon hooked on a piece of string, providing one less menace to the single pressed-and-starched white shirt, worn to the interview for the job that slipped more often than not, out of our grasp, since in these days, Inglann had not been accustomed to employing "*wogs*."

Sam did not have the same emotional reaction as I did, to the views expressed by Vidia on the BBC *Third Programme*, that Thursday night in 1965. Sam was not the kind of person to hold grudges, to express a deprecatory sentiment, nor evaluate, for the sake of comparison with his own work, the books of his colleagues. Sam was incapable of making, even by implication, a derogatory remark about his colleagues. And most ironical of all, he never was able, whether through self-assurance, or in the way he viewed his writing as work, as something he had to do, and was gifted in doing, he never discussed his work in the manner to establish his place in the spectrum of West Indian writing. During these years, the West Indian novel was the most impressive production, in worth and in quantity of creative writing taking place in the English-speaking world.

Sam was one of the heroes embraced by the Inglish. The Inglish however, using tactics reminiscent of their political philosophy of warfare and former colonialism, selected some (some would say, one, writer), and made him the representative of the entire body of writing coming from the pens of these literary and "lonely Londoners": Edward Brathwaithe, the poet; James Berry, the poet; Andrew Salkey, poet, novelist, and children's story writer; Jan Carew, poet and novelist; Wilson Harris, novelist; Edgar Mittelholzer, the novelist; Peter

Kempadoo, the novelist and herbalist; George Lamming, the poet and novelist; V.S. Naipaul, novelist and social commentator; E.R. Brathwaithe, the novelist; Michael Anthony, the novelist; Wallace Collins, the novelist—all these lived in Inglann at the same time. Their literal output in words, is phenomenal. And it spanned, for the main part of it, just ten years. And Samuel Selvon of course.

And then, the catastrophe of selectivity, the Inglish disposition for abandoning, happened. Inglann suddenly discovered Africa. And Heinemann and other publishers, acting in the same mode of political imperialism, decided there was more profits to be made from African literature, than they could get from that created by these West Indians.

This remembering of times, these journeys are not intended to be a critique of the comparative virtues of African literature (in English translation) as against West Indian literature. And I do not want to raise those emotional debates at this time: at this time of loss, and of joy for the contribution made by my friend, Sam; and for the tragedy of his early passing. But I shall say, that as in other times of similar choice made by an imperialist mentality, the supersession of African literature, with very few examples, was a decision to be praised more for its political and economical rewards, than for its purely literary and critical and intellectual argument.

The time was coming, when through systematic neglect, (books not being reviewed—except Vidia's), these "lonely Londoners" had to choose the routes of another journey, another immigration, and look to the New World, even although they themselves had originated from there.

They had been got accustomed to: like the imposing billboard advertising marmalade with the symbol, the grotesque illustration, of the golliwog. They themselves, through a second Notting Hill Riot, and more racial unpleasantness, and with the declared sentiment that they were no longer wanted, that they should be sent back, as Anthony Powell, MP, had argued in the safe atmosphere of the British House of Commons, had already considered the greener pastures of Amurcan universities and factories.

Here was official declaration of war; or as the black Amurcans would say, the opening of hunting season. And as the West Indian writers provided a vanguard for the new awareness and the demand for recognition and dignity that ought to have been given to their presence upon that London landscape, so too were the writers themselves in the first wave of turned-back immigrants, seeking a safe and a more materialistically profitable place to live and to write. They turned their attention to Canada and to Amurca.

But for the time being, there was still more of the sociology in Sam Selvon's work to be experienced and studied. I could see this sociology as the sightseeing tourist sees it. I was a tourist only because I was there for a fortnight. I could not be termed an immigrant. But I was an immigrant too, in the sense that for those two weeks, I was perceived as a London "wog." I wanted to make the most of my thinned time in this place, seen through the words of Samuel Selvon's, drawn with such honest positive illustration.

And I wanted too, to touch that segment of West Indian society in London, the student, who would be returning, some by choice, others with no choice, to the West Indies, to tell us, with their new education, how to run our lives.

The West Indian Students' Centre is housed in an imposing building, much different from the smallness and the cramped dinginess of the immigrant's attic and basement room. Here, they could, like future members of the West Indian aristocracy, and through their Inglish book learning, behave in precisely those discriminating ways with which they were born, and which they would use, some of them, in spite of their proletarian backgrounds back in the hot islands.

There was a palpable quality to their views and their antics and their postures. And I feel that this was possible because of the success of their exclusion from any real aspect of Inglish life; that this had segregated them back onto themselves; had made them, within this restrictiveness, obliged to work out a hierarchy, a modus operandi, the success of which, was almost a faithful replica of the class-and-colour-based conclusions they would have made back in those islands.

367

I could never discuss these matters, in this way, with Sam. He was not interested in this kind of sociological and racialistic dissection of matters. It was as if he had written his words in his "new" language, and through the mental and creative exhaustion that that had caused in his writing of it, he was now too weak to tamper and concern himself with these mundane things, these intellectual things. For his contribution, when the day had ended, was the epitome of creativity, the word stripped bare of any sophistications that might have taken away from its inherent force and essence.

When I had called Sam back that night of the *Third Programme*, to talk about Naipaul's contribution, he said simply, "Well, boy, you know Vidia! Vidia does-do his thing. That is Vidia." My disappointment was as alarmed as my discontent with Vidia's own views expressed on the program. "Is all right, yuh know, boy. Vidia does-do his thing, and thing ..." It seemed he was anxious to get back to another chapter in his chronicling of the real "lonely Londoners"; and any interruption, any digression to discuss points of view not germane to this essential portraiture of the realism of life in this strange, cold, inhospitable land, was irrelevant.

Now with Handrew, it was different. There was fierceness in Handrew's disapprobrium; passion in his deep disappointment with a "brother" gone wrong, with a friend who had misunderstood the Inglish congratulation, and had mistaken it for acceptance. "Rass!" Handrew said. "Bro', what you expect from the rass-man?" There was no need, in either case, from either evaluation, for further enlargement.

These certainly must have been my thoughts, as I travelled in the summer twilight, in the company of my Harrison College friend, Greville Clarke, a cousin; and Richard Small of Jamaica, a barrister in training, and Coolie Hewitt, who was preparing to be an accountant, to the frightening engagement of giving a talk at the West Indian Students' Union Centre.

My reservation was based upon the chilling fact that C.L.R. James was going to be in the audience. CLR, as he was endearingly known, was a man who knew everything. I knew that George Lamming's outstanding book of criticism, *The Pleasures of Exile*, is, in my view, based upon intimate and very intellectual conversations, mental exchanges that he must have had with CLR. For CLR, a Trinidadian, would have known Lamming when he taught English to Spanish immigrants living in that bordering country; and he would have been a regular at CLR's soirees during the long cold winters in London. Again, CLR had written the monumental volume *The Black Jacobins*, and would, during those gatherings, have imparted to Lamming (if he needed it!) a special, new Marxist view and interpretation of what was in *The Lonely Londoners*. CLR was going to be there. And all the new, rising, West Indian intellectuals, to listen to the words of a Barbadian, who did not even live in the centre of things, in this 1960s vortex of racial, intellectual, and political affairs.

But my trump card, which turned out to be no card at all, was that I was more radical than any of them; closer to the hub of the new black cultural nationalism; had already interviewed all the main personalities in the Civil Rights Movement and in the Black Power Movement. I had talked with Stokely Carmichael, Roy McKissick, Malcolm X, LeRoi Jones (Imamu Baraka), Rap Brown, Roy Innis, Larry Neal, John Henric Clarke, Abby Lincoln, Paule Marshall, Black Mother Africa, the followers of Father Divine, Louis Farrakhan, Toni Cade Bambara, Max Roach. The outstanding exception was Dr. Martin Luther King Jr. I missed him only because his predilection for the secretary at the CBC's New York studios was greater than his enduring another half hour of questions, following his re-recording the prestigious Massey Lecture for that year, for which he

368

had been honoured to give! I had, in the later words of Martin, "seen the moun-taintop," so far as this kind of black consciousness was concerned. And I could, off the top of my head, tell them tales of horror, tales of frustration, tales of the disillusionment of following the Southern Christian Leadership Conference's phi-losophy of turning the other cheek, of being logical in my arguments about white racial violence. I could give them a "heavy rap." I could talk in a way, devoid of the West Indian's characteristic for reason. I could snow them over.

For how was I to match my puny intellect with CLR's, and with him in the audience, in the front row, his visage exuding sagacity, doubt, and skepticism, that this young man could marshal and was qualified to talk with a profundity that CLR was capable of: CLR had already demonstrated superiority in these matters. I fell into the acolyte's trap of thinking that because Notting Hill did not have the drama, did not have the same negative possibility of détente as did any of the "uprisings" or "rebellions" that had taken place so close to the Canadian border, or the border of Canadian sensibilities, in the Amurcan cities of Harlem, Detroit, Selma, Augusta, Atlanta and, indeed, Washington D.C. itself, that I was bearing a heavier, more "relevant" dramatic evidence of racialism. I was representing the victim's point of view. And none of them, including CLR, himself, had this first-hand authority! How could I not mention by the dropping of names, the personages known even to those in benighted London, of "leaders" I knew personally? The "lec-ture" descended into the trough of a harangue. Instead of analyzing the conservative approach of blacks in London, whose philosophy was similar to the Ghandi-like non-violent approach of Dr. Martin Luther King Jr., I berated them for this conservatism and screamed at them because they were not burning down London town. I lost my temper, meaning I lost my cool, my rationality. Reason went out of the room of civilized discussion, and it came down to nothing more than a "rap."

I had known "raps." They were interminable sessions whose purpose seemed only to put your opponent off balance: to oppress him by "relevant" terminologies; to "come down on him heavily." Any audience, preferably a white liberal audience, would be slapped with the latest "black rhetoric." The latest black shit. I was, in the contemporary terminology, "heavy." Meaning, I was vacuous. I apologize now, too late perhaps, for that liberty taken, for that rudeness, for that stupidity, taken in the pres-ence of a man, CLR, whom I extol now, even in his death. He had given us *The Black Jacobins*, we West Indians whose dulled appreciation of the harsh French colonialistic savagery we had contrived to associate with that writing and symbiotic "fraternity." He had given, through those intellectual discussions with Lamming, Lamming's own

The Pleasures of Exile; and also, *Water With Berries*. And in a strange way (for he too, held Sam in high regard), he had given us, through his nurturing, the solid intellectual foundation of West Indian thought. I know that Sam regarded CLR, "as a giant"; and national chauvinism has nothing at all to do with this acclamation.

But there were salvaging moments to the evening of my failed opportunity to demonstrate to these West Indian intellectuals, the analytical aspect, the intellectualism of the Civil Rights Movement and the Black Power Movement about which I had talked. The salvaging lay in the sociology of life for the black Londoner. These matters have a more significant importance to me, a humanist like Sam, than the tortuous, academic breaking of ideas and points of view. I was, and still am, more interested in how people behave in their environment; how they interact, how they hold their forks, how they wear their shirts, and how their ties are knotted, than any intensive scrutiny into their character; for I think that *character* is exposed by these natural, human idiosyncrasies. I was therefore, under the spell of Sam's "lonely Londoners."

West Indian hospitality withstands any extremity of weather, of social circumstance, of the meanest existence. And it was obvious therefore, that after my failed "lecture," I would be lionized, in the "digs" of one of the students. After all, my intellectual shortcomings could not be so enormously appalling, that the rum would not be brought out, after midnight; and we could assuage the taint left by me, upon their association with me; that we could not meet, as a tribe, "as Bajans," and talk, not only about the more formal aspect of my visit to the Students' Union Centre, but as "immigrants" share the more important aspects of their life in a foreign country, with all its romantic notions of alienation. And we could also "old-talk" about what Sam so characteristically called, "things, and thing and thing."

So we gathered after the Students' Union had to close, in the flat of the student of accountancy, after I had impressed them with my unquenchable appetite for their Inglish pints of bitter. I did not find it bitter at all. I doubted they were poured in the legal measurement of "pints." But at the flat of the student, I was poured more generous portions of Mount Gay Rum. It had probably been sent up from Barbados to the customs of Inglann, and its alcoholic content lied about; and I drank it until the time for departure came. And when it did come, no one moved. No one went to the clothes cupboard to get his coat or windbreaker, or sweater or scarf to protect himself against the chilliness of Inglann's "summer."

I was offered a couch. Actually, a place on a large couch. It reminded me of the ones we in Toranno bought second or third hand from a place called Crippled

Civilians. One student was already stretched at full length on the hard wood floor. From his manner of getting immediately comfortable, and with no apology for his relaxed manner—his shoes already off, University tie loosened; his tired body already burrowed into the imaginary trough of the cold, hardwood floor, it seemed as if he was remembering mattresses made of cush-cush grass stuffed into a case, back in the island. He all but yawned his good nights to us. Then, came the turn of my cousin, Greville Clarke. He looked at me, inviting me to acknowledge this custom, and surrender myself to the dictates of the late night. The double-priced taxi fares, the end of the public bus transportation had to be balanced against the realism that if a "lonely Londoner" does not, like Sam's Rackley, who had to wait for "Auntie to cough," catch that last bus going to the ends of the earth, to his address, then he is doomed to sleep either in the tube, or in the street, as he had already been thrown out of the visited house.

We, back home, have always gone home, no matter how late the hour. No matter how compelling the sexual inducement. No matter how hospitable the hostess. But here, in London, one had to behave like a Barbadian Leghorn fowl, and "sleep where night catch you, boy!"

Greville was married, and lived far away. And our host, the student account- 371
ant was married. His flat did not provide the space or the privacy, in case he was peckish that night and desired the enticing bosom of his wife, a desire shipwrecked through his own West Indian generosity. As the distinguished guest, I feared I would be contributing to an inconvenience. Greville was my responsibility. I had pounds, sterling. "Whatever it costs, whatever it could cost, we going home in a taxi. After you drop me off in Maida Vale, take the blasted taxi home." He lived a "far way off." I didn't know the district. But Inglann is not so large, that he could not have walked the distance. Except, that he, a Londoner, would know the idiosyncrasies of the London Bobby better than I would, and might have exposed himself to some horrible indignities. Notting Hill was still on everyone's mind.

It was like this, this amazement by my friends at the largesse I was willing to dispense with, for my friends. I had not seen most of them since we had finished the Sixth Form at Harrison College. Sam, in Trinidad, was not known to me in this way: but he was close in this friendship, perhaps closer, from the Sunday nights on "Caribbean Voices"; and even in his fiction the humour had made the deprivation of immigrant life more palatable. Had he accepted my invitation to attend the talk at the Students' Union, I would not have permitted him to bunk on a stranger's couch, merely because the tube had stopped.

My amazement at what they called my largesse, my generosity, came to a head, at the late dinner I hosted, following my publisher's reception in Mayfair. Heinemann and my employers, the CBC in Toranno, had both contributed generously to my expenses for this working holiday. We had dined at one of the favourite eating spots in London, a Chinese restaurant. The best in the City, they said. But I found the food to be mediocre. Even in those days, we in Toranno were spoiled by the superb Chinese cuisine, of many regions and cultures that we had then. And the bill, measured in Canadian funds was not particularly exorbitant. But to my guests, it was a small fortune. We were certainly not so far from Berkeley Square in London, where there were more pigeons for the traps laid by the immigrants in Sam's brilliant short story.

"Man, you just paid, for this dinner, the equivalent of two weeks rent for my flat!" Greville said.

His wife, more sophisticated, said "Grevvie always said what a generous person you are."

It was probably that I liked her for that; that I knew how much she loved Greville and cared about his career in the Law; and that she was somewhere, alone, lost amongst the rubble of London, in some small, cramped flat. It was probably that I felt she was unprotected for the duration of his time away from home, that I insisted we take the taxi and he drop me off in Maida Vale, and then have the taxi proceed with him to his overpriced small flat, somewhere between the Students' Union, and the suburbs where Sam lived.

The Lonely Londoners had described it: this bunching together of immigrants, through economic necessity. The social and personal inconvenience of this unnatural burgeoning of the family of strangers would have to be stomached; and the cause of his new camaraderie, this taking on of an African tribalism, provided the basis, on this small model of personal encounter for the later "federation" of students back home, and put into operation the possibility that the West Indies political Federation which had been written on paper and signed, and had started to function, could with this "new wine" of political and social consciousness, be at least discussed again.

The Lonely Londoners had depicted the physical restrictiveness of immigrant life. And Sam himself was, in his personal life, a first-hand witness to this. We must have been drinking quite a lot of beer when I was in Sam's home in the suburbs. The necessity to go to the bathroom, arising out of the urgency of that abhorrent beer, demanded that I visit the bathroom. With West Indians, or I should say, with Barbadians of a certain social class, it is not normally proper to ask to use the bathroom, even if you are in the home of a friend. I do not know what the sociologist would say about this peculiarity. It must have to do with the psycho-sexual significance of the function of the body. It may be that we regard this request as an imposition, for it could expose the social status of the person asked the question. It may be, too, that when the request is made, no Christian-minded Barbadian would have the lack of decency to refuse you the use of his facilities. But the point lies precisely in the facilities. We are talking about a time when not all people in London, even those of some social substance, had running water *inside* their houses.

The beer, which was served warm, warmer than in Toranno, worked its magic upon my body and my irrigation system, and I had to go. I had to ask. I had to forget my Barbadian prudity. I could not keep the weight.

"Boy," Sam said. He seemed relieved that I was a boy and not a girl. For he would have been faced with a different sense of the propriety of the host. "It have shithouse here in Inglann, just like back in the West Indies, yuh know!" I was not prepared for this. Not in the Mother Country. The Mother Country had mothered us into believing, like her famous writers, E.M. Forster, Rudyard Kipling, and D.H. Lawrence, upholders of the ethic of paramountcy in empire and imperialism, that all things, including bathroom facilities were "bright and beautiful." We the "coloured members of the Empire always were taught our 'place' in that empire."

In Toranno, some upper-class friends of mine, take pride in leaving their gracious homes in the city, to go to the cottage, and live in this "natural state." The outhouse. The outdoor washroom. There is no water running in pipes, from the lake to the cottage. And in Barbados, a man who has grown up in that unnatural primitiveness, is bound there in this regard because modernity is circumscribed by his economic ability. And in Toranno, on Brunswick Avenue, in the Annex, an upper-middle-class residential community, the running water inside the house is taken for granted. It is not even to be regarded as a symbol of that gracious living.

But to think that in Inglann, in London in 1965; in the heart of the old Empire—and perhaps, the heart was not functioning in the way it was represent-ed and reflected back to us in the West Indies as a good heart—to think that in this day and age, as my mother would say, that "they don't have decent facilities for people to number one, and number two in! Especially to number two? That isn't like the way these Inglish people behave when they was around us, yuh!"

Sam, with some knowledge of our different circumstances, showed me the short passage from where we had been sitting, through the small kitchen, to the back door, and pointed at a structure within the palling of the property.

"Suppose, just suppose, it was winter and I had just come home, with some liquor in me, and I had just come in, and did-want to number two, and the temperature was below zero, and I had to walk through snow high as the blasted house! Suppose, I had just stepped outside, and fall down, and was buried in the blasted snow! But suppose, that I didn't have-in my 'darrou' in sufficient quantity to make me real drunk, and I just wanted to number one, pee, piss, fire a pee ... and as I unbutton my trousers, and let out my 'bird,' and the water not only freeze before it hit the blasted ground; but my 'bird' freeze-up and turn stiff, like a piece o'iron? Suppose, also, that there ain' no pailing separating my place from the neighbour's place, and I walk, with my liquors under my blasted belt, and as a drunken man does-walk, like a sailor just off a ship, from side to side, and I walk-in the neighbour's place, and thing and thing ..."

No, *Lonely Londoners* had not prepared me for this. And if it was winter, and I had had the urge to go, I know now that I would have held it, as I had to do, for many hours, always on Sunday, when I was a choirboy in the St. Michael's Cathedral Church, walking the *Twelve Stations of the Cross*, singing the interminable strains of Handel's *Messiah*, not daring to break down, not daring to break the water, like a woman on the verge of delivery from her pregnancy, not daring to break the news of my incontinence to the boy next to me.

In those days of my adolescence, when I would stupidly restrain myself from visiting the toilet, preferring even to wet my trousers, I would hold the water for many hours until we unrobed, when I would rush to the Urinal, and roar the water out.

But not only had *The Lonely Londoners* not prepared me for this natural exigency; and I have to admit neither did the novels of Jane Austin that were forced upon me at Harrison College in Barbados; not Thackeray, Dickens the greater describer of social conditions in Inglann in the nineteenth century; nor Goldsmith, not the poets, Keats, Wordsworth, not even John Milton with an obvious devout disposition; and certainly not the editions of Shakespeare, dramatist, and actor himself, a man who could on that Elizabethan stage have taken the radical step in his staging, and have given us a hint of the way it was done in those days. And it amazed me that in all this body of literature the Inglish have been able to conceal the facts about this natural function, and the arrangement they had to make to make the function work, hiding it all these years, leaving it only for the "weird," the maudlin, the sexually and socially deviant to wonder why this important aspect of life, the *essential* aspect, was left out of all those novels which have been acclaimed as touching the human spirit in its deepest realism? It probably was not human to succumb to natural bodily functions in that kind of literature.

But the Latin texts I studied, came closer to revealing this naturalness of life.

Back in Barbados, we boys at Harrison College used to amuse ourselves by inventing and imagining ways by which the Queen dealt with this natural problem, even when it was not an emergency, and in particular when she was inspecting guards of honour, when she was out shaking hands, and could not be within striking distance of her chamber and her pot!

We had chamber pots back in Barbados. In Toranno, we have chamber pots too, but they are used in the new chic manner appropriate to the collector of antiques. They are filled these days, with dried flowers, or Brazil nuts at Christmas. Their natural use has been wiped from the drawing-rooms of our sanitized sensibilities.

Someone told me, years and years ago, that the reason Victorian (and earlier) homes were decorated with such heavy, concealing velours, especially beside the huge dining rooms that held dinners that lasted for hours and into the dawn, with the huge amounts of food that the richer classes consumed, with the wines and ports, that these velours were more pragmatic than interior design and decoration. It was the curtain, the blind, the censor's hand in the case of the literature written in and about those times, it was the means of hiding the arrangement of "firing a pee," or "taking a shit." Behind the velour was a line, straight as a column of the Light Brigade, in single stiff file, covered with the best damask napkins, in which the gentlemen, and the ladies, "did their business" to alarming explosions, particularly when the food induced that condition in the bowels.

375

Why therefore, can I watch an Amurcan "western" whose theatrical time is days or weeks, and never do I see an "outhouse" on the screen? Or in those glamorous hotels when the men are drinking beer, and fighting, why do I never see a door marked "*Men*" or "*Women?*" And in the films that deal with the outdoors, with camps of the Amurcan Cavalry, why is the essential architecture omitted?

It was *one* cowboy movie, made by a comedian, and starring a black Amurcan, which was the first to bring this into our consciousness; the director had most of his actors farting in the way we sometimes hear men fresh from construction sites belch and fart!

Of course, we all live in polite society. And there is absolutely no need to be so realistically illustrative. This kind of realism is regarded as maudlin, crude, and improper.

But thinking about it is intriguing. We have been shown only part of the photograph. For if we can illustrate the shedding of blood in cowboy movies, especially those with Indians, why have we disdained comment on this function of the body, which in some societies is regarded as a gesture of acknowledgement that the hospitality extended was pleasant?

The Lonely Londoners predicted the exodus of the "new-wine" chroniclers of Inglish society, now profoundly tampered with, and tempered with that infusion of the West Indian sensibility. It had been already accomplished in cricket, the one activity that is the most Inglish.

The "Londoners" were leaving. Not because they had outgrown the landscape; not because there was nothing more, nothing so important as when they had first arrived, to write about; but they were leaving because they had to do so: forced by the new iciness of hospitality; by the blatant expressions of disrespect in the House of Commons; by the repudiation of "citizenship" which during the Empire of old, was extended to anyone who lived in the lands, colonies, dominions, beyond the seas. And of course, in those days unnecessarily glorified by E.M. Forster, Rudyard Kipling, and D.H. Lawrence, the "sun never set on the British Empire," and Britons "never, never-never-never shall be slaves."

Let the slaves of the twentieth century, and the sons of slaves of the nineteenth, many of whom had been bondaged by the Britons themselves, find a new world, and a new way of seeing and writing about things...

I returned to the CBC with two one-hour tapes of the interview I had recorded in Sam's house, in London, in 1965. But before I had left London, I spent an evening with Michael DeFreitas, in the mansion he shared with his Canadian "roommate," whose charm and hospitality was as large as the Prairie province from which she had come. Over dinner with wine, and good conversation in which Michael explained his relationship with Rachmann the slum landlord, for whom he admitted working and using strong-armed tactics to rip the rents from the West Indians, overcrowding those rooms meant for one or at the most two inhabitants, he talked at this incipient stage about the political situation of West Indians and other black people in Inglann. His views were not sharpened by any ideology. Not yet. For he had not met Stokely Carmichael and Malcolm X at this time. But he was touched by the ideas of liberalism instilled into him no doubt by his Canadian "roommate" a woman of great intelligence, who would, through her Canadian experience have been in a position to inform him of the Canadian attitude towards black people. Canada, could, then claim as she cannot claim now, to treat black people with more dignity than they were experiencing in Amurca.

From the dining table, as a good host, he took me to Notting Hill and to Brixton, two of the fields on which the recent racial wars had been staged. And he showed me the homes owned by Rachmann, and for which he was responsible for squeezing rents from West Indians and other inhabitants.

And then we descended steps that led into a different world. We were in a speakeasy, owned by an African, who was as tall and dignified as a Zulu. Instead of silver bangles he wore a gold Rolex watch. A man was dressed like an Oxford graduate headed for the House of Commons, who wore a Savile Row suit and spoke with an accent of the upper classes. I had never before ventured into such a "den of iniquity," as mother would term this liberalism. And because I was doing it in a country she did not know, and behind her back, I was wallowing in my own new licentiousness and freedom.

There was a slot machine. I had to be told what to do with the handle. And I did just that. And when it was all over, the florins or guineas had come falling into the tray like manna from heaven, and I imagined that I was in heaven, that I had been blessed by this heavenly spirit of fortune, with the glitter and the sound mesmerizing me, and when I recovered from this shock of fortune, I began to praise Inglann and London. I began repenting for the unforgiving comments and sentiments I had made about Inglann to friends, strangers, and colleagues. And I wondered what was the purpose of going back to Canada and Toranno?

When I left, I left like a tourist: laden down with gifts. I bought a pair of suede boots, made to measure. I can still feel the master craftsman's hands moving over my feet, touching corns and enlarged bunions, soothing veins and moving lightly over the "ash" on my feet that James Baldwin talked about; and in that moment I could understand and appreciate the life that those men, in books by Dickens and Thackeray and Jane Austin which told of such things, those men who sat at the interminable dinner table, beside the imposing, thick, concealing velour blinds.

I paid in guineas. No self-respecting gentleman, worth his oats in sophistication and class, would ever quote a price, or a fee, in any denomination less than guineas. I was learning fast.

I had been taken to Cambridge by my editor, who had studied there before going into publishing. I walked those Cambridge streets I had read about in books we had to study in Barbados. I punted on the Cam. I had supper beside the Avon.

377

I breathed in the same air as Shakespeare. And I dined in a cottage turned into a restaurant where Shakespeare himself must have eaten roast beef and Yorkshire Pudding, if it was invented then. Later, in the afternoon, I browsed through Heffers for rare books; after having been measured for a suit at a gentleman's outfitters.

If Sam could see me now!

The book I brought back to Canada with me and purchased from the loot in guineas, from the jackpot I had won at the after-hours speakeasy "club," was a leather-bound copy of *Othello*, printed in the old fashion, making it slow reading because I had to remember that an "f" was an "s" in those days, in sixteen hundred and something.

And for Mrs. Clarke, I brought back a blue-grey formal dress made of the best silk that would have come from China, or India and turned into the beautiful cloth I held in my hand, in one of the sweating factories somewhere outside of Sam Selvon's London.

The two-hour taped interview, was with others, cut and edited and turned into a program for the CBC, "Project 65," and played on a Sunday. We called the program, "London's Lonely Pilgrims." And as I write this, I remember, that I had bought a second leather-bound book, just as richly and beautifully turned. *The Canterbury Tales*.

I was thinking of Chaucer in the same sense of his chronicling those pilgrims as I had been thinking of my new friend, Samuel Selvon, and his "lonely Londoners."

He wrote his letters to me, in the same idiom, speech I had heard in bustling Port of Spain streets, when he worked as reporter for the *Trinidadian Guardian*. He wrote them in a sometimes difficult to read script, and with a ballpoint pen. Between 1972 and 1979 he wrote me ten handwritten letters and eight that were typed. They are masterpieces of conversation. He wrote as he spoke. Sam's letters are short, but grand and glorious stories. Details about his life, which to me, remained by comparison regimented to his large, old, manual Underwood typewriter; about his family of which he was very protective; of the difficulty of concentrating on his work, on the withering away of critical notice and attention— he foretold the colossal disregard by the Inglish for West Indian literature—and he anticipated, with more graciousness than I, the supersession of the Africans; about cricket; and about Naipaul: "*Boy, you know Vidia! Vidia does-do his thing, so, let the boy do his thing, eh! ...;*" about money, so necessary to the writer, for living, and for time in which to dream. He wrote about the Guggenheim Foundation grant that he had won. And I knew that he would turn his attention after this, to testing the waters, to live in North America.

He was always offering advice. Why didn't I try his publishers, who at that time, were treating him with more courtesy than they would in years to come? Why didn't I think of coming over again, for London was still the mecca for West Indian writers?

Handrew and I began a correspondence at about this time, so we had a triangular literary route, in which I learned from two points of view, what was happening to Sam—and to Handrew—and about the unsettled states of their lives. And in the one-pronged correspondence coming from Sam, I detected early, from a hint, that his health was not good. It had to be the Inglish weather, seeping into his bones, like a destroying virus. I thought of him, often, at night time, in December and January and February and March, when in Toranno, the temperature can fall with an abysmal heaviness and reach minus 20 degrees. It is *cold*. And cold is cold, in any measurement of coldness, if you are a West Indian. He had said as much in *Lonely Londoners*. If it wasn't the "system," it surely would be the climate that would get him.

And when it would take me a few seconds from my study on the second floor 379 of this large house in the Annex, to walk the few feet to the bathroom which was "indoor," he would, in Inglann's corroding dampness, have to work up the courage to dress, put on a wind-breaking coat, gloves, winter boots, and face the longer journey to the "outhouse." And how did he manage? Did he not, in a fit of temper, or a fit of drunkenness, the companion of the writer, *attempt* to postpone the urge and the urgency of that natural function? Was he the type who could postpone it till the morning, with hope of clemency? With a Victorian sensibility of civilized topics, we never talked about this in our letters, but it was uppermost in my mind, whenever the thermostat dropped. It is not something you discuss even with a close friend. We adopted this Victorian sense of prudity with which we had been brought up back there in those hot islands, and therefore understood the reason for the omission from the works of the Victorians, why we never were informed of this natural function.

These are romantic notions about the hardened ground, made more intractable by the freezing season of the winters spent in London. I was leaving to return to a more socially hospitable place, in the sense of facilities. And even that type of convenience, made it seem to me, at the end of that Inglish summer, that I was going to a better place.

Sam too, had at least contemplated that there were better places than the London of his loneliness. In *The Lonely Londoners*, the discussion of the choice of a better place is couched in the peculiar ambivalence of the man who finds himself living in the home of another man, not certain of his welcome, not certain of his own choice to be a visitor, wondering if time and circumstance and condition are tougher than the realism of readjustment, of taking the long journey, another Middle Passage, another working out of the peripatetic nature of those of us, who had been wrenched from home and made to travel to the home of others, no home that, but made into something resembling one, through the creative talent of our own improvisation:

"I would advise you to hustle a passage back home to Trinidad today," Moses say, "but I know you would never want to do that. So what I will tell you is this: take it easy. It had a time when I was first here, when it only had a few West Indians in London, and things used to go good enough. These days, spades all over the place, and every shipload is big news, and the English people don't like the boys coming to England to work and live."

"Why is that?" Galahad ask.

"Well, as far as I could figure, they frighten that we get job in front of them, though that does never happen. The other thing is that they just don't like black people, and don't ask me why, because that is a question that bigger brains than mine trying to find out from way back."

"Things as bad over here as in America?" Galahad ask.

"That is a point the boys always debating," Moses say. "Some say yes, and some say no. The thing is, in America they don't like you, and they tell you so straight, so that you know how you stand. Over here is the old English diplomacy: 'thank you sir,' and 'how do you do' and that sort of thing. In America you see a sign telling you to keep off, but over here you don't see any, but when you go in the hotel or the restaurant they will politely tell you to haul—or else give you the cold treatment."

"I know fellars like you," Galahad say in turn. "You all live in a place for some time and think you know all about it, and when any green fellars turn up you try to frighten them. If things bad like that, how come you still holding on in Brit'n?"

Island Wings

CECIL FOSTER

Cecil Foster was born in Barbados in 1954, twenty years after Austin Clarke, and his 1998 work *Island Wings: A Memoir*, from which this is taken, provides a different genera- tion's perspective. Like Clarke, Foster lives in Toronto.

SOLDIERS AND SEDITION

"So you're back from Jamaica," Prime Minister J.M.G.M. "Tom" Adams said in the friendliest of voices. As he spoke, he stretched out on the big desk in front of him, his head resting in the crux of his right arm, a very relaxed man. "And now you are writing some good things in the newspaper."

We were sitting on the second floor of the Barbados House of Assembly, an imposing weather-beaten limestone building, the third oldest legislature in the west- ern hemisphere, predated only by the Bermuda Legislature and the House of Burgesses in Virginia. This was the parliament the original colonists had fought and received a guarantee for in 1652 as a protection of liberties. The house that was the prototype for so many parliaments in the New World. Tom Adams had been three years in office and was still fighting to put his imprint on the island, for the legacy of his father, Sir Grantley Adams, and that of his nemesis, Errol Barrow, were still strong. These men had made their names in this building, in this room. Adams's task was to live up to the high expectations of his father and to match Barrow, who, even though he had been kicked out of office, was still very popular. Partially to undermine Barrow's pop- ularity, Adams had called a commission of inquiry into the "financial mismanagement and infelicities" of the previous government, a report that essentially exonerated Barrow and perhaps even further enhanced his image and popularity.

Mere weeks after my return to Barbados, on the first day of the new sitting of the House of Assembly, with all its pomp and circumstance, I was sitting across the desk from the prime minister, informally talking, as if I were an insider.

It was not by accident I was meeting with him. In the chair next to me was Glyne Murray, my editor at the Barbados *Advocate-News*, the man I had been recruited to replace. Murray was a very political editor. His weekly columns were controversial, setting a new style and standard in partisan politics. Tom Adams and his Barbados Labour Party loved them. Errol Barrow and his Democratic Labour Party hated them, even suggesting that Adams wrote, or at least dictated, the columns. When I returned from Jamaica, Robert Best, managing editor of the *Advocate-News*, one of the oldest newspapers in the region, had outlined his plans.

"We know that Glyne will be going on to bigger things soon," he said to me in the interview. At that time, there were rumours Murray was to be posted as a diplomat to Toronto or New York as reward for his service to the party. "So we are going to need an editor to replace Glyne." I was offered the job, raising the prospects that at twenty-four years old, I was going to be one of the youngest, if not the youngest, editor of a major newspaper in the Caribbean.

The first weeks on the job, I shadowed Murray. One of the big assignments was to report on a significant by-election that was to be the first test for the new BLP government at the polls since general elections in 1976. Although the by-election was in a DLP stronghold, the outcome was significant. The DLP not only retained the seat but now had in the winner a charismatic young doctor, Richie Haynes, a potential rival for Tom Adams. Murray's last job was to take me into the prime minister's chambers and generally make provisions for the passing of the torch to me, even if I was not told this was the specific reason. "Come and meet Tom," Murray had said to me. This accounted for my spending the luncheon break with a very relaxed Tom Adams.

"You have been doing some good writing," Adams said, punctuating his words with his trademark snort and snuffle. "I've been reading your stuff." Then he went on to talk more specifically about what I had written, especially my political columns. According to the plan, I was also to take over Murray's spot as the lead columnist in the Sunday newspaper. Flattering me, Adams asked what I thought about the day's proceedings in parliament. He said the opposition had made a strategic mistake. They had not milked the opening of parliament and the presentation of their victorious candidate for their full public relations impact.

"When Richie came into the courtyard of parliament, he had his supporters there. He should have walked through them. Stop and hugged them. Have one of them, a woman, give him a big bunch of flowers. Instead, he walked from the leader of the opposition's office into parliament, not stopping, only waving his hand as he went in." Tom Adams had worked for the British Broadcasting Corporation when he studied law in England. Obviously, he knew the power of the media, especially in a country like Barbados. A winning strike for him came during a televised debate prior to the last general election, a performance that was to become legendary on the island. Accusing the government of corruption, he dramatically produced a series of cancelled cheques incriminating the government, using the moment and the live political broadcast to the maximum, assured of parliamentary privilege against prosecution, and making a name for himself as a master public relations strategist. The performance set him on the way to winning the government.

"But what do you think about your time in Jamaica?" he asked.

Jamaica, especially the capital, Kingston, had been an eye-opener for me, the equivalent of a country boy going to live in the city. Yes, there were so many things that were the same as in Barbados, but still so many things different, the pace of life so much faster, the gulf between the richest and the poorest so wide. It was in Jamaica that I became a man, living on my own, having to budget and plan my life on a daily basis. But it was also where I quickly became aware of many of the harmful effects of political strife and violence and how political instability can destroy a society.

I was taking a taxi from the Kingston airport to the Mona Campus of the University of the West Indies when I got my first culture shock. This was mere hours after arriving on the island. The car was passing through what I later knew as a small community called Halfway Tree when it turned onto the main road to the university. I must have nodded off, for suddenly I was looking at a small park, with what looked like a statue of a man looking down on the streets, holding a gun. I looked again. It was not a statue, but a soldier standing in green fatigues, the gun pointed down on the streets and the people below. I was startled. I had never seen anything like this. In Barbados, police didn't even carry guns. There wasn't anything seriously considered an army, although the government was in the process of setting up a defence force. I soon found guns were everywhere, with the police and defence forces always having their weapons on display as a show of force, many of the weapons looking well-used with the paint rubbed off the barrels where they were palmed.

Jamaica was very different. This was the late 1970s and the battles between the socialist and capitalist forces were fought with real guns. Violence was a way of life, spilling over even onto the university campus, where the local bank and bookstore were knocked off from time to time. On weekends, I wrote for the Caribbean News Agency, hanging out in the offices of the *Jamaica Daily News*, catching up on the latest unravelling of law and order and the frantic efforts of the government to cope.

On campus, we were warned not to travel late at night and never alone. I noticed that on nights, drivers did not stop at street lights, not even when they were red. Everyone was talking about *the gunman*, a ubiquitous political animal given to a life of crime and intimidating supporters of rival political parties. And the government of the day was giving increased powers to the security forces and the regular courts, and was setting up a special gun court, to deal with the escalating violence. We talked about these developments in our classes, about how, as journalists, we should cover them—whether we should be bold enough to apportion political blame for what was happening. We feared what we were seeing in Jamaica was soon to arrive in the rest of the Caribbean. After all, this might be part of the maturation process as the region asserts its independence and right to self-determination, a test of our political systems.

384

One night, I was watching television in the common room of Irvine Hall, where I lived on campus, when I had a frightening experience. On the television was the minister of defence, a very blunt-talking Dudley Thompson. He was wearing his trademark black beret and he was speaking directly to *the gunman*. "We are going to come and get you. And when we get you, we will deal with you." The minister said words to this effect "We'll deal with you. We'll shoot you in the gutter. We'll shoot you in your home. We'll shoot you on the streets, wherever you are." The minister was declaring war on *the gunman* and gangsters. Either they surrender and put down their guns or risk a violent crackdown by the security forces. This must be how some civil wars begin, I thought, but I was so frightened listening to this minister of the Crown that I straightaway left the common room and went to my bed. The threats, however, didn't seem to have much effect on *the gunman*, as the carnage continued.

Life in Jamaica was hard for other reasons. Whenever we got the chance, we left the campus and the city to enjoy the beauty, size, and diversity of the country. But we were always looking over our shoulders. This was the era of political destablization, according to then prime minister Michael Manley. For this he

pointed a finger at the United States. It had decided to undermine the local economy because the Jamaican government was socialist, because it was non-aligned in
international politics, because Jamaica had nationalized the assets of American and
foreign companies, because the United States did not like the temerity of Jamaica,
Barbados, Guyana, and Trinidad and Tobago opening diplomatic relations with
Cuba, essentially breaking the American trade embargo against Cuba and asserting
their right to choose their friends, because America and its cronies in the World
Bank and the International Monetary Fund wanted to punish Jamaicans for voting
socialist by undermining and devaluing the local currency, wanted to pave the way
for the election of a more amenable government, wanted to prevent the influence
of the Cubans from spreading beyond Jamaica and Grenada.

These and many more reasons were given for this destabilization, a word I
had first heard in Barbados in the dying days of the previous government. Late at
night, we used to hear planes flying into Barbados. These were Cubana planes
refuelling in Barbados, supposedly transporting farmers to Angola. The passengers
that got off the planes in Barbados to stretch their legs looked amazingly fit and
young for farmers and they were all dressed the same way, in formal suits that
appeared to have been cut by the same tailor. And rarely were there any women.
As this was usually the last flight before the airport closed for the night, only a
few customs and immigrations officials saw these farmers.

As it turned out, the Americans were onto what was happening. They didn't
like the idea of Barbados being a refuelling station for Cuba's sending soldiers
across the Atlantic to Africa. The U.S. State Department would later claim that
Cuba had deployed up to fifty-thousand troops in Angola, much of the early
deployment coming through Barbados. These soldiers helped liberate Angola and
Mozambique in their wars of independence and were responsible for inflicting the
first major defeat on the vaunted South African Army, essentially making one of
the earliest strikes militarily against apartheid. Barbados becoming a refuelling
point was one of the results of the decision by these Caribbean nations to open
diplomatic relations with Cuba—a decision that had some deadly consequences
when Cuban exiles living in Miami, and later identified as operatives for the
Central Intelligence Agency, placed explosives on board a Cubana plane that blew
up in mid-air shortly after a refuelling stop in Barbados, killing all on board.

The United States protested and flexed its muscles over Cuba's making the
transatlantic stops. The Barbados government, having been caught out, claimed it had
a choice: either stop the flights or have Uncle Sam destabilize the local economy, the

385

same way it was hitting Jamaica. The prime minister of Jamaica, Michael Manley, and the prime minister of Barbados, Errol Barrow, were close friends and had supposedly learned their socialism at the London School of Economics, where they were colleagues of the man who was to become prime minister of Canada, Pierre Elliott Trudeau, who also refused to go along with American policy on Cuba. Tom Adams sided with the Americans. With the issue too hot for him, the Barbadian prime minister stopped the flights through Barbados. Obviously, this was a lesson for the learning: despite all the talk of independence, some countries simply did not have the free choice, or clout, to follow an individualistic foreign policy. And yes, to answer some of those questions raised during the independence debate, size did matter, as did the presence of a powerful military.

But destabilization, or just poor economic management, as claimed the main opposition, was destroying life in Jamaica. The economy was grinding down, with many of the intellectual and moneyed classes fleeing to Miami, New York, Toronto, or wherever. Airlines were operating shuttle services to Miami, taking people and large bank accounts. Food was in short supply, so that at university we were constantly complaining of a diet of primarily plain rice; we were subject to several electrical blackouts or brownouts as the Jamaican refineries ran out of fuel. Even laundry soap was in short supply.

Jamaicans were divided on just about every issue. They were solidly in two camps: the socialists with Michael Manley and his People's National Party and the capitalists rallying behind Edward Seaga and his Jamaica Labour Party. In the classroom or in discussions around the campus, we heard the heated debates, and we listened to the phone-in talk shows on the radio. Political disunity seemed to be the main cause of all problems in Jamaica. One of the high points of my stay was the euphoria over a peace rally at the National Stadium in Kingston. This produced the memorable picture of reggae great, Bob Marley, raising the hands of Prime Minister Manley and his opponent Seaga in a peace symbol. That euphoria quickly gave way to more violence, much of it the result of partisan politics.

Ruthless partisan politics was not unique to Jamaica. In our classroom at university we talked about the situation in Guyana and Trinidad and Tobago. In these countries, partisanship was compounded by race. In Guyana, the party of President Forbes Burnham was essentially black, while the opposition was supported by the majority Indian population. We had discussed how, in a bid to hold onto power, Burnham had resorted to rigging elections, primarily by introducing overseas voting. I knew a lot about the situation in Guyana. Over the years, I had interviewed

386

Guyanese opposition leaders in Barbados, where they always complimented us for having a free press. One of these leaders was Dr. Cheddi Jagan, the Marxist chased from power by Britain and the United States to make way for Burnham, but who would later die as president of the Guyanese republic. Jagan always warned us to fight to ensure press freedom, noting that under Burnham he could not even buy newsprint to publish his party newspaper. And in one of its most dastardly deeds, the Burnham regime was suspected of killing one of its main foes, Dr. Walter Rodney, when a bomb exploded in his car. This was the same Rodney for whom many people across the region had protested a decade earlier when he was deported from Jamaica.

In Trinidad, the ruling party which had been in power for an unbroken twenty-five years was also supported by blacks, while the majority Indians were splintered among smaller parties. In both countries, the party in power made no bones about offering jobs and whatever support was necessary to its partisans, often deliberately leaving opponents without. A similar situation existed also in Antigua, where the Bird family had used patronage to ensure a long rule. The rule was broken for five years when George Walters became premier. First thing back in power, the natural governing party in Antigua brought corruption charges against Walters and sent him to prison, essentially removing the only real challenge to the family. Just about everyone in the Caribbean believed Walters's biggest sin was to oppose the Bird dynasty. Partisan politics was his ruin. Added to this was the coup in Grenada where an elected government was overthrown and the ruling cadre appeared unwilling to call new elections, where for the first time the Caribbean had political prisoners. It seemed as though violence in its many disguises would wreck the region unless the people were to take control.

387

Prime Minister Adams said he agreed with my analysis and that Barbados should not fall into such instability. The Barbadian electorate was too smart and there was the legacy of respecting political institutions on this island. And while partisanship was strong in Barbados, its practice was nothing like what was the norm in Jamaica. Barbadians might disagree politically but they would not settle their difference with violence. Barbadians did not use politics as a weapon to hurt one another. And this, he said, was a legacy we must be careful to protect.

At this point the bell sounded, recalling parliament into session. "Well, I have to go now," Prime Minister Adams said, picking up his navy blue jacket "I want to wish you all the best as editor of the newspaper when you take over from Glyne. We should have these chats from time to time."

I went into the House of Assembly for the first reporting stint after the luncheon break. Within hours, I had blown any chance of becoming editor of the *Advocate-News*. Events were now set in motion for my eventual departure from Barbados.

STARVING FOR THE CAUSE

"Did Lammie Craig really say this?" managing editor Robert Best asked across the newsroom, his natural instincts as a long-time newsman pricked by what could only be the makings of a good controversy.

The question was directed at me. We were racing against deadline for the next day's newspaper. Best and his team of copy editors huddled around a table editing the raw news copy, with Best deciding on the spur of the moment where to place the story in the newspaper. "Did he really say this in the House today?" Best asked, his head down as he scratched his editor's notes on the paper with my story.

"Yes," I said, assured by my notes. "He said it."

"Okay, then," Best said, "if you say he said it, it is on the front page. Let's see what will happen."

We did not have to wait long. The next morning all hell broke loose. The island was in a political controversy and I was at the heart of it.

Minutes after leaving the prime minister's chambers, I was sitting at the reporters' table in the House of Assembly, a privileged position on the floor of parliament and ideal for monitoring the cut and thrust of debate. The session was raucous. The opposition, basking in the glow of its by-election victory, was going after the government. It was accusing the ruling party of trying to punish those who didn't vote for it by replacing hundreds of casual workers at the Parks and Beaches Commission with government lackeys. These workers kept the beaches spruced up to enhance the tourist industry. It was not exactly back-breaking labour and few of the workers seemed to put in a full day's effort. Undoubtedly, there was a lot of featherbedding, a way for the dominant political party to reward supporters by putting them on the government payroll. Now, it was the turn of ruling Barbados Labour Party to prune opponents from the ranks and replace them with its supporters. For this the opposition was self-righteously crying foul.

Suddenly, the government's chief firebrand was on his feet. Lionel Craig was the minister of housing and labour. In political terms, he was a partisan street

388

brawler, not one of the smoother debaters who had received the finishing touches of university or of an upper-middle-class background. Craig learned his politics
on the streets, having to sit out in personal hard times the fifteen years in the
wilderness as he waited for his party to return to power. In the bad days for his
party, often he was one of the few to be elected in opposition to the DLP. He
had learned to survive by playing tough partisan politics. His initial instincts were
to defend his government's record in the face of this assault and to point out that
his party's patronage appointments were simply a continuation of political politics
on the island. To the victor goes the spoils was the gist of his speech.

But this soldier of many political battles did more. Egged on by the taunts of
the opposition, the minister launched into a partisan rant. His government would
not offer assistance in any form to opposition supporters. His government would
offer jobs and assistance only to those who supported the ruling party. Supporters
of his party were to get preference in every way. As far as he was concerned,
people who supported the Democratic Labour Party should starve. Indeed, he was
going to be so partisan that if anyone approached him and had the misfortune of being
named Douglas Leopold Phillips, DLP for short, then that person should starve,
would get no work from him. That's how partisan the government would be.

Eventually, a government backbencher, realizing the minister of housing and
labour was straying too far, suggested nobody should be allowed to starve in
Barbados because of government policy. But, in the heat of battle, through various asides, Craig disagreed with his colleague and other members of his party too
timid to be as plain-spoken as he. Yes, they should starve, he insisted. As the minister responsible, he would deprive them of jobs and housing, just because they
were associated with the DLP.

As he spoke, I took notes and followed the debate. My colleague from the
competing *Nation* newspaper, Albert Brandford, promptly put down his pen and
sat back, watching events unfold. This was theatre of the highest. Several times
the House had to be brought to order. I was aghast at this behaviour. After all,
this was the venerable parliament, the one that we claimed with such pride as the
repository of all our rights and freedoms, a place where government ministers
announced and set policy, where ultimately they are held accountable. Craig was
one of the most senior parliamentarians. He knew the importance of parliament
and the significance of what he was saying. Here were all the elements for a good
news story, if not to inform the public of an apparent new government policy but
to indicate the level of debate in this august House.

389

When I returned to the office, I paraphrased in a story what Craig had said. My lead, front-page story the next day emphasized the Let-Them-Starve portion of the speech. I followed up the report with an editorial arguing this display of partisanship was responsible for violence and instability in Jamaica and should not be condoned in Barbados. For, in my mind, wasn't this what Tom Adams and I had discussed only minutes before this disgusting speech? One member of Craig's party had even disagreed with him in the House. My report was going to be a reminder of the need to maintain the integrity of the House and, as the prime minister had said to me earlier, to make sure Barbadians didn't descend into the kind of partisanship a minister of government was now proposing. How naive I was!

As to be expected, the opposition jumped on the story. Former prime minister Errol Barrow, who had been at the centre of the debate, said he was surprised to see a journalist with the temerity to write the truth. Various opposition members embellished the story, suggesting I had left out even more incriminating parts of the speech. With great glee, they pointed out that the *Nation* newspaper had reported nothing. For them, this was not only a sign that my presence was like a breath of fresh air in local journalism, as they put it, but proof that the entire media were partisan and censored themselves. And nobody even questioned why the government-owned radio and television service or the local Rediffusion also did not report the speech, for it was expected that they would act this way.

These were heady times for a young reporter. It seemed just about everyone who mattered on the island knew my name. And I felt I was making for myself a reputation that was going to serve me well in the editor's chair. People had to realize that not only did I spot good stories, I was showing I was non-aligned in local politics, a journalist following the age-old professional credo of unbiased reporting and independence of thought. Or so I thought.

It was a different story from the government. When parliament resumed, Craig walked through the courtyard of the building, hand-in-hand with his wife, Maria. Scores of partisans were on hand. He slowly walked through his throng of supporters, stopping to hug some of them, finally receiving a big bunch of flowers, all of this happening as the news photographers snapped away. Who would have been the mastermind choreographer? Inside the House, the opposition demanded a suspension of the day's regular business. They wanted a discussion of urgent importance because of a newly announced government policy on job patronage that would lead to people starving.

Craig said he had been badly misquoted and that his privilege in parliament had been violated. Various government members rose on points of privilege demanding that I be punished for an erroneous report, also for breaching their privilege as Members of Parliament, for to breach the privilege of one was to do it to all. This precedent had been set so many hundreds of years ago, they claimed, citing the various parliamentary traditions going back to the Magna Carta in England and possibly beyond. The solution, they suggested, was to call me before the bar of the House, when the entire parliament became a court, to deal with my transgression. There I was to be charged with contempt of parliament, the government members argued, with the possible punishment that I be held in prison indefinitely until I was purged of my contempt. I sat at the reporters' table, writing down all that was being said about this article, which was according to parliamentary parlance a published report purporting to be a true report of what had happened in the House and supposedly written by one Cecil Foster, or some-one claiming to be a Cecil Foster, or some stranger to the House named Cecil Foster. I was uncertain of what was to happen next, but I knew that matters could not get too far out of hand, as the prime minister had not spoken on the issue and had not even turned up in parliament. After all, in light of what we had dis-cussed, how could he not understand why I wrote the story or even defend me behind closed doors, if not publicly?

Prime Minister Adams soon let me know how he felt about the story. The following evening I was reporting on a speech he gave at a local hotel. When I arrived, I ran into Lady Grace Adams, mother of the prime minister and my for-mer teacher. She was cool and distant, but at least we talked, never mentioning the controversy of the day. When the prime minister finished speaking, a group of reporters approached him and I asked for a copy of his notes. "I don't think you'd be interested in anything I had to say. In it nobody didn't say anything about letting anybody starve." He fixed me with a deep gaze, the light dancing off his wire-rimmed glasses, the lenses of which were always well-polished. It was a wilt-ing look.

With the pressure building on me, fate intervened to give me a temporary respite. The opposition barbs that the *Nation* newspaper was in the government's pocket, and that this accounted for his ignoring Craig's statement, stung Albert Brandford. He decided to strike back by proving that he had not really missed a major story but that I might have been deluded or simply made too much of a non-issue. His solution was to publish a copy of Hansard, the official verbatim record of the day's sitting. The *Nation* carried the official report, and there was no mention of the controversial words *let them starve*. This might have been a result of some timely editing. In accordance with parliamentary tradition, MPs are given a draft of their speeches, called the blues (originally, from the colour of one of the layers of the paper on which the speech had been typed in triplicate). They can edit or add to the speeches. The approved and possibly sanitized version of the speech is entered as the record and later issued as a document of the House. Only then is it the record official.

By publishing the speech, Brandford ran afoul of the Speaker of the House for not getting permission to publish the early versions of Hansard. In a fit of rage, the Speaker imposed a ban for life on Brandford. By now the controversy had truly deepened. It was now not only a question of partisan politics but of press freedom. Could a Speaker unilaterally ban anyone for life, possibly flouting parliamentary tradition by binding future Speakers with his decision: and whose life was he talking about, the life of the reporter, the life of the Speaker or the life of the current parliament? As the focus shifted to discussing the niceties of parliamentary tradition, giving credence to those who argued that political independence showed we were simply mimic men and women, some of the heat was taken off me, if only temporarily. More importantly, it was because of the heavy-handedness of the Speaker and the resulting public outcry that I was spared the threat of being officially hauled before the bar of the House of Assembly.

Instead, I felt the suffocating pressure of government in other ways. Everything I wrote was scrutinized by the government and the opposition. Every morning the prime minister's office called to complain to the publisher about my stories. Monday morning complaints were less subtle. The prime minister's press secretary, Denzil Agard, often turned up in person to meet with the publisher to complain. People in the business were asking me to "cool it" for my own good. I should take the sting out of my writing until the situation settled. They reminded me of two important things. First, there were limited job opportunities on the island for anyone on the wrong side of the government. The government owned outright the sole television station and one of the two radio stations. It had the other radio station on a short leash, awarding it one-year licence renewal. The *Advocate-News* was under pressure to fire me and it was unlikely I would be employed by the *Nation* because its ownership was supposedly government supporters.

Second, they reminded me of what had happened to two other journalists on the wrong side of the government. A brilliant young journalist and friend, Yussuff

Haniff, had to seek refuge at CANA when his job prospects dried up after he criticized the government. So, too, did Trevor Simpson, fired by the government from his news anchoring job at the local television, and also seeking refuge at CANA [The Caribbean News Agency]. It was unlikely CANA could take a third refugee. Just as important, some nasty rumours were sweeping the island of what could happen to opponents of the government. The police were dealing with two high-profile murders and had failed to make an arrest in either case. Rumours suggested that the victims had paid the ultimate price for tangling with the government. Supposedly, this was not a government to mess with.

It was not easy reporting from Parliament. While I sat in the House of Assembly, government members often made snide remarks, as if inviting me to respond and run afoul of the rules of the parliament. With this pressure, I was very conscious of what I wrote, for I was often reminded by them that many on the government benches were lawyers and that they were willing to sue me if I ever misquoted them. Obviously, I was not bearing up well under this relentless pressure.

One night Parliament met late, and I suffered through many of the taunts and asides. On my way out, Henry Forde, the backbench lawyer who had tried to steer Craig back to safety in the initial debate, offered me a ride home. We talked candidly. He told me to be careful and to take the advice of "cooling things" and said that I should try not to get hit by the crossfire between the two parties. And he seemed to be saying that he liked the integrity I was bringing to the job, but that sometimes it was better to retreat to fight again. So I should let things cool down, he suggested. Over the years, I wondered whether Forde, who later became one of the finest Attorneys General on the island, a leader of the party, and was finally made Sir Henry, was acting on his own or whether my family had spoken to him. An aunt was one of his strongest supporters and canvassers in his constituency. I figured my name and her connection to me must have come up when they spoke.

But the issue of my reporting and Craig's statement had taken on a life of its own. One night I was walking towards a public meeting by the opposition DLP when I heard in the distance the former prime minister talking disparagingly about journalists on the island. "Cecil Foster is the only journalist among them with any sense." I stopped in my tracks. The statement reverberated for miles around, possibly picked up by government. This was like pouring gasoline on fire. Now I was likely to be even more marked by the government, I thought. Worse, the DLP had taken to publishing columns in the local newspapers and to claiming they were

393

written by someone named Douglas Leopold Phillips. Almost twenty years later, the party was still using this pen name. Douglas Leopold Phillips had entered into the local folklore. Then, two things happened in quick succession to make me realize I was really in big trouble with the government.

Robert Best strolled into the newsroom talking at the top of his voice. We heard him before he physically entered the room.

"Okay, Cecil. I know what I am going to do," he announced to one and all. "'Cause this is *bere* foolishness. They have to realize there is a difference between them as a government hitting out at you and your criticizing them. So from next week, I'm going to take you out of the line of fire. You ain't going into the House any more."

The next week, I was transferred to the courts. I also gave up my political column. It was some time before I found out what had caused this sudden change, before some media officials attending let me in on a secret.

Prime Minister Adams had gone on national television to warn of an attempt to overthrow his government. A gunrunner, Barbadian Sydney Burnett-Alleyne, who supposedly had never forgiven Adams for creating a public scandal by dramatically revealing on television, from parliament, cancelled cheques from Burnett-Alleyne to former government members, had been arrested in Martinique with a shipload of weapons. Apparently, he claimed he was planning to overthrow the Adams government. In light of what had happened in Grenada and in Dominica, where a group of white-power racist mercenaries from North America was intercepted on route to attacking the government, the threat announced by Adams was taken seriously.

Before going on television, Adams called the top media officials on the island for a meeting. Those attending were sworn in under the Official Secrets Act, which prohibited them from divulging what was said behind closed doors. Adams took them into his confidence over the threat against his government and suggested that they temper their reports so as not to spook the general population. Finally, he suggested that the meeting might be a good opportunity for the government and media to mend fences and to enter a period of co-operation. These had been testy times for all, with the banning of reporters and discussions about the erosion of press freedom, he said.

"Well, it's not only the banning of one reporter," one of the journalists said. "What about the treatment of Foster?"

"Foster is a different story," Adams said. "We will get even with him."

Although he never explained it, Best was responding to this statement when he came into the newsroom and assigned me to the courts, hoping the fury would blow over with me no longer a political reporter. Switching me to the court beat didn't change much, although it got me out of the line of political fire. For the change was too sudden and it became as much political fodder as what I used to write about. The issue of press freedom was raised among politicians and other government critics. The government didn't like getting blamed for forcing this change and I became even more of an albatross for them.

In the courts, some of the leading legal minds in the country befriended me and we would discuss my situation in the corridors. Of course, most of these lawyers were themselves politicians. One of them was Bobby Clarke, a friend of Maurice Bishop, then prime minister of Grenada. Another was the garrulous and plain-speaking lawyer and one-time luminary in the former government, Frederick (Sleepy) Smith. His advice to me the first day I showed up to report from the courts was always to make sure I reported both sides of a case and not to fall into the trap of presenting the Crown's case only. The case of the Crown should always be suspect until proven and I should remember the defence also had its own story. Failure to present both sides—something many reporters often did, according to him—could leave me open to a charge of contempt of court. Having narrowly missed a charge of contempt of parliament, I took to heart his advice. Sir Frederick, later knighted for his outstanding legal work, went on to become the chief justice of the Eastern Caribbean, but I will always remember him for that morning he purposely came over to me sitting in the press section, perhaps looking bewildered at all that had suddenly enveloped me, and offered his support and a figurative pat on the back.

Eventually, Glyne Murray decided to leave the newspaper and to accept the government's patronage appointment. Everyone was invited to a farewell party at a house about five minutes' walk from an apartment I was renting. I turned up at the party.

About midnight, with the music wailing, people dancing, and the food and drinks flowing, Prime Minister Adams showed up. Like me, he was not much of a dancer and eventually the two of us were standing side by side across from the dance floor.

"You are not a bad reporter," Adams said. "But I do think you are easier on the opposition than you are on the government." He proceeded to tell me of all the stories I had written, recalling from memory minute details, slights of his government and praise for his opponents, suggesting that like most reporters on the island I had missed the salient points of the commission of enquiry that essentially exonerated members of the previous government of corruption. We chatted for a long time, with Adams suggesting it was time for us to forget our differences. Ever conscious of the pressure on me, this was music to my ears. I wanted to be free of this war of attrition.

"With the estimates coming up we have some initiatives you might find interesting to write about," he said. "You might want to report on them." Once again he tried flattery, suggesting I was a natural political reporter and better understood what was happening on the island than many of the reporters. For this reason, he wanted to see me return to what I did best.

As we talked, we watched Lionel Craig, minister of labour and housing, waltzing *pretty*, *pretty* across the floor, the perspiration flowing down his face and soaking his multicoloured shirt. Craig had steered his partner in front of us and was within listening distance over the blaring music.

"Lionel," Adams called to him. "Lionel, I was telling Mr. Foster here about some of our plans. You might want to explain to Mr. Foster some of the finer points of the initiatives for your ministry that we are planning."

"Mister P.M.," Craig shouted, ending his dance and stylishly taking a handkerchief to wipe the sweat from his face. "I ain't having nothing to do with that man. 'Cause I'm going to get even with him. He writing that I say let people starve. Well, I am going to get even with him." Still wiping his face, he started talking directly to me. "If you ever cross my path, it's good night nurse. I'll feed you with a long spoon. It's going to be *bere* pressure in yuh chest from me. 'Cause you hurt me and I'm going to hurt you back and I'm going to hurt you worse than you hurt me. If I ever catch you on the wrong side, it's all over, lights out for you. If you or any member of your family get into my way, it's all over for them, too."

It must have been the alcohol in my head, but I was not backing down from Craig. We were standing toe-to-toe shouting at each other and ready to come to blows. The party was now stopped. Everyone was looking on. We were standing, waiting for one of us to throw the first blow. Suddenly, I was saved. I felt several strong slaps on my shoulder. Someone was saying "Cut this out. Cut this out. Cut this out. This is not the place for this kind of behaviour. This is not the place for this kind of discussion. Cut this out." The strong hand steered me away. It was Robert Best. I looked for Prime Minister Adams. He had gone, slipping away and disappearing into the night. I could never decide whether he had deliberately set me up for the confrontation with Craig.

Robert Best took me away to a corner, while talking loudly to defuse the situation. It must have worked and sobered me up. For standing in the corner, I realized I was never much of a fighter and the thought of fighting with a cabinet minister was indicative of what the daily pressures were doing to me. It was at that point that I realized I was in really big trouble.

When nobody was looking, I slipped into the darkness and walked home, looking over my shoulder frequently to make sure nobody was following me. Errol must have been sleeping when he answered the telephone in Toronto.

"You *gotta* help me get off this island," I said as soon as he answered. With that, I explained what had happened. I needed him to sponsor me to Canada and could he possibly make some enquiries soon with Canadian Immigration, perhaps as soon as the sun came up in a few hours.

Errol promised to act right away and asked me to take care of myself. But before hanging up, he asked questions that of late I had been asking myself. "Why didn't you keep your mouth shut like everybody else? Why did you have to write that story, let them starve? Why couldn't you be like that reporter who wrote nothing?"

I had no answers. Must have been something I had learned in school, something about being a maverick, the lone wolf, and feeling compelled to speak truthfully. Perhaps something ingrained in me that we, the young people of a young nation, had been entrusted with the fragile future of a country others didn't believe, I had taken perhaps too seriously the admonition that we had to consciously fight and sacrifice to build a better society. Within the people and their institutions had to be the checks and balances. In the schools, they had told us these things. I was a product of the new and supposedly post-colonial education system. I would not have become a reporter and columnist, someone talking and arguing about matters of state with prime ministers and men and women on the streets, someone considered by the leaders of my nation and some of the best minds among us as having some potential, if I had not been rescued by education. But in my frightened state, even that wasn't an adequate answer. For once again, I was back to yearning deeply for the opportunity to flee my island and to have a new start in somebody else's country.

FLYING ALONE

Within days Errol got back to me by phone and said he and his wife had visited Canadian Immigration in Toronto, filled out some forms and were told there shouldn't be much problem sponsoring me to come to Canada.

And sure enough, a few weeks later I received a letter from the Canadian High Commission in Bridgetown, setting a date for an interview with the Canadian officials. I felt the pressure easing off me. Still, there was no guarantee of a visa to Canada, so I told only my immediate family about my plans. I went to the headquarters of the Royal Barbados Police Force and had the mandatory fingerprints taken and an affidavit saying I had no criminal record. For the interview I took along my bank statement book showing I had the equivalent of $750 U.S..

The interview was with a bearded Canadian who nonchalantly smoked his pipe. It did not last long. Working from a long form, he ticked off some questions and filled in some spaces, then consulted a manual that told him how many points to award me for job prospects and work experience, for my education, my ability to speak English and to understand a few words and phrases in French, and for having a brother willing to assist me.

"Well, you qualify for a visa as an independent immigrant," he said. "Now, you can take your medicals and when everything is complete we'll send you your visa. I hope you like it in Toronto, Mr. Foster."

I walked out of the interview with a load lifted off my shoulders. The medical examination should be no problem and wasn't. Still, I decided not to tell anyone of my plans to immigrate to Canada. However, to save money, I moved back home. Although they never told me this, I got the feeling that members of my family were glad to have me back under their roof, perhaps so they could keep an eye on me until I was out of the country.

In an unexplained move, Robert Best sent me back to report from parliament. I was extremely cautious in my reports and when I saw colleagues put down their pens, I did likewise. Often, I put down my pen before they did. Still, there was controversy, even if I had nothing to do with it. One day I was sitting at home when a vendor came around selling a sensational newspaper from Trinidad called the *Bomb*. Everyone in Barbados was talking about what the *Bomb* was reporting. The newspaper claimed it had uncovered evidence of a political scandal in Barbados, information that it claimed the local journalists were afraid to touch. As I sat reading, obviously engrossed and even intrigued by the report, I heard the stern voice.

"You are not going to touch that one, you hear me? You will not write about that." It was Mervin. "Let somebody else write about them things. You've done your bit." Mervin had never spoken to me like that before even though he was essentially the only man in any of the houses I grew up in. It was the voice of

398

someone who genuinely cared, who didn't want me to feel some misplaced obligation to get involved and bring further grief on myself. At that moment he sounded just like what in my mind I figured a father would, the right mixture of concern and firm authoritative reproach.

"No, I won't," I mumbled. "I'm just reading."

We said nothing more about the subject I was not going to create waves. Unfortunately, everybody did not trust me not to make trouble, which meant my trials weren't over just yet.

The House of Assembly was to resume sitting after the luncheon break. We were walking to our positions at the reporters' desk, a route that took us directly behind the government benches. The voice was loud and clear and what it said was so unexpected it startled us and froze me with fear.

"Mr. Foster," it thundered. "So you planning to go up to Canada. I hear that before you leave you plan to write some bad things about me and my government. Well, let me tell you, if you think you can write anything bad about my government and run away to Toronto, Canada, I want you to know we can reach you up there. We can get you up there. All I can say is good riddance to you and the sooner you get out the better, but don't think you can say anything bad about me or my ministers and run. We'll get to you." It was Prime Minister Adams, standing in the place reserved for holders of his office in parliament.

"Wow," said Trevor Simpson, a reporter with the Caribbean News Agency and a news anchor with the government-owned Caribbean Broadcasting Corporation television station until he was fired at the bidding of this prime minister. "I wish I had what he just said to you on tape. That would be such a story. A prime minister saying that to a member of the press. But you know how these people are. If you don't have them on tape, they'll deny it and say they never said it."

To be threatened so openly was not the only reason I was scared. My mind kept wondering how the prime minister of Barbados knew I was planning to immigrate to Canada. I had told nobody but family members, had not even informed Robert Best that I was quitting the job, and I believed the Canadian High Commission handled all applications in confidence. Why would a prime minister be so interested in my plans and what else did he know? At that moment, all the warnings from people telling me to be careful and to cool things overwhelmed me. I decided to take everybody's advice, especially the prime minister's.

For that afternoon, I simply listened to the debates. My pen spent most of

399

the time resting on my notebook. The next day, I called the Canadian High Commission to ask if there was any word on my visa.

The officer handling the case wasn't in a great mood when the receptionist put through the call to him. He didn't like having to field these calls, he said, and apparently there were many. When everything was ready, he said, the visa will be sent to me from Trinidad. "In any case, it's winter in Toronto," he offered. "You wouldn't want to be walking the streets of Toronto looking for a job in winter. Spring would be a good time to be in Toronto. So relax and wait." If only he knew the reason for my urgency.

Returning from lunch, I found a note waiting for me with the receptionist at the *Advocate-News*. I had received my visa and was marking time until I left for Toronto. Errol had told me to telephone him when I got my visa. He had sent me the dates he was planning to vacation at home. We could fly to Toronto together. But I couldn't wait to double-check anything with him when my landed immigrant papers arrived. I straightaway booked a flight on Air Canada—one way—to leave on the day Errol planned his return from Barbados to Toronto. I assumed that naturally Errol was going to travel on Air Canada. Wrong, he was travelling on the charter airline Wardair and it was too late to change tickets. Now, everything was in place for me to leave.

The message left with the receptionist was scribbled in pencil. "Mama real bad in hospital. Help us how you can." It was signed Jasmine, Aunt Princess's real name. Later, David confirmed the bad news. Grandmother was terminally ill in hospital with cancer. He was visiting her every day, but the doctors had given up hope. David also told me of plans well underway for him to immigrate to New York and join his mother. Both of us were looking forward to new beginnings in North America. We said our goodbyes, realizing we might not see each other before I left and promising to keep in touch when we both were up north. I also promised to visit Grandmother before leaving.

I walked into the public ward at the Queen Elizabeth Hospital, having put off visiting until the very last moment. I never liked hospitals or their strange disinfectant smells. Something about them always reminded me of my friend Ian Nurse. The nurse on duty pointed out the cot to me. I approached gingerly. Stretched out on the cot was a figure I didn't recognize. It was in a white gown, the face turned away from the direction in which I was approaching. The person looked emaciated, not the strong Grandmother I knew. She had a scarf tied loosely around her head, but I could tell she had no hair, possibly from the radiation treatment. The woman on the cot must have been in a light sleep; for she was groaning and rhythmically raising one foot and letting it drop.

I stood next to her cot for a while. I had no voice. I stood and watched her, her foot rising and falling, groaning. Then I turned away.

"What happened? Didn't you say you came here to visit Mrs. Goddard?" the nurse asked.

"Yes. But I can't wake her."

"Why not? She might only be sleeping."

"I don't have the heart to wake her," I explained in an uncertain voice, hoping the conversation would not wake the woman on the cot. "Could you give her a message for me? Tell her for me that her grandson, Cecil, was here to see her."

"You sure you don't want to tell her yourself? Go ahead, man, wake her," she said.

"No, no, no. I can't Tell her for me that on Sunday I am going to Toronto, Canada, to live and that I came by to say goodbye but that she was sleeping."

"I am sure she would be glad to hear you tell her that yourself. Especially since you're going away for good." The nurse was speaking gently. "But if you can't ..."

I shook my head, wrote my name on the piece of paper the nurse handed me, wiped from my eyes whatever was causing them to mist up and walked away, unable to look back. I knew I was never going to see Grandmother again. David would write me in Toronto and tell me she had died. I didn't want to see Grandmother so frail. That was not the memory of her I wanted to take away with me, not when I was so unsure of my future.

I wanted to remember Grandmother as the strong woman of my early years in Lodge Road, of the endless times I fell asleep on her lap, making her a surrogate mother; when she joked and often stole from her pot the wet rice that she mixed with salted butter and gave me to eat when I was too hungry to wait for the full meal; when she always promised me with such surety that I would grow up to be a strong young gentleman who would go overseas and make her proud, as long as I kept asking God to grant me wisdom and understanding. I wanted to remember the Grandmother before the pressures of trying to survive in this society changed her, some of the same pressures I had handled just as badly and which were forcing me instinctually to return to those early dreams she instilled in me. I wanted to remember those dreams of succeeding overseas, of how moving to a foreign country would ease my pains and stop me from crying. I needed to adopt her strategy of appearing brave and strong on the outside when bullies threatened and frightened us, when the powerful made us cower at night, but in the morning we had to awake with a smile on our face and try to get through another day. I wanted the strength of this woman when she was really strong, and I hope she forgave me for not waking her and saying goodbye.

Easter Sunday 1979, we are assembled for the family lunch. Aunty Ann was putting on a spread. Easter is a day of celebration in Barbados, part of the Christian tradition of celebrating rebirth, resurrection, and new life. A day of hope. This lunch was traditional, but also different. It was to be the final time for only God knew how long that all of us who had shared this small house in Kendal Hill over the past fourteen years were going to be sharing a meal. Errol and I were leaving for Toronto in hours. The atmosphere was tinged with sadness. Grand-Grand was invoking God's blessing on me and suggesting that in all things I put God first. She, too, was happy to have me leaving the island. It was for the better, she promised.

402

After the meal, with the planes already waiting at the airport about half an hour's drive away, our luggage packed, it was time to bid farewell to those members of the family and close friends not going to the airport.

"Don't worry about Cecil," Errol said, speaking directly to Aunty Ann. "I will take care of him in Toronto. He will do well in Toronto once this is behind him. He will enjoy Toronto."

"I hope so," Aunty Ann said, trying to force a laugh. "I know you'll take care of him."

"But I know you'll worry," he said.

We hugged all around and headed with our luggage for the cars taking us to the airport.

Errol's flight on Wardair left first. Minutes before boarding, he came over to me. "Don't worry. I'll see you in Toronto. If for some reason your flight arrives before mine, wait for me. Otherwise, I'll come over from my terminal to yours and get you." Then, he reminded me to buy from the duty-free shop the maximum amount of rum I was allowed into Canada. Friends in Toronto will be expecting that much, he said.

Finally, it was time for me to leave. Stephen hugged me. "Do you realize this is the first time the three of us who were left behind are really going to be separated, and this time I'll be the one still left behind." He was trying to joke and lighten my spirits. "You will do well in Canada," he said. "Remember when that headmaster at Harrison College said you weren't good enough for his school? You will do well. All I ask of you is that you always remain humble and have humility, let us always remember where the three o' we came from." Then, he tried for another joke. "Now you are going to be living in Canada, you can go and try out for the Canadian cricket team. You know, you weren't all that bad as a batsman and it looks like just about anybody can make the Canadian cricket team."

We hugged again. I smiled and waved at my family. Then, I turned and walked through security and onto the tarmac, but not before stopping by the duty-free shop.

At the top of the stairs to the aircraft, I stopped for a moment to take one last look at the island and to wave to my family. As a little boy, I had always wondered what would be my thoughts as I entered an aircraft knowing I was leaving the island permanently. I didn't expect to have so many mixed feelings. I was looking forward to living in a new country, but I knew it was not going to be easy. I was not a Canadian. I was a very nationalistic Barbadian and Caribbean person. I knew few people in Toronto. The most I could hope for was that I would land quickly on my feet, maybe, if I were lucky, getting a job as journalist. In my luggage was a folder with clippings of various reports.

But I also knew this was not the way I had hoped to leave Barbados. I never believed I would be on the run. Even as I was boarding the plane, I was hoping that I would soon return to Barbados, even if friends had told me to rest a while in Toronto until the political situation blew over. (Meeting months later with Grenada's prime minister, Maurice Bishop, in Toronto, he said, "Fost, man, Bobby Clarke tells me Tom Adams ran you out of the country. Do you know you are probably the only Bajan in political exile?" Bishop was joking, or that was what I wanted to believe, for he and Tom Adams had become enemies, publicly denouncing each another. Adams had taken to accusing Bishop of having political prisoners in Grenada. Still, his statement hurt, for I could not make up my mind if I had been in physical danger. Perhaps I was still too naive. There was a lot of truth in the joke and it hurt.)

But I also realized that in my lifetime something profound had happened on this island. While life looked casual in Barbados and the Caribbean, big and possibly lasting changes were at work. The people of the region and my island were adjusting to the harsh realities of living independently on their own, like the children who had left home with so many ideas and dreams swimming in their heads, but who had to face up to the stark reality of their times, of trying to remain committed to their dreams while trying to earn a living. Yes, they were standing on their own, but life was tough, even if there had been improvements in our lifestyle and the style and numbers of our creature comforts.

I could think of my own case, how for me education had offered so much. There was a time when for most the dream was to pass the Common Entrance Examination and get to a grammar school, then to get a few passes at the General Certificate of Education examination to get a civil service job or to work in a bank.

But in only a decade since independence, life had changed remarkably. The dreams were bigger, and more people were jumping over the bars that previously looked so high and insurmountable, but which now looked so narrow and unchallenging. A short while earlier, a young woman and I were the first to pass five GCE subjects at Christ Church High School and that was considered historic in terms of the school. Since then, many more students from the same school had surpassed us. The same had happened at the various schools across the country. Education and the ability to see dreams within reach were now available to just about everyone.

404 But while an independent Barbados was producing a better educated and qualified population, it still was not generating the number of jobs to satisfy the demand; the jobs still weren't challenging enough. Many of us still had to consider immigrating. For some, even a university degree was no longer a guarantee of a good job and income. Many with well-trained minds were left with the luxury of time to question the society and what it offered, to analyze the lots of certain groups and to more aggressively agitate in institutions they better understood for improvements. The calibre of politicians, if not always the level of discussion, had risen.

The push out of the island for ambitious young men and women was still just as strong as when my mother and father looked to England for their self-fulfillment. And there were the political tensions. It appeared to me that the political leaders of the day were lacking vision, unable or unwilling to galvanize and unite the people behind a single idea or concept, such as how independence was more than just an idea, but also a reason for enduring tough times because independence promised a better day. It raised expectations, even if the expectations were different from person to person, from class to class. At least everybody seemed to be talking about and even working for the same purpose.

There wasn't the excitement of reaching for a goal, no flamboyant display of pride like what had first roared through the island and region when new flags first flapped in the air, seemingly daring the world to accept us, to notice our arrival. Ten tough years of adjusting and living on our own had wrung dry some of that enthusiasm. Politics seemed to be concerned with the mundane, as politicians readjusted their philosophies and looked for solutions to seemingly intractable problems such as solving high unemployment and diversifying the economy from its dependence on one crop or industry.

And there was a sense of anger in the region. A bloodless coup had over-thrown a government in Grenada, there was talk of attempted or planned coups against governments in Barbados, Dominica, and Trinidad and Tobago. Jamaica was battling with all sorts of domestic and imported problems. In Guyana, human rights and the standard of living were in sharp decline. Even one island, Anguilla, had voted to go against the trend of political independence by choosing to remain a British colony.

The region appeared headed for an explosion, perhaps as momentous as the eruption of Mount Soufrière in St. Vincent that dumped tons of ash on us in Barbados and neighbouring islands days before I left, the same kind of anger that erupted into a bottle throwing incident in Barbados when spectators abruptly ended a cricket test match between the West Indies and Pakistan. They had dis-agreed with an umpire's decision. And this was in Barbados, an island where the people were supposedly so placid, tolerant, and law-abiding.

405

The Caribbean and my island appeared to be at a juncture: they could slide into what might be considered to be typical Third World disease of lawlessness, as some had predicted before independence, or they could adjust and realign expectations with reality. Whatever the choice, I realized I was going to view it through the filter of distance. I was not going to be one of the young reporters chronicling the first draft of history. I was not going to be one of the voters mak-ing the decisions.

Still, it was Easter, a time of new beginnings, at least for me. I took one last look at the island, took a deep breath, and entered the aircraft. As we travelled across the Atlantic, the captain drew to our attention the ash from Mount Soufrière that providentially seemed to be travelling out of the region, going with us to North America.

Over the decades, thousands of us escaped this way. We always took some-thing with us—a defiance and a strong belief in ourselves, something that appeared peculiar to Caribbean people who tended to arrive in their adopted country with the strong belief that they belonged, that they can contribute, make changes to benefit everyone and then, if all went well, go back home in retirement. A belief that brought self-assuredness, no different from the visionaries, who from international capitals dreamt about a post-colonial nirvana in the Caribbean and returned to instill the dream in the young.

It was no different from those who from foreign lands looked back and felt a strengthening of the bond with those back home, who felt that to claim sovereignty and political independence was the culmination of one long struggle, perhaps going back as far as in 1651 in Barbados in Oistins, a small town on whose beach I used to walk. A struggle that took the peoples of this region through emancipation from slavery and indentured service, through riots for the right for poor people to vote, to the day when they not only voted but could be elected to parliament, when they could aspire to be their own rulers, prime ministers, presidents, and Governors General.

This was why other blacks living in North America for several generations considered those of us from the Caribbean as uppity, as the King George Negroes, as Coconut Heads, as we were called by African-Americans in the United States and by blacks in Canada. This early social and political training was partly why Caribbean blacks were considered so assertive.

Six hours later I was in Toronto. It was just over two decades since my father and then my mother had left Barbados, and now I was finally leaving, too, carrying on my search for some ties that could bind me to anyone, or anything. Perhaps I had finally taken my island wings. At various times, I had dreamt that my future rested with a new country, *new* not only in terms of remaking or modernizing the old, but as in different. *New* as in the type and choices of opportunities available to me. This was still the case. Except that the country in which I hoped to spread my wings and soar was now Canada.

Always Give a Penny to a Blind Man

ERIC WRIGHT

Eric Wright is one of the country's best-known writers of crime fiction. His Charlie Salter series of police procedurals is particularly popular. Wright came to Canada in 1951 from London, where he was born in 1929. He thus was an adolescent in Britain during the Blitz and the other terrors and deprivations of the Second World War, a period that is the subject of his only non-fiction work, *Always Give a Penny to a Blind Man: A Memoir*, from which this is taken. The book was published in 1999.

THE BOATMAN

After infants' school, everybody went to Fortescue Road Junior School until they were eleven, then they went to Singlegate Senior, except for the ones who got scholarships to the grammar school.

My first teacher at Fortescue Road when I was six was Mr. Young; I sat next to Mabel Tucker, who had brown curly hair. I woke up thinking about her in the morning and got to school early to make sure no one else sat next to her. Mr. Young used to smell of the paste we used to stick paper together with, and on Friday afternoon, if we had been good, he told us a story, an adventure story he made up.

After Mr. Young we had Miss Wait, but I still sat next to Mabel Tucker. Miss Wait had a cane like Charlie Chaplin's walking stick and one day she caned a boy named Arthur twice on each hand. Each time she hit him he shouted at her that he would bring his mum up to the school and she would bash Miss Wait, but she just waved for him to put his hand out again. Once, a boy wouldn't put out his hand to be caned, so Miss Wait fetched Mr. Jones, a knobbly old man who was the head teacher, and he took the boy away and when he came back he was crying.

When we were nine, Mr. Thomas took over the class and kept it until the scholarship exam which qualified you for grammar school. In the whole class of about thirty, ten of us were separated off by Mr. Thomas and trained for this exam. I didn't sit with Mabel now, though we were still pals, because her family didn't let her sit for the scholarship. Lots of the parents didn't want their kids to try for the scholarship. They said that too much education made kids grow away from their families, and they weren't having it. A lot of people thought that. One of them paid a special call on us to tell my mum that her son was just as clever as me but she didn't want a grammar school snot-nose in the house, one who would end up looking down his nose at his own family. My sister said she was probably protecting the boy because she thought he might not pass the exam if he took it.

When this woman came, my mum didn't even know I was in Mr. Thomas's scholarship group. She had just made sure I went to school clean and fed, and left it up to the school to know what to do with me after that. When she found out about the scholarship group she wanted to take me out of it because she saw it as special treatment for me, and she didn't allow that in the family, but my sisters told her to let me try, so I stayed in it even after the war started.

408   First, though, I was evacuated to the country.

Up until now, the countryside was something that filled up the space between Colliers Wood and the seaside, a view of trees and fields and cows, like a picture framed by the train window, to be looked at on our way to the seaside. The country was a desert of grass, without buses or shops or even proper pubs. What pubs there were were humpy, my mum said, full of local yokels, all men, who talked funny and stared at you, nothing like London or seaside pubs, which were sociable places, a bit noisy and some of them a bit rough, but still, more lively after a hard day's work than the dead-and-alive holes in the country. They didn't even have lights in the country, and not even real streets in some places. The only time the country was all right was during hop-picking when you could take the whole family and live in a big tent, using your holidays to earn a bit of extra money.

Vi lived in the country now. Before we moved from the Buildings, she went on holiday to Cornwall and met a sailor, an officer in the reserve navy, and married him, and he got a licence to run a pub in the country and they ran it for three or four years until the war came along. "The George," it was called, Loddon Bridge, Nr. Reading, Berkshire, the address was. It was very old by Colliers Wood standards; my sister May said it was a George IV hunting box, a story that she had heard from the local vicar. It seemed to have been put together by hand, any old how, so that upstairs all the rooms were on different levels and the floor of the landing sloped every which way.

Vi's husband was one of the first to go to war, before it even started, and then Vi ran the inn herself, and in the summer of 1939 when it was obvious there was going to be a war she offered to take me for the duration as her personal evacuee. The thing was, she had two bedrooms to let that might have been commandeered by the billeting officer who had to house the evacuees that were coming down from London, so it was better to have me than some stranger. She put me in one bedroom and our sister May and her husband and baby in the other. May's husband worked for a timber merchant who travelled back and forth to his work in London by train. May used to wait outside by the river to wave at him as his train crossed the railway bridge on his way home.

The River Loddon runs into the Thames, and where it runs past The George it's wide enough and deep enough to drown in. I couldn't swim then, but I only fell in once and my brother-in-law got me out with a boathook. The George had a big vegetable garden at the back with an orchard with enough trees to nearly fill the pavilion, a big storage shed, with russet apples. On one side, between the pub and the river, Vi had a tea garden on a lawn, with iron umbrella tables painted white and those little iron fold-up chairs. In the summer, people could order tea and cakes to be brought out there in the afternoon, and drinks at night when the bar was open.

409

Three young ladies appeared one afternoon and asked me if they could have some lemonade. I ran to tell Vi, who lifted down a bottle of Schweppes lemonade, divided it into three glasses, and put them on a tray for me to take out. "What do we owe you, young man?" one of the young ladies said. She was joking—I was just a boy, but she was being nice, and I ran back and asked Vi who said I should charge four pence a glass.

"But that's a shilling!" I said. "That bottle of lemonade only costs four pence ha'penny!"

"It only cost *me* tuppence ha'penny, my lad, but those misses are getting waited on. You pay for service. Off you go."

I ran back. "Four pence each. A shilling." I held my breath.

"There you are, then." She handed me the shilling, smiling.

When they had gone I collected up the glasses and found two pennies under hers. I ran after her but they were already in their car. I told Vi.

"That's a tip," she said. "For you. See? There's money in this game."

I saw. But I soon saw that there was more money in the boats.

The river ran for miles in both directions. Robbie and I used to go over to Tooting Bec park sometimes on Sundays and hire a rowboat on the pond there, so I knew how to row. Vi had a little rowboat I used to take out to see how far I could go but I always got tired before I got to a weir or anything like that. Vi had a lot of boats that she used to hire out, punts, with cushions, and some skiffs for those who fancied themselves as rowers. The punts had to be paddled because the bottom of the river had too many holes for poling, and mostly it was young couples who hired them for courting. They used to paddle out of sight of the inn and tie the boat to a branch of a tree and spend all the afternoon kissing each other.

I was the boatman. Vi had a gardener, Mr. Foster, a fierce little ginger-haired man in Wellington boots who kept telling me to leave the apples alone when he saw me in the orchard. Vi told me to be polite to him because soon gardeners would be hard to find. When Vi's husband went off to sea, Mr. Foster helped out with the boat-hiring at first, but he told Vi that was not his trade and she should find someone else. When I came, she got me to do it.

410

I thought it was smashing. We charged a shilling and six pence the first hour and a shilling an hour after that, and sometimes they would owe three and six pence or even four and six pence on a sunny afternoon. I used to write up the time they went out with a piece of chalk on the slateboard inside the boathouse, and the time they came back. They often gave me tips. The change from two forms for three hours was six pence, and I learned to be slow handing it to them to give them time to tell me to keep it. Sometimes, if they had had a nice afternoon kissing, I would get more.

Six pence bought a lot, all the sweets I could eat, but I had to be careful. Vi sold chocolate and potato crisps in the pub and I didn't want to be seen eating anything that she sold and might have thought I had nicked from the pub. Ice cream was safe, as was licorice, sherbet, and the loose sweets sold from large glass jars. Any chocolate I bought I ate on the way home from the sweet shop, in Earley. Probably Vi would have believed me that I had bought the sweets from my tips, but she might have told my mum who would have been more suspicious, so I didn't say anything. Vi also gave me pocket money for looking after the boats and that and the tips was what she thought I was spending.

So I was as happy as a prince, having this important job, making tons of money, and spending it on sweets and comics which I could buy in Earley. I used

to walk to Earley in the mornings when there weren't many customers. If someone wanted a boat when I wasn't there, Mr. Foster would look after them.
Sometimes I went for a row in the small rowboat, which we never let out because
I might have to row after a punt that got loose, or look for one that should have
come back. Sometimes people got out of their punt farther along the river and
walked away so as not to have to pay.

Vi and May were smashing cooks compared to my mum. I had an egg for breakfast every morning, always butter on the bread, never margarine, and two courses for dinner which May called lunch, with ham or pork pie for tea. Vi and May
also set about teaching me the manners they had taught themselves since leaving
the Buildings, like cutting the top off my boiled egg instead of tapping it and picking the shell off in bits; and breaking off a bit of bread with my fingers instead of
taking a bite out of the slice. Dry bread, that is, the kind you got with soup. It
was all right to hold a slice of bread and butter in your hand.

I had my own bedroom with a big sweet-smelling bed, and at night I could
hear customers in the pub downstairs, and Vi's shout at closing time—"Come on
you blokes," she shouted two or three times—and the traffic on the road past the
inn, and the lights of the cars went across the ceiling in patterns that followed
each other. Vi bought me pyjamas, which I'd never had before, none of us had.
In Kennington and Colliers Wood we slept in our shirts.

Although Vi was my sister, she was gone from the Buildings before I knew
her so she was a bit of a stranger, and I was on my best behaviour all the time.
One night the door to my room jammed because it was so old and warped out
of shape, and I wanted to pee but couldn't get out, so I peed in the copper kettle
in the fireplace. The next day I tried to wait until the coast was clear to empty it,
but there was always someone about so I left it. I could have told my mum about
it, and if it had been Gladys or Doris I was staying with, I could have told her, but
I was too shy to tell Vi because I didn't know her very well, so I left it there.

The other thing about it was that it got a little bit lonely having no mates
around, especially Robbie. After a while, Vi realized this and she got one of the
people who worked for her to send his son over to play with me, and that was
all right. I liked him, although he was a bit of a yokel, I thought, and he didn't
even have as good manners as I had in Colliers Wood, before May taught me. He
ate with his mouth open, with his knife and fork in the air, and didn't ask to be
excused before he got down from the table, and he always said yes if he was

offered more and wanted some. (My mum taught us all to say "No, thank you," to be polite.)

Still, we played a lot of good games together, in the orchard and along the river bank, and we tried to sink one of the punts, jumping up and down on one end, until Mr. Foster stopped us. But I was still on my own a lot.

The only time the war came near was one afternoon when I was in the apple-scented pavilion, lying in a hollow on a great pile of russet apples, where I thought no one could see what I was doing, and a German bomber came over and dropped a stick of bombs, four, I think, that went crump, CRUMP, CRUMP, crump as they straddled the inn and me. I thought God had been watching and sent the bomber to punish me.

CRIME AND PUNISHMENT

In the meantime the boats were very busy and sometimes I collected a lot of money. Did I ever think of stealing some of it? Did I ever *not* think of stealing any? I was from Colliers Wood by way of Kennington, and nicking stuff was as natural as breathing, so long as it was absolutely safe. It wasn't morality that kept us honest. You didn't steal because your family—my mother—had done a good job of letting you know the penalties: from being skinned alive by her, then handed over to your father when he came home to finish the job, then off to Borstal where you would be fed bread and water and knocked about continually by the jailers, and finally kicked out of the house—"I'm not having thieves in this house!"

That was why I didn't try to swindle my mother when I was sent to buy an egg. Rendell's, the shop around the corner from Colwood Gardens, sold four kinds of eggs: penny-farthing eggs, penny-ha'penny ones, penny-three-farthing ones, and tuppenny ones. They went up in size but the penny-farthing eggs were the same size as the penny-ha'penny ones. The difference was that the penny-ha'penny ones were guaranteed. If it was bad when you got it home, Rendell's would change it. But with a penny-farthing egg you took a chance. They were usually all right, but you took a chance. The thing was you could buy a golly bar, a stick of toffee the size of your finger, for a farthing, so if you were sent to buy a penny-ha'penny egg, you could buy a penny-farthing egg and a golly bar and hope the egg was good. If it wasn't, then you were caught because you couldn't take it back and change it. Although I got very close, I never got up the nerve to buy a penny-farthing egg.

The closest I got to stealing outside the house—apart from shoplifting chocolate bars with Robbie—was one afternoon after Sunday school. Sunday school was held in a community hall on the other side of the rec. We all had to go until we were about seven or eight; my mother treated it as a kind of inoculation, a "just-in-case" measure. "You never know," she used to say. Normally, no one in my family, or any other I knew of, ever went near a church, although all of us felt that the church was the only proper place to get married in, to die from, and, for some, to get christened in. ("I never had the last three christened: that new vicar got up my nose—kept coming round, collecting for this and that and wanting to see us in church. The old vicar left you alone. He was a nice old boy.") We were sent off to Sunday school to find out what it was all about (but never to speak of it inside the house, like sex).

There were two kids in Sunday school, Ernie and Ray, brothers, thieves, sort of mates of Robbie's from one of his other worlds. They were a bit common: once, in their house, I heard them all—mother, Ernie, Ray, and two sisters—sing a rollicking version of "Mademoiselle from Armentières," which opened with the line, "A fart went rolling down the hill, parley-vous ..." I felt very embarrassed, as if the mother had come downstairs in her knickers in front of us.

Ernie and Ray had noticed that the ha'pennies we took to Sunday school went into a little wooden box which was left in a small back room. Ernie, the elder brother, had also seen that the window of the toilet was always left open, and had found out that once you were in the toilet you could break into the small back room with no trouble. After Sunday school was over and the teachers had gone home the three of us ducked back through the bushes and made sure that we were out of sight of anyone walking down the path to the rec.

To get in the window, Ray, the younger brother, would have to stand on Ernie's shoulders; I was the lookout. "We'll share the money out equal," Ernie said. Then Robbie came along the path that led from the rec and was invited to join in. He listened to what we were planning, then flicked his head at me, ordering me to go along with him, saying to the others, "His dad sent me to find 'im."

"My dad's *asleep*," I protested, once we were away from the brothers. "He's always asleep on Sunday afternoons. Besides ..."

Robbie interrupted. "If you get caught, they'd say you was the one who did it. I know them. Don't listen to them."

And the next day we heard that they did get caught. Someone saw them breaking in and the police arrived and they were had up before the magistrates.

But I was still inclined towards stealing, most of us were if it could be done in safety, and the boat money was irresistible. Even if I was caught, my sister wouldn't send me to Borstal. So, from the time I saw the opportunity, I never considered not stealing some of it. And besides, I'd found a need for the money. The tips were all right for sweets, but I had started a stamp collection, and I took the bus into Wokingham as often as I could to buy stamps. The ones I wanted cost more than I could get from tips.

And so I took the next step. Five boats had been hired by a party of "young hounds" (Vi's word) and each other's sisters. Vi had gone to London, leaving the pub in the charge of the woman who helped out on Saturdays. I chalked up the time the five boats moved off, and when they came back, collected the money, walked twice round the garden to make sure Mr. Foster hadn't looked in on his day off, wiped out the record of the fifth boat, and put a mere fourteen shillings in the cigarette tin where we kept the day's take, pocketing the three and six pence, to be hidden later in the actual, real, hollow tree I had discovered on the other bank of the river.

And so it started. The swag grew until there were two or three pounds in a little leather bag I once kept my marbles in, tucked away in the old hollow tree, more money than I had ever handled. Now I had to spend it. Apart from stamps, I wanted a big Meccano set. Vi had bought me a starter set, with enough wheels and tiny girders to make a model handcart, but the set came with a leaflet picturing what could be done with a giant set: gantries, windmills, trucks—the possibilities were unlimited. But it was out of the question; I could never have accounted for it. So I had to be satisfied with buying stamps. I already had a little collection, bought in Colliers Wood with halfpence, mostly German inflationary issues, printed in the millions. I knew what I really wanted, not penny blacks or cape triangulars, but those gorgeous ones of the British colonies, the King's head in one corner of a beautiful picture of a giraffe (Kenya, Uganda, and Tanganyika), and all the other works of art from Africa, the Caribbean, and the South Seas.

Then, in Wokingham, I found a dealer and began to spend my money. One by one I brought them home and fixed them carefully in my stamp album. There was no need to show them to anyone yet; I could do that later, at home, when I saw Robbie again. For the time being I could enjoy gloating over the little Stanley Gibbons album I kept in the cardboard suitcase under my bed along with the two lead soldiers, the propelling pencil I found in one of the boats, and the army badges.

And then, one day, the stamp dealer asked me my name, and I thought I'd been caught. "William Brown," I said.

"Where's all the money coming from then, William?" The stamp dealer with a look invited his hovering wife to listen.

"My paper round."

"You're not from around here. You're a Londoner. You don't have a paper round."

I looked out the window, thinking. "That's my Dad," I said and ran.

For three days I lived in fear, but the dealer never appeared at the inn. Nobody set any traps, like they did in the stories I was reading, and no one asked me why I rowed over to the old hollow tree every day. No, this was how it happened.

After a few days the habit of stealing some of the boat money came back, but I didn't take as much as I did before because now that I couldn't buy stamps I didn't know what to do with the money. Then, one day, the fair came to a field in Earley and my sister gave me a shilling to visit it. It had been a quiet day on the river and all I had in my pocket was a six penny tip. Of course, it occurred to me what a good time I could have at the fair with the hoard from the old hollow tree, but Mr. Foster was looking after the boats for the afternoon, and with him watching I couldn't think of an excuse to row across the river before I went to the fair.

Even so, one and six was a lot of money and I was surprised how quickly it disappeared. Two rides, a go on the shooting gallery, and a coconut shy, and I only had three pennies left. I stopped by a stall in a round tent where you could roll pennies down a wooden slot in the hope of landing on a winning square. On the second try my penny rolled into a six penny square. The gypsy lady in charge dealt me six pennies and moved on. The booth was large and busy, and the gypsy had to circle around the inside, picking up the losing pennies and paying out the winners. I rolled down another penny and won six more; I did it again, and again, and again, until I was out of breath with excitement. There was a tiny warp in the surface of the table just beyond my wooden chute, and if my penny reached this warp, travelling at the right speed, it fell over into the square. I won about eight times, and then, deliberately, under her eye, put the penny too high in the chute and lost. I left the booth for a while and threw some more balls at the coconuts, but nothing compared with winning pennies.

When I went back, another gypsy had taken over and I won another four shillings before she started to watch me and I had to deliberately lose again. Now

I developed a system, winning a couple of times, going for a walk, coming back to win again as soon as my chute was free. Soon, both my pockets were crammed with big copper pennies, and the attendant in charge of the tent with the slot machines changed some of them for me into silver, and most of the rest I spent on rides, shooting ranges, and the other games, until I'd had enough, and I walked home with a story to tell.

I arrived back at The George, passing through the saloon bar to get to the living room behind. The barman was behind the counter, talking to a customer. His face was serious. "Your sister wants to see you," he said. "In the back room."

The customer turned round and I nearly swooned when I saw the face of the stamp dealer from Wokingham. I thought it was the end for me. But the man just said, with a sly look, "Who's this, then?"

"Her brother. Staying with her for the duration."

"Has he got a name?"

"Eric."

"Lucky boy, living in a pub." The dealer took a swig. "Interested in stamps, son?"

"Not much."

"I thought you collected them," the barman said, holding up the flap of the counter to let me through.

"Used to. Don't now."

The dealer smiled, picked up his change, winked at me. "Cheerio," he said, and left.

"She's waiting."

I ran through, dizzy with relief at the dealer's strange loyalty, and slipped into the living room where my sister was waiting with the woman who helped out on Saturdays.

"Come here," my sister said. "Turn out your pockets." She said it sort of sadly, kindly.

Now it looked as if the dealer had told on me after all, as was natural. The scene in the bar had been a tease, a cat-and-mouse scene, while all the time the dealer knew what waited for me in the kitchen.

My sister pointed to the kitchen table to show me where to put the money from my pockets.

"Don't have to," I mumbled.

"You want me to tell Mum?"

416

Threat enough. I emptied both pockets; I still had a dozen pennies, and several of the shillings that I had changed back. It was a pile the size of a fist. My sister looked at the money without saying anything. The face of the woman who helped out on Saturdays was shining.

"Where'd you get it?" my sister said at last.

"Won it."

Headshakes.

"I'll ask you again. Where'd you get it?"

"Won it."

Now she'd used up the threat of telling mum; it wouldn't have been fair to use it twice. She tried to shame me. "Don't tell lies," she said. "Don't *lie*," she said like a schoolteacher.

This wasn't fair. *Everybody* from Kennington lied to the authorities. She knew that. She'd lived there once. She had no right to be on the other side.

"I'm not lying. I won it."

The woman who helped out on Saturdays said, "They don't let you win. Only once or twice p'raps. Our Fred lost six bob on that roll-the-penny game." She gleamed at my sister, encouraging her to carry on.

"You took it out of the boat money, didn't you?"

"No. I won it."

And then I saw what she needed. A little brother who stole was one thing, a thief *and* a liar shown up in front of the woman who helped out on Saturdays was something else. I could feel her wanting me to tell the truth.

"Some of it was tips," I said.

"Not that much." She looked at the pile on the table. "Elsie, here, watched you all night. You went on all the rides."

"Spent a fortune," the woman said.

So it had been *this* rotten cow. The dealer had kept quiet, after all.

"Some of it probably *was* tips," my sister offered. "Not all of it, though, was it?"

"Not all of it, no."

"Some of it was boat money, wasn't it?"

I nodded, a quarter of an inch.

"Make 'im say," the woman who helped out on Saturdays said. "Go on."

"That's all right, Elsie," Vi said. "Leave us alone now."

"Make 'im say," the woman repeated as she went through the door.

"Don't tell Mum," I said, when we were by ourselves.

417

She shook her head. "What are we going to do with you, then?" I could feel her yearning across the space between us. We'd never touched each other; you didn't hug in our family. "Will you promise never to take the boat money again?"

"Oh, yeah." Then, suddenly, "I don't want to look after the boats any more."

"You can still look after the boats ..."

"I don't want to."

"What do you want to do, then? Help Mr. Foster?"

And then it came. "I want to go home," I said, and as I said it I did, want to go home, back to bread and margarine, back to the other liars and thieves on Colwood Gardens, back to a world of crime and punishment I understood, back to Robbie's world. "I want to go home," I said again. "Let me go home."

"P'raps that's best. Don't say I sent you, mind. If I take you up to London and put you on the right tube, can you manage?"

"'Course I can." We used to ride all day on the tube for a penny, changing trains. She was treating me like a kid. "You don't have to come up to London, even. I can go on the train myself." Then, to be certain, I said again, "Don't tell Mum."

"No, she'd kill you. What'll we say? You got homesick?"

"That'll do. In the morning, then?"

She sniffed and looked down at her hands.

"It's not *your* fault," I said. "I'll just say I got homesick."

She nodded and sniffed again. "I thought p'raps you might want to stay on here, even when the war's over. We would have sent you to Reading Grammar School," she said.

It was tempting because I was right in the middle of my schoolboy-story period, the *Hotspur* stories especially, stories that all took place in schools like Reading Grammar. But Colwood Gardens won. The thing was, I wasn't at home at The George. My sister was nice to me but we weren't friends—there was twenty years between us—and she wasn't trying to be a mother. She was just an old sister I didn't know very well, and though I knew she was trying to get me to better myself, like her, I found it a strain.

She did my washing and ironed it herself, and drove me to Earley station the next afternoon, and I caught the train to Waterloo.

I didn't row across the river first and get the money out of the old hollow tree. If I'd been caught doing that, I think Vi *would* have told my mum. She thought I'd just nicked the odd six pence or shilling, but the leather bag was nearly full. As far as I know, it's still there, like the pee in the copper kettle.

MR. THOMAS

It was smashing being back in Colliers Wood. The war hadn't properly got going yet, although Joe had been called up because he was in the Territorial Army, so I still went to Fortescue Road Junior School, and played out on the street with the same gang. Robbie was a year older than me and he was gone now, to Singlegate Senior School until he was fourteen, and he had some new mates from Singlegate, though we were still mates on Saturdays and Sundays because he still lived just round the corner on Clarendon Road.

It was smashing being back at school, too, because I worshipped Mr. Thomas. Everybody did. When he came out of Colliers Wood tube station in the mornings there was a gang of kids waiting to run alongside him as he walked to school through the rec, asking him questions like, "What were you like when you were our age, Mr. Thomas?" and "Where do you go on your 'olidays, Mr. Thomas?" and "Do you have any brothers or sisters, Mr. Thomas? What are their names?"

Anything to be noticed.

Mr. Thomas didn't just teach us our lessons; he tried to teach us everything he thought we needed. He told us all to buy toothbrushes and he used to look at our teeth every morning to make sure we had cleaned them. A few of the kids already had toothbrushes—I didn't—but if any of the others said they didn't have the money, he bought them one himself. This got him into trouble with some of the parents when the kids took their toothbrushes home, because they didn't like the idea that some schoolteacher was pointing out a deficiency in their upbringing, and besides, in one or two cases, they didn't agree with teethbrushing.

We bought little pink cakes of Gibbs dentifrice for a ha'penny each, and some of these Mr. Thomas paid for, too. Once he used me as an example of what would happen if we didn't use our toothbrushes.

Every year a woman we called Nitty Nora came round looking for fleas and lice on our heads, and also sometimes a dentist from the council looked at our teeth. One day when the dentist came to me he said I had to have all my back teeth out. My mum took me up to St. Thomas's, which was near Kennington, a long way from Colliers Wood, but it was always our hospital. My mum didn't trust the local hospital; St. Thomas's had looked after Ron's double pneumonia, May's diphtheria, Gladys's scarlet fever, and sewed Len's finger back on when he had chopped it off in the coal cellar. And the time May poured the boiling cabbage water over my arm when Mum was ill in bed, and my arm turned into a

419

big blister all the way from my shoulder down to my elbow, Mum made her take me up to St. Thomas's, never mind the dinner still cooking. You couldn't beat St. Thomas's.

The night after they took my teeth out I woke up with a mouth full of lumps of clotted blood, and my pillow was soaked with it. My mum gave me a piece of clean cloth to hold over my mouth and we walked to Robinson Road, where the all-night trams turned round, about a mile away, and caught the tram to St. Thomas's, an hour's journey away. There the night doctor, with a nurse alongside, lifted out the bloodclots, pulling them free from my gums, and told me to spit it all out. But there was nowhere to spit. I looked at my mother, because she was the one in charge of where I could spit, and she looked at the nurse, who nodded, and my mum whispered, "It's all right," and I spat it all out on the clean, disinfected marble floor. The doctor pulled all the rest of the loose bits away from my gums and made me spit them out, too, and the nurse called a skivvy over to clean up the floor.

We took the tram back only as far as Stockwell, because I kept falling asleep and choking, and my mum left me to stay the night with Aunt Rose, who lived in Stockwell, while she went home to see to the rest of the family. When I woke up the next day, Aunt Rose made me a bowl of warm bread and milk, but it was so much like the stuff I had left on the hospital floor—not the taste, but everything else about it—that I couldn't get it down, so she gave me a cup of tea and a digestive biscuit, and I managed that all right. Then she wrapped my face up in a clean piece of cloth and tied a scarf round my head to keep it in place and put me on the tram home.

Mr. Thomas told us that plimsolls, or gym shoes, were bad for our feet, and we should ask our parents for shoes or boots. (I always wore shoes because my mum thought boots were common, and only very poor kids wore plimsolls.) Some of the kids stayed away from school when their boots were being mended. That was always an acceptable excuse for Mr. Thomas.

He asked us not to fart in his classroom—"blowing off," he called it—and to bring a piece of rag to school to use as a handkerchief. All winter he taught us everything he thought we should know—arithmetic, spelling, drawing, the names of the continents and the seas—all that—and that was the best year I ever had in school. He made the ten scholarship pupils sit in a special section of the class and gave us extra spelling tests and extra arithmetic, and general-knowledge tests. He gave us little cards to take home at night with ten questions on them, and we had to write out the answers neatly in whole sentences in our exercise books for the next day. That was my first homework.

The war was very quiet at first. Some of the kids who had been evacuated when war broke out came back a few weeks later, and everything carried on as normal, except for the rationing, which we didn't notice much at first. Joe came home on embarkation leave with a pal from Croydon, before they went to France "to hang out their washing on the Seigfried line." He was one of the first soldiers on our street, and we were all proud of him. Then, just as the scholarship exam was getting near, Hitler seemed to be winning the war and there was talk of being invaded and the school closed because a lot of the kids were being sent away again. The fire brigade used the playground to practise rolling dustbins across it with their hoses.

Because of Mr. Thomas, what was left of the scholarship group still got lessons in the houses of some of the pupils, mostly in Kenny Field's house where his mum gave us milk and cake after the lesson. My mum said she was too busy to do anything like that but I think she was just nervous of strangers inspecting the inside of her house, especially Mr. Thomas.

In the spring of 1940, when the time came, we took the 152 bus to Mitcham County School at Fair Green to write the scholarship examinations, in English, general knowledge, and arithmetic, I think. They told us to bring a pen, a pencil (my sisters had bought me a Platignum pen-and-pencil set), a ruler, and a bottle of ink. That was my first examination and because of Mr. Thomas's teaching I thought it had been specially composed for me.

Four or five of Mr. Thomas's stars won scholarships, including me. When the letter came, my sisters got excited because my mum still wasn't sure if she wanted me to go even now I had won it. ("There'll be no money coming in from him until he's sixteen," my "uncle" said, when he heard. "It'll be all pay out with that one.") My sisters insisted, but my mum was afraid now that she might not have done a good job in teaching me the proper manners for a grammar school. She was nervous for herself and her house, too, about keeping her end up if I brought any "college" boys home. My sisters argued with her, and in the end my mum walked me to the corner of the street to post the letter. Just before we dropped it in the letter box, she made one last try to make sure I knew what I was taking on. "Now you be sure," she warned. "Sure you want to go. You can't drop out if you don't like it. You have to go for five years. You can't chop and change about." Back to the other stream, she meant, to Singlegate, and leave school at fourteen.

But I was too full of Billy Bunter stories not to want to go. I wanted a school uniform and a cap and to buy stuff at a tuck shop. And because of Mr. Thomas, I wanted to stay in school for the rest of my life. "I want to go," I said.

"You sure?"

"Yeah."

"No going back, mind."

"I know."

"Put it in the box yourself, then."

And I did.

Then I got my last lesson from Mr. Thomas, the first one in this new world. On a warm evening in the early summer I was playing football in the street with the kids I would soon leave behind, when Mr. Thomas appeared on a bicycle and called me over. Seeing Mr. Thomas out of school was so strange that the other boys stopped playing to watch and listen.

"Have you heard the results of the scholarship exam, yet?" he asked.

"Yeah."

"Did you pass?"

"Yeah."

"When did you hear?"

"Last week."

"You didn't come and tell me, did you?"

No one had taught me to. I couldn't say that to him but I had no other answer. I knew right away, though, that I should have. "I forgot," I said.

"All the others came to see me, to tell me they had passed. Anyway"—he put out his hand for me to shake—"well done. But I wish you'd come and told me yourself."

He didn't smile, but I understood that he wasn't telling me off. I'd just let him down by not going to the school to tell him, because it was *his* exam that I had passed.

He cycled away, and I never saw him again.

"Who was that?" my mother called from our front gate.

"Mr. Thomas, our teacher."

"What did he want?"

"He wanted to know if I'd passed."

"Didn't he know?"

"Course he did."

"Then what did he really want? Did you say thank you?"

"Course I did," I lied, shouting, nearly screaming at her, knowing immediately that I could not face all the "Why didn't you's?" from her, all the instructions to "Run after him and do it now," or "You'll have to go to school in the morning and tell him." She'd even make sure what words I would say as if I didn't know.

I turned back to the game. It wasn't my fault, I told myself. Nobody had told me that's what you're supposed to do. But that didn't stop me from feeling rotten. I looked for someone to punch but in the end just pushed a kid away from the ball, hoping he would push back and we could have a fight.

From now on I was on my own. My family had no idea what went on at a "grammar" school. (It was a county school, really, not a proper grammar school.) My mother had taught me everything she knew about manners, mostly to keep my mouth closed when I ate, and to refuse second helpings of anything. She had tried to get me to sign off my rare letters—"And oblige"—but even at eleven I knew she was the only one still saying that; Mr. Thomas had taught us to write "Yours faithfully." (My father wanted me to sign off, "Your humble and obedient servant," which he insisted was the proper way to end any letter.)

423

Then there was Dunkirk. Joe came home from the evacuation of Le Havre, and he sat in the corner, looking, my mother said, "like a tiger." She meant "like a cornered animal," I think, but she read almost nothing and had very few clichés to hand. Joe was one of the last off the beach. Because of varicose veins, he never got into the infantry proper, but was recruited into the service corps, looking after the equipment and supplying the kitchens with stores. He never realized until then how hard Dad worked, he said, lifting frozen sides of beef all day. But when the Germans rolled over the Maginot line and the French packed it in, the main thought of the English generals was to get as much of the army back across the Channel as they could, for the invasion they felt sure was coming. So they evacuated the fighting troops and left the odds and sods, like Joe and his mates, as a rearguard, to slow up the tanks. Eventually Joe and his mates were the only ones left and they got permission to leave themselves. Joe couldn't swim but he waded out to a small boat with his pal from Croydon who could, and then when they got to the boat his pal went under and never came up. When he came on leave, Joe had to go and visit his pal's parents to tell them how it had happened.

A neighbour over the garden fence said, "We might lose this one, ever thought of that?" My father said, "No, and we're not bleeding well going to, either, so sling your fucking hook out of here with that kind of talk and don't come back."

I'd never heard him swear like that before.

Six of them were gone now, and finally the rest of us each had our own bed.

All that summer we looked up to the sky and watched the Battle of Britain. And then came the Blitz. But first there was the Mitcham County School for Boys.

My mother applied to the local council for a grant for my uniform, and they gave us two guineas, and we went up to the official school shop in Mitcham and bought the shorts, the socks, the shirts, the tie, the blazer, and the cap, all in the school colours, and the shorts and singlets for gym. While we were in the shop, she also bought me some underpants "like the other boys will be wearing," in case the ones I had were the wrong kind. Once, two or three years before, I had gone to a Boy Scout camp in Ashtead Forest and I saw that all the boys except me had underwear on. When I came home I asked my mum if she would buy me some underwear like the other kids, and right away she put on her hat and coat and took me on the tram up to the co-op in Tooting Broadway, where she bought me some underpants. She didn't say much, but she was in a funny state, I could tell. Later on she told my dad she was "mortified"—one of her favourite expressions—but I don't know what she was mortified about.

My sisters bought me a satchel, and on a morning in September I caught the 152 bus to Fair Green, along with half a dozen other boys of different sizes.

On our first day a boy went home at dinnertime and it took a week to coax him back. There were no Mr. Thomases here that I could see, and none appeared in my time. Everyone seemed to be waiting for me to do something wrong; masters wore gowns and looked like jailers; the older boys, from the sixth-form prefects all the way down to the twelve-year-olds in the next form above us, tried to look superior in front of the new boys. I wondered where these older boys came from. There were no young gents like that in Colwood Gardens. Then, in the playground, as we were waiting to be called in, a boy standing next to me shouted, "'Ere, Jonesy," to a passing youth in long trousers who looked irritated at being called out to. The boy turned to me. "He lives on our street. His name's Bernard, but he asked me not to call him that here. What's your name?"

424

"Eric."

He shook his head. "Your proper name."

"Wright."

"That's it. Say that. Wrightie. Mine's Munnings. My father's a printer. What's yours?"

"He's a furniture mover. He's got his own van. He can carry a piano downstairs on his back." Everyone admired the story of my grandfather, so I gave it to my father.

"All by himself? Cor! Let's sit together."

And so we did for the few days until the place was familiar. Munnings saw right away how things worked, or he was told how by Jonesy. At any rate, he made it a lot easier than it would have been without him. After a week, Munnings and I parted because by now I had found a couple of mates and in those days he was essentially a cheerful loner, but we stayed on good terms.

Right away I stumbled badly in most of the subjects except English, and I never properly recovered. I missed Mr. Thomas very much. For one thing, he knew that everything was up to him, that it was a rare boy at Fortescue who had a parent who could help his upwardly striving ten-year-old son with his schoolwork. But at Mitcham they gave us homework that I had to do at the dining-room table with five or six other people in the room, listening to the wireless. Mum wouldn't allow any other lights in the house, even if the other rooms were warm enough. I could have done it for Mr. Thomas, but the thing was these new teachers didn't teach us— they taught *at* us, so you could look at them and think about something else, which you couldn't with Mr. Thomas. The French teacher was French, and I couldn't understand a word he was saying. The only one I took to was Mr. Stevens who taught math, and made sure you were listening. Because of him, I was good at math, though I wasn't naturally clever at it. The worst news was "PT."

425

PT was taught by an instructor who liked to put boys through their paces, as he called it. My clearest memory of PT is of him slashing repeatedly with a swagger stick (he was some kind of ex-serviceman) at the legs of a boy on a high beam. The boy was terrified of heights and terrified of the teacher and he shook so hard as he straddled the beam ten or twelve feet up in the air that the whole structure rattled, and still the teacher slashed away, shouting, "Come on, boy, get moving." He only stopped when Mr. Perry, the caretaker, looked in the door to see what the noise was all about. The same teacher liked to set up boxing matches among the older boys, and if they didn't mix it up properly, he put on the gloves himself and showed them how to knock each other about.

One big benefit of PT was the showers, the first constant hot water I had known, water that cleaned you off and warmed you up after a freezing two hours on the playing fields. And with two PT classes a week and the afternoon games, you didn't need any more to go through all that hot-water-heating palaver involved in having a bath at home, at least until you left school and started thinking about girls.

Almost as soon as the term began, the blitzkrieg started and the school was evacuated to Weston-Super-Mare on the Bristol Channel. Some of the families, ours included, refused to let us go and the ones who stayed behind were split up among the schools that stayed open to teach these boys like us, boys whose families had elected to stay together. ("If a bomb *does* drop, our Ken's better off dead with us than being an orphan in one of those homes.") More of the younger boys stayed at home, and there were enough first- and second-formers to make up a class of each and these classes were sent to the local girls' school where we stayed for the next two years. (Another reason for not letting me be evacuated, not talked about except at home, was that my mum couldn't be sure I had the right manners yet. I didn't eat with my mouth open, but I did drink my tea with the spoon still in the cup until my sister stopped me. And apart from my table manners, there were all kinds of areas where I might betray my origins. How did other boys tell their parents that they were constipated? Had she taught me to get in the corners of my ears properly, with the face flannel? Weren't there kinds of food that had to be eaten in a special way? My mother had been concerned enough about behaving properly in the new world of Colliers Wood; she was even more wary of the world I had shot up to, so I wasn't evacuated.)

THE GIRLS' SCHOOL

We very quickly acquired a distinct feeling that the Mitcham County School for Girls, though it was a county school and the parallel step for girls on the educational ladder, was superior to the boys' school. The war had not taken away their best teachers, of course, but it was also a question of tone, and of the physical plant and setting.

Inside the gates of the girls' school, there was a long drive edged on both sides with big plants with shiny dark green leaves, though in the early autumn there didn't seem to be any flowers. At the end of the drive the school faced the playing fields on one side and more bushes at the back, where we went in. The boys' school playing fields, on the other hand, had been laid out a long way from the school on a bit of waste ground where the dirt left over from tunnelling Morden station had been dumped and smoothed over, and to get to the playing field you cycled for a mile across Mitcham Common. The boys' school was surrounded by an asphalt area, much like Fortescue Road's playground, with a steel mesh fence separating it from an alley.

And the ambience of the girls' school was distinctly classier. We'd only been at the boys' school for a few weeks, but long enough to see that the girls' school dinners (called "lunch" in the girls' school) were not as good as ours. They went in a lot for fish pie and macaroni cheese and salads of wedges of slug-laden lettuce and pieces of tomato covered in "salad cream," while the boys were used to a fair number of meat pies and gravy, tastily seasoned by Mrs. Perry, the caretaker's wife, who knew what she was doing. The boys got cabinet pudding for afters, too, with custard, while the girls ate tapioca with a spoonful of jam in the middle, which when mixed together was christened "dragon sperm" by a witty second-form boy.

But although the food was rotten, the service was clearly superior. Instead of lining up and being given a plate of food through a hatch, as in the boys' school, the girls were served by a prefect at the end of each table of eight, a senior girl to whom we passed our plates in turn. Then the prefect would lead us in conversation. Even the grace was different. Instead of "forwhatweareabouttoreceivemaytheLordmakeustrulythankfulamen" bellowed from a raised podium at the end of the hall, followed by the clash of steel on a hundred and fifty plates, each girl prefect, when her table was ready, said a nunlike blessing, in Latin, and picked up her own tools as a signal for us to dig in. Our prefect was called Jean and she was thin, with dark hair caught up behind, terrifically feminine, with very white teeth that had a mother-of-pearl look about the front ones. She swelled gently, dovelike, under her gym tunic, and smelled of carnations. At the end of term she appeared one lunchtime in civilian dress, a blouse open enough so that when she leaned forward to hand you the soup you got a flash of breast, enough at twelve years to make me look at my soup in embarrassment. I had no desire to stroke her; I just wanted to kill on her behalf, animals if possible, people if necessary.

427

The boys were segregated into our own classes, a first form and a second form. Almost our first impression of the classroom in this new school was created by the geography mistress on the morning of day one. She walked in, sniffed the air, winced, and ordered the boys closest to the windows to open them wide. And that was before Munnings farted.

We understood perfectly what the geography mistress was saying, that we were from the element that smelled, unlike her girls. Munnings's instinctive response, "a voice from the gallery," as a wit named Kelly called it, was to give her something to complain about. (Later he said he never planned to let go such a ripsnorter; a short raspberry was what he was after.) The geography mistress could not ignore it, nor could she cope with it. She ran from the room and reappeared with one of the two masters we had brought with us from our own school. "I'll deal with this," he said and showed her to the door, closing it behind her.

"Right," he said, rummaging through the desk and finding a plimsoll which he slapped against his palm. "Own oop now"—he was from Yorkshire—"Who made a disgoosting noise?"

No one spoke.

428

"Right, then. I shall have to take hostages. Coom up alphabetically, and bend over this chair." He banged the slipper on the desk. "You first, Atterbury. Oop you coom."

When Atterbury was in place, and the master was measuring the blow, like a golfer lining up a five-iron, Munnings said, "It was me."

"Aye. I thought you might break down. Not lost to all decency, I take it. Coom oop, then. Back to your seat, Atterbury." He waved the slipper about some more. "So, tell me, Munnings. Do you make disgoosting noises at home, too?"

Munnings, seeing at that moment that the master was involved in something other than beating him—the man could barely keep from laughing—said, "No sir, it was an accident."

"In that case, it may not be all your fault. You may not be wicked, just not used to controlling yourself. Perhaps you're badly brought up. Is that it? Are you badly brought up?"

"Yes, sir."

"I'll tell Miss Haggard she was right, shall I? In the meantime we must make up for lost time. Learn to control ourselves. Coom round here." He led Munnings around the desk so that he was shielded from the view of Miss Haggard who was watching through the glass door. The slipper came down and we all winced but

Munnings did not flinch. The master proceeded to pantomime five more ferocious strokes which bounced lightly off Munnings's bottom. "Right," he bellowed. "Get back to your place." He waggled the slipper at the door and at the face of the geography mistress, who now came into the room, looking white at the terrible punishment she had caused to be inflicted on Munnings.

"You'll have no further trouble with this lot," our master said. "If you do, I'm just down the hall." He looked round the room, catching the eye of each boy in turn, lingering on Munnings, sending a message. Next time for keeps.

Munnings was incapable of restraining the spontaneous gesture. Music appreciation was taught by an enthusiastic twinkly little woman named Miss Dinn whom we liked, especially when she got all thirty of us proficient enough at the descant recorder to give a concert to the parents, with Kelly on piano. But that didn't stop Munnings from turning her piano into a barrel organ. He did it well. She was explaining the clever way Bach had put some piece of music together, and every time she played a few bars, Munnings, sitting at the end of the piano, out of sight of her but in full view of the class, turned the imaginary handle, stopping when she stopped, and even improvising a comic flourish in the style of Harpo Marx, looking amazed at the piano when she began to play before he had started to turn the handle, then giving a few quick turns to catch up, as it were.

429

Eventually, even our teacher realized something was going wrong as the class collapsed in hysterics, and then, the funniest moment of all, as she continued to play but looked around the corner of the piano to see what we were laughing at and saw Munnings, who was now playing the organ-grinder's monkey, holding out his cap to collect our change, enjoying himself so much he didn't notice he'd been rumbled.

This time the male teacher, who also liked Miss Dinn, was not amused. When she returned with him he hit Munnings so hard he lifted him out of his chair. When Munnings got to his feet, holding his ear, the master hit him through the door and they disappeared down the hall to the sound of Munnings's head being slapped.

If you were away for a day, you had to report to the headmistress the next morning with a note from your doctor or parent. I had had a day off with a cold and the next day I knocked on her door, was told to come in, entered, and handed her the note. As I turned to go, she said, "Come here."

In all the time we were there I never saw the woman smile and she was unsmiling now. "Come round here," she said, indicating the side of the desk. I went closer. "Show me your hands. Let me see your wrists. Now bend your head." She leaned over and looked inside my shirt collar. "Do you wash your neck every morning?" Her tone made it clear that it wasn't a real question.

"Yes."

"Not very well, I think."

Humiliation, rage, hatred. Did she think I didn't mind her insults? Wasn't I human? Was she running a workhouse? Would she have spoken to one of her girls like this? Or was this simply the natural way for a headmistress of a girls' county school to deal with a dirty little boy from the slums, the kind that had no feelings.

She gave me a problem. One way to show her what was what would have been to tell my mother, and let the headmistress feel the edge of the tongue of a respectable working-class woman who was trying to move us up in the world and was extremely sensitive to any charge that one of her kids had fallen short. She would have taken the headmistress's head off. The trouble was that she would have expected me to repeat what the headmistress had said in front of her and that would have meant ... God knows what it would have led to. And there was the other certainty, that my mother would first make sure she was in the right, and I foresaw a scene in the bathroom with my mother, holding my head in the sink and scrubbing my whole body raw, in cold water and probably with a bit of pumice stone, before marching me back to the school and inviting the headmistress to inspect me from arsehole to breakfast-time. So I kept my mouth shut. All I did at the time was try to work on the right insult, the worst one I could think of. I looked for an answer in my experience, a reply we would make when some kid on the street told you you had a snotty nose. The right response was "And you've got a dirty bum." That's what my training taught me to say to someone who told me I had a dirty neck. I toyed with the idea of telling the other boys that I *had* said it, but they wouldn't have believed me. I enjoyed thinking it, though.

Two years later, in the middle of the war, when the Germans had given up trying to bomb the civilian population into submission, the rest of the school returned from Weston-Super-Mare and we reassembled on our own premises, but our two co-educational years made it difficult for some of us to settle down and readopt the culture of the boys' school. We returned to the "normal" world at a rebellious age—fourteen—having had a couple of years of the civilizing experience of pretty women (the prefects, mainly, though I was in love with the art mistress, too) and some good teaching. We were like the soldiers when they returned from the war, no longer willing to accept uncritically the values of a society we had swallowed whole in our young days, and beginning to develop the vocabulary to criticize it.

We found a focus for our discontent in the struggle to be allowed to continue to play soccer, the only field sport that could be adapted to the hockey pitches of the girls' school. The official sport was rugby, of course, the sport of the public schools that the county schools were trying to emulate. One of the virtues of making working-class boys play rugby was that it created a sharp separation between the world of the county school and the world most of the students came from. In the old world, most of them had been playing soccer since they could run, in the street with a tennis ball mainly, but you couldn't play rugby in the street, and no one tried.

An important difference between the two games is that soccer can be played and enjoyed by boys, and girls, who are neither talented nor physically impressive. Rugby, although it has its own skills, can also be played by the untalented, but it is a bruising game, and other things being equal, the bruisers have the advantage. Thus it was that Alan Simpson organized a petition and collected fifty names which he took to the headmaster in support of allowing soccer as an option to rugby. The petition was denied and the rebellion crushed in a single interview with the headmaster who thus made outsiders of us all.

We didn't blame ourselves for hating rugby, as the misfits of previous generations might have done. We blamed rugby, and the school for offering it as socially superior to soccer, and we took some pride in refusing to play up and play the game. When we were forced to turn out for rugby, every Tuesday afternoon, a few of us took care to be picked last for the worst teams, and so were regarded with contempt by the keener boys, a contempt we reciprocated. By now Russia was in the war and socialists were agitating for a second front, an invasion of Europe to relieve the pressure on the eastern front. Communist sympathizers painted slogans on walls, demanding that we assist our Russian allies. Kelly, the class wit, joined us in not wanting to play rugby, or anything else, and kept on his woollen gloves and his overcoat even when picked for the seventh game, maintaining his identity by running up and down the touchline, shouting one of the Left's most popular slogans, "Strike now in the West and finish the job," whenever our team got the ball. (Kelly was the first person I ever heard use the response "I couldn't care less." That was in 1944. He was the class wit as well as the musician, like Oscar Levant.)

Another middle-class sport was cross-country running, so once a year we were made to run across Mitcham Common and back, with no previous practice or rehearsal or training, perhaps the dreariest effort to create a school spirit by means of athletics ever devised. The whole school ran, and the staff assembled at the finish line to cheer us home. They waited a long time to see some of us finish. As soon as we were out of sight of the school, our crowd turned it into a Sunday stroll, and made our way across the common chattering about soccer and the latest Bob Hope film, while being passed by smaller and smaller boys grimly responding to the spirit of the day. One bunch from the fifth form trotted briskly out of sight until they reached the first clump of bushes where they could safely stretch out for a smoke and a chat. You had to check in, though, so, late in the afternoon, the finishing line approaching, we broke into a trot, ironically aping the exhaustion of those who had arrived earlier.

This spirit of anti-establishmentarianism spread to other things—infected our lives, making us hostile to the brainwashing we were being subjected to. When we realized that we were being groomed to be middle-class supporters of the Conservative party, some of us became socialists. We used to mock the prefects with affected accents, accents they had adopted to assist them in their careers. One prefect we called Lord Haw-Haw because he sounded like the Nazi propagandist we listened to on the radio. No one we knew spoke like that. We watched each other for signs that we were succumbing to their culture and jeered at any conscious vowel-shift we overheard. At the same time, the system was performing its silent ministry, and while we were quick to jump on accents we felt had been acquired too easily and from too far up the ladder, already none of my cronies shared the same vowels as their fathers. The scholarship examination was doing its work. Within two years, Robbie and I were strangers.

In the area of manners appropriate to a young gentleman, the school carried on where Mr. Thomas and my sister had left off. So Dickey Bird, our English master, now gave us a lesson on how to manage our knives and forks. ("The tines of the fork always pointing down, unless you shift your fork into the other hand when you may reverse it; bread to be broken, never cut—cutting is for the French and Americans ...") We laughed but I was grateful for the advice, then and later, because I had more to learn than most, in spite of what May had shown me. Even to flout the rules (if you had the courage) you needed to know them.

432

They did not actually give us lessons in elocution, but we all knew from the first day to pronounce our aitches. Some of us were better at faking it than others: a boy called Churcher who later became my pal was sneered at in front of the class for having the wrong accent by Gaffer Cook, an old man who was hired to teach history. When Cook asked Churcher where he learned to speak like that, Churcher made the mistake of telling him, and Cook made fun of him, poncing about in the front of the classroom, saying, "'Ackney, sir. I'm from 'Ackney," to make the creepers laugh.

Afterwards, when Churcher and I became mates, he told me he really came from Bethnal Green, but he had only said Hackney because he thought it sounded better, a subtlety well beyond Gaffer Cook.

One of our troubles was that the war had taken away our role models. All the healthy young male teachers had disappeared into the armed forces, and their replacements were a mixed lot, some of them untrained women. One, Jesse Jewett, was the best history teacher I have ever had, and we were lucky to keep our maths teacher, Mr. Stevens: he was past retirement but he stayed on for the "Emergency." The others we just put up with. English was a subject that I could teach myself. Although there were only two books in our house—one was by Ouida, and the other was a Richmal Crompton "William" book with most of the pages torn out and the rest scribbled on—I was now borrowing ten books a week from the public library, using cards that I made my family apply for. I wish I could have taught myself French, Latin, science, geography, woodwork, music, and art, in all of which I had a lot of trouble. Part of the trouble was that I had discovered the cult of the amateur, that if a thing was difficult it wasn't worth doing. Only English and history were easy. And there was no one at home or at school perceptive enough to smack my head for being such an affected little twerp, or even to point out what I was really doing.

433

Many of the new teachers were not teachers by training or vocation but former travel agents and such, and sometimes a teacher would go missing, unable to face us any more. We had four geography teachers one year, refugees from Hitler mostly, including one who was said to be an Estonian diplomat, who told us stories about the countries he had lived in. One substitute geography teacher shrieked at us continually to use some initiative. It was his favourite word, and he used it at least once in every class, getting on our nerves until someone hit on the notion of privately substituting the word "shit" for "initiative." It was exactly the right level of gag for our age. "Sir, how shall I attach the map to my essay when I hand it in?" "Oh, use a bit of initiative," came the invariable reply. We rolled about in hysterics, leaving him blinking, mystified.

Between teachers, the headmaster sometimes filled in himself. This gave him a chance to show how teaching should be done. For a couple of classes he would improvise talks that were lively and entertaining, but he soon became bored and then a prefect would appear to keep us quiet while we did our own thing, under the guise of "reading ahead."

That headmaster was something of a showman, and every year he produced a very enjoyable Gilbert and Sullivan operetta which most of us sang in. I would have admired him more if he had not given off the air of having come down in the world in heading Mitcham County School, as he probably had. I had almost no contact with him in the time I was there until right at the end, when he told my mother that I should regard myself as lucky to have been there at all.

One day he went round the school, speaking to each class during the period set aside for religious instruction. Hands behind his back, going up and down on his toes, he said, "Piss, shit, fuck, arsehole, prick, cum—these are the words you have scratched on the walls of the latrine to illustrate the cave drawings you have engraved. As you see, there's nothing clever about knowing these words. I know them. Everyone does. But it is not the kind of language to be expected at a school like this. The latrines will be repainted in the holidays. Any boy caught defacing the walls in future will be caned and expelled, back to the gutter where he belongs."

Mouthing all those rude words was only a bit of showmanship, as we could see at the time, but we were struck dumb. Such language we only heard when the pubs turned out, certainly not in the gutter outside our homes, and never indoors. We had seen the words, of course, written on lavatory walls, put there, we believed, by the local kids who used the schoolyard at night after the government took the iron railings away to melt them down for munitions. We were embarrassed, then, not *by* the headmaster, but *for* him, a fully grown man using language like that in front of a class of young boys.

THE BLITZ

The war itself, though it affected our education, hardly interfered with our lives. Brothers and sisters went off and came back on leave. Len went into the navy after conducting a long campaign of non-violent resistance to the authorities who wanted him to stay in the munitions factory, a job classified as essential to the war effort which exempted him from military service. But Len had heard the call of the sea and stayed in bed until they agreed to let him heed it. They refused for a long time, and he refused to go to work at the munitions factory. He engaged in, for me, a wearisome campaign to get the authorities to give up. I shared a bedroom with him, and every morning I was awakened by the sound of my mother calling from the next room, "Len! Len! You up?"

"All right, all right. I'm up."

Two or three minutes later. "Len! Len! Are you up?"

Then I, who did not have to get up for another hour, chimed in from the other bed, "Len! Len! Get up! She's not going to stop. Come on. Get up!"

"Who do you think you are? Sod off!"

Then, "Len! Len! You up yet?"

On and on until she came in with a saucepan of cold water. "You want this poured over you? Get up!"

"Oh, bloody hell, all right." And he would get up, but not necessarily to go to work. From time to time two men in raincoats would appear, looking for him, because he had not been to the factory for a week. They explained to my mother that he could go to prison for refusing to do war work. This appalled my mother. Trouble with the law was what she thought she had left behind in Kennington.

"Speak to him, Jack," she exhorted my father when he came home from work. "Make him mind."

"He won't mind me. You see."

He didn't. The men in raincoats came back and found Len at home. They tried the same threats that had frightened my mother.

"What's so important about me doing war work?" Len wanted to know.

"Because it's vital, son."

"Yeah? You do it then, you look strong enough. A cripple could do our job. I want to go into the navy. Defend my country, like."

In the end they gave in, as Len, advised by his mates who were more in tune with the realities of the wartime world than my mother, knew they would. Why put a bloke in prison who wants to go in the navy? Makes no sense. Be in all the papers.

He spent the rest of the war on a minesweeper in the North Sea, under Mad Jack, as Len christened him, a former trawler skipper. The minesweeper had been converted from a trawler by mounting a single machine-gun above the deck. The purpose of this gun was to be able to make some response to attacking aircraft, but according to Len, Mad Jack saw it as an assault weapon with which he attacked

German minelayers. He prowled the North Sea, looking for vessels to shoot at, or, Len suspected, ram, if they were too big.

I think Len wanted to get into the navy because it had a more convivial image than the other services. The air force was full of "Brylcreem Boys," so called after the hair cream they were supposed to affect, and gave them a slightly prettified image to Len and his mates. The image of the army, on the other hand, came to him through our father—stories of a life in the trenches, waiting in the mud to go "over the top" and meet a lot of Germans drunk on schnapps, carrying bayonets. But the navy's image was of "Jolly Jack" the sailor, a couple of weeks at sea with a gang of pals, then ashore into the arms of the girls who were waiting on the dock at every port. I thought they would reject him because he couldn't swim, but that turned out not to be a qualification.

So I got a bedroom to myself, except when someone came home on leave. In fact, the war saved me from the embarrassment of being part of such a large family. I had sisters as old as most people's mothers, and under normal circumstances I would have been sharing a bed with a least one brother, and probably two. As it was, with all my brothers in the services, three of my sisters married, and one in the Women's Auxiliary Air Force, there was just me and one older and one younger sister, which meant I got Joe's old room, the tiny box room, all to myself, just like my school friends. Had there been no war, I would never have taken a friend home because of the stories he would have carried back about the way we lived.

At the beginning of the war, if the alert sounded, we lay down under the dining-room table, and slept there until the all-clear. A few people, noticing that when a house got a direct hit sometimes only the staircase survived, took to sitting under the stairs during a raid, but there wasn't room for all of us under the stairs, and you couldn't stay there all night. Grandma Wright in Westminster had died, and soon after my grandfather was bombed out of his rooms and came to live with us. He died one night early in the Blitz, peacefully in his bed, while we were still sleeping under the table. My father crept downstairs to let my mother know. "Daisy," he said, in a large whisper, "he's gorn."

"Gorn? Gorn where?"

"*Gorn!*"

"How was I supposed to know? Creeping down here, saying, 'He's gorn!' like that. All right. Don't wake everybody up. I'll see to it in the morning."

But we were awake, and giggling. We replayed the scene often, creeping in on each other (when my mother was elsewhere) to whisper, "Daisy, he's gorn." "Gorn where?" "*Gorn!*"

During the Blitz, many of our neighbours slept in the nearby underground station, a natural air-raid shelter, but there was as much chance of getting my mother to go down there, among a lot of strangers, as there was of getting her to camp out in Piccadilly Circus, and we spent the nights in our own Anderson shelter. This was a corrugated-steel affair issued by the government to be erected in the backyard. It came in sections, which, when bolted together, formed a small hut with a curved roof, about seven feet long, five feet wide, and high enough in the centre for a man to stand upright in. There was an open entrance at one end. The head of the house was supposed to dig a pit three or four feet deep and set the shelter in it, then cover the hut with a foot or so of earth as additional protection. A hole about three feet square and two feet deep was then dug in front of the entrance. To get into the shelter, you had to step down into this hole, stoop, then step down the remaining distance. Inside, four bunks were attached to the walls, two on each side. Once ours was built my mother and my sisters had the lower bunks, Jean sharing a bunk with Doris, and Len and I had the upper. My father stayed in the house, because he preferred to sleep under his own roof, in his own bed.

Some of the handier neighbours lined their shelters with concrete, built blast walls of brick in front of their doorways, and even made little flights of steps down to the shelters. They often fitted up the interiors with shelves and lights to make them more comfortable, and the more elaborately finished shelters were as compact and self-contained as one-room apartments.

Ours was not one of these. My father still had none of the suburban skills of his neighbours. That the shelter was erected at all was a miracle. Digging the hole was no problem—my father was probably the strongest man on the street—but after that he was just guessing. He piled up a small hill of earth and rocks in place of a blast wall, and never bothered about steps. He put an apple box inside the shelter to step down on, and hung a piece of sacking over the doorway. In wet weather, the approach became one long, greasy slope. I used to go first and help my mother and sisters from inside. Sometimes I literally caught them, like a playground director at the foot of a children's slide. The floor was rude earth, and as a result of faulty measuring the shelter was never quite straight, so that it looked as though it had been through one bombardment already. My mother had no real faith in it. She was convinced that her husband had made such a mess of putting it up that it was useless, and the only reason she stayed in it was because she did not want to show my father up in front of the neighbours.

When dusk came, other families along the street trooped down their garden paths with flashlights, wireless sets, cards, dominoes, books, vacuum flasks, and all the other stuff they needed for a cosy evening, but for us, dusk meant total extinction for the night. When it rained, there was two inches of water and mud on the floor, and we climbed immediately into the bunks. My mother stretched a piece of wood across the space between the two lower bunks, on which she kept a candle and her purse. For a while, we relied on the one candle for illumination. Then some local milquetoast told her that a candle used up all the oxygen, and after that our evenings were spent in darkness, my young sister and I playing an imaginary game of I Spy (we couldn't spy anything except the corrugated iron over our heads), and my mother trying to remember if she had turned off the gas stove. On really wet nights, when the water was a foot deep, I took a few pebbles to bed with me, because it was fun to drop them over the edge of the bunk and hear the *ploomp* they made in the dark waters below.

438 My dad would see us safely into the shelter, and then go back to the house to sleep. The idea of him asleep at the top of the house used to drive my mother mad. Not only was he a really sound sleeper, but because of his practice of piling three or four overcoats on top of the bedcovers to keep out the cold and the incidental noise of the raids, it took a specially heavy anti-aircraft barrage to get through to him. My mother used to fret about that. At the height of a raid, she would sit up in her bunk. "Listen to that. *Listen* to it," she would urge us. "The whole place being blown to bits and that bloody man asleep upstairs! *He* doesn't care."

This wasn't quite true. There was an anti-aircraft gun a few hundred feet from the house, and when this started up, my father would usually wake up with a guilty conscience, knowing that my mother was also awake, and angry. He would immediately hurry downstairs and make a cup of tea, and a few minutes later the sacking over our entrance would be pulled back, and there he would be, whispering hoarsely (so as not to wake the children), "Daisy! Daisy! Are you all right? I brought you a cup of tea."

The sky behind him would be a blaze of searchlights and shellbursts and, once, a flaming barrage balloon, and my mother would grab the tea. "All right? All *right?* Course I'm all right. Go back inside. What's the matter with you? You gone daft? Go inside!" And the sacking would fall into place again as my father returned to bed.

Eventually he got a job as nightwatchman in his own stables in Kennington, one of the most heavily bombed parts of the city. That way he could sleep at home during the day, when there weren't many air raids, and it was less nerve-racking keeping the horses calm during a raid than trying to assure my mother both that he was safe and that he knew it was dangerous to be outside. My young sister and I missed him a lot. We used to enjoy those visits, when the lifted cloth gave us a glimpse of the fireworks outside. For us, the whole terrible struggle was reduced to a familiar domestic argument—a kind of storm in which my father didn't have enough sense to get out of the rain.

The war wasn't nearly as important to me as the ordinary life at school. The only actual war incident I was part of happened one night when I answered a knock at the door to find a tramp there with three days' growth of beard and a sack on his back. Because of the blackout regulations I had to draw the curtain behind me before I opened the door wide, so there was no light for enemy bombers to see me by. The street lights were out, of course, and there was no moon or stars, so he was indistinguishable, too.

"Ullo, son," he said, and smiled.

It was as frightening as the appearance of Magwitch in David Lean's film version of *Great Expectations* but I stood my ground and asked him what he wanted. "I want to come in," he said.

And then, just as he was telling me, my mother came into the passage to find out what was going on and reacted with a scream, "O Gawd, it's Ron," and pushed past me to let him in.

Ron's ship, part of a Murmansk convoy, had been sunk near Archangel, but he had been rescued and taken ashore in Russia. In time, he joined a home-going convoy and returned to a survivors' camp in Scotland. The survivors were supposed to recuperate until they were fit to be seen by the civilian population, but Ron, being Ron, just walked out of the camp and hitchhiked home.

My mother fed him most of the food in the house, which he ate while she heated the water for a bath, and he washed himself and went to bed for sixteen hours, then got up and ate the rest of our week's rations and went back to bed for another eight hours. Then he had to go back to Scotland.

After that he went on the Atlantic run, on oil tankers, but he survived the U-boats and came home safely.

After Dunkirk, Joe was sent to Greece in time to cover the retreat of the fighting troops, and moved on to take part in the evacuation of Crete. Once again he found himself part of the rearguard covering the embarkation of the Welsh Guards or some such crack regiment, and found a place on one of the last landing craft to leave the beach. From here he went to Libya to be fattened up for the next battle.

Mad Jack repeatedly tried to get Len drowned in the North Sea but Len survived like his brothers. Gladys came as close as any of them to not coming home when she was machine-gunned on a Bournemouth street by a stray German aircraft. She escaped by lying in the gutter, as she had been instructed.

And then, one day, while we were in class, Mr. Gush, the French master, was called to the door of the classroom to hear something from the headmaster. When he returned he looked solemn but happy. "This morning," he said (in French), "the Allied armies crossed the Channel and landed on the beaches of Normandy. At this moment they are fighting to secure a beachhead. The second front has begun."

There was a breathless hush, mainly because even after four years of French classes, we couldn't understand what he was saying. He made the announcement again, more slowly, emphasizing the key words, pointing to a map of France on the wall to indicate where the troops had landed, and miming the firing of a Sten gun until we got it. It was probably the most momentous announcement of the war for a group of fifteen-year-olds, many of whom had fathers or brothers who would be involved. We knew it meant the beginning of the end.

For the civilians, nothing much more happened until the V-1 bombs appeared on the scene. These "buzz bombs" sometimes approached before the sirens could give warning, but you could tell roughly where a V-1 would land from its position in the sky when the engine cut out. One sunny afternoon, I was playing soccer in the rec when one of them appeared. We ran to shelter, and I saw it dip and heard the roar of the explosion, which came from the direction of our house. I raced home and found the house a shambles; the blast had taken out most of the windows, and tiles from the roof were strewn across the street. My mother was already at work trying to clean up the mess. I started to help when she suddenly screamed, "Your dad—he's upstairs!" Running up to the bedroom, we plunged into a choking cloud of plaster dust that had fallen on the bed, covering it completely. We tore off the mess of plaster and laths, which seemed about a foot thick, and when we eventually uncovered my father we found him dazed but not unconscious. My mother immediately assumed he had slept through the whole business (he *looked* as though he had), and she collapsed, sitting down on the bed, in tears for the first time I had seen her, but also furious, blaming him for the fright his appearance had given her.

Leaving School

Like everyone else over the age of ten, I had to earn my own pocket money, and I had a morning paper round during the first year of the Blitz. The papers had to be delivered between the end of the raids, after the all-clear had sounded, and getting ready for school. This was the best time for picking up shrapnel from the anti-aircraft shells, some of it still warm to the touch. Later in the war, shrapnel fell out of favour as a souvenir because it got rusty too quickly. A brand new gleaming piece of twisted metal would start to rust in a day or two and soon lose its attraction. The best finds were the brass nose-cones, and on one gala morning I found three. Sometimes, after a bombing, you couldn't deliver all your papers because the police would be clearing up an area that had been hit, but there wasn't much damage on my round. Ray Hampton found a whole house missing one morning when he tried to deliver a paper. The front door was still there, he said, but there was nothing round it or behind it, just a gap in the street with a door frame and a door.

I only delivered papers for a year. When I stopped, my father assumed I was lazy, a quitter, made soft by too much "eddication" (I had got out of a warm bed every morning in one of the coldest winters of the age and shivered my way round the dark streets without missing a single day for nine months, but that didn't count. Eventually my "quitter" streak showed through, just as he suspected it would.) It wasn't true. I just couldn't face the medical again. Boys who wanted to deliver papers had to be examined every year by a doctor to certify that they were fit to do the job. The doctors examined our chests for signs of tuberculosis, and felt the walls of our abdomens to make sure we didn't have a hernia. So, before I could start my round, a woman doctor listened to my chest with a stethoscope and then unbuckled my trousers and fumbled with my balls as if they were made of steel like those sold in Chinese novelty shops for reducing stress. She took a very long time to establish what she was looking for and sure enough, by the time she was finished, I had my first externally activated non-spontaneous erection, though the cause wasn't sex but friction and embarrassment. It soon faded but it was a real horn while it lasted, and my face was black with shame as I tried to step away. But she hung on gamely, saying, "It's all right," fumbling away for several more seconds before she let me go. "It's perfectly natural," she said, tapping me lightly on the head with her pencil and smiling.

For her, maybe, because she knew nothing about the way it was in Colwood Gardens, but not for me. I might have had to stay away from women doctors for the rest of my life, but I told Robbie when I saw him and he set me straight, told me it would have happened to anybody; he thought he might try to get a paper route himself, he grinned, but there were no vacancies. But a year later, I could not bring myself to be examined again, or tell my parents why I was quitting the paper route, so I had to get a job working all day Saturday in a banana factory, a dark steamy warehouse where bananas were ripened, to earn some money. (I got six shillings a week for the paper round, including the Saturday morning collection, a sum hard to replace.) It meant giving up my free time with my mates, but I had no choice.

Bombs killed two boys I knew, one only fifty yards from our house as he was cycling home for his Sunday dinner.

I was frightened once in the Underground when the train stopped, the lights went out, and some fool shouted that the tunnel was flooded.

And once, walking home from school, having spent my bus fare on toffee, I passed two old women on Western Road, near the gasworks, as one was saying to the other, "A landmine, they say, and if it goes orf, it'll take you, me, the gasworks, and most of Mitcham with it. Could go any minute. Come on." And they scuffled off down a side road. There was no one else about and I ran like hell, expecting any second to be plucked out of my clothes and deposited a mile away, naked and dead. (Those same two old women, or two very much like them, appeared several times later in my life. Once I came home from school to find them drinking tea with my mother. That time, after learning who I was, they looked at me closely, and one said to my mother, "I don't think he'll make old bones, Daisy." Often they waited for me on street corners, going silent as I approached, then watching me, shaking their heads as I walked past them and on down the road. They could tell I had been up to something.)

Otherwise, the war, for a schoolboy, was the background; the foreground was school.

In the summer of 1944 the school pitched some tents on a farm near Cheddar in Somerset and we helped to get in the harvest. I was fifteen now, and becoming aware of passages. Two of my cronies, Ray Hampton (now known as Hambone) and Bert Churcher (newly christened Peastick by us because he was tall and thin) had left school, both of them believing that life had to be more interesting and pleasanter elsewhere, and that made me aware that school would not go on for ever. Hambone said later that the stay at the girls' school had spoiled him. It was altogether a more civilized environment than the boys' school—the physical setting, the teaching, and the agreeableness of the senior girls who we found out afterwards had been asked to mentor us. Hambone got lucky and was looked after by Lucy, who we were all soft on. As for Peastick, when we returned to the boys' school he was separated from all his friends and put into a different form for no good reason, so it was like his first week of school all over again. And Hambone and Peastick hated rugger as much as any of us.

I understood why they went, and I was sorry because they were both cronies of mine now and would be hard to replace. But I didn't feel tempted to join them. I had begun to feel apprehensive about the future, which seemed to promise nothing, and I began to take some responsibility for my performance at school. I began to wonder, prompted into it by a new friend, Stan Yass, whether if I did some work, I might become a student, and I found the idea attracted me slightly. It was almost too late, but I set myself a couple of small academic tasks and achieved them. I thought about the sixth form, admiring a boy who had decided at the last minute to study languages and set himself the task of learning School Certificate Latin in one year. I could do that, I thought, if I took myself seriously, though perhaps not in Latin.

443

The closeness of living six to a tent in the harvest camp brought out the beginnings of a tolerance for each other which we were old enough to allow, an awareness of the sheer interestingness of boys whom I had dismissed as drips for the last four years. The old cliques broke up and were replaced by new friendships, some of them enduring. We worked in the fields, stooking, haymaking, and, if we could not avoid it, thinning root crops, the most back-breaking work of all. We worked alongside Italian prisoners of war, surely the most pleasant enemies any country ever had, or so it seemed to us. They had no money, so many of them turned to making things they could sell, women's jackets out of old blankets, and wallets and purses from scraps of leather. The Italian war effort had collapsed and Italy was about to surrender and some of the prisoners were beginning to wonder if they would not be better off staying in England than returning to a ravaged homeland. In the end, they all had to go back, and I put one of them in a book forty years later when I needed an Italian peasant with a fair command of English. All of the prisoners we worked with seemed to speak English fluently.

In 1945, as the final victory in Europe approached, so did the School Certificate examinations. I still led the class in English, and history and mathematics had remained interesting enough, but nothing else did; no one made me work hard. I had no self-discipline (my father was right about that). In spite of feeling the beginnings of a desire to achieve something, I was heading for ignominy. But that new friend, Stanley Yass, the only Jewish boy in the school, now took me seriously in hand.

Stan was not in my form but in the rival form, 5B. I had noticed him in the air-raid shelters when roll was being called to make sure the whole class had transferred from school to shelter intact. There was another boy in 5B at the end of the alphabet, a boy named Yapp, and Yass and Yapp entertained each other and their classmates by replying to the roll with each other's names: "Yapp?"—"Yass," then "Yass?"—"Yapp." I heard it in the shelter for the first time and thought it hilarious.

Stan was the first boy I had met who worked hard to get B grades who wasn't a drip. Stan said, "If you don't get your School Certificate, you'll be a bus conductor." I hadn't thought about it like that. I applied myself a little, just in time, and got my School Certificate with failures in art and music and Latin, but enough other passes to scrape by, including a distinction in English literature.

The same headmaster assembled us all in one room to hear the results. To put us out of our misery quickly, he had memorized the important result, whether we had passed or failed, and rapidly ran round the room saying, "Passed, passed, failed ..." etc., to a lot of boys, some of whom he hardly knew. It was a tricky performance because he must have taken some trouble to memorize us by our faces, and he meant well.

I had passed. Then he read out how we had done in individual subjects, going slowly round the room and I was in agony to confirm the mark in one subject. When he came to me, he looked at the marks and stopped, puzzled. He knew me well enough because I had been a policeman in his *Pirates of Penzance*. Then he read out the English mark—"A." There was a note of slight doubt in his voice.

"That's right," I said, a bit too quickly. I knew it was coming—the exam had been a piece of cake—and his pause made me belligerent. He looked down at the marks to be sure, and looked at me again, before he moved on. I had distinguished myself for the first time in my life, in however small a way, and congratulations were in order. But he just looked at me, thoughtfully, and moved on.

It was a bleak period. I did not seem to have felt as much of an outsider within the school as Peastick or Hambone, although there was no chance of that headmaster's ever choosing me as a prefect, because I certainly lacked the right attitude; for him, I was what was wrong with the school, perhaps he found me common. But, probably, fear of the world outside, perhaps some slight encouragement by Dickey Bird, the English master, a small genuine desire to remain a student—all of these combined as I offhandedly, casually, mentioned to my mother that Derek Ockenden and Len Dunkley, two of my school friends whom she knew and admired, were continuing on to the sixth form with the idea of going to university.

"You can put that out of your head," she snapped. "Right now. You've already been allowed to stay in school far longer than anyone else and now it's time to start paying it back."

I had not expected or deserved anything else. For her, I was one of the lucky ones, but all good things had to end. I couldn't lay in front of her or the rest of my family a burning ambition to be or do something that required more training or education. My one area of excellence seemed valueless, like being good at music appreciation. I had no mentors or advisers except Stan, and he was being apprenticed to a quantity surveyor. Fortunately even this was outside my reach, because the weekly stipend for a student in the minor professions—surveying, accountancy, and such—was intended only as pocket money, making even this level of qualification unavailable to someone who had to pay his own way from now on. I say *fortunately* because otherwise I might have been thwarted when I did finally become seized with an irresistible ambition to take ship somewhere.

It was time to leave. The sadness that always accompanies the end of an academic year was made more intense by the knowledge that this was the last. I had no affection for the school, but I was not looking forward to the future. I needed a job, and I couldn't think of anything I wanted to do. Before I started work, there was one last summer of harvest camp. They pitched our tents on Viscount Cowdray's estate near Midhurst in Sussex, and we swam in the pool of Midhurst Grammar. Midhurst was a distinctly superior school to Mitcham County in every way, but the war temporarily allowed for some fraternization among classes, here as elsewhere, though the viscount kept his distance. It was the custom to swim naked at Midhurst Grammar; the summer was very hot and we had a fine time aping our betters in that pool, as, I suppose, did that old master, a naturalist, he called himself, who sat naked, sunning himself in a corner of the wall surrounding the pool, watching us play in the water, smiling.

One day I had an appointment in the headmaster's study, along with my mother, for a five-minute counselling session which would settle the rest of my life. I sat there, ashamed of my mother for being a shabby little woman with a cockney accent, and hating the headmaster for knowing it, and for having trained me to be ashamed, and furious with her for whispering to me loudly, "Say, 'Sir,'" every time I spoke to him, as she had been doing since I was five.

He had a list of job vacancies and from that he suggested two, both clerkships, one with the United Dairies Company, and the other with the Asiatic Petroleum Company. The choice was easy: the petroleum company had its offices in the City of London, whereas the milk company had its offices in the next suburb. I was very keen both to sample the London I was already reading about in novels, and to get out of Colliers Wood as much and as often as I could.

LONDON

In Colliers Wood, in 1945, clerkships at the Asiatic Petroleum Company were reckoned to be good jobs, available only to those with School Certificates. A medical was necessary because you had to join the pension fund, and a bank account so your salary (not wages) could be paid into it, monthly. Bank accounts were very rare in Colliers Wood; when the county council awarded me a grant of two guineas a term to subsidize the cost of my school uniform, it came in the form of a cheque that was uncashable without a bank account, so we had to take it to the corner grocery shop, Rendell's, and spend some of it on milk and bread and tea. This was standard practice: no one else we knew had a bank account, except Vi, of course, for The George, but she only visited us about once a month, and The George was too far for one of us to go just to cash a cheque. Some people had Post Office savings accounts, but in our family any surplus money was kept in cash, in my mother's purse. My father kept his personal savings in one-pound notes in a shopping bag in the wardrobe.

So getting a bank account and a chequebook (and paying a stamp tax on every withdrawal) was pretty heady stuff. It was also absurd. My salary was a hundred and sixty pounds a year, paid monthly. In terms of paying the rent, buying a season ticket on the Underground, and so on, I lived weekly, so I had to be very careful to get fifty-two weeks' expenses out of twelve paycheques, by allowing for two or three extra days in every cheque, except February. In practice, on the day they deposited my salary into my account, I, along with most of the other junior employees of the Asiatic Petroleum Company, lined up, wrote a cheque, and drew it all out. I then lived carefully for three weeks and was impoverished for the rest of the month.

I used to think that the only possible reason for paying our money into a bank account, rather than giving us cheques, was to show us how we had come up in the world by joining the Asiatic Petroleum Company. The working class got wages and kept their savings in the Post Office; the genteel classes, including the lower middle class which I had now joined, earned salaries and kept their money in bank accounts. But any real workers I knew—plumbers, bricklayers, and so on— regarded my little salary as a joke, and the fact that it was paid monthly they saw as a swindle to rob me of four weeks' pay a year. Their unions wouldn't have stood for it. But the real reason, of course, was that it was more convenient for the Asiatic Petroleum Company, and we didn't have a union to complain to.

I was the office boy in the insurance department. No attempt was made to interest me in insurance, or to train me in any way whatever. As a sixteen-year-old, I was marking time until I did my two years of national service, which would begin at eighteen. There was no point in training me until that was finished, so I, along with all other sixteen-year-olds, faced the prospect of kicking my heels for four years until life started properly. The position was so empty of any interest or challenge that it performed the useful function of leaving me free to daydream and discover in myself a determination, when I finished my national service, to avoid any future involving the Asiatic Petroleum Company or any company like it. Mostly, along with two or three other office boys, I spent my time plotting how to get away. The army would be my first escape. After that I would see.

In the meantime the social struggle continued. It was just as necessary to conceal one's origins around Bishopsgate as it had been at school. Some of the juniors in other departments had actually been to minor public schools, and some others sounded as if they had. You were expected to wear a suit and a tie from Monday to Friday; on Saturday mornings you could wear a sports jacket and grey flannel trousers and a tie. Fortunately clothing was rationed, so there was plenty of excuse for shabbiness, but you had to observe the forms. One Saturday, one of the older office boys in another department visited me in the insurance department, wearing a parody of an overcoat with wide lapels and a pinched waist that looked like the costume for a stage bookmaker. It must have been handed down

447

to him by a flashy uncle. Nobody said anything to his face, but one of the older men in my department, who should have known better, thought he was being very witty by singing, apparently to himself, the first lines of "Knocked 'Em in the Old Kent Road." ("Last night, down our alley came a toff/Great, big, geezer wiv an 'acking cough ...") The boy was a pal of mine, so I didn't laugh, but I didn't encourage him to hang about in the office, either.

The world of sports continued to sort us out. Many of those who had played rugby at school continued to play in Old Boys clubs, and the sports club of the Asiatic Petroleum Company fielded its own teams. I, alone among my peers at the office, was a football fan, specifically a fanatical Chelsea supporter. I would not have actually denied being a Chelsea supporter if an office colleague had asked me; I simply didn't brag about belonging once a week to the cloth-cap brigade, even though Chelsea supporters were in the upper ranks of football society.

I had supported Chelsea for as long as I could remember, ever since Joe had taken me to a game when I was about seven or eight. By the time I was four-teen, and in full opposition to the rugby crowd at school, I was cheering from the terraces of Stamford Bridge every other Saturday afternoon. When I first started going, the war was on, and a lot of players from other teams who were now in the services were temporarily joining local teams where they happened to be sta-tioned. Sometimes the difficulty of fielding a full side was so acute that clubs had to appeal to the crowd on the terraces for able-bodied players to help out for the afternoon. I was hoping the war would last ten more years so that I could step forward, because I had not yet admitted to myself that I was really no good at all at the thing I most enjoyed doing besides reading.

Thus my heroes included George Hardwick, who came from Middlesborough, and played for England; and Charlie Mitten, from Manchester, I think, and many other imports. But the greatest player of all, more revered by me than the great Stanley Matthews himself, was Tommy Walker, the Scottish international inside right, whom even at that age I would cheerfully have followed into battle. The afternoon when Tommy Walker led Chelsea in an 11–2 victory over Crystal Palace was, up to that point, the happiest afternoon of my life. Never mind the lopsided score, which reflected the play; the afternoon was a ninety-minute demonstration by Walker of what you can do with a football. Most of the people who rave about the later demonstration that Stanley Matthews put on against the Russians (which was brilliant, I was there, I wouldn't dream of denying it) do not think anyone else could have done it. I think Tommy Walker could have.

Since I only began watching football during the war, I assumed that the conditions under which it was played were normal, that is, that the teams were divided into northern and southern divisions. But this was a temporary arrangement designed to cut down on travel. When, after the war, the old leagues (or some form of them) were resumed, I discovered that the war had obscured the football league's own class system, that my team had been playing some very lower-class clubs like Millwall, Charlton Athletic, and Brentford (especially Brentford) simply because the war had made it necessary. These were third division clubs that properly played among themselves, except once a year when they were given a chance in the Football Association Cup (if they survived the first two rounds) to play a game with aristocrats like Chelsea and Arsenal. The Football Association also relieved the social pressure by providing a minimal form of upward mobility in the league play; at the end of the season two clubs were promoted into the class above and two demoted, but the records show that if any of the real aristocrats like Chelsea slipped, it was usually only for a season or two.

Much of this has changed. Wimbledon is now in the premier division. In those days I would have as soon expected to see Tooting and Mitcham there.

449

There was no money. I had to contribute to the house, and pay my fare to the office, and I was left with about a pound a week to spend. During the day I wore shoes with pieces of linoleum in them to keep out some of the rainwater. I owned one office shirt with two collars which I changed (the collars—the shirt I kept on all week) on Wednesday or Thursday, depending on what I was doing at night. I went without gloves in winter because I couldn't afford a pair of leather ones and woollen ones marked you as a weed. And so on. But at night, for the first three weeks of the month, it was another thing. How could we carve out our nights from the scraps left from days lived like this?

Like this: the Asiatic Petroleum Company supplied luncheon, free, three courses—typically, Windsor soup and bread, toad-in-the-hole (sausages baked in Yorkshire pudding) with potatoes and cabbage, cabinet pudding with custard, and coffee. A free lunch from the employer was standard in those days and formed an important addition to the food rations; if employers were too small to have their own dining room and kitchen, then they supplied luncheon vouchers, worth half a crown, to be spent in any restaurant that honoured them, as most did. Free luncheons made it possible to stay in town after work for the evening, because if we ate as much as possible at lunch (if you went to the last sitting, you could sometimes get seconds of the cabinet pudding), and brought sandwiches from home for dinner, all we needed was the price of a cup of tea to wash the sandwiches down. Tuppence. Then your season ticket on the Underground, which got you to work and home, also covered most of your travelling at night. You might have to pay three ha'pence to buy a ticket to get you past the turnstile but, then as now, once on the platform no one could tell where you had come from, so you could get home free.

I set aside ten shillings for Saturdays—football and the Saturday night dance—and spent the rest on theatres, concerts, and cinemas. You could get into the galleries of a lot of theatres for a shilling, and you could get into the upper circle of Covent Garden Opera House for half a crown. From here I first saw *Rigoletto* and *La Bohème*, and got angry at the money I had wasted on some Wagner rubbish. But most of all, from here I had a musical experience the like of which I have never had since. The opera was *La Traviata*, the company, the San Carlos Opera Company, and the singer was Margherita Carosio, whom I have never heard since. That night, when I was sure there were to be no more curtain calls, I rushed around to the stage door to get as close as I could when she came out. She appeared from the stage door, looked frightened at the mob of faces, said, "Please," in a soft little voice from under her big black hat, and we let her through. I walked out to the Strand and onto Waterloo Bridge, where I hung over the parapet for half an hour, waiting for the excitement to die down. Eventually I walked over the bridge and caught the tube home. I think Stan was with me.

Opera and opera singers have never had that effect since.

We heard a lot of concert music, too, the whole Beethoven symphony cycle, conducted by Victor de Sabata, at the Albert Hall. During this period a nice man in the office, overhearing me rave about some opera I had heard, tried to mentor me by inviting me to his home and playing music at me for four hours one bank holiday afternoon, while his wife fed us tea and cake. But he was something of a musicologist and I wasn't ready for his level of understanding—it was another twenty years before I discovered chamber music. My colleague had mistaken my enthusiasm for the easy passions of opera for a genuine ear which he wanted to educate. All afternoon he played his favourites at me, lecturing me on the intellectual subtleties of what I was hearing—at one point, I remember, he was explaining the quarter tones to be found in Arab music—while I tried to respond. But it was no use; I couldn't hear what he was talking about, and as the afternoon wore on it grew more and more difficult to manufacture a polite, *interested* response to each piece, until finally he released me, nearly paralyzed with the effort I had been making, and I staggered off. Until that day, he had been glad to have a chat as I delivered his mail on my rounds, but he dropped me after that.

So once a week we saw and heard the best from the back of the gallery. We attended the theatre indiscriminately: Naunton Wayne in *Arsenic and Old Lace* or Paul Muni in *Death of a Salesman*—it was all grist to us. On Mondays we went to the pictures at the local cinemas, and on Saturdays we went to a dance hall in the doomed quest of a nice girl who went all the way. It sounds now like a very rich life, but it was only a rich seam, made possible because it was so cheap to do, and because we spent every penny we had on it, for the first three weeks of the month. Everything else was beyond me; we never visited a restaurant, not even for baked beans on toast, and it would have taken a year of not going out at night to save up the money for a spare suit.

In all this, Stan Yass was my constant companion and adviser. After we left school we formed a mutual exploration society, walking, learning to smoke, talking, trying to think. Only sex remained to be experienced and that was coming, Stan assured me, himself reassured by his elder brother. This brother had been a captain in the army and was now a chartered accountant, a very upwardly mobile type who had a lot of advice for Stan which Stan passed on to me, mostly about behaviour.

The proper word for Stanley and his brother is *aware*. They were conscious of what was going on around them whereas I lived unthinkingly until Stan pointed out what was happening. I knew nothing of his religion or culture for a year because there was no overt sign except that their food was better than I was used to, English but with a hint of garlic and a touch of pickled fish: tastier than ours. And then one Friday evening I called in to his house, noticed that the candles on their supper table were badly arranged and regrouped them as I had seen them arranged in the restaurants in Hollywood movies. No one said anything then, but later on, walking over the common, Stan explained the significance of the arrangement of candles in a Jewish house on a Friday night.

At the time it was no more or less interesting than if he had told me he was a Christian Scientist or a Quaker or Welsh. It was just something he reminded me of from time to time later on—when his mother wanted him to marry a nice Jewish girl, for example—to show me the difference between his family and mine.

451

The daytime poverty was made bearable by rationing, which excused any shabbiness in our clothes (but not the wearing of bookmakers' overcoats). Rationing had other benefits. My spinster aunt said that she never lived so well as she did during the war. Everybody had a job, Aunt Rose said, and the government made sure you had enough to eat. She regarded ration coupons not as limiting the quantity of food you could buy, but as guaranteeing that you would get something to eat, associating them with the only time of full employment she had ever enjoyed. She had been a chambermaid before the war at St. Ermine's Hotel in Victoria, often suddenly laid off in slack times and then having to choose between going in arrears on her rent, if her landlady let her, or going hungry. For her, it was worth being bombed occasionally to be sure of food and lodging. Peace, to her, meant being unsure you would have enough money for tomorrow's dinner, and when the war ended she left St. Ermine's and, on the advice of a pal of hers, took a job as an attendant in a public lavatory, where she found the work easier, the job permanent and pensionable, and the customers more agreeable.

Aunt Rose was a bit "slow," and may really have had the impression that ration coupons were a form of money. Certainly her limitations helped her to enjoy the happiest senility I have ever known of. She lived alone in a tiny basement in Stockwell. She visited us and my by-now-married sisters in rotation, every Tuesday afternoon for tea, so that if she failed to appear at the right house every six weeks or so, my brother Ron would check up on her. He generally looked in once a week anyway to make sure she had enough coals and kindling, and one night during a very fierce winter he found her unconscious, near death, suffering from hypothermia. She had become ill and unable to keep her fire in, and the cold added to her distress until she stayed in bed and nearly died. Ron got her to a hospital, and from there to a nursing home. When he next visited her, she no longer knew him, and she told him that now she was in heaven she was glad she had died; she had feared it before. Apparently when she woke up she was surrounded by figures in white, offering her cups of tea. This was so unusual for her that she assumed she was in paradise, and continued to believe that until she died, a year later. She left a very clear will, distributing all of her money among her nieces and nephews equally. We got forty-two pounds each. It was my first and last legacy, not an important sum, but not yet absolutely trivial, either, and I used it to buy a piece of costume jewellery for my wife in memory of my aunt.

Aunt Rose became a kind of political litmus test for me. After that, whenever I had doubts, I remembered that I should vote for the party that would guarantee the Aunt Roses of society enough to eat (without declaring a war) and a warm place to sleep, access to proper medical care without worrying about the cost, and at the end, a decent hospice when their wits are gone.

It wasn't only the Aunt Roses whose diets benefited from the war. The minister of food, I have read, was in 1938 preparing to use the coming war as an excuse to impose a better diet on the working class, by severely rationing tinned food, sugar, sweets and chocolate, butter and other fats, and by making it illegal to bleach the nutritional value of bread. Everyone grew vegetables—DIG FOR VICTO-RY was the nation slogan—and so, as well as good bread, even in winter, pota-toes and the horrible Brussels sprouts were always available. Some things like orange juice were available only for children, and children were issued a third of a pint of milk twice a day at school. And if you went to a county school, you got a large hot dinner at noon, which not only supplemented the rations, but in many cases improved the diet. In 1940, after Dunkirk, a famous American war corre-spondent remarked on what poor physical specimens the British prisoners of war were, compared to their German captors. The war was won by a generation of soldiers who had grown up on white bread, fried meat, and tinned vegetables, fol-lowed (on Sundays) by tinned fruit. But the children of my generation were as fit as Hitler's youth as, finally, because of the war, we got enough to eat.

453

Part Four:

Tragedies, Choices & Losses

Paper Shadows

WAYSON CHOY

Wayson Choy's first book, the novel *The Jade Peony*, published in 1995 when he was fifty-six, won the City of Vancouver Book Award and shared Ontario's Trillium Prize with a work by Margaret Atwood. While he was doing a publicity tour for *The Jade Peony*, he learned that he was adopted. This startling revelation so comparatively late in life led him to write the memoir *Paper Shadows: A Chinatown Childhood* (1999), of which this forms part.

"I saw your mother last week."

The stranger's voice on the phone surprised me. She spoke firmly, clearly, with the accents of Vancouver's Old Chinatown: "I saw your *mah-ma* on the streetcar."

Not possible. This was 1995. Eighteen years earlier I had sat on a St. Paul's Hospital bed beside Mother's skeletal frame while she lay gasping for breath: the result of decades of smoking. I stroked her forehead and, with my other hand, clasped her thin, motionless fingers. Around two in the morning, half-asleep and weary, I closed my eyes to catnap. Suddenly, the last striving for breath shook her. I snapped awake, conscious again of the smell of acetone, of death dissolving her body. The silence deepened; the room chilled. The mother I had known all my life was gone.

Eighteen years later, in response to a lively radio interview about my first novel, a woman left a mysterious message: URGENT WAYSON CHOY CALL THIS NUMBER.

Back at my hotel room, message in hand, I dialled the number and heard an older woman, her voice charged with nervous energy, insist she had seen my mother on the streetcar.

"You must be mistaken," I said, confident that this woman would recognize her error and sign off.

"No, no, not your mother"—the voice persisted—"I mean your *real* mother."

"My first crazy," I remember thinking. *The Jade Peony* had been launched just two days earlier at the Vancouver Writers' Festival, and already I had a crazy. My agent had, half-whimsically, warned me to watch out for them. The crazies had declared open season upon another of her clients, a young woman who had written frankly of sexual matters. I was flattered, but did not really believe that my novel about Vancouver's Old Chinatown could provoke such perverse attention. Surely, my caller was simply mistaken.

"I saw your *real* mother." The voice emphatically repeated the word "real" as if it were an incantation.

My *real* mother? I looked down at the polished desk and absently studied the Hotel Vancouver room-service menu. My real mother was dead; I had witnessed her going. I had come home that same morning eighteen years ago and seen her flowered apron folded precisely and carefully draped over the kitchen chair, as it had been every day of my life. I remember quickly hiding the apron from my father's eyes as he, in his pyjamas and leaning on his cane, shuffled into the kitchen. Seeing that the apron was missing from the chair, he began, "She's ...?" but could not finish the question. He stared at the back of the chair, then rested his frail eighty-plus years against me. Unable to speak, I led him back to his bed.

458

The voice on the hotel phone chattered on, spilling out details and relationships, talking of Pender *Gai*, Pender Street, and noting how my novel talked of the "secrets of Chinatown."

I suddenly caught my family name, pronounced distinctively and correctly: *Tuey*. Then my grandfather's, my mother's, and my father's formal Chinese names, rarely heard, sang into my consciousness over the telephone.

"Those are your family names?" the voice went on.

"Yes, they are," I answered, "but who are you?"

"Call me Hazel," she said.

She had an appointment to go to, but she gave me a number to call that evening.

"Right now, I can't tell you much more."

"Oh," I replied lamely, "I understand."

I did not understand. I meant it as a pause, a moment in which to gather my thoughts. I wanted to learn more. Provoked and confused, I said what came immediately into my head:

"Where should I begin?"

The line went dead. Hazel was gone.

That afternoon, in my fifty-seventh year, a phone call from a stranger pushed me towards a mystery. The past, as I knew it, began to shift.

When I think of my earliest memories, I do not worry about family history, nor do I think of the *five-times-as-hard* hard times my parents endured.

I think, instead, of first hauntings.

At the age of four, something vivid happened to me. I woke up, disturbed by the sound of a distant clanging, and lifted my head high above the flannelled embankment that was my mother's back to see if a ghost had entered the room. Mother rolled her head, mouth partially open, sound asleep. I rubbed the sleep from my eyes to survey the near-darkness. What I saw, reflected in the oval mirror above the dresser, was the buoyant gloom alive and winking with sparks. A cloud of fireflies.

The wonder of it jolted me fully awake.

The clanging began again. Then it ceased.

For a moment, I forgot about the noise. Mother's soft breathing pulled at the silence, stealing away a bit of my nameless fear. As I shook Mah-ma to wake her so she could see the fireflies, there was a rush of wind. I turned my head to look at the windows. A strong breeze lifted the lace curtains and fluttered one of the three opaque pull-down shades. Pinpoints of outside light sprayed across the room and spangled gems across the ceiling. I looked back at the wide, tilted mirror, at the reflected lights dancing within. I remembered how fireflies came together to rescue lost children in the caves of Old China. Mah-ma, her back to me, mumbled something, then receded into sleep.

I sank into the bed and leaned tightly against Mah-ma's great warmth. The clanging grew louder. A monster was approaching. My mind conjured a wild, hairy creature, eyes like fire, heaving itself, and the chains it was dragging, towards our bedroom cave. I turned to stone.

My child's wisdom said that Mah-ma and I had to lie perfectly still, or the monster would veer towards our bed, open its hideous wet mouth and devour us. Rigidly, I watched the pinpoints of light crazily dancing up the wall and across the ceiling.

Suddenly the wind died.

The blind hung still, inert.

I looked up. A ceiling of stars shimmered above me. The monster would be dazzled by the stars. It would be fooled. It would turn away from us. We were sky, not earth. I shut my eyes and whispered, "Go away, monster! Go away!"

There was rattling and banging, a clinking, and then a crescendo of sharp, steady *clip-clop, clip-clops*.... The monster, now frustrated by the lack of prey, shuddered—and turned into the milkman's old chestnut horse, its chains into *clink-clanking* bottles.

When I told Grandfather the next day how Mah-ma and I had escaped the hairy monster, he laughed. He said I was very smart to lie very still and not wake Mah-ma, who had been working two shifts and was tired. When I told Fifth Aunty, who often took care of me, she smiled, pinched my cheeks and said, "You lucky boy. Fireflies and stars always fortunate."

This haunting, Grandfather and Father both assured me, was only a child's dream. Many years later, Fifth Aunty reminded me of the old horse, how one late morning, when the milkman came to her alleyway door to sell her a strip of milk tickets, she had lifted me up to the animal's large, snorting head, and I, squirming in her arms, trembling, let it snatch a carrot stump from my palm.

"Only an old mare." She laughed.

Fifth Aunty told everyone how I had wiped the horse saliva on her face. I remembered none of it.

460

At five, I had my second haunting. This one, I recall clearly.

The distant clattering and clanging began again. I knew by now it was the sound of the approaching milkman. I lay still, listened for the comforting sound of the old horse, its hooves going *clip-clop, clip-clop* on the cobblestones, a rhythmic drumming that I can still hear today.

I sat up, not letting go of Mah-ma. She stirred and her breath deepened. My mother and I were utterly alone in the island kingdom of the double bed. Father was away again, on one of his frequent alternating three- and five-week stints as a cook on a Canadian Pacific steamship liner.

For my own amusement, I dared to imagine a slimy three-eyed monster somewhere in the dark outside, coming towards us, dragging its clanking chains.

I was lucky. I was brave. At will, I could render the great monster harmless and go back to sleep in the comfort of my own created magic. The chain's rattling had become as familiar as the sound of a chopstick hitting a milk bottle.

But that morning, for a reason I could not understand, I did not go back to sleep. From somewhere within me, a nameless fear slithered up my spine and gripped me by the nape of my neck. Then it began to pull me down. During the summer evening, the blanket and sheet had been pushed away. My pyjama top, rolled up, exposed my back. I could not reach the bedding wadded below my feet. I clung to Mah-ma, my cheek tight against her flannel nightgown. Her body heat and sweet salty smell anchored me.

As the morning sun began to bleach the darkness from the ceiling, the pinpoints of light faded. I needed to pee. But I did not get up and go down the hall, as I had been taught to do. An odd feeling fettered me, made me feel inadequate, like a helpless baby. And yet I knew that a big boy doesn't cry out for his *mah-ma*.

Carefully, I sat up.

A faint, distant clattering came through the open window: the milk wagon was lumbering down the street. I pushed myself off the big bed. The cold linoleum floor tickled my soles. I listened. The milk wagon halted. Except for Mother's breathing, and a scattering of birdsong, there was no sound. The world seemed to me to have suddenly altered, slipped into enchantment, like in a Grimm fairy tale.

In the near-dark, the scratched oak dressing table stood with squat authority. On its polished top lay a cluster of bottles filled with mysterious amber liquid, tortoiseshell combs, silver-topped jars, and fancy cylinders holding fragrant talc. I resolved to go there, pull out the seat, and climb up and play with the bottles. But then the single opened window dispatched a rapid tattoo of clopping hooves. The wind rose. The window shade lifted like a hand and beckoned me.

461

I was tall enough to lay my head on the window sill. Standing there, I then turned my head and stuck my tongue out to lick the rough, paint-flaked wood. It was real enough. I stared at the pull-cord ring swinging from the blind. When the wind faltered, the beige wooden ring *click-clicked* against the glass. Outside, the milkman's horse whinnied and shook its bells. The wagon stopped, started, stopped, started. My heart thumped against my chest. But I was not afraid of the milk wagon. It was something else I feared.

I turned my head and glimpsed, in the dresser mirror, my mother, a length of warm shadow stretched out along the far edge of the bed. From where I stood, I could not see the rise and fall of her back. Suddenly, I could not breathe: she seemed too still.

I swallowed hard and stared at her.

The milk wagon clattered on, the bump, bump, bump of the wheels on the cobblestones fading into nothingness. I did not cry out.

This is all I know of the second haunting.

To this day, the vision of that moment—me with my head on the window sill, breathless, watching my sleeping mother—has not left me. Whenever this image comes to me, unbidden, my heart pounds, my lungs constrict. I taste a second or two of panic, then, catching my breath, I tell myself I am being foolish.

Years after that moment, at the age of thirty-seven, I was at my mother's funeral, and Fifth Aunty was saying how pleased my mother must be that her last ride was in a Cadillac, and that Father had bought her such a fine oak casket.

"The lid good enough for a dining table, Sonny," she said, using my English name. "First class!"

Fifth Aunty leaned on my arm as we walked to my cousin's car. She looked up at the bright, cloudless sky and frowned. She had almost tempted the gods: if she made the funeral sound too perfect, the gods would humble us. She had to find something wrong. She stopped, casually curved her finger into her mouth and popped out her ill-fitting false teeth. They dropped into a Baggie. The handbag snapped shut. Fifth Aunty sighed; she was stalling, thinking how to tell me (as family should tell each other) what had gone wrong. She would have to be diplomatic, yet frank.

462

"Oh, but if you win the lottery, Sonny, you remember: I want a horse-drawn hearse. More fancy." She stopped, cleared her throat carefully. "Everything should take longer, Sonny. Cadillac so fast! Service too fast! Even your dear *mah-ma*, why so fast! Today everything too fast."

I laughed—exactly what Aunty wanted me to do. She went on, cheeks flapping. "If up to me, I order, you know, an *old* horse and a shining first-class wagon with lace curtains!"

Fifth Aunty touched my shoulder with her cane and giggled. Death never scared her. She had seen too much death in Old Chinatown. I told her that, if I won the big lottery, I would see her ride into the sunset in the grandest, and slowest, horse-drawn hearse.

"Remember that day you little boy and saw your very first one, Sonny?" she said. Aunty always went back to the old days.

"No, I don't," I said. "I remember big wagons."

"Yes, yes, you remember," she insisted. "We stand on Hastings Street, I hold your hand, and your aunty finally tell you that black thing no fancy milk wagon." Fifth Aunty broke into toothless laughter. "Oh, you looked so surprised that people died, just like your goldfish."

"What did I say?"

"You cry out, *'Mah-ma won't die!'*"

I think of that morning of the second haunting, when I was five years old—the haunting that has never left me. In my mind's eye, the looking glass reflects half the bed where my mother lies; its cool surface mirrors the dappled wall where my shadow first ambled towards the morning light.

As Fifth Aunty gets into the car, I know now why I stood there at the window, unable to speak. My cousin's car drives away.

I listen.

There is birdsong.

There is silence.

That early memory, that haunting, sends me on a search for other remembered moments. Some come in dreams, mere fragments, weighted with a sense of mystery and meaning. At such times, a sadness pervades me. I close my eyes: older, long-ago faces, a few of them barely smiling, push into my consciousness. I hear voices, a variety of Chinatown dialects, their singsong phrases warning me: "You never forget you Chinese!"

Now I am a child stumbling against Mother in an alley barely wide enough for two people, my three-year-old legs scooting two or three steps ahead of her. I am jerked backwards. "Walk properly," Mother says. I jump a few steps more, her arm extends and she tugs me back. I look up at the wintry strip of sky. We are going to visit someone who lives up the stairs at the back of the building.

"Remember what I told you to say," Mother cautions.

I nod, laughing.

"No"—her tone is solemn—"*no laughing.*"

At the end of the narrow alley, Mother stops walking and kneels beside me. She wets her fingers and brushes down my cowlicks. Other people angle themselves to pass us. A damp wind whistles above us. Mother pulls me closer to her. A man wearing a black fedora pats my head and tells me I'm a good boy. Two women push by us. Each speaks a few words to Mother, and their long, dark coats brush against my face. Everyone is going in the same direction. Mother shakes me to get my attention.

"Whisper to me what you are going to say."

I whisper. Every word. Clearly.

"Good," Mother says, wetting her fingers to push back a lock of hair that has fallen over my eye. "Remember. No laughing."

We follow some people up the stairs to the second or third floor of the building. A long hallway holds cardboard boxes the size of me; the cartons are piled on top of each other against one wall. As Mother and I walk down the dim corridor, the two women in the dark coats, single-file ahead, look back at us, as if to make sure we are safely following them. I do not laugh. It does not feel like a place for laughing.

"She's in here," one of the women murmurs to Mother, and the two women step aside to let us through. Mother holds my hand as we enter a tiny room that smells of incense and medicine. On one side, a big woman bends over someone on a bed and whispers, "He's here."

Mother lifts me up. I see a lady with damp black hair straining to raise her head and focus her eyes on me. The pillow is embroidered with flowers. Mother says, "What do you have to say, Sonny?"

I gulp. I know what I have to say, but I can't understand why the lady does not ask me anything. I am not afraid, but what I was told to say sounds, to me, like an answer. And an answer needs a question. Finally, the lady on the bed smiles and nods at me. I am satisfied.

"I'm fine," I say. "My name is Choy Way Sun and I'm a good boy."

The lady on the bed breathes heavily and closes her eyes. Mother puts me down. Whatever was to be done is done. We walk out of the room and down the two or three flights of stairs, pushing against people coming the opposite way.

"My, my," a voice exclaims. There is whispering.

Mother says nothing, only pulls me along and back out onto Pender Street. I blink.

The street is filled with a bluish light.

After that strange visit, Mother bought me an ice-cream cone and a paper snake with a wiggling clay head. At Ming Wo's hardware store, I sat on the oak counter in my new clothes, and Helena Wong popped a hard candy into my mouth. She distracted me with some nails she was weighing out for a customer. While my head was turned, another lady came and took Mother's place.

"Where's Mah-ma?" I ask.

Mother is not beside me, but I feel safe with Chulip Sim, one of Mother's best friends. She always smells of perfume and gives me squeezing hugs, and makes funny faces until I laugh aloud.

"Your mother will be right back," Chulip Sim says, but she does not hug me or make any funny faces. She holds me, as we both stare at Mother climbing quickly up the mezzanine staircase. I remember that I did not lick the ice-cream cone or even notice the paper snake bobbing its head. I remember watching Mother wipe her eyes with a handkerchief.

"I'm fine," I whisper. "I'm Choy Way Sun and I'm a good boy."

Chulip Sim gives me a big hug.

These are the documented facts that I have known all my life: I was born Choy Way Sun, on April 20, 1939, in Vancouver, in the province of British Columbia, to Nellie Hop Wah, age thirty-eight, and Yip Doy Choy, age forty-two, the *gai-gee meng*, the *false-paper names*, officially recorded in my parents' immigration documents. A midwife, listed as Mrs. Eng Dick, attended the birth.

"We waited a long time for you," Father used to say to me. Mother always pointed to my baby picture, that pudgy baby that was me, and shook her head.

"You were *soooo* big!" she would say. "Weighed eight or nine pounds!"

"Why didn't you have more?" I'd ask.

"You were enough." Then Mother would laugh. "I was too old to try for another one!"

Father always joined in the laughter.

Years later, after I knew something about how babies arrived into the world, I asked Mother about my delivery. How did she manage with an eight- or nine-pound baby? The year was 1967 and I was twenty-eight; my friend Donna Alexander and I were talking about a mutual friend who had endured a difficult labour. Mother was cutting up the homemade upside-down cake Donna had brought us for tea. The fresh pink roses my friend had brought for the house perfumed our kitchen.

"Were there any problems?" I asked. "Was it a difficult birth?"

"*Ho-naan wahtak teng*," Mother continued in Toisanese. "*Not easy to say for certain.*" Mother handed me a slice of cake. "*Aiihyaah: too long ago!*"

I translated into English for Donna.

"Sonny, your mother has small, delicate hips," she said, and gently laughed. "You don't have to ask your poor mom if it was difficult."

Mother never liked to discuss bodily matters of any kind, so I wasn't surprised she would rather not remember. She looked down, hesitated, then shifted the conversation.

"You remember how you got your name?"

465

"Think about your Chinese name," Mother always said to me, tapping my head. "Think what it means. Your grandfather came from Victoria to give you your name."

Six weeks after my birth, Grandfather left Grandmother and his family in Victoria and took the overnight ferry to Vancouver, where he proudly pronounced the formal name he had selected for his first grandson:

"Choy Way Sun."

A half-dozen jade and gold baby bracelets ringed my crib as he said my new name aloud three times to a gathering of friends and relatives.

The two Chinese characters Grandfather selected for my name form a political motto: "*Way Sun*," that is, "*to rehabilitate*," was an epigram in Old China, a promise "to reform old ways through peaceful means."

When Grandfather informed my parents of the name he intended to give me, Mother mentioned to him, very gently, how it seemed too distinctive, too unlike the usual names for boys; Father as well politely hinted that the reform sentiments might prove to be more of a burden than a blessing for his First Son. Even Third Uncle came on his day off to suggest that "Way Sun" was perhaps too idealistic for a *Gim San*, a *Gold Mountain*, child. The name "Gold Mountain," what the Chinese, during the fabled gold-rush days, called North America, was a symbol for those who craved or dreamed of earning lucky fortunes. No one in our family had had any such luck.

Grandfather did not reply. With an air of authority, he picked up his brush and dipped it into the prepared ink stone. With exquisite strokes of black ink, Grandfather slipped onto the surface of the vermilion-coloured paper the two characters of my name. He held the lucky-coloured sheet up for all to witness. At once, everyone, even Third Uncle, joined in the chorus of approval:

"Yes, yes! Fine, very fine!"

Grandfather's generation believed that names were potent, significant. In Old China, the act of naming a First Son, a First Grandson, involved the advice of numerologists and astrologers, fortune tellers divining appropriate meanings and symbols. The "right" name assigned to the "right" child is an invocation against bad fortune. Grandfather's naming me, following tradition, could not have been a shallow or pointless act. But I wonder if the old man had reflected upon his own failed dreams in naming me, or if he had just looked to his heart and simply knew: *this name and no other.*

On my desk, I have a family photograph from 1939, taken in Chinatown's Yucho Chow Photo Studio, shortly after the naming ceremony.

The chubby three-month-old baby propped cozily against his mother is Choy Way Sun, soon to be called by his English nickname, "Sonny," because his parents had been fond of Al Jolson's rendition of "Sonny Boy," and because, as a child, he had a sunny disposition.

Looking beautiful, Lilly Choy (also Nellie Hop Wah), her makeup fresh, is holding her son securely on her lap.

Toy Choy (also Yip Doy Choy), stands proudly behind his wife and his new son, their only child. In the tradition of Old China—for the child's long life and for his good fortune—a jade bracelet encircles the tiny wrist.

"You remember that house in the three-hundred block Keefer?" Fifth Aunty asked.

"Yes," I said. I remembered. "The house with the ghost."

After three years of living on the third floor of the Kam Yen Jan Chinese sausage factory, in overcrowded rooming-house conditions, Mother had demanded of Father that we rent a house all to ourselves. I was getting to be a handful, banging my toys in the hallway and always crying for attention. When I had just turned three, we moved into the narrow pine house on Keefer Street that was also home to a sort of ghost.

Years later, Mother told me Father took that house because it was so cheap. No one else wanted to live in it. Mother was desperate to escape the confines of the sausage factory, desperate to live in her own home. Ghost or not, Father went to the bank and showed the manager his seasonal-work contract with the Canadian Pacific Railway. He came home with the rent deposit and told Mother to start packing. He might even have said, "Beggars can't be choosers."

We left our cramped quarters at 223 Keefer Street and moved into my parents' first house, a block east of the sausage factory. Father and Mother had finished the packing, and Third Uncle had helped us settle in. Mother's adopted sister, whom I called *Dai Yee, Great Aunty*, helped, too. Dai Yee and Mother had met on the ship coming over and swore they would take care of each other in Gold Mountain, like sisters. Dai Yee always stiffened her face and narrowed her eyes at any of the misbehaving children at the sausage factory, and scared us straight. Her daughter, Lena, was my favourite sitter, but I always had to behave when her stern-faced mother showed up. Dai Yee was two years older than my mother; she had a strong voice and a tough attitude, and her eyes never let you forget that.

Everyone worked. Unpacking straw-filled boxes of dishes. Organizing stacks of shoeboxes stuffed with documents and letters. Emptying two steamer trunks

467

and three suitcases of camphor-scented clothes. Washing floors and walls. My job, Father said, was to keep out of the way, and I mostly did. Dai Yee would just look at me, start narrowing, and I'd immediately grab my tin trucks and run them through a wall of alphabet blocks and over my lead soldiers.

Third Uncle and the sausage factory's supervisor, Jim Lee, borrowed a delivery truck from the factory and helped Father transport our few pieces of furniture. Mother and Dai Yee set up my second-hand foldaway child's cot. Dai Yee had heard the rumours about the ghost, and she was not too happy about the house, but Father told her not to worry. Father went away to do a three-week shift for the CPR, leaving Mother to unpack, and to clean up the mess. I had new rooms to explore.

Our house was the second in a tight row of detached old two-storey houses on Keefer Street, just a few blocks east from the heart of Chinatown. They all had small alcove porches jutting out at varying angles, and matching second-storey windows topped by pitched cedar-shingled roofs. Gingerbread trim sheltered nesting birds and gnawing grey squirrels. Each house had its own rickety wooden steps leading from the sidewalk to the porch and, whenever it rained, slippery snail-silvered lines trailed across the planks.

Before my father ended his shore leave, my parents must have discussed how secure Mother might feel, living in a house for three or five weeks alone with a three-year-old, and with a ghost.

During the war years, Chinatown women left alone commonly feared strangers appearing at their front doors, especially at night. Stories were told of wayward drunks slamming themselves against closed doors, clever hoodlums picking flimsy locks, immigration officials showing up unannounced. One could never be too cautious.

Our front door had one key lock; one inside chain lock; and two bolts, one ten inches from the top of the door and the other six inches from the bottom. Mother sometimes used to let me play a game with her at bedtime: *On your mark, get set ...* and on my shout of *GO!* we would race to lock the door. She raised her arm high to pull the top bolt and I yanked shut the bottom one. She always let me win by seconds.

If a stranger knocked, and if Mother felt insecure about peering through the glass panel in the front door, she would very quietly take me upstairs with her and, together, we would look down to see who was knocking. We rarely were able to see any faces.

"Is that Third Uncle's hat?" she would ask me.

If we couldn't recognize the caller, Mother would kneel and hold me close to her and whisper, "*Shhhhh*, no noise." And I understood from the intensity of her grip that I should keep as still as possible, to outwit the stranger with silence.

Slim notebook in hand, a stranger might ask too many questions. Immigration officials chasing *gai-gee yung, false-paper citizens*, or city health inspectors hunting TB cases might come knocking at our door. Mother's responses to English speakers were limited to "Thank you," "No, thank you," "Yes," "No," or a blank fixed smile if the English words came too quickly at her.

Because of the war, the door's single six-by-ten-inch panel of glass was blocked by a thick curtain. Blackout flats, as well as curtains and blankets, darkened all the front windows. The demons in the sky could drop their bombs on Vancouver if they saw our lights. That was why, Father told me, the Japanese people were moved away from *Hahm-sui-fauh, Salt Water City*, the Chinese name for Vancouver.

Mother went to great trouble to protect the city. A length of heavy towelling was draped over the mail slot, to prevent someone peering through the opening and to keep the light from betraying us to the enemy. I remember a few evenings when the air-raid sirens sang out and Mother rushed me into the kitchen to stand with her by the back door.

"Here," she said. "We can get out fast."

She must have assumed that, if the enemy landed, they would come through the front door. Or that bombs falling from the sky would be aimed at the road, blasting through our parlour or front bedrooms, like the torn fronts of huge buildings in England shown on the newsreels.

When the sirens screamed, Mother lit a candle and shut off all the lights, slumping into a chair in the dim, stove-lit kitchen to sit and wait. She rubbed my ears, which I suppose was intended to distract me from sensing her fear, but it just hurt. Once I was awakened from a nap, and Mother, holding me tightly against her warmth, was shaking the ashes at the bottom of the stove. She lifted me up and told me not to worry. All the blackout curtains, draped blankets, and black-papered flats, were on our windows, even the street lights were out—the dark, a shield against sudden death.

I was not scared. Using an iron handle, Mother hooked the round fitting on the stove-top and set it aside so I could see the fire. Flickering flames from the burning sawdust tinted the kitchen walls with an orange-yellow glow. The fire snapped and crackled. Everything felt dreamlike until Mother began a singsong refrain——*Hm-mo pah, hm-mo pah ... No worry, no worry*—absentmindedly rubbing my ears. I wailed.

After the first series of blackout nights, the fear that enemy planes all the way from Japan would bomb Vancouver dissipated and we were allowed to take the blackout frames down. Not sure whom to trust, having seen too many newsreels of the bombing of Shanghai and Nanking, Mother kept the flats standing beside every window. After a Japanese submarine shelled Estevan Point on June 22, 1942, rumours flared around Chinatown: the Japanese were ready to land at any minute.

The blackout curtains went up again. Only when Father was home, or when we had visitors, did Mother let in the daylight. Otherwise, the front of the house was in a constant gloom.

In our new house, I would dream of the Cantonese opera and wake Mother up with my singing, or I would dream of the trick-playing Monkey and the shape-changing Fox from the ghost stories Great Aunty used to tell me at the Kam Yen Jan factory. The creature-ghosts made me kick my feet. But, because of Father, I was not too afraid of ghosts.

470

In Old China, when Father was a thirteen-year-old student in the village district of Sunwui, a fortune teller had told him he had a special gift: malevolent spirits were afraid of him. The fortune teller, a village crone, had observed wild dogs running away from him. And wild dogs, as everyone knew, were often the manifestation of evil spirits.

Though Father meant the circling, growling dogs no harm, as he hurried to school he would stop and look at them directly, staring each one down.

"The dogs would scatter," Father told me, still astonished, "their tails between their legs."

Few men were born with a *chee*, an *aura*, like this.

"Nothing to be afraid about," Father assured Mother, as he also assured Great Aunty when he told her this story. Great Aunty repeated it twice to me, and whenever I grew too frightened of her ghost stories, she would say, "No worry." Then with a laugh and a roll of her narrow eyes: "You like your father. Demons scare of you."

Throughout Vancouver at night during the war years, the streetcars and other vehicles had their headlights taped up, so that only a slit of light shone through. No one was allowed to drive faster than fifteen miles an hour. Glowing slit-eyes prowled city streets like unknown creatures, tail lights like the red eyes of tigers.

In the distance, snake-long trains rumbled; foghorns wailed; a patrolman sometimes blew his whistle sharply. Gradually, silence wrapped around our tiny house. I slept, and no bombs fell.

But a ghost came.

The rooms of that house I recall most vividly were the small front parlour, and the smaller dining room, with its shelved rows of wedding-gift silver, ornamental china, and English serving plates ranked according to size. On a middle shelf, collectable British bone-china teacups sat in a row. Some of the cups, with their delicate winglike handles, were gifts celebrating Mother's marriage to Father, and a half-dozen or so came from birthdays and anniversaries. Many of them came from the first-class store called Birks, on Granville. Whenever Chinatown ladies saw the familiar blue box from that store, their eyes would light up.

Neatly dividing this glittering collection of Mother's English-style teacups in two was my oversized clay piggy bank, a gift from Aunty Freda. I had insisted Piggy share the same space with Mother's prized Royal Doulton porcelain cups and saucers and, after some discussion, there it sat, a grinning pink pig among the flowery Staffordshire and Crown Derby cups. At night, as I waited for sleep, I imagined it sauntered about the lavish pasture of delicate Spode and Minton florals. Piggy, after all, had a hand-painted flower on each pink flank. It belonged.

Father always gave me some of his coins and lifted me up so that I could drop money into Piggy.

"Be careful," Father would say. "Don't knock over Mother's teacups."

The English teacups glittered in the morning light, as fragile as butterflies. I'd take Father's hand and we'd go down the hallway, then turn and climb the stairs.

As he pushed open a second-floor window, Father's eyes shone with satisfaction at the sight of similar houses built on higher ground across the street.

"Good air," he said.

Standing beside him, I took a deep breath. Father stood so assertively, looked so boldly, that I imagined yelping four-legged demons darting away.

One day, Dai Yee brought us a bag of red apples, three oranges, and a rare pomegranate. "Not to worry," she said. "Eat, eat, eat." When she saw Piggy on the shelf among Mother's collection of English teacups, she gave me three nickels and lifted me up to feed him.

"Careful," Mother said, watching my fist wavering over her prized collection.

"Not to worry," Dai Yee said. "Bless the house with good fortune, Sonny."

I slipped the nickels into Piggy.

"Don't worry?" Mother said. "I thought I heard something last night."

Dai Yee lost her stern look.

"What do you mean, Lilly?"

"At the front door," Mother said.

Dai Yee raised an eyebrow. Mother looked at my big ears and said nothing more.

There was a small kitchen in the back of the house. Against one wall, a great iron-black stove sat on thick-clawed legs. It had two rings of gas jets on one end, and, on the other, widely separated by a lampblack top and a steel-edged oven door, a sluggish sawdust feeder that burped loudly when you banged it during cold days. A pot of heated water always sat on the sawdust-burning side of the stove. Whenever Mother readied to turn on one of the gas elements, her mouth tight with tension, I always told her to wait. I liked to see the tiny blue pilot flame *poof* into a halo of fire and to watch Mother jump back.

But how utterly small that first house was!

To my three-year-old eyes, accustomed to exploring the long hallways and endless rooms of Kam Yen Jan, I suspect everything seemed lacking in that first house.

Shortly after we moved to that Keefer Street house, Mother took me to a family celebration held in the Wing Sang Block, a three-storey, bay-windowed building fronting on Pender Street that belonged to one of the richest merchant families in Chinatown. It must have been a truly festive occasion, an anniversary of sorts, for almost all the Chinatown families were invited to attend. There were tables and tables of food, and colourful paper chains and lanterns hanging over everything. Incense was burned, and the children, me included, got red packages of lucky money.

The man who built the Wing Sang Block, Yip Ch'un Tien, or Yip Sang, was a successful, shrewd, and obviously astute and extraordinary man. Yip Sang held together a complex of business ventures and, with amazing harmony, supported three wives in Vancouver, his first wife having died in China. He eventually fathered an official count of twenty-three children—nineteen sons and four daughters. These local-born sons and daughters eventually married, and many of them lived in the building with their children, some of whom were around my age.

The older children played games that imitated our working parents, games like Laundry Man, Cook, or Waiter. They played Grocery Store or Herbal Store, or they pretended to be behind the ornate iron-grilled counter, like the clerks at Wing Sang, and made us younger children line up to buy steamship or railway tickets, or pick up our mail or send remittances back to China.

In one of the many Wing Sang family rooms, Mother sat at a table to gossip and play mah-jong with the Yip women she knew, while I was merrily tempted away by a trio of their older daughters to play House with them. In exchange for being their play child, I got to explore what seemed to be an emperor's palace of countless rooms. One "room" was actually an auditorium/gymnasium. From there, the three older girls, myself, and one other dawdling boy roamed through long hallways, storage areas piled high with sealed trunks and hemp-tied boxes smelling of dried herbs, sacks of rice and silvered tins with colourful labels. Turning ill-lit corners and heading down deeper hallways, we eventually found a door that opened into a mysterious room with long windows. Panes of glass portioned off rooftops and bright sky. A strong arm gathered me up and lifted me so I could see. I gripped a thin wooden ledge, leaned way out, and glimpsed how high the open window stood above Pender Street. At first, I leaned heavily against the slim body that prevented me from falling away and dropping into the street. I caught my breath and giggled with wide-eyed wonder.

473

"Let go," the girl said to me. "I've got you." My fingers detached from the ledge and my hands flew skyward. I had never been up so high or felt so precarious.

Arms out, I gazed across at the windows of smaller buildings, watched a few men looking back to wave at me. I could see the whole length of Chinatown stretching east, towards Main Street, a vista dotted with straw hats and vegetable wagons, open stalls, and rows and rows of awnings billowing in the breeze like red and green sails.

In the distance were merchant ships docked like toys in blue slices of False Creek. Above Chinatown, the sky was streaked with a green and yellow chemical smog from the refineries. Seagulls launched upon unseen currents of wind and floated above us, their beaks pointing left, then right, wings outstretched. If only I could fly!

Suddenly, the Yip girl jerked me forward as if she were going to toss me out the window. I burst into tears.

"Oh, don't be a crybaby," she said, pulling me down from the window and making it clear that our fun was over.

Without a second's thought, I abruptly lifted my foot, kicked her, and sprinted away. I could not fly, but I giggled with the freedom of a child. There was nothing to be afraid of, except being called a crybaby.

I was caught, of course, by a big boy coming down the stairs who lifted me up, laughed, and turned me over to my chaperone.

"Don't be such a brat," she said, limping. I could sense she had decided to treat me with some caution. After all, I might squeal on her.

"Do you want to see more?" She took the hand of the other little boy.

"Yes," I said. "Everything."

We were friends again.

At Wing Sang, there were numerous front, side, and back staircases to climb, and multiple household kitchens to visit for what seemed like endless treats. Some pantries were small enough to contain only a hot plate and cupboards; others were much larger than our own kitchen: the one built for the preparation of banquets was at least ten times the size of our own tiny scullery. There were bedrooms of every size and condition; what I assumed were playrooms, but probably were storage areas, filled with mysterious boxes smelling of camphor, and oily machinery that had moving arms, iron chains with hooks, and iron wheels; and rooms with padded doors I was told were forbidden for children to enter. From some rooms came the sound of a Victrola playing big-band music. A king and queen lived here, I thought.

474

A pleasant mixed scent of damp wood, pungent herbs, ointments, and jasmine incense drifted after us as we walked from room to room. There were motes of dust floating in the rays of sunlight that crossed our path. We stopped to rest in one of the smaller family rooms.

"I live here," the boy holding the Yip girl's hand said to me.

It was my first taste of envy. A little boy just like me lived in this wonderful maze of rooms, and could dash about adventurously and see the world from high above Pender Street, higher even than our second-floor window. I wanted to live in countless rooms and roam miles of hallways and staircases—in a building like Wing Sang.

"You live here?" I said to the boy, incredulous. When he nodded so vigorously, the paper lanterns blinking triumphantly over his head suddenly made me want to cry. Instead, I punched him.

Mother took me away, dragging me down long flights of steps while I tried to get away. I would never forget Wing Sang.

Visiting Wing Sang had seeded me with dissatisfaction, but all that changed when I learned why our house had stood empty for so long before we moved in, with no one willing to rent it. I overheard Mother telling Dai Yee our house had a ghost.

"Does Wing Sang have any ghosts?" I asked.

Dai Yee narrowed her eyes and said, "Of course, plenty of ghosts in Wing Sang!" and Mother said, "Chulip Sim saw one in the storage room in the basement!"

I never quite longed to live in Wing Sang again. If our tiny house held a single ghost, a possible demon ghost, how many more must haunt that vast building?

I could have boasted of "our" ghost to the little boy I'd met at Wing Sang, but I was too scared and perplexed to dwell on the mysteries of the unseen world. And, really, no one in their right mind, especially not a child of Chinatown, would dare to talk to just anyone about seeing ghosts. That was for adults. When they told stories and plunged us into those other worlds of talking wolves and form-changing foxes, all of the children listened. Watched. Paid attention.

It wasn't until many years later—when I was fifteen and living in Belleville, Ontario, and had just watched a movie about a haunted house—that I even considered asking Mother about our Keefer Street ghost.

What happened between Father and Mother—and the tumbling, wall-shaking crashing that resulted—made us the talk of our neighbours.

Will Toy and Lilly Choy separate?

What will happen to their boy, Sonny?

475

The neighbours might have blamed the incident on Mother's decision to stay out late playing mah-jong that night, or on Father's bad temper and his return from work a day early. These were reasonable interpretations, and wholly inadequate for me when I was a child. Even today, I can't imagine there was not a more significant cause, one that ran deeper than the mundane facts.

The house, after all, had an actual wraith, a ghost, that I could clearly hold culpable. I would have regarded sombre explanations such as "Your parents weren't getting along" or "Mother and Father had a misunderstanding" as a mockery of my universe. To me, our first big family disturbance was as startling as a typhoon or a volcanic eruption—calamitous, but a natural disaster, like any other.

Nearing my fifth birthday, I was already deeply influenced by Chinatown stories of ghosts and hauntings. I took it for granted that the Keefer house had a *kwei*, a *ghost*, that had provoked Father to turn into a demon.

In Chinatown, there were at least two categories of ghosts. The Chinese who died in Vancouver became harmless, familiar ghosts and belonged to the first category.

"Ghosts everywhere," Fifth Aunty told me. "All the time ghosts. Not to worry."

Generally, Dai Yee and Third Uncle told me these spirits were "lost China people."

"Why don't they go away?"

"They wait," Third Uncle explained, "for their bones to be ship back home."

"Home," of course, was always a village or city in Old China, the place where you were raised, where they still wanted you, even dead; where you belonged. For ever.

"Canada no want you," Dai Yee said, matter-of-factly, remembering both her and Mother's welcome-to-Canada three-week confinement together in the "Pig House" customs building in Victoria.

"Canada say, 'Go home, chinky Chinaman!'" Mother tapped my head, the better for me to remember. "You worry about being Chinese."

Dai Yee agreed with Mother. "*Gay-gai quaw kwei-ah?*" Dai Yee said. "*Why worry about ghosts?*"

But the two women furrowed their brows, and I guessed why they worried. Dai Yee and Mother both knew that our Keefer Street house was possessed. Our house had a *bak kwei*, a ghost from the second category—a *white man's ghost*, an apparition full of spiteful trickery.

476

The *bak kwei* in our house made its appearance only when Father wasn't home.

Years later, whenever Mother's mind grew hungry for the past, she would say, "Remember that ghost?"

And if I were being tolerant about such superstitious nonsense—for I had grown up by then and supposed every ghost story had a logical explanation—I would answer, "I remember that loud knocking downstairs."

With a sigh, Mother would begin: "Yes, you were only four then."

I never forgot. That banging downstairs. It was frantic. We agreed about that.

"Mommy?" I muttered, half-awake. "What's that?"

"*Shhhhhhhhh ...*"

Cushioned by darkness, Mother lifted me up and we eased over to the window ledge, my thin arms clutched about her neck. We both peered through the sheer curtains, studying the glimmer of moonlight that touched the alcove of our porch. There was no one there.

No one.

I clung even tighter as Mother bent down to see if whoever had been knocking might have stood aside. My head bumped the glass. Nothing.

Pushing aside another inch of window shade, Mother lifted up a bit of curtain. We looked again.

"Do you see anyone?" she whispered. Floorboards. Nothing more. Wooden planks and the moonlit metal grin of our mail slot. I rubbed my eyes and began to sniffle. When the doleful banging started again, Mother said, "It's just the wind."

But on all the nights that the banging occurred, there was barely any wind. Sometimes a draught, barely lifting the edges of the curtains. But no wind—at least not that either of us could recall.

When I was in my twenties, I decided this incident with Mother had a logical explanation. Vancouver is located on a fault line. The earth moves. The noise was the house settling, the foundation shifting.

"Think what you like," Mother said, unable or unwilling to let go of the *bak kwei*.

Years before we moved in, a labourer had been walking home from a shift late at night. Unknown to him, a robber with a knife had been following him. The man jumped the workman. A struggle followed. The knife plunged deeply— once ... twice. Bleeding profusely, the wounded man managed to struggle up the staircase at our house on Keefer, to the front door, and banged, *banged* for help. No one would open the door, and he died.

"Was there a newspaper report?" I asked.

Mother grew impatient. I was old enough to be dogged about evidence. Mother was dismissive. We were the fifth tenants in three years who reported to the landlord these strange night bangings. Why was I so thick-headed? Was I still missing the point?

"It was a white man. That's all anyone ever said."

A white man. What else was there to know? Dai Yee had told her that a white man's ghost meant a curse.

"The Wongs next door said it was the *bak kwei* making all that noise," Mother said. "Even they heard the banging sometimes."

I turned the pages of *Time*. Everyday facts. Everyday reality. People were sometimes knifed in city streets. Often there were earth tremors.

"Have it your way." Mother sighed. "It was the house."

Of course, I knew when I was four it was not the foundation or the earth shifting. If I had not grown up, I would have agreed with Mother: it was the *bak kwei*.

477

"I heard it again last night," Mother reported to Mrs. Chew, our neighbour across the street.

"Yes, yes," Mrs. Chew said, nodding. "But why worry? No harm came to you or Sonny. The Wongs told me they heard something, too."

When she told Father, he laughed contentedly. "You see," he said. "Nothing to worry about. Mrs. Chew says so, too."

"This time it woke Sonny," Mother said. "I don't like being by myself in this house."

"Then go out. You stay home too much."

As usual, Father and Mother stopped talking when I began to pay attention.

When Father suggested Mother "go out," he meant that she should mix more with her new friends, go out for an hour for afternoon tea or perhaps an early-evening visit. Vancouver was not like Victoria, the home of Grandfather and Grandmother and their family, where all the married Chinese women, often pregnant, locked themselves away.

Mother quickly discovered a coterie of women who loved to gossip and, even more, to play mah-jong. Mother began to socialize with the wife of her boss at Kam Yen Jan, who was soon as good a friend as Dai Yee. Mrs. David Lee, Leong Sim as she was called, looked as if she could be Mother's sister.

"Take some time for yourself," Leong Sim said, a mother of four and pregnant again. "I always go out whenever I can. Take in a few rounds of mah-jong. Bring Sonny along."

Our friendship with the Lee family was the result of the two women's love of mah-jong. During those social evenings, Garson, two years younger than me, came along with his mother, and I with mine. As we grew older, Garson and I ended up playing together with the other children, rough-housing behind the Pender Street alleyway apartments where the ladies often gathered. Leong Sim took to calling me Garson's *dai goh, big brother,* whenever we played together. If it was still daylight, Garson and I, and several other children, ran up and down Chinatown's streets, playing hide-and-seek, or we played kick-the-can at the False Creek vacant lot, our unofficial playground beneath the huge six-storey tank that ominously proclaimed, in ten-foot letters: GAS THE MODERN FUEL. We jumped over rainbow-streaked oily puddles, breathed into our lungs the toxic smells of nearby refineries, and ran around piles of rusty metal junk. As Garson's *dai goh,* I was to keep an eye on him, while much older kids, in fact, watched over both of us.

If Mother wanted to gamble longer, I would go home by taxi with Leong Sim and Garson, and stay overnight at the Lees'. When we moved just one block east of them, Mother and Leong Sim became best friends, and I was a constant visitor, sharing meals with Garson's household. Mother never thought there was anything wrong with her taking me out gambling. Her friends, including Leong Sim, Fifth Aunty, and Dai Yee, who brought along her son, King, did not seem to mind taking me home with them. She could stay out late and have a break from me as well. It made perfect sense.

Mother took to mah-jong and her mah-jong friends as happily as they took to her. Whenever Father was away, and only then, I was bundled up with every necessity, in case I went home with one of her friends, and Mother and I journeyed by taxi out for our long nights. The games were held at different houses, each family taking a turn at hosting. Leong Sim and the other women openly breastfed their youngest while briskly playing their game. There were also large curved woven baskets where sleepy babies might be rocked with one foot while their mothers went on clicking the game tiles into play. A few of the women also brought older children, counting on them to fall asleep on couches, divans, rocking chairs, and small mattresses placed on the floor. Soon, Mother hardly worried about me. I played with whoever was there, while she gambled and gossiped and ate the midnight meal with her friends. Mother fitted in perfectly. I did, too. I had all the playmates I wanted, and their toys to share. I fought sleep, but never succeeded in staying awake till the end of the mah-jong parties. In bright sunlight, I would struggle awake, already snuggled in my foldaway cot, staring up at our ceiling.

479

Mother grew to love the feel of the inch-high, ivory-and-bone mah-jong tiles, the sensual *click* of the played pieces, the quick exchange of cash and chatter at the end of every round. She had a knack for the game, whose strategies were as satisfying as those of bridge, and she often won.

"Smart play," someone said as Mother turned over her trumping hand.

"No, no," Mother would quickly respond, afraid to tempt the gods. "Luck. Just luck." And she would tip the hostess with three or four coins from the winner's pot.

Stepping out, at Father's urging, Mother forgot the *bak kwei*, who tended to visit around midnight. A different kind of spirit had distracted her.

Mother adjusted unwillingly to Father's long absences at sea. Each time he returned, she would wait up for him, however late his arrival. When thick fog or storms delayed him, she still waited up.

Mother knew she should be at home whenever Father came back and thought that a reasonable expectation.

But one day Father came home a day too soon. He arrived in the evening, carrying a stack of restaurant treats for Mother and me, and some extras—stale foodstuffs from the ship's pantry that the crew was allowed to buy cheaply or to take for free. Father must have opened the door with his key and shouted up the staircase. Seen the light at the end of the hall, glowing from the kitchen, which Mother always left on to mislead thieves. Shouted again. Listened. He may have assumed we were out for a little while and waited, thinking we would be home within twenty minutes or so. The night being cold, Father may well have turned to the bottle of whisky that sat in the oak cupboard, and poured himself a small glass to sip.

One or two hours dragged by. Mother and I were still not home. Father waited. And drank. And waited, pouring himself another shot.

When Tom's Taxi delivered Mother and me from her gaming place, it was 5 A.M. I could barely stand up as she set me down to reach into her purse for the house key.

480

The front door opened. Looking down the long, narrow hallway, we could see a light on.

Someone was sitting in the dining room. Through sleepy eyes, I recognized Father.

"So you're back," he said. There was a long pause. Then a glass exploded against the wall. The smell of alcohol filled the air.

"*You're drunk!*" Mother shouted.

A chair toppled over and Father staggered down the long hallway towards us. Mother slammed the front door shut, turned, and ducked up the stairs, yanking me along. In seconds we were in the bedroom.

From the time when our house was home to roomers, there was a key lock on the bedroom door, and a slot lock above and below. In the seconds before Father reached the door, Mother had turned the brass knob, and pushed the two bolts shut. Father stepped back, then threw his weight against the door.

"Stop it! Stop it!" Mother cried out.

The voice of a demon howled back. Mother put her hands over my ears. She held me tightly, waiting for the door to collapse.

"*Damn you!*" Father shouted. "*Damn you!*"

I imagined a red-faced, horned creature forcing its voice through Father's mouth. I saw the muscles of a demon tearing through Father's legs and arms. The battering lasted for several minutes, and then there was silence.

"Not to worry," Mother said, looking at me sitting on the big bed, frightened and amazed. She slumped down beside me, as if she were being struck, and I imagined the door buckling and bending, like cartoon doors. But it held.

Father spewed out more expletives. Curses. Obscenities. Demon oaths. Mother rubbed my ears.

The banging stopped. We heard his breathing, a sound like a beast foaming, clawing, snorting. Then all was quiet, but for my crying. Perhaps Father heard this, and my sobs stopped him from going further.

We heard him stomping down the stairs. Mother rocked me, and we waited. We heard Father stumbling back into the dining room. Again, silence.

"You see," Mother said, "everything's fine—"

And then a volley of crashing reached our ears.

The unmistakable sound of smashing plates and exploding glass rose from our dining room and began to shake the whole house. The racket lasted at least ten minutes. There were momentary silences when Father stopped to regain his energy, followed by the frenzy of another round of shattering china and glass.

"Not to worry," Mother kept saying to herself, as much as to me. "Not to worry."

Then there was a really long silence. We waited, barely breathing. Father's voice roared up the stairwell, "*Damn you!*"

"He's leaving," Mother said. "He's going to leave."

Father slammed the front door with such force that the glass in our second-storey windows rattled. Mother carried me over to the window. We saw Father's dark figure hurrying away into the night.

"Oh, Death." Mother sighed.

The *bak kwei*, I knew, had tricked Father, had driven him mad. Mother held me against the night. Father took the demon with him.

Exhausted, Mother and I fell asleep, leaning against each other.

Late the next morning, Mother changed into her house clothes, put me in a shirt and itchy pants, and walked me downstairs. When we reached the end of the hallway, she picked me up in her arms. "Look, look at that mess," she said. I looked. Broken glass and china lay everywhere. Mother swallowed, as if she were choking back tears.

481

Mother stepped carefully into the blind-darkened dining room. I put my arms around her neck and looked where she gingerly stepped, her slippered feet pushing aside shattered porcelain and splintered glass. Carefully, she manoeuvred her way to the dining-room window. She lifted the blind all the way up.

Sunlight glittered about us, reflecting off piles of broken plates, knife-edged crystal fragments, and the dented silver tray. The remains of flowered teacups, two bone-china teapots, spouts and gilt handles broken off—everything Mother treasured lay on the floor, cracked or totally demolished. Mother held me securely and neither frowned nor winced. But I could feel her heart hardening against Father.

I looked up from the floor and surveyed the long shelves where the silver serving set, the rows of crystal glasses, the china plates and the flowered teacups once sat. Father must have used his hand to clear off shelf after shelf.

Mother stepped back, and I could see at last the lower shelf where Mother's treasured English cups once sat.

We both saw, round and full—intact—Piggy looking back. Fifth Aunty was right: I had the same *chee* as Father.

"Piggy," Mother said, "buy me some new dishes."

Mother went to the pantry and took out the Quaker Oats to make me breakfast. We could still use the everyday kitchen bowls. She filled a pan with water and turned on the gas ring.

"Call me when the water boils," she said, tying on her apron.

Mother picked up the empty sawdust bucket and walked over to the closet for the broom and a dustpan. When she began sweeping, I knitted my fingers together.

Piggy stood on the shelf unharmed, watching the brisk swing of the broom. The broken pieces of Mother's treasures tumbled together, like madly clicking tiles.

My Father's House

SYLVIA FRASER

The controversial novelist and non-fiction author Sylvia Fraser (b. 1935) aroused great public attention with the 1987 book from which the following passages are taken—*My Father's House: A Memoir of Incest and Healing*. The title tells the outline of the story, but the book was interesting for its technique as well as for its traumatic subject matter. It uses italic for descriptions of the period in which the abuse took place (a period lasting until her teenaged years) and boldface for passages derived through recovered memory (a hotly debated subject ever since); the pieces that are merely descriptive and in the past tense are set in ordinary roman. The horrific upbringing Fraser describes has also found expression in some of her other work, especially *The Book of Strange: A Journey* (1992), a study of the paranormal and its uses, and the novel *The Ancestral Suitcase* (1996). 483 Indeed, her revelations have permitted readers to see some of her earlier work, particularly *The Candy Factory*, a 1975 novel, in a new and different light.

REVELATION
Satan's Child

W hen my father died, he came alive for me. A door had opened, like a hole cut in air. It yawned before me, offering release—from what to where?

Before I could pass through it to wholeness and health, my other self would have to give up her secrets. Was she willing to be dragged from her closet into the klieg lights? Exposure meant the death of her dreams as well as her fears, of the princess as well as the guilty child. It meant dying as a separate personality. As for myself, did I truly wish to open the Pandora's box under my father's bed? How would I feel to discover that the prize, after four decades of tracing clues and solving riddles, was knowledge that my father had sexually abused me? Could

I reconcile myself without bitterness to the amount of my life's energy that had gone into the cover-up of a crime?

Resolving that conflict took another ten years. During that time I lived an increasingly contented life within a network of close friends and wrote four novels, each rife with sexual violence that offended some critics and puzzled me. Where did this harsh impulse come from? I didn't know. Like the thirsty Tantalus floating in water he couldn't drink, I was compelled by an inner vision I couldn't see. From each book I learned something about myself that was of value, but I knew I was writing below my capabilities and that frustrated me.

I also felt drawn to read about, and to experiment with, various psychological disciplines. Through Freudian and Jungian analysis, I learned how to interpret dreams as messages from my unconscious. Through primal and massage therapy, rolfing, bioenergetics, yoga, meditation, I grew more in touch with my body and my emotions. Each discipline raised questions about my real past. Why had I been such an angry child? Why did I hate my father? What was the source of the icy terror I now sensed under that anger and hatred?

484

Unbeknownst to me, I was approaching a time when I would remember. The obsession of a lifetime was drawing to a close. My path of revelation was to be the path of dreams—dreams triggered by physical shock.

I believe many unexpected deaths occur when a person finishes one phase of life and must become a different sort of person in order to continue. The phoenix goes down into the fire with the best intention of rising, then falters on the upswing. And so it was with me. At the point of transition, I came close to dying along with my other self.

I have a pain in my womb. It doesn't go away. Two doctors say I must have a hysterectomy. My response is stoical, but I have bad dreams.

I ride the incline up the Mountain. As I fumble for my fare, my purse plummets into dense undergrowth. I scramble barefoot through brambles under the incline, begging everyone I meet: "Have you seen my purse?"

I find a cleft in rock. A voice intones: "This is where the evil comes from." A child's hand reaches out. It's covered in slime and blood.

I check into Women's College Hospital in downtown Toronto one blustery day in February 1983. My operation is scheduled for the next morning. As an orderly wheels me into the corridor, my anesthetist clasps my hand. "Nothing to worry about. We'll be going in soon."

I climb down the perilous passage into the cave. A blond child is curled like a cat around her swollen belly. A demon-monster raped her here many years ago by stuffing a giant white larva down her throat. Now it has lodged in her womb, threatening her life. I fetch a priest. Dressed in white robes and mask, he raises his silver dagger with both hands, then plunges it into the girl's abdomen.

My mind awakens from the anesthetic but my body does not. It refuses to do what I request it to do, what it has always done. Nurses hook it up to machines, which perform its functions, duly recorded by numbers on dials. Nature, it seems, abhors a vacuum. Where once I nursed fibroids the size of a five-month fetus, now I nurture a virulent infection.

Another operation is scheduled and performed. This time I awake in a private room, very weak and still attached to my machines. The body, whose goodwill I once took for granted, still refuses to function. Friends drop by with flowers and kind words. I see them indistinctly. Nurses hover. The dials on my machines still do not say the right things. Another doctor joins the team. I hear talk of a third operation.

Inside the blond girl's womb the priest finds a fetus, half-human, half-animal. He holds it up by one cleft foot. "See Satan's child."

485

Since this blonde girl produced it, she is responsible for it, even though she claims to have been under a powerful spell. A computer photo of the monster-father is released to the press. It is apelike, about three times human size and covered in shaggy fur. Its face is a devil's mask with holes for mouth and eyes. I am present as a reporter. I have an uneasy sense that I've seen this monster before, but how could that be?

The demon-monster lives on a grassy island. I cross the muddy channel, hand over hand, on a rope. It's even uglier than I thought, with scarlet mouth and bright green dangling warts. As I struggle back to the mainland, the monster comes shrieking in lust after me. Close up, he's more like an ordinary ape, but very savage, with vivid blue eyes and slathering razor teeth. He overtakes me when I'm still dangling over muddy water. I scream. The blond girl recalls him to the island, but not before he scrapes me with his filthy coat, leaving his rank smell on me.

Eventually my body does kick in, its function does become normal. The numbers on my machines stabilize, and the machines are removed. I'm dismissed from hospital. Yet, even back in my own bed, my dreaming mind continues its serialized hallucinations.

I am with my mother and sister in a shadowy garden in the woods. Snakes, the exact shade of the barky earth, lurk everywhere, and sometimes they strike. A huge, oily, black serpent menaces me from a tree.

The garden opens onto a beach. As I stare at an imprint in the sand, a frightening thought strikes me. "Imagine if this mark and the one a mile away are part of the same footprint. Imagine how big the monster that left it would have to be!" And that is how it turns out. An enormous black thing lurches up up up up up up out of a rocky passageway until it is the height of a tall building. It is smooth and rubbery like the snake on the tree, but in the shape of a hulking black man. Does it have a face? It's too dark to tell.

I awaken overwhelmed by the size of this unknown thing confronting me. Believing myself to be on the murky path to revelation, I conjure up the same black snake man before falling asleep the next night. I ask myself: what does this mean? What am I afraid of?

The black shape transforms into a castle, highly polished and carved out of a single piece of ebony, like a chess piece. It is without doors or windows—an impenetrable fortress. I have a feeling that something evil happened in this place, or maybe in another place still too dark to see.

On subsequent nights the castle becomes a Victorian house—Other Grandmother's house.

Aunt Estelle sits on the porch, her waist strung with chains and padlocks, guarding the door. She looks like the black queen, except her blind eye has been plucked from her forehead, leaving a nasty hole. The dead carcasses of her four monkeys lie strewn at her feet—see-no-evil, hear-no-evil, speak-no-evil, and the fourth with mutilated genitals.

I am a child of about eight. I go around and around the house with a flashlight looking for an opening. Though everything seems tightly boarded, I know I'll be able to sneak in through the cellar. In some way I already understand what is going to happen, but I must take this journey anyway. This house is just a starting place. I'm anxious to begin.

My dreams intensify, grow more specific.

I am outside my father's house. A lawn sign reads: "Home Truths." A man perches on the porch rail, dressed in whiteface, top hat, and tails. There's something tricky about this man, like the joker in a deck of cards. Beckoning me onto the porch, he says: "When people are blind, they have the death smell."

"What do you mean?"

"A blind person knows when someone is going to die. They can smell it. It's the death smell."

"Maybe that's because a blind person's other senses become stronger."

"Don't play stupid. Blind persons aren't those who can't see, but those who can't be seen. Like duck hunters, they duck behind a blind." He laughs, revealing pointy teeth.

"Someone who is hiding behind a blind is going to die, and someone who is blind will see. They are one and the same. YOU will see."

By now I have advanced onto the porch of my father's house. The door is ajar, the Joker is beckoning me through, but I am afraid. I know all the electrical wires have been cut, the phone has been disconnected, and the stove yanked from the wall. No communication exists between my father's house and the outside world.

I awake with a heavy sense of impending doom. I can't shake the feeling that I, or someone close to me, is about to die. Throughout the day, my stomach seizes every time the phone rings, as if I were anticipating bad news.

After a week in which I sleep heavily with no recall, I again awaken in the grip of a terror that doesn't dissipate. Again I have had a compelling dream about death, which I scramble to remember. All I know for sure is that I am repeating with great urgency: "THE PRINCESS WHO IS A PISCES IS TO BE KILLED." Tossing between consciousness and sleep, I piece together the rest of the dream as best I can.

I'm not exactly a child, but neither am I an adult. I have to break the news of the princess's death to both my parents, but especially to my mother. I shout my message over and over, not only to convince my parents but also to awaken myself so I'll hear it too. Finally I get the message across to my father. He ushers me in to my mother as if to say, "I think you'd better listen to this." Both my parents are very grave. I absolutely and completely have their attention about something I want to say more than anything before in my life. I shout: "THE PRINCESS WHO IS A PISCES IS TO BE KILLED."

487

And that is when I awaken, lying on my back with my hands clasped over my midriff as if on a bier. My breathing is sharp and shallow, and I'm crying tears of relief at finally having been understood. I sense something real and important has happened that goes beyond any dream. A song from *The Wizard of Oz* bubbles through my mind: "Ding dong, the witch is dead ... the wicked witch is dead."

I have one more dream that seems connected by emotion, though not by imagery, to the rest:

My mother is setting a table in the basement. She directs me to a seat beside my father where the tablecloth is stained with broken eggs. I break a goblet. When I try to hide it, I find a shelf of broken goblets with sharp V clefts, all crudely mended.

After recording this, I scrawl a footnote. "The worst part about this dream with its obvious sexual imagery is the sickening way it makes me feel—nauseated, right down into my gut." A second even shakier footnote: "I seem to be on the verge of remembering something sexual having to do with my father."

I now suspected I'd forgotten much that was vital about my earliest years. I also suspected something terribly wrong might have taken place, but I couldn't leap from suspicion to accusation, even in my own mind. I was never going to believe anything I dreamed to have literal truth, no matter how persuasive. *My insight and intuition could only prepare me to remember. They were my detectives who could uncover clues, but who couldn't deliver a confession. That had to come from my other self.* Yet, in getting rid of the gnarled tissue in my womb, I couldn't shake the disconcerting belief that I had aborted Satan's child.

The Joker

The memories of my other self are difficult to recapture because they are so fragmentary. Even in my father's house she remained hidden in her closet for months, even years, till daddy again beckoned her out. Her separate life was largely confined to a single room with a window that might suggest the season and time of day, but rarely the year or even her age. The deeds that involved only her were confusing, repetitive, shameful, and mysterious—she had much to fear. Like a small child playing hide-and-seek, she often tried to conceal herself by closing her eyes so that visual memories were sometimes not recorded.

488

For more than forty years the memories of my other self lay deeply buried in jagged pieces inside me—smashed hieroglyphic tablets from another time and another place. When finally I began excavation, I brought these pieces to the surface in random order, to be fitted into patterns and dated. However, the story of my other self—as I came to know it—started in a blaze of discovery that April afternoon in 1983 when I first learned of her existence. The setting was banal, the circumstances unlikely for the revelation of dark secrets, but the time had come. I was ready.

Tonya and Arlene drive from Hamilton to shop for furniture for Arlene's new house. We lunch at the Courtyard, a glass-roofed restaurant in midtown Toronto. Still convalescing from my hysterectomy, still more at home in the world of dreams than in the real world, my mind drifts lazily in and out of the conversation—about Tonya's new job, about Arlene's new house.

"Naturally Babs is heartsick but she's always been a survivor."

Their hushed tone catches my attention. "What's wrong with Babs?"

They look at me in surprise. "About Joker—uh, Gerald. Haven't you heard?"

"About 'The Nashery'? Has it been cancelled?"

"Jeez, no. Sorry, I thought you knew."

"It's so ghastly everybody's just sick about it."

"Gerald tried to sexually molest Babs's daughter. She's still not sure how far he went. The kid was hysterical. Babs didn't believe it at first but she confronted him and he broke down."

Let's take the part where the child is sexually assaulted by the breadman. Frankly, I don't believe for one minute that—

Feeling a snub-nosed bullet explode in my chest, I pick up a dinner knife with my left hand and stab the table. "I want to kill that bastard!" Dropping the knife, I apologize in the language of the eighties. "I guess I'm overreacting."

"No, I feel the same."

"Everybody does."

My chest continues to explode as the conversation flows around me.

For such a sexual assault to take place, we must look to the conduct of the child. Some little girls can be seductive at an early age.

I get up from the table, almost upsetting my water glass. "Excuse me."

Did such an incident ever happen to you?

No, I wouldn't know how to write about a child as emotionally damaged as that.

"What's the matter?" asks Arlene. "You look terrible."

I try to protest, but hysteria in my chest leaves me helpless and humiliated. Joker is breathing deeply, almost heaving. His once-florid complexion is now so pasty he looks cadaverous.

"Where are you going?"

My lips expand in a beatific smile. "I'm going crazy."

I walk towards the restaurant door. Tonya blocks my path. "What's wrong?"

"I think my father raped me."

"Is that supposed to be a joke?"

"I didn't know what I was going to say till I heard myself. Now I think it's true."

"Don't go. Let's talk."

"I can't. I have to go home."

"We'll walk with you."

"No. I have to be alone."

I walk out of the restaurant in a state of heightened consciousness, seeing the sky more luminous than ever before, the buildings a dazzling white, the people

489

cut out of glass and edged in light, feeling the sidewalk slide in a carpet of hysteria under my feet ... I think my father raped me.

Inside my apartment, I throw down my keys, lie on my bed, close my eyes, fold my hands, *the princess on her bier* ... waiting. Spasms pass through me, powerful, involuntary—my pelvis contracts leaving my legs limp. My shoulders scrunch up to my ears, my arms press against my sides with the wrists flung out like chicken wings, my head bends back so far I fear my neck will snap, my jaws open wider than possible and I start to gag and sob, unable to close my mouth— lockjaw in reverse. These spasms do not feel random. They are the convulsions of a child being raped through the mouth.

I am sobbing, my lips pressed in a downward bow like a child refusing food. I am trying to shriek NO! but without daring to open my mouth for that is the new organ of assault. My father's house is empty so what does it matter if I scream? For all my protests I'm afraid to strike my daddy with my fists. I'm still afraid of my daddy. I'm still afraid daddy daddy daddy won't love me love me love me. My arms are glued to my sides as he forces me back against his bed so that my knees buckle. The edge of the bed cuts into me. My daddy is pressing his belly against me. I can't breathe. My daddy is forcing his wet-ums into my mouth. I gag. I'm smothering. Help me! I scrunch my eyes so I can't see. My daddy is pulling my body over him like mommy pulls a holey sock over a darning egg. Filthy filthy don't ever let me catch you shame shame filthy daddy won't love me love me dirty filthy love him hate him fear don't ever let me catch you catch you dirty dirty love hate guilt shame fear fear *fear fear fear fear fear fear* ...

490

I recapture that moment precisely when my helplessness is so bottomless that anything is preferable. Thus, I unscrew my head from my body as if it were the lid of a pickle jar. From then on I would have two selves—the child who knows, with guilty body possessed by daddy, and the child who dares not know any longer, with innocent head attuned to mommy.

The episode ends. My head snaps forward. My jaws close. My arms unglue from my torso. My breathing deepens, opening a cavity in my chest. I return to the present, to my adult self, to my own Toronto bedroom. I return from time travel into my past to an April day in 1983, but I am no longer the same. One startling piece of information has been fed into my head like a microchip into a computer: I KNOW my father raped me. My brain is alive with new memories, with shocking insights. In seconds, my history as I have known it undergoes a drastic shift.

Joker Nash, dressed as a magician in whiteface, top hat, and tails, perches on the railing of my father's house. A lawn sign reads: "Home Truths." Beckoning me onto the porch, he says: "Someone who is hiding behind a blind is going to die, and someone who is blind will see. They are one and the same. YOU will see."

The Joker on my father's porch has at last delivered. And the true villain of the piece? Not the breadman, as I wrote in Pandora, but the breadwinner with the devil's hooked hand.

Deeply shaken, I phone my sister, needing to make contact but not sure what I'll say or even if I'll say. I don't get beyond the hellos before someone else seems to grab the receiver—my tongueless other self, at last finding the words and will to speak: "Daddy daddy daddy daddy daddy daddy daddy raped me."

My sister, herself a mother with a long history of sorting out a day's small tragedies with the dirty socks, struggles to separate the words. "Tell me that again."

Her corroboration—thank God!—is instantaneous. "I always felt something strange was going on." And then, with the same speed by which I made unthinkable connections: "Remember your convulsions? You used to hold your breath and gag and turn blue. I was supposed to run and get mother."

491

Ah yes, my famous fits. The bad child. As my mother later explained: "She would fall on the ground, screaming and choking and vomiting, unable to catch her breath. We were afraid she would swallow her tongue."

In gratitude I assure my sister: "I know I wasn't the only victim. I know you suffered as much as I, but in a different way." The rejected child, rejected from she-knew-not-what.

Now hers is the baby voice, managing through the cryptics of pain to condense her life story into a single sentence. "Yes. That's why I got fat."

I put down the receiver, still assuming that what happened between my father and me had occurred only once. Humane considerations aside, who could risk doing that over and over to a screaming child and expect to get away with it? Yet, the following week is full of other revelations, counterpointing my childhood memories of Sunday drives to the Stoney Creek Dairy for double-scoop cones and report cards with gold stars. I have more convulsions as my body acts out other scenarios, sometimes springing from nightmares, leaving my throat ulcerated and my stomach nauseated. So powerful are these contractions that sometimes I feel as if I were struggling for breath against a slimy lichen clinging to my chest, invoking thoughts of the incubus who, in medieval folklore, raped sleeping women who then gave birth to demons. Similarly, as my bed shakes with the violence of my fits, I recall the child Regan in the movie *The Exorcist*, riding her bed like a brass bronco, in the throes of demon possession. In a more superstitious society, I might have been diagnosed as a child possessed by the devil. What, in fact, I had been possessed by was daddy's forked instrument—the devil in man.

Though I maintain phone contact with my sister during this period of first impact, I choose to be alone. Already two people occupy my bedroom—my adult self and my child self, whom I name the Child Who Knows. Though my restored memories come wrapped in terror, it is a child's terror that I realize I must feel in order to expel. Thus, the adult me comforts the child, holds her hand, pities her suffering, forgives her for her complicity, assuages her guilt. She has carried the burden until I was prepared to remember our joint history without bitterness. I feel only relief, release, compassion, even elation. The mysteries of a lifetime, shadowy deeds dimly suspected, have been clarified.

492

Now I understand my hatred of my father, rooted so far back I couldn't guess the cause. Now I understand my childhood revulsion at sitting on his lap, coupled with a dim recollection that I had once enjoyed it. Now I understand the agitated child's drawings I found in a trunk. Now I understand my fear of pregnancy which, to my child's self, would have seemed like yet another physical invasion—a nine-month rape. Now I understand the obsessional affair in which I relived my relationship with daddy. Now I understand the fear of confession that kept me from my father's deathbed. Now I understand the powerful psychic connection I felt at his death, though I had shunned him for twenty years. Now I understand the exorcised house where I felt not-terror. Now I understand my sexually violent novels. Now I understand my strange yet purposeful dreams and my feeling that I had aborted Satan's child.

I am surprised to discover that I feel no anger towards my father. Little boys are taught to convert fear into rage or bravado. Little girls, to convert anger into fear. I was a hostile little girl, a furious teenager, and a frequently bad-tempered adult. Anger was my salvation, the way I survived in my father's house, but it became my prison, blocking softer emotions. Now, as that tough shell cracks, a more vulnerable self is released.

Exactly a week after the first revelations, I go to bed with a feeling that the past has been placed in decent perspective and that it's time to get on with the present. That night, I have another provocative dream:

I am trapped with Aunt Estelle in the cellar of Other Grandmother's house. I am about seven. The cellar is wriggling with slimy, luminous worms that fall down our necks and squeeze up through the floor while we frantically and futilely swat at them.

I awake shivering with goose bumps and repeating: "Aunt Estelle, Aunt Estelle, Aunt Estelle."

Though I have no proof, I now possess one more conviction of the Child Who Knows: Aunt Estelle and my father had once been lovers. In the twilight world of illicit passion in which that other part of me so intensely dwelled, this union was taken for granted in the same way as the wedlock of my father and mother was a fixture of the ordinary world of hymns and grocery stores.

My Aunt Estelle who shares the bloodstone. Aunt Estelle who is also a Pisces. "Thanks for coming, Estelle."

Mirror, Mirror

493

A tinted photograph of my sister and of me hangs on the bedroom door of my Toronto duplex. I put it there soon after I remembered my father had sexually abused me. Helen, age eight, and I, age four, are at Winona beach, where St. James' Church once had a camp. Both of us are in mother-knit bathing suits. I am standing in front, my blond hair tied with a pink bow, and wearing a big grin, with my eyes scrunched against the sun. She's standing behind, her auburn hair pulled behind her ears, her freckled face clouded by a frown.

A photograph album repeats these images—always the discomfited older child is behind the younger, who grins for the camera, her clothes exhibiting what might be called seductive details: an off-the-shoulder neckline, a jaunty ribbon, a trailing slip, the lace edge of a pair of panties. From time to time, I find myself staring into that cherubic face in the photograph. "Tell me, little girl, what do you still know that I don't know?"

I consult Dr. Steven, a Toronto hypnotherapist. "I believe my father sexually abused me as a child. So far most of my regurgitated memories are physical and emotional rather than verbal or visual. They're very vivid, everything fits, but even now the whole idea is so shocking that I ask myself: did this really happen?"

Dr. Steven directs me to an armchair then instructs me to stare fixedly at a tinfoil pyramid. "Your eyes are closing. You are perfectly relaxed, perfectly at ease. Now, tell me, what do you see?"

After several false starts, I begin: "I am a child in my father's house. My father sits on his bed in his underwear. I'm hanging around outside his door, scuffing my foot back and forth across the threshold. There's something coy about my behaviour. Part of me wants to go in, part holds back. What lures me is a confused mixture of mystery, adventure and, most especially, the desire for attention ... Now I'm sitting on my daddy's lap. I don't know whether I was invited in or whether I went in on my own. He's squeezing my legs between his thighs. I giggle, feeling giddy. He distracts me with nickels, or maybe it's with chocolate-chip cookies ... It's hard to recapture a single storyline—one similar incident seems superimposed on another like a double or triple exposure. Now I'm lying face down on my daddy's bed. He's rubbing against me in a strange way that confuses me. I seem to feel that if I don't look it isn't really happening. Instead I'm staring at the scrollwork on the headboard of my father's bed. I seem to be counting things, concentrating on that—sometimes it's the bites in the chocolate-chip cookie, sometimes I'm counting pennies. The scrollwork reminds me of my mother's lips saying 'dirty dirty.' I'm rather enjoying that—defying her. It's fear and pleasure mixed, like playing with fire. Mostly my feelings can't be classified because I have no framework of experience in which to place them or to judge them. I don't seem to be unhappy, but that's partly because I hold my breath a lot and that makes me dizzy, or light-headed, as if I were swaying in a hammock outside time and space."

494

On subsequent visits to Dr. Steven's office I produce other childhood memories in which I express a growing sense of panic and of wrongdoing, and then of abject helplessness. When I block, he suggests: "Try moving the image of yourself away from your house to some imaginary place that's safer."

"All right. I'm in a forest. I'm looking up through oak leaves into blue sky. The images no longer seem real—as if I'm in a fairy-tale forest. My mother is dressed like the witch in Snow White. She's dipping apples, or maybe it's tomatoes, into a steaming cauldron—something to do with her canning on our kitchen table, combined with jars of fruit in Other Grandmother's cellar. All this is very confused."

"Then take a different path."

"All right. It's growing darker. It's very dark. I seem to be lost ... lost and miserable. I'm walking with my hands held out in front of me, like Frankenstein. They strike something solid—some kind of barrier. It feels shiny, like a mirror. Yes, it's a mirror, an oval mirror—again, it's like the queen's mirror in Snow White—'Mirror, mirror, on the wall.' I see it in the moonlight, but I can't see what the child sees because now I seem to be the reflection in that mirror looking out at her ... that is, at myself. Wait a minute." Agitation jolts me out of hypnosis. "Something doesn't jibe. The child's too old—maybe eleven or even twelve."

"What's wrong with that?"

"My father didn't abuse me after I started school."

"How do you know?"

"Because as soon as I begin school my memories are very clear and detailed even now. I remember everything—all my teachers, what kids were in my grade one class and where they sat, what kids were in the school plays including the understudies. I'm lethal to have at a school reunion."

Dr. Steven is cautionary: "Are you sure you want to keep stirring up these old memories? Why not rest it a bit? Maybe you've had enough."

495

Reluctantly, I leave his office, but I don't wish to rest it. I've rested it for too many years. Taking a blanket, I lie down under the oak tree in my backyard. Overhead I see a complex tracing of copper-leafed branches—the same ones I conjured up in Dr. Steven's office as my dream forest. I concentrate on them, spontaneously moving back into that other forest ...

I'm a child alone. It's very dark. Again I am walking with my arms outstretched. Again, my hands strike something solid—another mirror, except this time it's the mirror from my attic bedroom with two sides that tilt inward to create a multiple reflection. The central glass is cloudy with smoke. Gradually, it clears. I see a five-year-old child with matted hair and blue fangs staring back at me. Around her throat is the bloody mark of a broken leash. She lays her outstretched palms against mine. They fit mine exactly. We are one. She says: "I love my daddy."

Before my eyes, the child grows older. Now she is eight, nine, ten, eleven. Now I am in Miss Buchanan's room. Now I'm in Miss Sissons's room ... now ... now ... now ... I see a gaudy cheerleader with brassy hair. She, too, wears the bloodmark of her daddy's leash. I try to pull my palms away to blind my eyes but they're stuck to hers. She says: "I love my daddy." She too is I, and I am she. All three of us—my adult self, the blue-fanged child, the gaudy teenager—are reflected in the triple mirror.

For a long, long time I lie on the ground staring up into the oak branches, trying to assimilate what I have just seen. I now know why the image of the abused child that I've carried in my mind over the past couple of months frequently seemed too old. I now know that my incestuous relationship with my father went on far longer than I had first grasped—all through a time when I remembered everything else but.

Imagine this: imagine you discover that for many years another person intimately shared your life without your knowing it. Oh, you had your suspicions—the indented pillow beside you, the toothpaste with a thumbprint that wasn't yours. Now it all fits, you know it's true, but during all that time you never actually saw this person.

And so it was with me. She was my shadow-self, unknown to me. She knew passion where I knew only inhibition, then grief where I knew guilt, then terror where I knew anger. She monitored my every thought, manipulated my actions, aided my survival and sabotaged my dreams, for she was I and I was she.

496

RESOLUTION
My Mother

When I first discovered the truth about my past the last thing I could imagine was telling my mother. However, as the days and weeks and months passed, I came to feel a powerful need to do so—not I, but the damaged child in me. Her last act: the need to tell mommy. I ignored this impulse as long as I could. Logic and humanity demanded it. What did an eighty-three-year-old woman need with such desperate information?

Yet the desire to confide would not leave me. A scream of grief had lodged permanently in my chest. It expanded inside me with the insistence of hemorrhaging blood. It was sorrow, anger, love, perversity, vindication, helplessness, guilt, anguish, confrontation, love, despair—everything. Gradually, these feelings articulated themselves into an internal gush of words:

"Mother, why didn't you protect me? The walls of my father's house were thin. A cardboard house. A house of cards. As soon as he put his foot over the threshold I could feel it tremble, become unsafe. How could you not know?

"I became the other woman before I was five. The one who shared his bed. Did my child's wilfulness contain the arrogance of that? Did some of the wronged and jealous wife in you respond to the gall of that? I suspect far more than esthetics was at stake in those pitched battles we waged over my flaxen curls, my main claim to princess status. How you yanked at them, taking control of them, insisting on the braids that I hated, threatening me with the scissors. When I, as a child of five, saw the queen in Snow White turn into the wicked witch, I feared what I was seeing—your other self, the witch in you, the Witch Who Knew.

"Since my father was an obvious and dangerous villain it was necessary for me to believe you were a saint, even if that meant blackening my own character to keep that myth going. It was safer to be a bad child with a perfect mother whom I failed to please, than to be a frightened child with a flawed mother who failed to protect me. And yet, and yet, now that I have rescinded the legend of your saintliness, you too are released to become more human, to be worthy of understanding and love.

"You were born at the turn of the century, when girls who did not marry were dismissed as spinsters. War and depression had delayed courtship for you, as it had for so many others. My father had what passed for a good job and a stable future. Through such conventions you acquired your lot in life. Your philosophy was to make the best of things, whether it be leftover potatoes, a hand-me-down coat or a troubled marriage. I saw only the fossilized remains of that—a petulant father who shouted all the time and a forbearing mother who savoured romantic novels, escaped to church where she found joy in service, who endured her days in my father's house by keeping busy busy busy. Still, you were a mother who was always cheerful, who sang hymns as you hung sheets on the line, who never allowed yourself a day of illness, who shouldered more than your fair share of community responsibility, who delighted in telling Sunday school stories to children. You were then, as you are now, the first to phone a sick friend or take a tray of cookies to a grieving neighbour, the first to volunteer for a difficult or tedious job both inside and outside my father's house.

"Divorce was a religious and a moral matter, as well as an economic one— the subject of horrified whispers. You had a strong need to do the right thing, and to be seen to do the right thing. Your oft-stated concern: what will the neighbours think? Not what is, but what is seen to be. Thus you elected to stay at your post, to refuse to see what was there to be seen and yet to pave my yellow-brick road to a better life with dollars saved on the price of eggs. Your best for my sister and for me.

"I suppose you felt powerless—not just in this one thing but from the beginning of time. A family of four girls, with you in the middle. Serious illness as a child. Immigration from an English mining town to North America. A father defrauded of his savings, depression in a strange land and no jobs to be had. Tragedy in your family—one sister and then another dead from diseases no one dies from today until you, with your bookkeeping job, were the sole support of your family. And then, that final death.

"Your mother says: 'He must be down in the garage feeding the pigeons.' You go down to the garage. You open the door and, yes, your father is there—hanging from the rafters, his feet twisting a foot off the floor, his forty-four-year-old face a strangulated mask never to be erased from your dreams. After seeing that, how many other things would you not want to see?

"Grandma clung to this shred: 'There must be a note.' Together you pulled the house apart slat by slat. Nothing. Only silence from that early grave.

"Yes, mother, you had much in your life you dared not see. So it comes to this: can I blame you for choosing selective sight, the same method of survival that I, your daughter, would choose? If some part of you knows, or suspects, the story I have to tell, then some voice inside you, too, must scream for release. Just as I have been split all these years, so have you. Knowledge is your karma, as well as mine—the natural, inevitable result of all your actions as well as mine. Finally, truth is the only thing worth saying, but even if that proves too harsh, I confess that I am bloody-minded enough to take that responsibility onto myself. I need a chance to heal, to be free. I've earned that right. Forty-seven years is long enough for the working out of any curse. The Child Who Knows-and-is-tired-of-knowing is about to have her *cri de coeur*."

I walk the familiar streets past Laura Secord Public School and St. Cecilia's Infirmary and the Goodfellows' little bungalow, now lawn-paved and insul-bricked. Green shoots glisten against decaying snow and oozy mud, ripe with promise. Lawns are fuzzy green and the forsythia bushes are golden. Always my mother's first words of spring, more reliable than the robin: "I cut some forsythia today."

I am returning to the scene of the crime: home for Easter, the chosen time. I'm glad my natal home is still standing, still inhabited, the rooms still intact—

the *corpus delicti* that the prosecuting attorney is keen on seeing before he'll believe there's been a crime. Although I suspect the door key is in the same place, I ring the bell, a visitor now.

My mother embraces me. "Good! You're early." As always she is overly glad to see me—overly glad in that her welcome outstrips anything I can muster. "Yes, I had a good trip. Yes, the weather is lovely. Yes, it's wonderful to see the crocuses and tulips. Yes, you've cut some forsythia today."

Now that my father's house has given up its secrets it has become an old friend, each room a scrapbook of my past, little changed but the flowers on the wallpaper—from roses, to lilacs, then back to roses. Once again I invent excuses to rove from room to room, almost a ritual now, wishing to repossess the territory of the child that was, to see it from her eyes, three feet up from the carpet, feeling an overriding curiosity. Will things look different now that I know, and know that I know? I, an opener of boxes, of closed doors, of secret compartments, of everything labelled DON'T, NO, or POISON, am turning into Pandora, my fictional name.

Here it is again, the attic where my bedroom used to be—the iron cot by the lace-curtain window; the arched mirror; the frog's-eye gable, now without its patchwork toadstool. In the cubbyholes are trunks for woollens laced in mothballs, card tables for ladies' teas and all those other accessories I, as a child, thought no one ever lived without, now permanent castoffs even in my mother's house.

Down down down I go to hang outside my father's bedroom—unoccupied now, like most of the house; a graduation picture of myself on one dresser, my sister on the other; the bed the same, with the same scrolled headboard—my mother's pursed lips.

She is calling up the stairs with the lilt and heft she used to fetch me from the street: "Time for church!" Church with my mother—something I haven't done for many years. The church where I was christened, the altar where I was married.

"Who gives this woman?"

"I do."

Here's the aisle my father strode with the collection plate, tramp tramp tramp as he and the other elders marched in twos. A big congregation then, now mostly widows with young marrieds drifting back with their children. Even female elders now, chalk one up for necessity and the women's movement. Even here things do change.

"It was sad when they cru-ci-fied my Lord ..."

I remember when it seemed a confession of poverty to attend Easter service without a new spring outfit. Now only a few have made the effort—old faces under new hats. I see Mrs. Lunt and think of Magda—a single parent long before it became fashionable and now a doting grandmother.

"He arose. He arose. Hal-le-lu-jah, Christ arose!"

Afterwards my mother parades me among her peers, proud of the rare opportunity to display a daughter home from foreign battlefields, from larger wars. I cringe, feeling like Judas with thirty pieces of silver lining my pockets, but also knowing I will carry through. I believe in my truth, in the need to speak. I believe in the power of truth to heal both ways.

Home again. I set the table, finding everything exactly where it used to be, where it always has been—the same worn silver, same plates, same cups, same pans, all glued and taped and soldered and wired. Opening a cupboard is like participating in an archeological dig.

Mother has cooked a ham, though there's only two of us. I try to carry on a normal conversation—whose gall bladder is acting up and what cousin's daughter has just married or had another baby—struggling to keep the names straight while my mother jumps up every few seconds to fetch something to the table.

As it happens we are still having tea, the last mouthful of apple pie still on the fork, the plates unstacked, when I blurt the unavoidable bad dialogue. "Mother, there's something I have to tell you ... something terrible." I offer the only reassurance I can. "Something that happened a very long time ago."

My mother puts down her teacup: "What is it?"

Forty years are swept away. I'm crying now, abandoned by my adult self when I need her most. "This will hurt you. It will hurt you a lot."

"What is it? Tell me. You must tell me."

"This will take all of your strength as a Christian."

She is full of concern, clear and firm. "Don't worry about me, just tell me."

I get up from the table. "Please, come into the living room." My mother follows. We sit on the same chintz couch I remember as a child, reupholstered by her after a high-school night course, then resuscitated with mock-leather paint, now also wearing thin. "You're going to be asked to forgive someone, someone I've already forgiven. I don't want to pass this on to you as a burden. I want us to dispel it together."

"Yes. You must tell me."

I deliver the rest of my speech, rehearsed but sincere. "If you're bitter then I was wrong to tell you. It will be my burden again."

My mother takes my nail-bitten hands in her gnarled ones. "Just tell me."

Despite my adult words it's clear I am the child here. At last my other self has a mother after four decades of wandering in the wilderness. Mother ...

My mother still holds my hand. "You must tell me. It's all right. Tell me."

I'm not exactly a child, but neither am I an adult. I have to tell both parents, but especially my mother. Both are very grave. I absolutely and completely have their attention about something that I want to say more than anything before in my life ...

"Remember those convulsions I used to have as a kid?"

She frowns. "Why, yes, you had trouble catching your breath. We were afraid you'd swallow your tongue."

Now I sound like a textbook: "Some psychiatrists see childhood convulsions as a sign of sexual abuse." I pause for this to sink in. "I was sexually abused as a baby."

My mother scarcely reacts. I wonder if she has heard, if she has allowed herself to hear. My other self is crying, I am crying as we await the inevitable next question.

At last she asks: "But who?"

"Who had access?"

"I don't know."

I press: "Who?"

Indignantly: "There wasn't anyone."

"Someone did. Who?"

"Well, I don't know. There was just your father."

"Yes!"

She is looking into the distance, still holding my hands, squeezing them.

I babble: "He was affectionate at first. It wasn't just once. It went on a long time."

"Well!" My mother is near tears but not crying. I am sobbing. We fall into each other's arms, comforting each other. I feel overwhelmed with gratitude and hence with love. I am believed! Again I am babbling: "Thank you, mother. Thank you for believing me." For accepting both of us—me and my other self.

My mother's body feels birdlike but strong. "Of course, I believe you. You're my daughter!"

She is still staring off into space, quietly picking up the pieces of her life as if it were another plate to be mended: "Your daddy and I ... I don't suppose we ever talked. Many's the time I was tempted to leave, but whenever I was most exasperated your daddy would turn around and do something really nice." She sighs: "I don't suppose I could forgive him if he were alive, but now ..."

My Father

I take out Pandora's box once more—ivory, the colour of dead corsages, of old bones, the box that once lay under my father's bed. Again I rifle through the pictures—myself in velvet formal, in cheerleading outfit, in bathing suit. At the bottom of that box lies one more picture—of my father receiving the Steel Company's gold pin for forty years' faithful service. He stands in semi-profile, eyes lowered, his expression one of modesty mixed with pride. In his view, he has accomplished something.

My father had other moments of pride—as a player on the Hamilton Rough Riders football team when it won a national championship in 1912, as a lieutenant during the First World War—yet it is in this gold pin photo that he comes closest to smiling for posterity. For forty-three years he put on his navy suit, white shirt and tie, then drove his second-hand car to his seven-to-three, three-to-eleven, eleven-to-seven inspector's job at the Steel Company. That gold pin is a medal for some kind of gallantry, I know that now. The platitudes offered up at my father's funeral held their own truth—this Christian man who didn't smoke or drink, who played no card games beyond cribbage or solitaire, who helped with the grocery shopping, who never took the Lord's name in vain; this good neighbour who tipped his hat on Sunday, who commented Monday to Friday on the weather, who kept his snow shovelled, his leaves raked, and his bills paid. Is it fair to dismiss all this as hypocrisy? Was this not a second reality, offsetting the pictures that do not appear in the box?

My father's rage was an impotent rage. He shouted and waved his fists like a child in a high chair. I know that now. He demanded and he was obeyed, but he was never heard. I know that now. The weaker he became, the less I was able to justify my rage towards him and the guiltier I grew. But my rage did not diminish. Our secret lived between us. It tainted every sentence we spoke. I couldn't share my father's house and function as anything but a zombie. I couldn't share the same room and breathe normally. I couldn't sit at his table without choking. Any fumbling attempt he made at rapport was turned aside with contempt. How much I made him suffer I have no way of knowing. Perhaps his hide was thick enough to withstand my condemnation. Perhaps his internal problems were so acute I could scarcely make a difference. I suspect he paid as dearly as I for the amnesia that was once his salvation. As in the child's game of statues, we remained frozen at our darkest hour, with no possibility of forgiveness or compassion or redemption while he lived. I know that now.

My sister remembers hikes with my father and picnics. I do not. Any normal pleasures have long since been blotted out by the ink stain our relationship became. My father had no friends except those he met at church. He was estranged from his relatives, and belonged only to groups to which my mother gained him entrance. Once ensconced in a chair beside a set of ears, he offered little beyond a parade of his ailments. He had no hobbies other than stamp collecting and perusing the newspaper for bargains. I can't even imagine the loneliness of such an existence. I can't imagine the frustration that caused him to do what he did or the agony that must have resulted. Did he pretend I was a willing victim? Did he think he had the right? Did he do to me what had been done to him? Did he know that I couldn't remember what we did in secret? Was he as profoundly split as I? Was there a Daddy Who Knew and a Daddy Who Did Not Know?

I ask questions of the past but I don't expect answers. Though I shared a house and a crime with my father, I scarcely knew the man. Mine is not a story of the boot, but of the imprint of that boot on flesh: imprinting.

This I do know: my father was not a monster. His life was a bud that never opened, blighted by the first frost. His crime became his prison, his guilt his bars. He served his sentence as I have served mine, but his was for life, whereas I got off after forty-seven years for reasonably good behaviour.

In my earliest memory I am an infant lying on my father's bed, being sexually fondled but blissfully unaware of any deception. Then I was treated with tenderness. That was my Garden of Eden. As in Genesis, pain came with knowledge and expulsion. Yet some remembrance of happiness remained. I felt I was special, the chosen child, the princess. That lie had some truth. That lie was a blessing as well as a curse. I know that now.

The force with which I came to hate my father was a measure of the love I and my other self once bore him. I know that now. Inarticulate with pain, my father expressed his love in a perverted way which was all he could manage. I know that now. I was a stand-in for a mother and a sister, but we are all each other's surrogates. All of us are born into the second act of a tragedy-in-progress, then spend the rest of our lives trying to figure out what went wrong in the first act. I know that now.

503

When I look at the picture of my father receiving his gold pin, I think of the blinkered donkeys who ground grain: around and around and around, dragging their millstones till they dropped in a grave carved by their own hooves. Though I don't understand him, I can pity him and forgive him. I forgive my father so I can forgive myself, so I can embrace with compassion that fierce and grieving child who held her tongue to save her cat and that frenetic and gaudy teenager who danced in the red shoes and the wilful princess who betrayed the white knight who saved her. I also forgive my father because I love him. That is the biggest shock of all. Not only that I once loved him but that I love him even now. So that is the last winged creature to fly out of my Pandora's box. For hope, read love. I love my daddy, I know that now.

I am walking through a forest wearing a sky-blue dress. I come upon a ragamuffin in a tattered sunsuit, hiding behind a tree. I extend my hand. Wiping sticky fingers on her sunsuit, she accepts it. Together we walk deeper into the forest.

We come to a clearing. My father is lying on a bier, hands folded across his navy vest. Through the glass floor of the forest I see the Xs and Os of a tic-tac-toe game. I lift up the child to say goodbye to her daddy. With her finger, she makes Xs and Os on the side of her daddy's coffin—hugs and kisses, goodbye, goodbye. Hugging the child, I assure her she has done her best, that she's a good child, a wise child, as all children are.... I feel her melt into my chest.

Now I close my father's coffin. I wave goodbye with a handkerchief. The handkerchief turns into a white bird, which grows larger and larger till I feel myself becoming that bird. Now I am flying, my wings strong and sure as they beat the air—a seabird on its way to the ocean. In my mouth I have a quill to be dipped into the sun, a quill to write with fire before plunging into the ocean.

So that is it. My other self is dead. My father is dead. The king is dead. The princess is dead. "Ding dong, the witch is dead." I have been released from the monster that never was. Now I can close the coffin, truly close it.

X X X X

O O O O O

Goodbye, goodbye.

POSTSCRIPT

My husband's way of surviving our marital breakup was to cut off the past. Because our divorce was uncontested, involved no children and no alimony, it was handled by mail in 1977 on the grounds of my desertion. I thereafter respected his wish for total privacy, though that seemed more like an amputation than a parting.

Only once did I glimpse Danny during the next ten years. One sunny Friday in 1978 I was shopping near our former apartment when I saw him park "our" red Jaguar, filled to bursting with white chrysanthemums. I had been told, several weeks before, that he was remarrying soon. Instinctively I knew he was festooning our former apartment with flowers for his wedding. My first impulse was to rush over to wish him well, but a wiser part of me held back, knowing I must not allow my shadow to fall across his wedding day.

That poignant image of the little red car, abloom with white flowers, stayed with me for a long time.

Frequently, over the next few years I dreamed about Danny. Not as he was, but as he had been—a mate and a trusted friend. This did not indicate to me any longing for the past in reality, only the honouring of our inner bond. On those rare occasions when I did dream of him as he was now—a man married to someone else—we would hug each other, weep with pleasure at our reunion, then go our separate ways.

My separate way included the revelations in this book. Three years ago, towards the end of 1984, I decided to retreat to a place where I could heal and integrate, and perhaps write a book. Before leaving, I had a strong desire to see Danny. I wanted him to know that he had been the best mate anyone could ever want; that I had been compelled to leave him to struggle with demons far nastier than we could have guessed; that he had made survival possible by giving me faith in myself.

We met at a downtown Toronto restaurant, full of dark panelling and good leather, one stormy afternoon in late November. He looked the same as always—handsome with an affable, almost cherubic smile, his light brown hair only slightly greyer and thinner. One thing was different and I noticed it immediately—a gold wedding band.

Danny's first question—"Do you still write?"—indicated this might not be the easy meeting I had hoped for. My career was a noisy one, spawned in the same

505

city. Such detachment seemed unnatural. When I offered him a copy of my latest novel, he politely declined with the reminder that we now lived separate lives. His avuncular stance was the sort used to humour a difficult client who insists on special attention. It seemed impenetrable.

I struggled to stick to my agenda. Eight months had gone by since my past had exploded into my present. I thought I had been over this ground often enough, with enough people, to be dispassionate—even clinical. However, this special telling, with this special person, touched on a level of grief so deep I found myself unable to speak without the certainty of breaking. Fumbling in my purse for a purple felt pen, I began writing on cocktail napkins in block letters: I HAVE SOMETHING STRANGE TO TELL YOU. Eventually, in this peculiar way, my story was related.

Afterwards, in a wet courtyard, just receiving the afternoon's first murky rays of sunlight, he held me tightly for several seconds. Then he touched my shoulder bag with a whimsical smile. "Thanks for my book."

Two years later, while I was preparing this manuscript for publication, an announcement appeared in a Toronto paper, making this day tragically different from any other: "Suddenly, on Tuesday, January 6, 1987 ... Loving husband of ... Dear father of ..." Danny—my Danny for twenty years—had died of a ruptured heart at age fifty-five.

Oh, Danny, now I know the meaning of the verb to keen—to wail, to lament. A friend had phoned me to spare me a colder shock. A quarter into a newsbox brings my confirmation. How important that quarter seemed as I fumbled it into its slot—twenty-five cents to purchase official word of a husband's death.

I pick flowers for you at the florist's—painted daisies, the same as I carried in my bridal bouquet. It seemed important to choose each one myself, then to circle our former apartment block, looking up at our twelve lighted windows.

The newspaper says your family is receiving at the funeral home from 2:00 to 4 P.M. and from 7 to 9 P.M. I arrange to be there at 5:00, supported by a mutual friend, who knew us as a couple, who even shared our wedding anniversary. No one else is in your lying-in room—a small chapel set with an elegant mahogany casket. At first, I think I've stumbled into the wrong place, the wrong life, the wrong death. I do not recognize the corpse in the coffin. Not even after staring. An old man with grey flesh lies in your place. Not one recognizable feature has made it through death and the cosmetician's art. How can this be? You looked yourself when I saw you two years ago.

I touch your hand. Your flesh is cool and dense. Dead, really dead. No comfort there. And yet, as I examine this mock-up of you, I realize your corpse is the best advertisement for "something more" that I have ever seen. Since my college days I have acquired far more patience with the mysterious, more reverence for the unknown. "He is not here. He has risen." You are not here. That I know for sure. I am looking at your remains—that which is leftover. Dead and *gone.*

I grieve over what you have left for us. I speak to your corpse as if my message might get through. I tell you once again how grateful I am for our twenty years of intimacy, fifteen of them as man and wife. I wonder: what did you make of our last meeting? Did you learn that it was no offence to your present loyalties to love me in my proper context, our past? I regret that you never knew my better, wiser self, yet even as I form this thought I know you were attracted to my troubled spirit. I, your flock of one, your rescuee, was also your shadow, your sinner, your way of contacting your own rebelliousness, too deeply buried to touch. You lost a vital and valid part of yourself on the slippery slope to perfection. That part you found in me.

507

Why do people have to die before we begin to see them whole? Well, we played happily together, we worked hard together, we had adventures together, we took risks together. We laughed at the same things, had dozens of private jokes and code words, spent hours and days and years with our hands on each other. You called me your Little Friend, and for many years I was. I sensed—as you did—that yours would be a short life while mine would not. Some fragility there, not a long-lived family, whereas my great-grandfather bought his last motorcycle at age eighty.

My companion joins me at the casket. She speaks of you as a gentleman. That epithet surprises me. It's a word reserved for our elders—but now, of course, we are the elders. I take a step back, see you through her eyes. Yes, it's the right word, meaning far more than your three-piece navy suit, your red tie and matching handkerchief. A gentle man. One who practised the truth of good manners—formalized compassion.

I take another step back to explore your habitat. A photograph offers the confirmation I have been seeking—there you are, exactly as you should be, beaming with optimism and good cheer, your arm proudly encircling your son, age six, with your young wife embracing a daughter, age four. I don't recognize many of the names on your floral tributes. That gives me no pang. It's as it should be. Another life.

You are to be buried at eleven o'clock the next morning. I wasn't going to attend; finally, to stay away is unthinkable.

Dressing for the occasion is fraught with pathos—the black bride, ritualistically preparing for her last date. The stockings I will wear, the dark print dress, the black velvet coat, black muff, checked scarf, black boots—all acquire a mystique through association. My companion picks me up in ample time for your service. At 10:48, we discover that we are at the wrong church. An anxious race across town brings us to the right church at the wrong time—simultaneously with the casket. I had intended to arrive with everyone else, sit towards the back, participate with stoicism and leave with dignity. Now, a side door allows us to slip into the very back row. Another friend, male, slides into the pew beside me. Your official mourners are on the aisle front left. I am on the aisle back right, supported in compassion by both the male and female principle. Appropriate, but a little too showy.

Yours is an Anglican church with Gothic ceiling and an altar arched in stained glass. Now your casket moves slowly up the long central aisle, led by a white choir carrying a golden cross. At the first sound of those voices, high and haunting, I am lost ... I am lost ...

The hymns are unfamiliar. Did they mean anything to you? Last I knew you saved your skepticism for heaven and your good deeds for the earth. Did you change? The eulogy, given by your legal mentor, gracefully states your creed. "Daniel loved people. He saw the best in everyone ..."

Your casket is drawn from the church, followed by your children, eyes sweeping the crowded pews, still unaware their father lies in that shiny box, stone cold. Your young widow is dressed in white. She has a lovely face, full of an unspeakable sorrow. I, above all others, know the measure of her loss. My grief today is sharp and deep and clean, like the cutting of a knife through flesh to bone. Her grief has yet to die a thousand deaths. For me, this is closure.

As your long procession of mourners passes, I see that most of their faces, like the names on your wreaths, are unknown to me. Legal faces, correct and clear-eyed, used to containing grief. A few dear friends from our past. Probably most don't even know you're dead. I am still trying to be inconspicuous, but so obviously in pain, as I grip one male hand and one female, that I'm becoming harder to miss. One or two mourners do make that difficult crossover from the

508

formal line to embrace me, to say: "I'm glad you came." Their unexpected kindness, though deeply appreciated, unhinges me. It's been a cruel time, as well as a sorrowful one. Nobody's fault, no callousness intended. Your death took us all by surprise. I'm one wife, one widow too many. No one knows what to do with me. I don't know what to do with myself. I'm not supposed to feel pain while your funeral procession, with measured step, marches over me.

The last mourner leaves the church. No more need for artifice. I break.

I'm going to the cemetery, against all advice. It's necessary to see your body go down into the earth. Both of my companions have other engagements. I'm left outside the gate of Mount Pleasant Cemetery, watching your long cortege, headlights lit, from the wrong side of the street. By the time I make it through the traffic, the last car is rounding the first turn. I struggle to catch up. Now that last car is rounding a second turn. Now I am running, in full awareness of my absurdity, spared nothing there, the shadow of the lady in white, stumbling after your hearse, twelve years late.

Dare I cut across the graveyard, avoid some of the loops of the road? Wouldn't that be even more absurd, to come groping through tombstones? What will the neighbours think?

The truth is, yours is the only prohibition still with the power to hurt. Yours was the voice that laughed away my social outrages, for which I'm sure this qualifies, yet yours is also the voice that told me I was no longer wanted in your life. And yet, and yet, no one can possess all of someone else. Not one wife or another. Not a mother or a father. Not a child. No one. I will be burying a different set of memories, a different person from everyone else. What I'm doing now is no one's business but my own. Not even yours.

The braking of wheels on gravel. I stop running, grab for the tag ends of dignity. A blue sports car, door open. "Come on. Get in." A colleague of yours, someone we both like. He rescues me, as I believe you would have done, drives me to the right place as your surrogate, steers me to the edge of the crowd gathered under your canopy while a few more words are said and your coffin plunges into the earth.

Afterwards, we talk about you.

It's not quite over, not yet, not this long day. I've finished with one funeral in time for another—a memorial service for the compassionate friend and fine novelist to whom this book is dedicated: Margaret Laurence, 1926–1987. Ironically, here I am to sit with the family. As I walk up the aisle, no longer needing to be invisible, I encounter a rope marking off the first four rows. Paralyzed, I stare at it, unable to breach one more barrier, feeling myself begin to faint. A friendly arm reaches out, pulls me in. Now I can cry fully and freely—for Margaret, for you.

I believe the only way to overcome loss is to absorb the good qualities of that which is lost. Surely that is the meaning of the Eucharist: "This is my body, this is my blood." I await the dubious blessing of old age with your gentleness smoothing my rough edges, with your voice still sweet and clear in my ear: "It's okay, Little Friend. Now, try again."

Looking at my life from one vantage point, I see nothing but devastation. A blasted childhood, an even worse adolescence, betrayal, divorce, craziness, professional stalemate, financial uncertainty and always, always a secret eating like dry rot at my psyche. That is the dark side, the story I have told in this book. Yet, like the moon, my life has another side, one with some luminosity.

510

I have been loved once, unconditionally, and I have loved in return. That, like the gift of air, can never be withdrawn. The disguises I assumed—cheerleader, philosopher, princess, journalist, author—all had something to teach me about sorrow and about laughter. Since I had early been damaged by love, my ruling passion became curiosity—the desire to experience and to know. Since I could not trust what happened inside my father's house, I turned for adventure outside it. Since I dared not parent children, I created books.

Mine was a story of early loss—of innocence, of childhood, of love, of magic, of illusion. It was a hazardous life, which began in guilt and self-hate, requiring me to learn self-forgiveness. This meant discovering the difference between fixing blame and taking responsibility. The guilty child was me, though I didn't know of her existence. Her actions were mine, for which I must assume responsibility.

My life was structured on the uncovering of a mystery. As a child, I survived by forgetting. Later, the amnesia became a problem as large as the one it was meant to conceal. However, I did not remember my past until the homemade bomb was defused, until the evil was contained, until I was stable enough and happy enough that sorrow or anger or regret or pain was overwhelmed by joy at my release. To reach this state, I needed the help of friends and healers. This I had in abundance.

Mine turns out to be a story without villains. Children who were in some way abused, abuse others; victims become villains. Thus, not to forgive only perpetuates the crime, creates more victims. Like Sleeping Beauty I was both cursed and blessed at birth. I was given the poison and the antidote at the same time and by the same people. The well that poisoned me also provided me with the ability to resist that poison. Specifically, I was of the first generation of my family to receive the education and the social resources and the personal support to fight back.

Mental institutions and prisons and hostels and shelters and addiction centres are full of persons who were sexually abused and who did not recover. Sex between an adult and a child always involves emotional and physical brutality. It is a crime that cripples, usually for life. That some people do survive, that emotional health often requires the abused to forgive the abuser does not make the crime more acceptable.

A volunteer at a women's shelter told me of discovering a nine-month-old girl who had been raped. The mother's live-in lover who did this was an alcoholic. The family was on welfare and the baby was undernourished. By contrast, mine is a middle-class story with built-in loopholes and rescue stations and options and timelocks and safeguards.

In retrospect, I feel about my life the way some people feel about war. If you survive, then it becomes a good war. Danger makes you active, it makes you alert, it forces you to experience and thus to learn. I now know the cost of my life, the real price that has been paid. Contact with inner pain has immunized me against most petty hurts. Hopes I still have in abundance, but very few needs. My pride of intellect has been shattered. If I didn't know about half my own life, what other knowledge can I trust? Yet even here I see a gift, for in place of my narrow, pragmatic world of cause and effect and matter moving to immutable laws, I have burst into an infinite world full of wonder. The whole mystery of the universe has my reverence. Nothing is sure but nothing can be dismissed. I pay attention.

All of us are haunted by the failed hopes and undigested deeds of our forebears. I was lucky to find my family's dinosaur intact in one deep grave. My main regret is excessive self-involvement. Too often I was sleepwalking through other people's lives, eyes turned inward while I washed the blood off my hands. My toughest lesson was to renounce my own sense of specialness, to let the princess die along with the guilt-ridden child in my closet, to see instead the specialness of the world around me.

Always I was travelling from darkness into the light. In such journeys, time is our ally, not our enemy. We can grow wise. As the arteries harden, the spirit can lighten. As the legs fail, the soul can take wing. Things do add up. Life does have shape and maybe even purpose. Or so it seems to me.

It is July 6, 1987. My mother debarks from a Greyhound bus after a weekend visit to her niece's. Typically, she has decided to walk the four blocks home instead of taking a taxi from the bus terminal. Though it's a muggy ninety degrees, she is wearing her raincoat so she won't have to carry it, and toting her overnight case. Her gait is slow, sometimes uncertain, as she greets acquaintances en route, complimenting them on their flowerbeds, making this small journey an occasion for the exchange of pleasantries, imbuing each moment and everyone encountered in it with a sense of importance as she always has.

My mother is enjoying the final years of a productive life, still supported by a network of aging friends stitched together—like everything in her house— by eternal optimism. Despite failing eyesight, she reads the newspaper each evening through a giant magnifying glass, then bundles it up with the rest for recycling, accompanied by the tin cans she has flattened in the basement. She climbs the stairs of her three-storey house a dozen times a day. Only reluctantly, in the past few years, has she given up shovelling snow and cutting grass. She still refuses a cane. When anyone suggests she slow down, she insists: "I'm fine! Don't worry about me." To my mother, approaching her eighty-eighth birthday, ninety seems old.

Now, as she turns the corner onto her own street, she looks with relief towards her home of more than fifty years, just a few doors away. The gradient, though not steep, has been steady, all the way from Main Street to the Mountain. Soon she is mounting her own front steps, three of them, to her veranda. She sets down her little embroidered case, frankly exhausted, slips her key into the lock, opens the door leading into the cool sanctuary of her own home. She sits down on her favourite chair, still wearing her coat, and unclasps her earrings.

In the next few hours, the phone rings several times, unanswered. Friends, well-rehearsed for catastrophe, are becoming alarmed. Simultaneously, a neighbour grows suspicious of that still-ajar door and investigates. My mother, her final journey completed, has run out of breath.

No Previous Experience

ELSPETH CAMERON

A book nearly as controversial as Sylvia Fraser's was Elspeth Cameron's 1997 work *No Previous Experience: A Memoir of Love and Change*, a story of a lesbian's coming-out after a series of failed heterosexual relationships. Cameron, who was born in 1943, is an academic by profession and the author of three full-scale Canadian literary biographies: *Hugh MacLennan: A Writer's Life* (1981), *Irving Layton: A Portrait* (1985), and *Earle Birney: A Life* (1994). The last two were highly contentious in their own right, playing up their subjects' sex lives while attacking their literary worth. Cameron lives in Calgary.

"There's something I must tell you."

My therapist—formerly our marriage counsellor—looks expectant. I had returned to her to try to find out what the hell had gone wrong in my marriage. To understand. She sits silent.

I can't speak. I can't get it out. Five minutes pass ... maybe ten. It is a risk involving nauseating fear. She's heard Paul accuse me of being lesbian. She's heard my denials. Now I must tell her and take the consequences. It's too important not to. It is a waste of her time and mine to conceal the question that consumes every thought: What will become of Janice and me? Still I can't speak. I am sweating the cold, sharp sweat of terror.

"I ... want to tell you about ..." I am determined to tell her, but I can't do it. I just can't do it. "I am in love," I state baldly.

"Yes?" She knows this is not all. She waits, silent.

"It's ... it's ... a woman," I say. I sound so foolish. So at fault. She waits. "It's ... it's Janice," I blurt out.

My turn to wait now, catapulted into a horrible limbo. What will she say? Will she turn on me disapprovingly? Will she loathe me? Will all the respect and care she's shown me disappear, leaving me not only without Janice but comfortless, a therapist's pariah?

I feel as if I will suffocate.

She looks right at me. "I'm not surprised," she says. "I felt it might be something like that." *Will she damn me to hell?* I am mentally poised for flight from her office, from intense distress. "It's wonderful," she says in a quiet voice. "Wonderful. You deserve to be loved. Tell me all about it."

So began the first of many conversations through December that led to the risk I never thought I'd take.

"What do *you* want?"

"I want to live with her."

"What's stopping you?"

"Her. She loves her husband, her boys. I don't blame her. David is kind. He's not at all like Paul. He knows we sleep together. Not the details, just that we share a bed sometimes. He doesn't ask, and he doesn't mind."

"Have you asked her?"

"Asked her what?"

"To live with you."

"No. I couldn't do that. I don't want to pressure her."

"Okay, so what's your bottom line?"

"Well, the longest I think I can go without seeing her is a month—maybe six weeks." I pause. She waits. "You mean I should tell her that? Try to work it out?"

"What do you gain by saying nothing?"

"That way I don't force her to say no. I can have some of her, even if it's not enough."

"What would be so awful if she did say no?"

I began to cry. "I want her so. I mean ... I want to live with her. If I can't live with her, I need to see her every month at least."

"What would you do if she said no? If she called you today and said she can't see you again? What would you do?"

I try to take in the question. I know it is *the* question. Tears keep coming and coming and coming. I say nothing. I try to think about it. What if that worst of all possible scenarios occurred? What *would* I do? I don't think I could bear it.

It took several sessions to figure this out. Rather, it took several sessions even to face the possibility.

What *would* I do?

Not suicide, that much was clear. I felt strong. I felt like a good person. I felt true to myself. Being loved by a woman had given me the deepest approval I had ever felt. Janice's love had helped me love myself. To love her had been to accept all women as lovable, including me. And the therapist's gentle acceptance of my choice, of what I had chosen as a new sexuality, gave me hope and confidence.

What would I do?

I would live comfortably alone—despite the loneliness I knew I'd feel. I would grieve for my loss. No one could replace Janice, I knew that. We had discovered this other love together. We had given birth to one another. We had broken through some barrier together into another world. It had been like waking with a third eye that sees what most others never see. A brave, new world of the heart. We had composed something beautiful and enduring—like a triumphal hymn with lilting themes, unexpected harmonies, exquisite reverberations. The coda too could be a thing of beauty.

Eventually, I would seek and perhaps find another woman to love. I was sure I could not love a man again. Could not allow men—with their rough bodies, their crude imaginations, their dangerous needs, their alien souls—close to me again. But I might find someone else, someone different from Janice. Someone whose love I could bask in in another way. At fifty-three I couldn't count on it. But inside I felt it could happen. That I had a good chance of finding what I needed, and part of what I needed was someone to give to.

I decided to get things clear with Janice. I knew the risk was that pushing now might end everything. Forever and ever. My model was my friend the painter Doris McCarthy, whose memoirs I had long ago reviewed. I admired her integrity in ending an affair with a married man when it became clear he would not leave his wife. She had managed to keep his friendship afterwards and to say nothing. Even in her recollection, she refrained from naming him.

"Darling, this is going to be a fairly serious message, so brace yourself," I e-mailed in mid-December.

I have been thinking about David. About how unfair this situation is to him. You and I have full information to work from. He doesn't. I'm not any longer comfortable with that. I am feeling apprehensive about coming there in January as planned. I cannot just enter your house as you entered mine in November. It's not just that I can't sleep with you (a major point), but that I am automatically the outsider.

The "couple" is you and D. I am the mistress. I've been here before. I recognize the feelings: exclusion, degradation, confusion. I tend to rationalize and adapt. I want to raise the possibility of telling D.: you, me, or both of us.

I have also been thinking about a remark you made: that you despair of having enough to give me. I think this is a serious problem. I love you terribly. When you left I missed you more than ever before. The more time I spend with you, the deeper my feelings go. The deeper my feelings, the more committed to you I feel. The more committed I feel, the more hurt I am when you go home. I am in danger of drawing back on the one hand, or of becoming masochistic on the other.

Right now I feel a 100 per cent commitment to you as my partner. You say you don't want to make a choice. But you HAVE made a choice. You have chosen the status quo. I don't mean this is good for you. You too show the strain. And given the fine person you are, you must be troubled too. You have said you are.

Wait for you, however long that takes? I don't see this as controlling, or even as a request. Just your wish. We must realize that my waiting might well be in vain, were I to do it. And how would I feel if I DID wait—say for ten years. Would I be resentful and angry? Would you respect me? Would YOU be willing to wait if the situation were reversed?

Deceiving D. or anyone else offers me nothing. I feel no shame, either in relation to family or friends.

You on the other hand say that your feelings for D. run as deep as those you have for me. (What you actually wrote was, "This man has been a partner of mine for over twenty years. We have built good lives together and produced good children. I do not know what the future holds, as I said, but I know I will always feel connected to this man, even after separation and death. My feelings for him have some of the same depth as my feelings for you.") This is chilling for me, Janice. In person you have told me things at odds with this—e.g., that you have never felt as connected to anyone as you do to me, that D. was always off in his own world, etc., etc., etc. You'll know what I mean. It's as if you are appealing to me to put up with having so little of your time because D. is so nice. Sorry. I believe there is something hollow about your marriage. Maybe the real point is your revised statement that you DID love D., not that you DO love him. You seem to make a case that you chose a good father and husband—in that order. That the job of childrearing is almost ended. That the father role is pretty much all that's left now. You feel a responsibility to keep up a fairly conventional (your words) façade. This is called an affair, Janice. This is called keeping a mistress (gender of course irrelevant). If I see your point, I'm expected to put my needs and wishes aside so you can fulfill a responsibility to a man you no longer love, who has not indicated he feels the same responsibility towards you. I'm not willing to put my needs and wishes aside for this reason. Sharing a good deal of your life is what I propose. And less than a quarter of your time is not enough for me. Forever and ever. E.

517

Having started on this route there was no turning back. I offered choices that were acceptable to me. She would not choose.

Because my plane was late, she wrote, she had told David that she would spend that night with me in their guest room. I said no. "Either I sleep with you during my visit or I use the guest room entirely," I wrote. She spoke vaguely of "evolution" and of "making everyone happy" and of how it would be "abusive to D. to tell him."

She decided I'd have the guest room.

I pressed further. "What I feel is disrespect for my behaviour and yours," I wrote.

All I can control is my behaviour. If we are talking many years— and you say a minimum of five, while I say two—I don't think I can continue to be hurt as I am each time you go home. You say "I'm not giving you anything D. wants" and "D. lets me do whatever I want." Okay. So I propose we spend summers, Christmas holidays, other holidays together as a couple. During the teaching year, you live with your family. If you decline, I want to forgo the intimate part of our relationship for the time being. This would make me feel better about myself, and about you. It would be a risk, of course. I might meet someone else and find the intimacy without strings attached that I want. You might also find someone (a woman probably) with whom you found the physical intimacy that is lacking in your marriage. Or you might revive that aspect of your marriage.

If we were to take this path—of limiting ourselves to a professional partnership and a friendship—there would be still a possibility of getting together in the future on equal terms. I am making you a proposal for partnership now. You see, I love you, but I love myself too and am going to protect and look after myself this time round, no matter what the outcome. E.

It looked like the end of what we called JE. JaniceElspeth. A unit. Soulmates.

Janice informed me matter-of-factly that she and her guys were making a Christmas trip. They were going to have their traditional Christmas Eve at the Pass House a day early. David would dress up as Santa, as usual, dispensing presents. Then they would drive on to visit David's relatives in Portland, Oregon. It would be a great chance for their sons to bond with David's relatives, she wrote me. What I interpreted this to mean was that Janice herself was consolidating the McGinnis family. Yet another chapter in the McGinnis Family Narrative, a chapter that clearly excluded me. I asked if I could phone on Christmas Day. Not possible, she e-mailed. They would be on the road.

I knew this plan was Janice's, not David's. He never spoke of his relatives, whereas she talked often of hers—of how mean and stubborn the Clarkes were, how off-the-wall funny the Bartletts, how taciturn the Dickins. Anatol was a Bartlett, she used to say. Leopold was like her—part Clarke, but mostly Bartlett. I knew David had almost no contact with his two sisters (his parents were both long gone). I imagined this trip as Janice's bid to make David feel important. It would be *his* family for once.

I could almost hear her building bridges: who resembled whom, who had inherited which character traits, what possibilities there might be for future visits so the boys could get to know their father's family better—for the first time, really.

The beginning of the end.

I arranged to have all three of my children for Christmas. Bea and her new boyfriend Peter would fly in from England. Hugo could take a train from Montreal. I also invited my sister from Ottawa and her husband. Together, we would go to Barrie to spend Christmas Day with my parents. I knew the hustle and bustle would keep thoughts of Janice at bay—a little, anyway.

Even so, I felt loss and grief. I had made a proposal and got several things clear, despite her evasiveness. Her response had been to ask me to pose no more "hard questions" and then retreat deeper into her family. I had little if any hope of commitment from her side, and decided for my own well-being to cancel the trip to Calgary in late January. I would explain when she got back after New Year's.

It was in this frame of mind that I decided at last to check out the Rose Café, a bar and dance spot for women. I knew my future was with the lesbian community. I wanted no one but Janice, but if she simply moved me back into friendship and recast our affair as an unwise fling, I would have to get on with my life without her. I needed to brace myself by checking out what this community was like. I had no intention of anything other than observation.

It took every resource I had to get myself there one slushy evening just before everyone arrived for Christmas. I phoned the day before to gather whatever information I could.

"Is this a bar just for women?" I asked, my heart gripped with apprehension. "Yes," answered a woman whose voice was noncommittal.

"When does it get busy?"

"People stop in for drinks anytime after seven o'clock or so."

I thanked her and hung up quickly.

Next day I drove past the place to see exactly where it was. In spite of my elaborate preparations, when the time came, I could hardly force myself through the door. It was dark inside, and it took my eyes a minute to adjust. Disappointment was immediate. I had expected a cheery group of women at tables or standing at a bar. Music probably. But the place was almost deserted, except for a small group of men and women who were chatting as if at a cocktail party. I sat down at the empty bar. Exposed. Uncomfortable. The woman tending bar asked me what I'd like. She didn't seem lesbian to me—I mean, I never would have thought so meeting her anywhere else. I ordered a draft beer.

I felt duped. Where were the women who supposedly dropped in for drinks?

What were all these men doing here? Well, I was in here now I would stick it out. I braced myself in case I met one of my students, or someone else I knew. I felt exposed. A reluctant exhibit in ... what?

I looked around. The place was divided into two levels. At one end was a disc jockey's booth, uninhabited for the moment. Soft non-stop mechanical disco thumped through ceiling loudspeakers wrapped with Christmas baubles. Near the booth a large TV displayed Madonna in a Wonder Woman bra and not much else, strutting to music that could not be heard. At the other end of the room on a raised floor were a few tables with chairs. A couple of women played pool in a desultory fashion. In between was an empty dance floor backed by a huge wall-size mirror. Nothing, I thought, could induce me to dance in such a setting.

One of the men from the cocktail group came over and sat on the bar stool next to me. He looked like a frog. I looked away.

"Wanna dance?" he said, taking a long drink from his glass.

I ignored him.

"Wanna dance?" he said, more loudly this time.

I looked right at him. "No thanks," I said.

"Ah, c'mon. Wanna dance?"

I felt anger surge up into my throat.

"No," I said. "What are you doing here anyway? This is a women's place."

"It's our Christmas party," he slurred, leaning towards me and grinning his frog grin. His eyes bulged like Peter Lorre's. I noticed he was wearing a wedding ring.

"Is your wife here?" I asked.

He looked startled, then confused. "Uh ... no."

"Why not?" I said.

"She doesn't like these office parties. C'mon, wanna dance?"

"No," I said, feeling like a vindictive missionary. "What do you think you're doing asking *anyone* to dance. You're married. Go home to your wife, if she can stand you." And, surprised by my self-righteous tone and the vehemence with which I had spoken, I left the bar stool, leaving the frog man opening and closing his mouth as if gasping for air.

On the edge of the dance floor where I now stood were a couple of young women—about the age of my students—chatting. They had drifted in with a few other women who now began to greet each other, hugging and kissing and talking in an animated way.

"The guy at the bar is bugging me," I said, in a panic. "Can I join you for a few minutes until he gets lost?"

"Sure, no problem," they said in stereo, looking me over curiously. I did not look like one of them at all. My tailored pants and jacket seemed somehow out of place. The shorter one was wearing a baseball hat backwards over a dark ponytail. She was tiny, elflike. Had she been bigger, she would have looked like a baseball player on his day off: sloppy sweatshirt, sleeves pushed up, over battered jeans. The other, a large, plump girl with a pink baby face surrounded by light ringlets, wore a frilly blouse and loose pants. They didn't seem like a couple, but how would I know?

They wanted to know who I was. Why I was there.

I said I was a teacher, hoping they wouldn't ask where or of what. People immediately clam up on learning I am an English professor. Mostly they make some excuse about their poor grammar or inability to write so much as a postcard. Did I have a partner? they wanted to know.

"Yes," I said, "but she lives in Calgary."

"Oh, God. Long-distance relationships are the pits," one of them said. "I got into one of those once. You can't trust anyone at that distance."

"Tell me about this place," I said.

The large one said, "Well, you have to be careful. Looks like you're new here." I nodded. "See that one at the bar—her and the one beside her?" She glanced at a woman in her forties wearing a leather jacket and jeans, and another beside her in a fringed jacket and pants and boots. "Like, don't *ever* get alone with those two, either one of them."

"What do you mean? Any woman has to be better than some of the men I've been involved with. My husband was violent."

They laughed. The little one twirled round impishly on one foot, then bent double. "You think *lesbians* are any better?" she said when she straightened up. "I tell you, those two could chew nails and spit rust. You'd better be careful. *Real* careful."

"Say, where do you teach?" she asked after a moment.

Here we go, I thought. "U of T," I said, in a tone of voice that implied it was some sort of junior high or community college.

"You do!" The little one was delighted. "Maybe you know my dad. He teaches there too. What department are you in?"

"English, but it's a huge institution. I'm sure I—"

521

"*English!* No way! That's my dad's department," she said, naming a colleague I knew well.

I felt ill. But before she could pursue this any further, the disc jockey arrived and began a loud spiel welcoming all the "ladies and ladies" to the Rose Café. Her words were soon drowned out in the deafening beat of disco. Women seemed to pour in now from the street: couples I recognized as butch and femme—the butches like tough motorcycle guys, the femmes in miniskirts and thigh-high stockings. Paul would have liked them, I thought. There were other couples I recognized from my readings as "Bobbsey queers"—girls with exactly the same clothes, haircuts, shoes, even jewellery. But mostly there were women of all ages in pants and shirts and no makeup. Women I would never notice as anything other than the secretaries, business women, professionals, or whatever they were by day.

My two young friends pulled me between them onto the now-crowded dance floor. "Dance with us," they laughed. And I did, moving in that crowd of women as if caught in some Dionysian rite. Suddenly, a couple of women broke from the pulsating mass and clambered up on two tiny platforms at either side of the dance floor. One was a stocky leather dyke with hair cut like James Dean who stomped and slicked her hair back. The other was a sinuous black girl in a tiny miniskirt and stretch halter top who undulated as if in a spastic trance.

I avoided using the washroom. Once it had been a refuge from men. Now it could be dangerous. I knew men had washroom sex—did women, too? What if I got stuck in there with one of the two dykes at the bar? After a few beers and a couple of hours of dancing, I'd had enough. I thanked the two young women, grateful to escape before my new friend offered to say hello to her dad for me. As I pushed my way through what was now a crowd of women at the doorway, I found myself face to face with one of my graduate students. "Hi," we both said, astonished. "I'm just getting out of here," I said awkwardly and hurried past her into the cold, damp street outside.

I wasn't sure what I'd learned from my night at the Rose Café. I was confused. This community didn't feel comfortable to me. It hadn't seemed much different from hetero bars. It was pleasant to see couples of women dancing together, talking affectionately, holding hands and gazing at each other as Janice and I had done. But it still felt dangerous, out of control somehow. A smoky flesh market with trance-inducing music. The kind of music that gives permission. It seemed to have nothing much to do with the deep soul connection I felt with Janice, nor with the life of embroidery, reading, gentle stroking, and intimate loving we had so often imagined for ourselves.

In the car on the way home I heard a song that somehow captured the terrible melancholy I felt. I listened carefully for the singer and song afterwards. Suzy Boggs, "What Have I Got to Do to Make You Love Me." The next day I got the CD and played it over and over and over. Yes, it was a sad, sad situation. I played this song and cried and cried whenever I was alone.

Grieving had begun.

Christmas was otherwise dampened. One after another we came down with a gutwrenching, feverish flu. My turn was last. After everyone had gone except Hugo, it hit me full force. I was in bed in a fitful achy sleep when Hugo called me to the phone.

"It's Janice, Mum. I told her you were sick and sleeping, but she said it was urgent. Sorry to wake you ..."

Janice? It was two days early. She wasn't due back until the fourth, the third at the earliest. I had fixed on the fourth to protect myself from disappointment. I was restraining myself from checking my e-mail until the fourth. I took the phone.

523

"Darling," she said. "Are you okay? Hugo said you're sick."

"Yeah," I said, befuddled with headache and fever and sleep. "Just the flu. You aren't supposed to be back yet, are you?"

"Nope. We hit some bad weather and changed our plans. I missed you. I can't wait to see you."

"Look," I said firmly. I had prepared this as my first speech to her. "Look, I won't be coming out there this month. I just can't visit casually any more. Sorry."

"Darling, I thought you'd say that. But listen. I've done a lot of thinking over the holiday. I can't accept your proposal. It would be too hard for me to have a double life."

It was what I'd expected. I just wanted to go back to bed. Nurse my flu. She went on, but I hardly heard her.

"I've decided to live with you, if you'll have me. If not, I'll live alone. I've told David I'm leaving him. That was important to me. To tell him before discussing it with you. I've told him I'm leaving whether you'll have me or not. I'm doing this for me."

Then silence.

"You see," she went on, "I saw this movie. You know, with Geena Davis? From *Thelma and Louise?*"

She paused. I couldn't take it in. A movie? *Thelma and Louise?* Told David? Living with me?

"Hey, *say* something, Cameron. I'm telling you I can't accept your offer, because I want more. I want the works. *Say* something, dammit!"

"I'm sick. I can't take this in. You want *what?*"

"You, babe. JE. Life together. I'm leaving David no matter what, anyway. What do you say?"

"I don't know what to say. Have you actually left?"

"No ... David and I have worked it all out. We aren't going to tell the kids until later. We want to pick a time that doesn't disrupt their school. After exams, I guess. I figure I can leave by May."

"May?" I was stunned. May? I counted out the months. Five. Could we really be living together in five months?

"Why? What made you decide?"

"I told you. It was this movie. We saw it over the holiday. *Speechless.*"

"Sorry, I just can't think what to say."

"No ... no, that's the *movie. Speechless.*"

I had never heard her talk this fast, sound this enthusiastic.

"You see, the Geena Davis character is engaged to this one guy—he's played by Christopher Reeve—and this *other* guy falls in love with her. Michael Keaton. Christ, the Reeve guy has been with her for two years and he not only doesn't know her, he doesn't even *try* to know her ... and the *other* guy gets her number right away and really respects her, really connects. See?"

She paused.

"No ... I don't get it. But you can tell me later. I'll go see it myself. So what's going on here? You mean you're leaving David? For good? Seriously?"

"Yes ... oh, darling, yes. Isn't it wonderful?"

I was ... speechless.

"Well ... *say* something, Cameron. For God's sake. I need to hear something, anything."

"Well ... that's wonderful," I managed to get out in my fluey voice.

I was scared.

"I want you," she said, serious now. "Really want you. I want years and years. I want to go places with you and see things and read things and talk and talk and talk. And hold you and be held. To wake with you beside me and know we have that day and the next and the next after that. To feed you and be fed. To sit at Stratford holding your hand—or in theatres or trains or beside fountains."

"Yes," I said. "Yes."

"But I want us to think carefully about how to do this," she went on. She was miles ahead of me on a trail of her own choosing. "Try to make it as easy as possible on the people affected. Our kids, David. Everyone. I need to keep talking to David about this. Work it out together. Choose the best time to tell your guys. Our parents. At the end of this term we can be together. We can go to that lighthouse in PEI you said you can rent. Oh, God! I love you so."

She paused.

Finally she said, "You know what David said when I told him? He sat there and thought for a while. Then he said, 'I'm going to miss your soups.' That was it. That was all he said."

Could a hiking trip on Kilimanjaro or Everest have been worked out with any more caution and precision? Like any major expedition, telling family and friends about JE was planned in meticulous detail.

We did not know where or how we were going to live. The coming year was my sabbatical. I had planned to leave Toronto no matter what, knowing what happened to professors who are glimpsed collecting their campus mail or are encountered at parties of colleagues. Their advice is sought. They find themselves on "just this one" committee. Graduate students phone to ask for "this special last-minute letter of reference." I had spent all my other sabbaticals and leaves looking after kids and supporting husbands' careers. This might be my last year off to do research and write. I intended to use it for myself.

Paul was dragging his heels on our divorce. But I would not let his delays ruin my sabbatical year. I would wriggle off the hook. I'd have to be available for examinations for discovery or a pretrial or trial, but if I didn't leave Canada, that could be worked out. He had ignored my second offer to settle, but he might suddenly speed up and push for settlement. As always, the only thing I could expect from him was the unexpected.

He had not been around most of the time over the year Henry and I had lived at home. Much of the time he'd been doing research in Africa, leaving no forwarding address or phone number for his lawyer or even for Henry. By the time my sabbatical began, I would have lived with Henry alone for fifteen months.

525

My first talk was with Henry. Already he'd complained that he hardly saw his father. Months before, I had suggested he ask for a week or two with him. He came to me in tears shortly after to say Paul had told him he couldn't afford it. That was absurd, I thought, but did not say so. A salary of almost $100,000? Fassiefern such a cheap place to live? All his expenses in Africa covered by grants?

I began after that to broach the subject of my sabbatical. Henry did not want to leave Toronto. He wanted to stay in the same school, spend time with his friends. I invited him to suggest options along with mine. Why not close off the stairs to the basement, he said, and let Paul live downstairs while I lived upstairs? That way he could go back and forth between the two of us. I recognized the painful fantasy of all divorced children: to bring their parents back together. Gently I explained that I could not live in close quarters with a man who had hit me. Henry, who unfortunately had seen some of Paul's tempestuous outbursts, understood.

Between us we came up with a plan that suited us both. I would leave Toronto for my sabbatical, and Paul would move into the house and support Henry for the next fifteen months. Henry wanted lots of phone calls and visits from me, but otherwise was happy at the prospect of "cooking with Dad in the kitchen." Because I had seen him stand up to Paul, I did not fear for him.

Now the e-mail flew back and forth. The decision with Henry cleared the way for other plans. I would spend my sabbatical in Calgary. This meant we would have to find a place to rent. I flew out in March to check out apartments with Janice. Up and down the streets we went, noting For Rent signs and following up newspaper ads. There were so many places available, at rents so much less than Toronto's, I was delighted. Janice wanted good light, preferably southwest. I wanted enough space to write. We needed a place for kids to stay over. She knew the city, which districts would be best.

It wasn't until we saw a tiny blue bungalow with a garden for sale that the thought of buying crossed our minds. This little house with its sunny rooms and quiet location looked like a home—could be *our* home.

It would hinge on David, Janice concluded. He wanted their Calgary house and wanted the boys to stay on with him. She was to have the Pass House. But if he would agree to sign for a second mortgage, there might be enough money for a down payment. The money we would be paying for rent could cover mortgage payments instead, even though I would be paying half the mortgage, insurance, and taxes to maintain my equity in the two Ontario properties until my divorce was settled.

"I'm sure David's *glad* I'm leaving," Janice kept saying. "He seems so happy. He's eager to help us out with a down payment. We'll have to figure the details, but I think it will work. Honestly, it seems like he's getting what he wants. He told me that all along he's been planning his retirement a year from now without me in the picture. Makes me angry. I wish he'd been upfront about his feelings. He must have switched off long ago. I mean, the man's shared a bed with me for over a year now without ever laying a hand on me."

The bungalow, we decided, was a money pit. We had both been through renovations. Never again, we agreed. But now that we'd figured out how to buy instead of rent, our search for a home broadened. As I returned on the plane to Toronto, round in my mind swirled the condo with the balcony, the house with the patio, the townhouse with built-in everything, the New York-style loft with the raised bedroom in the historic warehouse. But there was nothing I really wanted to own.

I didn't pay much attention to Janice's e-mail describing a wonderful townhouse with really interesting spaces. I was too busy ending my teaching term. I booked another flight to Calgary, hoping that this time we would find a place we both liked enough to buy.

We had agreed to tell our kids about us at roughly the same time. Janice had decided not to tell her guys until after Leopold finished his mid-term tests. So that was the day I told Henry. "We need another talk," I said. "Come on, sit down."

"I've decided where I'm going next year," I went on. "I'm going to Calgary."

He nodded. "Will you live with Janice?" he asked.

"Yes. She and I have decided to become partners. I want you to know that you can always count on me. On us. Anytime you want to live with me, you'll be welcome. You could finish high school there. Or go to university later. There'll always be a room for you if you want it."

"Nope," he said firmly, shaking his head. "I want to stay here where my friends are. I want to stay in my school. Will you visit? Can I come visit you?"

"Yes, of course. And we can be in touch as much as you like by phone."

"Mum ..."

"Yes?"

"I knew ... about you and Janice, I mean. When she was here in November. I mean, you were sleeping together."

"Yes," I said. "I thought you'd ask about it. Does this bother you?"

He began to cry. "I don't want you to take the cats," he said. "They're my girlie-girls. And I don't want you saying Anatol and Leopold are like sons to you. You have two sons—me and Hugo. Not them."

I hugged him and felt the familiar exchange of love. "Don't worry," I said. "You can keep the cats here. I know you'll look after them well. I'll take them if you ever want me to. And no one can replace you and Hugo in my heart. Bea, either. I love you."

"I love you too, Mum."

That night I called Hugo.

"No problem," he said. "I mean, I'm not homophobic or anything. But I don't especially like Janice. Where will you be living?" I told him, and explained about Henry.

"What do you dislike about Janice?" I asked.

"Don't know. I just trust my gut feeling on people."

"That's okay," I said. "I hope in time you'll change your mind. If not, it won't make a difference between you and me. I'll always love you and want to see you."

There was silence.

"Mum?"

"Yeah."

"I'm worried that if you're not dressing for men any more you'll lose your looks."

Bea took it better. "Wow, Mum," she giggled after I'd finished my long-distance explanation. "And now for something *completely* different!" She laughed. "I think it's *great*! Peter and I are musicians, so—trust me—we're used to gay people. Like, *lots* of gay people. But I haven't even *met* Janice. I want to meet her as soon as possible."

"Well, sweetie, that won't be for a while, unless you're planning a trip."

"Not until next March, probably," she said.

"Well, I'll send pictures. Meanwhile, I'm so glad you're not upset. Your acceptance of this means so much to me. What you say makes me feel really, really happy."

I felt dazed. Almost too dazed to get onto e-mail to see how Janice's guys were taking it.

"We had a family powwow," the message said.

David and I—actually David—told the guys what was happening. We started by telling them we were getting divorced. They were surprised, and immediately came up with lots of ideas about how we

528

could stay together. We just listened for a while before telling them, no, this is final. We told them they could choose whether to stay on at the house or live with us. Told them they'd have lots of time to decide. D. and I want them to see that we are friends. That over the next couple of months until I move out there are no fights or conflicts. That there are civilized ways of splitting up.

Then we got onto JE. How you and I would be living together, but that we'd still be seeing David and them. We'd be here in Calgary where they could visit and see me whenever they wanted. There was all this discussion. Leopold said, "But it's every man's God-given right to have a woman." Then he caught himself and said, "Oh my God, what am I saying." They wanted to know where we'd be living. I had to tell them we didn't know, but we'd try to find a place not too far away.

Finally, the penny dropped for Anatol, who, after all, is only twelve. Finally he looked around at us all and said, "You mean ... my mother is *gay?*"

529

Look, I think you'll like this townhouse. I took A. over with me to look again, and he loved it. The agent says it hasn't sold because the spaces are so quirky. I can't really describe. I hope it hasn't sold by the time you get here. I love it BECAUSE the spaces are so quirky. And the light is phenomenal. Gorgeous. The bedroom has a south AND a west window. Big elm tree outside. Bonus: it's only five blocks from D. and the guys. I'm so HAPPY. Can't wait to see you this time. Forever and ever, J.

Next were our parents. "I asked D. to tell them," she e-mailed.

We went over there today. They were fairly upset. Father went into his minister role giving us advice. I had to shut him down. Mother wanted to blame me, since she's convinced women cause all the trouble in the world. They both think this, actually. We didn't tell them about JE. One thing at a time. We just told them about separating. They like D. What I told them was that I expect them to continue to treat D. as one of the family, just as they always have. We explained that there were no fights. No conflicts. We would have no problem attending family events together. They were mystified, but relieved not to have to make choices, I think.

I drove to Barrie to tell mine. I decided to tell them separately. First my mother.

"Mum," I said. "I have something really important to tell you. Janice and I have decided to live together."

"Well, that will be nice," she said. "What about her husband?"

"They are getting divorced. Amicably."

"Well, it does make sense economically, I guess. And I hate to see you so lonely. I've been dreading your bringing another man home."

"Mum, I don't just mean sharing a house, sharing expenses. I mean ..."

"You mean you intend to live as a couple?"

"Yes."

530 "Well, don't tell your father. I can understand it. Though I won't tell my friends. I couldn't tell them. But don't tell your father. He's dreadfully opposed to homosexuality."

"I can't promise that, Mum. I want him to know."

Later I tackled my father. "Dad, I want to tell you something important."

He looked up from his ongoing game of solitaire quizzically. He was eighty-three and his memory was a bit unreliable.

"Do you remember Janice?"

"Yes. She's that nice dark girl. The lawyer, isn't she?"

"Yep. She and I have decided to live together."

"Live together? Seems sensible. Good."

Just then my mother walked in. "Yes," she said. "Donald ... they've ... made a commitment to each other. To live together."

He looked at me. He understood. It was all right.

"It's drink time, isn't it?" he said looking at the clock. It was early, but for once he'd break his rule: No drinks until the sun is over the yardarm. "I'd better get the single malt out." And he made his way into the dining room and emerged with his precious single-malt Scotch.

Next were Janice's brothers and my sisters. Each of us got the warmest response from the much younger siblings we'd helped raise. My younger sister was enthusiastic. "I felt there was something between you two when I met Janice. Great! She's very good for you. She seems like a soulmate." Janice's youngest brother simply said, "No problem here. Wendy and I will have you both over as soon as we can."

Our other siblings said nothing much at all.

Finally came our friends. We didn't want anyone we cared for to hear via the gossip we knew would race through the academic world. We *wanted* the gossip, wanted it to inform acquaintances and colleagues, but we wanted to tell our close friends in person first. That meant telling them as simultaneously as possible.

I invited each of mine to lunch on consecutive days. And almost every one said, "I'm not surprised." I was bewildered. *I* was surprised, very surprised. Why weren't they? Members of my women's group said they had picked up on the vibes between Janice and me the evening I took her to meet them. That group had fostered one partnership between two women who claimed they knew, had been certain, just seeing us together. They welcomed me into the sisterhood and eagerly extolled the joys of lesbian life.

Gail and her husband, who had helped me so much through all the pain of separating from Paul, said they knew how close Janice and I had become. They weren't surprised because they couldn't see how I could trust a man after Paul.

Another friend—much younger—said she wasn't surprised because she knew how much more intimate women friends can be than a man and a woman. She couldn't fathom the sex, but she could certainly see how sharing life with a woman might be wonderful. Before long she was speculating on who among her girlfriends she could imagine choosing.

The American lesbian couple Paul and I had known for years—a doctor and a writer/professor—travelled up to see me on their annual visit. I warned them I had something important to tell them. They sat in my kitchen while I explained. "See," Anita said. "I was right. I told you this would be what she had to tell us."

"How could you know?" I asked. "I never envied you as a couple. Never wondered about whether life with a woman would suit me."

"I always thought you could be a sister. Don't know why. Just did. I'm not surprised," said Anita.

"But you could knock me over with the proverbial feather," said Beth. And they both gave me big hugs.

531

There was one couple I could not pin down to a specific lunch date. Eventually, after I'd persisted without success, they asked me over to their place for dinner instead.

While Jack got martinis, Cindy asked me impatiently, "What *is* it? Have you met someone? Don't tell me you're getting married again."

"Well," I said, deciding to join in the twenty-questions spirit, "sort of."

"Sort of? What do you mean? Who is he? Is it someone I know?"

"Yes, you've met." I remembered bringing Janice along to their big annual garden party the previous fall.

"Not that historian." She named a colleague.

"No."

"Thank God! He'd be real trouble. Who *is* he?"

"It's not a he. It's a she."

Cindy was speechless for a moment. Her eyes widened. "A *she*? Who?"

"Janice Dickin McGinnis. I brought her to your party last fall, don't you remember?"

"Vaguely. A dark woman, interesting. Yes ... yes. I do. Wasn't she married?"

"Not now."

Cindy thought for a moment. Then she said, "Look, Elspeth. Are you sure this isn't some sort of intellectual experiment? Virginia Woolf ... that sort of thing? Lots of writers try this sort of thing out just to find out what it's like."

"No," I said quietly. "I love her."

"Jack will have a fit. He's put you on a pedestal for years. He thinks you're the quintessential blonde.

"Well!" she said, as Jack brought a tray of martinis into the room. "Jack, Elspeth has some *very* interesting news for you."

"She's not getting married again, is she?" he said in his urbane way.

"Sort of."

Jack perked up. He raised a sardonic eyebrow. "Who's the lucky guy? Anyone I know?"

"You've met," I said.

"Is it someone in academe?" Jack was my colleague at U of T.

"Yes."

"Social sciences?"

"Yes."

He looked to Cindy. She sat beaming, but didn't give him a clue.

"It's not ... what's-his-name."

"Nope," we said in stereo.

He smiled in the knowing way he had when he made jokes. "It's a woman, I suppose."

"Yes," we said, again in stereo.

He chuckled and went right on. "So is he one of our colleagues, Elspeth? Who's the lucky bugger?"

"Jack. Jack," said Cindy, "didn't you hear us? It *is* a woman. It's Janice ... what's her last name, Elspeth?"

"Dickin McGinnis."

"Janice Dickin McGinnis. Elspeth brought her to our party last fall. Remember? Interesting woman." Jack just sat there. He was white, crumpled somehow.

"So, where will you live?" Cindy went on. She was full of questions. How had we met. How had this happened. What was the sex like. Jack said nothing.

Eventually we all moved into the dining room. Jack was still silent. His colour had changed from white to grey. When Cindy got up to clear the table for dessert, Jack quietly left the room and went upstairs. Cindy called him when she had dessert ready, and he slowly descended the stairs wearing his pyjamas and dressing gown. He looked ill.

"Well, I can take a hint. I guess this means it's time to go," I joked to Cindy. I finished my dessert quickly, accepted a quick, warm hug from Cindy and drove home.

I never heard again from all those York couples I had entertained with Paul for fifteen years. All those parties. All that care taken not to intimidate the wives, not to flirt with the husbands. All those picnics, visits, chats about children. Gone. It would be a year before I stopped feeling that loss.

Janice lost two couples she'd been close to for twenty years. One told her what she was doing was wrong. The other never replied to her repeated invitations for lunch or coffee. A woman she described as her oldest friend also evaporated. But her other friends responded with good wishes and requests to meet me as soon as we got settled. Some colleagues avoided her. Most—especially those in women's studies—congratulated her.

The townhouse was still for sale when I returned to Calgary. I fell in love with it at once. It was the corner house of an eleven-unit complex around a European courtyard garden. Each white unit had a different-coloured door. Ours was blue. The effect was that of a Mondrian painting. "Connaught Gardens," as it was called,

533

after the Duke of Connaught who had visited Calgary more than once early this century, had won awards for its architect and designer. It would be by far the nicest place I had ever lived in. The price had dropped to within our range, and David came through with the financing we needed to buy it. In a matter of days "Blue Doors" was ours. We would take possession June 30, right after our month and a half in the lighthouse on the coast of PEI. Our honeymoon.

I was happy with a happiness I'd never felt before. I felt more real than I'd ever felt before. My hair was slowly returning to its natural colour—dark ash with streaks of grey.

Our life together began exactly four years from the day we met in Edinburgh. On the fourth of May, I met Janice at the Toronto airport, as I had done so many times before.

We clasped each other tight, saying nothing. Finally, she said, "Darling."

"Yes," I replied.

And we exchanged anniversary gifts as we had each year on the fourth of May. For her, my Aunt Winnie's 1921 diamond watch. "I loved seeing this on her small wrist. Now I can admire it on yours," I said.

534

And for me a Swiss Army knife for our hikes.

"No dyke should be without one," she said, laughing, and took me in her arms.

After Daniel

MOIRA FARR

Moira Farr (b. 1958) is an Ottawa writer whose book *After Daniel: A Suicide Survivor's Tale* (1999) is just what the subtitle suggests: a memoir of coming to terms with the suicide of one's mate. Daniel was Daniel Jones, a Toronto writer, poet, and editor who killed himself in 1994, age 34, leaving a twenty-one page suicide note. He had published one collection of poetry, *Only the Brave Write Poetry* (1985). Two works of fiction, *Obsessions: A Novel* and *The People One Knows: Toronto Stories*, have appeared posthumously. His suicide was the first notable one among his generation of Canadian writers and provoked a sense of public loss, apart from the sort of deep private grief that Farr writes of here.

535

DANIEL,
We Hardly Knew You

As the months and years have passed since Daniel's death, I have often looked back on those final days and wondered how it was that I never translated my inchoate fears of what might happen into the dreaded word "suicide." At worst, I thought that if Daniel's depressed mood continued to spiral downward, it would render him helpless to cope with living alone in his apartment and he would have to stay with me, or someone else who could help him recover. The most grim thought of all, I wondered if he would have to be hospitalized. That seemed like rock-bottom, and I was prepared to do what I could to make sure Daniel didn't hit it. I knew that his greatest fear was of a return to the severe terrors of agoraphobia he had experienced years earlier, when he was trying to conquer alcoholism. As he saw it, the drinking had merely masked the depression and phobia he had begun to suffer in his early teens, and that had laid in wait to pounce on him as he struggled to become sober.

The young American novelist Andrew Solomon, writing in *The New Yorker* in 1997, brilliantly described his harrowing bouts of depression at its most extreme—so paralyzing that he spent days in bed, lying in his own urine, rather than face the terror of even simple movement—in words that hauntingly echoed for me Daniel's own graphic accounts of the affliction. So far, Solomon remains alive, with the aid of medications, supportive friends, an extraordinarily nurturing father who literally spoon-fed and washed his thirty-one-year-old son when he could not do it himself, and an admirable, unsentimental desire to affirm the value of life. Still, he heard what he calls the "seductress" of the suicidal impulse in his darkest times, knows others who have surrendered to it, and does not smugly suggest the siren call could never tempt him again.

Yes, that's how bad it gets for some. And even then, survival is possible. Yet Daniel viewed the prospect of another round of alcohol abuse followed by the hellish symptoms of withdrawal as unendurable: "I'd rather chop my head off than go through that again," he once told me dryly, as we sipped coffee on the outdoor patio of the Café Diplomatico one balmy day in June. He had explored some of the more horrifying aspects of that nightmare in his novel *Obsessions*. At the time, he seemed determined to never again find himself in such darkness.

Now, I know that given Daniel's set of "risk factors," and the place he would come to occupy as a statistic, he was practically a textbook case of a suicide waiting to happen: a young white male with a history of depression, alcoholism (though sober for eight years), previous suicide attempts, with a recent marital split and financial difficulties. These latter problems he sought to solve by doing something else that is a telltale sign of suicidality: getting rid of possessions, in his case, an impressive collection of modern first-edition books. There were also strained relations and outright estrangement from some family members and friends, and a string of disappointments concerning his work. Of course, if Daniel was in one of the highest risk groups for suicide, it occurred to me later that I, as someone predisposed to fall in love with a young man of this description, by virtue of my own age and sex and more personal identifying markers, had also entered a high-risk group, poised to mourn the suicides of these men.

There are statistics, diagnoses, categories and risk factors, trends and theories, and then there are real people and their unique lives. It seems that many still lack a language with which to adequately express, even to themselves, the nameless, formless despair that feeds on itself and grows bigger and more dangerous, more self-destructive. We speak now commonly of "depression," though it is, as author William Styron writes in *Darkness Visible* of his own frightening bout of it, "a noun with a bland tonality and lacking any magisterial presence, used indifferently to describe an economic decline or a rut in the ground, a true wimp of a word." Forsaking any sense that profound feelings of sadness might have a spiritual dimension, a greater purpose, if only to alert us that something is very wrong internally and externally with our lives, with our whole beings, we seem to expect people armed with medical degrees and pharmaceutical compendiums—wisdom and compassion optional—to take away our pain, solve our problems, make us better with a scrawl on a prescription pad. But any understanding of depression (for lack of a better word) that reduces it to its organic causes and effects alone, and the people suffering from it to mere biological entities with lists of symptoms to be treated, is an impoverished one.

By all indications, however, suicide was always a possibility for Daniel. "It's like all the trains came into the station at once, and there just weren't enough tracks," mused a friend shortly after Daniel's death. The expanding freight of misfortunes culminated in what suicide experts refer to as a "triggering event." In Daniel's case, it was the news in early February that publication of his book of short stories scheduled in a matter of weeks—advance manuscripts of the work had been sent out to the media for review, and he was to read at Toronto's Harbourfront reading series in March—had been delayed indefinitely. It was a situation fraught with acrimony and complications that did not die with Daniel, and which it must be in hindsight a relentless course of escalating self-sabotage. As is clear from his suicide note, it felt to him like a final, stunning failure, one that he did not believe he had the strength to redeem.

537

Yes, I look at all this today and can practically see a large movie marquee blinking brightly in the darkness above Daniel's apartment, announcing:

VALENTINE'S DAY SPECIAL!
ONE NIGHT ONLY!
THE SUICIDE OF DANIEL JONES
STARRING DANIEL JONES

(This followed by, in much smaller letters, somewhere near the bottom: *and Moira Farr as the girlfriend—who didn't know.*)

In the context of statistics and risk factors I learned about after the fact, it seems odd that Daniel's suicide would shock anyone who knew him. Yet despite the risk profile he theoretically embodied, or the fact that his writing had always been rife with references to suicide—indeed, took the reader all too closely into the troubled mechanics of the suicidal mind—no flashing sign proclaimed the imminent event. During his final days, Daniel did and said things and behaved in ways that he must have intended to throw me and others off the suicidal scent. Again, this is a not uncommon pattern for suicidal people. Time after time, survivors report with heartbreaking irony that if anything, the depressed people they have lost seemed in better spirits than usual in the days leading up to their suicides.

Those who study suicide say that the energy required to carry one out usually comes only when the person's depression has lifted somewhat. What family and friends think with relief is a positive uplift in mood may only reflect the person's own relief that he or she will soon be dead; and therefore no longer burdened with intolerable pain—or "psychache," a term coined by Edwin Shneidman, the psychologist considered the founder of the field of suicidology. And so, all kinds of clues that seem so obvious once the person is gone add up to something quite different while he or she is still alive and functioning, doing it better than has been the case for some time.

And maybe that is true. In one of the most painfully resonant observations I have read on the subject, Alfred Alvarez writes in *The Savage God:* "A suicidal depression is a kind of spiritual winter, frozen, sterile, unmoving. The richer, softer and more delectable nature becomes, the deeper the internal winter seems, and the wider and more intolerable the abyss which separates the inner world from the outer." I felt a terrible sadness when I first read these words, for their implied interpretation of all the changes Daniel tried to make in the last year of his life. Perhaps his embarking on a new romantic relationship was partly a desperate effort to allay the deep depression that always threatened to terrorize him. Once the first glow of the romance began to dim a little, I wonder, did he feel a huge sense of disappointment and even fear? Did he ever articulate the thought to himself that even grand feelings of love weren't going to chase away his black dogs for good? Was this experience the painful backdrop for his unfolding suicidal plan? It hurts to think so, and for a time after his death, brooding on this fuelled much of my sadness and self-pity. Like the bumbling loser protagonist of E. Annie Proulx's novel *The Shipping News*, I flagellated myself with a series of incriminating headlines bannering my brain:

538

STUPID WOMAN WANTS TO SETTLE DOWN
AND LIVE HAPPY LIFE, FALLS FOR DEPRESSED WRITER

STUPID WOMAN FAILS TO SAVE SUICIDAL BOYFRIEND

SAVE SELF, FRIENDS, EXPERTS URGE STUPID WOMAN

For a time, I regarded with disgust a world that skips merrily along on unexamined romantic fantasies that love conquers all, love is all you need, love lifts us
up where we belong, any kind of love is better than no love at all, and so on. I
had so wanted to believe it. Daniel and I loved each other, no question of that.
But, contrary to the pop propaganda, love wasn't enough to obliterate despair,
saved no one, did not mean never having to say you're sorry, failed to lift us higher and higher, or coax us into believing that with this love of ours, which had no
beginning and had no end, we could make everything all right. I endured an
unpleasant period when I privately and bitterly seethed at those who believed that
love had gotten them or someone they cared for through a tough situation. I
envied them their unsullied faith in their own human powers, their sunny belief
in a mellow and benevolent God who, when not restoring fallen baby sparrows
to their nests, spends his time making everything nice for special little them. I
viewed with contempt their ability to embrace an expansive sense of love's capabilities at a time when mine had been thoroughly destroyed. If there were a
Heartbreak Olympics, I figured I deserved gold, and for a time, all I wanted to
do was to rest on my dubious, self-awarded laurels.

539

This kind of bitterness is not uncommon among the mourning and the traumatized. Any illusion that you have control over your life or that of another has
been viciously ripped away. Suddenly, you are cast out from the world of unrav-
aged souls able to trust their own good emotional navigation, their own personal
goodness, while you limp along, hopelessly flawed, a pariah, uninvited to the celebration of happiness you imagine everyone else is enjoying. If anything spurred
me to get serious about facing the grief, it was my shamed feeling that I couldn't
genuinely extend good wishes for happiness to others.

Owning up to the fact that I was wasting a lot of time and energy feeling
sorry for myself was humbling. "The world breaks everyone, and afterward some
are strong at the broken places," wrote Ernest Hemingway in *A Farewell to Arms*.
Perhaps his own eventual suicide indicates he did not include himself in the strong

"some." But it seems appropriate that a 1990 book heralding the new and widening focus on human "resilience," as opposed to dysfunction, in social work and psychotherapy, takes its title from this bit of Hemingway. The book's author, Linda T. Sanford, a Boston psychotherapist, interviewed people who had overcome extreme abuse and loss in childhood, many of whom had chosen work in helping professions. Some expressed dismay that their lives had been marked so severely by trauma, and wondered if they might have been different people, making different choices, if they had not had their bad experiences. But they were people who succeeded in spite of—indeed, because of—their wounds, people who tried to use their understanding and knowledge positively, genuinely believing they were wiser counsellors to the bereaved and traumatized owing to their own experiences. They could help others more effectively, since they could truly empathize with their pain; in this sense, something good had arisen from their own difficulties, something they came to accept and value on its own painfully born terms.

Healing, to be real and complete, doesn't mean that scars reminding you of severe past wounds disappear. It can and should mean a restoration of one's faith in the enduring possibilities of life and love: your life, your love. Tolstoy recognized this when he wrote, "Only people who are capable of loving strongly can also suffer great sorrow, but this same necessity of loving serves to counteract their grief and heals them." The wise novelist's words appear on the introductory pages of a well-regarded handbook for grief counsellors.

And so, though it stings to imagine it, for I naively assumed that the support and love I offered Daniel might at least offset some of his depression, I now wonder if he was playing some horrific game of chicken with himself in those final days. It is hard to read his suicide note's careful accounting of what he finally decided to do and why, hard not to turn away from the unforgiving glare of the words he wrote in a trembling script, less than two hours after our last goodbye:

> between 6:45 and 7:00 took approx. 45–50 Ativan (1 mg.) ...
> shaking all over, but fully conscious ... I would like to be nearly
> passed out before closing the bag(s) completely around my neck with
> the rubber bands. Will this happen? I have handcuffs, to cuff myself
> in a position where I am incapable of tearing the bags ... should I have
> to suffocate myself in full consciousness ... I will go through with it,
> but it seems extremely unpleasant ... I have long wanted to do it, but
> fear alone has prevented me.

I knew he was despondent over yet another rejected writing-grant application the previous week. He did not mention the postponed book to me, which he would have known about several days earlier. Yet he refers to it in his lengthy suicide note and, as though helpfully laying out evidence, he neatly compiled the terse, rejecting correspondence that must have stung so harshly in a prominent place on his desk. Lots of conflicting clues indicate now that he was enduring a kind of ambivalence towards life that is common among suicidal people, see-sawing between "I will/I can't" almost until his final hour.

Evidence suggests that the suicidal state is indeed hellishly Janus-faced. American journalist George Howe Colt, in his 1991 book, *The Enigma of Suicide*, cites many examples of people who, after surviving serious suicide attempts, express relief that they failed, and gratitude that their lives were saved—lives which, up to the very moment of their self-destructive actions, they apparently did not wish to continue. In one extraordinary instance, a man who survived a jump from San Francisco's Golden Gate Bridge (often referred to as the suicide capital of the world, though now fenced to prevent jumps, and routinely patrolled and monitored for would-be jumpers), explains how the moment he leapt off and was airborne, he understood with horror that he had made a mistake and suddenly felt a frantic desire not to die. Accounts such as these do nothing to comfort the loved ones of successful suicides, who may prefer to think that the deceased did not feel anything in the moments before dying or they were so sure of their course, they at least got their wish, and are no longer suffering. Painful though it may be to face, it is more likely that this is not so. It is standard now in the treatment and study of the suicidal to assume ambivalence, on one side of which is indeed a desire to live.

Those of us close to Daniel, and there weren't many at that point, hadn't been given enough overt reason to look seriously at how desperate he had become in so short a time. I had thought about calling his psychiatrist or one of his friends to confide my worries but didn't, considering that meddlesome. Daniel's psychiatrist, whom he liked and trusted, and had visited regularly for eight years, was stunned by the news of his death, and pored over his session notes from the previous weeks and months, vainly searching for decisive signs of Daniel's shift into crisis that he might have missed.

Even Daniel's efforts to divest himself of possessions and previous attachments, in one regard a classic precursor to suicide, could also be interpreted as healthy emotional housecleaning that he felt was overdue. Daniel had a rueful self-awareness of

541

the obsessive-compulsive underpinnings of his book collecting. While visiting my sister in London, England, the previous summer, we had stopped at a curio shop window in which were displayed an array of T-shirts adorned with witty cartoons and captions. One showed a nerdish fellow with a serious expression sitting at a table on which were spread small round objects. The caption underneath said, "Fred was upset to find a Rice Krispie in his Corn Flake collection." Daniel burst into a loud cackle of appreciation at this, tears forming at the corners of his eyes as we wended our way home. "I'm laughing because it's true! It's sick, that's how bad it is, this collecting business." (The next day, my sister went to buy the shirt for Daniel. It had already been sold; the problem is clearly endemic. Instead, she bought us each a T-shirt printed with the clean, green-and-white cover graphics of the original Penguin paperbacks—*The Thin Man* for Daniel, and *Farewell, My Lovely* for me. It was one of the first things I gave away after his death.)

And so, by Daniel's own account, the hobby that gave him pleasure could also be a burden, just one more thing for the mind to find fault with and patrol for disorder to a picayune degree. On one occasion, Daniel returned from a bookstore foray with a remaindered novel by William T. Vollman, which had been listed in a collectors' magazine as potentially valuable. Daniel had laughed as he showed it to me: "You see, I didn't buy it because I want to read it. I have no idea why it's considered valuable. But it was there, so I had to get it."

On another occasion, I was perusing Daniel's shelves and sat down on a box, one of many that littered the room, as he sorted through and put aside things he wanted to get rid of after he separated from his wife. "You're sitting on my *Tamarack Reviews*," he said, hovering behind me. I looked up, not sure what he meant. "It's a complete set. There may only be one other one in Canada." I stood, and Daniel, looking grave, took the box and placed it off in a corner, out of danger of being sat upon again. I couldn't help teasing him a little afterwards. "How about I sit on your *Tamarack Reviews*?" I would say, when he seemed unnecessarily bothered by some minor matter.

Daniel's obsessive-compulsive side also found expression in day-to-day routines. Unlike other men I'd encountered, Daniel was competent domestically, perhaps overly so, with a need to be surrounded by clean countertops and very organized shelves. Order comforted him, and his urge to stave off anxieties in this way was far greater than my own. My more laissez-faire style must have troubled him on some subconscious level. I had to smile at such times, as when, after I'd loaded a washing machine at the local laundry and slung the large canvas bag loosely onto a table, Daniel reflexively picked it up and folded it neatly.

Daniel himself was all too aware of the negative side of this compulsive obsessing over matters that pass almost unexamined through less fretful minds. There were occasions when he would explain some complicated situation to me, why he couldn't do this or that, the double, or quadruple edges of some decision that had to be made, the mutually exclusive options that were not options at all, the endless looping spirals of detail painstakingly discerned and teased out and closely regarded. Sometimes I felt I'd lost the thread of the thing entirely and wanted to scream in frustration. Daniel was expert at fashioning existential knots around himself, the kind that only tighten further each time you try to loosen and move free of them, while I stood on the outside wondering impatiently why they couldn't just be cut away altogether.

No, life was not simple for Daniel, and he lamented that himself, especially when it came to literary business. "I feel like I'm from the eighteenth century," he once commented with dismay, as he groused about some linguistic offence committed in print that he wished to protest formally in a letter. He feared he'd be made to feel foolish by people who either hadn't noticed or didn't care. He was punctilious about his own writing and editing, and could be savage about others' mistakes or sins of sloppiness.

If details threatened to swamp him, a larger part of Daniel's love of books and language was far from onerous. "I was aware of the delight that reading and purchasing books held for him. I was not, however, aware of his total passion for collecting until seeing his complete library," wrote a Toronto book dealer, Janet Fetherling, in a catalogue she compiled of Daniel's collection, which she bought after his death. "Here was someone who put his dust-jacket covers on with a folding-bone, owned specialised bibliographical reference material, and possessed a computer program for his records. Considering everything else he did, I don't see how he found the time." Daniel also found time to search out and read largely unknown works published by small Canadian literary presses. After his death, more than one writer remarked to me how pleasantly taken aback he or she had been to be approached by Daniel after publishing something in a chapbook or small-press edition, and how appreciative of his thoughtful comments and words of encouragement. The Canadian literary world can be a dispiriting place, where obscurity until awards have been won is the norm, sour grapes are a dietary staple, and praise where it is due a rarity. In this withering atmosphere, Daniel knew how much a small gesture could mean to a struggling writer. As he sorted through his books, he gave several to me that he thought I might like. The last one of these was *The Lover of Horses*, by Tess Gallagher, partner of the late American short-story writer and recovered alcoholic Raymond Carver, and herself a writer whom Daniel admired.

Even selling books could give him deep satisfaction. "Daniel enjoyed the disposal of books as well as the acquisition of them," Fetherling also observed in her catalogue. "I'm sure I'll buy more, and have just as big a collection sooner or later," Daniel told me wryly, as he prepared for the grand clearance. It didn't occur to me to confront him and say, "You're not selling these because you plan to kill yourself, are you?" Especially in the beginning of our courtship, this sorting and selling seemed something he wanted to do, a symbolic starting over, and I didn't question it.

Daniel had, after all, endured so much through his painful young years, and with immense effort, had survived serious depression, phobias, and the terrible places, both physical and emotional, that his alcoholism had taken him—alcoholism that functioned as a mask and a distraction from those other disorders. As is the case with hard-core addicts, once Daniel stopped drinking, he faced the real work of dealing with his fears and emotional problems. With much help from others which he acknowledged, he did that work, and had made his way. Without consulting a suicide risk-assessment checklist, there would have been no reason in the minds of his friends and colleagues to bring in the commital forms. Daniel would have vehemently rejected them anyway. In earlier poems and stories, he had captured the unique pathos of living in a mental ward. Daniel would have viewed a return there as a disastrous defeat and step backwards; for so long, he had moved himself away from that world, from that possibility.

When suicides happen, especially when we feel in hindsight that we failed to see what we should have seen, we must forgive ourselves. Demographers and various medical experts aside, we don't generally view the people we love as microdata units under the cold light of a larger statistical checklist of telltale signs, or assess them with clinical detachment ("I'm sorry, Daniel, but after consulting the *Diagnostic and Statistical Manual of Mental Disorders*, I've reached the conclusion that you are at a high risk for suicide. Get help, and goodbye"). Would the suicide rate be much affected if we did this? It's absurd to seriously imagine so on a sociological level, but naturally I have asked myself whether knowing what I know now, I might have responded differently to Daniel as he slipped further into his lonely decision.

544

Forming a relationship with Daniel's parents, in particular his mother, was one of the many unexpected things that happened after Daniel's death. Our bond was a painful one, but it was also healing in unforeseen and subtle ways. I can say with some certainty that this relationship would not have unfolded if Daniel had not died. In such strange twists does suicide throw a wild card into the deck you thought you knew well enough to predict, drawing you off in startling directions, challenging you to play an unfamiliar new hand.

Daniel had been estranged from his father for many years; there was only a handful of contacts between them after Daniel left home for university. Nor did his sister keep in touch with Daniel; I met her only once, at his funeral. Daniel was not comfortable visiting his parents home, and maintained a connection only with his mother, who met with him occasionally when she visited Toronto. Clearly, the reasons for this estrangement were a source of great pain to the family, and there was little of the difficult times of the past that they wished to discuss. I knew how Daniel viewed it, and it was in fact with considerable wariness that I approached his family at all. But I saw how his parents suffered, how deeply they grieved the loss of their son. Sustaining anger, blame, guilt, and shame aimed at ourselves or others would not bring him back. Painful and emotionally complicated though it will always be to consider the reasons why, the Joneses and I got to know each other.

There is a strong physical resemblance between Daniel and his father, gestures and expressions in common that were difficult for me to watch playing over Mr. Jones's face when I first met him. Daniel's mother was shattered by her son's death, and she and I tried in our different ways to support each other in the months just after his death. We were obsessed with its details, as though repeating it over and over in our minds, backtracking and probing around and reconstructing it would finally allow us to accept it as real. Those who study bereavement know there is a risk that grief-stricken people will become stuck in this phase of mourning, and counsellors gently steer people along this intense course. Yet fixating on the details of the death in the immediate aftermath of it is normal, even necessary for some. It constitutes a means of orienting the wounded heart and mind to the new reality that should not be suppressed.

Over lunches together, Mrs. Jones and I perused photos taken in the months and weeks before the suicide, and pored urgently over the events of Daniel's last days, as if our own lives depended on getting a clear and precise picture. In some ways, they did. We shed tears together. As time went on, we sent letters back

545

and forth, just to keep in touch, sometimes speaking of Daniel and the pain we felt, sometimes just sharing news of our lives. There were visits to the Joneses' home in a small community in southwestern Ontario. On one occasion Mrs. Jones and I knelt on the floor surrounded by photo albums and shoeboxes full of more photos and the usual parents' mementoes of a young son's or daughter's life: This was Daniel when, and here he is again, and again and again. A sweet-looking blond boy, swinging on swings, playing cowboy with his sister, opening Christmas presents, visiting the zoo, off to the high-school formal with a pretty girl.

Mr. Jones was less expressive of his emotions during our visits, yet he struggled to understand too. Ironically, he gave me one of the most tender remembrances of Daniel, as we stood by the open trunk of his car unloading an array of plants from a local nursery. "The first book he ever read was *Mrs. Duck's Lovely Day*," he told me. Daniel would sit on his lap as a child barely old enough to talk and recite the jolly little tale. He was so bright, Mr. Jones marvelled, so quick to memorize and read, so naturally good at every subject in school.

I ached with sadness listening to this. Such a grim, absurdly long way from *Mrs. Duck's Lovely Day* to *Final Exit*, the suicide recipe book the coroner found resting in plain view on a bookshelf near Daniel's body, the book that so helpfully provided the method of self-destruction Daniel had employed, as well as the template for his suicide note cum last will and testament. I share Dr. Sherwin Nuland's mixed feelings, outlined in his excellent work, *How We Die*, on the place of a book like *Final Exit* in our culture. Its claims of humanitarian concern for the pain of the terminally ill won it a long-standing spot on best-seller lists starting in 1991, and it is still available in glossy paperback. I have found myself hiding it behind other books when I come across it on bookstore shelves, a small personal protest that helps me more than it hurts sales of the book, I am sure. It continues to be implicated in the suicides of more and more depressed people, beyond the terminally ill population for whom it is supposedly intended. I sympathize with those who face lengthy suffering from terminal conditions, and I don't believe in censorship. Still, I find the book's existence and widespread availability an affront.

Now I want to know, how does a person travel in thirty-four years from such blissful innocence to a state of fear and self-loathing so powerful that it seems the only way out is to die? I know it happens all the time. Some people don't even make it to thirty-four. Some don't even get a grace period from too much knowing in their very infancies. Yes, unconscionable though the thought is, children, too, kill themselves.

546

Later, in my long quest to understand why this happened to Daniel, why it happens to anyone, I experienced a moment of epiphany while reading Alice Miller's *The Drama of the Gifted Child*. The renowned Swiss psychoanalyst explores the early underpinnings of adult neurosis, all the subtle and intricate familial and social pressures that lead a person from earliest infancy to squash his unique qualities and construct a "false self." This narcissistic self seeks to safely negotiate the world on the world's terms, craves to be loved, but fears to its core that this love, so essential for its very survival, will never be given if the true self is revealed in all its resplendent, yet apparently unacceptable, colours.

To a greater or lesser degree, we all fear this, moulding ourselves to fit the place we are given to occupy in the world, however accommodating or untenable it may be. If we're lucky, as we grow into adulthood, we find ways to adjust as necessary to live more comfortably in our own skins, and muster the courage to allow our real selves to emerge for others to accept or reject as they wish. As mature people, we manage to sustain a healthy, balanced sense of self, despite external judgments, good, bad, or indifferent. We know and accept who we really are. The not-so-lucky instead totter along a precarious course, swerving dizzily between inappropriate grandiosity ("I'm *great*, it's the world that's an ass and the cause of all my problems!") and vicious self-hatred ("Could there be a lower form of scum than me?"). Some get stuck in one or the other of these dead-end pathways, or make side trips down the more dangerous roads of addiction, mania, depression, and suicidality.

But even these hazardous states can eventually be transcended, Miller says. She includes an extraordinary quote from one of her patients, a woman who had survived a serious suicide attempt when she was twenty-eight years old, and reflects at age forty on how she came to view herself and her life differently over twelve years:

> The world has not changed, there is so much evil and meanness all around me, and I see it even more clearly than before. Nevertheless, for the first time I find life really worth living. Perhaps this is because, for the first time, I have the feeling that I am really living my own life. And that is an exciting adventure. On the other hand, I can understand my suicidal ideas better now, especially those I had in my youth—it seemed pointless to carry on—because in a way I had always been living a life that wasn't mine, that I didn't want, and that I was ready to throw away.

Often, this passage has floated up from memory to comfort and sadden me. On the one hand, it is a testament to the possibility of healing, growth, and transformation, irrefutable proof that a suicidal person can overcome and make sense of his or her self-destructive yearnings. It happens all the time. I've done it myself.

How often I have wished that Daniel could have done it too. In choosing suicide, it seems he was in some way attempting to kill off a false self that no longer served him well, that never had, really. If only the fog of depression clouding his mind had lifted enough in those decisive moments for him to see that it is possible to discard a false self metaphorically, spiritually, that killing off the body that houses the self is literally a case of overkill. It is part of the human condition to transform ourselves. Less violently, we shuck off old ways of being, false or otherwise, and ease into new ones throughout the span of our lives. To let go of the past, however, you have to imagine that something is there to succeed it, and in the end, Daniel, regrettably, lacked that sense. For him, it seems, change equalled trauma, growth equalled terror. In such a state, paralysis and suicidal depression don't seem so out of place.

I believe that for a time, Daniel had faith in the future, but when a pattern of disappointment kindled despair, he felt himself pulled back into the past, overwhelmed by its echoes. Touchingly, he still grappled with the yearning to redo his early years. "Sometimes I feel like I'm 110 years old," he plaintively told me once, "and sometimes I feel about eighteen." Daniel expressed this in his short story "A Torn Ligament," from his last collection, *The People One Knows*, published posthumously:

> I was an alcoholic for ten years. I have not had a drink for six years. The story I am writing is not a complicated one. It has been written before. I am a writer in my early thirties. I want to capture on paper those years when I was still young, before I wanted to be a writer. I want to do this because I wish I could live those years again. I want those years back that I wasted as an alcoholic. I want to be twenty again, not in my early thirties.
>
> The difficulty—and this is why I must rewrite the story, to get this right—is that I can write the story about my past, but I can no longer feel what I felt then. I want to say: This is how it was to be young and to think I was in love. But I no longer know how it was. I cannot remember. If I say, This is why I drank, this is what it felt

like to be young and to think I was in love—if I say this—I know
that the story will be a better story, but also that it will be a lie.

In the story, the woman whom I call Assa is portrayed as if she
does not love the narrator—does not love me. But is it not the alcoholic young man—me—who is unable to love Assa? Is it possible that
I was not able to love her, that I hurt and rejected Assa? Could the
story have turned out differently? I do not know. I do not know.

Painful as it is to read Daniel's precisely executed fiction, I force myself, and it
reveals much. It often strikes me that in his writing, he operated with the cool-
eyed detachment of a coroner, performing the autopsy on his own life and dutifully reporting the findings, however unpleasant. To write so clearly of such obsessive solipsism—to observe and comment so subtly on one's own failure of imagination—takes some richness of imagination, an impressive level of creative intelligence. Daniel had to have achieved some protective distance from the self he
wrote about in order to perceive the young narrator's dilemma with such acuity.
But not quite enough distance, it seems in hindsight, to move safely beyond the
emotional paralysis that set in with all that looking backward. In the eyes of a man   549
in a state like that, there could be, literally, no future. It's no coincidence that
"no future" was one of the original punk movement's most famous anthemic asser-
tions—a recent book that explored the early years of punk is entitled *Please Kill
Me*. Daniel, as a fiercely troubled, talented young man determined to drink himself to death, was inexorably drawn to the scene's nihilism, which he documents
with raw force in his novel, also published posthumously, *1978*.

I think of Alice Miller's false-self theory as well when I look at the last photos of Daniel, taken a few weeks before his death by a friend. There is Daniel,
all leather jacket and buckles, his ears multi-pierced, his head recently shaved bald,
his demeanour alienated young-mannish. But for me, the Daniel in these pictures
is a disturbing pastiche, a jumble. His large, expressive eyes belie the toughness I
assume he meant to project. The first time I saw the images, they troubled me,
even before his death. The tragically hip image he seemed to aim for simply
didn't convince, not me anyway. After his death, the photographs struck me even
more as gravely out of kilter, images of a man not sure just who he is or who he
wants to be, a thirty-four-year-old who's really eighteen going on 110—a bit of
a mess.

Now it is an overcast day in late September, eight months after Daniel's death. I am standing with Mr. and Mrs. Jones at the gravesite where their son's ashes are buried, a family plot in a sprawling cemetery in Hamilton, Ontario, where a tree has been planted, and where a salmon-pink marble bench, JONES carved simply into it, sits on the well-tended grass. Jones, of course, is the family name, but also the one-word moniker that Daniel used to go by as a young poet, and with which many are still in the habit of referring to him, though he added "Daniel" later, and regretted having used only his last name as an affectation of youth. (The Library of Congress, he discovered to his chagrin, will not change the names of authors, ever, for any reason, and so he is "Jones" and only "Jones" in that system forever and ever, amen, based on the entry for his first book of poems, *The Brave Never Write Poetry*. Live and learn. His later books appeared with his full name despite this.)

Standing silently at the memorial spot, seeing the name stark like that, it is these echoes I hear, of this old Jones—"Jonesy," even, to some of his former cronies—that Daniel despised and seemed so driven to kill off. No, that Jones was not a very attractive character, although he certainly had his admirers, people who revelled in the outrageous rebellion of the bad-boy poet, the drunk punk who dared pull down his pants at a public reading, who made rude scenes challenging those he found pompous or otherwise objectionable, who wrote defiantly obscene poems, such as the one still considered a classic by some, "Things I Have Put into My Asshole." (These things include the CN Tower.) Though it would without doubt pain Daniel to know, this youthful rant against authority and convention, Toronto-style, written more than a decade earlier, got posted by an anonymous fan on telephone poles and buildings around downtown Toronto after his death, and on several anniversaries thereafter.

Oh, Daniel. I know this is not what you planned, I couldn't help thinking as I stood there, *not what you would have wanted to be most remembered for, nor to rest into eternity in a cemetery in the hometown you didn't remember fondly (though where else, I wonder—in an urn sitting on the counter of the Bar Italia, where you used to like to meet people and drink coffee?). It was your friend Kevin Connolly who made a remark to me, a little angry at you and protective of my sanity when I was too far gone in my grief as a tangled group of friends and colleagues waded through the mire of decisions about how your work would be handled after your death:* "Maybe he should have thought of this and stuck around. I think the living have some rights here."

It saddened me that people who hadn't been a part of Daniel's life for years rushed to publicly eulogize the young man they remembered from ten or twelve years earlier. Of course, they were and are entitled to their memories. I had also known, or more accurately known of, Daniel back in those days, when we were both students at the University of Toronto's University College—we even won the same college literary award one year, a fact that made me laugh when many years later I saw listed on Daniel's resumé the esteemed Norma Epstein Award for Creative Writing. As wide-eyed, bright young things from modest homes in provincial towns, where higher education is not a given, and only a few high-school students considered odd in some way leave to pursue it (and to escape feeling odd), we shared the experience of navigating an unfamiliar groves-of-academe world that operated on social formulas and codes of which we were painfully innocent. We traded recollections of our days slouching miserably through the same Victorian hallways with our knapsacks of literary anthologies and fat old novels during the late seventies and early eighties. Daniel's fictionalized account of these years appear in his novel *1978*. If I was a typically gloomy female undergraduate, scribbling my Plath-inspired poems, drawing liberally on all manner of death imagery, Daniel experienced feelings of alienation, anxiety, and depression to a far more alarming degree. Passages of *1978* that describe the narrator at his most stone-drunk and debased, barely able to dress himself properly or function in his job as a kitchen helper at the college's dining hall, are chilling.

Why did this young man carry so much anger? It seemed Daniel by then felt extremely alone, at odds with the steel-town, working-class reality he had recently come from, while furiously unable to fit into the culturally complacent world of middle-class student life, such as it was at a rather stuffy Canadian university that still served afternoon tea in china cups at the genteel Women's Union reception room, and retained its share of aging, duffer faculty members. It is no wonder that a whip-smart, creative, and undeniably fucked-up boy like Daniel would do the emotional equivalent of sticking his finger in a light socket during these years. He wasn't the only one—*1978* is also a document of the brutal world occupied by young punk wannabes, many of them primally screaming their complicated emotions, produced by family dysfunctions, a fragmented society that seemed to reward the compliant and marginalize the less acquiescent, and in which questing, sensitive young people might well conclude they had "no future." If the alcohol-dazed Daniel found any kind of home in those days, any kind of resonance between his inner self and outer reality, it was in the stark, violent, unforgiving culture of punk.

Our paths hardly ever crossed, except one night at a party I attended in the tiny apartment of a friend in 1982. The place was overflowing with hopelessly jejune university students, mostly in their early twenties. It was hardly a salon soirée or Dadaist happening, but all of us were doing our best to pretend that our avant-garde activities were on a par with those of the artistic denizens of Paris in the twenties, or some other bohemian, and of course better, time and place. There were poetry readings, some dance, or at least, movement, performances, much drinking, and smoking dope. I noticed the tall, skinny, blond guy with rather fierce eyes, the skin dark beneath them, sitting in a chair to the side. I recognized him from around the campus. Tonight he was talking loudly, bossing people around, acting like he owned the place. A young man and woman moved to the centre of the living room and began playing cello and violin. They were not very good, and the little crowd looked bored. The blond man began waving his hands at them like some ill-tempered stage director. "Oh, oh, you're awful," he said, fixing them with a heavy-lidded, contemptuous stare. "That's really bad, do you think you could stop? Really."

I remember being amazed anyone could be so bold and so cutting. Abysmal the pair might have been, but it would have been kinder to just grin and bear it. People began snickering and murmuring among themselves. There was no way the two could continue playing; they quietly packed up their instruments and skulked away. *What an asshole*, I thought. For the rest of the night, he buzzed around, exuding an air of being far above everyone else. In hindsight, I imagine that he was masking the fact that he was scared shitless, of everything and everyone.

"Who was that?" I remember asking a friend some time afterwards. He told me he was Jones, the poet, and regaled me with further tales of his legendarily atrocious, alcohol-fuelled misbehaviour. I was indignant at some of the stories, particularly descriptions of at least one violent public fight with his girlfriend at the time. I told my friend that if he ever hosted another gathering that Jones would be attending, he could count me out.

I forgot about this Jones over the next few years. Eventually, I stumbled on his writing again, found some of it good, some of it not to my taste. I also heard somehow through the grapevine that he had given up drinking, had married, was getting his act together. I would see him now and then bouncing along with his distinctive jackrabbit gait around the College Street West neighbourhood and environs where we had both ended up living. When we met up again in 1993 and I told Daniel of my less than fond memories of him, he was mortified. He said later that he assumed I would never want anything to do with him, and admitted that it was all true, just how bad he was back then. But it was hard to make the connection between the younger, disturbed character I'd heard of and observed myself, and this kind, generous, attentive, rather subdued man in his thirties. Our numerous long and candid conversations convinced me that he had indeed grown and changed.

After his death, every time I read or heard a remembrance that disregarded the man Daniel was trying to become, I marvelled at the blindness that allows someone to imagine that nothing of importance happened in another person's life once they, the eulogizer, were no longer a substantial part of it. While these people mourned the past, I was mourning the present, real time, and a future that was never going to be.

"He was a predator," one woman who had apparently dated Daniel briefly more than a decade earlier was quoted as saying in one newspaper column. I shook my head, recalling the man who had stood on my doorstep one day the previous spring, a box of custard tarts from the Portuguese bakery down the street held in one hand, and a bag of fresh, blushing apricots in the other, how he'd smiled and practically said "Aw, shucks, ma'am," as he handed me these offerings; and came through the door and into the kitchen. He scooped up my cat and began stroking her ears. There was nothing insincere or aggressively louche about this Daniel I got to know. Any revelations about his past behaviour came from his own mouth; he was quite capable of beating himself up over it with no posthumous help from others.

Was it only "Jones," the angry young drunk who would be remembered now? I stared at what seemed to me distorted tributes, and thought of one of the pieces of writing he was working on when he died, an essay on male alcoholic writers. He believed they tended to be celebrated and admired for all the wrong reasons. He had felt his own alcoholism as a yoke, a burden, something he had had to break free of before he could write anything he could respect. I struggled to figure out myself how best to honour the memory of the sober, still conflicted, older man I watched struggling so hard to mature and transform himself. This was one of the cruellest ironies of all surrounding Daniel's suicide; that the old, alcoholic self he did not value, the false self he most wanted to kill off, was the self that was immediately, publicly, ghoulishly, resurrected.

DEAD POET SOCIETY, screamed the headline on the cover of the entertainment weekly *eye*, beside a huge photo of Daniel, two years after his death. In the article, former cronies whinged about his work, in their judgment gone downhill since the heady days of their association with him. From the two-hour conversation I

553

had with the reporter, he extracted one sentence fragment, in which I'd divulged that Daniel left a note tacked to the locked door of the room in which he'd killed himself. The story seemed to have been written, complete with yellowed snapshots, long before the young reporter asked for an interview. Jones the outrageous stalked the world again. It was a sad and incomplete portrayal, a projection of spurious, romantic notions of what it means to live "on the edge," with the appalling implication that once Daniel had stopped abusing himself with alcohol, he lost his inspiration—even, preposterously, "sold out."

It wasn't the first such inane projection to surface. "He could have been a Jean Genet," went one wistful musing in a previous tribute, suggesting that if only he'd been more diligent and patient, he could have realized his talent, and that it was simply a hissy fit over not getting enough attention that had sparked his suicide. When I read this, I thought, what utter horseshit. He could have been Daniel Jones, and that was good enough! I grew irritated with the repulsive drive to situate his death as a literary event, which he in some ways had succumbed to himself. I wanted to shout, Don't you see, it wouldn't have mattered a good goddamn if he never wrote another word—his life had value beyond his literary efforts, and it's a crying shame he didn't see that himself.

These were the raging thoughts that plagued me in the confusion after his death, and again during the week, two years later, when every time I passed a café or corner store, Daniel's photo, trapped with the dead poet society headline in unforgiving newsprint, stared up at me from leftover *eyes* strewn in their racks throughout the city for all to see. I recalled the relaxed July morning that photo was taken by Sam Kanga, a young photographer, with Lynn Crosbie and Clint Burnham posing along with Daniel at the pool tables at the Bar Italia for the cover shot of *The People One Knows*, everyone chatting comfortably, hamming around for the camera. "I've never seen him so serene," Lynn told me that day as we sat sipping coffee afterwards. "When he called and sang 'Happy Birthday' to me on my answering machine, I knew he must be in love," she teased. Her friend was usually so much more reserved and serious, his leisure pastimes more along the lines of perusing the Grand and Toy catalogue, dreaming of new office supplies. Before he'd gone away for the weekend with me in Killarney, he had called Lynn to tell her that he was doing this unusual thing, perhaps hoping for moral support and sisterly approval from a fellow depressive. "Your books and catalogues will still be there when you get back," Lynn had counselled. "Just go have some fun."

Now I avert my eyes from that summertime photo of Daniel the serene.

"Don't let other people taint the sense of love and significance you feel about your time with Daniel," advises Daniel's psychiatrist. "He loved you," he assures me. But this is not much comfort, no shield against others' twisted, hurtful perceptions.

Contemplating the long remove between the fantasies people have about death, especially suicide, and the paradoxical reality of it always saddens and angers me. Daniel, of all people, understood how little glory there is in depressive illness, and admitted to the end that he feared pain and regretted what he was doing, even as he did it, arguing to himself and anyone who read his note that he had no other option. Yet possibly he wished to the end that he could still, maybe, find one. A poet from Daniel's former circle began cynically referring to his suicide as a "career move." He even wrote a bitter little poem about it. It appalled me that someone who'd once counted himself a friend of Daniel's would display such callous disregard for his final tragedy, but it should not have surprised me. People naturally seek to distance themselves from horror with this kind of glib, black humour. It is easier to bend someone into unflattering caricature without thought for the impact it might have on those he knew and loved.

Several rumours circulated after Daniel's death: He had just found out he had AIDS; he had plagiarized his forthcoming book of short stories; he'd been serious- ly hitting the bottle for months, and had been spotted getting hammered in various bars; as editor of the literary magazine, *Paragraph*, he'd planned to include in the last issue he edited before his death a series of photographs taken by a friend in which she depicts herself as a character in various suicidal poses. Actually, Daniel had long admired her surreal and haunting photography on a wide range of themes. She has since won international acclaim for her work. She later told me how stunned she was to be approached by someone who remarked, "I guess you must feel bad about those photos," as if they had somehow instigated her friend's suicide. Had someone also relayed to me that Daniel had been spotted slaughtering goats on the waterfront one midnight by the full moon, I would not have been surprised.

It was hard to take the rumours seriously, disheartening to imagine them believed. When the coroner's report from the obligatory autopsy cited "traces" of alcohol, some swooped in to say "Aha!" The finding confirms nothing. There was no alcohol in Daniel's apartment, save mouthwash and possibly cough medicine, and Daniel hadn't left the place for several days before his death. He was no Aqua Velva man (Hermit Sherry had been his plonk of choice at his worst point a decade earlier), though he might have gargled. It would have been difficult for someone who hadn't had a drink in eight years to suddenly start a wild binge, yet hide it entirely from someone with whom he had almost daily contact. There is no good cause for such speculation; at most, Daniel's fear, justified or not, that he might return to a life of alcoholism would have been just another reason in his mind to kill himself.

For some, though, suicide equals melodrama. There must be some obvious cause and effect, some single coherent reason why it happened, someone to accuse. I was myself accused of all manner of baroque nastiness, from murder to bad manners, and of anonymously penning a story sympathetic to Daniel and critical of his publisher in the national satirical magazine, *Frank*. To this day, I have no idea who wrote the curious squib in question. It might have been well-meant, but was filled with sloppy factual errors, and caused more problems than it solved.

When the prosaic truth fails to live up to expectations, overheated imaginations are brought into play. This impulse to embellish is linked, I think, to the ambivalence we all feel, yet may not wish to acknowledge, about the person who has left this way, surely making a statement, a damning comment, a "take *that*," or a "woe is me, and here is the final proof." It's easier to respond with a black-and-white theory, to fashion a coherent narrative momentum and linear chronology for the person's life, which stops with the resounding THE END of his suicide— and the epilogue containing the final judgments of the living.

"Ah, the 'pitchfork'/'halo' scenario," said Karen Letofsky, executive director of the Survivor Support Program in Toronto, during a counselling session after Daniel's death. There was comfort in learning that these kinds of stark, cartoonish reactions are quite common, as people seek to either sanctify the deceased or throw him into the burning fires of hell. Short shrift is given to the irresolute, contradictory nature of suicide—the person's motives, the circumstances surrounding the event, our responses.

If the living must live with mere interpretations, speculative and incomplete, they must also live with a burning curiosity about just how the person who did the deed interpreted the suicide himself. This is certainly the case in the period immediately following the death. Marc Etkind, author of a slim yet astonishing volume of collected suicide notes entitled ... *Or Not To Be*, describes himself as a television documentary producer who, "except for a handful of coroners and psychologists ... has probably read more suicide notes than anyone else," and suggests that virtually everyone on the verge of suicide, certainly those who leave notes behind, has a distorted perception of what he or she is doing, and the impact the suicide will have.

If suicide notes are indeed attempts at communication, then they are dismal failures. We all hope that as we near death, we'll have a moment of understanding, where our thoughts crystallize and we can sum up our existence with eloquence. But if the suicide attempter had this moment of understanding, he probably wouldn't kill himself. And there lies the ultimate paradox of the suicide note: If someone could think clearly enough to leave a cogent note, that person would probably recognize that suicide was a bad idea. Or as Edwin Shneidman writes, "In order to commit suicide, one cannot write a meaningful note; conversely, if one could write a meaningful note, one would not have to commit suicide." Suicide notes, written when people are at their psychological worst, are anything but the voice of clarity. Instead they are bizarre, rambling, angry and, above all, sad documents of disturbed minds.

While I agree that people who kill themselves are at their psychological worst, I would also argue that the notes they leave behind are not entirely meaningless. A suicide note can be rife with meaning—just not the one solely intended by the deceased. It would be hard to top "Dear Betty, I hate you. Love, George," one of the shortest notes Etkind includes in the book, for succinct conveyance of a point; indeed, the essential marrow of meaning at the heart of an entire life, that may have eluded both poor George and Betty, but not a distant reader of such a compact novel in a note.

However dubious on an emotional level, suicide notes require a certain degree of rationality to write, and have been recognized in law numerous times as "holographic" wills, that is, legitimate statements of the last wishes of the deceased. It is this principle that guides the concise instructions for writing a suicide note in the form of a legitimate will in *Final Exit*. And so, Daniel, capable of reading a book, absorbing the information it contained, and acting on it, was executing a relatively straightforward series of physical steps in a logical fashion, including the writing of a suicide note. In it he says that he hadn't planned to write it, just scribbled it "off the cuff." It does not surprise me that Daniel, being a writer, would join the fewer than one in five suicides, according to Etkind, who leave suicide notes. And for someone who had not intended to write a note, he certainly picked up a head of steam quickly enough upon beginning the task. Along with its expressions of self-loathing and extreme psychological suffering, the note is filled with instructions that detail, with characteristic punctiliousness, if not always straightforward logic, what he wanted done with his work. He also revealed his self-doubts: "To plan my final publications is a bit self-centred—I will be dead; the work may not be any good."

Difficult though reading this in the days after his death was, it was Daniel's situating of his suicide in a literary context that I found hardest to accept. I empathize with any writer's frustration, even despair, over how difficult it is to fashion a writer's life, particularly in Canada, where to sell a few thousand copies of a work of fiction or poetry is to be a roaring success, and to sell a few hundred is more the norm. Yet I cannot accept that this was worth dying for. Nor can I accept Daniel's placement of his suicide in linked formation with suicides of the past (he dedicated his note to the late Robert Billings, another Canadian poet who combatted mental problems and killed himself amid a turmoil of bad relations with friends and publishing colleagues), thereby somehow dignifying the act beyond its depressive underpinnings. In this, I believe Daniel was dead wrong. Others too viewed Daniel's suicide as in some way redeemed by its larger literary import, even went so far as to hope that his suicide note would eventually be published as a literary text, a final addition to his oeuvre.

I found it all offensive. The one thing I will not do is make Daniel's death lyrical. There is nothing exalted about death, particularly suicide. It is grossly physical, ugly, and monstrously intrusive, from the finding, removal, and identification of the body, to the autopsy, the funerals, and memorial services, the morbid tasks that must be performed far longer than anyone imagines could possibly be endured. Suicide is also so terribly banal, the moment of death itself mechanical, mundane, more anticlimactic than anyone's "Goodbye, Cruel World" fantasies would have it. I think most of us, in our death-denying culture, don't like to ponder how close our living selves are always, potentially, to death. How fragile we are. One moment, a man is standing in his bathroom flossing his teeth, or filling a coffee pot at the kitchen counter; the next, he is downing an overdose of pills and placing a plastic bag over his head; moments later, life unceremoniously transforms to death. Daniel's autopsy report itself I only scanned quickly before stuffing it into a file folder for good, and have had to block it from my mind. The thought of a young body clinically invaded that way, let alone one I knew intimately, surpasses my ability or desire to imagine.

It is the living who must cope with the horror and absurdity of it all. One of the most helpful books I read in the aftermath of Daniel's death was *Words I*

Never Thought to Speak, a collection of interviews with suicide survivors at various stages of their grieving. For me, the most moving and comforting anecdotes were those that revealed the awkward and ludicrous moments that seem so at odds with the magnitude of the tragedy: Imagine Alvin and the Chipmunks singing Wagner's Ring cycle. My heart went out to the son who told of how his family sat in charged silence as they drove to Dad's funeral, in the car in which he had only days earlier gassed himself to death; the young bride who, after scattering the ashes of the man she'd married less than a year earlier, stands by the ocean, wondering anxiously what to do with the plastic baggie that had contained them. Who wouldn't feel for the daughter of poet Anne Sexton, agonizing over whether to honour her mother's quixotic wish to have the palindrome "Rats live on no evil star" as her gravestone's epitaph? (After much soul-searching, the young woman, who'd endured her flamboyantly narcissistic mother's suicidal behaviour from childhood until her late teens, when Sexton finally succeeded in killing herself, in the end opted against it. It is hard to fault her in that decision.)

Now, I can only conclude that if Daniel the writer put his faith entirely in words, placing his very life in their power, Daniel the man was summarily betrayed by them. I believe he might still be alive if he had learned to define himself as something more than a writer—as "something human," to quote the final words of his short story "A Torn Ligament." To me, there is one thing he did reveal in his final note, in the very fact that he wrote it at all. As he sat in that dark corner of his life, feeling lost without words, taking pen to paper, he asked that his grammar and spelling be cleaned up (he was acknowledging the growing influence of the tranquillizers he had swallowed before he sat down to write), should anyone ever publish the note. He envisioned a future, even if he did not imagine that he would be there. It mattered to him enough to try to shape that future in some small way, with words, to the end.

Those who write of the future must possess a shred of hope and faith, a sense of connection, that there are things they would like to have happen, and things they would not. And anyone with this hope, no matter how strong their desire to die, probably also harbours somewhere within themselves a desire to live. Whether he intended it to or not, Daniel's suicide note, all twenty-one scribbled squares of notepaper tells me that. Yet whatever future Daniel imagined, it was not the one that came to pass. Ultimately, words failed him.

Eventually, I accepted that just as the dead typically don't get all their wishes, or leave the legacy they envisioned, if they envisioned one at all, so their survivors

559

cannot control what people say or think of the event either. This is nowhere more obvious than in the extraordinary case of the late English poet Ted Hughes, who wrote publicly in his 1997 collection *Birthday Letters*, for the first time in thirty-seven years, and in the year of his own death from cancer, about his wife Sylvia Plath's life and suicide. In an article accompanying excerpts from the book in *The New Yorker*, his friend and colleague Alfred Alvarez wrote that Hughes was always grimly aware of being, in his own words, "a projection post" for the many who preferred their own invented narratives, with him as unmitigated villain, to the thorny truth. Hughes was right: The sweeping condemnation of him, driven by what seems a childish, knee-jerk-feminist spin on the tragedy, went into full throttle on several chat sites and forums on the Internet after the publication of *Birthday Letters*, as the incensed gathered to discuss the scourge of Hughes, and further sanctify the divine Sylvia.

These people have forgotten that the woman they so admire attempted suicide long before she met Hughes, and wrote compellingly about her youthful depression in her powerful novel *The Bell Jar*. As Germaine Greer suggests in her study of female poets, *Slip-Shod Sybils*, Plath wrote in the context of a female aesthetic of self-destruction, well-developed by then, that nurtured her primal urge towards death. Plath was profoundly, pathologically depressed, living in a cold, foreign country, feeling alone and overwhelmed by motherhood and marital difficulties. She had easy access to a means to an end. The famous poet was not the only person to die by household oven, before the lethal gas that made it possible was removed from the mix by the companies that produced it.

For some reason, we often forget that writers are in fact also human beings. I sometimes wonder whether the notion that writers suffer from depression in greater proportion than others is wrong-headed. Is it not only that because they are writers, they write about their experience, finding expression for their pain in a way that a nurse, a policeman, a dentist, or an abused aboriginal foster child would not? The gifted Sylvia Plath expressed her darkness and pain with accomplished literary brilliance. Yet, regardless of her ability to articulate her experience in language that would be widely admired, even revered as a result of her tragedy, she was still a young woman suffering from what we call depression. In this she was quite ordinary.

Given what I know of surviving suicide, no one need worry that Ted Hughes didn't suffer enough. (His second wife also killed herself, murdering their three-year-old child before doing so.) His pain and his love for his former wife radiate through *Birthday Letters*. It is a work of grand and astonishing intimacy I found deeply moving. During my most intense grief over Daniel, it did occur to me painfully that while I would one day be an old woman, Daniel would remain forever the young man he was when he died. In my aging memory, he will inevitably change, and I wondered how he will seem to me as time passes. Even after five years, I think of him in a more distanced way, as a younger man I once knew, whose plight I witnessed and which still elicits sorrow and pity. Though his death is no longer the centre of my life, he holds a place in my heart, despite changes in my life, my relationships, my shifting self.

Often, after an apparently sudden suicide, people say things like, "We had no idea he was *that far gone*." The difficult truth is, maybe he, or she, wasn't. Maybe that person has lived through far worse times, but this time, there was a gun handy. Maybe just a momentary feeling, a perverse and bleak impulse coupled with a convenient means removes a person from life when a moment later, the same person might have reconsidered, as he or she has countless times before. Living with depression and suicidal feelings is like that. The man who lost his desire to jump from the Golden Gate Bridge the moment he'd done it was lucky to live. Countless people reconsider mid-attempt, begin to approach an awareness that the act, however firm or feeble, is metaphorical in some way, the proverbial cry for help, and live to be thankful they did.

561

The recent, award-winning Iranian film *A Taste of Cherry*, an unusually subtle cinematic exploration of suicide, makes this point powerfully. The main character, a middle-aged man who no longer sees the point of living, drives through the desolate Iranian landscape surrounding Teheran in a Range Rover, picking up three different passengers he hopes will bury his body by the side of the road once he has killed himself. All three refuse his strange request, and in the course of their rides with the suicidal protagonist, they engage him in philosophical debate over the question of whether to be or not to be, arguing persuasively for the former.

His final passenger, a grizzled, gravel-voiced old man, relates the story of his own attempted suicide, when he was a younger man, eking out a marginal existence with his family on a failing farm. He had gotten up one day at dawn, walked with a rope to a nearby orchard, and climbed into a cherry tree. He fashioned his noose, placed it around his neck preparing to jump from the limb, when he noticed the exquisite ripe fruit suspended from a nearby branch glowing in the morning light. He was captured by the beauty of the succulent blossoming clusters and could not resist popping one in his mouth. As he felt the cherry burst against his teeth, he was filled with sensual bliss, and knew in that instant that he did not want to die. Instead, he dismantled his noose, picked a handful of cherries, and carried them home, where he placed them in a bowl and took them to the bed where his wife still lay sleeping. The woman was lulled into the day by the delightful scent of the fruit he had brought her, never knowing what a momentous turn of events her husband's gentle act represented. "A cherry saved my life," says the wise old man, with a can-you-believe-it? shrug, to the suicidal one.

Abbas Kiarostami's extraordinary film is banned in Iran; strict Islamic law, like most religions, forbids suicide, and the censors there fail to see that a film like this might be one of the most powerful suicide prevention messages they could allow to be disseminated. Secular and modern in tone and presentation, its wisdom apparently cannot be allowed voice among people who would surely find themselves reflected there.

In contemporary Western culture, Spalding Gray's tragicomic musings on suicide are as wise and revealing as any. Gray has spent his life in the shadow of his mother's suicide, a grim reality he explores to great humorous effect in his mono-logue *Monster In A Box*. In his later work, *It's A Slippery Slope*, he recounts a moment out hiking on a high cliff with his girlfriend, when he feels a nearly irresistible urge to leap over the edge. He was not particularly depressed at the time, he just feels the seductive pull of the abyss more strongly than most others, the option of suicide never far from the edge of his consciousness, perhaps utterly central to it, something he is compelled to dance incessantly around. What stops him in the end is the look of horror he imagines would cross his girlfriend's face as he hung momentarily in the air just before falling to his death. With comic self-mockery, he implies that it may be more his feeling that he couldn't live with that on his conscience for the last few seconds of his life, than concern for his girlfriend, that stops him. He saunters peacefully on, his girlfriend oblivious to all that just didn't happen.

These particular contemplations of suicide struck a deep chord in me. They reveal the uncomfortable truth that all around us, within us, at any time, more lives than we care to imagine hang in the balance, spiritually, emotionally. Who can say what small blessing or absurdity will determine the ultimate call? Many who live with suicidal feelings say that, ironically, it is only the comforting knowledge that if their pain became too great to bear they could end their lives that gives them the strength to carry on living. Without that imagined escape hatch, they say they would succumb to paralyzing despair, rather than the mild to chronic depression that defines most of their days.

Yet the immutable fact of a suicide seems to herald our worst assumptions about the person's mental state, the horrible things that must have driven him or her to it. But this doesn't answer the question of why it is that many people live through the most abysmal realities, surviving with grace and courage, while others seem unable to cope with comparatively mild adversity. Some people will live with depression and its disastrous fallout for years, never acting on suicidal feelings, doing so perversely at a time when life seems to be going better than ever for them.

It is a less than encompassing general understanding of the sometimes depressingly flimsy and random dynamics of suicide that has made many a suicide survivor, particularly parents, feel tarred and feathered by social stigma that carries an implicit accusation: Your son/daughter killed him or herself, therefore whatever happened in your family must have been infinitely worse than what happens in families where all the kids survive. It isn't quite so simple. Certainly, it's difficult to dispute the link between childhood adversity and adult emotional troubles that can lead to suicide. "That the early social environment of suicidal individuals is often markedly disorganized is well established in an extensive literature on suicide and attempted suicide," writes psychiatrist Kenneth S. Adam of the University of Toronto in a 1986 article entitled "Early Family Influences on Suicidal Behavior," in the journal *Annals New York Academy of Sciences.* "Disorganized" in this context may mean, explains Adam, "marital conflict, parental hospitalization, parental alcoholism, and mental illness ... along with the more obvious family disruptions caused by parental deaths, separations, and divorce. More subtle variables such as covert hostility, isolation, and rejection by parents have also been found."

Distinguished pioneer suicidologist Ed Shneidman, in his 1996 book, *The Suicidal Mind*, brilliantly condenses a four-decade career's worth of observations and reflections, based on literally thousands of "psychological autopsies" and case studies of suicide. He writes, powerfully:

> I am totally willing to believe that suicide can occur in adults who could not stand the immediate pain of grief or loss that faced them, independent of a good or bad childhood or good or bad parental care and love. But I am somewhat more inclined to hold to the view that

563

the subsoil, the root causes of being unable to withstand those adult assaults lie in the deepest recesses of personality that are laid down in rather early childhood.... It is not possible to be robbed totally of one's childhood, but what does happen can seem to be just as bad. One can have one's childhood vandalized. Perhaps—I do not know—every person who commits suicide, at *any* age, has been a victim of a vandalized childhood, in which that preadolescent child has been psychologically mugged or sacked, and has had psychological needs, important to that child, trampled on or frustrated by malicious, preoccupied, or obtuse adults.

Obviously, it would be painful for a parent to read such words after the suicide of a child. In many cases, hard observations like these of Adam and Shneidman are without a doubt true. But in what family is there not some amount of covert hostility? If divorce in and of itself caused suicide, the suicide rate would be catastrophically higher. Clearly, there are subtleties here that have to be taken into account when drawing conclusions about cause and effect involving suicide. I have met many loving parents devastated by the suicides of their young sons and daughters, parents who were not alcoholics, not divorced, not malicious vandalizers of their children's early years—including parents of offspring with such illnesses as schizophrenia or manic depressions who did everything humanly possible to help their suffering children before losing them in cruel and violent ways; and parents who, in the wake of their personal tragedies, were motivated to educate themselves and help others.

It has been in part that frustrating sense felt by many survivors of suicide that they have been condemned, misunderstood, and neglected by mental-health professionals that has led them to form their own support groups over the past decade or so. Now, their numbers and degree of organization amount to a vocal movement. Not surprisingly, while more doctors, social workers, and bereavement specialists are gaining a greater understanding of the unique aspects of grief experienced by survivors of suicide, tensions exist between the two groups, and they were obvious at the conference of the American Association of Suicidology conference I attended in Memphis in 1997. At times, I felt like a double agent. As a journalist, I found that doctors and counsellors of all kinds were willing to speak to me, and even though I was upfront about also being a suicide survivor, they were frank in airing reservations about allowing what has been an organization of professionals in many disciplines, researching all aspects of suicide, to include a new contingent of mostly lay people whose chief focus is their own loss and bereavement. Meanwhile, survivors warmly welcomed me into their comforting circles, and spoke openly of their own concerns about the condescending desire for exclusivity of some of the professionals.

I came to feel that both groups had their points. Sometimes, watching the psychologists, psychiatrists, and social workers make their complicated presentations, complete with dizzying successions of graphs and bar charts projected onto screens, I wondered if they hadn't strayed a little too far from the humanity of the people that were the ostensible focus of all this theorizing. On the other hand, I was taken aback to learn that a group of survivors wished to reroute the AAS quarterly research journals that came to them automatically when they joined the organization, from their homes directly to local libraries, because they found reading them "upsetting." Better they go to libraries than into the garbage, but I did wonder if this wasn't a variation on a Groucho Marx joke about masochism—why join a club whose members espouse ideas you have no interest in exploring, or outright reject before you've even considered them? Perhaps both sides need to sit down and listen to each other with more open minds, and concede a few points; sometimes a suicidal person's best hope is medical intervention, but sometimes too, all the drugs and professional expertise in the world can't stop a suicide. Sometimes parents do indeed break their children's spirits; and sometimes, children of decent, loving parents kill themselves too. Not one of us has the definitive answer to all the questions that still surround suicide.

Each person grows in the world with a unique combination of genetic propensities, environmental influences, familial relationships borne along on wonderful and dreadful moments, and a relationship to society that may be nurturing or destructive, depending on how the former factors play themselves out. Of course, it benefits everyone to minimize the things in life that cause emotional pain—the unholy trinity of child abuse, addiction, poverty, numerous other related ills—to educate ourselves about the signs that a person may be depressed or suicidal, and to know how to act if so. It's a matter of paying attention, of taking the time to develop an understanding of how complex suicide can be. Social and cultural conditions beyond family can indeed play a part in tipping someone over the emotional edge and into the suicide danger zone: Fisheries fail, leaving entire towns with skyrocketing suicide rates. Gambling fuels economic development, street drugs and guns proliferate, and we see the casualties rise. Japan's suicide rate has escalated in the wake of its recently plummeting economy.

Focusing only on organic, individual causes for suicide to the exclusion of all other factors, and scurrying away in fear and dismissal from social responsibilities and community interventions, will not make it go away. Many people want to uphold a blinkered biological approach to depression: We live in an age of antidepressants of ever-more-refined design, yet the suicide rate is not commensurately lower. If all it took was a pill, a lot of people now dead would be walking around alive and well, perhaps including Daniel, who was on antidepressants at the time of his death. Drugs do play a role for many people, but they are not necessarily the entire answer to a person's malaise. A suicidal person may pitch from doctor to doctor, pill to pill, only to find his or her appetite for life restored by a lucky break on a job, a new relationship, an unexpected turn of fortune for the better. Touching stories abound, like that of the heroin addict in Winnipeg, who while walking down a street in rock-bottom despair one day, heard the cries of an old woman in a burning house, and without thinking ran through the thick smoke to break a basement window and pull the woman out. Interviewed later, her face glowed with pride and astonishment that she, the worst person on earth in her own eyes, had saved a life—two, including her own. Six weeks after the event, she was clean of drugs, and still visiting the grateful old woman. A depressed mother of two toddlers wrote a letter to Oprah Winfrey, telling her that she was just in the process of putting her kids to bed so that she could kill herself, when she happened to hear the talk-show host interviewing Maya Angelou. Something the poet said struck such a chord, the woman fell to the floor sobbing in gratitude, no longer wishing to die. Corny, but better than years of Prozac.

I write this at a time when the government of the province in which I live, Ontario, is closing several mental-health treatment clinics for children and dismantling a host of related services designed especially for emotionally disturbed children and adolescents. Even the provincial government's own child advocate has said publicly that the state of mental-health-care services for children is "in crisis," and that the lack of proper childhood care often leads to later tax-burdensome incarceration in correctional institutions. The untreated mentally ill or emotionally disturbed eventually lash out. We are regressing in dealing with these matters, in a way that can only lead to more tragedy.

Still, with every good intention, and adequately funded, well-designed and managed public mental health programs in place, we cannot definitively predict who will be felled by suicidal feelings and who will overcome them. As with something as basic and life-saving as cardiopulmonary resuscitation (CPR), we can train people to know what to do in a suicidal crisis. At the same time, suicide prevention training for individuals will not in and of itself reduce the prevalence of those factors that lead to suicide, any more than prepping a population to know how to massage suddenly failing hearts can do much to stop people from doing things that lead to heart attacks. As with CPR, when it comes to suicide there is no guarantee that someone with the knowledge to prevent it will be around when the crisis happens. I have met people from families plagued by suicide, in which every member was an alcoholic or drug addict except that one person; people who have survived unspeakable torture in prisons foreign and domestic, severe sexual abuse, violent assaults, their own addictions, and yet who maintain a happy view of life, or have recovered enough to reach out to others. I have met people who have shown me photo after photo of their beloved dead, a person unmolested or traumatized in any obvious way, who put a gun to his head after a romantic rejection or a failed exam or a rough call from a collection agency about a credit-card debt.

I recall suicidal moments of my own, several months after Daniel's death. I had gone to dinner at a friend's. It had been a lovely evening of good company and good food. The moment I was alone again, heading home, a frightening numbness set in, and a blunt thought crossed my mind: *If I had a gun, I would shoot myself right now. Why not? What is the point of anything?* The aggressive impulse was strong and lasted well after I got home and had crawled into bed. What saved me, aside from not having a gun, was the fact that part of me knew why I was having these feelings. By then, I had read of how common it was for people to feel suicidal after a loved one's suicide. I recognized it as a passing part of the grief.

If I'm honest, I realize it was a feeling I have had before in my life, long ago, in my twenties, that same disconcerting "I'm fine as long as I'm with people, desperate when alone" chronic depression, complete with "suicidal ideation" that had beset me for several terrifying months. So when it reappeared, even briefly, I knew I had to, and could, wait it out. Who knows where this strength comes from, what allows people to go on? But it did. I did. It's not something to feel smugly proud of, it is simply a reality. Those feelings vividly recalled, although experienced so long ago during that youthful depression, that primal darkness that seemed to seep through my blood, slowing me, making me turn hatred on myself, had a weird and horrible power. Then, as mysteriously and randomly as they had arrived, the feelings dissipated to nothingness. Eventually I could say I was no longer depressed, and could tell the difference between depression and grief, ordinary sadness and a hormone-driven PMS fit of teariness, anxiety, and irritability. This is what living with depression means. Not necessarily getting rid of it, or its potential to return, but learning to know it, identify it, grapple with it like an old enemy, let it run its course, refuse to give it the upper hand. Millions of people learn to do this. Daniel did, too, for a while.

I can probably anticipate that Daniel will always be with me, somehow, and that at times, I will find myself addressing him directly. Nearly everyone I have spoken with who has lost someone to suicide admits that at some time or other, perhaps quite regularly, they speak to their dead. More than three decades after his wife's death at age thirty, Ted Hughes, then in his late sixties, still addressed her directly—the poems are almost all to "you," the beloved, troubled, and tragically lost Sylvia. He imagined a dialogue with her, an eternal bond. In these fiercely loving poems, there is the world, and then there they are, separate from it, together on their own small planet, Ted and Sylvia, sharing a unique, intimate knowledge. And so it is expressed, in a poet's tough and beautiful language, this searing truth—as the living person's narrative moves along, the absent person remains vibrantly real, a thread, thinning perhaps as time unfolds, new relationships evolve, and old age encroaches, but strong as spun gold nonetheless, running through the story that continues to write itself.

For better or for worse, denied or acknowledged, that connection to the dead is an integral part of the survivor's life.

January 1994. We go to see a movie called *True Romance*. We eat dinner first, sharing a dish of Love Spice Shrimp in a Vietnamese restaurant near the theatre on Bloor Street west of Ossington. It's freezing outside. We shiver and run. We sit in the balcony, you put your arm around me. My hand languishes comfortably over your knee. We like the movie. We talk about it in the café next door afterwards. You wonder whether it has achieved Baudrillard's fifth simulation. I can't help laughing and teasing you about the pretentiousness of such a statement, and soon, you are laughing too. Words flow easily, endlessly between us. We run back to your apartment, cursing the cold. "I feel so close to you," you say with intensity, as we lie huddled together.

What is it that we gave each other, anyway? What is it that we "loved"? How did we manage it when we encountered each other, when our broken attempts at lasting connection pitched us back into the unenviable state of searching singlehood, our longings and regrets rather too obvious to ourselves and, we suspected, to others, despite our brave faces? Somehow we did manage it. Even though in the beginning we might have doubted that we had anything of value to offer, there were found bits and pieces, discarded or neglected parts of ourselves we might have forgotten or never realized were there at all. Suddenly, we saw these things in each other with exquisite clarity, and weren't afraid to feel again as we picked them up like unexpected treasures on a beach, and let them shimmer and play in the new light. It is difficult to understand why or how this happened. When it did, we couldn't believe our luck. It was the thrilling, elusive thing we all hope for, that deep erotic bonding between lovers, and compared by every modern psychologist from Freud on, to the "oceanic" feelings between mothers and infants. Babies must bond to survive; in "romantic" love, adults seek to duplicate the wonderfully fulfilling sensations of that long-ago connection. On rare occasions, it goes beyond the sexual and hits on something far more profound. It's what is missing from those dreary, awkward dates from which we slink away with mutual embarrassment, to crawl into our beds alone, telling ourselves wryly that it might be best to pack in this fruitless search, imagining that the kind of connection that we want, that we dream of, does not exist.

For a time with you, Daniel, it did. That you should choose to die in the midst of such hope and promise, such renewed faith in life and its possibilities, is for me the saddest thing of all.

You killed yourself a month after that lovely, light evening. This is not something a person "gets over." It is just something I live with.

May 1994. I am driving west along Bloor Street. It's warm and sunny. Chestnut trees are blooming and swaying in the light breeze, and though I am still caught in grief I notice that it makes me happy, somehow, the sun, the balmy wind, the blossoming trees and flowers after such a long and terrible winter. I know it would do nothing for you, or so you always claimed about your indifference to trees and other simple, natural beauties.

Without warning, I catch sight of the theatre in the distance as I approach Dovercourt Road. Suddenly I feel a confused dread, remembering what might have been the last good time out we had together, when we talked and talked, and you said you felt so close to me. So close. What *did* you mean? If you were still alive, I'd know. Or at least I would have the innocent luxury of imagining I did.

I see for the first time that the theatre is called The Paradise. Some strange sound comes from my mouth when I also see on the marquee, where a movie title should be, three words stacked on top of each other:

WE

NEVER

DIE

I forget about the chestnut trees, the warm, gentle air. As I pass the theatre, I am leaning slightly in my seat against the door, resting my elbow out the window, my hand holding my head, my fleeting springtime serenity dissolved. I'm resisting something, as if I can't decide whether what just happened is terrible or comforting.

It's both.

Thanks for the ironies, sweetheart.

Your parents and I don't say much as we stand awkwardly together at the place where your ashes are buried. What is there to say? Eventually, we get back in the car and begin driving along the gently looping roads of the vast, pristine graveyard, all whispers, cut grass and carved stone. Your mother is crying. I sit in the back seat trying to hold back my own tears. Your father looks over at your mother, with an expression on his face so like yours. He reaches over to put his arm around her.

I close my eyes.

Remembering Marian Engel

MARGARET ATWOOD

Marian Engel (1933–85), whose best-known work of fiction is the novel *Bear*, died of cancer the year that Daniel Jones published his first book, and was mourned by a different generation. In this memoir written for *Saturday Night* after Engel's death, Margaret Atwood (b. 1939), Canada's-best known living author at home and elsewhere, remembers her colleague and friend in a characteristically generous and unflinching way.

He speaks in his own voice. She sat up and said that out loud.   571

——MARIAN ENGEL, *BEAR*

We're all wrecks when it comes to it, but some of us have written books and I think we should be given credit for that.

——MARIAN ENGEL, IN A LETTER

She understood that he would never be with her more than at the present moment. The surprise to come was that he wouldn't be with her less.

——ALICE MUNRO, *WHO DO YOU THINK YOU ARE?*

I first saw Marian on a book, hers. It was called *No Clouds of Glory*, and on the front there was a coffee-cup ring you thought was real until you tried to wipe it off. The back showed the author, a tomboyish but pretty young woman with a gamine haircut, her top buttons undone, holding a cigarette and caught in the act of inhaling, looking sideways at the viewer with a grin that was amused, mischievous, even, you might say, provocative. Marian didn't like that picture, for some reason. (Also she didn't like the title, which wasn't hers. As soon as she got the chance, with the paperback, she put her own back on: *Sarah Bastard's Notebook.*)

I didn't know that at the time. I thought it was a good picture. I was a young author myself, and conscious of others, especially women. I read the book, looked at the picture, thought: *She'd be too much for me.* As it turned out, Marian thought the same thing about me; so after we'd gone through that, we could become friends.

The last picture I saw of her she did like. It's the one on *Room of One's Own*, Engel issue, summer of '84. There was some doubt as to whether she'd be alive to see it but she was. Those were the months when she waxed and waned. ("Very complimentary," she said. "Probably because of the state I'm in." She was pleased, but nothing escaped her. However, she did not say *dying*.)

In the picture, she's sitting in a chair in her living room, looking good enough. You can't tell she could hardly walk. She showed me the picture and then turned the magazine over. On the back was the rest of the picture: books piled up and spilling over, a table heaped with objects. "The usual chaos," she said. She liked having it in the picture, because it was true, not airbrushed, not artist-as-icon. None of her heroines are bodiless wisps, and several are downright sloppy, a condition she was, as a writer, excellent at describing.

Alice Munro, writer: "When I was young, in the 1950s, I used to sit around in kitchens with my married girlfriends; there would be exchanges, revelations, a kind of desperate honesty, a subversive wit. When I first read Marian's books—particularly *The Honeyman Festival*—I had the same sense of release and exhilaration. She'd caught something that was like the tone of those early conversations; it wasn't just an extension, it was a *vindication* of all that talk. It was the *way* she wrote. That sort of material wasn't commonly used; domestic material was either sentimentalized and sugared over, or it was turned back on itself, filled with irony and self-deprecation. She used it as straight literary material, and she made me see that it was possible to use it."

She thought she was untidier than that mythical beast, "other people." She had some ideal of perfection she felt others embodied but she fell short of. Maybe this came from her shattering early childhood, maybe it was part of that cleanliness-oriented, small-town, Ontario, Protestant upbringing provided by her adoptive parents. Whatever it was, it was always getting her into trouble with interviewers. She felt a need to be forthright with them, to show herself to them as fully human, dirty dishes, empty bottles, and all; or maybe she was in the grip of that modest self-disparagement small towns require. So she would tell stories on herself, times when she'd done things she regretted or made a fool of herself, and of course the interviewers would print these stories and present them as the whole truth and then she'd get mad, at herself as much as anyone. She was no saint, nor in her opinion was anybody—saintliness irritated her—but this other thing wasn't the real picture either, and she knew it. She had, among other things, a sense of decorum, and it was hard for her not to let that stifle her as a writer.

Timothy Findley, writer: "She used to pull her head in like a turtle when she laughed, because laughing out loud wasn't something one did, not according to her upbringing and mine as well. Once when I was chairman of the Writers' Union I was getting an ovation for something or other, and Marian was sitting in the front row. She pointed her finger at me and said, 'Look at you!' Because we both knew this was something that wasn't done.

"There was always that conflict—the 'lady' she'd been taught to be, and the bohemian thing. As a student she was defiant about which boys she'd go out with—she'd choose the offbeat ones on purpose; but the 'lady,' the inhibiting background, was never stamped out. Writing *Bear* nearly killed her; she was astonished by her own daring. 'I put that *word* on the page,' she'd say to me."

573

She knew why the dishes were dirty: she was a professional writer, not a professional housekeeper, and few can afford to be both. She thought of writing as an honourable profession. But she felt that Canada didn't really have a language for that yet. During her years in France, she met a man who asked her what she did. She told him. "*C'est un bon métier,*" he said. It was one of the stories from her past that she liked, especially the word *métier*. Such a word released the writer from the ranks of jugglers and personalities, those who made faces for a living, and instead took writing seriously.

Along with this professionalism (for although the dishes may have been undone the deadlines were met) went her obsession with supporting herself, difficult though this habitually was.

"Don't tell anyone I've got cancer," she said to me early on.

"Why not?" I said. She was nearly broke, as often: I could see some advantages, and anyway it was the truth.

"I might not be able to get another job."

She didn't want perks, special treatment. Also she didn't want deathbed condolences. A dying person can be thought of as dying or as living. Marian thought of herself as living.

She did not deny what was happening to her. She just didn't want it to interfere with her enjoyment of life, which, at its height, was vast. So when we did talk about her illness, we talked practical arrangements: reclining beds, tilting tables you could screw a typewriter onto. Damned if she'd give up writing. Nor did she.

Two months before she did die, she planned to go to Paris, with her two teenaged children and a wheelchair. By that time she could no longer walk and was living on painkillers, but she wanted to revisit the city where she'd made so many important discoveries for herself, twenty-five years or so before. All her friends cheered her on, aware that she might not make it there, let alone back. But her own stance was jaunty, "full of courage and comedy," as George Woodcock has put it. Or it appeared to be.

"Even towards the end," says Jane Rule, the writer, "there was that larkiness and hilarity. She wrote me from Paris: 'You haven't lived until you've gone over the cobblestones of Paris in a wheelchair.' She sent me a postcard. It was a view of a Paris street, taken from inside a basement, looking up through bars. She wrote on it: 'The Engel view—always looking up.'"

574   Which was not always entirely true. For us she brought back a more prophetic gift: a scented candle in a glass container which said on the outside: FOIN COUPÉ (CUT HAY).

There are a lot of stories that epitomize her, because she had a lot of friends. One comes from Bob Weaver, the former producer of the CBC radio program *Anthology*, and patron uncle of many writers. When she could still walk, although with a cane, she met him for lunch. Halfway through she said, "Oh my God."

"What?" said Bob, fearing a medical crisis.

"I've come here with my dress on inside out."

"Oh," said Bob, seeing that it was so.

"Usually my daughter checks me over. But she was out. What'll I do?"

"You have three choices," said Bob. "You can change it here, you can go to the washroom, or we can brazen it out."

"We'll brazen it out," said Marian.

When they'd said goodbye on the street, she called after him. He looked back and saw her leaning on her cane, waving.

"You can use this in your memoirs," she shouted.

She didn't always give such permission. "Copyright, eh?" she'd say, when telling something from her life that she wanted to save up and use herself. She knew the hazards of having other writers for friends.

Byrna Barclay, writer: "When Marian Engel began publishing I was up to my armpits in diaper pails and the other domestic symbols she wrote about. When I read *The Honeyman Festival*—in the bathtub, my favourite escape then—I almost drowned myself in the artistic statement she created about all our lives. Years later, after she won the Governor General's Award and I dared to fulfill my own writing dream, I met Marian at a conference on regional literature in Banff. At the banquet she told me—and the other people at our table—a story about winning the coveted GG. She had fifteen invitations to pass out, but no one to take to the official ceremony. She had bought a red evening gown. On the day of the awards, she was told it was an afternoon garden party, and she had nothing else to wear. She wore the red dress anyway and, flanked by her mother and her analyst, went to the garden party. No one else would talk to her. Except Joe Fafard, the sculptor, who arrived in a blue jean suit. It seems to me that red evening dress should hang in a writers' hall of fame."

We often talked about writing. Not the content of it, nor the craft, but about how one managed to do it at all. For her, given the circumstances of her life, which even before her illness were often prohibitively painful and difficult, this was a major subject. I was often astonished that she was able to write as well, as much, and as uncomplainingly as she did. She made me feel lazy, and somewhat spoiled.

Once, during a fragmented period in my own life, she gave me two pieces of advice. "Don't let other people take advantage of you." And: "Steal time."

David Young, writer: "It was difficult for her to take gifts from people or to allow herself things. She was a real string saver, she had a tremendous sense of thrift. But in the last few years that eased up—she made a garden out of what used to be a junk heap, in her backyard. It was a scaled-down version of something quite grand; she got infinite pleasure out of it. If you were over visiting her she'd make you pull out the weeds, at the back, where she couldn't get to them herself.

"She was stubborn and she had a temper, she'd give you both barrels if necessary. She could be abrasive and undiplomatic, in her official dealings, but she was idealistic and persistent too—in cultural politics, for instance. She served as first chairman of the Writers' Union of Canada, and she decided that Payment for

Public Use—of writers' books, in libraries—was what she'd go for, and she never gave up on it.

"She phoned me at midnight two weeks before she died. 'This pain isn't going to get better,' she said. And that was it. She'd decided."

Graeme Gibson, writer: "The time before, in July, when she almost died, I'd just come back from England. I went to see her in the hospital; she looked terrible. 'I wanted so much to be well for your return,' she said. I sat with her and after a while she apologized for not being entertaining, and I realized I'd better leave, because as long as I was there she was going to exert herself, for me."

Once, during a bad spell, I was visiting her in hospital, and a medical crisis really did strike. Buzzers were sounded, nurses hurried in, and I had to leave. As I did—as she was being lifted, stuck with needles—in the midst of all that, she winked at me.

This wink demolished me. It was so typical of her, but also so gallant and doomed, bagpipers going into battle, the Polish cavalry charging the tanks on horseback. It was meant, I knew, to cheer me up, but it said other things too: that no matter how gruesome things were, they had a funny side; that there was a conspiracy going on, between us, behind the doctors' backs. The doctors and her body were engaged in some solemn business or other that was of concern to her, but it wasn't the whole story.

Despite the alterations made in her by illness and drugs, here was the same expression I'd first caught her at, on that book cover: mischief, fun. *Relish* was a word she liked; "I've been naughty," she would say, with some pleasure. So there was something to be had, savoured, seen, understood, even at such a moment.

She would not have found this wink of hers courageous. Unless somebody else had done it, of course.

Suggestions for Further Reading

CANADIAN MEMOIRS: A SELECTED LIST

Appignanesi, Lisa. *Losing the Dead: A Family Memoir*. Toronto: McArthur & Company, 1999. Following the death of her parents in Canada, the author comes to terms with being the child of Holocaust survivors.

Barclay, Linwood. *Last Resort*. Toronto: McClelland & Stewart, Ltd., 2000. A memoir of growing up in the 1960s both in Toronto and at a trailer park run by his family in the Kawartha lakes region.

Butala, Sharon. *The Perfection of the Morning: An Apprenticeship in Nature*. Toronto: HarperCollins Canada, 1994.

Campbell, Maria. *Halfbreed*. Toronto: McClelland & Stewart, Ltd., 1973.

Coffey, Maria. *A Lambing Season in Ireland*. Toronto: McArthur & Company, 2000. A B.C. writer's travel memoir.

Cohen, Matt. *Typing: A Life in Twenty-Six Keys*. Toronto: Random House Canada, 2000. The novelist's professional memoir, published posthumously.

Doucet, Clive. *Notes from Exile: On Being Acadian*. Toronto: McClelland & Stewart, Ltd., 1999.

Edelson, Miriam. *My Journey with Jake: A Memoir of Parenting and Disability*. Toronto: Between the Lines, 2000.

Fiorito, Joe. *The Closer We Are to Dying*. Toronto: McClelland & Stewart, Ltd., 1999.

Foran, Charles. *The Story of My Life (So Far): A Happy Childhood*. Toronto: HarperCollins Canada, 1998.

Garebian, Keith. *Pain: Journeys Around My Parents*. Oakville: Mosaic Press, 1999. A

Canadian writer of mixed Indian and Armenian heritage writes of growing up in Bombay.

Gildiner, Catherine. *Too Close to the Falls*. Toronto: ECW Press, 1999. A physiologist's memoir of growing up in the Niagara region during the 1950s.

Gillmor, Don. *The Desire of Every Living Thing: A Search for Home*. Toronto: Random House Canada, 1999. A family memoir stretching from Scotland to Winnipeg.

Hillen, Ernest. *The Way of a Boy: A Memoir of Java*. Toronto: Penguin Books Canada Limited, 1995. A memoir of three and a half years in a Japanese internment camp in Indonesia during the Second World War.

————. *Small Mercies: A Boy after War*. Toronto: Penguin Books Canada Limited, 1998. A sequel to the above.

Houston, James. *Hideaway: Life on the Queen Charlotte Islands*. Toronto: McClelland & Stewart, Ltd., 1999. A memoir, by the person who created the international vogue for Inuit art, of life in a cabin in the Queen Charlottes.

Israel, Charles. *Son's Eye, A Memoir*. Oakville: Mosaic Press, 1999. A mature man's attempt to remember and reconstruct the life of his father, who died when the writer was twenty.

Johnston, Wayne. *Baltimore's Mansion, A Memoir*. Toronto: Knopf Canada, 1999. An award-winning memoir of Newfoundland.

Karafilly, Irena F. *The Stranger in the Plumed Hat: A Memoir*. Toronto: Penguin Books Canada Limited, 2000. A Montreal writer's memoir of her mother's struggle with Alzheimer's.

Kogawa. Joy. *Obasan*. Toronto: Lester & Orpen Dennys, 1981. A famous Japanese-Canadian memoir.

Kurelek, William. *Someone with Me*. Toronto: McClelland & Stewart, Ltd., 1973. A memoir by the Canadian visual artist.

Kwan, Michael David. *Things That Must Not Be Forgotten: A Childhood in Wartime China*. Toronto: Macfarlane Walter & Ross, 2000.

Laurence, Margaret. *Dance on the Earth*. Toronto: McClelland & Stewart, Ltd., 1989.

————. *The Prophet's Camel Bell*. Toronto: McClelland & Stewart, Ltd., 1963.

Lavut, Karen. *Simple Things: The Story of a Friendship*. Toronto: Mercury Press, 1999. A memoir of the late Canadian painter Christiane Pflung.

Layton, David. *Motion Sickness: A Memoir*. Toronto: Macfarlane Walter & Ross, 1999. A memoir by the son of the poet Irving Layton about the difficulties of being the child of bohemian parents.

Macfarlane, David. *The Danger Tree*. Toronto: Macfarlane Walter & Ross, 1991. A family memoir.

Mezlekia, Nega. *Notes from the Hyena's Belly: Memories of My Ethiopian Boyhood*. Toronto: Penguin Books Canada Limited, 2000.

Moir, Rita. *Buffalo Jump: A Woman's Travels*. Regina: Coteau Books, 1999. A memoir of driving through Western Canada in search of female ancestors.

Plaskett, Joseph. *A Speaking Likeness*. Vancouver: Ronsdale Press, 1999. A Canadian expat in Paris.

Porter, Anna. *The Storyteller: Memory, Secrets, Magic and Lies*. Toronto: Doubleday Canada, 2000. A Canadian book publisher's account of growing up in Hungary in the years before the 1956 revolution.

Scofield, Gregory. *Thunder Through My Veins: Memories of a Métis Childhood*. Toronto: HarperCollins Perennial Canada, 2000.

Stafford, Ellen. *Always and After: A Memoir*. Toronto: Penguin Books Canada Limited, 1999. An octogenarian's reflects of her marriage and her generation.

Stegner, Wallace. *Wolf Willow*. New York: Viking, 1962. The esteemed American novelist's memoir of childhood years spent on the Canadian Prairies.

Winter, Michael. *This All Happened*. Toronto: Anansi, 2000. A "fictional memoir," in journal form, of a writer's life in St. John's, Newfoundland.

Wiseman, Adele. *Memoirs of a Book-Molesting Childhood*. Toronto: Oxford University Press Canada, 1987.

CANADIAN LIFE-WRITING CRITICISM

Buss, Helen. "Canadian Women's Autobiography: Some Critical Directions," in *A Mazing Space: Writing Canadian Women Writing*, edited by Shirley Neuman and Smaro Kamboureli. Edmonton: Longspoon/NeWest, 1986.

————. "The Different Voice of Canadian Female Autobiographers," in *Biography* 13:2, Spring 1990.

————. *Mapping Our Selves: Canadian Women's Autobiography in English*. Montreal: McGill-Queen's University Press, 1993.

Heidenreich, Rosmarin. "Mothers, Daughters, Writers," in *Literary Review of Canada* 1:7, July 1992.

Heilkman, Robert B. "Theatre, Self, and Society: Some Analogues," in *A Political Art: Essays in Honour of George Woodcook*, edited by W.H. New. Vancouver: UBC Press, 1978.

Hinz, Evelyn J., ed. *Data & Acta: Aspects of Life Writing*. Oakville: Mosaic Press, 1978.

Jackel, Susan. "Canadian Women's Autobiography: A Problem of Criticism," in *Gynocritics: Feminist Approaches to Writing by Canadian and Québécoise Women* edited by Barbara Godard. Toronto: ECW Press, 1987.

Kadar, Marlene, ed. *Essays in Life-Writing*. Toronto: Robarts Centre for Canadian Studies, York University, 1989.

————, ed. *Essays on Life Writing: From Genre to Critical Practice*. Toronto: University of Toronto Press, 1992.

New, W.H. "Glimpses, Shadow, Fool," in *The Inward Journey*, edited by Elizabeth Alley. Wellington, New Zealand: Daphne Brasell, 1994.

————. "Notes for a Decade to Come," in *Temoinages*, edited by Shirley Neuman and Louise Marcil. Ottawa: Canadian Federation for the Humanities, 1993.

Stich, K.P., ed. *Reflections: Autobiography and Canadian Literature*. Ottawa: University of Ottawa Press, 1988.

Woodcock, George. "Don't Ever Ask for the True Story; or, Second Thoughts on Autobiography," in *Essays on Canadian Writing* 29, Spring 1984.

Permissions

Every effort has been made to contact copyright holders; in the event of an inadvertent omission or error, please notify the publisher. Grateful acknowledgement is made to the following for permission to reprint previously published material:

Atwood, Margaret, "Remembering Marian Engel." Copyright © by O.W. Toad Ltd., 1985. Originally published in *Saturday Night*. Reprinted by permission of the author.

Callaghan, Barry, "Barrelhouse Kings." Copyright © by Barry Callaghan, McArthur & Company, 1998. Reprinted by permission of the author and McArthur & Company, Toronto.

Cameron, Elspeth, "No Previous Experience." Copyright © by Elspeth Cameron, 1997. Reprinted by permission of Penguin Books Canada Limited.

Choy, Wayson, "Paper Shadows." Copyright © by Wayson Choy, 1999. Reprinted by permission of Penguin Books Canada Limited.

Clarke, Austin, "A Passage Back Home." Copyright © by Austin Clarke, Exile Editions Ltd., 1994. Reprinted by permission of the author and Exile Editions Ltd.

Farr, Moira, "After Daniel." Copyright © by Moira Farr, 1999.

Findley, Timothy, "From Stage to Page." Copyright © by Timothy Findley, 1996.

Foster, Cecil, "Island Wings." Copyright © by Cecil Foster, 1998.

Fraser, Sylvia, "In My Father's House." Copyright © by Sylvia Fraser, 1989. Reprinted by permission of Sterling Lord Literistic, Inc.

Gidlow, Elsa, "I Come with My Songs." Copyright © by Elsa Gidlow, Celeste West, 1986. Reprinted by permission of Celeste West and Booklegger Publishing, P.O. Box 460654, San Francisco, CA 94146. (415) 642-7569.